WHY FORESTS?
WHY NOW?

WHY FORESTS? WHY NOW?

The Science, Economics, and Politics of Tropical Forests and Climate Change

Frances Seymour and Jonah Busch

Center for Global Development

Copyright © 2016
CENTER FOR GLOBAL DEVELOPMENT
2055 L Street NW
Washington DC 20036
www.cgdev.org

Library of Congress Cataloging-in-Publication data

Seymour, Frances.
    Why Forests? Why Now? The Science, Economics, and Politics of Tropical Forests and Climate Change / Frances Seymour, Jonah Busch
        p.   cm.
    Includes bibliographic references.
ISBN: 978-1-933286-85-3

9 8 7 6 5 4 3 2 1

Contents

vii   *Foreword by Alec Baldwin*

ix   *Foreword by Lord Nicholas Stern*

xi   *Preface by Nancy Birdsall*

xiii   *Acknowledgments*

1   CHAPTER 1. **Introduction**

27   CHAPTER 2. **Tropical Forests**
A Large Share of Climate Emissions; an Even Larger Share of Potential Emission Reductions

59   CHAPTER 3. **Tropical Forests and Development**
Contributions to Water, Energy, Agriculture, Health, Safety, and Adaptation

89   CHAPTER 4. **Monitoring Tropical Forests**
Advances in Tracking Emissions, Sequestration, and Safeguards

121   CHAPTER 5. **Cheaper, Cooler, Faster**
Reducing Tropical Deforestation for a More Cost-Effective Global Response to Climate Change

149   CHAPTER 6. **Making Forests Worth More Alive than Dead**
Carbon May Succeed Where Other Values Haven't

185   CHAPTER 7. **How to Stop Deforestation**
Experience from Brazil and Beyond

219   CHAPTER 8. **Global Consumer Demand**
A Big Footprint on Tropical Forests

249   CHAPTER 9. **The International Politics of Deforestation and Climate Change**
Two Problems with a Common Solution

287   CHAPTER 10. **Forest Politics in Developing Countries**
Tipping the Balance Away from Deforestation as Usual

325   CHAPTER 11. **The Politics of REDD+ in Rich Countries**
Broad Constituencies in Favor, Small but Vocal Opposition

359   CHAPTER 12. **Finance for Tropical Forests**
Too Low, Too Slow, Too Constrained as Aid

401   CHAPTER 13. **Conclusion**
A Closing Window of Opportunity

416   *Index*

Justin Jay

Foreword by Alec Baldwin
Actor and Activist

In 1995, while shooting a documentary in the Peruvian rainforest about the illegal importation of exotic birds, I first became truly interested in the desecration of the Amazon rainforest. In recent years, that concern has grown through my work with the United Nations Development Program and their mission regarding the rights of indigenous peoples. As someone who cares about the threat of climate change, it has become impossible for me to decouple these issues.

It is clear from this remarkable book that we simply cannot meet global climate goals without greater investment in forest protection and restoration. When you look at who is protecting many of the world's remaining tropical forests, it is indigenous peoples and local communities.

I have been moved by the experiences of communities from all over the world struggling to defend their ancestral territories from the ravages of loggers, miners, and the expansion of commercial-scale agriculture. Efforts to silence their voices of protest have included ruthless violence. I have been inspired by the hundreds of community-level initiatives to develop new models of economic development that respect the ecological, social, and cultural values supported by standing forests.

I understand that the success and sustainability of community-based efforts depend on broader changes at national and international levels. For example, communities need national governments to recognize their local land rights and enforce the rule of law. They also need domestic and global markets to block access for illegal timber and other goods produced in ways that damage forests and overwhelm the people who depend on them for livelihood and identity.

The great news is that there is a viable way forward. As is clearly laid out in the pages that follow, those of us in wealthy nations have a responsibility to help by being mindful consumers of products that cause deforestation. And a particularly promising way that wealthy nations can reduce threats to forests and forest peoples is through global efforts to combat climate change. Because tropical deforestation generates a large share of global carbon emissions, international agreement has been reached on how wealthy nations can pay for reductions in forest-based emissions by developing countries. By offering serious funding to reward successful efforts to reduce deforestation—including the recognition of indigenous peoples as the world's first and best forest stewards—wealthy nations can provide incentives for developing countries to move forward with necessary actions, while also shouldering their fair share of reducing overall emissions.

Why Forests? Why Now? offers a superb introduction to the science, economics, and politics behind forest protection by two of the world's foremost authorities. The book provides clear, compelling, and timely solutions in prose and info-graphics that are accessible to non-experts and experts alike. It gives an honest and vivid portrayal of the struggle for forest protection and shows how governments, companies, and the international community can either foster or obstruct the protection of standing forests with their policy choices. In each chapter, stories and summaries of relevant research findings are used to build the case that international cooperation to protect forests is urgent, affordable, and feasible. It answers basic questions like: Why not just plant more trees? What causes deforestation? And if payments to developing countries for reducing deforestation are viable, why hasn't it already happened? This book should be mandatory reading for people who already care deeply about tropical forests, as well as for those who remain not yet convinced. It will no doubt attract and inspire a whole new generation of forest advocates and for that I am deeply grateful.

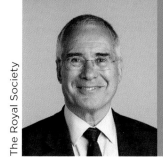

Foreword by
Lord Nicholas Stern

IG Patel Professor of Economics and
Government, London School of Economics
President of the British Academy

Poor people are hit earliest and hardest by the effects of climate change, including, for example, floods, droughts, extreme weather events, transformations in the monsoons, changing growing conditions, and heat stress. They also have so much to gain directly by more sustainable ways of organizing our economic lives, including, for example, efficiency in the management of water and energy or decentralized solar power. And, in particular, and the subject of this study, poor people stand to benefit from the better management of our forests, grasslands and other ecosystems. Climate change makes the climb out of poverty much more difficult for poor countries and poor households. Development, mitigation of emissions, and adaptation to climate change are inextricably intertwined across economic activity, and especially in relation to forests.

The analysis presented in *Why Forests? Why Now?* makes clear that reducing greenhouse gas emissions is only one of the many pathways through which standing forests contribute to human well-being in developing countries. Seymour and Busch describe the many goods and services provided by forests and how they are seldom taken into account in economic decision making. The economic values of forests are ignored despite the evidence that they are not only very large but also are often disproportionately important to poor people, including as a buffer to the impacts of climate change already being experienced around the world. A key message of this book is that forests contribute to a better climate globally as well as to a better economy locally.

This book will be a valuable primer for readers interested in economic and social development and especially those seeking to understand the critical connections among tropical forests, climate change, and development. It should be required reading for scholars and policy makers around the world and particularly for anyone in a position to influence the financial commitments that rich countries make toward the objectives of protecting the climate and achieving the Sustainable Development Goals agreed at the United Nations in September 2015.

I first studied the importance of tropical forests to climate change more than a decade ago, when I led a review on the economics of climate change. The magnitude of greenhouse gas emissions resulting from the clearing of tropical forests for activities, many of which were of low economic value, was both striking and worrying. Not least, the magnificent Amazon rainforest was being converted to pasture on which one lonely cow per hectare grazed, a stunning example of market failure with globally significant consequences. Our 2006 report concluded that reducing tropical deforestation was an essential element of any credible strategy to address climate change.

That conclusion remains robust. *Why Forests? Why Now?* brings together a new generation of research and experience that reaffirms and strengthens the case for protecting tropical forests as a climate mitigation strategy. Seymour and Busch pick up where the Stern Review left off: they update the science on the linkage between forests and climate change, stressing the potential of forest protection not only as a way of reducing emissions, but also forests' role as a safe and natural technology for carbon capture and storage. The agreement reached under the UN Framework Convention on Climate Change (UNFCCC) in Paris in December 2015—which came into force in November 2016—committed to a global balancing of sources and sinks for emissions by the second half of this century; such balance is vital to the stabilization of temperatures and likely impossible or very difficult without an expansion of existing forests.

Seymour and Busch demonstrate the power of spatial econometrics—now made possible by a revolution in forest-related data—to estimate the costs and benefits of protecting forests. And they analyze the political interests in industrialized and developing countries that made negotiations about forests one of the rare "win-wins" that contributed to the successful conclusion of the Paris Agreement.

Seymour and Busch make a compelling argument that rich countries should reward developing countries for their success in slowing deforestation as good economics, management of public goods, and promotion of economic development and social justice. It is a clear and sound application of the "Cash-on-Delivery" approach to international cooperation promoted by Nancy Birdsall and her colleagues at the Center for Global Development. Although results-based finance for reducing emissions from forests has been agreed under the UNFCCC, *Why Forests? Why Now?* explains why it remains a great idea that has yet to be implemented at scale. Their prescription for more—and more performance-based—finance, channeled through mechanisms other than traditional development aid agencies, is a timely recommendation as the global community gears up to deliver on the climate commitments made in Paris and on the Sustainable Development Goals.

These two sets of commitments represent the first truly global agenda since those made at the end of the Second World War. And the proposals here should be at the heart of the delivery of that agenda.

Preface by
Nancy Birdsall
Founding President,
Center for Global Development

Climate change threatens to upend decades of gains in global development. The benefits of consumption and production based on fossil fuels accrue mostly to the world's rich, while poor people in poor countries bear a disproportionate share of the resulting costs: rising seas, bigger storms, more severe droughts and floods, tougher living conditions.

This book is a wakeup call for development thinkers and climate advocates. On what can sometimes seem a lost cause, Frances Seymour and Jonah Busch have a good-news story to tell: tropical forests are a potentially huge asset in the fight against climate change. They constitute safe, natural carbon capture and storage. Their protection and management are affordable and available at a large scale.

While tropical forest protection is not enough to prevent climate disaster on its own, a global effort focused on forests would be cheaper and faster than most "energy" solutions. Furthermore, that global effort would confer major and direct benefits—in terms of justice and better livelihoods for many of the world's poorest and most vulnerable

people—while contributing to progress on Sustainable Development Goals related to water, energy, food, health, and safety.

Seymour and Busch show there is now an opportunity like never before to capture these development and climate benefits. In a world in which globally traded commodities drive deforestation, new technologies, and changing norms are making a difference. Satellite monitoring of changes in forest cover, higher standards for acceptable corporate behavior, and widespread recognition of the rights of forest peoples are all contributing to a healthy realignment of accountabilities among governments, corporations, and citizens.

In addition—and this is a change from even just a decade ago—the 2015 Paris Agreement on climate change has blessed a new model of international cooperation. Under this model, a few rich countries are now paying a few developing countries for the global climate services tropical forests provide. As a partnership among equal parties, this pay-for-performance approach has the potential, with more payers and more recipients, to liberate forest finance from the traditional fetters of most foreign aid programs.

At the Center for Global Development, we've long understood climate change to be a first-order way in which the policies and practices of the rich world affect the lives of poor people in developing countries. William Cline's *Global Warming and Agriculture* (2007) was among the earliest economic analyses of the disastrous effects of unabated climate change on agriculture in both rich and poor countries. Aaditya Mattoo and Arvind Subramanian's *Greenprint* (2012) called for a new narrative in which key developing countries would take a lead on climate change mitigation. David Wheeler's pioneering work on Forest Monitoring for Action (FORMA), now part of Global Forest Watch at the World Resources Institute, produces online satellite alerts of deforestation in near-real time. *Why Forests? Why Now?* builds on the tradition set by these and other works on climate by the Center of clear-eyed analysis with a focus on solutions.

It also builds on our "cash-on-delivery" approach to making development assistance more effective, and on the evidence that development is better served when donors shift their focus toward paying for outcomes, such as children educated or diseases avoided, rather than reimbursing for inputs, such as schools or hospitals built. The analysis provided in this book of experience with payments for performance for tropical forest conservation holds important lessons for development finance more broadly.

This book arrives at a timely moment. In December 2015, the world celebrated the historic diplomatic achievement of the Paris Agreement on climate change. Now countries are grappling with how to turn the ambitious promises of Paris into domestic laws, policies, and greenhouse gas emission reductions. In alerting the world to the potential of tropical forests to fight climate change and promote sustainable development, *Why Forests? Why Now?* charts a timely path forward.

A book like *Why Forests? Why Now?* does not come along very often. It is authoritative, well researched, accessible, and passionate. I expect it will change the way you think about forests, as it has done for me. After making an initial policy splash, *Why Forests? Why Now?* will assuredly have a long half-life, remaining a primer on tropical forests and climate change for years to come.

Acknowledgments

Why Forests? Why Now? would not have been possible without the generous contributions of many colleagues, to whom we express our gratitude.

We are indebted to the authors of the more than twenty papers in the CGD Forest and Climate Paper Series from which this book draws much of its material and many of its insights: Sérgio Abranches, Nancy Birdsall, Katrina Brandon, Ann Carlson, Robin Davies, Alaya de Leon, Metta Dharmasaputra, Kate Dooley, Kimberly Elliott, Jens Engelmann, Kalifi Ferretti-Gallon, Scott Goetz, Rosa Goodman, Matthew Hansen, Sean Hecht, Sabine Henders, Erlend Hermansen, Martin Herold, Cara Horowitz, Richard Houghton, the late Sjur Kasa, Thomas Kastner, Laura Kiff, Antonio La Viña, Nadine Laporte, Donna Lee, Alice Lépissier, Jesse Lueders, Katrina Mullan, Smita Nakhooda, Marigold Norman, Charlie Parker, Edward Parson, Martin Persson, Till Pistorius, William Savedoff, Ade Wahyudi, Wayne Walker, and Michael Wolosin.

These papers can be found at http://www.cgdev.org/page/wfwn-paper-series.

We are grateful to those expert reviewers who participated in an in-person review meeting and/or provided valuable written feedback on the full manuscript: Masood Ahmed, Nancy Birdsall, Artur Cardoso de Lacerda, Michele de Nevers, Kimberly Elliott, Alan Gelb, David Kaimowitz, Ravi Kanbur, Inge Kaul, Kenneth Lay, Michael Levi, Lawrence MacDonald, and Smita Singh.

We thank the many expert reviewers whose thoughtful insights, corrections, or suggestions on early drafts of one or more background papers or chapters strengthened the book: Sérgio Abranches, Stefan Agne, Naikoa Aguilar-Amuchastegui, Arild Angelsen, Nazanin Ash, Juliano Assunçao, Charles Barber, Ed Barbier, Owen Barder, Sebastian Bauhoff, Andrew Bishop, William Boyd, Duncan Brack, Josefina Braña Varela, Maria Brockhaus, Benjamin Bryant, Derek Byerlee, Ken Chomitz, Michael Clemens, Matt Collin, Erin Collinson, Edward Davey, Eric Davidson, Penny Davies, Robin Davies, Crystal Davis, Alaya de Leon, Michele de Nevers, Shanta Devarajan, Kate Dooley, Anthony Eggert, Christiane Ehringhaus, Chris Elliott, Kimberly

Elliott, Jens Engelmann, Victoria Fan, Dan Farber, Kalifi Ferretti-Gallon, Greg Fishbein, Sean Frisby, Omar García-Ponce, Ivetta Gerasimchuk, Amanda Glassman, Peter Graham, Nancy Harris, Erlend Hermansen, Daniel Honig, Richard Houghton, Ronald Hutjes, David Kaimowitz, Peter Kanowski, Rodney Keenan, Charles Kenny, Gabrielle Kissinger, Kaisa Korhonen-Kurki, Linda Kreuger, Gina Lambright, Deborah Lawrence, Sam Lawson, Kenneth Lay, Donna Lee, Nancy Lee, Ben Leo, Alice Lépissier, Thais Linhares-Juvenal, Alexander Lotsch, Ruben Lubowski, Simon Maxwell, Desmond McNeill, Rajesh Mirchandani, Scott Morris, Todd Moss, Anit Mukherjee, Smita Nakhooda, Deepa Narayan, Marigold Norman, Jimmy O'Dea, Manuel Oliva, Mead Over, Charlie Parker, Subhrendu Pattanayak, Martin Persson, Till Pistorius, Billy Pizer, Francis Putz, Vijaya Ramachandran, Peter Riggs, Claudia Romero, Michael Ross, Justin Sandefur, William Savedoff, Neil Scotland, Frank Seifert, Douglas Sheil, Sudhir Shetty, Sergei Soares, Souleymane Soumahoro, Marc Steininger, Fred Stolle, Jon Strand, Charlotte Streck, Kimberly Todd, Obbe Tuinenburg, Louis Verchot, Ade Wahyudi, David Wheeler, Michael Wolosin, and Heather Wright.

We are grateful to the members of the CGD Working Group on Scaling Up Performance-Based Transfers for Reduced Tropical Deforestation, chaired by Nancy Birdsall and Pedro Pablo Kuczynski and managed by Michele de Nevers, discussions with whom helped us refine the messages of this book: Arild Angelsen, Owen Barder, Andreas Dahl-Jørgensen, Robin Davies, Christine Dragisic, Gwen Hines, Kevin Hogan, Ingrid Hoven, Bharrat Jagdeo, Harrison Karnwea, Carlos Klink, Benjamin Knoedler, Rezal Kusumaatmadja, Gavin Neath, Per Pharo, Nigel Purvis, Artur Runge-Metzger, Juliana Queiroz Santiago, William Savedoff, Dorte Verner, and Michael Wolosin.

We are deeply grateful to our colleagues at the Center for Global Development. Nancy Birdsall was the original proponent of the book and a continual source of inspiration, insight, and encouragement. Sara del Fierro coordinated every aspect of book production over the course of more than two years and made an orderly handoff to Emily Foecke, who got us over the finish line with the help of Kathryn Brown. Jens Engelmann and Kalifi Ferretti-Gallon provided essential research assistance, while Alice Lépissier contributed critical analysis. Kinshuk Chatterjee fact-checked nearly every sentence, though the authors are solely responsible for any remaining errors of fact or interpretation. Michele de Nevers, William Savedoff, Kimberly Elliott, and other colleagues provided helpful advice at many stages. Lawrence MacDonald, Rajesh Mirchandani, John Osterman, Stephanie Brown, Erin Collinson, Lauren Post, Forrest Rilling, and Kate Wathen assisted with communications. Michael Clemens oversaw and Cynthia Rathinasamy and Marla Spivack coordinated the review of commissioned papers.

We thank the members of the team at Bittersweet Creative who produced the infographics that appear throughout this book.

We apologize in advance to any contributors we may have inadvertently omitted above.

We are pleased to acknowledge financial support from the government of Norway's International Climate and Forest Initiative that made our research possible.

Finally, we thank our friends and family members—especially our partners Ariana Alisjahbana Busch and Mike Kopetski—for their patience, support, and encouragement throughout the production of this book.

Frances Seymour and Jonah Busch
November 2016

CHAPTER 1

Introduction

For six long days at the end of October 1998, Hurricane Mitch lashed Central America with gusts of wind over three hundred kilometers per hour. Waves as high as thirteen meters crashed onto the shore.[1] Dubbed a "Category 5 Monster," the worst Atlantic storm in more than two hundred years spread death and destruction across the region. Millions of people were displaced, and eleven thousand died. In countries where two-thirds of the population lived on less than four U.S. dollars a day,[2] the economic damage was estimated to be at least $5 billion.[3]

While El Salvador, Guatemala, and Nicaragua suffered significant loss of life and decimation of bridges, roads, and crops, Honduras bore the brunt of the hurricane's impact. Although a storm of Mitch's magnitude would have caused destruction under any circumstances, Honduran life and property were especially vulnerable to its wrath because of deforestation.[4] As the country's hillsides were drenched by up to 1.9 meters of rain,[5] too little vegetation was left to hold the soil. Floods and mudslides washed away villages, destroyed 80 percent of the country's infrastructure, and damaged one-third of all buildings in the capital city of Tegucigalpa.[6]

Honduras's remaining forests were not spared. The pine, hardwood, and mangrove forests of the Bay Island of Guanaja were "utterly flattened,"[7] with mangrove trees suffering 97 percent mortality.[8] Mangroves throughout the region, which otherwise provided protection from coastal storms, were severely damaged by high winds and waves and buried in sediments that washed down from the hillsides.[9]

In the year following Hurricane Mitch, the economy of Honduras contracted by 4 percent.[10] More generally, natural disasters can knock rich and poor countries alike off paths toward greater prosperity. Research on the impacts of thousands of cyclones over almost sixty years found such storms have a dramatic, long-term effect on economic development. Following the most extreme disasters (that is, those in the worst 10 percent), national income declines from its pre-disaster trend and does not recover within twenty years.[11]

The U.S. National Oceanic and Atmospheric Administration (NOAA) predicted Mitch's rank as the Western Hemisphere's second deadliest hurricane (after the Great Hurricane of 1780) would "likely stand for a long, long time."[12] It might not stand for as long as we'd like, though. With climate change, such tropical cyclones are expected to become more severe, and the most severe storms are predicted to become more frequent.[13]

In the meantime, tropical deforestation—which continues in most developing countries, including Honduras—is a key source of the greenhouse gas emissions that cause climate change. When forests are cleared and trees are burned or decay, the carbon stored in trunks, branches, leaves, and roots is released into the atmosphere. When disturbed, the carbon-rich soils beneath peatland and mangrove forests are among the world's most potent land-based sources of greenhouse gas emissions. Removal of tree cover affects the climate through other pathways, as well, such as increases in surface temperature and disruptions to rainfall patterns.

Direct human action—such as the cultivation of hillsides in Honduras, the conversion of Amazon forests to cattle pastures and soybean fields, and the draining of Indonesia's peatlands for oil palm and timber plantations—is the primary cause of emissions from deforestation. Those emissions are augmented by damage to forests from acute events linked to climate change—such as when Hurricane Mitch stripped mangrove trees from the island of Guanaja—as well as from the increased vulnerability of trees to drought, fire, and other sources of climate-induced stress.

Thus, deforestation contributes to climate change and erodes resilience to it, while climate change undermines development and damages forests. Figure 1.1 illustrates some of the ways deforestation and climate change are intertwined in a vicious cycle that exacerbates poverty. The good news is that this cycle can be arrested, and possibly even reversed.

The purpose of this book is to make the case that rewarding developing countries for protecting their forests is an urgently needed, affordable, and feasible strategy for rich countries to support reducing the emissions that cause climate change, while at the same time providing significant direct contributions to development.

In this introductory chapter, we summarize why forests are so important to meeting goals related to both climate change and the reduction of poverty and why the current moment is ripe for action. We then explain why we believe the book will be useful to readers interested in climate change or development and provide a road map to its contents.

Figure 1.1: Deforestation and climate change drive a vicious cycle that exacerbates poverty.

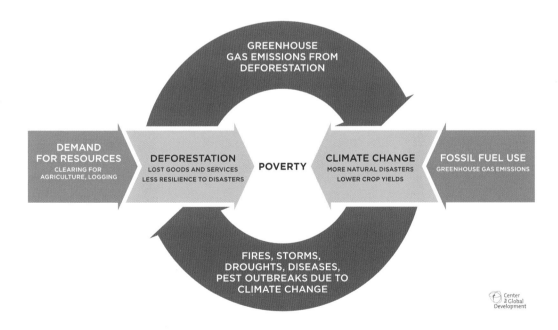

Climate Change Threatens Development and Poverty Reduction

The lives and livelihoods of poor people are especially dependent on a stable climate. In Latin American cities such as Rio de Janeiro and Bogota, the houses of poor families perch on steep, often unstable, hillsides. Across dryland Africa, the crops cultivated by poor farmers fail if the rain is too little or arrives too late. Along the coastlines of Asian countries from India to the Philippines, the safety of poor households depends on calm seas, and their livelihoods depend on productive fisheries.

Everywhere, the lives and livelihoods of poor people are threatened by a changing climate. Climate change amplifies extreme weather events, such as periods of intense rainfall that cause landslides, months without rain that lead to droughts, and high winds whipping up waves that destroy coastal communities and coral reef ecosystems. The places where poor people live and the sources of their income often place them on the front lines when societies face the impacts of floods, droughts, and storms. Because they are less likely to have savings, insurance, access to modern health care and other services, or the ability to migrate to safer or more resilient communities, poor people are often the least able to recover when disaster strikes.

On a broader scale, the development prospects of poor countries are threatened by climate change. It's not just that a tropical cyclone like Hurricane Mitch can deal a long-term setback to growth; even in the absence of such a disaster, a less predictable climate raises the costs of achieving food, energy, and water security. Infrastructure for transpor-

tation and irrigation can be overwhelmed by too much rain; infrastructure for hydropower and drinking water can be rendered useless by too little.

Indeed, climate change is regressive. In other words, its effects will make poor households and countries not just worse off, but disproportionately worse off than better-off families and nations. While climate change will be disruptive and expensive for rich households and rich countries, for the poor it will be catastrophic.

In its Fifth Assessment Report in 2014, the International Panel on Climate Change (IPCC) detailed the many ways climate change will adversely affect the well-being of poor people and developing countries, including increasing risks to their incomes, health, safety, and food security. The IPCC concluded, "Climate-change impacts are projected to slow down economic growth [and] make poverty reduction more difficult."[14] Figure 1.2 provides a summary of those impacts.

Hunger caused by crop failure and drought, destruction of housing and infrastructure by storms and floods, disease spread by insects and water scarcity—all of these development challenges are exacerbated by climate change. For poor households and poor countries alike, an increasingly warm and unstable climate steepens the climb out of poverty. Achievement of development objectives will be much easier in a stable climate.

Why Forests?

Reducing emissions from the burning of fossil fuels such as coal, oil, and gas is, of course, central to any global climate mitigation strat-

Figure 1.2: Poor people are most at risk from climate change.

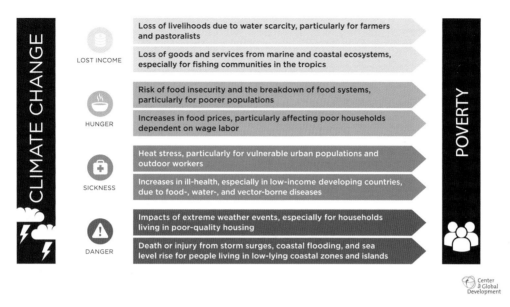

Source: C. B. Field et al., eds., *Climate Change 2014: Impacts, Adaptation, and Vulnerability.* Part A: Global and Sectoral Aspects. Contribution of Working Group II to the Fifth Assessment Report of the Intergovernmental Panel on Climate Change (Cambridge, UK, and New York: Cambridge University Press, 2014).

egy. Emissions from fossil fuels make up the largest and fastest growing share of carbon being released into the atmosphere. Furthermore, industrialized countries and richer households are disproportionately responsible for such emissions, and they are in a better position than poor countries and households to limit their emissions.

But alongside reductions in emissions from fossil fuels through shifts to clean energy and transportation systems is a poorly recognized opportunity to reduce emissions from tropical deforestation. Reducing emissions from tropical deforestation is essential to any strategy to achieve climate stability, and maintaining forests contributes to the achievement of many sustainable development goals. Lowering deforestation rates

offers many developing countries the single most attractive option for contributing to reduced global emissions in a way that is compatible with their own development objectives and one that is particularly aligned with the interests of their poorest citizens.

> Tropical forests are undervalued assets in addressing two of the most significant challenges of our time: climate change and development.

Tropical forests are, thus, undervalued assets in addressing two of the most significant challenges of our time: climate change and development. The chapters in this book present evidence that a major international initiative to reduce deforestation is urgently needed, affordable, and feasible.

Action to Protect Forests Is Urgently Needed

Preventing the warming of global temperatures by more than two degrees Celsius—the upper limit agreed on at the 2015 climate talks in Paris—is not possible without protecting forests. If tropical deforestation were a country, its annual contributions to the emissions that cause climate change would be greater than those of the European Union. Efforts to avert catastrophic climate change are unlikely to succeed without reducing both forest and nonforest emissions.

According to the IPCC, global net emissions from forests and land-use change—mostly tropical deforestation—accounted for 11 percent of total human-caused emissions as of 2010. That percentage is misleadingly small for two reasons. First, while emissions from deforestation have continued apace in recent years, emissions from all other sources have increased dramatically, reducing forests' share of the total. Second, growing tropical forests compensate for a large proportion of current emissions, pulling carbon out of the atmosphere and into vegetation, a safe and natural carbon capture and storage technology. Thus, forest destruction not only generates carbon emissions; it diminishes nature's capacity to absorb them.

IPCC numbers suggest that if deforestation ended today and degraded forests were allowed to recover, tropical forests alone could reduce current annual global emissions by 24 to 30 percent.[15] In other words, tropical forests hold the potential to constitute somewhere between one-quarter and one-third of the near-term solution to climate change.

According to the IPCC, all scenarios for staying below the two-degree limit include assumptions that deforestation is halted and reversed. And yet satellite imagery analysis makes clear that tropical forest loss is occurring today at an *accelerating* annual rate, with an area the size of Austria cleared each year.[16] Modeling past deforestation trends into the future suggests that, without countervailing action, in thirty-five years the world will lose 289 million hectares of tropical forests—an area about the size of India. Furthermore, deforestation will release 169 billion tons of carbon dioxide, thus using up fully one-sixth of the remaining emissions budget allowable under a scenario that keeps global warming under two degrees.[17]

The longer the world waits before reversing current deforestation trends, the more the capacity of the remaining forests to serve as a natural carbon capture and storage system is eroded. And as climate change progresses, even intact forests will be damaged by such effects as more frequent and severe droughts and fires. Such damage could tip forests from being a large part of the solution to being a larger part of the problem. The window of opportunity is closing.

Action to Protect Forests Is Affordable

Among the many strategies available to reduce the emissions that cause climate change, protecting tropical forests is among the most affordable. Modeling suggests cutting emissions from tropical deforestation in half would make it 28 percent cheaper to keep global warming below two degrees Celsius. Alternatively, cutting emissions from tropical deforestation by between one-third and one-half could lessen global warming by 0.15°C to 0.82°C and hasten by two to five years the time when global greenhouse gas emissions start decreasing, without raising the overall cost of fighting climate change.[18]

Furthermore, modeling that simulates response to a price on carbon suggests that forest conservation represents more than half of the lowest-cost opportunities for emission reduction in developing countries other than China. In a scenario in which developing countries use payments for forest conservation to influence land-use decision making, the same analysis estimates a $20 per ton price on carbon dioxide could generate 41 billion tons of avoided emissions from 2015 to 2050.[19] That price is significantly less than the U.S. Environmental Protection Agency's estimates of the economic benefits of emission reductions over the same period at a 3 percent discount rate.[20] The cost of an equivalent quantity of emission reductions in Europe or the United States would be far higher.[21]

Yet the actual cost to developing-country governments of reducing deforestation could be far lower than those generated by the simulation for a number of reasons. The governments, for example, need not compensate land users for the large portion of forest clearance that is illegal. In recent years, forest-rich developing countries have offered emission reductions as part of bilateral and multilateral payment-for-performance agreements for as little as $5 per ton—a bargain compared to many other emission abatement options.

Developing-country governments are also increasingly recognizing the economic justification for protecting forests based on the domestic value of the many goods and services forests provide beyond carbon capture and storage. Wild products gathered from natural forests contribute, on average, more than one-fifth of household incomes in nearby communities—second to the proportion contributed by agricultural crops.[22] Serving as "green infrastructure," forested watersheds save tens of millions of dollars by preventing sedimentation, which extends the lives of hydroelectric dams and irrigation systems.

Farmers and researchers have long known forests provide services to nearby agricultural fields by regulating stream flows, providing shelter from wind, and supporting pollination from birds, bats, and bees. Evidence is now accumulating that they also support agriculture at continental scales by bringing rainfall to inland farmers. A study published in 2014 shows forest loss leads to warmer, drier conditions, both locally and at great distances.[23]

Recent studies are also illuminating the linkages between forests and health, beyond the provision of pharmaceutical compounds from medicinal plants. Forests provide clean water by filtering out pollutants, and intact forests have been associated with decreased incidence of malaria; conversely, air pollution from forest fires is estimated to result in hundreds of thousands of premature deaths each year. New research is also substantiating the role of forests in making communities more resilient to costly natural disasters, such as fires, floods, droughts, and the landslides and waves generated by storms like Hurricane Mitch.

Most of these goods and services from forests are disproportionately important to people who live in the poorer communities in and around them, with the abovementioned result that deforestation is often regressive. Yet because the benefits generated by forests have not been systematically integrated into national accounts, they are invisible to economic development planners.

Action to Protect Forests Is Feasible

Tropical deforestation was long considered an intractable problem, and international cooperation to address it was particularly fraught. But over the past decade, innovations in policy and technology have converged to demonstrate that slowing deforestation is feasible, and to show how international support can help.

Utilizing a combination of land-use planning and recognition of property rights (including designation of protected areas and indigenous territories), law enforcement efforts, and market incentives, Brazil has dramatically lowered the deforestation rate in the Amazon, even as agricultural production has continued to rise. Brazil pioneered the use of remote sensing technology to track and respond to illegal forest clearing in remote forest areas. By slowing deforestation in the Amazon by some 80 percent in the decade starting in 2004, Brazil has made the single largest contribution to reducing the emissions that cause climate change of any country in the world.[24] And the out-of-pocket costs to federal, state, and municipal budgets are estimated to have been only a few dollars per ton of avoided emissions.[25]

While Brazil's achievement was driven primarily by leadership from within Brazilian society, key elements of that success illustrate the potential contribution of international cooperation to complement domestic political will. First, researchers and activists, empowered by new norms of transparency and widespread Internet access, raised international awareness of Brazil's high rate of deforestation and effectively mobilized pressure on government and corporate actors to take action. Civil society groups took advantage of Brazil's participation in international environmental forums to advance the domestic policy agenda.

Second, Brazil's experience—which included a voluntary moratorium on forest clearing by the soy industry—illuminated the changing drivers of tropical deforestation. In the past, forest loss was blamed on the clearing of land by poor farmers for subsistence. Now, a large and increasing portion of deforestation across tropical countries is driven by forest clearing—much of it illegal—to cultivate globally traded commodities, such as soy, beef, palm oil, and fast-growing timber to make pulp and paper.

Expansion of the area dedicated to production of those commodities has occurred at the expense of carbon-dense forests. An analysis of 2000–2009 data reveals that forest clearing to produce four commodities in only eight countries was responsible for one-third of all emissions from tropical deforestation.[26] Furthermore, fully one-third of those emissions were embodied in international trade, a proportion that is certainly larger today, as exports of those commodities have increased since 2009. Market signals from international traders and buyers, as well as policy signals from consumer countries, can provide incentives for legal and "deforestation-free" production of food, fuel, and fiber.

Third, just as the more timely availability of satellite imagery helped Brazil crack down on illegal forest clearing, advances in the spatial resolution of remote sensing data now also enable more precise measurement of the amount of climate emissions avoided by reducing deforestation. Brazil has been a pioneer in an internationally agreed-on approach to international cooperation on forests, described further below, in which rich countries finance forest emission reductions in developing countries on a payment-for-performance basis. As of 2016, more than $1 billion in results-based payments from the governments of Norway and Germany had contributed to consolidating domestic support for forest conservation.

Why Now?

International concern about tropical deforestation dates back at least 165 years, when a "denudation crisis" in India raised alarm in the United Kingdom about looming shortages of timber and fuelwood. A century ago, French colonial officials noted the urgency of addressing the disappearance of dryland forests in West Africa, a concern that reemerged in the 1970s following droughts in the Sahel.[27]

In the mid-1980s, rapid loss of tropical rainforests, deemed "the lungs of the Earth," fueled an outpouring of activism, international initiatives, and donor funding, with a special focus on protecting the biological and cultural wealth of the Brazilian Amazon. A United Nations–sponsored Tropical Forestry Action Plan (TFAP) called for some $8 billion in pledges

from donor countries to save the rainforest. In 1988, U.S. ice cream maker Ben and Jerry's introduced a popular new flavor with cashew and Brazil nuts: Rainforest Crunch.

But fashions change in both ice cream flavors and favored development topics. Ben and Jerry's dropped Rainforest Crunch from the menu less than a year after introducing it, and donor-funded forest initiatives proved more difficult to carry out than originally thought. At the 1992 Earth Summit in Rio de Janeiro, negotiators failed to conclude a convention on forests, largely because developing countries perceived the proposed agreement as an attempt to limit their sovereignty over domestic natural resources needed for development. The TFAP ended in acrimony, without reducing deforestation or reaching agreement on the best way to do so.

Funding and political attention focused on forests gradually dissipated. Development finance institutions, such as the World Bank, began disengaging from the forestry sector after being burned by allegations that their lending for business-as-usual timber extraction damaged ecological systems and harmed indigenous peoples. Other imperatives arose on the international agenda, and the individuals and organizations devoted to conserving tropical forests struggled to maintain support for their work into the 2000s.

Now, however, developments in the science, economics, and politics of tropical forests and climate change over the past decade have created a new opportunity for action. Culminating in the 2015 Paris Agreement, the world has recognized that deforestation and climate change are two problems with a common solution.

A New Framework for International Cooperation Has Been Agreed On

Ten years ago, tropical forests catapulted back to the top of the international agenda, this time due to the discovery of their importance to climate change. The surge of energy and enthusiasm unleashed by this linkage is difficult to exaggerate. Between the climate negotiations in Bali in 2007, when forests were formally incorporated into tracks for negotiation, and the 2009 summit in Copenhagen, when a global climate deal was expected to be struck, mobilization around the agenda to stop deforestation reached fever pitch.

Negotiations toward a framework eventually known as REDD+ (described in box 1.1) to support mitigation of forest-based emissions through results-based payments emerged as the most constructive area of annual discussions under the United Nations Framework Convention on Climate Change (UNFCCC), as negotiators worked through how to manage various risks to the interests of rich-country financiers and stakeholders in recipient countries. Donor agencies returned to the forestry sector with replenished checking accounts. And the thinned ranks of forest-related government officials, practitioners, researchers, and advocates, thrilled by the prospect of rapid policy development and significant financial support for their work, launched a new generation of initiatives ranging from village pilot projects to national strategic planning efforts.

The rebirth of tropical forest protection as a climate mitigation strategy in the first decade of the 2000s, in parallel with shifts in forest governance norms toward transparency and recognition of indigenous rights,

---

Box 1.1: What is REDD+?

REDD+ stands for

- **R**educing
- **E**missions from
- **D**eforestation and forest
- **D**egradation
- **plus** conservation, sustainable management of forests, and enhancement of forest carbon stocks.

REDD+ is the international framework agreed on for including forests in strategies to reduce the emissions that cause climate change. It was negotiated under the UN Framework Convention on Climate Change (UNFCCC) over the past decade, and was endorsed in the 2015 Paris Agreement. Through REDD+, industrialized countries can provide financial incentives to developing countries for reducing forest-based emissions and enhancing the carbon capture and storage functions of forests.

The key distinction between REDD+ finance and previous international flows of funding to address deforestation is the explicit intention to progress toward results-based finance. In other words, developing countries can receive ex-post payments for verified emission reductions, which can be financed either from public funds or carbon markets.

According to the Warsaw Framework for REDD+, which was agreed on under the UNFCCC in 2013, a developing country must have in place the following to qualify for results-based finance:

- A national strategy or action plan for reducing forest-based emissions
- A system for monitoring and reporting forest cover change and associated emission reductions
- A baseline (reference level) against which progress in reducing emissions will be measured
- A safeguards information system (SIS) for reporting on how measures to protect against environmental and social harm are being implemented[a]

Developing countries can get access to "readiness" funding to help them meet these requirements ("phase 1") and investment funds to address the drivers of deforestation ("phase 2") to qualify for payments based on performance in reducing emissions ("phase 3").

Many early activities initiated under the banner of REDD+ took place at the level of individual projects managed by nongovernmental organizations (NGOs) or private sector entrepreneurs hoping to sell forest carbon credits to buyers in the voluntary carbon market. But consistent with the outcome of international negotiations, the current focus of results-based finance for REDD+ (and of this book) is on the "jurisdictional" scale. The few large-scale, results-based financing agreements to date have been concluded between rich-country governments, on the one hand, and developing-country governments and/or subnational state or provincial governments, on the other.

While the Paris Agreement allows for the "international transfer of mitigation outcomes"—which would allow rich countries to purchase REDD+ credits to offset their own emissions—none of the few REDD+ agreements concluded to date have included such transfers, nor have any compliance-driven carbon markets yet allowed REDD+ offsets (although as of mid-2016 the state of California was considering doing so). As a result, international REDD+ finance at the jurisdictional scale has been limited to commitments from donor-country aid budgets.

The term "REDD+" is often used broadly as shorthand for the objective of reducing emissions from deforestation and forest degradation, rather than more narrowly as the framework negotiated under the UNFCCC and associated activities. It is also commonly used as a label for the many projects, national strategies, bilateral agreements, and multilateral initiatives spawned while negotiations were still going on. In this book, we attempt to use the term in its narrower sense as far as possible.

a. United Nations Framework Convention on Climate Change (UNFCCC), "Decision 9/CP.19: Work Programme on Results-Based Finance to Progress the Full Implementation of the Activities Referred to in Decision 1/CP.16, Paragraph 70," from "Report of the Conference of the Parties on its Nineteenth Session, Held in Warsaw from 11 to 23 November 2013 Addendum Part Two: Action Taken by the Conference of the Parties at Its Nineteenth Session," Warsaw, Poland, January 31, 2014.

has led to a realignment of interests and constituencies that is more supportive of international cooperation. Within the UNFCCC, countries from both North (industrialized countries) and South (developing countries) recognized reducing emissions from deforestation as a rare "win-win." At the climate conference in Warsaw in 2013, negotiators agreed on REDD+ as the framework for rewarding developing countries for reducing forest-based emissions, and it was later incorporated into the 2015 Paris Agreement.

Recent Advances in Remote Sensing Technology Enable Measurement of Forest Emissions

A previous constraint on the incorporation of forests into climate change mitigation strategies was the difficulty of measuring changes in forest cover and associated emissions. Rapid technological change has now enabled satellites orbiting the Earth to generate pictures of sufficiently high resolution to pinpoint changes in areas the size of baseball diamonds. In 2008, the U.S. government made its archive of such images available for free.[28] This wealth of data, combined with increased computing power and lower cost, has made it possible to map and analyze deforestation around the world with a degree of precision that was unthinkable only ten years ago.

Increasingly refined satellite imagery to measure forest cover change has been accompanied by the deployment of new laser technologies to assess carbon density. In combination, these technologies make possible the estimation of carbon emissions from deforestation with a high degree of accuracy. Such measurements can, in turn, serve as the basis for financial rewards to developing countries, based on their performance in reducing emissions by protecting forests.

Payment for Performance Promises Better Outcomes

In parallel to the development of REDD+ as a climate mitigation strategy over the last decade, a new approach to foreign aid has been percolating in development policy circles. The 2005 Paris Declaration on Aid Effectiveness and the subsequent Accra Agenda for Action placed new emphasis on developing-country leadership of development policies and strategies and managing such policies and strategies for results.[29] Our colleagues at the Center for Global Development have translated these principles into a practical proposal for a cash-on-delivery approach to development cooperation.[30]

The cash-on-delivery approach focuses on payment for performance in generating results rather than specifying the necessary inputs or strategies to achieve development objectives. Donors agree, for example, to pay a fixed amount for each child reaching an agreed-upon level of educational attainment, rather than financing the building of schools or the training of teachers. A number of benefits are expected from such a "hands-off" role for donors:

- Greater leadership and coordination of development strategies on the part of developing-country governments
- Greater accountability of governments to their citizens, as a result of the transparent reporting of progress
- Greater flexibility, for learning by doing and adjusting strategies rather than being tied to a project blueprint
- Less risk of corruption, as diversion of funds to the point of jeopardizing outcomes would result in nonpayment

Results-based finance is, arguably, particularly appropriate for reducing emissions from deforestation for a number of reasons.

The recent developments in remote sensing technology described above make it possible to measure outcomes and independently verify results in ways not available to other sectors, such as health and education.

Furthermore, the complexity and political sensitivity of the forestry sector indicate the limitations of donor-designed approaches to addressing deforestation, which have not succeeded in turning the tide of deforestation at scale. While compliance with internationally agreed-on safeguards is essential, due deference to developing-country stakeholders as to how results can be achieved is otherwise in order. Paying only for results is attractive to rich-country politicians and the taxpayers they represent. Perhaps most important, payment-for-performance agreements reframe financial transactions as equal partnerships rather than charitable gifts, a more politically acceptable mode of cooperation for developing countries.

REDD+ agreements constitute a significant portion of the few genuine experiments with results-based finance between governments now underway, and they are already generating experience of broader relevance to improving aid effectiveness.[31]

Developing Countries Are Lined Up but Losing Hope

In developing countries, domestic constituencies for forest conservation were once small and often politically constrained, and agencies charged with forest management focused most of their attention on exploiting rather than conserving forest resources. In international negotiations related to forests, developing-country governments jealously guarded national sovereignty and resisted taking on international obligations.

In recent years, domestic and international factors have intertwined to pique a new appetite for international cooperation on forests. Domestically, democratic transitions in countries such as Brazil and Indonesia have empowered environmental advocates and social movements, while new technologies (see above) have increased the transparency of forest-related information and decision making. Advocates' numbers have been augmented by those whose rights or livelihoods are threatened by forest loss, such as rubber tappers and indigenous peoples. Natural disasters such as droughts, floods, and fires have called national political attention to the linkage between forest protection and national well-being.

In addition, risks to their international reputations have helped motivate political leaders to address high rates of deforestation, starting with initiatives begun under President Luiz Inácio Lula da Silva in Brazil. When President Susilo Bambang Yudhoyono of Indonesia announced the first voluntary emission reduction targets from a developing country in 2009, he demonstrated the potential of forests as a vehicle for developing countries to show leadership in the climate protection arena. Both presidents were among the first to enter into bilateral payment-for-performance REDD+ agreements with the government of Norway.

Since then, dozens of other developing-country governments have initiated REDD+ programs with international support. But the large-scale, results-based finance from rich countries initially envisioned for REDD+ never materialized. The failure to conclude a binding agreement to reduce climate emissions at the UNFCCC summit in Copenhagen in 2009 had nothing to do with forests. In fact, negotiators had continued their steady progress in resolving contention concerning how to integrate forests into such an agreement. But just as the linkage to climate change had helped put tropical forests back on the international agenda, it also punctured the inflating expectations for large-scale forest finance based on demand for emission reductions. The sudden dimming of the possibility that such demand would emerge in the absence of a global climate agreement marked a stunning reversal for all those who had pinned their hopes on an international cap-and-trade system to generate the finance necessary to stop deforestation.

The Copenhagen disappointment was soon followed by others. In 2010, U.S. climate legislation, known as the Waxman-Markey Bill when it had passed the House of Representatives in June 2009, died without a vote in the Senate. The legislation would have generated demand for up to 1.5 billion tons of reductions in forest-based emissions annually, as well as separate funding for forests at a level of $3 billion per year. With no prospects for crediting in compliance markets, demand for forest carbon offsets from avoided deforestation on the voluntary market softened and fell by 8 percent in 2011 alone.[32]

Many worthwhile initiatives launched between 2007 and 2009, when expectations were peaking, continued to muddle along. Although some early REDD+ projects folded, proponents of others soldiered on in the face of challenges, such as insecure land tenure and insufficient finance, that extended beyond project boundaries.[33] The $2.5 billion pledged by the government of Norway at the 2007 negotiations in Bali buoyed progress in addressing deforestation by offering performance-based finance to a handful of countries and making grants to numerous civil society groups.

But even Norway's "rainforest billions" were insufficient to meet the expectations of the dozens of developing countries that signaled their intent to reduce emissions from deforestation in return for finance. Without compliance markets for forest carbon offsets, allocations of public funds for performance-based payments fell far short of what was required if the efforts of those countries to reverse current deforestation trends were to be successful.

Many political leaders and project entrepreneurs in developing countries who had taken political and financial risks with the expectation of a robust global willingness to pay for reduced emissions from deforestation found themselves tethered to a gradually deflating balloon, and a "narrative of disappointment" in the promise of REDD+ began to take hold.[34] In August 2014, twenty-three governors from forest-rich states and provinces signed on to a commitment to reduce deforestation in their jurisdictions up to 80 percent by 2020 in return for guarantees of adequate, performance-based financing, while expressing their frustration at having seen so little finance so far.[35]

We Are at a Watershed Moment

Despite all this, 2014 also brought a palpable regaining of momentum in efforts to stop tropical deforestation. At the UN secretary-general's Climate Summit 2014 in September, a critical mass of governments, private companies, nongovernmental organizations, and indigenous groups came together to endorse the New York Declaration on Forests, committing to contribute to a goal of halving deforestation by 2020 and ending it by 2030.[36] Later that year, at the UNFCCC negotiations in Peru, a group of forest-rich developing countries endorsed the Lima Challenge, offering to increase their ambition to reduce deforestation in return for greater incentives from rich countries.[37]

In the meantime, private sector support for ending forest loss was growing. An initial trickle of private businesses making commitments to get deforestation out of their supply chains turned into a gush, with companies ranging from Mondelez to McDonald's signing on to pledges. As recently as mid-2013, activists had seen global commodity traders as opaque corporate behemoths with no interest in or incentive to reduce the tropical deforestation powering their businesses. By early 2015, following commitments by Wilmar International, Golden Agri Resources, Bunge, Cargill, and other traders, some 90 percent of the global trade in palm oil was covered by corporate pledges to remove deforestation from supply chains.[38]

Momentum continued to build in the run-up to the 2015 climate summit in Paris. In June, Pope Francis delivered his encyclical calling for action on climate change, giving particular attention to the importance of conserving forests.[39] In September, 193 countries adopted a new set of global sustainable development goals (SDGs), one of which includes halting deforestation by 2020.[40] And in Paris in December, heads of state from Brazil, Colombia, the Democratic Republic of Congo, Ethiopia, Gabon, Indonesia, Liberia, Mexico, and Peru joined a pledge to intensify their efforts to protect forests, while many countries included forests in the national plans for emission reductions they lodged at the conference.

Still, despite a prominent role for forests in the Paris Agreement itself and a new pledge of $5 billion in funding from the governments of Germany, Norway, and the United Kingdom, the need remains for large-scale, results-based finance to realize the promise of REDD+.

We are now at a watershed moment. Most of the pieces are in place: international consensus on a framework for REDD+; forest-rich countries and subnational jurisdictions making commitments contingent on additional finance; private corporations pledging to do their part; technology that enables accountability; and support from a broad base of civil society groups, including representatives of indigenous peoples. The one vital piece missing from the puzzle is a significant response from rich countries to meet this opportunity with tangible incentives, including increased finance, market demand for averted forest emissions, and demand-side trade and public procurement policies to complement corporate commitments.

Without such a response from rich countries, the fragile progress achieved in developing countries could slide backward, as the narrative of disappointment takes hold among early proponents of forest protection linked to performance-based finance for emission reductions, and the proponents of business as usual reassert themselves. Tropical forests could again slip from the international agenda, and lost momentum would be difficult to regain. Deforestation would continue, accelerating the rate of climate change through continued emissions and diminished carbon capture and storage capacity. Climate change in turn would undermine the ecological viability of the world's dwindling tropical forests, with devastating consequences for both the climate and the world's poorest communities.

The science, the economics, and the politics are now aligned for a major international effort to conserve tropical forests, with finance the missing piece.

A brighter scenario is possible. With political and financial support from rich countries, decision makers in developing countries who plan to clear their remaining forests could be encouraged to reconsider. Rich countries could help support decisions to protect forests by providing more, more certain, and more performance-based funding than is available today to reward successful efforts to reduce emissions from deforestation. International cooperation on protecting tropical forests could prove the key to maintaining momentum on efforts to protect the climate by providing a politically attractive and economically feasible bridge to broader and more aggressive efforts to implement the Paris Agreement to reduce emissions, while at the same time improving the lives of billions of people in developing countries.

In short, the science, the economics, and the politics are now aligned for a major international effort to conserve tropical forests, with finance the missing piece.

Why a Book, and Who Should Read It?

Although some world leaders noted the linkage between tropical deforestation and climate change as early as the late 1980s, concerted international effort to reduce forest loss as a climate change mitigation strategy has ramped up only within the past decade. In late 2006 and early 2007, three analyses propelled forest-based emissions onto the global climate change agenda:

- The IPCC Fourth Assessment Report identified deforestation as a major source of the emissions that cause climate change, estimating that forest-based emissions comprised more than 17 percent of total annual emissions from all sources. This share was more than that of all the cars, planes, trains, and ships that constitute the global transportation fleet, which together were responsible for just over 13 percent.[41]
- Lord Nicholas Stern's economic analysis of climate change mitigation options, in a study commissioned by the British government, identified reducing deforestation as one of the most cost-effective strategies for reducing emissions. The study concluded that reducing emissions from deforestation had to be one of four pillars of any international framework to address climate change,

along with emissions trading, cooperation on technology, and adaptation.[42]

- A World Bank report on the relationship between deforestation and poverty identified North–South finance to reduce deforestation as an "international arbitrage opportunity" between the value of avoided emissions to the global climate protection effort and the relatively lower value of alternative land uses to local forest stewards. North–South transfers to slow deforestation could both protect the climate and promote development.[43]

Over the ten years since these reports were published, understanding of the science, economics, and politics of reducing deforestation as a win-win opportunity to address both climate change and development has advanced dramatically. New data on the extent of deforestation, new analysis of the economic drivers and consequences of forest loss, and early experience with new modes of international cooperation are among the resources now available. As the chapters that follow elaborate, recent research across disciplines further strengthens the case for a major international effort to maintain the world's remaining tropical forests.

Alongside the frenzy of activity in policy circles and among practitioners catalyzed by renewed attention to tropical forests late in the first decade of the new century, research, writing, and publication related to forests and climate change also flourished. In academia, a cohort of graduate students across disciplines selected this topic as the focus of their dissertations. Think tanks and advocacy groups churned out materials targeting negotiators and policy makers as well as forest management practitioners. As of mid-2016, a search on Google Scholar on the key words "reducing emissions deforestation" unearthed more than seventy-eight thousand articles.

So why does the world need a book on forests and climate change? First, we see a need to articulate the role of rich countries in reducing tropical deforestation as a strategy to promote global prosperity and climate stability, and in ways that go beyond traditional development aid. In particular, we present analysis designed to illuminate the gap between the potential of international results-based finance as an incentive for forest conservation and its actual deployment to date. While we provide evidence of the effectiveness of various domestic policy tools for slowing deforestation, we do so to instill confidence among rich-country audiences that success is possible, rather than to instruct developing countries on what to do. Indeed, a tenet of the payment-for-performance approach is that actors within countries are best positioned to figure out what works and ask for help when they need it.

A second reason for the book is that the recent outpouring of information and analysis on tropical forests has been consumed almost entirely by audiences within "Forestry World"—the policy makers, practitioners, researchers, and activists whose professional concentration is on forests. Key messages have not yet reached similar professionals in "Climate World" or "Development World." Forest-related panel discussions held on the sidelines of annual climate negotiations are attended almost exclusively by those already focused on forests. Climate-related negotiators, advocates, and practitioners who specialize in climate finance, clean energy, or sustainable transport often have only vague and sometimes incorrect impressions about the potential of maintaining forests as a climate change mitigation strategy.

Similarly, many experts in "Development World" remain largely unaware of the evidence that conserving tropical forests serves many of their objectives. To the contrary, the myth that zero-sum trade-offs exist between forest conservation on the one hand and economic development, agricultural production, and/or poverty reduction on the other is remarkably persistent. We have been dismayed to discover how many experts working on global health issues are unfamiliar with the concept of "ecosystem services" and how such services might relate to their agendas. Although forest conservation would serve many of the U.N. Sustainable Development Goals formulated in 2015, the text describing them and their associated targets is mostly silent on the potential contributions of forests.[44]

In short, despite the near-total domination of "Forestry World" by the focus on reducing climate emissions from deforestation in recent years, there is abundant evidence that the denizens of both "Climate World" and "Development World" do not yet fully appreciate the relevance of tropical forests to their objectives.

Misconceptions about the implications for action abound. For example, when alerted to the benefits of forests for climate and development, many people assume the best way to reap them is to plant trees. Planting trees is often a good thing to do, but it is not a substitute for reducing emissions from deforesta-

tion: when forests are cleared, emissions are released in a large pulse to the atmosphere right away, while newly planted trees accrue carbon in small increments over many years. In addition, planting trees cannot compete with maintaining existing natural forests as a way of conserving biodiversity and producing ecosystem services.

The knowledge gap has been exacerbated by the rate of change in relevant technology, analysis, and experience. Because the science, the economics, and the politics of conserving tropical forests are evolving so quickly, debates that took place less than ten years ago on issues such as the potential for measuring forest degradation, the feasibility of slowing commodity-driven conversion, and the risks to indigenous peoples from forest protection initiatives must now all be revisited in the light of new facts.

Even the professionals in Forestry World have lots of new information to assimilate. The rapid accumulation of new research, early experiences with REDD+, and broader changes in global economics and politics that have occurred since tropical forests recaptured the imagination a generation ago—and especially since the issue reemerged within the last decade—have rendered much conventional wisdom obsolete. Some changes—for example, the boom in profitability and production of commodities, such as palm oil, that destroy or degrade forests—have made the objective of protecting tropical forests harder to attain. But many goals that seemed hopelessly expensive, difficult, or risky not long ago now appear affordable, feasible, and prudent in the light of new information and experience.

Accordingly, this book synthesizes the latest evidence on the importance of tropical forests and the potential of international cooperation to conserve them, in a way that is accessible to people in both "Climate World" and "Development World." Below we summarize some of the perceptions common in each of these worlds that we aspire to challenge.

Why Climate World Undervalues Forests

Since international discussions on climate change began in the run-up to the 1992 Rio Earth Summit, negotiators, advocates, and academics have focused most of their attention on reducing emissions from fossil fuel use. The problem of emissions from land-use change has been recognized from the beginning of those discussions, but it has seldom taken center stage as the focus of mitigation strategies. More recently, developing countries have insisted on increasing attention to adaptation to climate change, but the role of forests in helping maintain the resilience of households and countries has been similarly underplayed.

Forest protection formally entered climate negotiations in 2007, and, by 2013, the parameters of a framework to finance protection—in the form of REDD+ (see box 1.1)—were largely agreed on. But the allocation of climate finance does not yet reflect the scientific and economic analysis of the importance of forests nor the political consensus on how to promote their protection. For example, while tropical forests constitute somewhere between a quarter and a third of the solution to climate change in terms of potential mitigation of current total emissions, decision makers in Climate World allocated to REDD+ only about 10 percent of the $35 billion in "fast-start finance" pledged for 2010–12.[45]

Some reasons for this mismatch stem from persistent misunderstandings and myths. International climate negotiators, for example, first considered "avoided deforestation" as an emission mitigation strategy during discussions that led to the Kyoto Protocol in 1998 and with respect to determining the kinds of projects eligible for the Clean Development Mechanism in 2001. At that time, protecting forests was relegated to the "too-hard basket," in part because of the limited ability to measure and monitor changes in forests and thus to make sufficiently accurate estimates of avoided carbon emissions. Many people still believe REDD+ cannot advance until elaborate national-level monitoring systems are in place, even though the aforementioned improvements in remote-sensing technologies are already making available sufficient data to get performance-based payments for reducing deforestation underway.

A second misunderstanding is apparent in the confusion regarding the significance of deforestation to climate change, which has been generated by statistics that combine the dual roles of forests as both sources and sinks for carbon emissions. Because periodic reports by the IPCC present the share of emissions from forests as a net number (that is, the difference between emissions from deforestation and emissions sequestered by forest regrowth), the number presented is smaller than forests' mitigation potential (which is the sum of emissions and sequestration). In other words, the IPCC number takes emissions from deforesting countries such as Indonesia and reduces them by the amount of reforestation and regrowth taking place in countries such as China. And yet reducing deforestation in Indonesia and continuing to plant trees in China are both part of the solution.

Third, myths persist among climate policymakers that emissions avoided by leaving forests standing are somehow less valuable than those avoided by leaving fossil fuels in the ground, even though their impact on the atmosphere is the same. In fact, forests left standing are arguably more valuable for the climate than fuels left underground, as they continue to serve as a natural carbon capture and storage system in a way shale oil and coal deposits do not.

Finally, another myth holds that "REDD+ has been tried and it didn't work." But if a key component of REDD+ is the certainty of large-scale, performance-based finance to reward reductions in deforestation, it has hardly been tried: only about $4 billion in results-based finance has been made available to developing countries over the past decade, mostly through bilateral agreements, and only 11 percent of the total funds pledged for multilateral REDD+ finance had been disbursed as of 2014.[46] The certainty of large-scale, performance-based finance has so far been offered to only a handful of countries.

Why Development World Underinvests in Forests

Decision making in Development World suggests similar blinders are in place to the significance of forests for development objectives. Chronic and acute setbacks to poverty eradication and growth objectives caused by forest mismanagement have seldom penetrated the boundaries between forestry and other sectors. For example, although thick smoke from periodic forest fires in Indonesia routinely closes airports and sends people to hospitals due to respiratory distress, transportation and health sector planners rarely speak up for improved forest management.

Experts in Development World can be forgiven for not seeing these linkages, because they are largely invisible. Neither subsistence income from the harvest of wild forest products nor the value of forest-based ecosystem services is captured in national statistical accounts (although World Bank initiatives are striving to remedy these omissions).[47] Standing forests are thus effectively given a value of zero in country-level economic analysis and decision making.

In addition, many elements of the conventional wisdom about the role of forests in development are incorrect. A fundamental misconception is that standing forests do not make significant contributions to development objectives. In fact, research shows that wild products collected from forests constitute an average of 21 percent of household income in communities that live in and around forests, ranging as high as 63 percent in parts of Bolivia where households gather valuable Brazil nuts.[48] Significant headroom remains to act on the evidence that forest-based ecosystem services are important to agriculture and health and support the resilience of transportation, irrigation, and hydropower infrastructure.

Thirty years ago, poor people were widely believed to be the primary agents of deforestation. Since then, the drivers of deforestation—and our understanding of how they interact—have changed. Commercial-scale clearing for agriculture is now the primary driver, and studies show higher poverty levels are more often than not associated with less rather than more deforestation.[49] But the myth about poor people as the main cause of deforestation has been stubbornly persistent.

Many development professionals believe clearing forests for agriculture is necessary to achieve food security and reduce poverty, and as of around 2005, no large, forest-rich country had yet successfully slowed deforestation before most of the forest was already gone. Brazil's success in reducing its deforestation rate in the Amazon by some 80 percent over the ensuing decade proved deforestation could be decoupled from agricultural production, with greater gains from intensifying cultivation in an area than from increasing the area under cultivation. New science is revealing the significant role of forests in maintaining the cooler, wetter climates that support agricultural productivity at continental scales, in addition to providing local hydrological, pollination, and other services.

Another challenge is the reputation the forestry sector has gained among donor agencies for being difficult. Indeed, donors have tended to avoid engaging in forest-related activities precisely because of perceived risks of association with the corruption and land rights conflicts endemic to the sector. While forests do, indeed, present challenging and complex issues, such perceptions may overestimate the risks to investing in the sector compared to those of undertaking other strategies to address climate or development goals. Of more than one hundred claims brought to the World Bank's Inspection Panel over its twenty-two-year history, only five concerned forestry projects, while another eight involved the impacts on forests of lending in other sectors, such as mining and hydropower.[50]

Early in the development of REDD+, some were deeply concerned about the risks of unintended negative consequences of assigning monetary value to forest carbon, especially for indigenous communities. The slogan of indigenous activists at the 2007 climate negotiations in Bali was "No Rights, No REDD." While some indigenous groups remain opposed to REDD+, and in particular to private markets for forest carbon offsets, many have cautiously embraced the potential of valuing their forests for global climate protection as a way of strengthening their rights and generating revenue.

Furthermore, early experience with REDD+ initiatives suggests engagement on a payment-for-performance basis can promote improved governance, because it requires transparency and the clarification of responsibility for forest management outcomes. Indigenous peoples in several countries, for example, are using the political processes and funding flows opened by REDD+ to assert their customary rights over forests.

Indeed, many of the actions needed to reduce deforestation are the same as those needed to promote improved governance. Increased transparency and accountability in land-use decision making, for instance, reduces opportunities for corruption, and clarification of land tenure can help strengthen the rights of indigenous peoples and reduce rural conflict.

In sum, the purpose of this book is to provide an understanding of the science, the economics, and the politics of mobilizing tropical forests in the service of climate change mitigation and development. In both climate and development policy arenas, large gaps remain between the implications of recent research and current actions to incorporate those findings into decision making. By raising awareness of the importance of tropical forests to both climate and development goals, we aim to help close those gaps. Our hope is that greater understanding will stimulate action on the most promising ways forward—especially scaled-up payment-for-performance finance—with a focus on what rich countries can do.

Road Map to the Rest of the Book

The rest of this book comprises three sections summarizing the science, economics, and politics of international cooperation to protect forests for climate and development, plus a chapter on REDD+ finance and a final chapter on the way forward.

The Science

Chapter 2 explains the biophysical relationships between tropical deforestation and the greenhouse gas emissions that cause climate change. The chapter emphasizes how forest loss is a significant source of global emissions, while standing forests offer a safe and natural carbon capture and storage system.

Chapter 3 presents the rapidly evolving science linking tropical forests to the achievement of goals related to development and poverty reduction through the provision of ecosystem services. The chapter synthesizes studies describing how forests provide benefits to water, energy, agriculture, health, safety, and climate adaptation.

Chapter 4 describes how forest monitoring has undergone a "data revolution" in less than a decade. Technological advances in remote sensing are enabling increasingly precise and timely measurement of changes in forest cover and associated carbon emissions.

The Economics

Chapter 5 analyzes the costs of forest emission reductions relative to reductions in other sectors and discusses the uses and limitations of marginal abatement cost curves to assess emission mitigation options. The chapter presents fresh analysis confirming that the inclusion of forest conservation in climate mitigation strategies is a "best bet" for achieving more, cheaper, and faster global emission reductions.

Chapter 6 summarizes the accumulating evidence of the economic value of the direct contributions tropical forests make to development objectives. The chapter discusses the reasons monetizing forest-based ecosystem services, such as regulation of the quantity and quality of water, has proved difficult and why carbon might be different.

Chapter 7 provides an analysis of how Brazil succeeded in taming deforestation in the Amazon. The chapter also synthesizes decades of research on what causes and what slows deforestation, illuminating the policy levers that can be pulled to reverse forest loss.

Chapter 8 describes how the expansion of land area devoted to the production of globally traded commodities is now the leading driver of tropical deforestation. The chapter explains how the policies of consumer countries related to biofuel subsidies and imports of illegally produced forest products can either accelerate or attenuate forest loss.

The Politics

Chapter 9 analyzes how the international politics of protecting tropical forests have shifted from North–South antagonism in the 1980s to global agreement on REDD+. It analyzes how the linkage to climate change has created the most favorable environment for international cooperation on forests than has ever existed.

Chapter 10 describes how the politics of forest exploitation and conservation has evolved within forest-rich developing countries over the past generation, with a special emphasis on Brazil and Indonesia. The chapter explains how international political support and finance can interact with domestic political forces to tip the balance away from deforestation as usual.

Chapter 11 summarizes how political constituencies in selected donor countries have aligned to support international cooperation to protect tropical forests. The prospect of cost-effective climate emission reductions has been layered onto other motivations for helping developing countries improve forest management, including domestic and colonial-era forest histories, concern about threats to biological diversity and indigenous cultures, and desire to protect domestic forest industries.

Chapter 12 assesses the state of international REDD+ finance. The chapter documents how funding has been too low, too slow, and too constrained by the politics and procedures of development assistance, and it highlights prospects for alternative sources of finance that are better fitted to the purpose.

In Chapter 13, we summarize the key conclusions from previous chapters and their implications for actions needed from rich countries. We argue that current approaches to international cooperation to protect tropical forests are badly out of date. Tropical forests should be much higher on the list of funding priorities for climate protection and development, and a larger share of such finance should be provided on a payment-for-performance basis.

Notes

1. National Oceanic and Atmospheric Administration (NOAA), "Mitch: The Deadliest Atlantic Hurricane since 1780," National Climatic Data Center, January 23, 2009, http://www.ncdc.noaa.gov/oa/reports/mitch/mitch.html.
2. World Bank, "Poverty and Equity Regional Dashboard: Latin America & Caribbean," October 9, 2014, http://povertydata.worldbank.org/poverty/region/LAC.
3. Ibid. All dollar signs indicate U.S. dollars unless otherwise noted.
4. K. Brandon, "Ecosystem Services from Tropical Forests: Review of Current Science," CGD Working Paper 380, Center for Global Development, Washington, DC, 2014.
5. NOAA, "Mitch."
6. Ibid.
7. C. Humphrey and A. E. Robertson, *Honduras and the Bay Islands* (Berkeley, CA: Avalon Travel, 2009).
8. D. R. Cahoon and P. Hensel, "Hurricane Mitch: A Regional Perspective on Mangrove Damage, Recovery and Sustainability," USGS Open File Report OFR 03-183, U.S. Geological Survey and U.S. Department of the Interior, 2002.
9. Ibid.
10. World Bank, "GDP Per Capita Growth (Annual %)," World Development Indicators, World Bank, Washington, DC.
11. S. M. Hsiang and A. S. Jina, "The Causal Effect of Environmental Catastrophe on Long-Run Economic Growth: Evidence from 6,700 Cyclones," National Bureau of Economic Research, NBER Working Paper w20352, 2014, 1–69.
12. NOAA, "Mitch."
13. S. I. Seneviratne et al., "Changes in Climate Extremes and Their Impacts on the Natural Physical Environment," in *Managing the Risks of Extreme Events and Disasters to Advance Climate Change Adaptation: A Special Report of Working Groups I and II of the Intergovernmental Panel on Climate Change (IPCC)*, ed. C. B. Field et al., 109–230 (Cambridge, UK, and New York: Cambridge University Press, 2012); A. Sobel et al., "Human Influence on Tropical Cyclone Intensity," *Science* 353, no. 6296 (2016): 242–46.
14. C. B. Field et al., eds., *Climate Change 2014: Impacts, Adaptation, and Vulnerability. Part A: Global and Sectoral Aspects. Contribution of Working Group II to the Fifth Assessment Report of the Intergovernmental Panel on Climate Change* (Cambridge, UK, and New York: Cambridge University Press, 2014).
15. R. Goodman and M. Herold, "Why Maintaining Tropical Forests Is Essential and Urgent for a Stable Climate," CGD Working Paper 385, Center for Global Development, Washington, DC, 2014.
16. See M. C. Hansen et al., "High-Resolution Global Maps of 21st-Century Forest Cover Change," *Science* 342 (2013): 850–53. According to Hansen and colleagues, annual tropical deforestation (using a 25 percent threshold for tree cover) is approximately eighty-five thousand square kilometers. The size of Austria is eighty-three thousand square kilometers.
17. J. Busch and J. Engelmann, "The Future of Forests: Emissions from Deforestation With and Without Carbon Pricing Policies, 2015–2050," CGD Working Paper 411, Center for Global Development, Washington, DC, 2015.
18. Ibid.
19. Ibid.
20. U.S. Environmental Protection Agency, "The Social Cost of Carbon," updated February 2016, https://www3.epa.gov/climatechange/EPAactivities/economics/scc.html.
21. Busch and Engelmann, "The Future of Forests."
22. A. Angelsen et al., "Environmental Income and Rural Livelihoods: A Global-Comparative Analysis," *World Development* 64 (2014): S12–28.
23. D. Lawrence and K. Vandecar, "Effects of Tropical Deforestation on Climate and Agriculture," *Nature Climate Change* 5, no. 1 (2015): 27–36.

24. M. Wolosin and D. Lee, "US Support for REDD+: Reflections on the Past and Future Outlook," CGD Policy Paper 48, Center for Global Development, Washington, DC, 2014.

25. F. A. Fogliano de Souza Cunha et al., "The Implementation Costs of Forest Conservation Policies in Brazil," *Ecological Economics* 130 (2016): 209–20.

26. U. M. Persson, S. Henders, and T. Kastner, "Trading Forests: Quantifying the Contribution of Global Commodity Markets to Emissions from Tropical Deforestation," CGD Working Paper 384, Center for Global Development, Washington, DC, 2014.

27. Ibid.

28. U.S. Geological Survey, "USGS Landsat Global Archive," http://landsat.usgs.gov/USGSLandsatGlobalArchive.php.

29. Organisation for Economic Co-operation and Development (OECD), "The Paris Declaration on Aid Effectiveness and the Accra Agenda for Action," Paris, France, 2005/2008.

30. N. Birdsall and W. Savedoff, *Cash on Delivery: A New Approach to Foreign Aid* (Washington, DC: Center for Global Development Books, 2010).

31. R. Perakis and W. Savedoff, "Does Results-Based Aid Change Anything? Pecuniary Interests, Attention, Accountability and Discretion in Four Case Studies," CGD Policy Paper 53, Center for Global Development, Washington, DC, 2015.

32. M. Peters-Stanley and D. Yin, "Maneuvering the Mosaic: State of the Voluntary Carbon Markets 2013," Forest Trends' Ecosystem Marketplace and Bloomberg New Energy Finance, 2013, http://www.forest-trends.org/documents/files/doc_3898.pdf.

33. W. Sunderlin et al., "The Challenge of Establishing REDD+ on the Ground: Insights from 23 Subnational Initiatives in Six Countries," CIFOR Occasional Paper 104, Center for International Forestry Research, Bogor, Indonesia, 2014.

34. The authors first heard this expression used by Donna Lee in September 2013.

35. Governors' Climate & Forests Task Force, "Rio Branco Declaration: Building Partnerships & Securing Support for Forests, Climate & Livelihoods," Rio Branco, Brazil, August 11, 2014.

36. Signatories of the New York Declaration on Forests, "UN Climate Summit: New York Declaration on Forests," United Nations, New York, September 2014.

37. Signatories of the Lima Challenge, "Lima Challenge," United Nations Framework Convention on Climate Change Conference of Parties, Lima, Peru, December 9, 2014.

38. R. Butler, "Palm Oil Major Makes Deforestation-Free Commitment," Mongabay.com, February 3, 2015, http://news.mongabay.com/2015/0203-ioi-group-palm-oil.html.

39. Pope Francis, Encyclical Letter Laudato Si of the Holy Father Francis on Care for Our Common Home (Vatican: The Holy See, 2015).

40. United Nations, "Historic New Sustainable Development Agenda Unanimously Adopted by 193 UN Members," Sustainable Development blog, September 25, 2015, http://www.un.org/sustainabledevelopment/blog/2015/09/historic-new-sustainable-development-agenda-unanimously-adopted-by-193-un-members/.

41. R. K. Pachauri and A. Reisinger, eds., *Climate Change 2007 Synthesis Report: Summary for Policymakers* (Geneva, Switzerland: Intergovernmental Panel on Climate Change Secretariat, 2007).

42. N. Stern, *The Economics of Climate Change: The Stern Review* (Cambridge, UK: Cambridge University Press, 2007).

43. K. Chomitz, *At Loggerheads? Agricultural Expansion, Poverty Reduction, and Environment in the Tropical Forests* (Washington, DC: World Bank, 2007).

44. F. Seymour, "SDG Fifteen: Four Observations on Forests," Global Development: Views from the Center blog, Center for Global Development, April 6,

2015, http://www.cgdev.org/blog/sdg-goal-fifteen-four-observations-forests.

45. S. Nakhooda et al., "Mobilising International Climate Finance: Lessons from the Fast-Start Finance Period," Overseas Development Institute, World Resources Institute, Institute of Global Environmental Strategies, and Open Climate Network, 2013.

46. M. Norman and S. Nakhooda, "The State of REDD+ Finance," CGD Working Paper 378, Center for Global Development, Washington, DC, 2014 (updated 2015).

47. See, for instance, the Wealth Accounting and the Valuation of Ecosystem Services (WAVES) initiative at e. For more information on the initiative, visit http://www.wavespartnership.org.

48. A. Angelsen et al., "Environmental Income and Rural Livelihoods."

49. K. Ferretti-Gallon and J. Busch, "What Drives Deforestation and What Stops It? A Meta-Analysis of Spatially Explicit Econometric Studies," CGD Working Paper 361, Center for Global Development, Washington, DC, 2014.

50. World Bank Group, *World Bank Group Forest Action Plan FY16–20* (Washington, DC: World Bank, 2016).

Forest fires light up the night sky in Thailand.
Credit: KobchaiMa/Shutterstock

CHAPTER 2

Tropical Forests

A Large Share of Climate Emissions; an Even Larger Share of Potential Emission Reductions

ndonesia, 2015. Between January and October 2015, more than 127,000 fires broke out across Indonesia,[1] burning an area larger than the state of New Jersey.[2] On many days, the fires generated more greenhouse gas emissions than the whole economy of the United States.[3] Why was the world's third largest expanse of tropical rainforest going up in flames?

Large-scale fires in 1982–83 in East Kalimantan—a province in the Indonesian portion of Borneo—provided an early clue. A weather pattern called *El Niño* (Spanish for "the boy," a reference to the Christ child, due to its tendency to arrive on the west coast of South America at Christmas time) had prolonged the dry season that year, but that was not sufficient to explain the fires. Historically, Indonesia's rainforests had proved resistant to burning, even during exceptionally long dry seasons. Traditional swidden agriculturalists—whose method of farming relies on the rotational cultivation of small forest plots—had to work hard to fell and burn areas of mature forest so they could clear land to grow upland rice.

But in the decades preceding 1982, East Kalimantan's forests had been opened up to industrial-scale logging. Openings in the canopy caused by road building and the felling of tall dipterocarp trees had allowed the fierce equatorial sun to dry patches of the forest floor. Large volumes of logging waste—stumps, treetops, and branches left behind when logs were hauled away and smaller

trees pulled down by vines or damaged by bulldozers—provided abundant tinder.

The next *El Niño* event came in 1997–98. In the intervening fifteen years, logging had continued to degrade and fragment remaining forests across the Indonesian archipelago. In addition, large areas of peat swamps had now been disturbed, exposing to the air previously waterlogged organic matter—peat—that had accumulated over hundreds or even thousands of years to a depth of several meters. Peatlands are among the world's most carbon-rich ecosystems, and, when drained, they become extremely flammable.

Especially on the island of Sumatra, peatland forests were cleared, drained, and converted to oil palm and fast-growing timber plantations. In addition, a million hectares of peat swamp forests in Central Kalimantan—an area the size of Jamaica (see box 2.1)—were slated for conversion into rice paddies as part of an ill-fated effort by the Suharto regime to ensure Indonesia's food self-sufficiency. Over the course of eighteen months starting in January 1996, big yellow machines cleared the forest and dug some four thousand kilometers of canals to drain the swamps.[4]

Under these conditions, fires set to clear land in 1997 quickly spread out of control. While intact forests remained relatively resistant to burning—with only 5.7 percent of their area affected, compared to 59 percent of logged forests in East Kalimantan[5]—by October 1997, Indonesia's damaged forests and drained peatlands had ignited on a vast scale. What was possibly the largest tropical fire in history engulfed 9.7 million hectares[6]—an area the size of South Korea—and continued burning into the early months of 1998.

This chapter draws heavily on a background paper by Rosa Goodman and Martin Herold synthesizing the science on the linkages between deforestation and climate change.

Misery inflicted on local communities by the fires and thick smoke (euphemistically called "haze") was extreme. Some 15,600 child, infant, and fetal deaths were attributed to respiratory distress caused by the smoke, with impacts worse in poorer areas.[7]

The fires and smoke also affected Indonesia's neighbors. One study estimated that residents of Kuala Lumpur experienced a 7 percent higher risk of mortality during the fires due to the high concentrations of particulates.[8] Soot created a haze so thick and expansive that the low visibility closed airports and caused flight cancellations in neighboring Malaysia and Singapore, causing "severe" losses to the tourism sector.[9]

The impact of the fires extended globally, as well. Supercharged by the carbon-rich peat soils, the climate change potency of the smoke from Indonesia's fires was espe-

Figure 2.1: Deforestation remains a significant contributor to climate change even as emissions from other sectors have grown faster.

Total annual greenhouse gas emissions 1970–2010

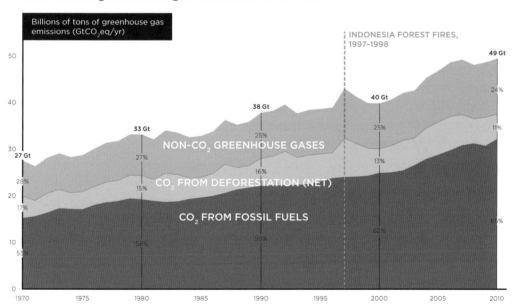

Source: O. Edenhofer et al., eds., *Climate Change 2014: Mitigation of Climate Change.* Contribution of Working Group III to the Fifth Assessment Report of the Intergovernmental Panel on Climate Change (Cambridge University Press, Cambridge, UK, and New York: Cambridge University Press, 2014).

Note: Deforestation represents net emissions from gross forest cover loss and degradation less removals by forest regrowth.

How large is . . . ?

1 hectare = baseball or rugby field
1,000 hectares = large university campus
1,000,000 hectares = Jamaica
1,000,000,000 hectares = Canada

How much is . . . ?

1 ton of CO_2 = emissions from a typical U.S. household's monthly energy consumption
1,000 tons of CO_2 = emissions from a passenger airplane flight across the United States
1,000,000 tons of CO_2 = annual emissions from the Maldives
1,000,000,000 tons of CO_2 = annual emissions from Japan

Source: Authors' calculations.

cially intense. In fact, the greenhouse gas emissions released by the Indonesian forest fires of 1997–98 represented 13 to 40 percent of annual emissions from fossil fuels.[10] This contributed to the discernible spike in global emissions seen in figure 2.1—the largest annual increase of carbon dioxide in the atmosphere in history.[11] Estimates of the total economic costs of the fires ranged between US$4.5 billion and $6.3 billion.[12] Distressingly, the 2015 fires were even more damaging, costing the Indonesian economy more than $16 billion.[13]

As it would in 2015, the massive scale of the Indonesian forest fires in 1997 caught the world's attention. International news networks carried heartbreaking images of singed baby orangutans, accompanied by the voices of breathless reporters. Meanwhile, the degradation, clearing, and burning of tropical forests that were proceeding in significant, if less spectacular, fashion in many other countries received little, if any, media attention. Yet each time a forest was burned, converted to another land use, or depleted by the removal of timber and fuelwood, the carbon previously stored in the trees would be released into the atmosphere.

The climate damage from this deforestation and forest degradation was and remains massive (see definition of deforestation in box 2.2). As shown in figure 2.1, net emissions from deforestation constitute more than 10 percent of total global emissions, most of which comes from tropical regions.[14] While this percentage has fallen over time, this is not because deforestation has diminished. Rather, it is because emissions from burning fossil fuels have risen more quickly.[15]

Meanwhile, the potential contribution of tropical forests to fighting climate change is considerably larger than deforestation's share of emissions. That's because emissions from deforestation can be not just driven to zero, but made negative. As this chapter will explain, halting all tropical deforestation while allowing damaged tropical forests to recover could reduce global net emissions by as much as 30 percent.

Altogether, emissions from tropical deforestation and degradation exceed those of the European Union. Nobody would suggest fighting climate change without addressing the emissions of a bloc the size of Europe, yet in both Europe and the United States, tropical deforestation is routinely omitted from discussions of climate change or is treated as an afterthought. True, the geography, politics, and industries involved are different; but, as with the need to address Europe's emissions, the climate problem simply cannot be solved without tackling tropical deforestation. Indeed, according to the Intergovernmental Panel on Climate Change (IPCC), every scenario in which the world stabilizes global warming below 2°C (3.6°F) involves halting and massively reversing deforestation.[16]

People in Europe, North America, and other developed countries are rightfully concerned about what they can do to fight climate change at home—by using clean energy, fuel-efficient vehicles, and so on. But fewer are aware that additional, attractive action can be taken by conserving and restoring forests in tropical countries. People living outside the tropics may be less familiar with the phenomenon of tropical deforestation than they are with burning fossil fuels. After all, for many, cars, factories, and power plants are fixtures of modern life, while tropical forests are the stuff of nature documentaries. In this chapter we aim to bring readers up to date on the rapidly advancing science of tropical deforestation and climate change.

Climate change stems from two problems: a well-known energy problem and a lesser-known land problem. No aspect of the land problem is more significant than tropical deforestation. We begin this chapter by summarizing the latest science on how tropical deforestation and forest degradation contribute to the climate problem and how halting and reversing forest loss can contribute to the climate solution. We explain why tree-planting programs are no substitute for reducing deforestation. We present the recent distribution and trends in tropical deforestation. And we discuss the potential impacts of climate change on tropical forests.

Forests: The Other Half of the Climate Story

Many people in developed countries know only half of the climate story. It's the half that involves fossil fuels, and it goes like this:

When plants and animals that lived millions of years ago died in swamps or shallow seas, their remains sank and were buried under layers of mud. Over the course of eons this buried organic material was compressed and heated underground, where it formed into vast deposits of solid coal, liquid oil, and methane gas.

People realized as long ago as ancient Chinese and Roman times that they could obtain more energy from burning fossil fuels than they could from burning wood or charcoal. They've been burning them ever since, with a steep acceleration since the Industrial Revolution. Today the world burns tens of billions of tons of fossil fuels every year to fire power plants, run factories, fill gas tanks, and much else.

The carbon that was pulled from the atmosphere by prehistoric plants and captured undergroud over millions of years is now being released back to the atmosphere within a geological blink of an eye. And every atom of the carbon that's burned combines with two atoms of oxygen, meaning that every ton of carbon burned on the ground emits 3.67 tons of carbon dioxide (CO_2) gas to the atmosphere. All this burning has raised the concentration of carbon dioxide in the atmosphere from 275 parts per million in preindustrial times to 400 parts per million in 2016, and it continues to climb.

Once in the atmosphere, carbon dioxide traps solar energy that would otherwise return to space, heating the earth like a blanket. A hotter planet leads to bigger storms, rising sea levels, tougher growing conditions for crops, and other problems. As discussed in chapter 1, the impacts of climate change hit developing countries especially hard.

This part of the story is well known, but another side to it is less widely recognized. As illustrated in figure 2.2, less than half of the carbon dioxide that's emitted by burning fossil fuels actually accumulates in the atmosphere; just over a quarter goes into the ocean. And it turns out that the ocean isn't a very good place for carbon dioxide to accumulate, either. When carbon dioxide dissolves in seawater, it forms carbonic acid, which breaks down the calcium carbonate marine animals

Figure 2.2: Since 1750, deforestation has been responsible for one-third of emissions; forests have been responsible for half of natural uptake.

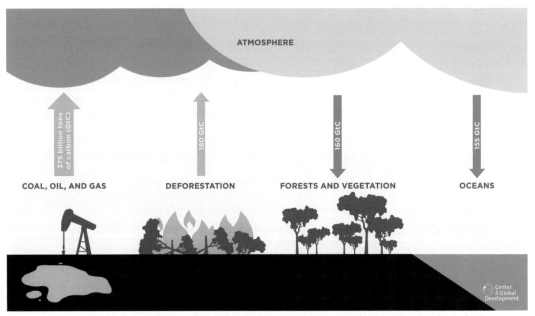

Source: P. Ciais et al., "Carbon and Other Biogeochemical Cycles," in *Climate Change 2013: The Physical Science Basis.* Contribution of Working Group I to the Fifth Assessment Report of the Intergovernmental Panel on Climate Change, ed. T. F. Stocker, D. Qin, G. K. Plattner, M. Tignor, S. K. Allen, J. Boschung, A. Nauels, Y. Xia, V. Bex, and P. M. Midgley (Cambridge, UK, and New York: Cambridge University Press, 2013).

need to form hard shells.[17] Ocean acidification threatens the marine life that billions of people depend on for food.[18]

The remaining quarter or so of carbon dioxide emissions that don't go into the atmosphere or ocean are taken up by forests and other vegetation. Because of the emissions going into forests and the ocean, the concentration of greenhouse gases in the atmosphere is increasing by only two parts per million each year rather than four parts per million.[19] Together with the ocean, forests form a natural buffer against climate change.[20]

Unlike the atmosphere or ocean, forests are a good destination for excess carbon. Forests are a safe, natural, available "carbon capture and storage" (CCS) system.[21] Not only that, but forests provide many side benefits, or "co-benefits," for development, as we discuss at length in chapters 3 and 6. They clean water for downstream irrigation and hydroelectricity production; they are a source of lifesaving medicines; they buffer towns from the impacts of deadly storms.

A logical response to climate change would be to take more carbon out of the atmosphere by preserving and enhancing forests on a massive scale. But instead we're still doing the opposite. Every year from 2000 to 2014, the world cleared forest from areas totaling the size of North Dakota, of which half, an area the size of Maine, was in the high-carbon tropics.[22]

When forests are burned and cleared to be turned into cropland or pasture, carbon dioxide in the atmosphere rises three times over, as shown in figure 2.3. First, a net flow of carbon from the atmosphere into forests is ended. Trees take carbon dioxide out of the atmosphere as they grow, capturing carbon through photosynthesis and turning it into trunks, branches, leaves, and roots. When trees die and decay, they release this carbon back to the atmosphere. In a mature forest, growing trees absorb slightly more carbon than dying trees release, with excess carbon going into the soil as dead vegetation decomposes. Individually, big old trees actually remove carbon from the atmosphere faster than smaller, younger trees[23] —a discovery made in 2014 that overturned long-standing conventional wisdom. When forests are cleared, this "sink" steadily absorbing carbon from the atmosphere is lost.

Forests are a safe, natural, available "carbon capture and storage" system.

Second, deforestation causes the rapid release of the massive stock of carbon that has accumulated over decades or centuries in trees and soil. In the tropics, this typically happens through burning, as smallholder farmers and large agribusinesses alike set fires deliberately as a profitable and immediate way to clear forests and maintain fields. Fires can also start inadvertently, either because intentionally set fires escape or because openings in the forest canopy allow sunlight to penetrate and dry out vegetation past the point of flammability. Intense fires can even burn the soil. Burning forests release not only carbon dioxide, but more potent greenhouse gases such as methane, nitrous oxide, ozone-forming compounds, and black carbon (soot). Even when forests are cleared without

Figure 2.3: Natural forests capture CO$_2$; deforestation releases CO$_2$.

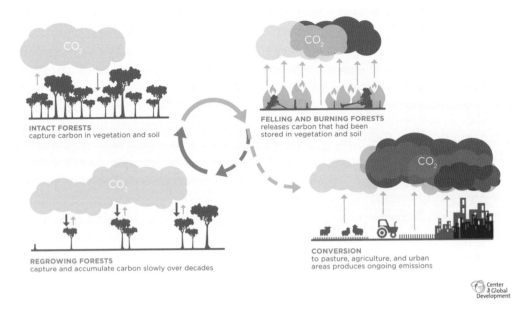

INTACT FORESTS
capture carbon in vegetation and soil

FELLING AND BURNING FORESTS
releases carbon that had been
stored in vegetation and soil

REGROWING FORESTS
capture and accumulate carbon slowly over decades

CONVERSION
to pasture, agriculture, and urban
areas produces ongoing emissions

Center
& Global
Development

using fire, their carbon still reaches the atmosphere eventually when dead trees decompose.

Finally, the land uses that replace forests following deforestation, such as growing crops, grazing animals, and mining, are all sources of carbon dioxide and other greenhouse gases. Deforestation is closely linked with agricultural expansion, as agriculture accounts for around 85 percent of forest clearing in the tropics, and half of all new agricultural land comes at the expense of tropical forests.[24] Agriculture itself is a major contributor to climate change, responsible for about 11 percent of global greenhouse gas emissions during the first decade of the 2000s.[25] Mining and urban expansion account for a smaller portion of deforestation but can be extremely damaging.[26] These activities contaminate the soil to the point where even serious afforestation or reclamation efforts may be unable to bring the forests back.[27]

Deforestation heats the planet in several other ways not directly related to carbon dioxide. Deforestation changes the amount of heat that land absorbs from sunshine, which as explained below has a warming effect in the tropics. Deforestation can cause localized warming by altering weather patterns.[28] Conversion from forests to agriculture can release greenhouse gases other than carbon dioxide; much of the damage to the atmosphere from agriculture comes from methane and nitrous oxide from livestock, rice paddies, fertilizers, and other sources.[29]

All in all, deforestation heats the planet by eliminating carbon sinks, releasing carbon stocks, and making way for new carbon sources, as well as by increasing local heat absorption, altering local weather patterns, and producing noncarbon dioxide greenhouse gases. Of these harms, the largest is the rapid release of the carbon stock from forests to the atmosphere. It is this harm we refer to explicitly throughout the book, while recognizing that the other harms occur as well.

Of course, forests are not just damaged and destroyed; they also can and do regrow. When damaged forests are left to regenerate naturally, or once-forested fields are replanted with trees, carbon gradually returns to the forest. In this respect, forests are different from industrial sources of emissions, which are effectively a one-way street by which carbon travels to the atmosphere.

But in the tropics, forests aren't usually left to regrow after they are cleared.[30] Deforested land is usually permanently converted to pasture or cropland. Traditional swidden agriculture, which allows for regrowth through rotation, is responsible for only a small portion of tropical deforestation. Rotational timber plantations, while on the rise, are still far less common in the tropics than in temperate countries.

Since the carbon dioxide that is emitted from deforestation or sequestered—that is, captured—through forest regrowth is completely identical on a molecular level to that released from burning coal, oil, and gas, tropical forests are equally worthy as a target for efforts to reduce emissions. This is the case even though forests that are conserved today might still be cleared later. A parallel can be drawn to fossil fuels: slowing down the burning of fossil fuels is good for the climate, even though large reservoirs of coal, oil, and gas remain underground for potential use in the future. The same holds true for forests—slowing emissions to the atmosphere from deforestation is of value even though the stock of carbon in conserved forests remains at risk.

Just as some fossil fuels are worse for the climate than others—burning coal produces more carbon dioxide per unit of energy than burning natural gas, for example—the same is true of deforestation. Burning and clearing tall, dense forests produces more carbon dioxide emissions per unit of land area than clearing low, sparse forests. Forests around

---

Box 2.2: Definition of Deforestation

Despite decades of debate among scientists and policymakers, "deforestation" has no universally accepted definition.[a] In this book, we use the term to describe any loss of forest—that is, any change from land covered by trees to land with no or few trees. This so-called "land-cover change" definition differs from a "land-use change" definition, in which the term "deforestation" is only applied if land stripped of trees is subsequently converted to farms or other uses. In 1999, forester Gyde Lund recommended the UNFCCC use the land-cover change definition, as it is both more appropriate for measuring changes in carbon stocks and more intuitive to the general public.[b] We agree.

a. E. Romijn et al., "Exploring Different Forest Definitions and Their Impact on Developing REDD+ Reference Emission Levels: A Case Study for Indonesia," *Environmental Science & Policy* 33 (2013): 246–59.

b. H. G. Lund, "A 'Forest' by Any Other Name," *Environmental Science & Policy* 2, no. 2 (1999): 125–33.

the world vary widely in terms of their carbon content per area of land, or "carbon density." Generally, tropical forests store more aboveground carbon than temperate forests, which in turn store more carbon than high-latitude boreal forests. Even within tropical forests, tremendous diversity exists. Wet rainforests store more carbon than dry forests; lowland forests often store more carbon than forests at higher elevations. Forests also vary in the services they provide, as elaborated in chapter 3. For example, high-altitude cloud forests provide water; riparian forests stabilize stream banks; and mangrove forests protect coastlines.

Deforestation takes a particularly severe toll on the atmosphere when it happens on carbon-rich peat soil.[31] Peat is a thick, waterlogged organic soil in which partially decomposed plant material has accumulated over centuries.[32] Peat swamps are found across much of Indonesia and Malaysia, as well as parts of Africa, South America, and elsewhere.[33] When peat swamps are stripped of their protective forest vegetation and drained of water by canals, previously inundated soil is left exposed above the water table, where it comes into contact with air and sunlight. The carbon in this newly exposed soil oxidizes and decays, leaking greenhouse gases to the atmosphere for decades. And there's a lot of carbon to leak—peat swamps can contain two thousand tons of carbon per hectare below ground. As illustrated in figure 2.4, this is an order of magnitude more than in tropical forests' aboveground vegetation. Peatlands cover just 3 percent of global land area, but they store 20 to 25 percent of all soil carbon.[34]

Even worse, when peatlands are drained, they become dry and flammable—and peat fires are fiendishly difficult to extinguish.[35] They can burn underground for years, reigniting periodically, until the land is rewetted by blocking up canals; this is the case with the peat fires in Indonesia described at the beginning of this chapter. Massive fires have recurred in Kalimantan and Sumatra nearly every year since 1997, with particularly severe outbreaks in 2002, 2005, 2006, 2009, 2013, and 2015.

Another type of deforestation especially damaging to the climate is the destruction of mangrove forests, which fringe many tropical coastlines. Mangrove forests store an average of one thousand tons of carbon per hectare in their soils.[36] They are also nurseries for offshore fisheries, and they protect coastal villages from storm surges and tsunami waves, as described in chapter 3. Mangroves are being cleared two to four times as fast as inland tropical forests for shrimp farms, tourism, and other coastal uses.[37]

In addition to full deforestation, the atmosphere suffers from so-called "forest degradation." In forests that are left standing, logging, fuelwood extraction, fires, and grazing often wear down carbon stocks faster than they can naturally recover. Emissions from degradation are around 12 to 16 percent as large as emissions from deforestation, with substantial variation across countries.[38] As well as causing climate emissions in its own right, forest degradation can be a precursor to outright deforestation. Logging roads increase the vulnerability of forests to fire and make it easier for people to gain access to them and convert them to pasture or cropland.

Figure 2.4: Conversion of peat forests releases large volumes of carbon from below ground.

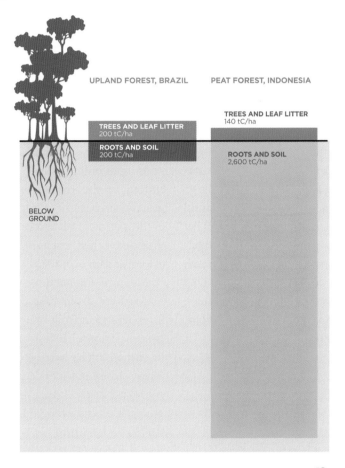

UPLAND FOREST, BRAZIL   PEAT FOREST, INDONESIA

TREES AND LEAF LITTER
140 tC/ha

TREES AND LEAF LITTER
200 tC/ha

ROOTS AND SOIL
200 tC/ha

ROOTS AND SOIL
2,600 tC/ha

BELOW
GROUND

Center for Global Development

Sources: Y. Malhi et al., "Comprehensive Assessment of Carbon Productivity, Allocation and Storage in Three Amazonian Forests," *Global Change Biology* 5, no. 15 (2009): 1255–74; J. Jaenicke et al., "Determination of the Amount of Carbon Stored in Indonesian Peatlands," *Geoderma* 147, no. 3 (2008): 151–58.

Why Focus on Tropical Forests?

Developed countries in temperate latitudes have been clearing their forests for centuries. Forests once blanketed nearly the entirety of Europe,[39] and it is said that at the time of European settlement in North America, a squirrel could hop from the Mississippi River to the Atlantic Ocean without ever leaving the treetops.[40] Centuries of clearing forests, however—first for firewood and timber and later for farmland—transfigured the landscapes of Europe, North America, Australia, and East Asia. Temperate forests today cover only half as much land as they did originally, and just

1 percent or so of the forest cover has been left in its original state.[41]

Several centuries of temperate deforestation have taken a major toll on the climate. Until 1912, changes in land use, not fossil fuels, were the predominant source of annual greenhouse gas emissions. Not until the 1960s did fossil fuels surpass land use as the largest cumulative contributor of greenhouse gases to the atmosphere.[42] Even today, about one-third of all cumulative, human-caused greenhouse gas emissions have been from changes in land use. While combustion of fossil fuels has produced about 375 billion metric tons[43] since 1750, net land-use change has produced around 180 billion tons over the same time period, as shown in figure 2.2, with deforestation before 1750 contributing another 27 billion tons.[44] Much of this land-use change took place in Europe, North America, and temperate Asia.

Looking just at net emissions from deforestation underestimates the potential contribution of forests to reducing greenhouse gases in the atmosphere.

Earth's original temperate forests are mostly gone now, with the majority of remaining old-growth forests inside scattered protected areas. Deforestation in temperate latitudes has given way in recent decades to rotational forestry, in which timber companies plant about as many trees as they cut. This type of land use is far more benign from a climate standpoint than permanently converting forest to other uses, since forest regrowth nearly neutralizes net carbon emissions from timber harvest.[45] For the past twenty-five years, nearly all temperate countries have reported stable or increasing forest cover.[46] Although temperate forests often suffer severe losses to wildfires or pest outbreaks,[47] many tree species in them are adapted to fire, so, unlike tropical trees, they are more likely to regenerate after such events.[48]

In contrast, ever since the 1960s, the chainsaws and bulldozers of deforestation have shifted to the tropics, where deforestation greatly outpaces forest regrowth.[49] About half of the world's gross deforestation (that is, total forest-cover loss) but less than one-third of forest-cover gain occurs in tropical countries.[50]

Hectare for hectare, the damage to the atmosphere from tropical deforestation is far worse than from temperate deforestation because tropical forests are so much richer in carbon.[51] The average hectare of tropical forest stores 164 metric tons of carbon aboveground in trees and vegetation—2.7 times as much as the average temperate forest (61 tC/ha) and 3.5 times as much as the average boreal forest (47 tC/ha).[52] All in all, tropical forests contain approximately 470 billion tons of carbon—more than half the world's terrestrial carbon, and nearly twice the amount that has accumulated in the atmosphere since the Industrial Revolution (240 billion tons).[53]

Deforestation warms the planet more when it takes place in the tropics for another reason as well, related to the reflection of sunlight. Because of the "albedo effect," dark surfaces absorb more heat than light ones, as anyone who has worn a black outfit during summertime understands. The thick white clouds generated by tropical rainforests reflect the sun's warming rays back to space. When tropical forests are cleared and cloud cover dissipates, the exposed ground absorbs more sunlight and heat.[54] This is in contrast to temperate forests, where deforestation replaces dark, cloud-free forests with comparatively light ground.

Furthermore, deforestation that takes place in the tropics is often harder to reverse. Abandoned farmland in Indiana will naturally begin to revert back to oaks and maples within a few years as seeds are scattered by birds and wind. The same is true in Costa Rica, where unused pastures will regrow, first as tangled jungle and later as mature forest. But throughout much of the tropics, forest regeneration is unlikely to occur naturally. In the African Sahel, deforested soil rapidly degrades and hardens; in Southeast Asia, deforested land is frequently overgrown with flammable *imperata* grass, so forests can only regrow if the land can be protected from fire. Large mammals are vital for dispersing the seeds of many forest trees, and if these mammals have been hunted out, the ability of the forest to recover is threatened.[55]

Several other circumstances, beyond their biophysical differences from temperate and boreal forests, warrant greater policy attention to tropical forests. First, as described in chapter 3, tropical forests are far richer in biodiversity, providing habitat to two-thirds of land-based plants and animals. Second, tropical forests make outsized contributions to the health and welfare of people living in developing countries, as described in chapters 3 and 6. Finally, existing international climate policy agreements already encourage forest conservation and restoration in devel-

oped countries, while the nascent framework for reducing tropical deforestation and degradation—REDD+, described in chapter 9—remains woefully underfunded to date.

For all these reasons, a focus of global policy on tropical forests in particular is justified. That's where we devote our attention for the rest of this chapter, and for the remainder of this book.

Tropical Deforestation Is a Large Part of the Climate Problem

Every day in Europe, five hundred million people in some of the world's wealthiest and most industrial societies power factories, heat and cool buildings, drive cars and trains, and run tractors by burning fossil fuels. In 2012, all the carbon pollution produced from every smokestack, tail pipe, and chimney from Aberdeen to Athens added up to 4.4 billion tons of carbon dioxide.[56]

That's a lot of carbon dioxide—about a tenth of the annual world total. But it's less than what was emitted from tropical deforestation, as shown in figure 2.5. As mentioned above, the world burns down an area of tropical forest the size of Maine every year, and, on average, every square mile (2.59 square kilometers) of tropical forest that's burned releases as much carbon dioxide as driving the typical American car to the sun and back, twice.[57] All *those* emissions added up to 4.8 billion tons of carbon dioxide in 2012.[58]

The emissions from tropical deforestation, degradation, and peat during the first decade of the 2000s have been quantified by more than a dozen studies, listed in table 2.1. While measurements have become more precise over time, estimates vary because dif-

Figure 2.5: If tropical deforestation were a country, its emissions would be greater than those of the European Union.

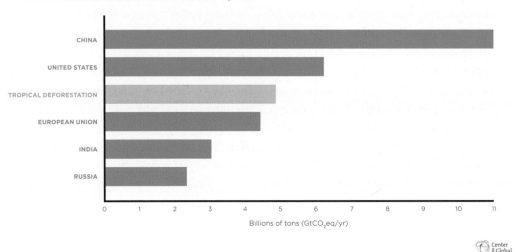

ANNUAL GREENHOUSE GAS EMISSIONS, 2012

Billions of tons (GtCO$_2$eq/yr)

Center for Global Development

Source: Data from CAIT v2.0, "Total GHG Emissions (Excluding LUCF)," World Resources Institute, Busch and Engelmann (2015).

ferent studies have analyzed different years, used different data and methods, and include different scopes of emissions. Nonetheless, all the studies agree that emissions are enormous. At the high end, ecologist Yude Pan and her colleagues estimate tropical deforestation produces more than ten billion tons of carbon dioxide emissions annually, nearly equaling emissions from China.[59] At the low end, ecologist Nancy Harris and her colleagues estimate only three billion tons are emitted from tropical deforestation—a mere India.[60] The median estimate comes in at around five billion tons of CO$_2$ a year—higher than the emissions of the European Union.

Forest degradation is responsible for around one billion tons of annual carbon dioxide emissions—as much as total emissions from Japan.[61] And one billion to two billion tons of carbon

dioxide a year is released from the decay and combustion of peat soils—as much as from Japan or Russia.[62] The rapid destruction of mangrove forests results in emissions of up to 440 million tons of carbon dioxide each year.[63]

Meanwhile, during the first decade of the 2000s, regrowing secondary forests and plantations in the tropics absorbed an estimated 4.4 billion to 6.3 billion tons of carbon dioxide from the atmosphere a year—nearly as much as the United States pumped in—while carbon absorption by mature tropical forests pulled out an additional 1.7 billion to 3.7 billion tons.[64]

From the standpoint of climate science, a useful calculation is the net flux in carbon dioxide emissions from tropical forests to the atmosphere. Net emissions are calculated as gross emissions (all the carbon dioxide that is released to the atmosphere when tropical

Table 2.1. Gross annual pan-tropical emissions during the 2000s, by study

Study	Gross emissions (GtCO$_{2(-eq)}$/yr)	Time period	Scope
Zarin et al. 2015	2.3	2001-2013	Selected deforestation
Harris et al. 2012	3.0	2000-2005	Deforestation
Achard et al. 2014	3.2	2000-2010	Deforestation
Liu et al. 2015	3.6	2000-2005	Deforestation
Tyukavina et al. 2015	3.7	2000-2012	Deforestation, degradation
Busch & Engelmann 2015	3.9	2001-2012	Deforestation, peat
Tubiello et al. 2014 (FAOSTAT)	4.9	2000-2009	Deforestation, degradation
Tubiello et al. 2014 (Houghton)	4.9	2000-2009	Deforestation, degradation
van der Werf et al. 2009	5.5	2000-2005	Deforestation, degradation, peat
Tubiello et al. 2014 (EDGAR)	6.5	2000-2009	Deforestation, degradation
Grace et al. 2014	7.4	2000-2010	Deforestation, degradation, peat
Baccini et al. 2012	8.4	2000-2010	Deforestation, degradation
Pan et al. 2011	10.3	2000-2007	Deforestation

Study	Removals (GtCO$_{2(-eq)}$/yr)	Time period	Scope
Baccini et al. 2012	-4.3	2000-2010	Reforestation and regrowth of secondary forests
Grace et al. 2014	-4.8	2000-2010	Reforestation and regrowth of secondary forests
Pan et al. 2011	-6.2	2000-2007	Reforestation and regrowth of secondary forests

forests are burned and cleared) minus gross removals (all the carbon dioxide removed from the atmosphere by tropical forests that are replanted or allowed to regrow). If gross emissions are larger than gross removals, as is currently the case, then net emissions are positive. But if gross emissions are less than gross removals, as can potentially be achieved by halting and reversing deforestation, then net emissions would become negative. Net emissions vary from year to year and are higher in years with *El Niño* events and large fires.

Net emissions were calculated in 2014 by the Intergovernmental Panel on Climate Change (IPCC), the Nobel Prize–winning volunteer effort by thousands of scientists to synthesize the scientific literature on climate change. The studies synthesized in the IPCC's Fifth Assessment Report showed an estimated 8.4 billion to 10.3 billion tons per year of gross emissions and an estimated 4.3 billion to 6.2 billion tons per year of gross removals, or 4.1 billion tons per year in net emissions.[65] This figure is around 8 percent of annual net global greenhouse gas emissions circa 2010 or, as shown in figure 2.1, 11 percent when forest losses outside the tropics are included as well.

Tropical Forests Are an Even Larger Part of the Climate Solution

While net emissions from forests to the atmosphere are relevant for climate *science*, what matters for climate *policy* is the potential scope to reduce emissions and increase removals. The 2015 Paris Agreement on climate change aspires to bring overall emissions and removals into balance. When it comes to forests, there's no floor at zero on net emissions—they can be made negative if regrowing forests absorb more carbon than cleared and degraded forests release. For this reason, looking just at net emissions from deforestation underestimates the potential contribution of forests to reducing greenhouse gases in the atmosphere.[66] Forests are different in this respect from the energy, industry, building, and transportation sectors, all of which pump emissions into the atmosphere in a one-way flow.

From a policy standpoint, forests can be used to reduce greenhouse gases in the atmosphere in two ways: by avoiding deforestation and by letting them regrow. These can be thought of as largely independent approaches to reducing overall emissions, or "mitigating" climate change, since for the most part deforestation and reforestation are occurring in different parts of the world. Roughly half of all tropical deforestation occurs in Brazil and Indonesia, while China and India have undertaken efforts to reforest large areas. As a result, greenhouse gas emissions from deforestation can be decreased in some places and removals by forest regrowth increased in others simultaneously.

There are some places in the tropics, such as timber plantations or swidden agricultural plots, where forest clearing is followed by regrowth in a cycle. Emissions and removals may balance out over time, but even in these forests the potential to mitigate climate change is greater than their current zero-net emissions. For example, a rotational logging site may currently be carbon neutral—that is, it has an equal balance between emissions from logging and removals from regrowing trees—but if the logging were ceased and the area left to regrow, it would become a carbon sink, absorbing carbon from the atmosphere.

A better estimate of the potential for tropical forests to contribute to climate change mitigation can be calculated by *adding* removals to gross emissions, rather than *subtracting* them. That is, rather than using the calculation of net emissions (gross emissions *minus* gross removals) to represent potential mitigation from tropical forests, the potential is calculated as the gross carbon dioxide emissions avoided by halting all tropical deforestation *plus* the carbon dioxide removed

Figure 2.6: Net tropical deforestation produces 8 percent of net emissions, but halting and reversing tropical deforestation could reduce total net emissions by up to 30 percent.

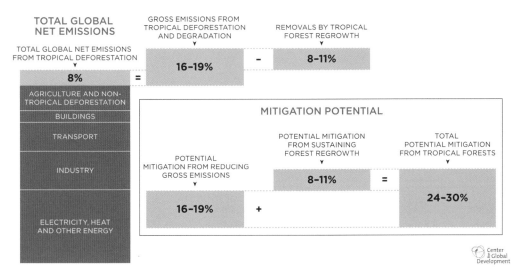

Source: Y. Pan et al., "A Large and Persistent Carbon Sink in the World's Forests," *Science* 333, no. 6045 (2011): 988–93; A. Baccini et al., "Estimated Carbon Dioxide Emissions from Tropical Deforestation Improved by Carbon-Density Maps," *Nature Climate Change* 2, no. 3 (2012): 182–85.

from the atmosphere by continuing to regrow tropical forests at the current pace.

Using the same numbers as the IPCC's Fifth Assessment Report for gross emissions (8.4 billion to 10.3 billion tons per year) and removals (4.3 billion to 6.2 billion tons per year), halting and reversing tropical deforestation could reduce net emissions by as much as 12.7 billion to 16.5 billion tons per year. This is equal to 24 to 30 percent of total annual emissions from all sources of greenhouse gases, as illustrated in figure 2.6. A third study published after the IPCC assessment report puts summed gross emissions and removals from tropical forests at 12.4 billion tons per year— 24 percent of total annual emissions.[67]

Why Forests Could Be Less or More than 24 to 30 Percent of the Climate Solution

A few caveats are in order regarding the estimated 24 to 30 percent for tropical forests' contribution to a climate solution. Three of these cautionary notes suggest a lower percentage, while three suggest it could be even higher.

Suggesting a lower percentage is, first, the fact that some deforestation and forest regrowth happen in the same place. As mentioned, a fraction of emissions and removals in the tropics comes from rotational forestry or swidden agriculture. In these places, ceasing deforestation also stops the potential for new reforestation to occur, diminishing total mitigation potential below 24 to 30 percent. It is not diminished completely, however: logging areas and swidden fallows that are left to regrow will continue to absorb carbon for decades, albeit at a slower rate than newly planted forests.[68]

Second, it's important to reiterate that regrowing tropical forests are *already* canceling out 8 to 11 percent of total greenhouse gas emissions every year. Only actions that increase carbon sequestration above baseline rates should be considered "additional" and eligible for the results-based carbon payments described elsewhere in this book. That doesn't mean regrowing forests can be taken for granted, however. Without continued human actions to sustain this current pace of regrowth, total emissions would be 8 to 11 percent higher, and this much more mitigation would have to come from somewhere else.

Finally, it would not be socially just or politically realistic to stop *all* deforestation—for example, countries may wish to allow traditional subsistence swidden farming, highly lucrative mining, or the building of infrastructure. For this reason and the two above, the potential for tropical forests to reduce total greenhouse gas emissions may be smaller than 24 to 30 percent.

On the other hand, tropical forests might actually offer *more* than 24 to 30 percent of the solution to climate change, again for several reasons. First, little is stopping reforestation from being increased above its current pace. Indeed, as discussed in the next section, many tropical-forest countries have pledged to do exactly that. The amount of land that could be reforested every year is nearly un-

limited from a biophysical standpoint, though practical considerations constrain how much can realistically be reforested.[69]

Then, too, changes in forest and land management can be achieved more rapidly than the transition from fossil to renewable fuels. Ecologist Richard Houghton and his colleagues compared ambitious mitigation trajectories for forests and fossil fuels consistent with a 75 percent likelihood of avoiding global warming in excess of 2°C. They assumed tropical deforestation could be halted and reversed by 2025, while fossil fuel emissions could be phased down by 80 percent by 2050. Under these conditions, tropical forests would provide around 50 percent of the cumulative reduction in net emissions over the next fifty years.[70] In chapter 5, we present a thorough analysis of how much more cheaply and rapidly emissions from forests can be reduced than emissions from fossil fuels.

Last, the figures above still don't capture the full contribution of tropical forests to fighting climate change. An additional 3 to 7 percent of emissions are absorbed every year by mature forests,[71] regardless of short-term human activity. These fluxes are very small on a per-hectare basis, but since they are spread over a very large area of mature tropical forest, they add up. In total, if all deforestation were stopped tomorrow, damaged forests were allowed to grow back, and mature forests were left undisturbed, tropical forests would absorb 27 to 37 percent of current annual net greenhouse gas emissions, or 30 to 40 percent of the remaining greenhouse gas emissions from sources other than tropical forests.[72]

Tree-Planting Campaigns Are Not Enough

Thirteen years after devastating fires raged across Indonesia under President Suharto, another Indonesian president, Susilo Bambang Yudhoyono, made an audacious pledge: Indonesia would plant one billion trees in 2010. "We are highly committed to protecting the environment," President Yudhoyono said of the program three years later. "We plant one billion trees every year in hope of growing a greener and healthier Indonesia in the next 30 years."[73]

It is easy to understand the appeal of tree-planting campaigns. Planting a tree feels good. Rolling up one's sleeves and gently placing a small seedling into the soil offers a tangible way to "do something" about climate change. People can plant trees in remote fields, or just as easily in backyards or urban neighborhoods. Planting a tree is an irresistible photo opportunity for politicians and Instagrammers alike. Best of all, the Saturday morning labor of planting a tree generally encounters no organized opposition, in contrast to the heavy work of halting bulldozers and chainsaws.

Certainly, planting trees is all well and good. In a world where carbon capture and storage (CCS) using industrial methods is at best a work in progress and at worst may not become economically viable for decades, trees are a cheap and readily available "negative emission technology."[74] But here's the thing: simply planting trees won't be enough to slow climate change as long as we're still rapidly burning down the forests we have now; and, unfortunately, forests are currently being cleared and burned far faster than trees are being replanted.

Since 2000, the world has lost an area of forest the size of all the United States east of the Mississippi River, while an area only one-third this size has regrown.[75] In the tropics, deforestation exceeds reforestation in area by a factor of four.[76] In Indonesia, reforestation constitutes a tiny fig leaf strategically placed over a much larger body of deforestation. Since the tree-planting program began in 2010, Indonesia has reported reforesting around 100,000 to 150,000 hectares of forest every year.[77] At the same time, though, the country was clearing around 1.5 million hectares of forest a year—ten times as much.[78]

When you compare deforestation and reforestation in terms of carbon dioxide instead of area, the picture looks even grimmer. A hectare of mature tropical forest may have built up more than two hundred tons of carbon through decades or centuries of growth;[79] a deliberate fire can release it all back to the atmosphere in one smoky morning.

A regrowing tropical forest sequesters carbon as it grows at a rate of about one to eight tons per hectare per year.[80] As shown in figure 2.7, it takes decades or even centuries at this rate for a forest to accumulate the same amount of carbon that was there originally.[81] Relative to the brief window humanity has to fight climate change, a century is a long time to wait for results.

In cases where forests are replanted with tree crops rather than native species, the long-term potential for carbon sequestration is diminished further. Replanted areas frequently bear little resemblance to the original forests. They might be planted as orchards, commercial timber plantations (which are nearly always monocultures),[82] or even oil palm plantations. Orchards and plantations can grow

Figure 2.7: The carbon released immediately from deforestation can take a century to re-establish through forest regrowth.

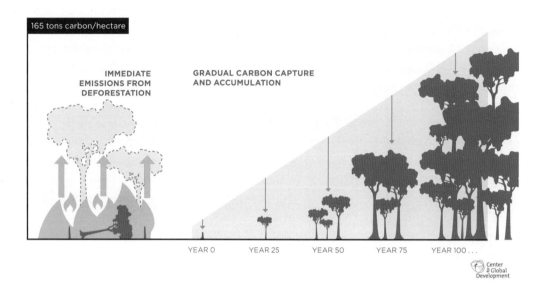

165 tons carbon/hectare

IMMEDIATE
EMISSIONS FROM
DEFORESTATION

GRADUAL CARBON CAPTURE
AND ACCUMULATION

YEAR 0   YEAR 25   YEAR 50   YEAR 75   YEAR 100 . . .

Center
for Global
Development

quickly and produce valuable products, but they store less carbon at maturity than the original forest. A typical full-grown oil palm plantation in Malaysian Borneo stores around 50 tons of carbon per hectare, or even less, while a full-grown timber plantation stores around 120 tons.[83] Meanwhile, unlogged forests in the same region store about 350 tons of carbon per hectare.[84] Since oil palm and timber plantations are cut and replanted periodically, the average carbon they store at any point in time is even smaller.[85]

Furthermore, the journey from announcing a goal to replant trees to reestablishing forests successfully can be surprisingly difficult. Although we could not find any publicly available data on the success of President Yudhoyono's tree-planting campaign, independent analyses suggest Indonesia's aggres-

sive industrial tree-planting targets yielded far smaller results than anticipated.[86] According to an Indonesian official close to the billion-trees initiative, most of the seeds counted toward the target were never actually planted.[87]

From time to time, a peculiar variant on the mitigate-climate-change-through-reforestation idea surfaces: accelerate timber harvesting and replanting and lock up the carbon in long-lived wood products, such as furniture and buildings. The math doesn't work out well, however. Harvesting wood is an inefficient process, and only a small fraction of the carbon from a logged forest ever makes it into products.[88] After a forest is logged, most of the carbon is left behind in branches, roots, and other unused parts of each harvested tree, as well as in nearby trees killed during the felling and extraction process. All this material eventually decays and releases carbon to the atmosphere. For the trees that are extracted, processing in inefficient mills produces further waste.

After accounting for collateral damage to nearby trees during logging and extraction, unused tree parts, the wood that is lost when logs are sawn into lumber, and the wood that ends up in landfills, the carbon that makes its way from harvested forests into long-lasting products is a tiny fraction of the carbon emitted during the process.[89] This is especially true in tropical regions, where the lowest proportion of timber ends up in long-lived wood products.[90] Removing old forests to plant young ones is simply not a legitimate climate strategy, although replacing pastures or croplands with timber plantations does have climate benefits.

Reforestation featured prominently in multiple national climate pledges submitted to the United Nations Framework Convention on Climate Change (UNFCCC) in 2015. Brazil, China, and India collectively pledged to replant an area the size of Texas. Cambodia, Honduras, and Vietnam were among the other countries with reforestation goals.[91] Outside of the UNFCCC, thirteen countries signed up for the "Bonn Challenge" to restore 150 million hectares of degraded forestland by 2020.[92]

While such initiatives are to be welcomed, reforestation is secondary to stopping the loss of forests that already exist today. Planting trees shouldn't be a distraction that allows politicians to divert attention from bringing deforestation to a halt. While reducing deforestation is more politically challenging than planting trees, as described in chapter 10, it is also far more urgent. And from Latin America to Africa to tropical Asia, deforestation rates are high and, in most places, increasing.

Distribution and Trends in Tropical Deforestation

Just over half (51 percent) of tropical deforestation and 41 percent of the emissions from deforestation between 2001 and 2012 occurred in Latin America.[93] Around half of this deforestation was driven by commercial agriculture, especially beef and soy, while subsistence agriculture accounted for a third. Mining, infrastructure, and urban expansion were responsible for the remainder. Industrial logging and timber operations were responsible for almost half the forest degradation in Latin America, while fuelwood collection, fires, and grazing also contributed.[94]

About 30 percent of tropical deforestation between 2001 and 2012 occurred in Asia. Yet due to its carbon-dense peat soils, more emissions from deforestation came from Asia (44 percent) than any other continent.[95] Commercial and subsistence agriculture drove more than two-thirds of deforestation, much of it for industrial oil palm or pulpwood plantations, and forest degradation was dominated by industrial timber operations.[96] Also occurring in Asia was more than half of all peatland drainage.[97]

About 19 percent of tropical deforestation from 2001 to 2012 took place in Africa, producing around 15 percent of emissions from tropical deforestation.[98] Compared with deforestation on other continents, that in Africa is driven less by export crops and more by small-scale farming of staple crops and livestock,[99] and degradation is more significant relative to deforestation. Forest degradation

Figure 2.8: Nine countries produced 77 percent of emissions from deforestation from 2001–12.

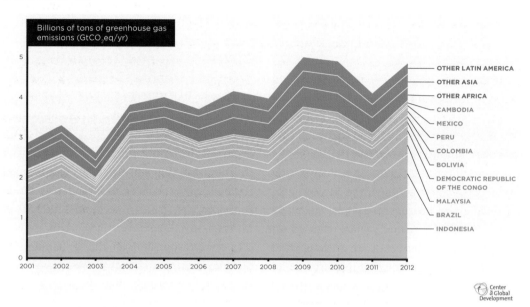

Note: Emissions from deforestation refers to gross emissions from tropical forest cover loss and peat conversion.
Source: Busch and Engelmann (2015).

in Africa is led by fuelwood collection and charcoal production, with industrial timber a secondary contributor.[100]

In total, half of gross emissions from tropical deforestation and peat conversion from 2001–12, as shown in figure 2.8, came from just two countries—Indonesia and Brazil. The next seven combined (Malaysia, Democratic Republic of Congo, Bolivia, Colombia, Peru, Mexico, and Cambodia) accounted for another 27 percent. The remaining 23 percent of emissions were spread across nearly one hundred other tropical countries, none of which individually contributed more than 1.5 percent of the total.

The concentration of emissions from tropical deforestation in a handful of countries makes it tempting to focus policy and finance efforts on a few countries and commodity

supply chains. As we discuss in chapter 8, just four commodities (beef, soy, palm oil, and wood products) in eight countries were responsible for one-third of all tropical deforestation from 2000 to 2009.[101] Yet broad participation by many tropical countries in forest conservation efforts is still important to prevent "leakage" of deforestation activities from one forest to another. As Indonesia takes steps toward growing oil palm without clearing new forests, for example, efforts are needed to ensure oil palm expansion doesn't simply relocate into forests in other countries.

With one notable exception, trends in deforestation during the twenty-first century are not encouraging. The bad news is that satellite data show deforestation to be stable or accelerating in nearly all tropical countries, led by Indonesia, Malaysia, Paraguay, Bolivia, Zambia, and Angola. The good news is that it fell in Brazil, as a result of strong antideforestation policies discussed at length in chapter 7. But since deforestation decreased in Brazil by just half the amount it increased elsewhere, deforestation across the tropics rose by an average of 2,200 square kilometers a year (about 2.6 percent a year) between 2001 and 2014.[102] For a comparison of these rates with figures self-reported by countries, see chapter 4.

In the absence of policy interventions, there is every reason to expect high rates of tropical deforestation to continue.[103] If current trends persist for the next thirty-five years, an area of tropical forest about the size of India will be lost by 2050, according to an analysis undertaken for *Why Forests? Why Now?* discussed at length in chapter 5.[104]

This future loss of tropical forests would have a big effect on the climate, by itself burning through one-sixth of the planet's remaining "carbon budget" needed to avoid breaching the 2°C target of dangerous climate change.[105] At the same time, future climate change is expected to affect the world's tropical forests.

The Effect of Climate Change on Tropical Forests

The amount of carbon stored in any given forest fluctuates through time. Forest carbon decreases when trees are logged, burned, or die natural deaths. It increases when trees grow or recover after damage.

On the whole, mature tropical forests have been gaining more carbon than they have been losing.[106] The rate at which forests have been pulling carbon dioxide out of the atmo-

sphere has been increasing over time, with most studies speculating that rising carbon dioxide levels have been contributing to this trend through increased photosynthesis (so-called "carbon dioxide fertilization").[107] Carbon dioxide fertilization may be responsible for nearly half of the carbon mature forests accumulate every year.[108]

But whether the amount of carbon that forests contain will continue to rise in coming decades as climate change intensifies is uncertain. In the most extreme climate change scenarios, by late in the century forests might even start putting more carbon back into the atmosphere than they take out.[109] Whether such a scenario comes to pass depends on two uncertain effects: carbon fertilization and fires. The carbon fertilization effect might weaken over time, if it hasn't already; uncertainty about future carbon fertilization is high.[110] In addition, as climate change intensifies, fires and drought could take a more severe toll on forests, causing them to lose carbon. In years with normal rainfall, moist tropical forests are not susceptible to fire because of their high moisture content.[111] But logging, droughts, and fires kill trees, thin the canopy, and allow more heat to reach the forest interior, all of which reduces forests' resistance to further fires.[112] Forest fires have been growing larger and more common due to droughts and deforestation, and it may become increasingly difficult for forests to recover.[113] As with fertilization, however, enough complicating factors exist to make projections of future fire risk highly uncertain.

One particularly feared effect of climate change on tropical forests is "Amazon dieback," in which a vicious cycle of dry conditions and forest fires would gradually turn the Amazon from a rainforest into a savanna.

The carbon released from such a transition would be monstrous, constituting a planetary tipping point toward runaway climate change. Fortunately, according to the IPCC, the likelihood of Amazon dieback by 2100 is lower than previously thought, and climate change alone will not drive large-scale forest loss in the Amazon this century.[114]

Insect pests and diseases, which have recently ravaged forests in Western North America as a consequence of warming temperatures, are less of a concern in hyper-diverse tropical forests. A pest affecting a single tree species that can devastate a forest containing only a few tree species would have little effect on a tropical forest containing hundreds or thousands of species.[115] Furthermore, in temperate zones some pests are kept at bay by seasonal cool temperatures. As climate change makes cold snaps less cold or less frequent, pests proliferate. But in most tropical forests, the spread of pests is not currently limited by cool temperatures.[116]

Amazon dieback and pests aside, climate change is expected to be unkind to tropical forests. In a vicious cycle, climate change diminishes the rate at which forests take carbon out of the atmosphere, which in turn accelerates climate change. But it is possible to arrest this cycle, by protecting forests from deforestation and by reducing greenhouse gas emissions from all sources. In this way, forests will continue to be a natural buffer against climate change.

Conclusion

The clearing of tropical forests contributes to climate change by eliminating a safe and natural carbon sink, releasing large stocks of carbon from the earth into the atmosphere, and allowing new sources of emissions to take the forests' place. Yet while net tropical deforestation is responsible for nearly one-tenth of the annual greenhouse gas emissions causing climate change—more than the European Union—tropical forests offer up to a third of the climate solution. By halting deforestation and letting damaged forests regrow, this massive source of carbon dioxide to the atmosphere can be turned into a massive sink pulling carbon from the atmosphere. Doing so would reduce annual global greenhouse emissions from all sources by an estimated 24 to 30 percent, which would constitute a giant step toward realizing the global aspiration, agreed to in Paris in 2015, to balance emissions and removals.

Subsequent chapters describe the tremendous opportunities humanity has to reduce tropical deforestation through satellite monitoring (chapter 4), economic incentives (chapter 5), national policies (chapter 7), supply chain initiatives (chapter 8), political will (chapter 10), international cooperation (chapters 9 and 11), and finance (chapter 12).

Slowing climate change is one reason to conserve tropical forests, but many more exist. Tropical forests contribute to the livelihoods and well-being of people who live in and near them in many ways, from cleaning water to suppressing malarial mosquitoes to buffering homes and infrastructure from the impacts of deadly storms. We describe these and many other benefits of tropical forests in chapter 3.

Notes

1. N. Harris et al., "With Latest Fires Crisis, Indonesia Surpasses Russia as World's Fourth-Largest Emitter," World Resources Institute blog, October 29, 2015, http://www.wri.org/blog/2015/10/latest-fires-crisis-indonesia-surpasses-russia-world%E2%80%99s-fourth-largest-emitter.

2. S. Mollman, "Indonesia's Fires Have Now Razed More Land than in the Entire US State of New Jersey," *Quartz*, November 2, 2015, http://qz.com/538558/indonesias-fires-have-now-razed-more-land-than-in-the-entire-us-state-of-new-jersey/; A. Garbillin, "Lapan: Tahun ini, dua juta hektar hutan hangus terbakar," *Kompas*, October 30, 2015, http://nasional.kompas.com/read/2015/10/30/13070591/LAPAN.Tahun.Ini.Dua.Juta.Hektar.Hutan.Hangus.Terbakar.

3. Harris et al. (2015).

4. H. D. V. Boehm and F. Siegert, "Ecological Impact of the One Million Hectare Rice Project in Central Kalimantan, Indonesia, Using Remote Sensing and GIS" (paper presented at the 22nd Asian Conference on Remote Sensing, Singapore, November 5–9, 2001), http://www.crisp.nus.edu.sg/~acrs2001/pdf/126boehm.pdf.

5. F. Siegert et al., "Increased Damage from Fires in Logged Forests during Droughts Caused by El Niño," *Nature* 414 (2001): 437–40.

6. P. Peduzzi et al., "Wildland Fires: A Double Impact on the Planet," *Environment Alert Bulletin*, United Nations Environment Programme—GRID-Europe, June 2004, http://www.grid.unep.ch/products/3_Reports/ew_fire.pdf.

7. S. Jayachandran, "Air Quality and Early-Life Mortality: Evidence from Indonesia's Wildfires," *Journal of Human Resources* 44, no. 4 (2009): 916–54, cited in K. Mullan, "The Value of Forest Ecosystem Services to Developing Economies," CGD Working Paper 379, Center for Global Development, Washington, DC, 2014.

8. N. Sastry, "Forest Fires, Air Pollution, and Mortality in Southeast Asia," *Demography* 39, no. 1 (2002): 1–23, cited in Mullan, "The Value of Forest Ecosystem Services."

9. P. M. L. Hon, "Singapore," in *Indonesia's Fires and Haze: The Cost of Catastrophe*, ed. D. Glover and T. Jessup (Singapore: Singapore Institute of Southeast Asian Studies, 1999).

10. S. Page et al., "The Amount of Carbon Released from Peat and Forest Fires in Indonesia during 1997," *Nature*, 420 (2002): 61–65.

11. M. Harrison et al., "The Global Impact of Indonesian Forest Fires," *Biologist* 56, no. 3 (2009): 156–63.

12. All monetary values in this chapter and in this book are reported in U.S. dollars at the time of the publication of the source article, unless otherwise indicated. J. Schweithelm and D. Glover, "Causes and Impacts of the Fires," in Glover and Jessup, *Indonesia's Fires and Haze 2006*; L. Tacconi, "Fires in Indonesia: Causes, Costs and Policy Implications," CIFOR Occasional Paper 38, Center for International Forestry Research, Bogor, Indonesia, 2003.

13. World Bank, "Indonesia Economic Quarterly: Reforming Amid Uncertainty," December 2015.

14. R. Goodman and M. Herold, "Why Maintaining Tropical Forests Is Essential and Urgent for a Stable Climate," CGD Working Paper 385, Center for Global Development, Washington, DC, 2014.

15. Ibid.

16. P. Smith, M. Bustamante, et al., "Agriculture, Forestry and Other Land Use (AFOLU)," in *Climate Change 2014: Mitigation of Climate Change. Contribution of Working Group III to the Fifth Assessment Report of the Intergovernmental Panel on Climate Change*, ed. O. Edenhofer, R. Pichs-Madruga, Y. Sokona, E. Farahani, S. Kadner, K. Seyboth, A. Adler, I. Baum, S. Brunner, P. Eickemeier, B. Kriemann, J. Savolainen, S. Schlömer, C. von Stechow, T. Zwickel, and J.

C. Minx, 811–922 (Cambridge, UK, and New York: Cambridge University Press, 2014).

17. S. Doney, V. J. Fabry, R. A. Feely, and J. A. Kleypas, "Ocean Acidification: The Other CO_2 Problem," *Marine Science* 1 (2009): 169–92.

18. O. Hoegh-Guldberg, P. J. Mumby, A. J. Hooten, R. S. Steneck, Paul Greenfield, E. Gomez, C. Drew Harvell, et al. "Coral Reefs under Rapid Climate Change and Ocean Acidification," *Science* 318, no. 5857 (2007): 1737–42; I. Nagelkerken and S. D. Connell, "Global Alteration of Ocean Ecosystem Functioning due to Increasing Human CO_2 Emissions," *Proceedings of the National Academy of Sciences* 112, no. 43 (2015): 13272–7.

19. C. Le Quéré, "Global Carbon Budget 2014," *Earth System Science Data Discussion* 7 (2014): 521–610; C. Goodall, *Ten Technologies to Fix Energy and Climate* (London: Profile Books, 2008).

20. Goodman and Herold, "Why Maintaining Tropical Forests Is Essential"; O. Phillips and S. L. Lewis, "Recent Changes in Tropical Forest Biomass and Dynamics," in *Forests and Global Change*, ed. D. A. Coomes, D. F. R. P. Burslem, and W. D. Simonson, 77–108 (Cambridge, UK, and New York: Cambridge University Press, 2014).

21. Goodman and Herold, "Why Maintaining Tropical Forests Is Essential"; F. Seymour, "What If We Had a Safe and Natural Way to Capture and Store Carbon?," Center for Global Development blog, November 4, 2014, http://www.cgdev.org/blog/what-if-we-had-safe-and-natural-way-capture-and-store-carbon.

22. World Resources Institute, "Global Forest Watch," 2014, www.globalforestwatch.org, based on M. C. Hansen et al., "High-Resolution Global Maps of 21st-Century Forest Cover Change," *Science* 342 (2013): 850–53.

23. N. Stephenson et al., "Rate of Tree Carbon Accumulation Increases Continuously with Tree Size," *Nature* 507 (2014): 90–93.

24. N. Hosonuma et al., "An Assessment of Deforestation and Forest Degradation Drivers in Developing Countries," *Environmental Research Letters* 7, no. 4 (2012): 044009; H. K. Gibbs et al., "Tropical Forests Were the Primary Sources of New Agricultural Land in the 1980s and 1990s," *Proceedings of the National Academy of Sciences* 107, no. 38 (2010): 16732–7.

25. Goodman and Herold, "Why Maintaining Tropical Forests Is Essential."

26. Ibid.

27. R. F. Huttl, "Forest Ecosystem Development in Post-Mining Landscapes: A Case Study of the Lusatian Lignite District," *Naturwissenschaften* 88, no. 8 (2001): 322–29; V. Sheoran, A. S. Sheoran, and P. Poonia, "Soil Reclamation of Abandoned Mine Land by Revegetation: A Review," *International Journal of Soil, Sediment and Water* 3, no. 2 (2010): 13; G. Asner, W. Llactayo, R. Tupayachi, and E. Raez Luna, "Elevated Rates of Gold Mining in the Amazon Revealed through High-Resolution Monitoring," *Proceedings of the National Academy of Sciences* 110, no. 46 (2013): 18454–9.

28. D. Lawrence and K. Vandecar, "Effects of Tropical Deforestation on Climate and Agriculture," *Nature Climate Change* 5, no. 1 (2015): 27–36.

29. K. H. E. Meurer et al., "Direct Nitrous Oxide (N_2O) Fluxes from Soils under Different Land Use in Brazil—A Critical Review," *Environmental Research Letters* 11, no. 2 (2016): 023001; Smith et al., "Agriculture, Forestry and Other Land Use."

30. M. C. Hansen et al., "High-Resolution Global Maps of 21st-Century Forest Cover Change," Science 342 (2013): 850–53.

31. Goodman and Herold, "Why Maintaining Tropical Forests Is Essential."

32. S. E. Page, J. O. Rieley, and C. J. Banks, "Global and Regional Importance of the Tropical Peatland Carbon Pool," *Global Change Biology* 17, no. 2 (2011): 798–818, doi/10.1111/j.1365-2486.2010.02279.x/full.

33. Food and Agriculture Organization of the United Nations (FAO), "Harmonized World Soil Database v 1.2," Rome, Italy, 2012, http://www.fao.org/soils-portal/soil-survey/soil-maps-and-databases/harmonized-world-soil-database-v12/en/.

34. Smith et al., "Agriculture, Forestry and Other Land Use."

35. Smith et al., "Agriculture, Forestry and Other Land Use."

36. D. Donato et al., "Mangroves among the Most Carbon-Rich Forests in the Tropics," *Nature Geoscience* 4, no. 5 (2011): 293–97.

37. N. Duke et al., "A World without Mangroves?" *Science* 317, no. 5834 (2007): 41–42.

38. M. Huang and G. P. Asner, "Long-Term Carbon Loss and Recovery Following Selective Logging in Amazon Forests," *Global Biogeochemical Cycles* 24, no. 3 (2010): GB3028; R. Houghton, "The Emissions of Carbon from Deforestation and Degradation in the Tropics: Past Trends and Future Potential," *Carbon Management* 4, no. 5 (2013): 539–46; T. Pearson, S. Brown, and F. M. Casarim, "Carbon Emissions from Tropical Forest Degradation Caused by Logging," *Environmental Research Letters* 9, no. 3 (2014): 034017.

39. J. Kaplan, K. Krumhardt, and N. Zimmermann, "The Prehistoric and Preindustrial Deforestation of Europe," *Quaternary Science Reviews* 28, no. 27 (2009): 3016–34.

40. F. X. Faust, C. Gnecco, H. Mannstein, and J. Stamm, "Evidence for the Postconquest Demographic Collapse of the Americas in Historical CO2 Levels," *Earth Interactions* 10, no. 11 (2006): 1–14. See, for example, G. Scherer and M. Fletcher, *Who on Earth Is Aldo Leopold? Father of Wildlife Ecology* (New York: Enslow Publishers, 2009).

41. P. B. Reich and L. Frelich, "Temperate Deciduous Forests," *Encyclopedia of Global Environmental Change* 2:565–69 (Chichester: John Wiley, 2002).

42. R. Houghton, "Balancing the Global Carbon Budget," *Annual Review of Earth and Planetary Sciences* 35 (2007): 313–47.

43. "Tons" refers to metric tons throughout this book.

44. P. Ciais et al., "Carbon and Other Biogeochemical Cycles," in *Climate Change 2013: The Physical Science Basis. Contribution of Working Group I to the Fifth Assessment Report of the Intergovernmental Panel on Climate Change*, ed. T. F. Stocker, D. Qin, G. K. Plattner, M. Tignor, S. K. Allen, J. Boschung, A. Nauels, Y. Xia, V. Bex, and P. M. Midgley (Cambridge, UK, and New York: Cambridge University Press, 2013); J. Pongratz, T. Raddatz, C. H. Reick, M. Esch, and M. Claussen, "Radiative Forcing from Anthropogenic Land Cover Change since AD 800," *Geophysical Research Letters* 36, no. 2 (2009): L02709.

45. R. Houghton, "The Emissions of Carbon from Deforestation and Degradation in the Tropics: Past Trends and Future Potential," *Carbon Management* 4, no. 5 (2013): 539–46

46. Food and Agriculture Organization of the United Nations (FAO), *Global Forest Resources Assessment 2015*, Rome, 2015, http://www.fao.org/3/a-i4808e.pdf.

47. Hansen et al., "High-Resolution Global Maps."

48. T. T. Kozlowski, ed., *Fire and Ecosystems* (New York, San Francisco, and London: Academic Press, 1974).

49. Houghton, "The Emissions of Carbon"; Goodman and Herold, "Why Maintaining Tropical Forests Is Essential"; R. Houghton, J. I. House, J. Pongratz, G. R. Van der Werf, R. S. DeFries, M. C. Hansen, C. Le Quéré, and N. Ramankutty, "Carbon Emissions from Land Use and Land-Cover Change," *Biogeosciences* 9, no. 12 (2012): 5125–42; Hansen et al., "High-Resolution Global Maps."

50. Hansen et al., "High-Resolution Global Maps."

51. Goodman and Herold, "Why Maintaining Tropical Forests Is Essential."

52. Y. Pan et al., "A Large and Persistent Carbon Sink in the World's Forests," *Science* 333, no. 6045 (2011): 988–93.

53. Ciais et al., "Carbon and Other Biogeochemical Cycles."

54. G. Bala, K. Caldeira, M. Wickett, T. J. Phillips, D. B. Lobell, C. Delire, and A. Mirin, "Combined Climate and Carbon-Cycle Effects of Large-Scale Deforestation," *Proceedings of the National Academy of Sciences* 104, no. 16 (2007): 6550–55.

55. C. A. Peres, T. Emilio, J. Schietti, S. J. M. Desmoulière, and T. Levi, "Dispersal Limitation Induces Long-Term Biomass Collapse in Overhunted Amazonian Forests," *Proceedings of the National Academy of Sciences* 113, no. 4 (2016): 892–97; J. A. Lindsell, D. C. Lee, V. J. Powell, and E. Gemita, "Availability of Large Seed-Dispersers for Restoration of Degraded Tropical Forest," *Tropical Conservation Science* 8, no. 1 (2015): 17–27; J. Dew and P. Wright, "Frugivory and Seed Dispersal by Four Species of Primates in Madagascar's Eastern Rain Forest," *Biotropica* (1998): 425–37; J. Ganzhorn et al., "Lemurs and the Regeneration of Dry Deciduous Forest in Madagascar," *Conservation Biology* 13, no. 4 (1999): 794–804.

56. Data from CAIT v2.0, "Total GHG Emissions (Excluding LUCF)," World Resources Institute, EU-28, 2012, available at http://cait.wri.org.

57. Authors' calculations based on aboveground carbon density of 165 tCO$_2$/ha, using U.S. Environmental Protection Agency greenhouse gas equivalencies calculator: https://www.epa.gov/energy/greenhouse-gas-equivalencies-calculator.

58. Busch and Engelmann, "The Future of Forests."

59. P. Ciais et al., "Carbon and Other Biogeochemical Cycles"; Y. Pan et al., "A Large and Persistent Carbon Sink."

60. N. L. Harris et al., "Baseline Map of Carbon Emissions from Deforestation in Tropical Regions," *Science* 336, no. 6088 (2012): 1573–76.

61. J. Grace, E. Mitchard, and E. Gloor, "Perturbations in the Carbon Budget of the Tropics," *Global Change Biology* 20, no. 10 (2014): 3238–55.

62. G. R. van der Werf et al., "Estimates of Fire Emissions from an Active Deforestation Region in the Southern Amazon Based on Satellite Data and Biogeochemical Modelling," *Biogeosciences* 2, no. 6 (2009): 235–49; Grace et al., "Perturbations in the Carbon Budget"; Busch and Engelmann, "The Future of Forests."

63. See, for example, Food and Agriculture Organization of the United Nations (FAO), "The World's Mangroves 1980–2005," FAO Forestry Paper 153, Rome, 2007; Donato et al., "Mangroves among the Most Carbon-Rich Forests."

64. Pan et al., "A Large and Persistent Carbon Sink"; A. Baccini et al., "Estimated Carbon Dioxide Emissions from Tropical Deforestation Improved by Carbon-Density Maps," *Nature Climate Change* 2, no. 3 (2012): 182–85; Grace et al., "Perturbations in the Carbon Budget"; S. J. Wright, "The Carbon Sink in Intact Tropical Forests," *Global Change Biology* 19 (2013): 337–39.

65. Smith et al., "Agriculture, Forestry and Other Land Use."

66. Goodman and Herold, "Why Maintaining Tropical Forests Is Essential"; R. Butler, "Protecting Rainforests Could Sequester Equivalent of a Third of Global Emissions Annually," Mongabay.com, June 13, 2014, http://news.mongabay.com/2014/06/protecting-rainforests-could-sequester-equivalent-of-a-third-of-global-emissions-annually/; J. Busch, "Tropical Forests Offer Up to 24–30 Percent of Potential Climate Mitigation," Center for Global Development blog, November 4, 2014, http://www.cgdev.org/blog/tropical-forests-offer24%E2%80%9330-percent-potential-climate-mitigation; The Prince's Charities' International Sustainability Unit, "Tropical Forests: A Review," London, April 2015, http://www.pcfisu.org/wp-content/uploads/2015/04/Princes-Charities-International-Sustainability-Unit-Tropical-Forests-A-Review.pdf.

67. J. Grace, E. Mitchard, and E. Gloor, "Perturbations in the Carbon Budget of the Tropics," *Global Change Biology* 20, no. 10 (2014): 3238–55.

68. L. Poorter, F. Bongers, T. M. Aide, A. M. A. Zambrano, P. Balvanera, J. M. Becknell, V. Boukili, et al., "Biomass Resilience of Neotropical Secondary Forests," *Nature* 530, no. 7589 (2016): 211–14.

69. See, for example, R. Chazdon et al., "Carbon Sequestration Potential of Second-Growth Forest Regeneration in the Latin American Tropics," *Science Advances* 2, no. 5 (2016): e1501639.

70. R. A. Houghton, B. Byers, and A. A. Nassikas, "A Role for Tropical Forests in Stabilizing Atmospheric CO_2," *Nature Climate Change* 5, no. 12 (2015): 1022–23.

71. Grace et al., "Perturbations in the Carbon Budget"; Pan et al., "A Large and Persistent Carbon Sink"; Baccini et al., "Estimated Carbon Dioxide Emissions"; Wright, "The Carbon Sink."

72. Goodman and Herold, "Why Maintaining Tropical Forests Is Essential."

73. *Jakarta Globe* staff, "Indonesian Growth Must Not Threaten Environment: SBY," *Jakarta Globe*, June 11, 2013.

74. B. Caldecott, G. Lomax, and M. Workman, "Stranded Carbon Assets and Negative Emissions Technologies," working paper, Smith School of Enterprise and the Environment, University of Oxford, February 2015.

75. Hansen et al., "High-Resolution Global Maps."

76. Ibid.

77. Badan Pusat Statistik, "Luas Kegiatan Reboisasi (ha), 2000–2013," 2016, http://www.bps.go.id/linkTableDinamis/view/id/860.

78. World Resources Institute, "Global Forest Watch."

79. Baccini et al., "Estimated Carbon Dioxide Emissions."

80. Pan et al., "A Large and Persistent Carbon Sink"; R. T. Watson et al., eds., *Land Use, Land-Use Change, and Forestry: Special Report of the IPCC* (Cambridge, UK: Cambridge University Press, 2001).

81. Goodman and Herold, "Why Maintaining Tropical Forests Is Essential"; Huang and Asner, "Long-Term Carbon Loss"; S. Riswan, J. B. Kenworthy, and K. Kartawinata, "The Estimation of Temporal Processes in Tropical Rain Forest: A Study of Primary Mixed Dipterocarp Forest in Indonesia," *Journal of Tropical Ecology* 2, no. 1 (1985): 171–82.

82. J. Nichols, M. Bristow, and J. Vanclay, "Mixed-Species Plantations: Prospects and Challenges," *Forest Ecology and Management* 233, no. 2 (2006): 383–90.

83. A. Morel et al., "Estimating Aboveground Biomass in Forest and Oil Palm Plantation in Sabah, Malaysian Borneo Using ALOS PALSAR Data," *Forest Ecology and Management* 262, no. 9 (2011): 1786–98; F. Agus et al., "Historical CO_2 Emissions from Land Use and Land Use Change from the Oil Palm Industry in Indonesia, Malaysia and Papua New Guinea," Roundtable on Sustainable Palm Oil, Kuala Lumpur, 2013.

84. A. Morel et al., "Estimating Aboveground Biomass in Forest and Oil Palm Plantation in Sabah, Malaysian Borneo Using ALOS PALSAR Data."

85. Agus et al., "Historical CO_2 Emissions from Land Use and Land Use Change from the Oil Palm Industry in Indonesia, Malaysia and Papua New Guinea."

86. L. Verchot et al., "Reducing Forestry Emissions in Indonesia," Center for International Forestry Research, Bogor, Indonesia, 2010; Forest Trends and the Anti-Forest Mafia Coalition, "Indonesia's Legal Timber Supply Gap and Implications for Expansion of Milling Capacity: A Review of the Road Map for the Revitalization of the Forest Industry, Phase 1," *Forest Trends*, 2015; K. Obidzinski and A. Dermawan, "Smallholder Timber Plantation Development in Indonesia: What is Preventing Progress?" *International Forestry Review* 12, no. 4 (2010): 339–48; personal communi-

cation with the author from Indonesian official, July 2015.

87. Anonymous, personal communication with one of the authors, July 2015.

88. J. Earles, S. Mason, and K. Skog, "Timing of Carbon Emissions from Global Forest Clearance," *Nature Climate Change* 9, no. 2 (2012): 682–85.

89. T. Abebe and S. Holm, "Estimation of Wood Residues from Small-Scale Commercial Selective Logging and Sawmilling in Tropical Rain Forests of South-Western Ethiopia," *International Forestry Review* 1, no. 5 (2003): 45–52; C. Lauk et al., "Global Socioeconomic Carbon Stocks in Long-Lived Products 1900–2008," *Environmental Research Letters* 7, no. 3 (2012): 034023; Pan et al., "A Large and Persistent Carbon Sink"; Goodman and Herold, "Why Maintaining Tropical Forests Is Essential."

90. Earles et al., "Timing of Carbon Emissions."

91. Intended Nationally Determined Contributions (INDCs) can be found at the United Nations Framework Convention on Climate Change website, "INDCs as Communicated by Parties," http://www4.unfccc.int/submissions/INDC/Submission%20Pages/submissions.aspx.

92. Global Partnership on Forest Landscape Restoration, "The Bonn Challenge," September 2011, http://www.bonnchallenge.org/content/global-partnership-forest-landscape-restoration.

93. Busch and Engelmann, "The Future of Forests."

94. Hosonuma et al., "An Assessment of Deforestation."

95. Busch and Engelmann, "The Future of Forests: Emissions from Deforestation with and without Carbon Pricing Policies, 2015–2050."

96. Hosonuma et al., "An Assessment of Deforestation."

97. Smith et al., "Agriculture, Forestry and Other Land Use."

98. Busch and Engelmann, "The Future of Forests."

99. Hosonuma et al., "An Assessment of Deforestation"; R. S. DeFries, T. Rudel, M. Uriarte, and M. Hansen, "Deforestation Driven by Urban Population Growth and Agricultural Trade in the Twenty-First Century," *Nature Geoscience* 3 (2010): 178–81; B. Fisher, "African Exception to Drivers of Deforestation," *Nature Geoscience* 3, no. 6 (2010): 375–76.

100. Hosonuma et al., "An Assessment of Deforestation."

101. U. M. Persson, S. Henders, and T. Kastner, "Trading Forests: Quantifying the Contribution of Global Commodity Markets to Emissions from Tropical Deforestation," CGD Working Paper 384, Center for Global Development, Washington, DC, 2014.

102. Authors' calculations based on World Resources Institute, "Global Forest Watch."

103. C. Pagnutti, C. Bauch, and M. Anand, "Outlook on a Worldwide Forest Transition," *PloS One* 8, no. 10 (2013): e75890; World Wildlife Fund and International Institute for Applied Systems Analysis, "Living Forests Report," World Wildlife Fund, 2011.

104. Busch and Engelmann, "The Future of Forests."

105. Ibid.

106. Le Quéré et al., "Trends in the Sources and Sinks of Carbon Dioxide," *Nature Geoscience* 12, no. 2 (2009): 831–36; Pan et al., "A Large and Persistent Carbon Sink"; S. Lewis et al., "Increasing Carbon Storage in Intact African Tropical Forests," *Nature* 7232, no. 457 (2009): 1003–6.

107. J. Settele et al., "Terrestrial and Inland Water Systems," in *Climate Change 2014: Impacts, Adaptation, and Vulnerability. Part A: Global and Sectoral Aspects. Contribution of Working Group II to the Fifth Assessment Report of the Intergovernmental Panel on Climate Change*, ed. C. B. Field, V. R. Barros, D. J. Dokken, K. J. Mach, M. D. Mastrandrea, T. E. Bilir, M. Chatterjee, K. L. Ebi, Y. O. Estrada, R. C. Genova, B. Girma, E. S. Kissel, A. N. Levy, S. MacCracken, P. R. Mastrandrea, and L. L. White, 271–359 (Cambridge, UK, and New York: Cambridge

University Press, 2014); S. Lewis et al., "Changing Ecology of Tropical Forests: Evidence and Drivers," *Annual Review of Ecology, Evolution and Systematics* 40 (2009): 529–49; R. Norby and D. Zak, "Ecological Lessons from Free-Air CO_2 Enrichment (FACE) Experiments," *Annual Review of Ecology, Evolution, and Systematics* 42 (2011): 181–203.

108. Pan et al., "A Large and Persistent Carbon Sink"; D. Schimel, B. Stephens, and J. Fisher, "Effect of Increasing CO_2 on the Terrestrial Carbon Cycle," *Proceedings of the National Academy of Sciences* 112, no. 2 (2015): 436–41.

109. J. Settele et al., "Terrestrial and Inland Water Systems."

110. Ibid.

111. M. Cochrane, "Fire Science for Rainforests," *Nature* 421, no. 6926 (2003): 913–19.

112. C. Uhl and J. B. Kauffman, "Deforestation, Fire Susceptibility, and Potential Tree Responses to Fire in the Eastern Amazon," *Ecology* 71 (1990): 437–49; L. M. Curran et al., "Lowland Forest Loss in Protected Areas of Indonesian Borneo," *Science* 303 (2004): 1000–1003; D. Ray, "Micrometeorological and Canopy Controls of Flammability in Mature and Disturbed Forests in an East-Central Amazon Landscape," *Ecological Applications* 15, no. 5 (2005): 1664–78.

113. O. Edenhofer et al., "Summary for Policymakers," in Edenhofer et al., *Climate Change 2014*.

114. Y. Malhi et al., "Comprehensive Assessment of Carbon Productivity, Allocation and Storage in Three Amazonian Forests," *Global Change Biology* 5, no. 15 (2009): 1255–74; P. Cox et al., "Sensitivity of Tropical Carbon to Climate Change Constrained by Carbon Dioxide Variability," *Nature* 7437, no. 494 (2013): 341–44; P. Good et al., "Comparing Tropical Forest Projections from Two Generations of Hadley Centre Earth System Models, Hadgem2-ES and Hadcm3lc," *Journal of Climate* 2, no. 26 (2013): 495–511; C. Huntingford et al., "Simulated Resilience of Tropical Rainforests to CO_2-Induced Climate Change," *Nature Geoscience* 4, no. 6 (2013): 268–73; J. Settele et al., "Terrestrial and Inland Water Systems."

115. J. Settele et al., "Terrestrial and Inland Water Systems."; Food and Agriculture Organization of the United Nations (FAO), Forestry Resources Division, "Pest and Disease Occurrence," in *Protecting Plantations from Pests and Diseases*, report based on the work of W. M. Ciesla, Forest Plantation Thematic Papers, Working Paper 10, Forest Resources Development Service, Rome, 2011.

116. J. Settele et al., "Terrestrial and Inland Water Systems."

Forested mountains surround rice fields in Lang Son, Vietnam.

Credit: Jimmy Tran/Shutterstock

CHAPTER 3

Tropical Forests and Development

Contributions to Water, Energy, Agriculture, Health, Safety, and Adaptation

Hispaniola. Three thousand meters above the Caribbean, a raindrop is streaking toward Earth at terminal velocity. It's heading for the Cordillera Central, the mountainous spine of the island of Hispaniola, and a small puff of wind could blow it in any direction. A slight draft to the east, and the raindrop will fall in the Dominican Republic. A gust to the west, and it will fall in Haiti. Whether this tiny drop of water will ultimately flow east or west will be determined by topography, wind, and chance; but whether it will bring comfort or provoke suffering will be determined by forests.

The mountains of the Dominican Republic are forested. Water falling on these slopes comes out clean, nourishing families that rely on it for drinking, cooking, cleaning, farming, and freshwater fishing. In stark contrast, the mountainsides of Haiti are deforested. Water that flows down brings misery by exacerbating erosion, triggering landslides, transporting diseases, and muddying the reservoir behind the country's largest hydroelectric dam.

The disparity in development between the Dominican Republic and Haiti is infamous. The United Nations Development Program rates the Dominican Republic's human development as "high," on par with the world average. Haiti's human development is "low"; outside of Sub-Saharan Africa, only Afghanistan ranks lower.[1] Poverty is greater in Haiti for many reasons, starting with its tortured political history. One of the other reasons is deforestation.

When Christopher Columbus first set foot in the New World, Hispaniola was covered nearly entirely by forests. After centuries of clearing to make way for agriculture, the forests on the Haitian side are now almost completely gone. Haiti reported in 2015 that its forest cover had plummeted to a shockingly low 3.5 percent.[2] The difference between Hispaniola's verdant east and denuded west is visible from space, as depicted in figure 3.1.

The human consequences of the deforestation of Haiti are far reaching. Eastern winds have always delivered more moisture to the Dominican Republic side of Hispaniola, but upland forests once regulated the uneven pattern of rainfall, making the Haitian side productive for farming. Without the forests, Haiti has become increasingly dry and desertified.[3] Topsoil has eroded and washed away from productive lands, and about 90 percent of the country's soils have become degraded, compared to 40 percent in the Dominican Republic.[4]

Farming is becoming increasingly untenable, leading to migration from the countryside to city slums.[5] Haitian novelist Emmanuel Védrine, returning to the village where he had grown up, recounted the devastation wrought on the landscape and its people during his lifetime:

> When I visited my village . . . it was all brown. No vegetation. Most of the trees I used to see as a boy had been cut down. The birds had left the village. No place to build their nests or for them to rest. No rainfall. The rivers were almost all dried out. My neighbors had moved to other areas . . . My village is like a desert.[6]

Deforestation has also caused the country's waterways to become badly silted. Bare slopes in the largely mountainous country are increasingly exposed to landslides and

---

This chapter draws heavily on a background paper by Katrina Brandon on the ecosystem services provided by tropical forests.

Figure 3.1: The difference in forest cover between Haiti and the Dominican Republic is visible from space.

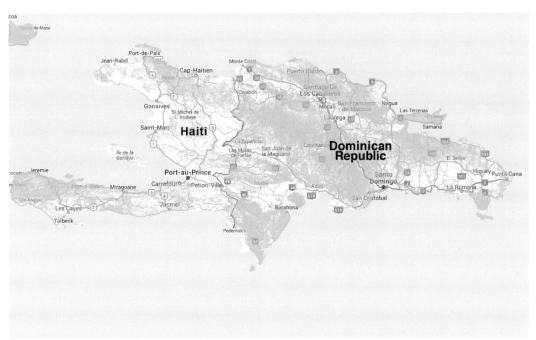

Source: World Resources Institute (WRI), "Global Forest Watch," 2014, www.globalforestwatch.org,

flooding after heavy rains during the rainy season.[7] "Just one day of continuous rain is devastating; it can cause catastrophe," observed Haiti's minister of agriculture, natural resources, and rural development, Jean François Thomas, in 2013.[8]

One casualty of deforestation is the Péligre Dam, Haiti's largest source of electricity. Erosion from the deforested watershed above the dam has steadily filled in the reservoir with more than six hundred million cubic meters of sediment, reducing its capacity by half and diminishing its value for irrigation and flood control.[9] As a result, Haiti's electricity consumption fell by half between 1990 and 2010.[10] Without costly dredging of silt from the res-

ervoir, the estimated lifespan of Péligre Dam has been shortened by a century.[11]

Deforestation has, at times, even sickened Haiti's citizens. Researchers from the University of Alabama at Huntsville and the Centers for Disease Control and Prevention (CDC) surmised that deforestation was to blame for an outbreak of hookworm in Haiti in the 1990s.[12] Deforestation led to more silt in the River Royone, producing soil conditions in the river delta conducive to the spread of the infection where it had never existed previously. Within six years, the prevalence of hookworm among children in the town of Leogane rose from zero to more than 15 percent.

In short, the destruction of Haiti's forests

has played a part in the decline of the country's agriculture, freshwater, electricity, and health and has increased the severity of natural hazards, all of which worsens poverty and political instability. The Dominican Republic has largely avoided this fate.[13] The island of Hispaniola provides a striking cautionary tale of how intact forests provide services to people and how deforestation puts lives and livelihoods at risk. Hispaniola is just a microcosm of the tropics as a whole.

Whereas carbon stored in the atmosphere or ocean is harmful, carbon stored in forests is beneficial.

All across the tropics, intact forests provide services to people with regard to water, energy, agriculture, health, and safety. Protected upland watersheds are a source of clean drinking water for citizens of Quito and Bogotá.[14] Forest plants are used in hundreds of natural medicines by villagers in Madagascar.[15] And forest birds and bats in Indonesia provide free natural pest control to nearby cacao farmers, increasing their yields by nearly half.[16]

Conversely, deforestation puts lives at risk. Deforestation in the Amazon is associated with local spikes in malaria.[17] Coastlines in South Asia that have been stripped of their mangrove forests are more exposed to the full force of storms and tsunamis.[18] And every year, hundreds of thousands of people in Southeast Asia and elsewhere die prematurely from breathing the smoke and haze from deliberately set tropical forest fires.[19]

In fact, tropical forest services contribute toward the achievement of the United Nations' Sustainable Development Goals (SDGs) related to agriculture (Goal 2), health (Goal 3), clean water and sanitation (Goal 6), energy (Goal 7), safety from disasters (Goal 11), and resilience to the impacts of climate change (Goal 13), in addition to the preservation of "life on land"—that is, the conservation of ecosystems and biological diversity (Goal 15). Forests are rarely the main means for achieving these goals, relative to vaccination campaigns or power plants, for example. But they can play a more significant role than is currently recognized by the SDGs, the targets of which focus on traditional interventions.

The underappreciation of forests notable in the SDGs, and, indeed, in broader development-related decision making, is forgivable. Scientific research on the importance of the services provided by tropical forests has proliferated rapidly but only recently, with the cumulative number of scholarly articles having doubled every three years since 2000—the year in which UN Secretary General Kofi Annan commissioned the influential Millennial Ecosystem Assessment.[20] While some benefits forests provide to people ("ecosystem services") have been known for decades, others are just coming to light.

In this chapter, we review the current state of science underpinning the many contributions of tropical forests to development. We first describe two superlative features of tropical forests that enable them to provide so many services: their complex physical structure and their extraordinary biological diversity. We then elaborate on tropical forests' contributions to cleaner water and more electricity, more productive agriculture, better health, and safer lives and property. Figure 3.2 depicts these contributions, as well as the adverse consequences of deforestation. We conclude the chapter by discussing forest conservation as an ecosystem-based action to adapt to the effects of climate change.

In describing the many benefits they provide, we do not mean to argue that forests are a panacea for meeting all development challenges—they aren't. Forests are just one means, and in some cases a relatively small or indirect one, for meeting development goals. Rather, we emphasize that whereas carbon stored in the atmosphere or ocean is harmful, carbon stored in forests is beneficial. And while some methods of combating climate change offer few benefits beyond preventing the release of carbon dioxide, forest conservation offers numerous attractive co-benefits.

We hope this review can shorten the lag between the publication of scientific papers and the adoption of development policy and practice that reflects their findings.

Finally, the review of forest services is complemented by analyses in other chapters of this book. We discussed in chapter 2 what is arguably the greatest service of tropical forests: carbon storage. We save until chapter 6 a discussion of the goods tropical forests provide (such as timber and nontimber forest products), as these benefits are better understood and appreciated than forests' services. We also wait until chapter 6 to discuss the valuation of forests' services—that is, the quantification of their economic contributions—and how these values have been widely omitted from economic indicators. Finally, we save until chapter 6 a discussion of

Figure 3.2: Forested landscapes provide services; deforestation puts lives and livelihoods at risk.

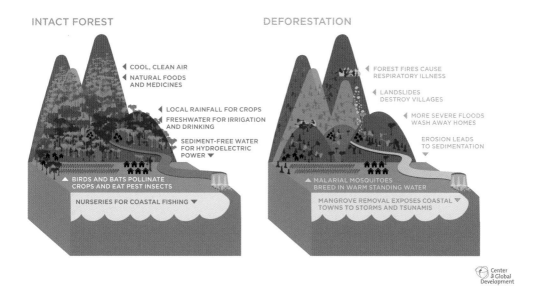

the distribution of forest services; the greatest harm from their loss generally comes to the poor and remote people who are most dependent on them.

Physical Structure and Biological Diversity of Tropical Forests

Tropical forests are superlative in two ways that enable them to provide many valuable services: their physical structure is more complex and their biological diversity is richer than those of any other ecosystem. We describe each feature in turn, starting with physical structure.

The tropics are ideally suited for plant growth. Warm temperatures, abundant rainfall, constant sunlight, and a year-round growing season coincide to let forests flourish in equatorial latitudes like nowhere else on the planet.[21] Forests form a thick green ribbon around Earth's midsection, spanning tropical Africa, Asia, and Latin America.

Tropical forests are the most productive ecosystems on Earth. The year-to-year rate at which wet tropical forests (that is, rainforests) turn sunlight, water, and carbon dioxide into biomass (that is, their net primary productivity) is nearly twice that of their nearest competitors, temperate evergreen forests.[22] While covering less than 12 percent of Earth's land surface, tropical forests generate one-third of the world's net primary productivity and store in their biomass nearly half its living terrestrial carbon.[23]

All this forest biomass is manifested in a dense, multilayered structure.[24] At the top of a mature tropical forest, trees strain skyward competing for light, their crowns forming a thick, multi-tiered canopy. Emerging above the canopy, the tallest trees soar more than sixty meters above the forest floor—as high as the top of a twenty-story building. Below it, other trees cluster in the shade. Hanging off the trees are vines and epiphytes—plants that grow on trees and may never even touch the ground. Near the ground are ferns, shrubs, and saplings, and at ground level is a thick mat of leaves and organic material, covering a dense underground network of roots, stems, and soil. So thick are the layers of vegetation above that the forest floor exists in near darkness even at midday.

The dense, layered structure of tropical forests is integral to regulating water flow. Forests buffer the impact of intense tropical rainfall. Their many leaves and branches act like umbrellas stacked at different heights, catching, softening, and distributing water.[25] Tropical soils are typically shallow and of poor quality, yet their diversity of plant life, including trees, shrubs, vines, and mosses, anchors the soil in place. Litter—dead plant material on the forest floor—also shields the soil from harmful impacts of rain. Underground, large root systems form the equivalent of nets, holding soil in place even on steep slopes.

Forests absorb the impact of tropical rainstorms better than other types of land cover.[26] Rainstorms in the humid tropics can drop massive amounts of water in short bursts. On forested hillsides, this stormwater can seemingly disappear within hours, absorbed into the soil or transpired back into the air.

In contrast, on deforested hillsides raindrops strike directly at the earth with full force, damaging crops and soil. Rapid runoff can create deep gullies and mudslides and flood fields. Water rushing downstream often carries sediment and debris with it, threatening damage to downstream infrastructure.

Box 3.1 elaborates on the many beneficial roles tropical forests play in the water cycle.

The other feature of tropical forests that enables them to provide so many services is their extraordinary biological diversity (biodiversity). Trees in a tropical forest have different heights, root systems, transpiration rates, chemical compounds, and flowering and fruiting patterns. This variety creates many habitats and ecological niches that are filled by animals. Some animals disperse seeds; some pollinate plants. Some microorganisms fix nitrogen, while others decompose wastes. Leaves and bark are eaten by insects, which are eaten by small animals, which are then eaten by larger animals in a complex food web.

The range of biodiversity is exceptional not only within tropical forests, but also across them. The growth of tropical forests encompasses a wide range of altitudes, rainfall levels, soil types, and other conditions. They range from high montane cloud forests to lowland dipterocarp forests; from evergreen rainforests that see five meters of rain a year to dry, deciduous forests; and from seasonally flooded forests to brackish coastal mangrove forests. Each of these forest types has its own distinct array of plant and animal life.

Box 3.1: Tropical Forests and the Water Cycle

Tropical forests play a critical role in absorbing, cleaning, and recycling water in the following ways:

They catch what comes down: Trees intercept rain and fog. When a torrent of rain hits a forest, leaves and branches lessen its impact on any one spot by catching, spreading, and channeling the water.

They send moisture up: Forests return moisture to the sky through evapotranspiration. This refers to the moisture that evaporates directly off leaves and branches, as well as the water that falls to the ground, is absorbed by tree roots, travels up to leaves, and is transpired into the air as vapor.

They capture water underground: Forests are especially good at catching and storing water underground along root systems or in pockets left by bugs and animals. Forests provide greater potential for water to seep into the ground (infiltration) and travel to aquifers instead of flowing overland.

They slow flows: Forests' thick vegetation forms a series of obstacles to water flow, reducing soil erosion.

They clean and green: A highly diverse array of plants and animals in tropical forests clean water and remove pollutants as water slowly filters underground.

They recycle nutrients: Vegetation captures and reuses nutrients that are washed from higher ground and holds decomposing plant material in place.

They maintain weather patterns: The capture and release of atmospheric water by forests has been linked to the maintenance of current wind and weather patterns at local, regional, and even continental scales.

Source: Brandon, "Ecosystem Services."

As a result, the proliferation of plant and animal life to which tropical forests are home is astounding. They contain more than 40,000 species of trees, as compared to fewer than 1,000 tree species in North America and just 124 in Europe.[27] One square kilometer of tropical rainforest in Malaysia can contain more tree species than all of the United States and Canada; moreover, a single tree in the Peruvian Amazon may be home to more ant species than the entire British Isles.[28]

The prize for the most biodiverse area in the world may go to Madidi National Park in Bolivia, which is home to 1,088 bird species (11 percent of bird species worldwide), over 200 mammal species, 12,000 plant species, and 300 freshwater fish species, all living within an area the size of Slovenia.[29] By contrast, Yellowstone National Park, a high-biodiversity temperate protected area half the size of Madidi, has only one-third as many mammal species, one-quarter as many bird species, one-tenth as many plant species, and one-twentieth as many fish species.[30]

All told, tropical forests provide habitat to over two-thirds of all land-based species,[31] ranging from lowly and anonymous insects to some of the planet's most charismatic and beloved creatures: gorillas, jaguars, toucans, orangutans, and tigers. Many tropical forest species are endemic—that is, found in only one valley, watershed, or mountaintop, and nowhere else on Earth. Madagascar, for example, is striking for its endemism. The whole country has nearly 14,000 plant species, 95 percent of which are found nowhere else.[32]

Scientists' understanding of the diversity of life in tropical forests is far from complete. While most birds and mammals have been relatively well studied, little is known about many of the other "millions of species that are estimated to inhabit tropical rainforests, including almost all belowground, canopy, and aquatic species as well as most insects, fungi, parasites, lower plants, and microorganisms."[33] With the understanding of how they contribute to providing ecosystem goods and services so incomplete, their value is likely underestimated.[34]

These two attributes of tropical forests—their dense and complex physical structure and their extraordinary biodiversity—explain their importance in providing people with freshwater, food, health, and safety from natural disasters.

Forests, Water Use, and Energy

People's dependence on water goes far beyond quenching thirst. Every kilogram of food is grown with water, whether from rainfall, surface water, groundwater, or irrigation. Water is essential to cooking and cleaning, nourishment, and sanitation. Clean water is fundamental to health; dirty water can bring sickness.

Furthermore, water provides a major source of electricity. Access to energy is at the heart of modern economies and lifestyles, and in much of the world it comes from hydroelectric dams. Dams produce one-fifth of the electricity in countries outside the Organization for Economic Co-operation and Development (OECD), including two-thirds of all the electricity in Latin America.[35] Dams depend on water that is abundant, reliable, and clean. Low water levels during a dry season can reduce power generation. The reservoirs behind dams are vulnerable to being filled with sediment, which reduces generation capacity and necessitates costly repairs and dredging.

Two of the SDGs are related to clean water and access to modern energy (goals 6 and 7, respectively).[36] The development agenda in the water resources sector has traditionally emphasized hard infrastructure—dams, irrigation systems, and water treatment facilities—often with big investments and high-profile ribbon cuttings. Yet alongside these engineering triumphs, tropical forests can play key roles in ensuring both good water quality and reliable water supply, allowing people in developing countries to live healthier lives with more electricity.

Forests and Water Quality

Forests clean water in two main ways. The first is by preventing sedimentation. Erosion is a process in which land is stripped of soil by wind or water. Erosion occurs naturally, but it is worsened by human activities that remove the vegetation holding soils in place (such as deforestation) or that compact or harden soil (such as cattle grazing). Soil that erodes into water sources becomes sediment, which can

> reduce reservoir capacity; impair water for drinking and domestic or industrial uses; obstruct navigation channels; raise river beds, which reduces the capacity to handle water safely; adversely alter aquatic habitat in streams; fill the spawning grounds of fish; wear down turbine blades in power installations; and cause landslides, which damage people and their structures and block channels, resulting in floods.[37]

With their many pathways for slowing water flow, healthy tropical forests allow little erosion.[38] They are the most effective land cover in reducing sediments in water.[39]

Riverside (riparian) forests and mangrove forests are especially important for reducing sediment in waterways.[40] Riparian forests anchor soils and reduce erosion and sedimentation, especially from overland water flows.[41] Coastal mangrove forests trap sediment that has flowed downstream, preventing it from flowing offshore where it can damage coastal ports, transportation infrastructure, and fisheries. By trapping sediment, mangroves build shoreline, adding to their protective value in buffering coastal communities from waves and storms. Other forests reduce sediments as well, even if they have been partially logged.[42]

The second way forests clean water is by filtering out other pollutants. Water can carry chemicals, nutrients, sediments, salts, and pathogens, some of which have adverse consequences for human health. Trees remove pollutants from the water they return to the atmosphere through transpiration. They also filter pollutants from water that flows overland and into groundwater, as their vegetation, leaf litter, microbes, and soils all remove or biochemically transform contaminants.[43] Again, riparian forests are especially important for filtering out pollutants before they reach streams.[44]

In addition to providing direct cleaning of water, the maintenance of forest cover precludes other land uses associated with greater pollution, including pesticide and chemical runoff from agriculture, animal waste from grazing lands, and toxic tailings from mines. The conversion of Indonesian forests to oil palm plantations, for example, increased sediment by up to 550 times the amount found in natural forest streams, reducing the quality of freshwater for poor farming communities.[45]

For all these reasons, cities safeguarding municipal water supplies have long recognized the benefits of conserving healthy forests. Cities as diverse as Bogota, Harare, New York City, Quito, and Singapore have set aside protected areas in upland watersheds to preserve water quality.[46] In fact, about one-third of the world's hundred largest cities obtain a significant portion of their drinking water from protected areas.[47]

Forests and Water Availability

When rain falls on a forest, some of the water is recycled to the air through evapotranspiration, some filters underground, and some flows along the ground. In contrast, when rain falls on other types of land cover, more water flows overland.[48] In other words, forests distribute water more like a sprinkler system and less like a hose.

Both natural forests and tree plantations are associated with lower total flows than less-forested lowland tropical watersheds, according to a meta-analysis conducted by environmental scientists Bruno Locatelli and Rafaele Vignola.[49] Because most lowland tropical forests send less water in overland flows than deforested areas, they are said to "consume" water.[50]

On the other hand, high-altitude cloud forests "produce" water, intercepting fog from the air and converting it into available water on the ground. Cloud forests are of outsized importance for water availability in the tropics, especially during the dry season.[51] They are also of outsized importance for hydropower; although they occupy less than 5 percent of the land area that drains into dams in the tropics, they receive between one-fifth and one-half of the surface water of these watersheds.[52] Clearing cloud forests impairs the performance of dams downstream, while restoring such forests upstream can enhance dam functioning.[53]

The perception that tropical lowland forests are consumers of water has led some to suggest converting forests to other uses in places facing water scarcity.[54] The water that forests recycle to the air, however, is distributed downwind as rainfall, where it may be useful for agriculture, among other purposes. Fully understanding the influence of forests on water availability requires analysis of areas large enough to include both upwind forests with high evapotranspiration and downstream areas that receive more rain as a result.[55]

Two-thirds of the studies in the Locatelli and Vignola meta-analysis looked at watersheds smaller than one square kilometer. But studies that account for water recycling at the regional level tell a different story.[56] An analysis of the entire Xingu River basin above Brazil's Belo Monte dam complex, for example, found that upstream deforestation would increase water flow locally but decrease it regionally, compromising energy production from the dam.[57]

The conventional understanding that lowland tropical forests consume more water than they produce has recently been challenged by a new and still-debated theory called the "biotic pump."[58] According to biotic pump theory, the particles of dust and pollen that hover above forests cause condensation to form. This condensation lowers air pressure, which pulls moisture inland from oceans.

According to its proponents, the biotic pump theory can explain why rainfall in the forested Amazon and Congo basins does not diminish at increasing distances from the ocean. Uninterrupted expanses of forests act like a bucket brigade, passing coastal moisture from one stretch of forest to the next, deep into the continental interior. When forests in the middle are felled, the flow of moisture is broken, and the continental interior is left high and dry.

Forests distribute water not only across space but over time as well. Forests have been found to retain water in the wet season and release it in the dry season when it is needed most.[59] Studies from the Brazilian Amazon forest and Cerrado wooded savanna and from China's Yellow River found that deforestation extended the length of the dry season by as much as a month, with costs to agriculture and energy.[60] Reforestation can reverse this effect, with dry season river flows increasing after it is carried out on a large scale.[61] The Locatelli and Vignola meta-analysis found that natural lowland forests had higher water flow during dry periods ("base flow"), though the same was not true for tree plantations.[62]

Forests and Agricultural Production

Agriculture is the backbone of rural development, with farming providing the bulk of employment in many developing countries. Furthermore, food security looms large as a political consideration. High food prices are a notorious source of political instability; governments in developing countries have been overthrown when food prices spiked.[63]

The Sustainable Development Goal related to ending hunger (Goal 2) focuses on increased agricultural productivity and production, as well as on research, extension services, and well-functioning commodity markets.[64] Development planners have commonly sought to increase agricultural production by expanding areas that produce soy, beef, and palm oil, among other crops. As a result, most new cropland expansion in the tropics for the past two decades has taken place at the expense of forests.[65]

Forests shouldn't be seen as just an inconvenience getting in the way of grazing land or cropland, however—standing forests make substantial and largely unrecognized contributions to agricultural production in their own right. Forests are, as mentioned previously, a source of clean water for irrigation. Forests also influence the weather patterns that make land suitable for farming, both directly downwind and at great distances, and the bees, birds, and bats that live in them pollinate crops and control pests on nearby farmland. Forests directly provide a cornucopia of edible plants and animals, and forest cover contributes to the health of inland fisheries that nourish millions.

Forests, Weather, and Agriculture

Agriculture is highly dependent on favorable weather. Weather, in turn, is influenced by the geographical features over which air passes. Coastal Washington State and Oregon are lush because of wet winds off the Pacific Ocean, while the eastern parts of those states are bone dry because the towering Cascade Mountains block those same wet winds from advancing. Likewise, farmers across Brazil owe their rainfall to the moist air blowing in from the Amazon Forest.

Tropical forests recycle much of the rainfall they receive back to the atmosphere as moisture.[66] Winds that pass over forests produce more rainfall than those that pass over open land.[67] This phenomenon leads to cooler, wetter air downwind of forests, which is generally better for farming.[68] The moderating effects of moisture also mean farms downwind will experience fewer very hot days and very cold nights, either of which can be detrimental to crops.[69]

Forests generate cooler, wetter weather regionally as well as locally. Large-scale deforestation may lead to less regional rainfall and longer dry seasons, independent of the effect of carbon dioxide emissions from deforestation on the global climate.[70] The Amazon is particularly susceptible to deforestation-induced heating and drying, which could lead to declines in cattle and soy productivity.

Brazilian atmospheric scientist Antonio Nobre likens the water evaporated by the Amazon rainforest to a "flying river, which rises into the atmosphere in the form of vapour [and] is bigger than the biggest river on the Earth . . . . The Amazon is a gigantic hydrological pump that brings the humidity of the Atlantic Ocean into the continent and guarantees the irrigation of the region." He warns that deforestation of the Amazon will dry up the "river," leading inevitably to droughts in central and southern Brazil, including São Paulo's worst-ever drought and water shortage, which ran from 2013-2015: "The smoke from forest fires introduces too many particles into the atmosphere, dries the clouds, and they don't rain."[71]

Because atmospheric winds circle the globe, deforestation in tropical regions can change weather patterns on distant continents, too. Tropical forests influence climate and weather patterns in far-off locations through "teleconnections," affecting farmers as far from the tropics as Canada, China and Mongolia, northern Europe, Scandinavia, Siberia, and the midwestern United States and Texas.[72] A global climate model shows, for example, that deforestation in central Africa and the Brazilian Amazon decreases rainfall in the U.S. Midwest.[73]

Forests affect weather patterns even at the global scale. Complete deforestation of the tropics would heat the planet by 0.1 to 0.7°C, an estimate based on weather influences alone that does not even consider the effects of elevated concentrations of carbon dioxide. Thus, at the upper end, deforestation of the tropics would effectively double observed global warming since 1850. Warming would be especially severe across the tropics, as would drying.[74]

Pollination and Pest Control

Wild insects and animals living in tropical forests support global food production by pollinating crops and controlling agricultural pests. About 70 percent of leading global crops benefit from pollination by bees and other wild insects, which affects the size, quality, and likelihood of fruit and the stability of the harvest.[75] More than one-third of the global food supply depends on or benefits from animal pollinators.[76] Pollination is especially important for many higher-value crops, such as fruits and nuts. Pollination by wild insects is more than twice as effective as pollination by honeybees, suggesting that managed honeybee hives should be viewed as supplementing, rather than substituting for, wild pollinators.[77]

No data are available on the share of global pollination performed by wild forest–dependent pollinators. It may well be substantial, however, given the known preference of many species of wild pollinators (such as birds, bats, rodents, and lemurs) for forests. A global synthesis shows, for example, that 53 percent of all tropical bird species live only in forests, while only 3 percent prefer agricultural areas. Of the bird species that live in forests, a third will fly to agricultural areas, where they pollinate crops and eat pests.[78]

Forest animals that eat insects (insectivores) can also provide important pest control services, reducing or eliminating the need for pesticides.[79] Cacao yields in Sulawesi, Indonesia, for example, were found to be 45 percent higher in farms nearer to primary forest than those in distant areas, thanks to pest control services provided by birds and bats.[80] In an on-farm experiment in Costa Rica, native bird predators reduced damaging infestations of coffee berry borer beetles by 50 percent relative to coffee shrubs where nets kept birds out.[81] And in Mexico, certain hardwood trees host insects that attack fruit fly pests, reducing crop losses.[82]

The pollination and pest control services of forests come with a few caveats. For one, the effects forest animals have on agriculture are somewhat limited to areas near forests—say, within the natural flying ranges of birds or bats. For another, these effects aren't always good. Agricultural fields near forest edges can suffer depredations from such forest-based species as monkeys, wild pigs, or elephants.

Forest Foods

To those who know tropical forests, they are natural grocery stores containing a wide variety of edible fruits, nuts, vegetables, mushrooms, and meats. Forest foods account for nearly one-third of the income households living in and around forests derive from forest products, second only to wood fuels.[83] According to studies in twenty-two countries in Africa and Asia, agricultural and forager communities use an average of ninety to one hundred different food species at each site, with as many as three hundred to eight hundred species used in Ethiopia, India, and Kenya. Many of these food species come from seminatural, cultivated forest gardens or are actively managed species within natural forests, which suggests that in some cases the distinction between cultivation and wild foraging may be blurry.[84]

In remote areas where diets are limited, greater forest biodiversity has the potential to increase the variety of nutrients people receive, thus contributing to overall health. Across Africa, children living in forested areas have more diverse and nutritious diets, based on a positive relationship between tree cover and dietary diversity.[85] One study showed, for example, that children living in parts of Malawi with higher forest cover had a more diverse diet, were more likely to consume foods rich in Vitamin A, and had less diarrhea. Declines in forest cover were followed by drops in dietary diversity.[86]

Wild meats, known as bushmeat, are of great nutritional importance for many of the world's poor. The nutritional value of wild meats tends to be higher than that of plants, providing protein and fat, iron, zinc, vitamin B-12, and other micronutrients.[87] Unfortunately however, bushmeat harvest raises issues of sustainability and public health. While the hunting of fast-reproducing mammals such as deer or rodents is likely sustainable, the hunting of primates or other slow-reproducing species is less so. Bushmeat consumption also carries the risk of transmitting to humans wildlife diseases capable of causing pandemics.[88]

Wild foods can be especially important by providing a "safety net" in times of crisis. Farmers in Madagascar, for example, depend on wild yams from forests during lean seasons, when food is scarce or crops are damaged by cyclones.[89] Researchers have documented communities foraging for wild foods and products in forests as a natural insurance mechanism in dozens of locations across the tropics.[90] Still, while use of forests in times of crisis is widespread, it is not necessarily preferred over loans from kin or off-farm wage labor, meaning that gathering food and income from forests may be best viewed as options of last resort.[91]

Forests and Fisheries

The rich array of life in tropical forests extends to their waterways, as well. The rivers and streams of the Amazon Basin, for example, contain between 2,500 and 3,500 species of freshwater fish—possibly more than all the marine fish species in the Atlantic Ocean.[92] And these freshwater fish are eaten; freshwater yields comprise one-tenth of the global catch by commercial fisheries.[93] In 2008, the global value of inland captured fish, excluding aquaculture, was estimated to be between $5 billion and $18 billion, if not more.[94] In contrast to production from marine fisheries, which is often used for animal feed, inland fish catch is almost always for direct human consumption. The fish are caught mostly by small enterprises, and women harvest more than half.[95]

In some places, inland fisheries provide people's primary protein source; one is the Great Tonle Sap area in Cambodia, the world's fourth most productive inland fishery. Fish, crabs, and other inland aquatic animals account for 79 percent of animal protein consumed by people in the region.[96] In other places, inland fisheries fill seasonal gaps in food security.[97] Forest peoples in the upper Amazon region of eastern Peru, for example, turn to inland fisheries as a safety net in times of crisis, such as family illness or major flooding.[98]

The productivity of inland fisheries depends on the health of forests upstream. The leaves and fruits that fall from forests provide food for fish.[99] Deforestation can increase runoff and sediment and alter water flow patterns in ways that can diminish fishery productivity.[100]

Flooded forests are particularly important for inland fisheries. In broad areas of the Amazon Basin and much of the Mekong River Delta, forests that are flooded for all or part of the year act as nurseries and breeding grounds for highly productive fisheries, and removing them reduces the number of fish. The loss of forests in the Mekong River Delta has been paralleled by losses in fishery production.[101]

Forests are valuable to marine fisheries, too. Coastal mangrove forests serve as breeding grounds and nurseries for a wide variety of fish and other aquatic species.[102] The many tangled roots of mangroves keep young fish and crustaceans safe from larger fish and other predators. By the time small fish have grown enough to leave mangroves in search of additional food, they will have reached a size where they are more likely to survive. Mangroves also shelter small fish from strong waves and nurture them with steady supplies of nutrients and food. Fish that rely on mangroves at some stage of their life cycles are estimated to comprise 30 percent of the fish catch in Southeast Asia, 60 percent of commercial fish species in India, and 67 percent of the commercial fish catch in eastern Australia.[103]

Forests and Health

Worldwide improvement in human health has been one of the greatest development success stories of recent decades. Since 1950, global life expectancy has risen by almost twenty years, and since 1990, global child mortality has fallen by 50 percent.[104] Great progress has been made in eliminating diseases that once ravaged humanity, including smallpox, leprosy, river blindness, polio, and guinea worm.

Still, for all our successes, some diseases remain stubbornly persistent or resurgent. Health is still a top development priority, occupying a prominent place among the Sustainable Development Goals (Goal 3). Among the SDGs' many targets related to health are quests to combat malaria and to reduce deaths from air and water pollution. Vaccines and health clinics are central to meeting health goals, but forests can play a role as well.

Tropical forests make important contributions to health, and not just because forest foods contribute to more varied and nutritious diets. Tropical forests are the source of thou-sands of medicines, of both the traditional and modern pharmaceutical varieties. Deforestation is linked to increased incidence of malaria and other diseases. And the air pollution from forest fires associated with land clearing is a major cause of deaths and illnesses.

Forest Medicines

The extraordinarily diverse species inhabiting tropical forests are endowed with a vast array of chemical properties. Plants and animals produce chemicals to lure mates, attract pollinators, repel predators, or coagulate sap. Poison dart frogs produce powerful neurotoxins; salamanders can regenerate their limbs. Other plants and animals produce fungicides and antibiotics.[105]

People use many of these compounds in traditional medicines. The World Health Organization estimates that 70 to 95 percent of people living in developing countries (three and a half billion to four billion) rely chiefly on traditional medicines for their primary health care needs.[106] Despite few of them having been through clinical trials to prove their effectiveness, these traditional medicines continue to be used widely, for reasons discussed in chapter 6. One estimate suggests that, globally, fifty-three thousand plant species are used medicinally.[107] The share of these species that are from tropical forests is unspecified but is doubtless considerable. In just one relatively small rainforest watershed in Madagascar, Makira, 241 plants are used locally as medicines.[108]

Compounds from tropical forest plants and animals are used in modern medicines as well. One-quarter of all pharmaceuticals are created from wild plants or are synthesized based on the plants' molecular properties.[109] Nearly half the drugs approved to treat cancer are derived from natural products.[110] Scientists have identified thousands of tropical forest plants as having potential anticancer properties, and dozens have been shown to be active against cancer cells in clinical screenings. Vinblastine and vincristine, derived from Madagascar's rosy periwinkle, are routinely used to treat many types of cancer.[111]

Deforestation and Disease

Malaria, the third largest killer of children in the tropics after pneumonia and diarrhea, is responsible for more than half a million deaths per year.[112] A link between deforestation and malaria has been noticed for decades, ever since the prevalence of "frontier malaria" was observed among colonists clearing forests in the Amazon.[113]

Intact forests suppress the incidence and transmission of malaria through multiple channels. They have many insectivores that eat mosquitoes, cooler temperatures that slow the rate at which mosquitos mature, and more species competing within the ecological niche occupied by disease-carrying mosquitoes.[114]

In addition, a "dilution effect hypothesis" proposes that since forests contain more animals for mosquitoes to bite, the risk that humans will be bitten and infected is reduced. Furthermore, with more creatures being bitten, fewer will be reservoirs for malaria or other diseases, diluting the overall effect of the disease. This hypothesis is still a subject of debate, but it has found significant support in field-based studies.[115]

Conversely, deforestation improves the conditions for malaria. Small pools of standing water provide more breeding areas, and warmer temperatures mean faster larval growth. Roads, forest fires, and selective logging all heighten malaria risk.[116]

While deforestation is associated with greater exposure to malaria in Africa and South America, it has less predictable impacts in Asia.[117] Reforestation doesn't necessarily reverse the problem, as young, growing plantations can be havens for malarial mosquitoes.[118]

Deforestation has been linked directly or indirectly to increased incidence of other diseases, as well, among them chikungunya, dengue, hantaviruses, leishmaniasis, lyme disease, schistosomiasis, simian immunodeficiency virus (SIV), West Nile fever virus, and yellow fever.[119] The mechanisms for transmission vary by disease; often, human movement into forests changes pathways and vectors and exposes people to diseases with which they had little contact until they entered or disturbed forests. Yellow fever, for example, is passed in a cycle between tree-dwelling monkeys and mosquitoes.[120] When people disturb forests through hunting or fuelwood collection, they can become infected and transmit the disease to larger urban population centers.[121]

Between 60 and 80 percent of emerging infectious diseases are zoonotic in origin, meaning they come to humans from animals.[122] Many zoonotic diseases come from farm animals, but a sizable fraction come from tropical deforestation and forest exploitation.[123] Human consumption and trade of forest animals, especially with deeper encroachment into forests, have been linked to the start and spread among humans of HIV/

AIDS, severe acute respiratory syndrome (SARS), Ebola and other hemorrhagic fevers, Nipah virus, avian influenza, and pandemic H1N1.[124]

Without further research, these linkages imply little on their own about whether reducing deforestation can be an effective or cost-effective component of efforts to control these diseases. They do, however, suggest that conserving tropical forests for their carbon value can have side benefits for public health.

Forest Fires and Air Pollution

Forest fires rarely occur naturally in wet tropical forests because of their high moisture content, high rainfall, and high leaf-to-wood ratio.[125] Fires that occur naturally tend to be small, slow, and extinguished at night. Unlike in ecosystems where fire is a frequent part of natural cycles, a wet tropical forest may go thousands of years without a fire.[126]

For rainforests to get hot enough to burn, trees first have to be felled ("slashed"), dried, and sometimes stacked into piles.[127] When wet tropical forests do burn, it is almost always as the result of deliberate land clearing or logging. In a vicious cycle, deforestation increases the risk and intensity of future fires by creating more edges and gaps in the canopy, both of which increase drying of the forest.[128]

Smoke and haze from tropical forest fires release heavy metals, carcinogens, ultrafine particulates, and ozone-producing compounds, among other harmful substances.[129] Throughout broad swaths of the tropics, landscape fires produce particulate matter at average concentrations far above the level the U.S. Environmental Protection Agency con-

siders unhealthy.[130] Pollutants from fires can travel thousands of kilometers beyond their points of origin; fires in South America, for instance, have been observed to raise carbon monoxide levels over Australia.[131]

Air pollution produced by forest fires is responsible for hundreds of thousands of premature deaths every year. Globally, annual premature deaths from forest fires are estimated to range from 250,000 to 339,000 in typical years, to as high as 532,000 during the 1997–98 El Niño.[132] The haze from those fires resulted in increased cardiorespiratory ailments, as well.[133]

Forests and Safety

International news coverage is routinely dominated by shocking images of the death and destruction wrought by landslides, floods, storms, and tsunamis. These events prompt generous charitable giving in their immediate aftermath. The process of rebuilding lives and economies takes years or even decades after the event has dropped off the front pages. The largest storms can set back development prospects by decades, as described in chapter 1.[134]

The SDGs aim to reduce deaths and economic losses from disasters (Goal 11).[135] Good public planning and building codes are key. Where and how people build can save lives from disasters, as well-sited and well-built infrastructure can withstand impacts where poor construction is swept away. Similarly, forests are protective green infrastructure that can prevent damage from small disasters and lessen the impacts of larger ones, including landslides, floods, storm surges, and tsunami waves.

Deforestation and Landslides

Landslides are a natural occurrence that is especially common on mountainous slopes steeper than 25 degrees. They are usually caused by seismic activity but can also be triggered by heavy rains or fires. As small landslides move downslope, they can grow in size and impact as loose, unstable soils gather small trees and logs in their wake. As debris hurtles down hillsides it can rip away roads and houses in its path, and it may not stop until it reaches a plateau, valley, or river.[136]

The most extreme landslides result in high death tolls. A tropical storm that struck three Mexican states in 1999 triggered hundreds of landslides, affecting two hundred municipalities and nearly one and a half million inhabitants, resulting in 263 deaths. Engineer Irasema Alcántara-Ayala and her colleagues described deforestation as a causal "precursor" to these landslides—more than two-thirds occurred on slopes with less than 10 percent forest cover, many of which had been deforested during the previous decade.[137]

Forests can limit both small and large landslides and stabilize smaller debris flows in a number of ways.[138] First, forest vegetation shields soil from the damaging impact of hard and heavy rain.[139] Second, forested slopes are less likely to give way because of their soils' stronger cohesion and because forests quickly recycle excess water to the air through evapotranspiration or pull it underground.[140] Finally, when land does slip, root systems anchor the soil and act as brakes.

Deforestation can increase the intensity, frequency, and extent of landslides. Converting forests to pastures rapidly and permanently diminishes the stability of slopes.[141]

The higher that trees or vegetation are cleared on a hillside, the worse the impacts of debris flows are downhill, since they have room to increase in weight and size.[142] As previous landslides make revegetation more difficult and costly, they lead to future landslides' increasing in area and frequency, in a vicious cycle of ever-widening erosion.

Deforestation and Floods

Floods occur when large storms and heavy rains cause rivers to overflow their banks, as was the case with Hurricane Mitch, described in chapter 1. The conventional wisdom that has emerged from more than a century of study is that forests reduce and mitigate small floods.[143] They do so by pumping water into the air through evapotranspiration and into the ground through root systems, so less runs off as surface flow. Furthermore, less sediment is released into floodwater by forests' healthy soils than by the crumbly or compacted soils of deforested areas.

On the relationship between forests and extreme flood events, the jury is still out. Forests can potentially reduce the magnitude or severity of large floods in the same ways they mitigate small floods—through soil infiltration and evapotranspiration. Larger floods may overwhelm these functions of forests, however, allowing floodwaters to continue flowing downstream. While some studies have presented evidence that forests lessen the destructive impacts of large floods, this connection remains disputed.[144]

Deforestation can exacerbate floods in another way, too. When low-lying peat forests are cleared, the peat soil oxidizes, shrinks, and subsides. As land subsides, the risk of inundation increases. This dynamic has been well studied in temperate zones and is increasingly being observed in the tropics.[145]

Deforestation, Storm Surges, and Tsunami Waves

On December 26, 2004, at 6:58 a.m. local time, 160 kilometers off the coast of Sumatra, one geological plate slipped under another. The magnitude-9.1 earthquake that resulted triggered a tsunami, the enormity of which was nearly unknown in human history. Waves up to thirty meters high killed more than two hundred thousand people in fourteen countries. In regions closest to the tsunami's epicenter, little could have prevented catastrophic destruction. Farther away, however, mangroves and other coastal forests substantially mitigated the deadly impacts of the waves.[146] Similar protective effects of mangroves were observed after a supercyclone struck Odisha, India, in 1999 and after the Japan tsunami of 2011.[147]

Mangroves reduce the impact of waves from peak tides, storm surges, and even extreme wind-driven waves from tropical cyclones—events in which wave height is relatively small.[148] The mechanisms are straightforward: trees help dissipate tidal and wave energy. Coastal forests also trap sediments, increasing coastal elevations.[149]

How well forests slow waves varies, depending on the characteristics of both the forests and the waves.[150] During the most extreme storms and tsunamis, very high winds and waves may overwhelm and destroy mangroves and other coastal forests, as occurred in Honduras after Hurricane Mitch, although

evidence suggests that coastal forests may attenuate even the highest waves.[151]

Forests and Adaptation to Climate Change

In coming decades, advancing climate change will bring hotter temperatures, increased stress on water and crop production, larger storms, melting glaciers, and rising seas. In this future, many of the services provided by tropical forests will become even more important. Conserving and restoring forests is a type of "ecosystem-based adaptation"[152]—an important component of the package of measures people must take now and in the future to adapt to the effects of climate change.

As climate change advances, many of the services provided by tropical forests will become even more important.

Climate change is expected to make tropical agricultural lands hotter and, in many cases, drier. Scientists predict the best conditions for farming will shift away from the tropics toward the poles. Farmers can adapt to climate change by switching to more climate-tolerant crops, while agronomists can develop and promote more heat- and drought-tolerant varieties, and governments and insurance companies can provide safety nets for more turbulent farming conditions. In addition to these measures, people can adapt to climate change by maintaining forests above and throughout agricultural regions. In a world of drought and fire, the cool, moist air circulated by forests can provide some relief to farmers.

Climate change is expected to melt glaciers, while larger storms are predicted to become more frequent. The result will be more landslides and more floods. Sturdier construction of buildings, precautionary zoning, and disaster preparedness are all key responses to a stormier world. So, too, is the protection and restoration of forests. Forests on steep slopes can absorb heavy snowmelt and limit the extent and intensity of landslides, while forested watersheds can attenuate the impacts of small-, medium-, and (debatably) large-scale flooding.

Climate change is expected to raise sea levels and produce more large storms, battering shorelines with a one-two punch.[153] Sea walls, levees, pumps, and early warning systems can all limit destruction from these events. Alongside hard infrastructure, "green" infrastructure can often achieve the same goals. Mangrove forests elevate and protect coastlines from powerful waves, and, unlike cement sea walls, they also serve as fish nurseries and carbon sinks.

Various countries are already undertaking ecosystem-based adaptation using forests. Sri Lanka is protecting and restoring mangroves around its entire coastline.[154] Rio de Janeiro is reforesting steep hillsides to reduce landslides and flood risk.[155] And Kenya is promoting agroforestry throughout the Kikuyu Escarpment to diversify livelihoods, in preparation for future stress on agriculture.[156] The implementation of such measures implies that support for tropical forests should be a component of climate finance for adaptation, as well as mitigation, as described in chapter 12.

Conclusion

Tropical forests provide many benefits with regard to water, energy, agriculture, health, and safety. Their contributions are illustrated starkly on Hispaniola: in the Dominican Republic, citizens benefit from forests' services, while deforestation in Haiti has put lives at risk. As climate change advances, the value of the protective services provided by forests will increase, making forest conservation an important climate adaptation measure.

Whereas pumping carbon into the atmosphere or ocean is harmful, storing carbon in forests is actually beneficial. And while some emission-cutting methods offer few benefits beyond preventing the release of carbon dioxide, forest conservation offers many positive side benefits. Some of these have been well understood for decades; others are becoming clear only with recent scientific study.

Many of the services described in this chapter would benefit from further research to explore, solidify, and refine the connections with deforestation. One important component for such research is the availability of accurate and consistent spatial data on forest loss and gain. Fortunately, data on the state of forests are undergoing a revolution in quality and availability, as we describe in chapter 4.

Notes

1. United Nations Development Programme, "Human Development Index (HDI)," http://hdr.undp.org/en/content/human-development-index-hdi.

2. Food and Agriculture Organization of the United Nations (FAO), Global Forest Resources Assessment 2015: Desk Reference, Rome, Italy, 2015.

3. V. Williams, "A Case Study of Desertification in Haiti," *Journal of Sustainable Development* 4, no. 3 (2011): 20–31.

4. Ibid.

5. S. Alscher, "Environmental Degradation and Migration on Hispaniola Island," *International Migration* 49, S1 (2011): e163–88.

6. E. Vedrine, "Haiti and the Destruction of Nature," Hartford Web Publishing, November 10, 2002, http://www.hartford-hwp.com/archives/43a/254.html.

7. K. Than, "Haiti Earthquake, Deforestation Heighten Landslide Risk," *National Geographic News*, January 14, 2010.

8. R. R. Lall, "Haiti to Plant Millions of Trees to Boost Forests and Help Tackle Poverty," *The Guardian*, March 28, 2013.

9. J. Wells, "A Dam for the People, and a People Damned," *The Star*, November 21, 2010; Inter-American Development Bank, "Haiti: Water Management Program in the Artibonite Basin, HA-L 1087," proposal for non-reimbursable financing, 2013, http://idbdocs.iadb.org/wsdocs/getdocument.aspx?docnum=38234119.

10. M. Lucky et al., *Haiti Sustainable Energy Roadmap: Harnessing Domestic Energy Resources to Build an Affordable, Reliable, and Climate-Compatible Electricity System* (Washington, DC: Worldwatch Institute, 2014).

11. P. Howard, "Development-Induced Displacement in Haiti," *Refuge: Canada's Journal on Refugees* 16, no. 3 (1997): 4–11.

12. D. Taylor, "Seeing the Forests for More than the Trees," *Environmental Health Perspectives* 105, no. 11 (1997): 1186.

13. A. Martin, "An Island Divided: What We Must Learn from the Tragedy of Hispaniola," EcoWatch, April 5, 2014, http://ecowatch.com/2014/04/15/learn-from-tragedy-on-hispaniola/.

14. S. Postel and B. H. Thompson, "Watershed Protection: Capturing the Benefits of Nature's Water Supply Services," *Natural Resources Forum* 29, no. 2 (2005): 98–108.

15. C. D. Golden et al., "Rainforest Pharmacopeia in Madagascar Provides High Value for Current Local and Prospective Global Uses," *PLoS ONE* 7, no. 7 (2012): e41221.

16. B. Maas, Y. Clough, and T. Tscharntk, "Bats and Birds Increase Crop Yield in Tropical Agroforestry Landscapes," *Ecology Letters* 16, no. 12 (2013): 1480–87.

17. D. Sawyer, *Frontier Malaria in the Amazon Region of Brazil: Types of Malaria Situations and Some Implications for Control* (Brasília: World Health Organization and the Special Programme for Research Training in Tropical Diseases, 1988); S. Myers et al., "Human Health Impacts of Ecosystem Alteration," *Proceedings of the National Academy of Sciences* 110, no. 47 (2013): 18753–60.

18. S. Das and J. R. Vincent, "Mangroves Protected Villages and Reduced Death Toll during Indian Super Cyclone," *Proceedings of the National Academy of Sciences* 106, no. 18 (2009): 7357–60; N. Tanaka et al., "Combined Effects of Coastal Forest and Sea Embankment on Reducing the Washout Region of Houses in the Great East Japan Tsunami," *Journal of Hydro-Environment Research* 8, no. 3 (2014): 270–80.

19. M. Z. Jacobson, "Effects of Biomass Burning on Climate, Accounting for Heat and Moisture Fluxes, Black and Brown Carbon, and Cloud Absorption Effects," *Journal of Geophysical Research: Atmospheres* 119, no. 14 (2014): 8980–9002; F. Johnston et al., "Estimated Global Mortality Attributable to Smoke from Landscape Fires," *Environmental Health Perspectives* 120, no. 5 (2012): 695–701.

20. Authors' calculations, based on Google Scholar searches of "tropical forest" plus "ecosystem services" by year from 2000 to 2014.

21. K. Brandon, "Ecosystem Services from Tropical Forests: Review of Current Science," CGD Working Paper 380, Center for Global Development, Washington, DC, 2014.

22. H. Lieth and R. H. Whittaker, eds., *Primary Productivity of the Biosphere, Ecological Studies* 14 (Berlin, Heidelberg, and New York: Springer-Verlag, 1975).

23. M. C. Hansen et al., "High-Resolution Global Maps of 21st-Century Forest Cover Change," *Science* 342 (2013): 850–53; J. Roy and B. Saugier, "Terrestrial Primary Productivity: Definitions and Milestones," in *Terrestrial Global Productivity*, ed. J. Roy, B. Saugier, and H. Mooney, 1–6 (San Diego: Academic Press, 2001); C. B. Field et al., "Primary Production of the Biosphere: Integrating Terrestrial and Oceanic Components," *Science* 281, no. 5374 (1998): 237–40; S. Brown and A. E. Lugo, "The Storage and Production of Organic Matter in Tropical Forests and Their Role in the Global Carbon Cycle," *Biotropica* 14 (1982): 161–87.

24. Brandon, "Ecosystem Services."

25. Ibid.

26. Ibid.

27. J. W. F. Slik et al., "An Estimate of the Number of Tropical Tree Species," *Proceedings of the National Academy of Sciences* 112, no. 24 (2015): 7472–77.

28. F. Montagnini and C. Jordan, *Tropical Forest Ecology: The Basis for Conservation and Management* (Heidelberg: Springer, 2005).

29. WCS-Wildlife Conservation Society, "Amazing Photos Chronicle Staggering Diversity of Bolivia's Madidi National Park," *ScienceDaily*, September 12, 2012.

30. National Park Service, "Yellowstone National Park: Park Facts," U.S. Department of the Interior, 2014, http://www.nps.gov/yell/planyourvisit/parkfacts.htm.

31. P. H. Raven, "Our Diminishing Tropical Forests," in *Biodiversity*, ed. E. O. Wilson and F. Peter, 119–22 (Washington, DC: National Academy Press, 1988).

32. M. T. Irwin et al., "Patterns of Species Change in Anthropogenically Disturbed Forests of Madagascar," *Biological Conservation* 143, no. 10 (2010): 2351–62.

33. T. A. Gardner, J. Barlow, N. S. Sodhi, and C. A. Peres, "A Multi-Region Assessment of Tropical Forest Biodiversity in a Human-Modified World," *Biological Conservation* 143, no. 10 (2010): 2293–2300.

34. Brandon, "Ecosystem Services."

35. International Energy Agency, "Renewable Energy Essentials: Hydropower," 2010; B. Wheeler, "Hydro Powers Latin America," *Renewable Energy World*, June 21, 2012.

36. United Nations, "Draft Outcome Document of the United Nations Summit for the Adoption of the Post-2015 Development Agenda, Sixty-Ninth Session of the General Assembly of the United Nations," New York, 2015, http://www.un.org/ga/search/view_doc.asp?symbol=A/69/L.85&Lang=E.

37. L. S. Hamilton, "Forests and Water: A Thematic Study Prepared in the Framework of the Global Forest Resources Assessment 2005," FAO Forestry Paper No. 155, Food and Agriculture Organization of the United Nations, 2008.

38. I. R. Calder and B. Aylward, "Forest and Floods: Moving to an Evidence-Based Approach to Watershed and Integrated Flood Management," *Water International* 31, no. 1 (2006): 87–99.

39. Hamilton, "Forests and Water."

40. Brandon, "Ecosystem Services."

41. M. Acreman et al., "Report of the Work of the Expert Group on Maintaining the Ability of Biodiversity to Continue to Support the Water Cycle" (report to the Conference of the Parties to the Convention on Biological Diversity, Eleventh Meeting, Hyderabad, India, October 8–9, 2012).

42. J. R. Vincent et al., "Valuing Water Purification by Forests: An Analysis of Malaysian Panel Data," *Environmental and Resource Economics* 64, no. 1 (2015): 59–80.

43. K. A. Brauman et al., "The Nature and Value of Ecosystem Services: An Overview Highlighting Hydrologic Services," *Annual Review of Environment and Resources* 32, no. 1

(2007): 67–98; J. S. Hall et al., "The Ecology and Ecosystem Services of Native Trees: Implications for Reforestation and Land Restoration in Mesoamerica," *Forest Ecology and Management* 261, no 10 (2011): 1553–57; Acreman et al., "Report of the Work of the Expert Group."

44. Acreman et al., "Report of the Work of the Expert Group."

45. K. M. Carlson et al., "Influence of Watershed-Climate Interactions on Stream Temperature, Sediment Yield, and Metabolism along a Land Use Intensity Gradient in Indonesian Borneo," *Journal of Geophysical Research: Biogeosciences* 119, no. 6 (2014): 1110–28.

46. N. Dudley and S. Stolton, *Running Pure: The Importance of Forest Protected Areas to Drinking Water*, World Bank/WWF Alliance for Forest Conservation and Sustainable Use, 2003; Hamilton, "Forests and Water."

47. Dudley and Stolton, *Running Pure.*

48. Brandon, "Ecosystem Services."

49. B. Locatelli and R. Vignola, "Managing Watershed Services of Tropical Forests and Plantations: Can Meta-Analyses Help?" *Forest Ecology and Management* 258, no. 9 (2009): 1864–70.

50. Brandon, "Ecosystem Services."

51. M. Mulligan and S. M. Burke, "DFID FRP Project ZF0216 Global Cloud Forests and Environmental Change in a Hydrological Context," Final Technical Report, December 2005; M. Mulligan, "Modelling the Tropics-Wide Extent and Distribution of Cloud Forest and Cloud Forest Loss, with Implications for Conservation Priority," in *Tropical Montane Cloud Forests: Science for Conservation and Management*, ed. L. A. Bruijnzeel et al., 14–38 (Cambridge: Cambridge University Press, 2010).

52. M. Mulligan and L. Sáenz, "The Role of Cloud Affected Forests (CAFs) on Water Inputs to Dams," *Ecosystem Services* 5 (2013): 69–77.

53. L. Sáenz et al., "The Role of Cloud Forest Restoration on Energy Security," *Ecosystem Services* 9 (2014): 180–90.

54. V. Andréassian, "Waters and Forests: From Historical Controversy to Scientific Debate," *Journal of Hydrology* 291, no. 1 (2004): 1–27; L. A. Bruijnzeel, "Hydrological Functions of Tropical Forests: Not Seeing the Soil for the Trees?" *Agriculture, Ecosystems & Environment* 104, no. 1 (2004): 185–228; D. Kaimowitz, "Forests and Water: A Policy Perspective," *Journal of Forest Research* 9, no. 4 (2004): 289–91; I. Calder et al., "Towards a New Understanding of Forests and Water," *Unasylva* 58, no. 229 (2007): 3–10; S. Lele, "Watershed Services of Tropical Forests: From Hydrology to Economic Valuation to Integrated Analysis," *Current Opinion in Environmental Sustainability* 1, no. 2 (2009): 148–55.

55. D. Ellison, M. N. Futter, and K. Bishop, "On the Forest Cover-Water Yield Debate: From Demand- to Supply-Side Thinking," *Global Change Biology* 18, no. 3 (2012): 806–20.

56. J. A. Marengo, "On the Hydrological Cycle of the Amazon Basin: A Historical Review and Current State-of-the-Art," *Revista Brasileira de Meteorologia* 21, no. 3 (2006): 1–19.

57. C. M. Stickler et al., "Dependence of Hydropower Energy Generation on Forests in the Amazon Basin at Local and Regional Scales," *Proceedings of the National Academy of Sciences* 110, no. 23 (2013): 9601–6.

58. A. M. Makarieva and V. G. Gorshkov, "Biotic Pump of Atmospheric Moisture as Driver of the Hydrological Cycle on Land," *Hydrology and Earth System Sciences Discussions* 3, no. 4 (2006): 2621–73; D. Sheil and D. Murdiyarso, "How Forests Attract Rain: An Examination of a New Hypothesis," *BioScience* 59, no. 4 (2009): 341–47.

59. M. C. Roa-García et al., "The Role of Land Use and Soils in Regulating Water Flow in Small Headwater Catchments of the Andes," *Water Resources Research* 47 no. 5 (2011): W05510; F. L. Ogden et al., "Effect of Land Cover and Use on Dry Season River Runoff, Runoff Efficiency, and Peak Storm Runoff in the Seasonal Tropics of Central Panama," *Water Resources Research* 49, no. 12 (2013):

8443–62; J. Krishnaswamy et al., "The Groundwater Recharge Response and Hydrologic Services of Tropical Humid Forest Ecosystems to Use and Reforestation: Support for the 'Infiltration-Evapotranspiration Trade-Off Hypothesis,'" *Journal of Hydrology* 498, no. 19 (2013): 191–209.

60. D. Ellison, M. N. Futter, and K. Bishop, "On the Forest Cover-Water Yield Debate"; G. F. Pires and M. H. Costa, "Deforestation Causes Different Subregional Effects on the Amazon Bioclimatic Equilibrium," *Geophysical Research Letters* 40, no. 14 (2013): 3618–23.

61. G. Zhou et al., "Forest Recovery and River Discharge at the Regional Scale of Guangdong Province, China," *Water Resources Research* 46, no. 9 (2010): W09503.

62. Locatelli and Vignola, "Managing Watershed Services."

63. R. Arezki and M. Bruckner, "Food Prices and Political Instability," IMF Working Paper 11-62, International Monetary Fund, 2011; M. Lagi, K. Z. Bertrand, and Y. Bar-Yam, "The Food Crises and Political Instability in North Africa and the Middle East," working paper, New England Complex Systems Institute, 2011.

64. United Nations, "Draft Outcome Document."

65. H. K. Gibbs et al., "Tropical Forests Were the Primary Sources of New Agricultural Land in the 1980s and 1990s," *Proceedings of the National Academy of Sciences* 107, no. 38 (2010): 16732–37.

66. T. Kume et al., "Ten-Year Evapotranspiration Estimates in a Bornean Tropical Rainforest," *Agricultural and Forest Meteorology* 151, no. 9 (2011): 1183–92.

67. D. V. Spracklen, "Observations of Increased Tropical Rainfall Preceded by Air Passage over Forests," *Nature* 489 (2012): 282–28.

68. Y. Li et al., "Local Cooling and Warming Effects of Forests Based on Satellite Observations," *Nature Communications* 6 (2015): 6603; R. Alkama and A. Cescatti, "Biophysical Climate Impacts of Recent Changes in Global Forest Cover," *Science* 351, no. 6273 (2016): 600–604.

69. D. Lawrence and K. Vandecar, "Effects of Tropical Deforestation on Climate and Agriculture," *Nature Climate Change* 5, no. 1 (2015): 27–36.

70. Ibid.

71. J. Rocha, "Drought Bites as Amazon's 'Flying Rivers' Dry Up," Climate News Network, September 14, 2014, http://climatenewsnetwork.net/drought-bites-as-amazons-flying-rivers-dry-up/.

72. Brandon, "Ecosystem Services."

73. R. Avissar and D. Werth, "Global Hydroclimatological Teleconnections Resulting from Tropical Deforestation," *Journal of Hydrometeorology* 6, no. 2 (2005): 134–45.

74. Lawrence and Vandecar, "Effects of Tropical Deforestation."

75. T. H. Ricketts et al., "Landscape Effects on Crop Pollination Services: Are There General Patterns?" *Ecology Letters* 11, no. 5 (2008): 499–515.

76. A. M. Klein et al., "Importance of Pollinators in Changing Landscapes for World Crops," *Proceedings of the Royal Society of London B: Biological Sciences* 274, no. 1608 (2007): 303–13; J. Ollerton, R. Winfree, and S. Tarrant, "How Many Flowering Plants Are Pollinated by Animals?" *Oikos* 120, no. 3 (2011): 321–26; G. Lebuhn et al., "Detecting Insect Pollinator Declines on Regional and Global Scales," *Conservation Biology* 27, no. 1 (2013): 113–20.

77. L. A. Garibaldi et al., "Wild Pollinators Enhance Fruit Set of Crops Regardless of Honey Bee Abundance," *Science* 339, no. 6127 (2013): 1608–11.

78. Çağan Şekercioğlu, "Bird Functional Diversity and Ecosystem Services in Tropical Forests, Agroforests and Agricultural Areas," *Journal of Ornithology* 153, no. 1 (2012): 153–61.

79. F. Bianchi et al., "Sustainable Pest Regulation in Agricultural Landscapes: A Review on Landscape Composition, Biodiversity and Natural Pest Control," *Proceedings of the Royal Society of London B: Biological Sciences* 273, no. 1595 (2006): 1715–27.

80. Maas, Clough, and Tscharntke, "Bats and Birds."

81. D. Karp et al., "Forest Bolsters Bird Abundance, Pest Control and Coffee Yield," *Ecology Letters* 16, no. 11 (2013): 1339–47.

82. M. Aluja et al., "Pest Management through Tropical Tree Conservation," *Biodiversity and Conservation* 23, no. 4 (2014): 831–53.

83. A. Angelsen et al., "Environmental Income and Rural Livelihoods: A Global-Comparative Analysis," *World Development* 64 (2014): S12–S28.

84. Z. Bharucha and J. Pretty, "The Roles and Values of Wild Foods in Agricultural Systems," *Philosophical Transactions of the Royal Society B: Biological Sciences* 365, no. 1554 (2010): 2913–26.

85. A. Ickowitz et al., "Dietary Quality and Tree Cover in Africa," *Global Environmental Change* 24 (2014): 287–94.

86. K. Johnson, A. Jacob, and M. E. Brown, "Forest Cover Associated with Improved Child Health and Nutrition: Evidence from the Malawi Demographic and Health Survey and Satellite Data," *Global Health: Science and Practice* 1, no. 2 (2013): 237–48.

87. S. P. Murphy and L. H. Allen, "Nutritional Importance of Animal Source Foods," *Journal of Nutrition* 133, no. 11 (2003): 3932S–5S; R. Nasi, A. Taber, and N. Van Vliet, "Empty Forests, Empty Stomachs? Bushmeat and Livelihoods in the Congo and Amazon Basins," *International Forestry Review* 13, no. 3 (2011): 355–68.

88. W. B. Karesh et al., "Ecology of Zoonoses: Natural and Unnatural Histories," *Lancet* 380, no. 9857 (2012): 1936–45.

89. C. A. Harvey et al., "Extreme Vulnerability of Smallholder Farmers to Agricultural Risks and Climate Change in Madagascar," *Philosophical Transactions of the Royal Society* 369 (2014): 20130089.

90. S. Wunder, A. Angelsen, and B. Belcher, "Forests, Livelihoods, and Conservation: Broadening the Empirical Base," *World Development* 64 (2014): S1–S11.

91. K. McSweeney, "Forest Product Sale as Natural Insurance: The Effects of Household Characteristics and the Nature of Shock in Eastern Honduras," *Society and Natural Resources* 17, no. 1 (2004): 39–56; Wunder, Angelsen, and Belcher, "Forests, Livelihoods, and Conservation."

92. W. J. Junk, M. G. M. Soares, and P. B. Bayley, "Freshwater Fishes of the Amazon River Basin: Their Biodiversity, Fisheries, and Habitats," *Aquatic Ecosystem Health & Management* 10 (2007): 153–73; B. Matsen, *Jacques Cousteau: The Sea King* (New York: Vintage, 2010), 228.

93. G. D. Raby et al., "Freshwater Commercial Bycatch: An Understated Conservation Problem," *BioScience* 61, no. 4 (2011): 271–80.

94. R. E. Brummett, M. Beveridge, and I. G. Cowx, "Functional Aquatic Ecosystems, Inland Fisheries and the Millennium Development Goals," *Fish and Fisheries* 14, no. 3 (2013): 312–24; World Bank, *The Hidden Harvests: The Global Contribution of Capture Fisheries* (Washington, DC: World Bank, 2010).

95. R. L. Welcomme et al., "Inland Capture Fisheries," *Philosophical Transactions of the Royal Society B: Biological Sciences* 365, no. 1554 (2010): 2881–96.

96. D. C. Israel, M. Ahmed, and H. M. C. Yeo Bee Hong, "Aquatic Resources Valuation and Policies for Poverty Elimination in the Lower Mekong Basin," Department for International Development of the United Kingdom and World Fish Center, Penang, Malaysia, 2005.

97. N. Hanazaki et al., "Livelihood Diversity, Food Security and Resilience among the Caiçara of Coastal Brazil," *Human Ecology* 41, no. 1 (2013): 153–64.

98. O. T. Coomes et al., "Floodplain Fisheries as Natural Insurance for the Rural Poor in Tropical Forest Environments: Evidence from Amazonia," *Fisheries Management and Ecology* 17, no. 6 (2010): 513–21; Y. Takasaki, B. L. Barham, and O. T. Coomes, "Smoothing Income against Crop Flood Losses in Amazonia: Rain Forest or Rivers as a Safety Net?" *Review of Development Economics* 14, no. 1 (2010): 48–63.

99. L. Castello et al., "Lessons from Integrating Fishers of Arapaima in Small-Scale Fisheries Management at the Mamirauá Reserve, Amazon," *Environmental Management* 43, no. 2 (2009): 197–209; J. F. Gonçalves, Jr., et al., "Relationship between Dynamics of Litterfall and Riparian Plant Species in a Tropical Stream," *Limnologica-Ecology and Management of Inland Waters* 44 (2014): 40–48.

100. R. L. Welcomme et al., "Inland Capture Fisheries," *Philosophical Transactions of the Royal Society B: Biological Sciences* 365, no. 1554 (2010): 2881–96.

101. N. Van Zalinge et al., "Where There Is Water, There Is Fish? Cambodian Fisheries Issues in a Mekong River Basin Perspective," in *Common Property in the Mekong: Issues of Sustainability and Subsistence, International Center for Living Aquatic Resources Management Studies and Reviews* (Philippines: ICLARM, 2000), 37–48.

102. E. Barbier et al., "The Value of Estuarine and Coastal Ecosystem Services," *Ecological Monographs* 81, no. 2 (2011): 169–93; H. Van Lavieren et al., "Securing the Future of Mangroves," policy brief, UNU-INWEH, UNESCO-MAB with ISME, ITTO, FAO, UNEP-WCMC, and TNC, 2012.

103. P. Rönnbäck, "The Ecological Basis for Economic Value of Seafood Production Supported by Mangrove Ecosystems," *Ecological Economics* 29 (1999): 235–52.

104. World Health Organization, "WHO Traditional Medicine Strategy 2002–2005," WHO, Geneva, 2002, http://apps.who.int/medicinedocs/pdf/s2297e/s2297e.pdf; D. You et al., "Levels and Trends in Child Mortality: Report 2014," UNICEF and the Inter-agency Group for Child Mortality Estimation Child Mortality Report, New York, 2014.

105. Brandon, "Ecosystem Services from Tropical Forests: Review of Current Science."

106. M. M. Robinson and X. Zhang, "The World Medicines Situation 2011: Traditional Medicines—Global Situation, Issues and Challenges," World Health Organization, Geneva, 2011, http://digicollection.org/hss/documents/s18063en/s18063en.pdf.

107. A. C. Hamilton, "Medicinal Plants, Conservation and Livelihoods," *Biodiversity and Conservation* 13, no. 8 (2004): 1477–1517.

108. C.D. Golden et al., "Rainforest Pharmacopeia."

109. Robinson, and Zhang, "The World Medicines Situation 2011, Traditional Medicines: Global Situation, Issues, and Challenges."

110. Ibid.

111. M. Moudi et al., "Vinca Alkaloids," *International Journal of Preventive Medicine* 4, no. 11 (2013): 1231.

112. World Health Organization, "Child Mortality," updated September 2011, http://www.who.int/pmnch/media/press_materials/fs/fs_mdg4_childmortality/en/.

113. Sawyer, "Frontier Malaria."

114. Y. A. Afrane et al., "Effects of Microclimatic Changes Caused by Land Use and Land Cover on Duration of Gonotrophic Cycles of Anopheles Gambiae (Diptera: Culicidae) in Western Kenya Highlands," *Journal of Medical Entomology* 42, no. 6 (2005): 974–80; K. A. Lindblade, "Land Use Change Alters Malaria Transmission Parameters by Modifying Temperature in a Highland Area of Uganda," *Tropical Medicine & International Health* 5, no. 4 (2000): 263–74.

115. Myers et al., "Human Health Impacts"; C. L. Wood et al., "Does Biodiversity Protect Humans against Infectious Disease?" *Ecology* 95, no. 4 (2014): 817–32.

116. M. B. Hahn et al., "Influence of Deforestation, Logging, and Fire on Malaria in the Brazilian Amazon," *PloS One* 9, no. 1 (2014): e85725.

117. D. Sawyer, "Frontier Malaria in the Amazon Region of Brazil: Types of Malaria Situations and Some Implications for Control" (Brasília: World Health Organization and the Special Programme for Research Training in Tropical Diseases, 1988); S. Myers et al., "Human Health Impacts of Ecosystem Alteration."

118. D. Taylor, "Seeing the Forests for More than the Trees," *Environmental Health Perspectives* 105, no. 11 (1997): 1186.

119. B. A. Wilcox and B. Ellis, "Forests and Emerging Infectious Diseases of Humans," *Unasylva* 57, no. 2 (2006): 11, ftp://ftp.fao.org/docrep/fao/009/a0789e/a0789e.pdf; K. Campbell et al., "Strengthening International Cooperation for Health and Biodiversity," *EcoHealth* 8, no. 4 (2011): 407–9; Myers et al., "Human Health Impacts"; R. C. Sang and L. M. Dunster, "The Growing Threat of Arbovirus Transmission and Outbreaks in Kenya: A Review," *East African Medical Journal* 78, no. 12 (2001): 655–61.

120. D. J. Gubler, "Resurgent Vector-Borne Diseases as a Global Health Problem," *Emerging Infectious Diseases* 4, no. 3 (1998): 442; T. P. Monath, "Yellow Fever and Dengue—The Interactions of Virus, Vector and Host in the Re-emergence of Epidemic Disease," *Seminars in Virology* 5, no. 2 (1994): 133–45.

121. Ibid.

122. M. E. J. Woolhouse and S. Gowtage-Sequeria, "Host Range and Emerging and Reemerging Pathogens," *Emerging Infectious Diseases* 11, no. 2 (2005): 1842–48; M. E. J. Woolhouse et al., "Human Viruses: Discovery and Emergence," *Philosophical Transactions of the Royal Society B: Biological Sciences* 367, no. 1604 (2012): 2864–71;

123. Karesh et al., "Ecology of Zoonoses."

124. F. Keesing et al., "Impacts of Biodiversity on the Emergence and Transmission of Infectious Diseases," *Nature* 468, no. 7324 (2010): 647–52; Campbell et al., "Strengthening International Cooperation"; A. Cascio et al., "The Socio-ecology of Zoonotic Infections," *Clinical Microbiology and Infection* 17, no. 3 (2011): 336–42; S. S. Morse et al., "Prediction and Prevention of the Next Pandemic Zoonosis," *Lancet* 380, no. 9857 (2012): 1956–65; P. Rabinowitz and L. Conti, "Links among Human Health, Animal Health, and Ecosystem Health," *Annual Review of Public Health* 34, no. 1 (2013): 189–204.

125. M. Cochrane, "Fire Science for Rainforests," *Nature* 421, no. 6926 (2003): 913–19; W. J. Bond and J. E. Keeley, "Fire as a Global 'Herbivore': The Ecology and Evolution of Flammable Ecosystems," *Trends in Ecology & Evolution* 20, no. 7 (2005): 387–94; D. Bowman, J. A. O'Brien, and J. G. Goldammer, "Pyrogeography and the Global Quest for Sustainable Fire Management," *Annual Review of Environment and Resources* 38, no. 1 (2013): 57–80; V. Dantas, M. A. Batalha, and J. G. Pausas, "Fire Drives Functional Thresholds on the Savanna–Forest Transition," *Ecology* 94, no. 11 (2013): 2454–63.

126. J. B. Kauffman and C. Uhl, "Interactions of Anthropogenic Activities, Fire, and Rain Forests in the Amazon Basin," in *Fire in the Tropical Biota*, ed. J. G. Goldammer, 117–34 (Berlin, Heidelberg: Springer, 1990); Cochrane, "Fire Science."

127. R. Carmenta et al., "Shifting Cultivation and Fire Policy: Insights from the Brazilian Amazon," *Human Ecology* 41 (2013): 603–14; Q. M. Ketteringsa, "Farmers' Perspectives on Slash-and-Burn as a Land Clearing Method for Small-Scale Rubber Producers in Sepunggur, Jambi Province, Sumatra, Indonesia," *Forest Ecology and Management* 120 (1999): 157–69.

128. Brandon, "Ecosystem Services."

129. M. Yamasoe et al., "Chemical Composition of Aerosol Particles from Direct Emissions of Vegetation Fires in the Amazon Basin: Water-Soluble Species and Trace Elements," *Atmospheric Environments* 34 (2000): 1641–53; T. R. Muraleedharan et al., "Chemical Characteristics of Haze in Brunei, Darussalam, during the 1998 Episode," *Atmospheric Environment* 34 (2000): 2725–31; M. A. M. Costa et al., "Real-Time Sampling of Particulate Matter Smaller than 2.5×m from Amazon Forest Biomass Combustion," *Atmospheric Environment* 54 (2012): 480–89; B. Langmann et al., "Vegetation Fire Emissions and Their Impact on Air Pollution and Climate," *Atmospheric Environment* 43 (2009): 107–16.

130. F. Johnston et al., "Estimated Global Mortality Attributable to Smoke from Landscape Fires," *Environmental Health Perspectives* 120, no. 5 (2012): 695–701.; U.S. Environmental Protection Agency, "Fine

Particle Pollution: Basic Information," updated February 2016, http://www.epa.gov/pmdesignations/basicinfo.htm.

131. A. M. S. Gloudemans et al., "Evidence for Long-Range Transport of Carbon Monoxide in the Southern Hemisphere from SCIAMACHY Observations," *Geophysical Research Letters* 33 (2006): L16807, as cited in Langmann, "Vegetation Fire Emissions."

132. Jacobson, "Effects of Biomass Burning"; Johnston et al., "Estimated Global Mortality."

133. J. Mott et al., "Cardiorespiratory Hospitalizations Associated with Smoke Exposure during 1997 Southeast Asian Forest Fires," *International Journal of Hygiene and Environmental Health* 208 (2004): 75–85.

134. S. M. Hsiang and A. S. Jina, "Effect of Environmental Catastrophe on Long-Run Economic Growth: Evidence from 6,700 Cyclones," NBER Working Paper 20352, National Bureau of Economic Research, Washington, DC, 2014.

135. United Nations, "Draft Outcome Document."

136. Brandon, "Ecosystem Services."

137. I. Alcántara-Ayala , "Hazard Assessment of Rainfall-Induced Landsliding in Mexico," *Geomorphology* 61, no. 1–2 (2004): 19–40; I. Alcántara-Ayala, O. Esteban-Chávez, and J. F. Parrot, "Landsliding Related to Land-Cover Change: A Diachronic Analysis of Hillslope Instability Distribution in the Sierra Norte, Puebla, Mexico," *CATENA* 65, no. 2 (2006): 152–65.

138. R. C. Sidle et al., "Erosion Processes in Steep Terrain—Truths, Myths, and Uncertainties Related to Forest Management in Southeast Asia," *Forest Ecology and Management* 224, no. 1–2 (2006): 199–225; R. H. Guthrie et al., "An Examination of Controls on Debris Flow Mobility: Evidence from Coastal British Columbia," *Geomorphology* 114, no. 4 (2010): 601–13.

139. D. R. Greenway, "Vegetation and Slope Stability," in *Slope Stability: Geotechnical Engineering and Geomorphology*, ed. M. G. Anderson and K. S. Richards (Chichester, UK: John Wiley and Sons, 1987).

140. C. W. Runyan and P. D'Odorico, "Bistable Dynamics between Forest Removal and Landslide Occurrence," *Water Resources Research* 50, no. 2 (2014): 1112–30; R. M. De-Graaf et al., *Technical Guide to Forest Wildlife Habitat Management in New England* (Hanover: University Press of New England, 2006).

141. M. Guns and V. Vanacker, "Forest Cover Change Trajectories and Their Impact on Landslide Occurrence in the Tropical Andes," *Environmental Earth Sciences* 70, no. 7 (2013): 2941–52.

142. Brandon, "Ecosystem Services."

143. L. A. Bruijnzeel, "Hydrological Functions of Tropical Forests: Not Seeing the Soil for the Trees?" *Agriculture, Ecosystems & Environment* 104, no. 1 (2004): 185–228; Brauman et al., "The Nature and Value of Ecosystem Services"; W. F. Laurance et al., "The Fate of Amazonian Forest Fragments: A 32-Year Investigation," *Biological Conservation* 144, no. 1 (2011): 56–67.

144. C. J. A. Bradshaw, N. S. Sodhi, K. S.-H. Peh, and B. W. Brook, "Global Evidence That Deforestation Amplifies Flood Risk and Severity in the Developing World," *Global Change Biology* 13, no. 11 (2007): 2379–95; Y. Alila et al., "Forests and Floods: A New Paradigm Sheds Light on Age-Old Controversies," *Water Resources Research* 45, no. 8 (2009): W08416; Ogden et al., "Effect of Land Cover"; J. Tan-Soo et al., "Econometric Evidence on Forest Ecosystem Services: Deforestation and Flooding in Malaysia," *Environmental and Resource Economics* 63, no. 1 (2016): 25–44; Food and Agriculture Organization and Center for International Forestry Research, "Forests and Floods: Drowning in Fiction or Thriving on Facts," Bangkok, Thailand, 2005, ftp://ftp.fao.org/docrep/fao/008/ae929e/ae929e00.pdf; A. I. J. Van Dijk et al., "Forest–Flood Relation Still That Deforestation Amplifies Flood Risk and Severity in the Developing World,' by C. J. A. Bradshaw, N. S. Sodhi, K. S.-H. Peh, and B. W. Brook," *Global Change Biolo-*

gy 15, no. 1 (2009): 110–15; J. C. Bathurst et al., "Forests and Floods in Latin America: Science, Management, Policy and the EPIC FORCE Project," *Water International* 35, no. 2 (2010): 114–31.

145. J. Prongera et al., "Subsidence Rates of Drained Agricultural Peatlands in New Zealand and the Relationship with Time since Drainage," *Journal of Environmental Quality* 43, no. 4 (2014): 1442–49; K. Brouns et al., "Spatial Analysis of Soil Subsidence in Peat Meadow Areas in Friesland in Relation to Land and Water Management, Climate Change, and Adaptation," *Environmental Management* 55, no. 2 (2015): 360–72; A. Hooijer et al., "Flooding Projections from Elevation and Subsidence Models for Oil Palm Plantations in the Rajang Delta Peatlands, Sarawak, Malaysia," Deltares Report No. 1207384, 2015; E. Sumarga et al., "Hydrological and Economic Effects of Oil Palm Cultivation in Indonesian Peatlands," *Ecology and Society* 21, no. 2 (2016).

146. H. Yanagisawa et al., "Tsunami Damage Reduction Performance of a Mangrove Forest in Banda Aceh, Indonesia Inferred from Field Data and a Numerical Model," *Journal of Geophysical Research: Oceans* 115, no. C6 (2010): C06032; J. C. Bayas et al., "Influence of Coastal Vegetation on the 2004 Tsunami Wave Impact in West Aceh," *Proceedings of the National Academy of Sciences* 108, no. 46 (2011): 18612–17; A. L. McIvor et al., "Mangroves as a Sustainable Coastal Defence" (paper presented at the Seventh International Conference on Asian and Pacific Coasts [APAC], Nature Conservancy, University of Cambridge and Wetlands International, Bali, Indonesia, September 2013); M. B. Samarakoon, N. Tanaka, and K. Iimura, "Improvement of Effectiveness of Existing Casuarina Equisetifolia Forests in Mitigating Tsunami Damage," *Journal of Environmental Management* 114 (2013): 105–14.

147. Das and Vincent, "Mangroves Protected Villages"; Tanaka et al., "Combined Effects of Coastal Forest and Sea Embankment."

148. A. H. Baird and A. M. Kerr, "Landscape Analysis and Tsunami Damage in Aceh: Comment on Iverson and Prasad (2007)," *Landscape Ecology* 23, no. 1 (2008): 3–5; R. Cochard et al., "The 2004 Tsunami in Aceh and Southern Thailand: A Review on Coastal Ecosystems, Wave Hazards and Vulnerability," *Perspectives in Plant Ecology, Evolution, and Systematics* 10, no. 1 (2008): 3–40; Yanagisawa et al., "Tsunami Damage Reduction Performance."

149. McIvor et al., "Mangroves as a Sustainable Coastal Defence."

150. Ibid.; Das and Vincent, "Mangroves Protected Villages"; R. A. Feagin et al., "Shelter from the Storm? Use and Misuse of Coastal Vegetation Bioshields for Managing Natural Disasters," *Conservation Letters* 3, no. 1 (2010): 1–11.

151. McIvor et al., "Mangroves as a Sustainable Coastal Defence"; D. R. Cahoon et al., "Mass Tree Mortality Leads to Mangrove Peat Collapse at Bay Islands, Honduras, after Hurricane Mitch," *Journal of Ecology* 91 (2003): 1093–1105; Bayas et al., "Influence of Coastal Vegetation"; Tanaka et al., "Combined Effects."

152. International Union for Conservation of Nature, "Ecosystem-Based Adaptation," updated April 2016, https://www.iucn.org/about/work/programmes/ecosystem_management/climate_change/eba/.

153. J. H. Christensen et al., "Climate Phenomena and Their Relevance for Future Regional Climate Change," in *Climate Change 2013: The Physical Science Basis. Contribution of Working Group I to the Fifth Assessment Report of the Intergovernmental Panel on Climate Change*, ed. T. F. Stocker, D. Qin, G. K. Plattner, M. Tignor, S. K. Allen, J. Boschung, A. Nauels, Y. Xia, V. Bex, and P. M. Midgley (Cambridge, UK, and New York: Cambridge University Press, 2013).

154. M. Kinver, "Sri Lanka First Nation to Protect All Mangrove Forests," BBC News, May 12, 2015, http://www.bbc.com/news/science-environment-32683798.

155. City of Rio de Janeiro, Municipal Secretariat of Social Development, "Rio de Janeiro's Community Reforestation Project," UNFCCC Adaptation Ecosystem-Based Project 29, 2011, http://unfccc.int/files/adaptation/application/pdf/29eba.pdf.

156. Nature Kenya and Kenya Forest Service, "Kikuyu Escarpment Forest," UNFCCC Ecosystem-Based Adaptation Project 7, 2011, http://unfccc.int/files/adaptation/application/pdf/17eba.pdf.

Smoke from burning peatland blankets large areas of Indonesia.

Credit: NASA Earth Observatory

CHAPTER 4

Monitoring Tropical Forests

Advances in Tracking Emissions, Sequestration, and Safeguards

Bonn, Germany, July 2001. It was late in the day. Behind a closed ballroom door in the faded Hotel Maritim, United Nations climate diplomats negotiated the fate of tropical forests. Specifically, they were deciding whether the Kyoto Protocol to the United Nations Framework Convention on Climate Change (UNFCCC) would include provisions for avoiding tropical deforestation.

The Kyoto Protocol had been adopted four years earlier, but many issues remained unresolved. One related to its Clean Development Mechanism (CDM), which let developed countries meet their climate targets more cheaply by purchasing offset credits from projects in developing countries. Projects related to energy efficiency or fuel switching had already been declared eligible for the CDM; at issue now was whether those for "avoided deforestation" would be eligible, too.

The stakes for tropical forests were high. A "yes" decision would create a viable business model for companies seeking to generate carbon credits by conserving rainforest. A "no" decision would entirely exclude the second largest source of greenhouse gas emissions—tropical deforestation—from the international agreement on climate change.

The formal decision had been delayed from December 2000 in The Hague to May 2001 in Bonn, and then delayed again to July. Tensions ran high that day: bitterly divided environmental groups splintered into rival camps, and negotiators shouted each other down in the hallways.[1]

This chapter draws heavily on a background paper by Scott Goetz, Matthew Hansen, Richard Houghton, Wayne Walker, Nadine Laporte, and Jonah Busch on the current state of measurement and monitoring technology for forests.

When the ballroom doors opened, the decision was apparent to observers, based on which negotiators were upset and which were relieved. Advocates for tropical forests had lost. Tree-planting projects were in, but projects to address deforestation—a far more meaningful concern—were out.

Years later, environmental policy expert Tia Nelson of The Nature Conservancy remembered the decision as a disappointment but not a surprise. "It was a pretty lonely battle at the time," she told mongabay.com, an environmental science and conservation news outlet. "I was hopeful that we had a good case, but there were only a few voices arguing for avoided deforestation then."[2] In an irony that would persist for more than a decade, the UNFCCC sanctioned the generation of carbon credits from planting trees in tropical countries but not from preventing adjacent forests from being felled.

Many of the reasons delegates gave at the time for excluding avoided deforestation projects were technical. What if emissions prevented in one place just shifted somewhere else? What if the emission reductions would have happened anyway? What if emissions avoided in one year were simply deferred until a later year?

Such concerns, known in climate jargon as "environmental integrity," largely boiled down to an inability to confidently measure emissions from deforestation over large scales and long time frames. As veteran climate negotiator for the Philippines Antonio la Viña put it, negotiators in Bonn had reservations about "insufficient guidance and technology available to measure and validate emission reductions and ensure environmental integrity."[3]

The technical arguments against including avoided deforestation projects in the CDM likely masked political motives,[4] but they were not without merit. Monitoring emissions from deforestation in the late 1990s was, indeed, challenging. When the first of a series of Landsat Earth observation satellites was launched by the National Aeronautics and Space Administration (NASA) in 1972, a researcher needed the better part of a day to interpret by hand a single Maryland-sized image into areas of forest and nonforest. As late as 2008, each image cost more than $4,000 to acquire, and a researcher would need thousands of them to obtain complete cloud-free coverage of a country the size of Brazil.[5] Well into the 2000s, the state of forest monitoring technology, to paraphrase seventeenth century philosopher Thomas Hobbes, was pricy, tedious, and small. But that was about to change.

A Data Revolution for Forest Monitoring

Before 2008, information on the world's tropical forests was stuck in the Typewriter Age. High-quality satellite data on deforestation existed for just a handful of tropical countries for just a few time periods.[6] For the most part, cross-national data on the world's tropical forests were limited to the Food and Agricultural Organization's Forest Resources Assessment (FRA),[7] for which each national government would self-report its country's forest area once every five years.

But during the 2000s, forest monitoring began a data revolution, as space agencies from half a dozen countries launched new forest-monitoring satellites into orbit. In December 2008, an act of Congress made the United States Geological Survey's (USGS's)

entire archive of Landsat images available for free download.[8] Computing power grew, costs fell, and downloads increased one hundredfold.[9] Scientists devised automated routines for distinguishing whether satellite images showed dense forest vegetation or bare ground. And free access to many images of the same site over the course of a year gave analysts a far better chance of finding at least one cloud-free image from which to determine if deforestation had occurred.

The data revolution came to a head in December 2013, when geographer Matthew Hansen of the University of Maryland, together with colleagues at Google and elsewhere, devised an automated process to translate all those Landsat images into data points indicating where forests were present or not. They published a map in *Science*, reprinted in figure 4.1, showing everywhere on the planet that forest had been lost, every year from 2000 to 2012, at thirty-meter resolution—that is, down to squares (or pixels) thirty meters across, about the size of baseball diamonds.[10] The World Resources Institute then uploaded the map to Global Forest Watch, a website it runs with more than forty partner organizations, where it can now be freely downloaded by anyone with a computer and an Internet connection.[11]

It is hard to overstate how groundbreaking this research was relative to the previous status quo. The Hansen data represented a radical improvement over the Forest Resources Assessment in nearly every respect. Whereas the FRA listed a single forest area per country every five years, and previous efforts to measure forest loss from satellites relied on a few thousand sparsely sampled points,[12] the Hansen data presented a full-coverage map

Figure 4.1: Forest losses and gains have been mapped globally using data from satellites.

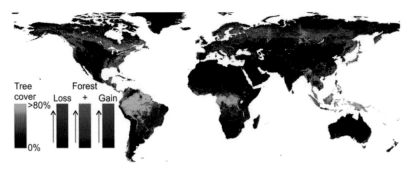

Source: M. C. Hansen et al., "High-Resolution Global Maps of 21st-Century Forest Cover Change," *Science* 342 (2013): 850–53.

of billions of pixels every year, at thirty-meter resolution. Whereas the methods, accuracy, and completeness of the FRA data varied widely from country to country—sometimes even for the same country at different points in time, and with numbers often just extrapolated from previous or subsequent data points[13]—the Hansen data were produced using consistent methods and provided complete coverage of all places and all years. Furthermore, the fact that the Hansen data were produced by independent scientists using uniform methods, rather than self-reported by agencies whose performance might be evaluated by stakeholders on the basis of the numbers they reported, alleviated suspicions of misreporting.

What Hansen's map showed wasn't good. The Earth lost 2.3 million square kilometers of forest between 2000 and 2012—an area about one-quarter the size of the United States—while gaining an area of forest only one-third this size. Not only that, but the pace of deforestation was actually increasing on the back of accelerating tropical deforestation. Increases in deforestation across many tropical countries more than offset a drop in deforestation in Brazil. This accelerating trend came as a surprise to regular readers of the FRA, in which countries had always reported their aggregate pace of deforestation in decline, both globally and across the tropics.

Despite its many advantages, the Hansen data set had limitations. As discussed later in this chapter, it did not distinguish natural forests from plantations or other tree cover, and its globally consistent methods meant it might or might not be as accurate in any particular location as a nationally calibrated map.[14] Still, it represented a vast advance over what came before, and global satellite data of this nature continue to improve.

The data revolution extended as well to the measurement of carbon in forests. In 2012, two research teams independently mapped the aboveground carbon stocks of the world's tropical forests: the NASA Jet Propulsion Lab, at one-thousand-meter resolution, and the Woods Hole Research Center, at five-hundred-meter resolution.[15] These maps of forest carbon stocks are also freely available and are rapidly being improved to cover the whole globe, every year, in ever finer detail.[16] For instance, the Woods Hole Research Center has now produced and made available a map of forest carbon stocks at thirty-meter resolution.[17]

In a related development, data collection by satellites has made possible detection of a deforestation event within a week or two of its happening. Such monitoring capacity is of particular interest to law enforcement agencies and independent monitors in tropical countries. In 2004, as part of a package of antideforestation measures (described in detail in chapter 7), Brazilian authorities began using biweekly deforestation alerts based on Moderate Resolution Imaging Spectroradiometer (MODIS) satellites to match illegal clearing in the Amazon to specific properties and enforce forest laws. Since 2014, a version of MODIS-based deforestation alerts for the humid tropics, called Forest Monitoring for Action (FORMA), has been made available on the Global Forest Watch website.[18] As a clickbait headline put it in 2014, "New Google Tool Lets You Watch the Forests Disappear in Real Time."[19]

The technological advances in forest monitoring led to political advances in international climate negotiations.[20] In 2005, the provisions for allowing avoided deforestation projects into the CDM that had met their demise in 2001 were reincarnated in the form of a proposal to the UNFCCC by Papua New Guinea and Costa Rica for compensating national-scale reductions in emissions from deforestation (RED).[21] Negotiations on RED, later expanded to REDD (Reducing Emissions from Deforestation and Forest Degra-

dation) and then REDD+, described in box 1.1, in chapter 1 were largely finalized in Warsaw in 2013, and, in Paris two years later, REDD+ was included prominently as Article 5 of the global climate agreement, as described further in chapter 9.

In just over a decade, then, tropical deforestation advanced from being left out of international climate negotiations entirely to being the issue that reached consensus most quickly. Key to this advancement were improvements in technology that enabled accurate monitoring and verification of forest-based emissions over large areas. These improvements enabled REDD+ programs to operate at the scale of entire countries or provinces—a so-called "jurisdictional approach"—rather than isolated islands of avoided deforestation projects.

Improvements in technology helped tropical deforestation advance from being left out of international climate negotiations entirely to being the issue that reached consensus most quickly.

In short, as a result of better monitoring capabilities, the technical challenges related to environmental integrity voiced in Bonn in 2001 were simply less of a concern. Instead of having to guess how much deforestation might have been displaced elsewhere by isolated forest conservation projects, countries could now observe deforestation everywhere across their entire territories. And because rates of emissions fluctuated less at the national level than at individual project sites, countries could set baselines for payments more confidently.

Technology and politics advanced in a virtuous circle. Just as technological breakthroughs energized negotiations, so, too, did the prospect of a United Nations climate mechanism for conserving tropical forests jumpstart a new era of forest measurement, monitoring, and analysis.

Why Monitor Forests?

As discussed in chapter 2, there are three ways people can enlist forests to reduce the level of greenhouse gases in the atmosphere. First, people can reduce the amount of forest that is cleared every year for agriculture, grazing land, or other uses, thereby preventing carbon from being emitted and maintaining forests' natural carbon capture and storage function. Second, people can reduce the amount of carbon emitted from within forests as a result of logging, forest fires, or other causes. And, third, people can replant forests or let damaged forests grow back, increasing the amount of carbon that forests remove from the atmosphere.

Of course, people can undertake these activities without sophisticated monitoring. But monitoring emissions and sequestration from forests is useful for several reasons. As described in chapter 2, monitoring provides climate scientists with an accurate picture of the emissions that cause climate change. As described in chapter 7, it helps governments design and evaluate programs for meeting national forest or climate goals, since, in the words of an old saying, "If you can't measure it, you can't manage it." And if internationally funded performance payments are

based on emission reductions, as described in chapter 12, then buyers will want to be confident they're getting what they've paid for. This is especially true if REDD+ payments are funded through carbon market offsets, in which emission reductions from forests can substitute for reductions from industrial sources, as described in chapter 9.

In this chapter we describe current technological capabilities to monitor forests, as well as prospects for further advances in the near future. We organize the bulk of the chapter around the types of measurements needed to operationalize each element of the United Nations framework for REDD+, shown in box 4.1: emissions from deforestation; emissions from forest degradation; sequestration by regrowing forests; and safeguards for natural forests and biodiversity (monitoring of social safeguards is not discussed here). We then discuss technologies to detect deforestation in near-real time to support law enforcement and independent monitoring. We conclude with a discussion of how much monitoring is enough.

Technological capabilities are now sufficient to monitor emissions from deforestation over broad areas and long time frames. For other areas of importance to REDD+, such as emissions from forest degradation, carbon sequestration by regrowing forests, and differentiation of natural forests from plantations, monitoring capabilities will be operational soon. Some key areas where large measurement uncertainties persist, such as where peat soils are and how much they emit, are benefiting from continued research. And new frontiers of research are opening up, including satellite monitoring of forest biodiversity.

Figure 4.2: Today's technology lets us monitor emission reductions from lower rates of forest loss.

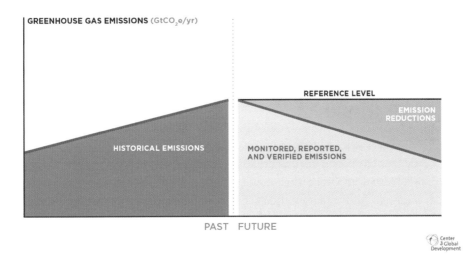

Note: Reference level depicted is an illustrative example; reference levels could be above, equal to, or below historical emissions.

Monitoring Emissions from Deforestation: The "First D" in REDD+

When forests are cleared, the carbon that was previously stored aboveground in tree trunks and branches is released to the atmosphere, as explained in chapter 2. Most is released immediately through burning, while the remainder is released more slowly through decomposition.

The amount of carbon emitted from deforestation—defined in this book as a removal of tree cover, regardless of subsequent land use (see discussion in box 2.2)—can be calculated by combining two pieces of information: the area of forest cleared and the carbon content of that forest before deforestation. Technologies for mapping both have evolved rapidly in recent years. Together they are enabling more accurate estimates of emissions from deforestation than ever before.

Mapping Areas of Forest Loss

Imagine a minister of forestry of a medium-sized tropical country who would like to know the answer to a deceptively simple question: how much of the country's forest has been lost in the last five years? To answer this question, the minister might dispatch field teams to walk the length and breadth of the country's forests. But this is hundreds of thousands of square kilometers of terrain, much of it inaccessible. Small planes might be sent to take aerial pictures that could be stitched together into a comprehensive mosaic. But the cost of so many flights and images would be prohibitive. And, even if the ministry could afford it, the minister would still be missing information on the status of the forest five years ago.

The minister needs a technology that can gather information over vast areas, repeatedly, at relatively fine spatial resolution, and at reasonable cost. The technology needs to be one that collects the same information about forests year after year and has done so for decades. The minister needs a satellite.

Of all the thousand or so working satellites orbiting the Earth, one is particularly well suited to the minister's task: Landsat.[22] Owned and operated by NASA and USGS, Landsat has been collecting data on the world's forests since 1972. Since 1999, it has been systematically taking pictures of every area of the Earth's land surface every two weeks, providing information on areas of land as small as thirty square meters. Its images are of consistently high quality, and NASA and USGS make them accessible in a user-friendly way.

Landsat, in addition to being the source for Hansen's global map described above, is used by some tropical countries to monitor their own forest loss. The standard setter is Brazil. The Brazilian National Institute for Space Research (INPE) uses data from Landsat and similar satellites to provide annual digital maps of deforestation for the nine states of the Brazilian Legal Amazon as part of its Program for the Estimation of Deforestation in the Brazilian Amazon (PRODES), included in box 4.2.

Satellites launched by other nations are also beginning to gather accurate and consistent records on forest cover and forest loss.[23] These include the China-Brazil Earth Resources Satellite (CBERS) and the European Space Agency's Sentinel series. Both Brazil and Europe have open and free data access policies. Australia, India, and a few other countries also have satellite-based deforestation mapping programs, but they do not yet provide maps to the public, as INPE does.[24]

Other satellites and airborne technologies can now take images of forests and forest loss at resolutions even higher than thirty meters—for example, Spot-5[25] and RapidEye[26] take images at five-meter resolution and Ikonos[27] and Quickbird[28] at resolutions below one meter. These satellites can provide detailed pictures but not of large areas, and not continuously. Globally, these technologies are useful for validating results from medium-resolution satellite images, like those from Landsat.[29]

Mapping Forest Carbon Stocks

The more carbon a forest holds in its tree trunks, branches, leaves, roots, and soil, the more carbon dioxide is released to the atmosphere by clearing it. The second step in cal-

---

Box 4.2: Selected Remote Sensing Technologies and Programs

A variety of technologies can be used to monitor changes in forests and forest carbon stocks, as described here.

DETER (Real Time System for Detection of Deforestation) is a program of the Brazilian National Institute for Space Research (INPE) that detects clearings within the Brazilian Amazon in near-real time using MODIS and sends biweekly alerts to federal and state law enforcement agencies.

FORMA (Forest Monitoring for Action) is a MODIS-based system that provides biweekly alerts of deforestation in the humid tropics, available on the Global Forest Watch website.

GEDI (Global Ecosystem Dynamics Investigation) is a NASA mission to install a lidar instrument on the International Space Station in 2018 that will let researchers measure the carbon density of the world's tropical and temperate forests far more accurately.

High- and Very High–Resolution Imagery is generated by sensors such as Spot-5, RapidEye, Ikonos, and Quickbird, which can provide detailed pictures, but not of large areas, and not continuously. Globally, these technologies are useful for validating results from medium-resolution satellite images like those from Landsat.

Landsat (Land + Satellite) is a satellite owned and operated by NASA and USGS that collects long-running, frequent, high-quality, and freely accessible images of the world's forests at thirty-meter resolution—that is, the smallest square in each image covers an area the size of a baseball diamond.

Lidar (Light Detection and Ranging) is an airborne remote-sensing technology that collects three-dimensional data on forests, which makes it particularly valuable for accurately mapping carbon stocks. Currently available only from airplanes, lidar flew on board the ICESAT-1 satellite from 2003 to 2009 and will be installed on the International Space Station in 2018 (see GEDI, above).

MODIS (MODerate spatial resolution Imaging Spectroradiometer) is a satellite instrument owned by NASA that collects biweekly information on the world's forests at resolutions of one thousand meters, five hundred meters, or two hundred fifty meters. MODIS has been used to map carbon stocks and send deforestation alerts.

PRODES (Program for the Estimation of Deforestation in the Brazilian Amazon) is a program of the Brazilian National Institute for Space Research (INPE) that uses data from Landsat and similar satellites to map deforestation for the nine states of the Brazilian Legal Amazon annually.

Radar (Radiowave Detection and Ranging) is a sensor that can penetrate cloud and canopy cover to provide estimates of forest carbon stocks. Radar on its own is most useful for measuring carbon stocks in low-carbon forests rather than carbon-dense tropical forests, but when taken together with data from lidar or other sensors, radar data can provide even greater advances in measurements of carbon stock change.

Sentinel refers to the European Space Agency's Sentinel missions, which are expected to provide free and open data on forests and forest cover change globally at up to ten-meter resolution using radar (Sentinel-1, launched in 2014) and optical imagery (Sentinel-2, launched in 2015).

culating emissions from deforestation, then, after mapping where forests have been lost, is estimating how much carbon those forests held before they were cleared.

Almost exactly half the weight of all plants, including trees (after subtracting water weight, which can vary substantially), is made up of carbon, while the other half is comprised of other elements. Heavier trees therefore contain proportionally more carbon, and knowing their weight, or biomass, is enough to know their carbon content.

The amount of carbon a hectare of forest contains varies widely across the tropics. A dry forest in Brazil may hold forty tons of carbon per hectare, while a rainforest in the Congo Basin may have over two hundred tons. Even within a single forest, the distribution of carbon stock can be uneven and patchy.

Carbon stocks have been meticulously calculated at thousands of field plots worldwide under the auspices of national forest inventories, scientific research, or other long-term monitoring programs. Field plots provide detailed and reliable information on the carbon content of particular sites, but they do not provide continuous coverage over large areas. Furthermore, these field plots are not necessarily a representative sample of forests as a whole; many, for example, have historically been located in primary forests undisturbed by human activity.

Because field measurements are time consuming, expensive, and unrepresentative, it is difficult to adequately determine spatial variation in carbon stocks across large and diverse tropical countries using field plots alone.[30] To obtain continuous maps of carbon stocks over large areas, measurements from field plots must be extrapolated through one of three methods: forest type, remotely sensed data from airplanes, or remotely sensed data from satellites.

The simplest way to map carbon stocks over large areas is to estimate the average carbon stock per hectare, or carbon density, for different types of forest, such as lowland dipterocarp forest, primary montane forest, or secondary dry woodland. Maps of this sort have been available globally since 2007 and have been produced in greater detail for particular countries, such as the Democratic Republic of Congo.[31]

While simple, the forest-type approach is somewhat limited in accuracy. Average carbon values for a particular forest type can be misleading. The field plots where carbon stock is measured may not be representative of the forest type, or the places where deforestation is happening may differ from the average forest of that type, or both.[32]

Carbon densities can also be mapped over large areas by combining measurements from field plots with remotely sensed information obtained from aircraft. An airborne remote-sensing technology called "Light Detection and Ranging" (lidar) is particularly valuable for mapping carbon stocks. Lidar sensors fire laser pulses down from airplanes to collect three-dimensional data on the forests below. Just as an X-ray can look through the skin into the human body, lidar can penetrate the upper forest canopy to reveal the density of the vegetation beneath, all the way to ground level.[33] Taken together, lidar estimates of canopy height, tree cover, and vertical structure are highly correlated with carbon density.[34]

Estimates of carbon density obtained from airborne lidar are far more accurate and precise than the forest type-specific averages described above. They are also sub-stantially more expensive, however. Mapping the carbon density of the entire tropics using aircraft would take four years and cost $250 million for a single snapshot.[35]

Finally, carbon densities can be mapped over large areas by combining measurements from field plots with remotely sensed information obtained from satellites. In 2012, research teams from the NASA Jet Propulsion Lab and the Woods Hole Research Center independently mapped aboveground forest carbon stocks across the entire tropics at five-hundred-meter resolution using information from two satellite systems in combination: Lidar data from the ICESAT-1 satellite-based Geoscience Laser Altimetry System (GLAS), which ran from 2003 to 2009 and was originally designed for ice sheet monitoring, and satellite-based MODIS.[36]

These maps of forest carbon stocks are shown in figure 4.3. The two maps have been used in combination to produce even more accurate maps of tropical forest carbon stocks.[37] Both are freely available to researchers and are rapidly being improved to cover the whole globe, every year, in finer detail. Similar maps have already been produced for large areas of Canada and Siberia.[38]

A significant advance in carbon stock measurement is expected in 2018, when scientists install a lidar instrument on the International Space Station as part of a NASA mission called Global Ecosystem Dynamics Investigation (GEDI).[39] Space-based lidar will generate densely sampled coverage of the world's tropical and temperate forests that will let researchers measure forest carbon densities far more accurately.[40] It will also vastly improve the potential to monitor losses and gains in

Figure 4.3: Forest carbon stocks have been mapped across the tropics using data from satellites.

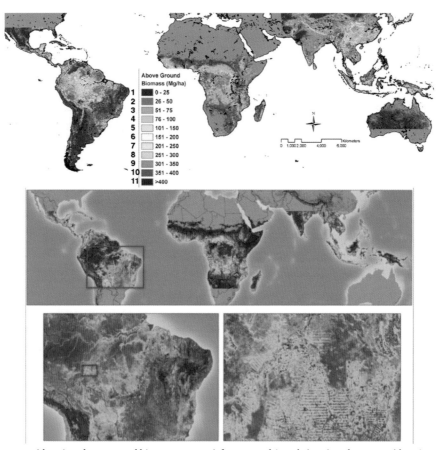

Source: Top map (showing aboveground biomass, c. 2000) from Saatchi et al. (2011). Other maps (showing carbon contained in aboveground live woody vegetation, c. 2007–08) from Baccini et al. (2012).

forest carbon stocks directly, as discussed below in the section on forest degradation.

Where available, another technology that can be used for measuring forest carbon stock is Radiowave Detection and Ranging (radar) imagery. Unlike optical imagery or lidar, radar can penetrate cloud cover, and images can be acquired day or night. The radar sensors currently operating have limited ability on their own to measure carbon stocks because they have difficulties differentiating among carbon densities greater than around one hundred tons per hectare, and most wet tropical forests have more carbon. When taken together with data from lidar or other sensors, however, radar data can provide even greater advances in measuring changes in carbon stocks than lidar alone.[41]

The European Space Agency, Indian Space Agency, and Japanese Aerospace Exploration Agency have all recently launched or will be launching satellites with radar sensors. In 2020, the European Space Agency's Biomass mission will launch a satellite-based radar system that will be able to measure carbon stocks at greater densities than is possible with currently operational radar satellites.[42] Together, GEDI and BIOMASS will provide unprecedented knowledge on forest carbon stocks globally.

As powerful as remote sensing technologies are, they can only measure carbon that is aboveground. In most cases this is adequate, since in most places 70 to 90 percent of carbon in forests on mineral (nonorganic) soils is concentrated in tree trunks, branches, and leaves, and it is this aboveground carbon that is most vulnerable to damage from logging, fire, storms, or conversion to agriculture.[43] The remainder of forest carbon is stored in roots and soils. On most soils, clearing forests releases only a fraction of this belowground carbon.[44]

Remote sensing technologies are unlikely to be able to measure belowground carbon in the foreseeable future. The only way to directly measure the carbon content of nonorganic soils is with soil core samples taken at field sites. Belowground carbon stocks can, however, be roughly approximated using simplified ratios of above- to belowground carbon that have been estimated for different ecosystems.[45]

For forests on organic soils, the story is more complicated. As discussed in chapter 2, carbon emissions from disturbing soils in peat-swamp forests and mangroves can be considerable. And while core samples or ground-penetrating radar can gauge the depth of peat soils, this information alone is of limited usefulness in calculating emissions, which depend on how much of the water table has been drained, what type of crops have been planted subsequent to forest clearing, and other factors. Scientists have produced rough estimates of average annual emissions from disturbed peat soils, but they are very uncertain.[46] The distribution of peat soils and emissions from their disturbance are both high priorities for future research, as mentioned in box 4.3.

Monitoring Emissions from Degradation: The Second D in REDD+

In addition to the carbon that is lost when forests are cleared ("deforestation"), carbon can be lost from within standing forests.

Box 4.3: Current and Near-Future Status of Forest Monitoring Capabilities

Technologies for monitoring changes in forests and forest carbon stocks have advanced rapidly in recent years, and are expected to continue advancing, as described here.

Forest cover losses have been mapped globally at thirty-meter resolution using the Landsat satellite. These data are freely available online and are regularly updated and improved. National governments can adapt them to meet their monitoring needs by combining them with country-specific information from forest inventories and aircraft.

Forest cover gains have been mapped globally at thirty-meter resolution based on imagery from the Landsat satellite. This map, however, excludes forests that had not yet reached five meters in height by 2012, as well as growth within forests that had already reached five meters in height by 2000.

Aboveground forest carbon stocks have been mapped across the tropics at five-hundred-meter resolution using the MODIS satellite. These data are freely available and are rapidly being improved to cover broader areas and longer time periods at higher resolution. National governments can adapt these data to meet their needs by combining them with country-specific information from forest inventories and aircraft.

Belowground forest carbon stocks can be extrapolated indirectly from aboveground stocks using published ratios combined with other spatial data, such as topography or known presence of wetlands. Remote sensing will unlikely be able to map belowground carbon stocks in the near future.

Emissions from degradation of peat soil have large uncertainties; the accuracies of their estimates will benefit from continued research.

Carbon stock losses within forests can be calculated indirectly by combining information on forest cover loss and carbon stocks. Forest carbon stock losses can be measured directly at the plot scale using repeated inventory data and at the country scale using repeated aircraft measurements. These data can be extended globally using moderate-resolution satellites (such as Landsat). In 2018, a lidar sensor on the International Space Station is expected to enable the generation of globally consistent time series of forest carbon stock losses.

Carbon stock gains within forests can be measured at local or regional scale by combining data from aircraft and forest inventories but not yet systematically at the country scale. Space-based lidar is expected to enable the generation of globally consistent time series of forest carbon stock gains, as well.

Natural forests can be distinguished from plantations by trained technicians using visual classification of high- or moderate-resolution imagery. Automated algorithms have been developed for some geographical locations and are being improved for global use.

Distributions of many plant and animal species have been modeled using biological and environmental information. Some characteristics related to the biodiversity of forests can be approximated using aircraft- or satellite-derived estimates of forest cover and density. These maps are improving with the development of measurements of three-dimensional canopy structure using lidar and radar.

Law enforcement agencies and independent monitors have taken advantage of biweekly deforestation alert systems based on MODIS satellites, such as the DETER system used in the Brazilian Amazon. Global biweekly deforestation alerts (for example, FORMA) are available online for the humid tropics and can be adapted for law enforcement or independent monitoring in other countries.

Source: Adapted from Goetz et al. (2014).

This is referred to as "forest degradation" in the context of REDD+. It can result from, for instance, selective logging, fuelwood collection and charcoal production, or forest fires. Forest degradation has been estimated to emit around 12 to 16 percent as much carbon dioxide as deforestation does pantropically, with large variations from country to country.[47] Note that in other contexts forest degradation can refer to the loss of biodiversity or the loss of capacity to provide goods and services.[48]

Emissions from degradation are harder to measure than emissions from deforestation for several related reasons. Carbon losses from degradation are inherently smaller than those from deforestation, since forests lose only some rather than all of their carbon when degraded. The effects of degradation may be hidden from view beneath a closed forest canopy, rather than showing up as large-scale changes on maps of forest area. And degradation can happen gradually over many years, while deforestation usually takes place suddenly. Furthermore, degradation often happens concurrently with some amount of forest regrowth.

As with deforestation, estimating emissions from forest degradation requires information about forest area and carbon stocks. But while emissions from deforestation can be estimated based on carbon stocks at a single point in time, estimating emissions from degradation requires knowledge of carbon stocks both before and after degradation has occurred. Fully accounting for net emissions from degradation requires measuring forest carbon stocks repeatedly over a long period of time.

It is currently difficult to detect degradation in which less than one-third of biomass is lost using any single remote sensing technology. The best way to detect low levels of degradation is to combine multiple sources of information: images of changes in forest area from very high–resolution optical satellites (such as IKONOS or Quickbird), plus repeated measurements of carbon stocks from field plots or lidar. Neither high-resolution satellites nor lidar-equipped airplanes currently capture areas of more than a few hundred square kilometers at a time, which limits the ability to detect forest degradation at large scales.

Advances are, however, on the way on both fronts. The European Sentinel-2 satellites launched in 2015–16 will be able to detect forest area changes at ten-meter resolution every five days across most of the planet.[49] Installation of lidar on the International Space Station in 2018 will broaden measurements of carbon stocks to the entire tropics, as well as to temperate regions.

Alternatively, emissions from degradation can be estimated using indirect proxy variables. This approach matches information on typical losses of carbon from particular activities such as logging, fuelwood collection, or disturbance along roadsides to maps of where such activities are taking place.[50] While this approach is quicker and easier and can cover larger areas than combined high-resolution imagery, it is far less accurate, and uncertainty ranges are difficult to know. Indirect proxy approaches are most useful for providing a first approximation of degradation, which can be helpful in planning more targeted observations using field plots, high-resolution images, or lidar.

Monitoring Forest Regrowth: The "Plus" in REDD+

Forests remove ("sequester") carbon from the atmosphere as they grow. This is true for both newly replanted forests and degraded forests that are allowed to recover. Sequestration by forest regrowth has been estimated to be equivalent to 23 to 46 percent of emissions from deforestation in the tropics, with regional concentrations in coastal Brazil, China, India, parts of Southeast Asia, and coastal West Africa, as shown in figure 4.1.[51]

Calculating how much carbon is sequestered by growing forests presents challenges similar to those of calculating emissions from deforestation and degradation, but in reverse and over longer time scales. A regrowing forest typically requires decades or even a century or longer to recapture the same quantity of carbon that was once stored in a primary forest.[52] Thus, forest regrowth has to be tracked longer than deforestation or degradation to confidently determine recovery to a forested state.

As with deforestation, newly established forest areas have been mapped globally using Landsat, as shown in figure 4.1. Forest growth was mapped over a twelve-year period (2001–12) rather than annually, as for deforestation, since forest regrowth happens so much more slowly. Even so, this map still doesn't include regrowing forests that were shorter than five meters in height as of 2012, nor does it show growth within forests that had already surpassed five meters by 2000.[53]

As with degradation, carbon gains within closed-canopy forests are difficult to observe using imagery alone, but they can be measured using imagery in combination with field plots, radar, or lidar. Significant advances in monitoring regrowth will also be possible when lidar is installed aboard the International Space Station.

Mapping Changes in Carbon Stock Directly

The distinctions among the different activities described above (deforestation, degradation, regrowth) are somewhat artificial. The threshold of loss in forest cover beyond which mere degradation is considered outright deforestation is arbitrary. Likewise, an area of forest can be losing carbon through degradation even as it is regaining some through regrowth. Even determining what counts as a forest is controversial; worldwide there are more than eight hundred official definitions.[54]

What matters for the climate is not definitional distinctions, but how much the carbon stored in forests is increasing or decreasing. Climate researchers would like to be able to measure changes in forest carbon stocks directly, whether or not they are associated with changes in forest area. They are currently prevented from doing so by technological limitations, so they resort, out of necessity, to combining data on forest area changes with data on carbon stocks.

But here, too, good news is on the horizon. As mentioned earlier, lidar sees through the canopy to take measurements of the entire forest profile. Lidar data are particularly useful for mapping carbon stock changes associated with forest growth and forest degradation. Repeated lidar measurements have been used to monitor carbon stock losses and gains, as shown in figure 4.4 for a landscape in Costa Rica.[55]

While the 2018 installation of lidar on the International Space Station will make it possible for researchers to measure tropical and temperate forest carbon stocks far more accurately, intense competition among scientific missions for slots on the station makes it uncertain whether the lidar sensor will operate more than a year or two. But even the 18 billion or so samples collected in the first year of operation will enable scientists to establish relationships between image data (from Landsat or Sentinel-2, for example) and data on carbon stocks. These relationships can then be used to infer changes in carbon stocks from image data alone.

Monitoring Safeguards on Conservation of Natural Forests and Biodiversity

As described in chapter 3, biodiverse natural tropical rainforests contain hundreds of tree species per hectare. Their many layers stretch from the ground to the canopy, and their tallest trees emerge from the canopy and soar more than sixty meters into the sky. Such forests provide habitat for thou-

Figure 4.4: Changes in forest carbon stocks have been mapped at the landscape level using data from sensors on airplanes.

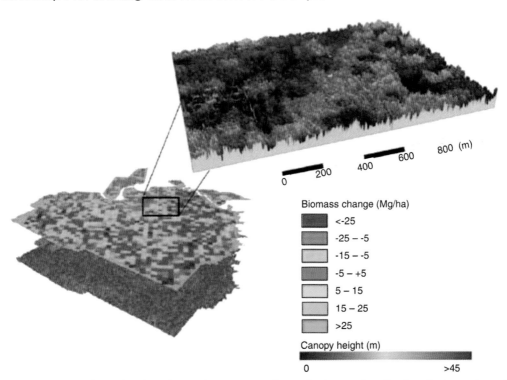

Source: S. Goetz and R. Dubayah, "Advances in Remote Sensing Technology and Implications for Measuring and Monitoring Forest Carbon Stocks and Change," *Carbon Management* 2, no. 3 (2011): 231–44.

sands of species of birds, mammals, and other animals. To people who know these forests well, they are a cornucopia of usable products such as fruits, nuts, and medicines. The services biodiverse natural forests provide include the provision of clean water and cool air.

On the other hand, a typical oil palm plantation contains rows of *Elaeis guineensis,* evenly spaced and of uniform height. While oil palm plantations produce a highly profitable product, they have less carbon, less wildlife, and dirtier water than mature natural forests.[56] Oil palm plantations have been rapidly displacing natural forests throughout Indonesia and Malaysia and, more recently, in parts of Africa and Latin America, as well.[57]

Most people wouldn't consider an oil palm plantation a forest. And yet, under the definition of forest used by the UNFCCC, a country is allowed to classify any area as a forest as long as it contains enough trees above a certain height.[58] The definition says nothing about the type of trees. A biodiverse natural rainforest meets the UNFCCC definition, but so does a eucalyptus plantation; and if the fact that palms are technically not trees is overlooked, so might an oil palm plantation.

The upshot of this is that a country could conceivably burn and clear vast swaths of natural forests to make way for oil palm or timber plantations and take advantage of a definitional loophole to claim no deforestation had occurred—that it had simply converted one type of forest to another. Some analysts interpret UNFCCC guidance to mean the country could count the lost carbon as "degradation" rather than "deforestation" and in doing so potentially leave the change off its balance sheets for REDD+.[59]

Climate diplomats could have closed this loophole by amending the UNFCCC definition of forest or by requiring that countries account for all emissions, whether from "deforestation" or "degradation." Instead, they enacted this safeguard on natural forests and biological diversity in 2010:

> Actions [should be] consistent with the conservation of natural forests and biological diversity, ensuring that actions [to reduce deforestation] are not used for the conversion of natural forests, but are instead used to incentivize the protection and conservation of natural forests and their ecosystem services, and to enhance other social and environmental benefits.[60]

This convoluted sentence is interpreted by many observers as intended to prevent the mass conversion of natural forests to plantation monocultures described above. It's one of seven "Cancun Safeguards" to prevent negative social or environmental consequences of REDD+ and promote positive synergies.

At the heart of monitoring the application of this safeguard is the technological capability to distinguish natural forests from plantations. Technology on this front is not as far along as it is for measuring the extent of deforestation or the density of carbon stocks, but it is advancing rapidly.

Distinguishing Natural Forests from Plantation Monocultures

Detecting the presence of plantation crops with remote sensing is not difficult. Oil palm or timber plantations can blanket hundreds or thousands of hectares, so moderate-resolution imagery such as that produced by Landsat or MODIS satellites can be used to detect their presence as easily as detecting the presence of a natural forest.

The challenge comes in distinguishing between plantations and natural forests. Growth rates of plantation species are fast across the tropics, so planted trees can quickly mature to form a closed canopy. To a moderate-resolution satellite, a closed-canopy plantation and a natural forest look similar.[61]

Their geometric patterns differ, however. Plantations are marked by long, even rows, while natural forests appear rough and mottled, as seen in figure 4.5. A trained technician, given a high-resolution lidar or radar image, can easily interpret the difference. But a computer can't. As with the CAPTCHA images used to protect websites from automated spammers, the human eye can instantaneously recognize patterns where computer algorithms fail.[62]

High-resolution images can be used to create local maps that distinguish natural forests from plantations, as in figure 4.5 (top), or to calibrate regional maps, as in figure 4.5 (bottom). Such mapping is most advanced in Southeast Asia, where rainforests are rapidly being cleared to make way for oil palm and fast-growing pulp and paper plantations. Mapping has also been undertaken in Brazil, Costa Rica, Ghana, and Peru.[63] Although no global maps exist yet, in 2016 researchers at the World Resources Institute and Transparent World distinguished plantations from natural forests in seven countries.[64] They found plantations make up 13 percent of the land area in Indonesia and 30 percent in Malaysia.[65]

Automated computer routines to distinguish natural forests from plantations are also advancing. These approaches can assess large areas by combining two types of imagery: high-resolution imagery that is interpreted by humans and moderate-resolution images that are available across large areas.

Storing, processing, and analyzing large amounts of high-resolution imagery is currently expensive, and using high-resolution imagery to map large areas (that is, thousands of square kilometers) routinely requires computing capabilities currently beyond the reach of many countries. Such capabilities are rapidly advancing, however, with computers becoming more powerful, costs falling, and more and more high-resolution imagery being acquired and archived. Some countries are building complete, or "wall-to-wall," maps of their forested lands. Some, including Mexico, are systematically acquiring high-resolution imagery to produce detailed maps of land cover, including for the purpose of distinguishing between natural forests and plantations.[66]

Monitoring Biodiversity

In addition to the language related to natural forests, the other piece of the Cancun Safeguard quoted above relates to biological diversity. Tropical forests are far more than just giant repositories of carbon; they provide habitat for two-thirds of all plants and animals that live on land.[67] This includes some of the most beloved species on the planet—orangutans, jaguars, gorillas, and birds of paradise. As discussed in chapter 11, preserving biodiversity has long been a primary motivation for wealthy countries to put money toward forest conservation initiatives in tropical countries, even while it has often been a lower priority in the tropical countries themselves.

Conserving tropical forests through REDD+ offers collateral benefits for biodi-

Figure 4.5: Oil palm plantations can be distinguished from natural forests in remotely sensed images.

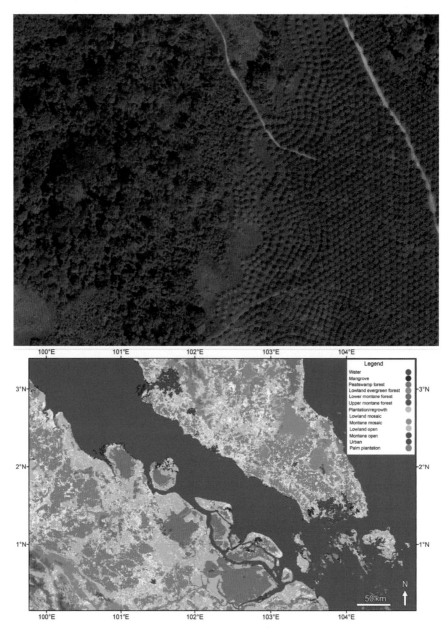

Top Image: Oil palm plantations (right) vs. natural forest (left) in Southeast Sulawesi, Indonesia. *Bottom Image:* Oil palm plantations (brown) vs. natural forests (green) in Peninsular Malaysia and Sumatra, Indonesia.

Source: Global Forest Watch, World Resources Institute. (www.globalforestwatch.org); J. Miettinen, C. Shi, W. J. Tan, and S. Liew, "2010 Land Cover Map of Insular Southeast Asia in 250-m SPATIAL RESOLUTION," *Remote Sensing Letters* 3, no. 1 (2012): 11–20.

versity.[68] With planning, forest countries can promote conservation in areas that are rich in both carbon and biodiversity. Doing so requires information on where species live.[69] Until recently, this information has been limited to static maps of the ranges of mammals, birds, reptiles, amphibians, and plants.[70] These maps are modeled on biological and environmental information, not on direct observations of where species are present or absent. They are also not routinely updated.

Mapping the distribution of forest species directly was long considered beyond the capability of remote sensing technologies, due to the complex structure of tropical forests and the high density of species living in them. But that may be changing, at least for some aspects of biodiversity.[71] Two types of remote sensing data, used alone or in combination, offer new information on the distribution of species and can be used to monitor changes in species distribution over time.

First, hyperspectral remote sensing, also known as imaging spectroscopy, can identify plant types based on their nitrogen concentration, leaf pigmentation, leaf water content, or other chemical and physiological "fingerprints."[72] Second, lidar can take detailed measurements of a forest's three-dimensional structure, which can be used as an indirect proxy for forest biodiversity.[73] Together these technologies can be used to infer tree composition, habitat diversity, and animal species richness, as well as changes in these attributes over time.

Flying planes with these technologies over large areas of forest is currently prohibitively expensive for most countries. Academic research has shown that studies using these technologies are possible at small scales, however, and technologies to monitor changes in forest biodiversity are also getting cheaper, becoming more accessible, and covering larger areas.[74] Scientists' ability to monitor biodiversity directly is expected to advance markedly with the launch of two satellites, the German Environmental Mapping and Analysis Program (EnMAP) in 2017 and the U.S. Hyperspectral Infrared Imager (HyspIRI) within a decade, as well as with new lidar and radar missions.

Real-Time Detection of Deforestation to Support Improved Forest Governance

In much of the tropics, deforestation takes place far from the watchful eyes of guardians of the public interest. When a tree falls in the forest with no one around to hear it, as the saying goes, it makes no sound, at least in terms of the attention of law enforcement. Logging and deforestation may be illegal on the books in a country's capital, but if law enforcers can't see it occurring they are powerless to respond.

Brazil addressed that problem in May 2004, when the Brazilian National Institute for Space Research (INPE) launched the Real Time System for Detection of Deforestation (DETER) program. The MODIS-based DETER system detects forest clearings in the Brazilian Amazon in near-real time and sends biweekly alerts to federal and state law enforcement agencies. The agencies then use this information to detect, rapidly respond to, and prosecute perpetrators of illegal deforestation. The launch of the DETER program was a key factor enabling Brazil's rapid and sustained drop in Amazon deforestation, as described in detail in chapter 7. In 2014, a DETER-like system was effectively extended to all humid forests of the tropics as part of Global Forest Watch's Forest Monitoring for Action (FORMA) program.

The launch of a real-time detection system was a key factor enabling Brazil's drop in Amazon deforestation.

Local guardians of forest resources, be they park wardens or indigenous communities, not only can take advantage of the real-time monitoring systems described above; they can also look to a wide variety of emerging technologies to detect deforestation at local scales. Motion-activated cameras currently used to monitor wildlife can also be used to detect people encroaching illegally on areas of forest.[75] Repurposed cell phones can be used to detect the sound of loggers' chainsaws or poachers' gunshots and transmit alerts.[76] Drones are currently being developed to do so as well, as are constellations of "micro-satellites"—clusters of small, light, cheap satellites purpose-built for specific tasks.[77]

Real-time information on deforestation is particularly useful when it is combined with maps of land ownership or concessional use rights, where such maps exist. This combination of information can help attribute deforestation to particular perpetrators and suggest policies for targeting the causes of deforestation and forest degradation. For example, Brazil created a rural property registry, the Rural Environmental Cadastre (CAR), as a means of enforcing its Forest Code; Indone-

sian organizations have used information on concessions and fires to identify companies responsible for areas where forest fires have been set illegally.[78] Maps of ownership or use rights can also be used to identify the key role of good forest stewards, as in the case of an analysis that shows more than 20 percent of the carbon in tropical forests is contained in indigenous territories.[79]

In many cases, these maps of ownership or use rights are informal, incomplete, outdated, contradictory, or otherwise unreliable, and they have often been overtaken in quality by maps of forests, forest loss, and carbon based on remotely sensed data.[80] Technology can be combined with social and legal processes to bring maps of ownership and usage up to date, however. Indonesia, for example, has undertaken an ongoing initiative called One Map to standardize and publicize concession boundaries; and indigenous peoples are using global positioning system (GPS) devices and Internet mapping applications to delineate the borders of their territories.[81]

Forest monitoring and demarcation of claims have benefits that extend well beyond tracking the reduction of carbon emissions. Good maps contribute to good environmental governance by providing access to information, offering recourse to justice in environmental matters and allowing public participation in decision making.[82] In these ways, the rapid advances in monitoring technology support good governance agendas as well.

How Much Monitoring Is Enough?

As described in the sections above, a variety of technologies are now available for monitoring forest carbon losses and gains. Most national governments, however, are not interested in simply importing the published output of outside scientists. Forest agencies understandably seek to do their own forest monitoring, especially when money and reputation are at stake. Different countries apply different definitions of what constitutes a forest or deforestation, as well. Fortunately, national government agencies can adapt the same raw data scientists use for global or pan-tropical analyses to meet their own needs by combining them with country-specific information from forest inventories and aircraft.

How much monitoring of forest carbon flows is really needed to underpin forest countries' REDD+ efforts? On the one hand, increased investments in monitoring technology can always improve the accuracy and precision of measurements, and their cost may represent just a small fraction of potential carbon payments received under a fully funded REDD+ program.[83] On the other hand, programs need to be operationalized quickly and affordably, and the fact that emissions must be not only *monitored* and *reported* but also *verified* by third parties argues in favor of simpler, more transparent methods.

Fortunately, two related concepts allow programs to be implemented quickly with available data while improving estimates of emission reductions over time. First, countries participating in REDD+ programs can start off simply, by developing reference levels and monitoring systems in a piecemeal fashion and expanding them as better data and cheaper methods become available. The UNFCCC agreement on REDD+ encourages such a "stepwise approach."[84]

And, second, funding countries can pay a premium for emission reductions that have been measured with greater precision. This "conservativeness approach," first articulated by scientist Giacomo Grassi and his colleagues, would allow performance payments to get off the ground without delay, while providing monetary incentives to improve monitoring capabilities over time.[85] Both these approaches were put into practice by Guyana and Norway in their landmark payment-for-performance agreement in 2009, as described in box 4.4.

There's another limit on the importance of obtaining ever more accurate and precise measurements, which is that calculating reductions in emissions involves more than just monitoring. As described in box 4.1 and shown in figure 4.2, the calculation also depends on reference levels. Depending on the REDD+ program paying for emission reductions, as well as the circumstances of the forested country in question, reference levels might take a number of forms. They might be simple averages of historical deforestation rates, which are used as the basis for payments into Brazil's Amazon Fund. They might be adjusted upward toward a tropical average deforestation rate, as in Guyana. Or they might represent projections of future deforestation rates, as allowed in some cases by the Forest Carbon Partnership Facility's Carbon Fund. One of the most prominent justifications for an adjusted or projected reference level is to enable potential finance for forest conservation in countries where deforestation has been low historically but is expected to increase in the future.[86] These adjustments are political as much as technocratic. To the extent reference levels rely on adjustments or projections in addition to historical measurements, the soundness of the

Box 4.4: Monitoring in Practice: The Guyana-Norway Partnership

Guyana has fewer than a million people and is one of the poorest countries in the Americas. Most citizens of the Kansas-sized country live along a narrow coastal plain, while the vast interior is almost entirely covered in rainforest inhabited by scattered Amerindian communities.

In November 2009, President Bharrat Jagdeo of Guyana and Prime Minister Jens Stoltenberg of Norway signed a landmark climate agreement, whereby Guyana would keep its rate of deforestation at near-zero levels. In exchange, Norway would pay up to $250 million, based on performance.

But how to monitor the terms of the agreement? Needless to say, Guyana has never had a space program. When the agreement was signed in 2009, like most tropical forest countries, it lagged far behind Brazil in its ability to monitor deforestation using remote sensing technology and forest inventories.[a]

On the other hand, not every country needs its own world-class space program to monitor emissions from deforestation. Guyana and Norway agreed to keep monitoring simple and move quickly, rather than wait for technologies that could count every ton of carbon perfectly. For the purposes of making results-based payments, the two governments agreed to assume a conservative value of one hundred tons of carbon per hectare of forest across the board, even though both knew that in most cases the carbon density was much higher than this.

Since then, the Guyana Forestry Commission has invested in systematic improvements to forest monitoring, using a mixture of local capacity and external consultants. Satellite-based maps of deforestation have become more accurate, more frequently generated, and produced at higher resolutions. In 2012 Guyana's maps improved from thirty-meter resolution Landsat imagery to five-meter resolution RapidEye imagery, which can detect many forms of forest degradation as well as deforestation.[b] The government of Guyana used these high-resolution maps to identify and start to address deforestation by the unregulated informal mining sector.[c] Carbon stock estimates have advanced from the simple, conservative assumption of one hundred tons per hectare to a six-stratum map of carbon density covering the whole of the country's forests.[d]

Both parties have upheld their ends of the bargain. Guyana's deforestation rate has remained extremely low by world standards, as reported in four annual monitoring reports.[e] Third-party consultants have verified Guyana's emissions estimates, with Norway making payments based on those results. By May 2015, Norway had made five payments in support of low-carbon development in Guyana, totaling $190 million.[f]

a. E. Romijn, M. Herold, L. Kooistra, D. Murdiyarso, and L. Verchot, "Assessing Capacities of Non-Annex I Countries for National Forest Monitoring in the Context of REDD+," *Environmental Science & Policy* 19 (2012): 33–48.
b. P. Watt, "Forest Area Change Assessment & Monitoring in Guyana as Part of the National Monitoring Reporting & Verification System," Indufor, 2015.
c. J. Busch and N. Birdsall, "Assessing Performance-Based Payments for Forest Conservation: Six Successes, Four Worries, and Six Possibilities to Explore of the Guyana-Norway Agreement." CGD Climate and Forest Paper Series 1, 2014.
d. Government of Guyana, "The Reference Level for Guyana's REDD+ Program," December 2014.
e. Guyana Forestry Commission, "Monitoring Reporting and Verification System: Interim Measures Report Year 5, Version 1, 1 January 2014–31 December 2014," October 7, 2015.
f. Government of Guyana, "Guyana Receives US$40 Million Payment from Norway for Climate Services and Continued Low Deforestation," PR Newswire, May 8, 2015.

rationales used for adjustments or the models used for projections is at least as important as the accuracy and precision of measurements.

Conclusion

Within the last five years, technology for monitoring forests has improved rapidly. It is now technologically feasible to monitor greenhouse gas emissions from deforestation over large areas and long time periods. Promising advances are also being made in monitoring forest degradation and sequestration by regrowing forests, distinguishing natural forests from oil palm and timber plantations, and even in tracking some components of forests' biological diversity, as shown in figure 4.6.

As technology has advanced, so, too, have international climate negotiations. In 2001,

concerns about environmental integrity capsized the prospect of including avoided deforestation projects in the Clean Development Mechanism. But the improved capability to monitor and verify emissions over large areas and long time periods enabled a consensus to develop around national- or jurisdictional-level performance payments to protect tropical forests. This consensus was realized in 2015 as an article on REDD+ in the Paris Agreement.[87]

Now that monitoring is no longer the barrier it once was, tropical countries can protect forests, with rich countries paying for the results. Why should they do so? For one reason, protecting and restoring tropical forests can make global efforts to prevent dangerous climate change cheaper, bigger, and faster, as we discuss in the next chapter.

Figure 4.6: Technology for monitoring tropical forests is rapidly advancing.

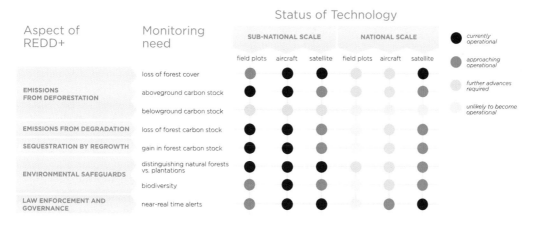

Source: Adapted from Goetz et al. (2014). National-scale degradation refers to an approach based largely on fine-scale forest-cover change while subnational scale degradation refers to a stock-change approach. National-scale regrowth refers to an approach based largely on mapping afforestation and reforestation while sub-national scale regrowth refers to a stock-change approach. Biodiversity refers to plant and animal species richness and diversity.

Notes

1. R. Butler, "Are We on the Brink of Saving Rainforests?" Mongabay.com, July 22, 2009, http://news.mongabay.com/2009/0722-redd.html.

2. Ibid.

3. A. G. M. La Viña and A. de Leon, "Two Global Challenges, One Solution: International Cooperation to Combat Climate Change and Tropical Deforestation," CGD Working Paper 388, Center for Global Development, Washington DC, 2014.

4. P. M. Fearnside, "Saving Tropical Forests as a Global Warming Countermeasure: An Issue that Divides the Environmental Movement," *Ecological Economics* 39, no. 2 (2001): 167–84; U.S. Geological Survey, "Fees and Landsat Data Products," 2014.

5. S. Goetz, M. Hansen, R. A. Houghton, W. Walker, N. Laporte, and J. Busch. "Measurement and Monitoring Needs, Capabilities and Potential for Addressing Reduced Emissions from Deforestation and Forest Degradation under REDD+." *Environmental Research Letters* 10, no. 12 (2015): 123001.

6. See, for example, National Institute for Space Research (INPE), "Projeto Prodes: Monitorament da floresta Amazonica Brasileira por satelite" [Prodes Project: Monitoring Forest in the Brazilian Amazon by Satellite], Instituto Nacional de Pesquisa Espaciaias, 2015, http://www.obt.inpe.br/prodes/index.php; G. Harper et al., "Fifty Years of Deforestation and Forest Fragmentation in Madagascar," *Environmental Conservation* 34, no. 4 (2007): 325–33; T. J. Killeen et al., "Thirty Years of Land-Cover Change in Bolivia," *AMBIO: A Journal of the Human Environment* 36, no. 7 (2007): 600–606.

7. L. Olander et al., "Reference Scenarios for Deforestation and Forest Degradation in Support of REDD: A Review of Data and Methods," *Environmental Research Letters* 3, no. 2 (2008): 025011.

8. U.S. Geological Survey, "Fees and Landsat Data Products."

9. Ibid.; U.S. Geological Survey, "Landsat Project Statistics," http://landsat.usgs.gov//Landsat_Project_Statistics.php.

10. M. C. Hansen et al., "High-Resolution Global Maps of 21st-Century Forest Cover Change," *Science* 342 (2013): 850–53.

11. To access Global Forest Watch, visit http://www.globalforestwatch.org.

12. F. Achard et al., "Determination of Deforestation Rates of the World's Humid Tropical Forests," *Science* 297, no. 5583 (2002): 999–1002; E. Lindquist et al., "Global Forest Land-Use Change 1990–2005," Food and Agriculture Organization of the United Nations (FAO) Forestry Paper, Food and Agriculture Organization of the United Nations/JRC, Rome, Italy, 2012, 169.

13. A. Grainger, "Difficulties in Tracking the Long-Term Global Trend in Tropical Forest Area," *Proceedings of the National Academy of Sciences* 105, no. 2 (2008): 818–23.

14. R. Tropek et al., "Comment on 'High-Resolution Global Maps of 21st-Century Forest Cover Change,'" *Science* 344, no. 6187 (2014): 981–81; M. Hansen et al., "Response to Comment on 'High-Resolution Global Maps of 21st-Century Forest Cover Change,'" *Science* 344 (2014): 981.

15. S. Saatchi et al., "Benchmark Map of Forest Carbon Stocks in Tropical Regions across Three Continents," *Proceedings of the National Academy of Sciences* 108, no. 24 (2011): 9899–904; A. Baccini et al., "Estimated Carbon Dioxide Emissions from Tropical Deforestation Improved by Carbon-Density Maps," *Nature Climate Change* 2, no. 3 (2012): 182–85.

16. Saatchi (2011) data available at: Improved pan-tropical forest biomass map at 1 km resolution for the year circa-2000. Created October 30, 2015. ArcGIS Storymap. http://www.arcgis.com/home/item.html?id=3e547458f4a14f62a481d6337184fbf5; Improved pan-tropical forest biomass map at 1 km resolution for the 2000's. Created October 30, 2015. ArcGIS Storymap. http://www.arcgis.com/home/item.html?id=ef85b

c1b7a8048079b8c1e959ed24573; ArcGIS Storymap. http://www.arcgis.com/home/item.html?id=ef85bc1b7a8048079b8c1e959ed24573. Baccini (2012) data available at http://www.arcgis.com/home/webmap/viewer.html?webmap=2332b43bc5454127bfde21e894c89a51.

17. D. Zarin et al., "Can Carbon Emissions from Tropical Deforestation Drop by 50% in Five Years?" *Global Change Biology* 22, no. 4 (2016): 1336–47; "Global Forest Watch: Climate," *Global Forest Watch.*

18. Developed at the Center for Global Development in 2009 by David Wheeler, Dan Hammer, and Robin Kraft, http://www.cgdev.org/initiative/forest-monitoring-action-forma.

19. L. Abrams, "New Google Tool Lets You Watch the Forests Disappear in Real Time," *Salon*, February 24, 2014, http://www.salon.com/2014/02/24/new_google_tool_lets_you_watch_the_forests_disappear_in_real_time/.

20. La Viña and de Leon, "Two Global Challenges, One Solution: International Cooperation to Combat Climate Change and Tropical Deforestation."

21. United Nations Framework Convention on Climate Change (UNFCCC), "Submission by the Governments of Papua New Guinea and Costa Rica: Reducing Emissions from Deforestation in Developing Countries: Approaches to Stimulate Action," FCCC/CP/2005/Misc.1, November 11, 2005, http://unfccc.int/resource/docs/2005/cop11/eng/misc01.pdf.

22. Goetz, Hansen, Houghton, Walker, Laporte, and Busch, "Measurement and Monitoring Needs, Capabilities and Potential for Addressing Reduced Emissions from Deforestation and Forest Degradation under REDD+."

23. Ibid.

24. Ibid.

25. Satellite Imaging Corporation, "SPOT-5 Satellite Sensor," Satimagingcorp.com, http://www.satimagingcorp.com/satellite-sensors/other-satellite-sensors/spot-5/.

26. Satellite Imaging Corporation, "RapidEye Satellite Sensor," Satimagingcorp.com, http://www.satimagingcorp.com/satellite-sensors/other-satellite-sensors/rapideye/.

27. Satellite Imaging Corporation, "Ikonos Satellite Sensor," Satimagingcorp.com, http://www.satimagingcorp.com/satellite-sensors/ikonos/.

28. Satellite Imaging Corporation, "QuickBird Satellite Sensor," Satimagingcorp.com, http://www.satimagingcorp.com/satellite-sensors/quickbird/.

29. Goetz et al., "Measurement and Monitoring."

30. Ibid.

31. H. Gibbs et al., "Monitoring and Estimating Tropical Forest Carbon Stocks: Making REDD a Reality," *Environmental Research Letters* 2, no. 4 (2007): 045023;

32. S. J. Goetz et al., "Mapping and Monitoring Carbon Stocks with Satellite Observations: A Comparison of Methods," *Carbon Balance and Management* 4, no. 1 (2009): 2; R. A. Houghton, F. Hall, and S. J. Goetz, "Importance of Biomass in the Global Carbon Cycle," *Journal of Geophysical Research: Biogeosciences (2005–2012)* 114, no. G2 (2009).

33. For meta-analysis, see S. G. Zolkos, S. J. Goetz, and R. Dubayah, "A Meta-Analysis of Terrestrial Aboveground Biomass Estimation Using Lidar Remote Sensing," *Remote Sensing of Environment* 128 (2013): 289–98.

34. G. P. Asner et al., "High-Resolution Forest Carbon Stocks and Emissions in the Amazon," *Proceedings of the National Academy of Sciences* 107, no. 38 (2010): 16738–742; R. Dubayah et al., "Land Surface Characterization Using Lidar Remote Sensing," in *Spatial Information for Land Use Management*, ed. M. J. Hill and R. Aspinall, 25–38 (Singapore: International Publishers Direct, 2000); E. Næsset and K. O. Bjerknes, "Estimating Tree Heights and Number of Stems in Young Forest Stands Using Airborne Laser Scanner Data," *Remote Sensing of Environment* 78, no. 3 (2001): 328–40.

35. J. Mascaro et al., "These Are the Days of Lasers in the Jungle," *Carbon Balance and Management* 9, no. 1 (2014): 7.

36. A. Baccini et al., "Estimated Carbon Dioxide Emissions from Tropical Deforestation Improved by Carbon-Density Maps," *Nature Climate Change* 2, no. 3 (2012): 182–85; S. Saatchi et al., "Benchmark Map of Forest Carbon Stocks in Tropical Regions across Three Continents," *Proceedings of the National Academy of Sciences* 108, no. 24 (2011): 9899–904.

37. V. Avitabile et al., "An Integrated Pan-Tropical Biomass Map Using Multiple Reference Datasets," *Global Change Biology* 22, no. 4 (2016): 1406–20.

38. J. Boudreau et al., "Regional Aboveground Forest Biomass Using Airborne and Spaceborne LiDAR in Québec," *Remote Sensing of Environment* 112, no. 10 (2008): 3876–90.

39. National Aeronautics and Space Administration, "New NASA Probe Will Study Earth's Forests in 3-D," September 8, 2014, http://www.nasa.gov/content/goddard/new-nasa-probe-will-study-earth-s-forests-in-3-d/#.Vl3bt3arSUk.

40. The instrument will sample about 1.7 percent of covered land area.

41. See, for example, Woods Hole Research Center, "Aboveground Forest Carbon Stocks in Mexico," http://whrc.org/publications-data/datasets/aboveground-forest-carbon-stocks-in-mexico/.

42. European Space Agency (ESA), *Report for Mission Selection: Biomass*, ESA SP-1324/1, 2012, http://esamultimedia.esa.int/docs/EarthObservation/SP1324-1_BIOMASSr.pdf.

43. M. Cairns et al., "Root Biomass Allocation in the World's Upland Forests,"*Oecologia* 111, no. 1 (1997): 1–11.

44. J. Powers, M. D. Corre, T. E. Twine, and E. Veldkamp, "Geographic Bias of Field Observations of Soil Carbon Stocks with Tropical Land-Use Changes Precludes Spatial Extrapolation," *Proceedings of the National Academy of Sciences* 108, no. 15 (2011): 6318–22.

45. R. B. Jackson, H. A. Mooney, and E. D. Schulze, "A Global Budget for Fine Root Biomass, Surface Area, and Nutrient Contents," *Proceedings of the National Academy of Sciences* 94, no. 14 (1997): 7362–6; H. K. Gibbs, S. Brown, J. O. Niles, and J. A. Foley, "Monitoring and Estimating Tropical Forest Carbon Stocks: Making REDD a Reality," *Environmental Research Letters* 2, no. 4 (2007): 045023

46. See, for example, D. Murdiyarso, K. Hergoualc'h, and L. V. Verchot, "Opportunities for Reducing Greenhouse Gas Emissions in Tropical Peatlands," *Proceedings of the National Academy of Sciences* 107, no. 46 (2010): 19655–60; and K. Hergoualc'h, and L. V. Verchot, "Greenhouse Gas Emission Factors for Land Use and Land-Use Change in Southeast Asian Peatlands," *Mitigation and Adaptation Strategies for Global Change* 19, no. 6 (2014): 789–807.

47. M. Huang and G. P. Asner, "Long-Term Carbon Loss and Recovery Following Selective Logging in Amazon Forests," *Global Biogeochemical Cycles* 24, no. 3 (2010); R. Houghton, "The Emissions of Carbon from Deforestation and Degradation in the Tropics: Past Trends and Future Potential," *Carbon Management* 4, no. 5 (2013): 539–46; T. Pearson, S. Brown, and F. M. Casarim, "Carbon Emissions from Tropical Forest Degradation Caused by Logging," *Environmental Research Letters* 9, no. 3 (2014).

48. Food and Agriculture Organization of the United Nations, "Forest Degradation," http://www.fao.org/docrep/009/j9345e/j9345e08.htm.

49. European Space Agency (ESA), "Sentinel-2: Changing Lands," http://www.esa.int/Our_Activities/Observing_the_Earth/Copernicus/Sentinel-2/Changing_lands.

50. See, for example, M. Herold et al., "A Review of Methods to Measure and Monitor Historical Carbon Emissions from Forest Degradation," *Unasylva* 62, no. 2 (2011): 238; P. Potapov et al., "Mapping the World's Intact Forest Landscapes by Remote Sensing," *Ecology and Society* 13, no. 2 (2008): 51; B. Margono et al., "Mapping and Monitoring Deforestation and Forest Degradation in Sumatra (Indonesia) Using Landsat Time Series Data Sets from 1990 to 2010, " *Environ-*

mental *Research Letters* 7, no. 3 (2012): 034010.; I. Zhuravleva et al., "Satellite-Based Primary Forest Degradation Assessment in the Democratic Republic of the Congo, 2000–2010," *Environmental Research Letters* 8, no. 2 (2013): 24034; M. Bucki et al., "Assessing REDD+ Performance of Countries with Low Monitoring Capacities: The Matrix Approach," *Environmental Research Letters* 7, no. 1 (2012): 014031.

51. M.C. Hansen et al., "High-Resolution Global Maps of 21st-Century Forest Cover Change," *Science* 342 (2013): 850–53; A. Baccini et al., "Estimated Carbon Dioxide Emissions from Tropical Deforestation Improved by Carbon-Density Maps," *Nature Climate Change* 2, no. 3 (2012): 182–85; J. Grace, E. Mitchard, and E. Gloor, "Perturbations in the Carbon Budget of the Tropics," *Global Change Biology* 20, no. 10 (2014): 3238–55.

52. R. Goodman and M. Herold, "Why Maintaining Tropical Forests Is Essential and Urgent for a Stable Climate," CGD Working Paper 385, Center for Global Development, Washington, DC, 2014; Huang and Asner, "Long-Term Carbon Loss"; S. Riswan, J. B. Kenworthy, and K. Kartawinata, "The Estimation of Temporal Processes in Tropical Rain Forest: A Study of Primary Mixed Dipterocarp Forest in Indonesia," *Journal of Tropical Ecology* 1, no. 2 (1985): 171–82.

53. A. Tyukavina et al., "Aboveground Carbon Loss in Natural and Managed Tropical Forests from 2000 to 2012," *Environmental Research Letters* 10, no. 7 (2015).

54. J. O. Sexton et al., "Conservation Policy and the Measurement of Forests," *Nature Climate Change* 6, no. 2 (2016): 192–96; R. L. Chazdon et al., "When Is a Forest a Forest? Forest Concepts and Definitions in the Era of Forest and Landscape Restoration," *Ambio* (2016): 1–13.

55. R. O. Dubayah et al., "Estimation of Tropical Forest Height and Biomass Dynamics Using Lidar Remote Sensing at La Selva, Costa Rica," *Journal of Geophysical Research: Biogeosciences (2005–2012)*, 115, no. G2 (2010).

56. D. P. Edwards, J. A. Hodgson, K. C. Hamer, S. L. Mitchell, A. H. Ahmad, S. J. Cornell, and D. S. Wilcove, "Wildlife-Friendly Oil Palm Plantations Fail to Protect Biodiversity Effectively," *Conservation Letters* 3, no. 4 (2010): 236–42.

57. J. Sayer, J. Ghazoul, P. Nelson, and A. K. Boedhihartono, "Oil Palm Expansion Transforms Tropical Landscapes and Livelihoods," *Global Food Security* 1, no. 2 (2012): 114–19.

58. United Nations Framework Convention on Climate Change (UNFCCC), "Report of the Conference of the Parties on its Seventh Session, Held at Marrakesh from 29 October to 10 November 2001," FCCC/CP/2001/13/Add.1, January 21, 2002.

59. N. Sasaki and F. E. Putz, "Critical Need for New Definitions of 'Forest' and 'Forest Degradation' in Global Climate Change Agreements," *Conservation Letters* 2, no. 5 (2009): 226–32.

60. United Nations Framework Convention on Climate Change (UNFCCC), "Outcome of the Work of the Ad Hoc Working Group on Long-Term Cooperative Action under the Convention," UNFCCC COP 16, 2012.

61. V. H. Gutiérrez-Vélez, and R. DeFries, "Annual Multi-Resolution Detection of Land Cover Conversion to Oil Palm in the Peruvian Amazon," *Remote Sensing of Environment* 129 (2013): 154–67; A. Morel et al., "Estimating Aboveground Biomass in Forest and Oil Palm Plantation in Sabah, Malaysian Borneo, Using ALOS PALSAR Data," *Forest Ecology and Management* 262, no. 9 (2011): 1786–98.

62. CAPTCHA stands for "Completely Automated Public Turing test to tell Computers and Humans Apart." It is commonly used in computing to determine whether or not the user is human.

63. Summarized in R. Petersen et al., "Mapping Tree Plantations with Multispectral Imagery: Preliminary Results for Seven Tropical Countries," World Resources Institute and Transparent World, January 2016, http://www.wri.org/sites/default/files/Mapping_Tree_Plantations_with_

Multispectral_Imagery_-_Preliminary_Results_for_Seven_Tropical_Countries.pdf.

64. Brazil, Cambodia, Colombia, Indonesia, Liberia, Malaysia, and Peru.

65. R. Petersen et al., "Mapping Tree Plantations with Multispectral Imagery."

66. Goetz et al., "Measurement and Monitoring."

67. P. H. Raven, "Our Diminishing Tropical Forests," in *Biodiversity*, ed. E. O. Wilson and F. M. Peter, 119–22 (Washington, DC: National Academy Press, 1988).

68. J. Busch, F. Godoy, W. R. Turner, and C. A. Harvey, "Biodiversity Co-Benefits of Reducing Emissions from Deforestation under Alternative Reference Levels and Levels of Finance," *Conservation Letters* 4, no. 2 (2011): 101–15.

69. K. M. Carlson et al., "Influence of Watershed-Climate Interactions on Stream Temperature, Sediment Yield, and Metabolism along a Land Use Intensity Gradient in Indonesian Borneo," *Journal of Geophysical Research: Biogeosciences* 119, no. 6 (2014): 1110–28.

70. J. Schipper et al., "The Status of the World's Land and Marine Mammals: Diversity, Threat, and Knowledge," *Science* 322, no. 5899 (2008): 225–30; Birdlife International World Bird Database, 2010, available at http://www.birdlife.org/datazone/index.html; Global Assessment of Reptile Distributions, available at http://www.gardinitiative.org; S. N. Stuart, J. S. Chanson, N. A. Cox, et al. "Status and Trends of Amphibian Declines and Extinctions Worldwide," *Science* 306 (2004): 1783–86; H. Kreft and W. Jetz, "Global Patterns and Determinants of Vascular Plant Diversity," *Proceedings of the National Academy of Sciences* 104, no. 14 (2007): 5925–30.

71. B. Leutner et al., "Modelling Forest Diversity and Floristic Composition: On the Added Value of LiDAR Plus Hyperspectral Remote Sensing," *Remote Sensing* 4, no. 9 (2012): 2818–45.

72. S. Ustin et al., "Using Imaging Spectroscopy to Study Ecosystem Processes and Properties," *BioScience* 54, no. 6 (2004): 523–34.

73. K. M. Bergen, S. J. Goetz, R. O. Dubayah, G. M. Henebry, C. T. Hunsaker, M. L. Imhoff, R. F. Nelson, G. G. Parker, and V. C. Radeloff, "Remote Sensing of Vegetation 3-D Structure for Biodiversity and Habitat: Review and Implications for Lidar and Radar Spaceborne Missions," *Journal of Geophysical Research: Biogeosciences (2005–2012)* 114, no. G2 (2009).

74. K. M. Carlson et al., "Hyperspectral Remote Sensing of Canopy Biodiversity in Hawaiian Lowland Rainforests," *Ecosystems* 10, no. 4 (2007): 536–49; G. Asner and R. E. Martin, "Airborne Spectranomics: Mapping Canopy Chemical and Taxonomic Diversity in Tropical Forests," *Frontiers in Ecology and the Environment* 7, no. 5 (2008): 269–76; K. T. Vierling et al., "Lidar: Shedding New Light on Habitat Characterization and Modeling," *Frontiers in Ecology and the Environment* 6, no. 2 (2008): 90–98; S. Goetz et al., "Lidar Remote Sensing Variables Predict Breeding Habitat of a Neotropical Migrant Bird," *Ecology* 91, no. 6 (2010): 1569–76.

75. See the website, "Wildland Security: Surveillance Technology Saving Wildlife," 2011, http://www.wildlandsecurity.org.

76. R. Butler, "Discarded Cell Phones to Help Fight Rainforest Poachers, Loggers in Real-Time," Mongabay.com, June 24, 2014, http://news.mongabay.com/2014/0624-rainforest-connection-interview.html.

77. L. P. Koh and S. A. Wich, "Dawn of Drone Ecology: Low-Cost Autonomous Aerial Vehicles for Conservation," *Tropical Conservation Science* 5, no. 2 (2012): 121–32; "Planet Labs," https://www.planet.com/; "Skybox Imaging," http://www.skyboximaging.com.

78. D. Nepstad et al., "Slowing Amazon Deforestation through Public Policy and Interventions in Beef and Soy Supply Chains," *Science* 344, no. 6188 (2014): 1118–23.

79. Environmental Defense Fund and Woods Hole Research Center, "Tropical Forest Carbon in Indigenous Territories: A Global Analysis," A report for the UNFCCC COP21, December 2015, http://www.edf.org/sites/

default/files/tropical-forest-carbon-in-indigenous-territories-a-global-analysis.pdf.

80. D. Gaveau et al., "Overlapping Land Claims Limit the Use of Satellites to Monitor No-Deforestation Commitments and No-Burning Compliance," *Conservation Letters*, no. 12256 (2016): 1–8.

81. T. Salim, "One-Map Policy Helps Resolve Land Disputes, Overlapping Permits," *Jakarta Post*, December 26, 2014; "Indigenous Communities Deploy High-Tech Mapmaking to Staunch Global Land Grab," at http://phys.org/news/2013-08-indigenous-deploy-high-tech-mapmaking-staunch.html; "Landmark: Global Platform of Indigenous and Community Lands," at http://www.landmarkmap.org.

82. United Nations Environment Programme, "Rio Declaration on Environment and Development" (1992); United Nations Economic Commission for Europe, "Convention on Access to Information, Public Participation in Decision-making and Access to Justice in Environmental Matters" (1998).

83. J. Pelletier, J. Busch, and C. Potvin, "Addressing Uncertainty Upstream or Downstream of Accounting for Emissions Reductions from Deforestation and Forest Degradation," *Climatic Change* 130, no. 4 (2015): 635–48.

84. United Nations Framework Convention on Climate Change (UNFCCC), "Report of the Conference of the Parties on Its Seventeenth Session, Held in Durban from 28 November to 11 December 2011, Addendum Part Two: Action Taken by the Conference of the Parties at Its Seventeenth Session," Decision UNFCCC 12/CP.17, FCCC/CP/2011/9/Add.2, March 15, 2012, http://unfccc.int/resource/docs/2011/cop17/eng/09a02.pdf.

85. G. Grassi, S. Monni, S. Federici, F. Achard, and D. Mollicone, "Applying the Conservativeness Principle to REDD to Deal with the Uncertainties of the Estimates," *Environmental Research Letters* 3, no. 3 (2008): 035005; Pelletier, Busch, and Potvin, "Addressing Uncertainty Upstream or Downstream of Accounting for Emissions Reduc-

tions from Deforestation and Forest Degradation."

86. J. Busch, B. Strassburg, A. Cattaneo, R. Lubowski, A. Bruner, R. Rice, A. Creed, R. Ashton, and F. Boltz. "Comparing Climate and Cost Impacts of Reference Levels for Reducing Emissions from Deforestation." *Environmental Research Letters* 4, no. 4 (2009): 044006.

87. United Nations Framework Convention on Climate Change (UNFCCC), "Adoption of the Paris Agreement," FCCC/CP/2015/L.9/Rev.1, December 12, 2015, http://unfccc.int/resource/docs/2015/cop21/eng/l09r01.pdf.

Soy fields fragment a forested area of Brazil.
Credit: Frontpage/Shutterstock

CHAPTER 5

Cheaper, Cooler, Faster

Reducing Tropical Deforestation for a
More Cost-Effective Global Response to Climate Change

Kemper County, Mississippi. Beneath the rolling pastures and yellow pines of eastern Mississippi lies a reservoir of coal. Soft, wet, crumbly, and low-grade, the brown coal of Mississippi has been described as "a step above dirt."[1] Compared to the older, denser, blacker bituminous coal that is mined in West Virginia and Wyoming, this brown coal when burned produces less energy, more air pollution, and more carbon dioxide. Since 2006, the Southern Company has had plans to strip-mine brown coal from up to 125 square kilometers of Kemper County to feed a 500-megawatt power plant.

The power plant planned for Kemper County, Mississippi, will be no ordinary facility—it is to provide the largest test case of a technology dubbed by its backers as "clean coal." Once operational, it will use a series of heated chambers to separate the coal into its component parts—carbon dioxide, pollutants, ash, and a cleaner-burning synthetic gas.[2] The synthetic gas will be burned to produce electricity, while the ash and pollutants will be solidified and disposed of separately. Up to two-thirds of the carbon dioxide will be captured, according to Southern Company estimates, resulting in greenhouse gas emissions comparable to those of a typical natural gas plant. The captured carbon dioxide gas will then be piped to depleted oil fields nearby, where it will be injected to extract more oil than would otherwise be economically feasible.

That's the plan, anyway. The project has

_____

This chapter draws heavily on two background papers: one by Jonah Busch and Jens Engelmann on the cost of reducing emissions from deforestation, and one by Jonah Busch, Jens Engelmann, and Alice Lépissier on the cost of reducing emissions from many sources.

not had smooth sailing. The "clean coal" project was originally slated for Orlando, Florida, in 2006, but it relocated to Mississippi when local legislators pulled their support.[3] The opening of the plant, originally scheduled for 2013, has been delayed by years.[4] Allegations of contracting scandals have swirled. Project partners have pulled out.[5] And construction costs have ballooned from $1.8 billion in 2006 to more than $6.1 billion by 2015. Southern Company has cushioned itself from the cost overruns through grants from the U.S. Department of Energy, federal tax breaks, and higher utility bills for local ratepayers. No carbon has yet been captured or stored.[6]

How much does it cost to keep carbon out of the atmosphere using "clean coal" technology? It's tough to know exactly, given all the uncertainties around this as-yet-unrealized technology, but one can hazard a guess. The Southern Company projects its plant will capture and store three million tons of carbon dioxide a year. If two-thirds of the carbon dioxide emissions saved at Kemper were cancelled out by extracting and burning additional oil,[7] the net carbon storage would be closer to one million tons per year. Over a half-century of operation, the plant would capture and store perhaps fifty million tons of carbon dioxide. That adds up to a cost of more than $100 per ton of avoided emissions, based on construction costs alone, which is consistent with other estimates of the costs of "clean coal."[8] After accounting for ongoing maintenance, costs would be even higher. If you are looking for a cheap, easy, quick way to fight climate change, "clean coal" isn't it.

San Martín Province, Peru. Ten thousand kilometers south-by-southeast from Kemper

County, Mississippi, is San Martín Province, Peru. Here, the Alto Mayo Protected Forest sits at the high western edge of the vast Amazon rainforest that stretches more than four thousand kilometers east to the Atlantic Ocean. This forest at the headwaters of the Alto Mayo River was protected in 1987 to provide clean water to downriver communities and to preserve the habitat of many unique local plants and animals, including three endangered species of monkey.

For decades, the law on the books in Lima said Alto Mayo was protected, but the reality in the forest on the far side of the Andes Mountains was quite different. Only three park rangers patrolled an area more than two and a half times the size of Singapore. Rules against settling within the park boundaries were poorly enforced, and thousands of farming families left dire conditions in the Andes Mountains in search of land inside the park. These new arrivals chipped away at the forest, carving out plots for coffee and cattle. The deforestation rate inside the park jumped by 68 percent between the periods 1996–2001 and 2001–6, then rose another 33 percent by 2008–12, sending increasing quantities of carbon dioxide to the atmosphere.[9]

But by the middle of the first decade of the 2000s, an intriguing new idea had begun catching on like wildfire in international climate circles: communities that protected tropical forests might earn income from the carbon they kept out of the atmosphere. Governments or companies in rich countries would pay for reductions in emissions from deforestation and forest degradation and for enhancing forest regrowth (REDD+). Suddenly, trees might be worth more alive than dead.

The international rules governing REDD+ transactions were years away from being finalized. Ultimately, as described in chapter 9, the UNFCCC would specify REDD+ as payments to national or subnational governments, leaving site-specific forest conservation projects to seek private funding from voluntary carbon markets. But in the absence of clear international rules, entrepreneurs around the world were taking an early chance that site-specific projects would eventually be eligible to sell forest carbon credits directly into international compliance markets. Conservation International (CI), a Virginia-based conservation group with offices in several dozen tropical countries, including Peru, placed a bet on Alto Mayo.

Climate benefits are identical whether emissions are avoided in Mississippi or Peru, but there's a big difference in cost.

In 2008, CI-Peru began offering local families technical support for cultivating premium shade-grown coffee in exchange for agreeing not to clear any more forest within the park. In 2012, the government of Peru and CI-Peru began co-managing the area, hiring more rangers and park staff and enticing families to relocate by building a clinic and high school outside the park. Funding for these activities was provided by the Walt Disney Company, which hoped eventually to use carbon credits generated by the Alto Mayo project to voluntarily offset emissions from its Disney Cruise Line. The work has shown signs of paying off: the deforestation rate in the park fell by 28 percent between the periods 2008–12 and 2012–14.[10]

Based on methods established by the private Verified Carbon Standard organization and validated by third-party auditors, Conservation International calculates the conservation activities in Alto Mayo prevented 1.7 million tons of carbon dioxide from entering the atmosphere during 2013–14.[11] That's almost the same as the estimated amount of annual emissions Southern Company's Kemper plant would avoid. The climate benefits would be identical whether emissions were avoided in Mississippi or Peru, but there's a big difference in cost. While Southern Company's "clean coal" reductions are projected to cost more than $100 per ton of carbon dioxide, Conservation International estimates its emission reductions in Alto Mayo work out to around $2 to $3 per ton.[12]

Any attempt to fight climate change without reducing tropical deforestation will be needlessly weak, slow, and expensive.

Fighting Climate Change Efficiently: Seeking Cheap, Plentiful Emission Reductions

No single action can deter climate change. Achieving a stable climate requires reducing emissions across many sectors, through renewable energy, clean transportation, forest conservation, and so on.[13] Still, nobody would want to throw money at a boondoggle while ignoring a bargain.

And, so, choices must be made as to how to tackle climate change. How much abatement should come from "clean coal" and how much from reduced deforestation? How much from solar panels, from geothermal plants, from electric cars, from nuclear power, or from no-till farming? In a world where resources are scarce, it makes sense to favor large, cheap, reliable solutions.

In this chapter, we first describe some of the conceptual issues associated with estimating the cost of reducing emissions from tropical deforestation as compared to other options. We then present results from a new model developed for *Why Forests? Why Now?* by Jonah Busch and Jens Engelmann of the Center for Global Development. Their new marginal abatement cost (MAC) curve (explained further below) improves upon previous models by considering how land users have historically responded to price incentives, based on evidence from agricultural markets. We combine this MAC curve with the SkyShares model developed by Owen Barder, Alex Evans, and Alice Lépissier of the Center for Global Development to simulate how much cheaper, bigger, and faster global climate change efforts could be made by including tropical forests. In addition, we describe how these results relate to policy options facing developing-country governments and the likely size of international payments needed to prompt effective action.

We find that using carbon payments to reduce emissions by conserving tropical forests would cost tropical governments less than one-quarter of what it would cost in the European Union or the United States to reduce emissions from industrial sources by the same amount. This means that, in addition to cutting carbon emissions at home, governments of rich countries could augment their contributions to climate stability by paying for relatively low-cost reductions abroad. By taking full advantage of the low-cost emission reductions from reduced tropical deforestation, the world's response to climate change could be 28 to 30 percent cheaper. Or, at the same cost, the projected increase in global temperature could be kept 0.15°C to 0.82°C (0.27°F to 1.3°F) lower (cooler), than would otherwise occur. Likewise, at the same cost, the year in which global greenhouse gas emissions stop increasing and start decreasing could arrive two to five years faster than would otherwise occur, as shown in figure 5.1.

The new analysis corroborates what previous studies have already suggested: reducing tropical deforestation offers a large, fast, and cost-effective means of reducing emissions, while any attempt to fight climate change without reducing tropical deforestation will be needlessly weak, slow, and expensive.

Uses and Limitations of MAC Curves for Estimating the Costs of Reducing Deforestation

Fighting climate change may well come to be seen as the defining challenge of the twenty-first century, but it is not the only important global challenge. The Sustainable Development Goals include sixteen other global goals, from expanding prosperity to billions of people currently living in poverty to vanquishing infectious diseases.[14]

In a world of competing priorities, it is essential to fight climate change as cost effec-

Figure 5.1: By reducing tropical deforestation, a cooler climate can be achieved more cheaply and quickly.

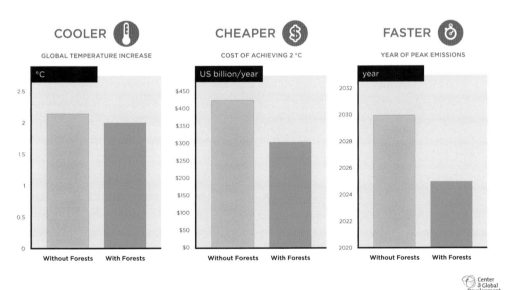

Source: Busch, Engelmann, and Lépissier (2016).

Note: "With Forests" refers to emission reductions from gross tropical forest cover loss and peat conversion; it does not include emission reductions from forest degradation or forest regrowth.

tively as possible so resources are available for other worthy ends. By taking advantage of low-cost emission reductions, people could achieve climate goals more cheaply, which would let them spend more money on other things. Alternatively, the cost savings could be used to go even further on climate, keeping the planet cooler at the same cost.[15]

Of course, while cost effectiveness is important, it's not the only consideration when prioritizing climate actions. Side benefits, or "co-benefits," of protecting the forests of Alto Mayo include providing clean water and protecting endangered species, among others. The Kemper "clean coal" plant, if it were ever to become operational, would result in less local air pollution than a conventional coal plant, although it wouldn't reduce the damage to the local environment from strip mines.

Much of the attraction of reducing tropical deforestation as a means of fighting climate change stems from its presumed low cost—its availability among many possible climate actions as "low-hanging fruit." Often, the land uses that replace thick, carbon-dense tropical forests provide scant economic returns, which implies that emissions from deforestation could be avoided at a cost of just a few dollars per ton—an order of magnitude cheaper than reducing them in industrial sectors. A case in point is the Brazilian Amazon, where four-fifths of deforestation has been caused by sparse cattle grazing.[16] At the other extreme, some deforested land provides very high monetary returns—for instance, land cleared for gold mines. In between are many land uses with middling values, mostly from growing crops of one sort or another.

In 2006, the Stern Review presented eye-catching figures showing how cheap it could be to halt tropical deforestation, with just $5 billion per year or so required to cover the opportunity cost of forest protection in eight countries responsible for 70 per cent of emissions.[17] Soon thereafter, more economic studies corroborated the thinking that "REDD+ is cheap." Cutting tropical deforestation in half would cost $17 billion to $33 billion per year by 2030, according to one study, $17 billion to $28 billion according to another.[18]

These studies and others like them have presented their findings in the form of marginal abatement cost (MAC) curves, a standard economic tool used to illustrate how many emission reductions could be achieved below a given cost, for one or more climate actions. They are useful for distinguishing climate actions that are cheap and large from those that are small and expensive.

Some MAC curves, such as the various studies of the cost of reducing emissions from tropical deforestation shown in figure 5.2, have been produced for a single type of action. In this type of MAC curve, the y-axis shows the cost of reducing carbon dioxide emissions by one ton, while the x-axis shows how many emissions can be reduced more cheaply. Moving from left to right along the curve, each successive ton of emission reductions becomes more expensive to achieve.

Other MAC curves compare costs across many different types of climate actions. Perhaps the most famous MAC curve comparing the costs of many climate actions, shown in figure 5.3, was produced by the consulting firm McKinsey and Company in 2009.[19]

Figure 5.2: Multiple studies have estimated the cost-effective potential of reducing emissions from tropical deforestation.

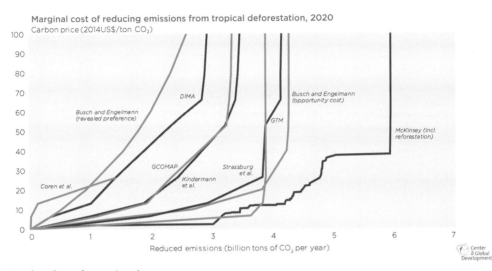

Marginal cost of reducing emissions from tropical deforestation, 2020
Carbon price (2014US$/ton CO₂)

Reduced emissions (billion tons of CO₂ per year)

Source: Busch and Engelmann (2015).

Note: All costs presented in 2014 U.S. dollars.

McKinsey analysts estimated the average cost of reducing a ton of emissions through any particular action and then lined up those actions as bars from left to right, from cheapest to most expensive. As shown in the figure, the height of each bar represents the average cost of the action; the width represents the quantity of emission reductions available.

At the far left are actions that could reduce emissions while saving money (for example, switching to more efficient light bulbs). At the far right are those that could reduce emissions at very high cost (for example, retrofitting power plants with carbon capture and storage). By working from the cheapest options on a MAC curve to the most expensive, policies would reduce emissions at the lowest overall cost. Actions associated with reducing deforestation and promoting forest regrowth comprise some of the lowest cost

options—far cheaper than carbon capture and storage, and cost-competitive relative to many other industrial options, as well. The McKinsey MAC curve, now more than seven years old, provides a concrete point of departure for discussing both the usefulness and the limitations of MAC curves more generally.

MAC curves are tidy, useful models. By comparing the costs of avoiding emissions through different climate actions, they can be used to direct scarce climate finance to the most cost-effective actions or places. Governments can use MAC curves to help them prioritize regulations; investors can use them to prioritize investments; and international funds, such as the Green Climate Fund, can use them to prioritize grants and loans. Furthermore, analysts can use MAC curves to simulate the workings of carbon markets, whether real or hypothetical.

Figure 5.3: Forests offer some of the most cost-effective potential abatement measures, according to McKinsey & Company (2009).

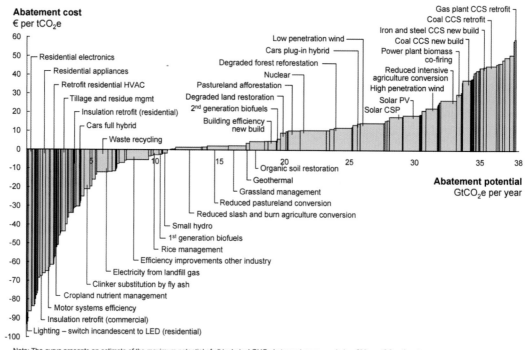

Global GHG abatement cost curve beyond business-as-usual – 2030

Note: The curve presents an estimate of the maximum potential of all technical GHG abatement measures below €60 per tCO₂e if each lever was pursued aggressively. It is not a forecast of what role different abatement measures and technologies will play.
Source: Global GHG Abatement Cost Curve v2.0

Source: McKinsey & Company. Exhibit from "Pathways to a low-carbon economy: Version 2 of the global greenhouse gas abatement cost curve," 2009.

As critics have noted, however, MAC curves have limitations.[20] This is especially true with regard to using MAC curves to estimate the costs of reducing emissions from deforestation. We discuss these caveats below.

Costs to Whom? Opportunity Costs to Land Users Versus Budgetary Costs to Government Agencies

Reducing deforestation imposes two distinct types of costs within a tropical forest country. The first is the opportunity cost of conserving forest—that is, the value of alternative uses, such as ranching or agriculture, that potential land users forgo when they keep land as forest. This opportunity cost represents the theoretical minimum amount that a holder of land rights would have to be paid to refrain voluntarily from deforesting. The second is the budgetary cost of deforestation prevention programs to government agencies, such as the cost of law enforcement or incentive payments. While MAC curves have typically focused on land users' opportunity costs, some government agencies may be more concerned with their direct expenditures than with the costs those policies impose on the people they regulate.

Note that where opportunity costs are based on the maximum value potential land users would give up by forgoing conversion, they commonly overestimate the values landowners could realistically obtain. In many cases, full exploitation may not be possible; depending on ownership and use rights, some types of conversion might be unlikely, illegitimate, or illegal. In tropical forests these rights span open access forests, highly restricted state-owned protected areas, privately owned land, indigenous land, communal land, and public land licensed out for private use under long-term leases. Often rights are unclear or conflicting. Even where landowners have full and clear rights, they may unable to put land to its highest value use, because of credit or irrigation constraints, for example.

Both opportunity costs and budgetary costs depend on the type of domestic policies put into place to reduce deforestation, and policies also depend on ownership and use rights. For example, payments might be appropriate for legal landowners, while law enforcement would be a more appropriate response to ranchers' illegally encroaching on an indigenous reserve. Depending on policy, opportunity and budgetary costs might not be correlated. For example, antideforestation restrictions that rely heavily on law enforcement might have low budgetary costs and high opportunity costs. On the other hand, a program that pays small farmers to maintain forests on their land might have high budgetary costs while providing net revenues to participating farmers.

Budgetary costs and opportunity costs would only be equal in the unlikely case of governments paying all land users their exact opportunity costs and nothing more. And, while it is theoretically possible to do so using reverse auctions, as practiced by the U.S. Conservation Reserve Program and Australia's Bush-Tender program, such programs are unusual in practice.[21] On top of the above-mentioned costs are the costs of setting up and implementing a payment system.

Cost of What? Different Policies Have Different Costs

To the extent that studies producing MAC curves have explicitly specified the policies involved in reducing deforestation, they've generally been consistent with carbon pricing policies, in which governments pay land users for reducing emissions from deforestation or tax land users for each ton of emissions resulting from deforestation. In reality, while carbon pricing policies are being introduced by a growing number of countries, they remain largely hypothetical in most developing countries.[22] Including forests in carbon pricing policies is likely to be particularly complicated or expensive across much of the tropics because of unclear property rights over forestlands. Programs showing how such carbon pricing policies might work include initiatives that offer payments for ecosystem services (PES) in Costa Rica and elsewhere and Brazil's land registration system (CAR), which makes possible the trading of forest restoration responsibilities in the Amazon. In chapter 6 we discuss the strengths and limitations of PES programs at greater length.

As an alternative to carbon pricing, governments in forest countries might instead turn to imposing direct restrictions on deforestation, like those enacted by Brazil in the Amazon. As described in greater detail in chapter 7, from 2005 onward Brazil designated large swaths of forest as protected areas or indigenous reserves, placing them off limits to large-scale ranching and agriculture. Backed by satellite monitors, police stepped up enforcement of existing antideforestation laws on private property. The country restricted rural credit to farmers in municipalities with high deforestation rates while, at the same time, its soy and beef industries issued moratoriums on purchasing commodities from farms involved in deforestation.

This raft of policies was remarkably effective. In the decade after 2004, deforestation rates fell by 80 percent, even while beef and soy production rose. Felipe Arias Fogliano and his colleagues estimate this set of policies cost the federal, state, and municipal governments of Brazil around $2 billion over nine years, which is undoubtedly small relative to the hypothetical cost of compensating all land users for forgone uses.[23]

Again, MAC curves have implicitly looked at just a single type of policy—carbon pricing—rather than exploring the multitude of possible domestic policies for reducing deforestation, with all their various costs to land users or government agencies. Furthermore, they implicitly assume countries will undertake the cheapest reductions first. To the extent that policies prioritize more expensive reductions, overall costs would be higher.

Costs to Whom? Domestic Costs Versus the Costs of Paying for Emission Reductions

Another important distinction is between the domestic costs of reducing deforestation (that is, the opportunity costs and budgetary costs discussed above) and how much buyers in rich countries would need to spend on payments for reduced emissions from deforestation. The amount one government would pay another depends on the outcomes of negotiations between the buying and selling governments.

MAC curves provide a starting point for thinking about the costs buyers would have to pay for reductions: the greater the domestic costs in forest countries, the higher the price necessary to justify a transaction. The price international "buyers" pay, however, might be more or less than "sellers'" domestic costs, depending on a variety of factors described in chapters 9 and 12. These include negotiated purchase prices; whether the baseline levels against which emission reductions are counted (that is, the "reference levels") are generous or stingy; and the extent to which payments are meant to compensate fully for costs or merely subsidize a tropical forest country's own policy efforts.

Evidence regarding the actual purchase price in international REDD+ transactions is just starting to come in. In the two government-to-government transactions to date, for example (between Brazil and Norway and Guyana and Norway, discussed further in chapter 12), emission reductions were priced at $5 per ton. This price was higher than the out-of-pocket costs roughly estimated by Fogliano and colleagues and was sufficient to motivate transactions in Brazil and Guyana.[24] It is difficult, however, to extrapolate just these two data points to the many countries where such transactions have not yet taken place. The prices necessary to justify transactions could be higher in countries where the land uses replacing forests are more profitable—for example, oil palm in Indonesia and Malaysia.

Much of the appeal of international REDD+ transactions is in the potential for carbon revenue to make reducing deforestation a financial win for all involved. Governments obtaining revenues from selling emission reductions face the challenge of determining how to share the benefits with the people who bear the costs of restrictions on deforestation. Such "benefit sharing" could take a number of forms. Governments might pay land users for reducing deforestation, in a sort of two-tiered "payment for ecosystem services" (PES) program; or an Alto Mayo–like project might be permitted to make direct international sales of emission reductions in a "nested approach"; or governments could distribute revenues by financing the programs of community and industry associations, as in Acre, or through investment in public goods, as in Guyana.[25] As with policies, MAC curves don't reflect the net costs or benefits arising from alternative forms of benefit sharing.

Nonmonetary Values, Market Feedback, and a Small Evidence Base

MAC curves are elegant in their simplicity: they consider costs and quantities of potential emission reductions. But they generally don't consider other nonmonetary benefits of climate actions, such as the value reducing deforestation provides beyond avoiding carbon dioxide emissions. As described in chapter 3, forests provide good weather patterns for farming; clean water for greater production by hydroelectric dams; and habitat for two-thirds of terrestrial plants and animals. The value of such services can be significant, even when they are challenging to quantify and rarely large enough on their own to sway land-use decisions, as discussed in chapter 6. Because the benefits from forests are often felt downstream or downwind rather than onsite, their value is more likely to be internalized at the scale of regions or nations than at the level of individual landowners. Were the value of forests' noncarbon benefits included in MAC curves, the benefits of reducing tropical deforestation relative to other climate actions would be even greater.

A variety of other kinds of market feedback are rarely touched on by broad-brush MAC curves. Might climate actions that appear inefficient now, such as experimentation with "clean coal," see costs fall or technologies improve over time?[26] Might aggressive reductions in one sector change the costs of actions in another sector? And so forth.

One final weakness of the cost estimates presented in MAC curves for reducing deforestation is that, to date, they have been largely hypothetical. They are based on assumptions about how land users would behave in response to forest conservation policies, rather than evidence from actual payments or policies. Many early projects in the vein of Alto Mayo are selling credits on the voluntary carbon market for prices below $10 per ton.[27] Even though government-to-government REDD+ transactions won't look like these, such projects still provide useful evidence on the costs to land users. But, as with international transactions, the relatively low prices paid in these transactions shed little light on the price of transactions that didn't happen, so they can't yet be used to trace out a MAC curve. Beyond direct carbon transactions, few impact evaluations of forest conservation policies have considered cost effectiveness. As more payments and policies to reduce deforestation are rolled out and evaluated for cost effectiveness, it will become more feasible to construct evidence-based MAC curves.

In summary, MAC curves consider costs to a particular group (land users) consistent with a particular policy (carbon pricing) for producing a particular service (reductions in greenhouse gas emissions). They don't reflect the full complexity of potential domestic policies, international transactions, and forest services, nor are they yet built upon a broad evidence base of actual payments and policies. Nevertheless, they provide a useful benchmark for comparing the costs of reducing deforestation with the costs of climate actions in industrial sectors, where many of these same caveats apply.

New MAC Curves for Tropical Forests

As input for this book, Busch and Engelmann produced a new set of MAC curves for reduced tropical deforestation.[28] They reflect a number of improvements over the previous generation of MAC curves published between 2006 and 2011. For one thing, they take advantage of the revolutionary new dataset on forest loss described in chapter 4.[29] While previous MAC curves relied on the nationwide forest cover estimates that countries self-report to the United Nations Food and Agriculture Organization (FAO) every five years, Busch and Engelmann used data on

forest loss from consistent, worldwide satellite observations the size of a baseball diamond every year between 2001 and 2012.

For another thing, the new MAC curves reflect Brazil's extraordinary success in reducing deforestation in the Amazon since 2005, as described in more detail in chapter 7. Where previous MAC curves used data that predated this drop, Busch and Engelmann revisited estimates of the quantity of available abatement from reduced deforestation in light of this positive development. Furthermore, Busch and Engelmann looked not just at payments, but at restrictive policies, such as those implemented in Brazil. Finally, Busch and Engelmann based their MAC curves on historical evidence regarding the effects of actual changes in agricultural prices on land-use decisions across the tropics—a technique that wouldn't have been possible before the release of high-resolution deforestation data.

These improvements brought MAC curves a big step closer to being based on actual behavior rather than assumptions alone. Even so, the MAC curves in this analysis still share many of the limitations listed above. The methods of this new analysis are discussed briefly in box 5.1 and presented more thoroughly, along with caveats, in a Center for Global Development working paper.[30]

Projections of Tropical Deforestation
From 2001 to 2012, the world lost 960,000 square kilometers of tropical forest—an area the size of France and Italy combined. As reported in box 5.2, Busch and Engelmann project that unless additional countervailing policies for forest conservation are put into place, the world will lose another 2.89 million square kilometers of tropical forest from 2016

Box 5.1: A Cheaper, Bigger, Faster Response to Climate Change: The Methods

How much cheaper, bigger, and faster can the global response to climate change be by including tropical forests? To answer this question we drew upon several studies, as described here:

Step 1: Busch and Engelmann calculated historical emissions from deforestation by combining tropics-wide satellite-based maps of deforestation[a] from 2001–12[b] with maps of how much carbon was released from trees and soils in the deforested areas.

Step 2: They constructed and validated a statistical model explaining how much deforestation occurred in any given location in any given year as a function of the location's slope, elevation, protected status, distance from a city, previous clearing, and suitability for agriculture, as well as the price of agricultural commodities that year.

Step 3: They used the statistical model to project historical patterns of deforestation and associated emissions into the future. According to their model, deforestation would proceed more quickly on land that is low, flat, fertile, and close to towns and existing farms, and more slowly on land that is high, rugged, arid, and remote. Their "business-as-usual" scenario assumed that no new forest conservation policies would be put into place, and that future agricultural prices would remain at average 2001–12 levels.[c]

Step 4: They simulated how much deforestation would be avoided in the future if the governments of forest countries were hypothetically able to make carbon payments to land users based on a uniform price per ton of carbon dioxide emissions avoided. In the absence of historical evidence on how land users responded to carbon prices, Busch and Engelmann turned to the wealth of data on how they responded to agricultural prices. Since land users deforested more when agricultural prices were higher because they could earn more income from selling crops, Busch and Engelmann assumed they would deforest less if carbon payments were higher, because they could earn more income from keeping forests standing. In addition, Busch and Engelmann simulated how much future deforestation would be avoided if every country enacted restrictive policies with effectiveness equivalent to those put into place by Brazil in the Amazon post-2005.

Step 5: Busch and Engelmann traced out MAC curves for reduced emissions from tropical deforestation by modeling for any given carbon price how many emissions would be avoided, by when, and from where. They did not consider emission reductions from forest degradation or carbon sequestration from reforestation.

Step 6: Busch, Engelmann, and Lépissier[d] compared the MAC curves for reduced deforestation in tropical countries to MAC curves for buildings, energy, industry, and transportation in all countries from the Global Climate Assessment Model (GCAM).[e] They excluded agriculture because GCAM presented a combined MAC curve for agriculture and forestry that did not split out a MAC curve for agriculture separately. This analysis suggests how, for example, a global fund for climate mitigation such as the Green Climate Fund should allocate its resources across sectors to achieve the greatest emission reductions at the lowest cost.

Step 7: Finally, Busch, Engelmann, and Lépissier translated different levels of global emissions into expected global temperature increases using the SkyShares model.[f] They compared scenarios in which global action on climate change did or did not include reducing tropical deforestation. The end result was a new estimate of the extent to which reducing tropical deforestation can keep the climate cooler, and how much cheaper and faster it would be to do so.

Selected caveats: Land users might not treat income from agriculture and income from carbon as equivalent. Future agricultural prices, as well as other future conditions, are, of course, uncertain. Emissions from disturbance of peat soils are uncertain. The sensitivity of the results to these and other uncertainties is described in more depth in Busch and Engelmann (2015).

a. In the absence of a universally agreed-on definition of deforestation (see E. Romijn, J. H. Ainembabazi, A. Wijaya, M. Herold, A. Angelsen, L. Verchot, and D. Murdiyarso. , "Exploring Different Forest Definitions and Their Impact On Developing REDD+ Reference Emission Levels: A Case Study for Indonesia," *Environmental Science & Policy* 33 (2013): 246–59), we use the term "deforestation" to describe forest cover loss, regardless of subsequent land use. For an explanation, see box 2.1.

b. Hansen et al., "High-Resolution Global Maps."

c. As suggested by OECD/FAO for the period 2013–22. OECD/FAO, "OECD-FAO Agricultural Outlook 2013–2022," Organisation for Economic Co-operation and Development (OECD), Paris, France, and Food and Agriculture Organization (FAO) of the United Nations, Rome, Italy, 2013.

d. J. Busch, J. Engelmann, and A. Lépissier, "Technical Background Note for Why Forests? Why Now? Chapter 5 Cheaper, Cooler, Faster: Reducing Tropical Deforestation for a More Cost-Effective Global Response to Climate Change," CGD Policy Paper 093, Center for Global Development, Washington DC, 2016.

e. Joint Global Change Research Institute (JGCRI), "Global Climate Assessment Model (GCAM)," University of Maryland, 2015; S. H. Kim, J. Edmonds, J. Lurz, S. J. Smith, and M. Wise "The ObjECTS Framework for Integrated Assessment: Hybrid Modeling of Transportation," *The Energy Journal*, special issue no. 2 (2006): 63–91.

f. A. Lépissier, O. Barder, and A. Evans, "Modelling SkyShares: Technical Background," CGD Technical Background Paper, Center for Global Development, London, 2015.

to 2050.[31] That's an area about the size of India or all of the United States east of the Mississippi River, plus Texas. It's one-seventh of the area of tropical forest around the year 2000.

If left unchecked, the rate of tropical deforestation will climb steadily in the coming decades, with currently remote areas in the Congo Basin, the Western Amazon, and the island of New Guinea coming under increasing threat. Since these forests are richer in carbon than the average forest cleared today, a projected 16 percent rise in annual deforestation between 2015 and 2050 corresponds to a projected 42 percent rise in annual emissions from deforestation.

If Brazil fails to sustain its remarkable achievements in slowing deforestation and instead reverts to the pre-2004 policy environment, deforestation across the tropics will be even higher, with 3.65 million square kilometers lost between 2016 and 2050. This is an area of forest loss not just the size of India, but of Pakistan, as well.

As discussed in chapters 3 and 6, losing an India-size area of forest would have massive effects on regional weather patterns, air and water pollution, and resilience to disasters. The habitat loss would threaten numerous extinctions among the two-thirds of all land-based species that live in tropical forests. But,

Box 5.2: Cheaper, Cooler, Faster: Key Findings

- If left unchecked, tropical deforestation is projected to rise steadily through the 2020s and 2030s and then accelerate in the 2040s, resulting in the clearing of an area of 2.9 million square kilometers by 2050. That's equivalent in area to India, or one-third of the entire United States.

- The carbon emissions from that tropical deforestation from 2016–50 would be 169 billion tons of carbon dioxide—the equivalent of running 1,270 typical coal plants for the same length of time.[a]

- If all tropical governments enacted restrictive policies as effective as those put into place by Brazil in the Amazon since 2005 (as described in greater detail in chapter 7), emissions could be reduced by around one-third.

- Emissions from tropical deforestation could be reduced by about one-quarter if governments in tropical countries were hypothetically able to enact carbon payments or taxes at a price of $20 per metric ton of carbon dioxide, equivalent to an average cost to land users of $9 per ton.

- Reducing emissions by conserving tropical forests using carbon payments would cost tropical forests less than one-quarter of what it would cost the United States or the European Union to reduce emissions from industrial sources by the same amount.

- Worldwide, reducing tropical deforestation represents one-third of low-cost emission reductions from all sources, including buildings, energy, industry, and transportation, but excluding agriculture.

- While deforestation constitutes around 15 percent of nonagricultural emissions[b] across developing countries, reducing tropical deforestation constitutes 43 percent of low-cost nonagricultural emission reductions. Outside of China, reducing tropical deforestation constitutes 61 percent of low-cost nonagricultural emission reductions in developing countries.[c]

- By taking full advantage of the low-cost emission reductions from reduced tropical deforestation, the world's response to climate change could be 28–30 percent cheaper. Or at the same cost, the increase in global temperature could be 0.15–0.82 °C (0.27-1.3 °F) cooler, and the year in which global greenhouse gas emissions begin decreasing could arrive two to five years faster.

a. Authors' calculations based on U.S. Environmental Protection Agency's greenhouse gas equivalencies calculator, available at https://www.epa.gov/energy/greenhouse-gas-equivalencies-calculator.

b. These comparisons include buildings, electricity, industry, and transportation (GCAM), in addition to forests from Busch and Engelmann (2015), but they notably exclude agriculture. Because agriculture and forestry were aggregated as a single land-use sector in GCAM, we excluded this sector to avoid double counting. If agriculture were included, the fraction of low-cost abatements comprising land use would be larger, and forests would be smaller.

most of all, this loss of forest would make a huge dent in humanity's chances of maintaining a safe and stable climate.

Emissions from Unhindered Tropical Deforestation

In the 2015 Paris Agreement on climate, nearly two hundred countries unanimously agreed to keep the increase in global temperature relative to preindustrial levels well below 2°C (3.8°F). The Intergovernmental Panel on Climate Change (IPCC) estimated in its Fifth Assessment Report that keeping the rise in Earth's temperature below 2°C will likely depend on emitting no more than one trillion tons of carbon dioxide from 2011 onward.[32] This limit has been dubbed the planetary carbon budget. All IPCC scenarios in which the world holds temperature rise below 2°C involve halting deforestation to near-zero levels, as well as reforesting on a massive scale.[33]

Busch and Engelmann project that unless new countervailing forest conservation policies are put into place, in the next thirty-five years tropical deforestation will release 169 billion tons of carbon dioxide, equivalent to what would be produced by running 1,270 coal plants for the same length of time. That amount of emissions alone will burn through one-sixth of the remaining planetary carbon budget. Carrying the projections out through 2100, unchecked tropical deforestation will release 410 billion tons, or more than one-third of the remaining carbon budget.

Reducing Tropical Deforestation as a Low-Cost Mitigation Option

Whether the world's carbon emissions continue to rise or begin to fall depends on millions of small decisions made by people around the world. A city council decides whether to purchase power from coal plants or wind farms. A commuter decides whether to drive or bike to work. An investor decides which new technologies to finance. A landowner decides whether to keep forest on her property or clear the land for cattle.

In each such decision, the deck is stacked against the climate. That's because the costs of reducing emissions are localized and personal, while the benefits from a stable climate are spread across everyone on the planet, including people who haven't been born yet. Some people might make climate-friendly choices based on feelings of civic responsibility, or because doing so benefits them for reasons unrelated to the climate. But civic-mindedness and co-benefits alone are unlikely to be sufficient to stabilize greenhouse gas emissions. That's why government policies are critical.

The Busch and Engelmann analysis considered the effect of two types of policies governments can use to reduce greenhouse gas emissions from an economy: direct restrictions and carbon payments. Other types of policies exist, too—information campaigns, research and development in cleaner technology, and so forth—but the analysis did not consider the effect of those.

With direct restrictions, government agencies prohibit particular greenhouse-gas emitting activities, and they enforce these prohibitions with legal consequences. A good example of direct restrictions with respect to tropical forests is provided by Brazil, which, as discussed above, introduced a raft of policies from 2005 onward to prevent deforestation in the Amazon.

The Busch and Engelmann analysis simulated that if all other tropical countries were able to implement restrictive policies on deforestation as successfully as Brazil did post-2005, around 58 billion tons of carbon dioxide emissions would be kept out of the atmosphere from 2016 to 2050—just over one-third of projected emissions from tropical deforestation.[34]

The benefit of direct restrictions such as those imposed in the Brazilian Amazon is that, since most forestland in the tropics is state-owned rather than private, they can often be accomplished quickly using existing laws. They are, however, blunt instruments; public authorities can't typically differentiate between land users who can reduce a lot of emissions cheaply and those who can only reduce a few emissions at great cost. So the overall cost to land users of reducing emissions is higher than it needs to be, and the overall benefits to the atmosphere lower. Furthermore, the land users who are regulated by direct restrictions only bear costs; they have no opportunity to receive benefits, which in some settings may be more appropriate.

For both of these reasons, governments might prefer to use carbon pricing as a complement to direct regulations. In forest countries, carbon pricing could take the form of a tax on deforestation or of payments to land users that reduce emissions below some benchmark level. Carbon pricing is more efficient than direct regulation, achieving greater emission reductions at lower overall cost to land users. Carbon pricing would give all land users the incentive to reduce emissions and to innovate low-emission ways of doing business, just as it would for regulated companies in other sectors. Depending on how much a carbon pricing system relies on payments rather than

taxes, it can create winners as well as losers. As mentioned above, however, the drawback of carbon pricing is that it requires institutions to allocate emission rights and monitor emissions, which would likely be cumbersome or expensive to create across much of the tropics.

To get a sense of the costs of reducing emissions from deforestation, Busch and Engelmann simulated a hypothetical scenario in which all tropical forest countries were able to put a price on carbon through some combination of payments and taxes. They projected that if all tropical forest countries put into place between 2016 and 2050 a carbon price of $20 per ton—an arbitrarily chosen point of comparison—about one-quarter of carbon dioxide emissions from deforestation—41 billion tons—would be avoided.

The regions with the greatest potential to avoid emissions from deforestation at low cost are spread across the Amazon and the Andes; Central America; the Guyana Shield; the islands of Southeast Asia; mainland Southeast Asia; and West and Central Africa. It is worth noting that the MAC curve Busch and Engelmann produced is more conservative than those of previous studies, which projected even greater emission reductions in response to a carbon price. For example, whereas Busch and Engelmann found a $20-per-ton carbon price would result in a reduction of 0.92 billion tons of emissions from tropical deforestation in 2020, the previous MAC curves shown in figure 5.1, after inflating to 2014 U.S. dollars, indicated it would reduce emissions by 0.8 billion to 4.4 billion tons.

How the costs and benefits of the hypothetical carbon price would be shared between land users and governments would depend on how much the policy relied on taxes versus payments. If the full $20 per ton took the form of a payment, the cost to land users of reducing emissions would average out to about $9 per ton. The difference between the $9-per-ton cost and the $20-per-ton payment price would accrue as profit to land users supplying emission reductions. In the case of a higher $50-per-ton carbon payment, nearly half of tropical emissions from deforestation—77 billion tons—would be avoided, with an average cost to land users of $21 per ton and a profit of $29 per ton.

The quantity of low-cost emission reductions available from reducing tropical deforestation through carbon pricing would compare quite favorably to opportunities to cut emissions in other regions. As shown in figure 5.4, while a carbon price of $20 per ton would reduce emissions from tropical deforestation by 923 million tons, the same carbon price in the European Union would reduce emissions from buildings, energy, industry, and transportation by just 206 million tons. In the United States, it would reduce emissions from the same sectors by 228 million tons.[35] Put differently, reduced emissions from deforestation would cost less than a quarter of equivalent reductions in the industrial sectors of Europe or the United States. Worldwide, a carbon price of $20 per ton would reduce emissions from buildings, energy, industry, and

Figure 5.4: Reducing tropical deforestation is a relatively low-cost way to fight climate change.

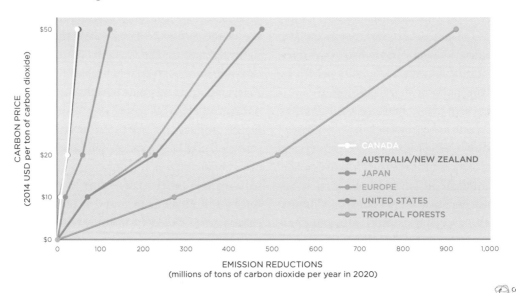

Source: J. Busch and J. Engelmann, "The Future of Forests;" Joint Global Change Research Institute, "Global Climate Assessment Model (GCAM)."

Note: "Tropical forests" refer to gross emissions from forest cover loss and peat conversion and exclude forest degradation and reforestation. Regions refer to emissions from buildings, energy, industry, and transportation, and exclude agriculture.

transportation by 1.9 billion tons,[36] meaning that reducing tropical deforestation would represent 33 percent of global, low-cost nonagricultural emission reductions.[37] If agriculture were included, the share of cost-effective emissions from forests would be somewhat lower, while the combined share from forests and agriculture would be somewhat higher.

Not only are the costs of reducing deforestation low relative to the costs of reducing emissions in other sectors; they're also low relative to the damage to the climate from continuing deforestation. The U.S. government estimates that in 2014, each ton of carbon dioxide emitted resulted in damage around $40 per ton of carbon dioxide, and that cost is rising over time.[38] If climate change negatively affects economic growth, the cost could be several times higher.[39]

The potential of tropical forests to supply relatively low-cost emission reductions should be of interest to institutions seeking a cost-effective global response to climate change, such as the Green Climate Fund (GCF). The GCF, an international financial institution based in Seongdo, Korea, was green-lighted by world leaders in Copenhagen in 2009 to channel "a significant portion" of finance for climate needs in developing countries—$100 billion per year by 2020, according to the same world leaders. The GCF faces many challenges, including raising capital and ensuring its funds are well spent. One of its most important challenges is deciding how best to allocate funds across many possible investments to prevent climate change.

In determining how to allocate funds, the GCF should consider cost effectiveness. The institution would get the most mileage from its money by channeling funds to the lowest-cost emission reductions. Across the developing countries where the GCF is mandated to spend, deforestation constitutes around 15 percent of nonagricultural emissions;[40] but Busch, Engelmann, and Lépissier project that reducing tropical deforestation would constitute 43 percent of low-cost (that is, below $20 per ton) nonagricultural emission reductions in 2020, as shown in figure 5.5. And, outside of China, reducing tropical deforestation would constitute 61 percent of low-cost nonagricultural emission reductions in developing countries in 2020.[41] If the GCF sought to spend half of the finance pledged in Copenhagen ($50 billion a year) on climate mitigation in developing countries in the most cost-effective way, it would spend 43 percent of its money on forests—about $21 billion a year.

This is even before considering that some part of the other $50 billion a year, intended for adaptation, ought to be directed to forests, too, since they provide ecosystem-based adaptation, as described in chapter 3. As climate change advances, tropical forests will become even more valuable for the services they provide in buffering against hotter temperatures, larger storms, rising seas, melting glaciers, and increased stress on crop production.

Cheaper, or Cooler and Faster at the Same Cost

Some level of global warming has become unavoidable. The greenhouse gases humanity has added to the atmosphere have already heated the planet by 0.85°C (1.5°F) above preindustrial levels. Even if all emissions were to cease immediately, Earth would continue to heat further as a result of past emissions.[42] But just because global warming is already happening doesn't mean it should

Figure 5.5: Reducing deforestation offers nearly half the potential low-cost emission reductions in developing countries.

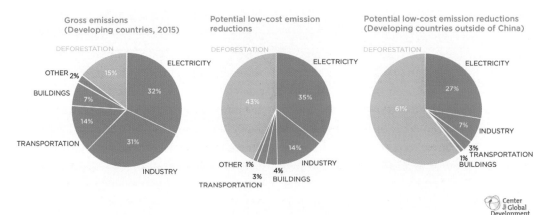

Source: Busch, Engelmann, and Lépissier (2016); Joint Global Change Research Institute (2015).

Note: Gross emissions and emission reductions refer to greenhouse gases excluding agriculture. Low-cost emission reductions refer to emission reductions available below a carbon price of $20/tCO$_2$ in 2014 U.S. dollars.

be allowed to proceed unhindered—each additional degree of temperature increase brings more severe harm than the last.

The IPCC gives a rough indication of the escalating consequences of heightened warming: 1°C (1.8°F) of warming portends high risk of heat waves and flooding, high risks for arctic sea ice, and high risks for coral reefs, upon which a large portion of the world's tropical fisheries depend; 2°C (3.6°F) portends high risks to crop yields and water availability, affecting the food security and livelihoods of millions of people; 3°C (5.4°F) threatens a collapse in biodiversity and a high risk of tipping points, triggering runaway irreversible climate change, regardless of future mitigation. [43]

Without action, the world is heading toward a temperature increase of around 4°C (7.2 °F).[44] But the more emissions are reduced, the more the risks can be minimized. By including tropical forests in the global response to climate change, emissions can be lowered more than they could be otherwise, at the same cost. The SkyShares model estimates, for example, that reducing emissions by 140 billion tons of carbon dioxide between 2016 and 2030 would set the world on a pathway to an increase of 2°C.[45] But if tropical deforestation were excluded from the climate response, the world could reduce emissions by only 93 billion tons at the same cost from 2016 to 2030, which would set the world on a higher temperature-increase pathway of 2.15°C, as shown in figure 5.6. Similarly, including forests in the portfolio of mitigation responses could let the world hit a pathway toward an increase of 3°C rather than 3.82°C, at the same cost from 2016 to 2030. Thus, reducing tropical deforestation can set the world on a pathway toward a future that is 0.15°C to 0.82°C cooler than it would otherwise be, at the same medium-term cost.

Similarly, the low-cost emission reductions from tropical forests could be used to help meet climate goals more cheaply. Getting on a pathway to a 2°C target, for example, would cost 28 percent less between 2016 and 2030 if reduced tropical deforestation were included in the global portfolio of climate solutions rather than relegated to the sidelines. Meeting a 3°C target would be 30 percent cheaper.

Previous analyses came to a similar conclusion: a 2013 review by economists Ruben Lubowski and Steven Rose found that including reduced emissions from tropical deforestation would lower the costs of meeting

climate policy targets by 25 to 40 percent.[46] The billions of dollars saved every year by including forests in the global climate response could be ploughed back into further reductions, or spent on other priorities.

Buying Time: Conserving Tropical Forests to Turn the Corner on Emissions Sooner

The aim of the Paris Agreement is for global greenhouse gas emissions to stop increasing and start declining as soon as possible, with the recognition that this will take longer for developing countries to achieve.[47] The G7 has set a goal of reducing emissions by close to 70 percent by 2050, with complete decarbonization by 2100.[48] In 2014, President Xi Jinping

Figure 5.6: Reducing tropical deforestation would let the world achieve a cooler climate more cheaply.

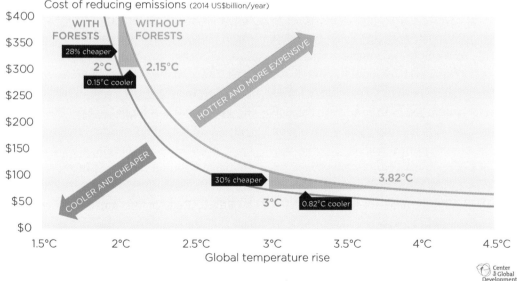

Source: Busch, Engelmann, and Lépissier (2016).

Note: Curves represent the theoretically minimum global cost of achieving a temperature target.

announced as part of a surprise diplomatic breakthrough with President Barack Obama that China would bring its emissions to peak and decline around 2030—an outcome some analysts think could happen even sooner.[49] President Xi's commitment would see China's emissions do an about-face, from an average increase of around 9 percent per year during the first decade of the 2000s[50] to negative growth by the end of the 2020s.

Yet for all these political commitments, phasing out fossil fuels has been compared to turning around a supertanker headed for an iceberg. The lifetime of a coal-fired power plant is more than thirty years, meaning that construction of such infrastructure today effectively locks in emissions for decades. Furthermore, many of the technologies necessary to power a low-carbon economy have not yet been invented or are not yet commercially viable.

In contrast, trees are ready today. Forests have been photosynthesizing for millions of years. And while fossil fuels are currently fundamental to the way the world produces energy, deforestation is a mere asterisk on the world's production of food. In 2012, fossil fuels powered more than 80 percent of world energy consumption.[51] In contrast, tropical deforestation expands the world's five billion hectares of agricultural land by around one-tenth of a percent per year.[52] Modest yield increases would be more than enough to make up for the forgone agricultural production from areas maintained as forests.

Of course, there would be costs to halting deforestation, to governments in the form of direct costs of law enforcement and to land users in the form of lost opportunities to use deforested land for crops or cattle. And, as discussed in depth in chapter 10, big money and powerful political interests are on the side of deforestation-as-usual. Nobody suggests stopping deforestation is easy. And yet all deforestation could, biophysically speaking, be halted overnight. In contrast to other industries, no physical or technological impediments stand in the way of everyone in the world resolving not to clear a forest today, not to clear a forest tomorrow, and not to clear a forest for the next thirty-five years. As former Norwegian prime minister Jens Stoltenberg once remarked, "Everyone knows how to not cut down a tree."[53]

The realization that reducing deforestation can be accomplished in the near term is reflected in international commitments. In the 2014 New York Declaration on Forests, more than thirty-five countries endorsed a timeline to cut deforestation in half by 2020 and strive to end it entirely by 2030, if supported by international finance.[54] In 2015, the broadly endorsed Sustainable Development Goals went even further, aiming to halt deforestation globally by 2020.[55] In contrast, few nations are contemplating phasing out fossil fuels as fully or quickly. The Paris Agreement strives for near-zero emissions by the second half of the century, while even the most optimistic projection scenarios don't envision eliminating fossil fuel use before 2050 at the earliest.[56]

Busch, Engelmann, and Lépissier calculate that the same amount of emission reductions that could be achieved from tropical forests in the five years from 2016 to 2020 would take sixteen years to achieve in the United States or eighteen years to achieve in Europe, at the same cost. They project that by including tropical forests in the global response to climate change, global emissions can peak and decline two to five years sooner, at the same cost from 2016 to 2030. If countries started cutting emissions in 2016 to keep global warming below 2°C, in line with the Paris Agreement, a portfolio of climate actions that included reducing tropical deforestation could see global emissions peak by 2020, while an equally costly portfolio that ignored tropical deforestation would not see that happen until 2022. Similarly, if countries started in 2020 on a pathway toward a 2.5°C increase, a portfolio of climate actions that included reduced tropical deforestation could see global emissions peak by 2025 instead of by 2030, at the same cost.

Of course, rapid decarbonization is needed across many sectors and many countries. Research and development is very much needed for all potential low-carbon or negative-emissions technologies, even "clean coal." But the world can't simply wait for new technologies. Every year of delay until global emissions peak will require steeper decarbonization thereafter to achieve the same temperature. That's what makes the plentiful, low-cost emission reductions that are available from forests in the near term so important: rapid action to reduce deforestation in the near term can buy time to make necessary reductions in other sectors where progress will take longer and cost more.

Forest conservation is not a distraction from industrial emission reductions, just as renewable energy is not a distraction from cleaner transportation. Reducing tropical deforestation offers the world a head start in tackling climate change. This extra time

is desperately needed for the longer, tougher challenge of decarbonizing modern economies from fossil fuels.

Conclusion

New analysis presented in this chapter confirms that tropical forests offer a plentiful source of low-cost emission reductions relative to other sectors. If carbon payments could be implemented in developing countries, reduced emissions from deforestation would cost less than a quarter of equivalent reductions in the industrial sectors of Europe or the United States. If forest countries implemented restrictive policies with benefit sharing from international carbon payments, emission reductions could be even greater.

Forests make up a large part of a cost-effective global portfolio for mitigating climate change: one-third of the lowest-cost nonagricultural emission reductions globally; nearly half of the lowest-cost nonagricultural emission reductions across developing countries; and three-fifths of the lowest-cost nonagricultural emission reductions outside of China. By taking full advantage of reduced tropical deforestation rather than leaving these low-cost emission reductions on the sidelines, the world's response to climate change can be 28 to 30 percent cheaper. Or, at the same cost, the climate can be kept 0.15°C to 0.82°C (0.27°F to 1.5°F) cooler than would otherwise occur, with emissions beginning to decline two to five years faster than they would otherwise.

A cost-effective global response to climate change would see global institutions like the Green Climate Fund prioritize tropical forests. Rich countries would supplement ambitious climate actions at home with purchases of emission reductions from forest conservation in tropical countries.

Like other MAC curves before it, the analysis in this chapter considers only the carbon benefits of conserving forests. But, as described in chapter 3, forests provide many other goods and services, too. Conserving forests for their carbon value will go a long way toward providing these other services, and carbon values have the potential to influence land users' decisions in a way the value of other services alone has not yet been able to do. We discuss measuring and internalizing the value of these other goods and services in chapter 6.

Notes

1. S. Bernard, "The Cost of Clean Coal," Grist, February 2015, http://exp.grist.org/clean-coal/.

2. KBR, Inc.,"Coal Gasification," updated 2016, http://www.kbr.com/Technologies/Coal-Gasification/; U.S. Department of Energy, National Energy Technology Laboratory, "KBR Transport Gasifiers," 2015, http://www.netl.doe.gov/research/coal/energy-systems/gasification/gasifipedia/kbr.

3. U.S. Department of Energy, "DOE Awards $235 Million to Southern Company to Build Clean Coal Plant," February 22, 2016, http://energy.gov/articles/doe-awards-235-million-southern-company-build-clean-coal-plant.

4. D. Samuelsohn, "Billions over Budget. Two Years after Deadline. What's Gone Wrong for the 'Clean Coal' Project That's Supposed to Save an Industry?" *POLITICO*, May 26, 2015, http://www.politico.com/agenda/story/2015/05/billion-dollar-kemper-clean-coal-energy-project-000015; C. Marshall, "Tech 'Challenges' Force Utility to Evaluate Kemper Schedule," *Greenwire*, January 8, 2016, http://www.eenews.net/greenwire/stories/1060030357.

5. D. Cusick, "Electric Power Association Pulls Out of Deal with Flagship Southern Co. Coal Project," E&E Publishing, May 22, 2015, http://www.eenews.net/climatewire/2015/05/22/stories/1060019000.

6. Bernard, "The Cost of Clean Coal."

7. Ibid.

8. M. Al-juaied and A. Whitmore, "Realistic Costs of Carbon Capture," Belfer Center Discussion Paper 2009-08, Harvard Kennedy School, Cambridge, MA, 2009.

9. Verified Carbon Standard "Alto Mayo Protected Forest," VCS Project Database, 2015, http://www.vcsprojectdatabase.org/#/project_details/944.

10. Ibid.

11. Conservation International—Peru, "Alto Mayo Conservation Initiative Monitoring and Implementation No. 2," December 2014, http://www.v-c-s.org/sites/v-c-s.org/files/AM%20Monitoring%20_%20Implementation%20Report%202014_12_18_final.pdf.

12. Agustin Silvani, personal communication, May 25, 2015.

13. S. Pacala and R. Socolow, "Stabilization Wedges: Solving the Climate Problem for the Next 50 Years with Current Technologies," *Science* 305, no. 5686 (2004): 968–72.

14. United Nations, "Sustainable Development Goals," https://sustainabledevelopment.un.org/?menu=1300.

15. R. Lubowski and S. Rose, "The Potential for REDD+: Key Economic Modeling Insights and Issues," *Review of Environmental Economics and Policy* 7, no. 1 (2013): 67–90; A. Angelsen et al., *REDD Credits in a Global Carbon Market: Options and Impacts* (Copenhagen: Nordic Council of Ministers, 2014); V. Bosetti et al., "Linking Reduced Deforestation and a Global Carbon Market: Implications for Clean Energy Technology and Policy Flexibility," *Environment and Development Economics* 16, no. 4 (2011): 479–505.

16. D. Nepstad et al., "The End of Deforestation in the Brazilian Amazon," *Science* 326, no. 5958 (2009): 1350–51.

17. M. Greig-Gran, "The Cost of Avoiding Deforestation: Report Prepared for Stern Review of the Economics of Climate Change," International Institute for Environment and Development, London, 2006; N. H. Stern, *Stern Review: The Economics of Climate Change* 30 (London: HM Treasury, 2006).

18. J. Eliasch, "Climate Change: Financing Global Forests," Office of Climate Change, London, 2008, https://www.gov.uk/government/uploads/system/uploads/attachment_data/file/228833/9780108507632.pdf; G. Kindermann et al., "Global Cost Estimates of Reducing Carbon Emissions through Avoided Deforestation," *Proceedings of the National Academy of Sciences* 105, no. 30 (2008): 10302–7.

19. T. Nauclér and P. Enkvist, "Pathways to a Low-Carbon Economy: Version 2 of the Global Greenhouse Gas Abatement Cost Curve," McKinsey & Company 192, 2009, http://www.mckinsey.com/~/media/mckinsey/dotcom/client_service/sustainability/cost%20curve%20pdfs/pathways_lowcarbon_economy_version2.ashx.

20. See, for example, F. Kesicki and Paul Ekins, "Marginal Abatement Cost Curves: A Call for Caution," *Climate Policy* 12, no. 2 (2012): 219–36.

21. R. Pirard, "Market-Based Instruments for Biodiversity and Ecosystem Services: A Lexicon," *Environmental Science & Policy* 19 (2012): 59–68.

22. N. Hohne et al., "State and Trends of Carbon Pricing 2014," World Bank Group and ECOFYS, Washington, DC, May 2014.

23. F. A. Fogliano de Souza Cunha et al., "The Implementation Costs of Forest Conservation Policies in Brazil," *Ecological Economics* 130 (2016): 209–20.

24. Ibid.

25. L. Pedroni et al., "Creating Incentives for Avoiding Further Deforestation: The Nested Approach," *Climate Policy* 9, no. 2 (2009): 207–20; A. Duchelle et al., "Acre's State System of Incentives for Environmental Services (SISA), Brazil," in *REDD+ on the Ground: A Case Book of Subnational Initiatives across the Globe* (Bogor, Indonesia: Center for International Forestry Research [CIFOR], 2014).

26. Al-juaied and Whitmore, "Realistic Costs of Carbon Capture."

27. See, for example, Stand for Trees, "How It Works," 2015, https://standfortrees.org/en/how-it-works.

28. J. Busch and J. Engelmann, "The Future of Forests: Emissions from Deforestation With and Without Carbon Pricing Policies, 2015–2050," CGD Working Paper 411, Center for Global Development, Washington, DC, 2015.

29. M. C. Hansen et al., "High-Resolution Global Maps of 21st-Century Forest Cover Change," *Science* 342 (2013): 850–53.

30. Busch and Engelmann, "The Future of Forests."

31. Ibid.

32. R. K. Pachauri et al., eds., *Climate Change 2014: Synthesis Report. Contribution of Working Groups I, II and III to the Fifth Assessment Report of the Intergovernmental Panel on Climate Change* (Geneva, Switzerland: Intergovernmental Panel on Climate Change, 2014).

33. O. Edenhofer et al., eds., *Climate Change 2014: Mitigation of Climate Change. Contribution of Working Group III to the Fifth Assessment Report of the Intergovernmental Panel on Climate Change* (Cambridge University Press, Cambridge, UK, and New York: Cambridge University Press, 2014).

34. Why one-third rather than a number closer to 80 percent? Because we compared average deforestation rates in the Amazon pre- and post-policy, not just from peak to trough, and because the large gains from implementing such policies in the Brazilian Amazon have already been realized.

35. Joint Global Change Research Institute, "Global Climate Assessment Model (GCAM)," University of Maryland, 2015, http://www.globalchange.umd.edu/models/gcam/; S. H. Kim et al., "The ObjECTS Framework for Integrated Assessment: Hybrid Modeling of Transportation," *The Energy Journal*, special issue no. 2 (2006): 63–91.

36. Ibid.

37. These comparisons include buildings, electricity, industry, and transportation (GCAM), in addition to forests from Busch and Engelmann (2015), but they exclude agriculture. Because agriculture and forestry were aggregated as a single land-use sector in GCAM, we excluded agriculture to avoid double counting. If agriculture were included, the fraction of low-cost abatement comprising land use would be

larger than one-third, and the fraction of low-cost abatement comprising forests would be smaller than one-third.

38. U.S. Environmental Protection Agency, "The Social Cost of Carbon," www.epa.gov, updated 2016, http://www.epa.gov/climatechange/EPAactivities/economics/scc.html.

39. F. C. Moore and D. B. Diaz, "Temperature Impacts on Economic Growth Warrant Stringent Mitigation Policy," *Nature Climate Change* 5 (2015): 127–31.

40. As noted previously, these comparisons include buildings, electricity, industry, and transportation (GCAM), in addition to forests (Busch and Engelmann), but notably exclude agriculture. Because agriculture and forestry were aggregated as a single land-use sector in GCAM, we excluded this sector to avoid double counting. If agriculture were included, the fraction of low-cost abatements comprising land-use would be larger, and forests would be smaller.

41. This calculation considers all emission reductions that can be made below the cost at which $50 billion is spent per year, excluding emissions from agriculture.

42. T. F. Stocker et al., eds., *Climate Change 2013: The Physical Science Basis. Contribution of Working Group I to the Fifth Assessment Report of the Intergovernmental Panel on Climate Change* (Cambridge, UK, and New York: Cambridge University Press, 2013), 1535.

43. Pachauri et al., *Climate Change 2014*.

44. Ibid.

45. A. Lépissier, O. Barder, and A. Evans, "Modelling SkyShares: Technical Background," CGD Technical Background Paper, Center for Global Development, London, 2015. Note that in the calculations that follow, we examine scenarios in which a 2°C increase is attained with 50 percent likelihood, rather than the 66 percent likelihood used in Edenhofer et al., *Climate Change*.

46. Lubowski and Rose, "The Potential for REDD+: Key Economic Modeling Insights and Issues."

47. United Nations Framework Convention on Climate Change (UNFCCC), "Paris Agreement," Paris, France, 2015, http://unfccc.int/files/essential_background/convention/application/pdf/english_paris_agreement.pdf.

48. Leaders of the G7, "Leaders' Declaration," G7, Schloss Elmau, Germany, June 7–8, 2015, https://www.g7germany.de/Content/DE/_Anlagen/G8_G20/2015-06-08-g7-abschluss-eng.pdf?__blob=publicationFile&v=5.

49. People's Republic of China, Department of Climate Change, "Enhanced Actions on Climate Change: China's Intended Nationally Determined Contributions," Beijing, June 30, 2015, http://www4.unfccc.int/submissions/INDC/Published%20Documents/China/1/China's%20INDC%20-%20on%2030%20June%202015.pdf.

50. See data analysis from the Oak Ridge National Library Carbon Dioxide Information Analysis Center, available at http://cdiac.ornl.gov/.

51. U.S. Energy Information Administration, "International Energy Outlook 2016," executive summary, 2016, http://www.eia.gov/forecasts/ieo/exec_summ.cfm.

52. Authors' calculations based on World Bank, "Agricultural Land (Sq. Km)," updated 2016, http://data.worldbank.org/indicator/AG.LND.AGRI.K2; and H. K. Gibbs et al., "Tropical Forests Were the Primary Sources of New Agricultural Land in the 1980s and 1990s," *Proceedings of the National Academy of Sciences* 107, no. 38 (2010): 16732–7.

53. J. Stoltenberg, "Speech at UN Climate Change Conference in Bali," December 13, 2007, https://www.regjeringen.no/en/aktuelt/speech-at-un-climate-conference-in-bali/id493899/.

54. United Nations, "New York Declaration on Forests," September 23, 2014, http://www.un-redd.org/portals/15/documents/ForestsDeclarationText.pdf.

55. United Nations, "Draft Outcome Document

of the United Nations Summit for the Adoption of the Post-2015 Development Agenda, Sixty-Ninth Session of the General Assembly of the United Nations," New York, 2015, http://www.un.org/ga/search/view_doc.asp?symbol=A/69/L.85&Lang=E.

56. United Nations Framework Convention on Climate Change, "Paris Agreement" (2015); see, for example, M. Jacobson, "100% Clean and Renewable Wind, Water, and Sunlight (WWS) All-Sector Energy Roadmaps for the 50 United States," *Energy & Environmental Science* 8, no. 7 (2015): 2093–2117.

The Sumatran village of Bukit Lawang sits next to Gunung Leuser National Park, home to a rich forest ecosystem.

Credit: Shanti Hesse/Shutterstock

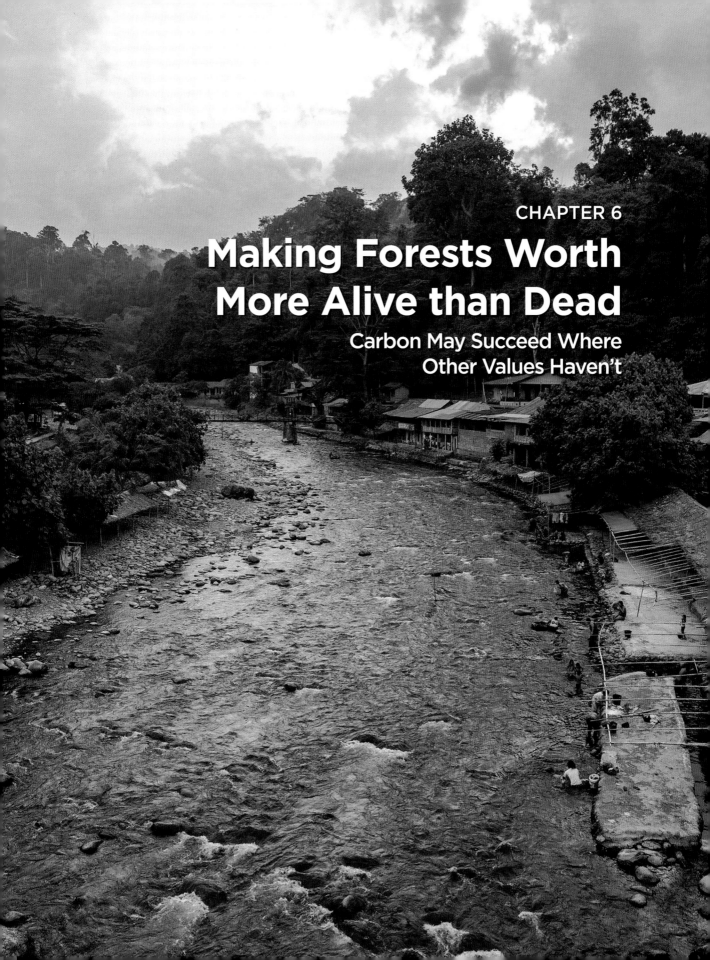

CHAPTER 6

Making Forests Worth More Alive than Dead

Carbon May Succeed Where Other Values Haven't

akira National Park, Madagascar. The island nation of Madagascar is home to so many plants and animals that live nowhere else on Earth that biologists have dubbed it the Eighth Continent.[1] In addition to the lemurs and baobab trees for which the world's fourth largest island is famous, Madagascar hosts colorful chameleons, bizarre see-through frogs, and a fierce overgrown mongoose relative called a fossa. Madagascar sits off the east coast of southern Africa, but it actually split off from what is now India nearly one hundred million years ago. Since then, its flora and fauna have evolved in nearly complete isolation from the rest of the world.

Madagascar's biological diversity is on full display at Makira National Park, a Rhode Island-size protected rainforest watershed in the country's remote northeast. The 140,000 people who live in and around Makira are well acquainted with the many plant species growing in the forest and surrounding fields, which they collect and use for medicine. In a fascinating study of the medicine usage patterns and preferences of thousands of local households, epidemiologist Chris Golden and his colleagues documented the use of 241 species of plants to treat 82 types of illness.[2]

Few, if any, of these medicinal plants have been tested by the U.S. Food and Drug Administration for efficacy and safety. Nevertheless, people in Makira consume natural plant-based medicines in large quantities. Many even prefer them to the Western medicines that are available from local hospitals

and pharmacies, at least for some ailments. While preferring Western medicines for headaches, coughs, and insomnia, they favor natural local medicines for stomachaches, fatigue, and back pain, in part because they are more familiar with dosages and possible side effects, can tailor their use to gender or other patient characteristics, and can be certain the medicines are fresh rather than expired.[3]

Best of all, the only cost of local medicines is the time spent gathering them. In 2012, Golden and his colleagues calculated how much it would cost people in Makira to buy at market prices the drugs they currently collect from the forest for free. They estimated that purchasing notionally comparable courses of treatment from a clinic at highly subsidized prices would cost families $30 to $45 per year, equivalent to 43 to 63 percent of median household income. If they had to buy their currently free medicines at U.S. prices, they'd spend $100 to $300 per year—more than the median income.

The 241 medicinal plants found in Makira are just a subset of the 3,500 found across Madagascar.[4] And Madagascar's forests not only provide economically valuable goods such as medicines; they also provide services, such as keeping water clean by anchoring soil in place.

Yet despite the value of its forest goods and services, Madagascar has long had some of the highest deforestation rates on the planet.[5] Deforestation in the highlands leads to mass erosion of sediment into rivers, which imposes costs on rice farmers downriver and damages irrigation projects.[6] In fact, so much red soil spills out from Madagascar's rivers into the surrounding sea that the plume is

---

This chapter draws heavily on a background paper by Katrina Mullan on the economic values of tropical forest services.

visible from space, likened by astronauts to "open veins bleeding the country to death."[7]

People clear forests in Madagascar to make way for growing rice, grazing cattle, and mining. These industries produce direct and substantial economic benefits, albeit often to people other than those who benefit from the forests. In a country that faces urgent and profound challenges to overcoming poverty, deforestation is unlikely to stop as long as forests are worth more dead than alive.

Invisible Forest Goods and Services

The same story is playing out all across the forested tropics. As mentioned in chapter 3, natural medicines constituted an $83 billion global market in 2008.[8] They are used for primary care by roughly 70 to 95 percent of people in most developing countries.[9] Globally, an estimated 52,885 plants are used in medicines—fully one-sixth of all plant species on Earth.[10] Many of these undoubtedly come from forests.

And medicine is just one of many goods people harvest from tropical forests. A meta-analysis in 2004 found that across the rural populations sampled in fifty-four site-level studies, environmental income from tropical forests comprised an average 22 percent of their total income, split evenly between cash and subsistence income.[11]

The sizable contribution of forest goods to rural livelihoods was corroborated ten years later by a large-scale, standardized survey of eight thousand households living in and around forests in twenty-four tropical countries.[12] Conducted by the Poverty and Environment Network (PEN) of the Center for International Forestry Research (CIFOR) and published in 2014, the study showed that, on average, 21 percent of household income across study sites came from forests, not including plantations. The share of household income from forests exceeded income coming from wages (15 percent), livestock (12 percent), and businesses (7 percent) and was second only to income from crops (29 percent). Although richer people gained the most income from forests in absolute terms, poorer people were most dependent on them as a share of household income.

It has been known for decades that forest income comes from many products besides timber.[13] In the 2014 PEN study, about a quarter of forest income for the households examined came from wood products and construction materials, but most forest income in all three major tropical regions came from other sources. In Africa and Asia, around 40 percent came from firewood and charcoal and around 25 percent from other plant and animal products. In Latin America, just over half came from plant and animal products. In all continents, just under 10 percent of household income from forests was derived from medicines, resins, dyes, fodder, and myriad other products. Production of these materials is not always sustainable—in some cases, forest resources are being extracted faster than they can regenerate.

Forests also provide many services to agriculture, energy, health, and safety, as described in chapter 3 and shown in figure 6.1. They provide cool, wet air that is favorable for farming and pleasant for people living downwind, they stabilize slopes in the face of land-

Figure 6.1: Tropical forests' goods and services contribute to development.

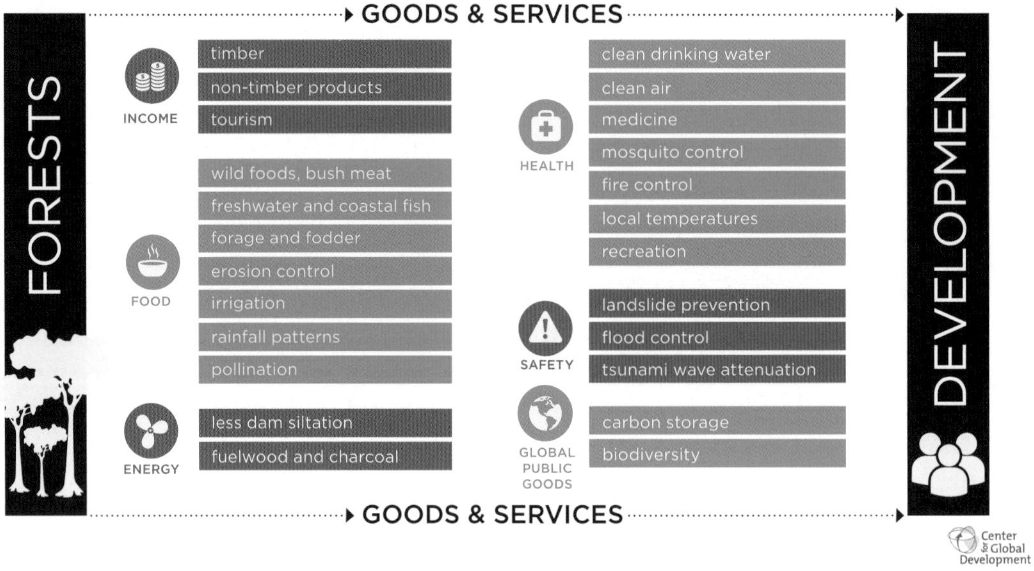

FORESTS	GOODS & SERVICES		DEVELOPMENT
	INCOME	timber	
		non-timber products	
		tourism	
	FOOD	wild foods, bush meat	
		freshwater and coastal fish	
		forage and fodder	
		erosion control	
		irrigation	
		rainfall patterns	
		pollination	
	ENERGY	less dam siltation	
		fuelwood and charcoal	
	HEALTH	clean drinking water	
		clean air	
		medicine	
		mosquito control	
		fire control	
		local temperatures	
		recreation	
	SAFETY	landslide prevention	
		flood control	
		tsunami wave attenuation	
	GLOBAL PUBLIC GOODS	carbon storage	
		biodiversity	

Center for Global Development

slides, and they keep water free of sediment, to mention just three examples.

Nevertheless, an area of tropical forest the size of Maine is cleared every year, largely for ranching and crop production and, as noted above, sometimes by different people than those who benefited from leaving the forests standing. This is happening in part because many of forests' values are not well known; or some of the values are known, but they are not very large; or some of the values are known to be large, but they are difficult to capture and translate into monetary benefit.

Certainly, in some instances, forest-dependent communities, and indigenous peoples especially, have conserved forests even in the absence of significant monetary benefits, with little fanfare. But for many others, economic motivations are important to decisions about land use. Many public policymakers might be more likely to conserve forests if they understood the full magnitude of forest values, while the prospect of obtaining sizable monetary benefits from conservation could be decisive for many land users who might otherwise clear their land of forest.

In this chapter we document the economic values of forest services and discuss initiatives to make them more visible to policymakers and more tangible to land users. We start by presenting three illustrative cases in which academics have quantified the dollar values of forest services or damages from forest destruction. Even in the best cases, valuations of forest services are often cruder than those in other fields of economics, as a result of challenges we describe. We also discuss the distribution of these service values between rich and poor.

As we then explain, the values of forest goods and services are mostly invisible to public planners. When forest goods are not transacted in markets, they are harder to detect and count in gross domestic product (GDP), the scorecard of development planners everywhere. Forest services are even less noticed in national accounts. Their invisibility gives development planners one more reason to promote industries such as agriculture and mining, which do show up on their scorecards, at the expense of forest conservation, which doesn't. We discuss fledgling efforts to make forest values more visible to public decision makers by including them in national accounts and poverty surveys.

The simple knowledge that forests provide services may not be enough to convince land users to protect them. Land users receive tangible and immediate benefits from converting forests to cropland or grazing land, while the benefits of maintaining forests are dispersed to other people living downwind, downhill, or downriver. To alter land users' economic calculations, forests' values need to be made tangible and substantial—that is, forests must be made worth more alive than dead.

We discuss the long history of efforts to capture forest values monetarily so that local land users can benefit financially from conserving forests. These initiatives include the marketing of sustainable timber and forest products, bioprospecting, ecotourism, and payments for ecosystem services. While some of these ventures have made modest progress in putting tangible values on some services, especially with relation to watersheds, collectively they have not yet succeeded in turning the tide of deforestation on a large scale.

Concern about preventing climate change has the potential to make tropical forest services visible and tangible in a way no other service has yet, however. As we discuss, carbon is easier to place a value on, demand for carbon storage is larger, and we have good reasons to expect demand for carbon storage will be easier to turn into hard income—for example, through international carbon payments at the scale of political jurisdictions (that is, REDD+; see box 1.1). We discuss potential obstacles to international carbon payments, as well. If carbon payments begin to make forests worth more alive than dead, they can bring along the provision of other forest goods and services as a bonus.

The Value of Forest Goods and Services

Forests provide valuable goods and services, while deforestation leads to economic damages. We present case studies at the local, regional, and international scales, respectively: mangrove forests in Thailand; forested watersheds above dams in China, Colombia, and Costa Rica; and forest fires in Indonesia.

Local Values of Forests: Mangroves in Thailand

Thailand is a nation blessed with abundant coastlines. Its east coast wraps gracefully for 1,670 kilometers around the Gulf of Thailand, while its 750-kilometer west coast faces the Andaman Sea.[14] Along these shores sit tens of thousands of households in thousands of fishing villages.

Thailand's coasts are naturally fringed by mangrove forests—dense tangles of low trees whose roots protrude above the seawater like interlaced fingers.[15] These saltwater forests support Thailand's fishing communities in a variety of ways. They provide products that people harvest: timber, fuelwood, charcoal, crabs, shellfish, and resins. They are nurseries for marine fish that will be harvested off-shore when they are old enough to leave the safety of the mangroves' root networks. And they buffer coastal villages from the impact of storms and high waves, as they did during the 2004 tsunami.[16]

In spite of their value, Thailand's mangroves are being cleared rapidly. From 1961 to 2004, Thailand lost between one-third and one-half of its mangroves.[17] More than half of the clearing was undertaken to build shrimp farms.[18] Clearing for tourist resorts was a major contributor to deforestation, as well; while mangroves have their own sort of brackish backwater charm, they don't attract international sunbathers the way powdery white beaches and coconut palms do. Clearing mangroves for shrimp farms and tourist beaches was systematically encouraged by public policies; lost ecological value barely factored into decision making.[19]

In 2007, economist Ed Barbier compared the net present value[20] of the natural services provided by mangroves to the net present value of shrimp farms.[21] He estimated the products harvested from mangroves by local villagers were worth about $500 per hectare in 1996 dollars, compared to a scenario without mangroves.[22] The contributions of mangroves to offshore fisheries amounted to around $700 to $1,000 per hectare. Finally, the value of mangroves in protecting coastal towns from storms, floods, and tsunamis averaged out to about $9,000 to $11,000 per hectare. If villagers tried to replicate mangroves' protective function by building seawalls, they would have to spend $68,000 to $82,000 per hectare.

All told, by Barbier's estimates, Thailand's mangroves provided goods and services worth about $10,000 to $12,000 per hectare in net

present terms. That's an order of magnitude higher than the $1,200 per hectare net present returns from shrimp farms, and it's even higher than the roughly $9,000 per hectare it costs to restore a mangrove forest on an abandoned shrimp farm. Considering the benefits to all villagers and not just aquaculturalists, protecting and restoring mangroves makes more economic sense than building shrimp farms. By quantifying and publicizing these values, findings such as Barbier's contributed to Sri Lanka's comprehensively protecting all its remaining mangrove forests in 2015.[23]

Regional Values of Forests: Watersheds and Dams in China, Colombia, and Costa Rica

It is impossible to talk about China's Three Gorges Dam without using big numbers. Its construction on the Yangtze River took fourteen years and displaced more than a million people.[24] It is the world's largest hydroelectric dam, with a capacity of over 22,000 megawatts from its thirty-two turbine generators.[25] It produced nearly 100 billion kilowatt hours of electricity in 2014[26]—as much as is consumed every year by Vietnam, or half as much as consumed by Australia. The dam provides electricity to tens of millions of people, and since 2011 it has earned a profit of $2 billion to $3 billion per year.[27]

All of that power flows from water, and the water flows from forests. As discussed in chapter 3, forests provide key services to hydroelectric dams. They limit the amount of sediment flowing into reservoirs, which keeps turbine blades functioning longer and averts costly dredging; and they are hydrological sponges, retaining water during wet periods and releasing it during dry ones. The forests above Three Gorges Dam provide both these services. Without them, the river would be muddier and its flow more erratic, reducing the dam's performance.[28]

Ecologist Zhongwei Guo and his colleagues estimated that forests in the three counties above the dam contributed services worth $35 million per year in 2004—about 6 percent of the dam's $600 million revenue that year. Of that amount, $20 million came from greater electricity production during the dry season, thanks to increased water flow; an additional $15 million came from avoided costs of removing sediment from the reservoir.[29] The value of the forest in Three Gorges' watershed has grown since then, as the number of operational turbines has increased from ten to thirty-two.[30]

The benefits from the 442,000 hectares of forests above the Three Gorges Dam average out to about $80 per hectare per year, compared to a scenario without forests. Unlike in the cases of medicines in Madagascar or mangroves in Thailand, however, little of this benefit accrues to people in the forested counties. Instead, it flows to consumers in Shanghai and other relatively wealthy regions in the form of cheaper, more plentiful, and more reliable electricity.

The forests upriver from the Three Gorges Dam are protected under China's 1998 Logging Ban, imposed in response to devastating floods.[31] To the people who live there, this ban represents an economic liability. The forests aren't devoid of economic activity—they are used for tourism, and they are a source of mushrooms and traditional Chinese medicines, which people gather and sell. Given the choice, however, many people might prefer to convert forestland to growing wheat or rape-

seed crops, which Guo and his colleagues estimate would produce revenue of about $3 million per year. At the time of Guo's article, China paid compensation of $10 per hectare per year to landholders in return for keeping or restoring their land as forest, which was less than potential income from crops. Guo and his colleagues estimated that if electricity consumers in Shanghai paid just an extra thousandth of a cent per kilowatt hour, they could more than make up the forgone benefits from agriculture.

Half a world away in Colombia, forests are also contributing to hydroelectricity generation. Hydroelectricity makes up 75 percent of installed energy capacity in the Andean country. The watersheds above Colombia's dams were once about two-thirds covered in cloud forests—as discussed in chapter 3, these are high-altitude forests with persistent cloud cover that pull in water from the atmosphere. But deforestation for cattle, mining, and illegal crops has depleted the original area of cloud forest by nearly half.

If the cloud forests above the dams were restored, hydroelectric production would increase.[32] Eco-hydrologist Leo Sáenz and his colleagues modeled the benefits that would accrue from reforesting the watershed above Calima Dam in the Colombian Andes. Using a string of sophisticated models, they estimated that restoring the watershed from its current forest cover of 54 percent to its original cover of around 90 percent would increase the amount of moisture intercepted from fog by 25 percent. This would increase water flow to the dam by 6 percent, which in turn would increase power generation by 4 percent and increase net revenue by 5 percent. Those estimates are for a year with normal water flow;

in a water-scarce year, the increase in revenues would be even greater.

Furthermore, restoring natural cloud forests to their original extent would reduce sedimentation by two-thirds, leading to lower dredging costs. All told, Sáenz and his colleagues estimated the benefits to the Calima Dam from restoring forests to their original extent would work out to about $300 per year in additional revenue per hectare of forest relative to current levels.

At Calima Dam, as at Three Gorges, payments from downstream electricity producers to upstream land users might make forest protection or restoration competitive with the revenues from current land uses—mostly cattle as well as coffee and sugar cane—before considering the upfront costs of forest restoration. But Colombia has taken a different approach than China. Downstream dams pay about 6 percent of annual electricity sales into a fund to improve upstream forest management. These payments are not performance-based—that is, they are not closely linked to the desired outcome of maintaining or restoring forest cover—and they are perceived as unsuccessful.[33]

A third example of the value of forests to downstream dams comes from Costa Rica. Three hydroelectric plants downstream of the Tapantí National Park spend $3 million per year battling sedimentation from erosion in deforested areas. Agronomist Florence Bernard and her colleagues estimated that these costs would be twice as high without the protected forests upstream.[34]

Since 1997, Costa Rica has taken an innovative approach to protecting forests, called "payments for ecosystem services" (PES).

Where China has protected upstream forests by "regulating and compensating," and Colombia's dams pay into forest management funds, the government of Costa Rica pays landowners for every hectare of forest they maintain on their properties. Making the value of forests tangible to local landowners through the PES program was one of many policies Costa Rica introduced while increasing its forest cover from a low of 20 percent in the mid-1980s to more than 50 percent by 2010.[35] We further discuss the effectiveness of PES programs below and in chapter 7.

International Values of Forests: Forest Fires in Indonesia

In 1997 and 1998, Indonesia was on fire. Towering flames raged across large swaths of Sumatra and Kalimantan, triggered by unusually dry conditions, an El Niño, aggressive rainforest logging and clearing (much of it illegal), and the draining of peat swamps. As described in chapter 2, the resulting haze blanketed the region, from Indonesia and Malaysia to Singapore and Brunei, and as far away as Thailand and Vietnam.

The haze shut down schools. It shut down airports. It sullied the air breathed by millions of people. Schoolchildren in Malaysia were issued masks. Hospital admittances soared. The spike in greenhouse gas emissions in 1997–98 was globally significant, amounting to between 13 and 40 percent of annual emissions from fossil fuels.[36]

The cataclysmic fires spawned a series of studies estimating the economic damage from various aspects of the fires and haze. They analyzed respiratory illnesses in Indonesia, early deaths among the elderly in Kuala

Lumpur, a drop in births in Indonesia, especially among the poor, and lost wages and illnesses in Brunei, among other damage.[37]

One of the earliest and most ambitious efforts to quantify comprehensively the damage from the fires and haze was undertaken by economist David Glover and environmental expert Timothy Jessup. In their 1998 book, *Indonesia's Fires and Haze: The Costs of Catastrophe*, reissued in 2006, they estimated the total economic losses to be more than $4.5 billion, in 1997 dollars: $4 billion in Indonesia, $400 million in Malaysia, and $100 million in Singapore. Selected costs in Indonesia included health damage ($924 million), agricultural losses ($470 million), timber losses ($494 million), lost tourism ($70 million), firefighting costs ($25 million), and losses to airports ($10 million) and airlines ($8 million).

Although the fire season of 1997–98 was the biggest ever, fires have recurred ever since. The 2015 fires cost the Indonesian economy more than $16 billion, according to a study by the World Bank—more than double any potential benefits arising from the conversion of burned land to oil palm.[38] Affected sectors included agriculture, forestry, trade, tourism, and transportation. Knowledge of the economic damage from the fires has broadened constituencies for forest reforms in Indonesia, as we discuss in chapter 10, even though the measures the country has put in place to try to contain deforestation and fires have not yet brought them under control.

Challenges to Quantifying Forests' Economic Values

The four examples presented above—medicines, mangroves, dams, and forest fires—represent just a few of the cases in which researchers have estimated the economic contributions of forest goods and services in monetary terms. Many others can be cited.

For *Why Forests? Why Now?* we commissioned an expert review of all studies of the value of tropical forests' services in developing countries. Conducted by economist Katrina Mullan, the review catalogued forty-five primary studies of the contributions of forests to health, safety, energy, and agriculture that linked changes in forest condition to changes in well-being, using economic techniques described below.[39] The magnitude of impacts found by these studies ranged considerably. Some were large, while many were modest. Not all were fully quantified, nor was causality always proved. The studies' findings included the following:

- The improvement in drinking water from protecting Chile's forested Llancahue watershed was worth at least $162/hectare/year in the summer and $61/hectare/year at other times of year.[40]
- Households in Vietnam were willing to pay up to 0.9 percent of their annual incomes to reduce landslide risk by reforesting hillsides upslope.[41]
- Establishing the Mantadia National Park to protect forests in eastern Madagascar reduced flood risk to downstream farmers, worth tens of thousands of dollars a year.[42]
- Cacao farmers in Indonesia were willing to pay up to 0.8 percent of their annual household incomes to increase by 10 percent the shade provided by forests.[43]
- Forest protection in Indonesia mitigat-

ed drought, with a 25 percent increase in forest cover leading to increases of 1 to 3 percent in annual farm profits, with variation across watersheds.[44]

- People in fishing villages in Micronesia were willing to pay up to 2.5 percent of their household incomes to protect 1,500 hectares of mangroves for the services they provide.[45]

Despite the few dozen case studies Mullan reviewed, valuation of tropical forest services remains the exception rather than the rule. The values of many of the services identified by scientists in chapter 3 have yet to be quantified by academic studies. Forest services that have been studied have been valued for only a handful of times and places, often using far cruder methods than economic valuations in other fields.

Forests have values, whether or not they have been quantified. Sadly, the paucity of valuation studies might lead public decision makers to overlook them. Why haven't more quantitative estimates been made of the value of forest services? It's worth considering a few of the barriers that make valuation so difficult, and hence so costly and rare.

Forest Services Are Not Marketed

Let's start with the obvious. Forest services aren't traded in markets. Hydroelectric companies can't buy a cubic meter of sediment reduction at Walmart; coastal villagers can't log on to eBay and purchase storm wave attenuation by the kilometer. Unlike with traded goods and services, economic researchers can't look to market prices for insights about the values of nature's untraded goods and services.

Instead, economic researchers can use three other techniques to infer these values.[46] First, where forest services are inputs to markets, they can analyze how the market quantities or values are affected by changes in forest condition. Forest insectivores, for example, control agricultural pests. The value of this service can be inferred from the higher crop yields and revenues on farms nearer to forests.[47] Similarly, cleaner water from forests can lead to better downstream health, which can be quantified through fewer sick days or less money spent on health treatments.[48] Or, the value of forest amenities can be estimated by observing how nearby real estate sells or leases at a premium. The advantage of this technique is that it directly relates to changes in human well-being. It is straightforward if the relationship between forest services and marketed goods and services is well understood. Data on this relationship are frequently absent, however.

Second, economic researchers can look at how much people are willing to spend in other markets to take advantage of forest values. For example, people's values for forest recreation are revealed by how much money and time they spend to visit a forest. Alternatively, forests' values can be inferred by calculating how much money people would have to spend in other markets to achieve the equivalent level of the services forests provide—for example, how much they would have to pay for health treatments from pharmaceuticals instead of forest plants or for storm protection from seawalls instead of mangroves.

Third, economic researchers can simply ask people how much they would be willing to pay to obtain forest services in a hypothetical market (a technique variously termed "contingent valuation" or "choice modeling"). This type of valuation, at least in principle, provides an indication of how much people would be willing to pay to retain those services, or how much they'd need to accept to be made whole if those services were diminished. Moreover, it can take into account people's full values for forests and their biodiversity, not just one particular good or service. Valuation through a hypothetical market is, however, potentially sensitive to a number of problems. People may be unfamiliar, for instance, with the services in question, or they may respond differently to a hypothetical questionnaire than they would act in real life. And, like actual markets, the method implicitly favors the preferences of people with more spending power. Nevertheless, a Blue Ribbon Panel that was convened by the National Oceanic and Atmospheric Administration (NOAA) in the wake of the 1989 Exxon Valdez oil spill and which included Nobel Prize-winning economists Ken Arrow and Robert Solow produced a set of best-practice methods for contingent valuation,[49] and hundreds of studies have been conducted using such methods since then.

The Chain of Cause and Effect Is Complex

Another reason forest services are difficult to value is because the chain of cause and effect leading to tangible benefits can be quite complex. Changes in management or policy lead to changes in forest conditions, which lead to changes in the provision of forest services, which in turn lead to changes in economic well-being. Quantifying each step of the chain requires data and, often, specialist knowledge spanning multiple disciplines.[50]

In the case of Colombia's Calima Dam, researchers used sophisticated vegetation and hydrological models to estimate how the increase in forest cover would lead to cleaner water and seasonal changes in river flow. They then used financial models to project how changes in water flow would lead to increased revenue and profit for the dam.

Since valuation studies are inherently multidisciplinary, they typically require collaborations among researchers familiar with both economics and the natural sciences. Such collaborations are more rare and often more costly than single-discipline studies. Furthermore, researchers often have few incentives to work across disciplinary boundaries, with economists particularly disinclined to do so.[51]

Because multidisciplinary studies are comparatively costly and rare, they tend to be geographically concentrated in a few places with available data or established researchers. Nearly half of the forty-five studies identified by Mullan were from just two countries—Indonesia and Brazil. Forests in poorer, more remote locations have been less studied.

Real-World Decisions Hinge on Marginal Values, Not Average Values

Many real-world decisions result in a little less forest here or a little more forest there. Regional development plans, forest restoration programs, investments in logging, or new national parks slow down or speed up deforestation incrementally. Few human decisions can completely eliminate forests from an entire region.

Thus, what's important for modeling the value of programs and policies is the change in service values arising from a relatively small change in forest cover on a landscape (that is, the "marginal value" of an additional hectare of forest).[52] None of the dam studies noted above did this kind of analysis. They compared the current value of forest services either to a scenario in which these watersheds were entirely denuded or to one where they were nearly entirely restored.

Omitting the calculation of forests' marginal values is common but misleading. In the study of medicines in Madagascar, the researchers calculated that the total value of medicinal plants from Makira's forests, as measured by avoided purchases of equivalent medicines from pharmacies, averaged out to $17 per hectare per year.[53] But total values don't necessarily say much about the lost value from deforesting a small amount of forest; if forest cover were diminished by 20 percent, for example, then access to medicinal plants might go down by just 5 percent.

One reason marginal and average values can differ is that forest services, like other services, can have diminishing returns. Barbier followed up the mangrove study from Thailand described above with another study looking at how storm attenuation varied with the width of mangroves along the shoreline. He found that a stretch of mangrove forest extending two hundred meters inland from the sea attenuated wave damage 36 percent as well as one extending a thousand meters inland.[54]

That relatively small amounts of forest can supply relatively large amounts of services is good news for local economies—it suggests the potential to expand some economic uses while retaining many of forests' most important services, as long as some threshold level of forest cover is maintained. But it presents a challenge for easy dollar-per-hectare extrapolations of forest values. One can't simply divide forests' total value by their area in hectares to calculate marginal value per hectare, nor multiply marginal value per hectare by forest area to obtain forests' total value.

Values Vary Widely across Space and Time

Another hurdle to overcome in valuing forest services accurately is that they are a moving target. Forest services can fluctuate widely across space and time even under undisturbed conditions.[55] The clean water forests provide to dams is more valuable during the dry season than the wet season, for example, and more valuable in low-flow years than high-flow years. The health damage caused by forest fires is more severe when prevailing winds blow haze over cities rather than out to sea.

Furthermore, forest values are greater when more people live where they can benefit from the services, be it onsite, downwind, downhill, or downriver. Mangroves provide greater protective services when more people live inland from them, and forests' role in cleaning water has a greater value the more people use the water downstream.

The value of forests also depends on the existence of technologies that can substitute for services. Makira's medicinal plants are less used, and therefore less valued, in villages where Western drugs are available from hospitals or clinics. The damage from Indonesia's fires was lower in households that could afford to buy appropriate face masks or air conditioning. On the other hand, technologies can also increase the value of forests; the clean water provided by the forests above

Three Gorges Dam increased in value after more turbines were installed.

Extrapolating and Aggregating Values Is Even Harder

As challenging as it is to credibly value one forest service in one place and time, extrapolating values elsewhere or aggregating the values of multiple services is even harder.[56] As just mentioned, the value of forest services is highly context specific, depending on where and when these services are provided and to how many people and the extent to which technologies act as a substitute or complement. Values expressed in dollars per hectare can't simply be transferred to other locales, where services may be affected by different landscape characteristics (such as topography, wind direction, or soil type), different beneficiary characteristics (population size, wealth, or employment), or differing use of technologies that substitute for or complement forest services. For example, Sáenz and his coauthors were quick to point out that the values of forests to Calima Dam can't be extrapolated to other forests, even in adjacent watersheds. Such values are dependent not only on aspects of the topography and microclimate of the forested watershed, but also on the capacity of the dam and the preexisting sedimentation of its reservoir.

Where estimates of benefits are transferred from one study area to another, it is best to stick to similar contexts and control for differences in relevant characteristics.[57] Generally it does not make sense to transfer benefits between very different contexts—for example, between tropical and temperate forests or between developed and developing countries.

Furthermore, summing values across multiple goods and services generally doesn't work if there are trade-offs between one good or service and another. Since the collection of fuelwood, for example, comes at the direct expense of carbon storage for a given area of forest, it makes little sense to sum these two values as if they were independent.

An oft-referenced 1997 study by ecological economist Robert Costanza and his colleagues tallied the value of the world's ecosystem services to be $33 trillion per year in 1995 dollars.[58] A 2012 update revised the figure upward to $72 trillion per year in 2007 dollars, and it valued the flow of services from tropical forests at $5,300 per hectare per year.[59] These analyses arrived at their numbers by violating nearly every single one of the above provisos—by conflating average and marginal costs, extrapolating values across wildly different contexts, and summing the values of contradictory services, to name a few. For this reason, the attention-generating studies have been heavily critiqued.[60] A different meta-analysis that attempted to account for geographical variation found a lower average value of tropical forest services: $1,300 per hectare per year.[61]

Why have we discussed at such length the challenges associated with valuation? Certainly not to say researchers shouldn't try to quantify the value of forest services. To the contrary, researchers should undertake more valuation studies, in more places and more times, and in more sophisticated ways. Indeed, the breakthroughs in fine-scale satellite data described in chapter 4 enable researchers to examine as never before the relationships between deforestation and phenomena such as diseases or hydropower production.

Rather, we have discussed these challenges for two reasons. The first is to explain why studies of forest values have been so few and far between. That forest values have so frequently remained unquantified doesn't mean they don't exist. In fact, these values can be considerable. But the scarcity of credible estimates of forests' values have rendered them all but invisible in economic decision making. The second reason is so we can show later in this chapter how carbon values are easier to quantify than the values of most other forest services.

Concentrated Values Are Small; Large Values Are Infrequent or Dispersed

A few themes recur throughout academic studies of the values of forest services.[62] First, forest services exist, and they come in all shapes and sizes, from providing shade and pollination to nearby coffee farmers to affecting air quality several countries away. Heightened recognition of forest services empowers the beneficiaries—be they people farming downstream or people breathing air downwind—to press for forest protection, as described further in chapter 10.

Second, compared to the revenue that can be obtained from farming or ranching, the locally received values of forest services are often small. As a result, ecosystem services are rarely the decisive factor in decisions about whether or not to deforest. They are either collateral damage of a decision to deforest or the icing on the cake of a decision to conserve.

Third, where forest service values are large, they are usually infrequent, as in the case of protection from tsunami waves, as shown in figure 6.2. Or they are dispersed across many beneficiaries, as in the case of

clean water. Or they are both infrequent and dispersed, as in the case of preventing air pollution from forest fires.

Because the beneficiaries of forest services are dispersed, infrequently served, and often unaware they even are beneficiaries, it is hard for them to coalesce into organized political constituencies in support of forest conservation. In contrast, farmers or loggers benefit directly and tangibly from clearing forest. It's easy to figure out which group has the advantage politically. We discuss the politics of deforestation in tropical countries in far greater depth in chapter 10.

Loss of Forest Goods and Services Is Regressive

Across the tropics, poor and economically marginalized people are often the most dependent on forests' goods and services. Likewise, they are the most vulnerable to negative impacts of deforestation. This is the case for a number of reasons:[63]

- Remote areas with poor infrastructure and little market access often have both high forest cover and high incidence of poverty.
- Many of the benefits from forest goods and services amount to a few dollars per household per year. Such small amounts are negligible to richer households but can comprise a significant proportion of annual agricultural profits for poor farm households.
- The benefits from disease prevention or mitigation of natural disasters may be greater for poor households because their baseline vulnerability is higher. For example, the impacts of the Indonesian

Figure 6.2: Forest services have been difficult to monetize because most large economic values are either dispersed widely or occur infrequently.

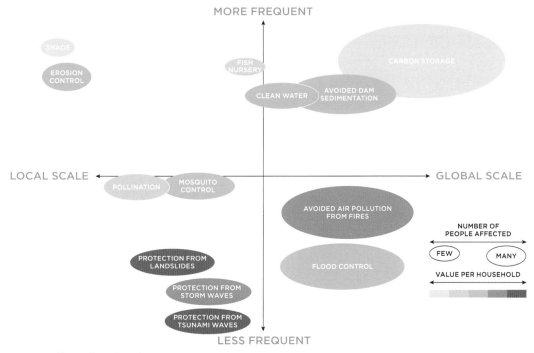

Source: Mullan, "The Value of Forest Ecosystem Services."

forest fires were most severe for the poor, the young, and the elderly.[64] Similarly, poor households were most severely affected by, as well as least able to recover from, the 2004 Indian Ocean tsunami.[65]

- Poor people are less able to afford substitutes for forest goods (such as clean water, wild fish, and meat) or services (such as disease control and pollination).
- Finally, poor people may be consuming forest goods because they are poor, turning to the forest for their livelihoods as a last resort.

Similarly, the loss of forest goods and services has the potential to worsen gender in-equalities, due to differences across genders in occupations and household decision making.[66] For example, a CIFOR study of forest-dependent communities in Pará, Brazil, found that men generally placed a greater value on timber, which provides greater cash value, while women generally placed a greater value on forest plants that could be harvested for food or medicine.[67] According to anthropologist Lorena Aguilar, "Globally, women's heavy dependence on forests and their associated products means that they often have more at stake than men when forests are degraded or when forest access is denied."[68]

For all the reasons listed above, deforestation is regressive, hitting the poor hardest. In contrast, the economic benefits that come from new land uses, such as agriculture, mining, or logging, may or may not be pro-poor—that is, improving the condition of poor people the most. Some people will clearly win from a transition from forests to fields and may be able to afford market substitutes for the services they once obtained from forests. But others will be harmed by the transition, losing access to forest services while remaining excluded from the new economic activities. Scientist Samuel Myers and his colleagues described an "ecological transition" in which,

> over the course of economic development, people replace complex, natural systems with engineered infrastructure and markets as the source of food, water purification, shelter, fuel, clothing, and protection from natural hazards and infectious disease. A majority of people are able to make this transition and reap the benefits [of economic development]. However, the poorest and least entitled may fail to make the transition successfully, unable to access either the engineered infrastructure or markets. They are left with degraded natural systems but little with which to replace them.[69]

Myers and his colleagues suspected that roughly one billion people worldwide come out on the losing end of the ecological transition. In cities, these are slum dwellers lacking access to basic services, while in rural areas they are the resource-dependent poor faced with inexorably degrading soils, water, forests, and fish, in a "quiet erosion of natural infrastructure."[70]

How much poor people gain from the economic activities that replace forests varies considerably from place to place. In Madagas-

car, poor, smallholder farmers growing rice are responsible for a large portion of deforestation. On the other hand, in the Brazilian Amazon, a large portion of forest is cleared by large wealthy ranchers and soy growers, as described in chapter 7. In Indonesia and Malaysia, the conversion from forest to oil palm generates considerable employment and revenue in aggregate, but local people may lose livelihoods from forests without benefiting from new employment opportunities on plantations.[71] One recent study found 85 percent of cash flow from oil palm accrued to "local elites and plantation developers," rather than to farmers or land clearers.[72]

Economist Ken Chomitz reviewed the complex relationship between forests and poverty in *At Loggerheads?* in 2006.[73] Since then, the predominant driver of deforestation has continued to shift away from smallholder farming to large-scale commercial plantation agriculture. We are not aware of any more recent comprehensive review of winners and losers from the transition from tropical forests to agriculture, and we see this as a high priority for future research.

That forest services tend to benefit poor people disproportionately takes on special importance with climate change. As discussed in chapter 3, forests are expected to help people adapt to climate change by lessening the impact of storms, floods, landslides, droughts, and fires. In some cases, they may be able to do so more cheaply than engineered infrastructure, as in the case of mangroves and seawalls in Thailand. Forests also can provide a natural safety net when crops fail. Both of these helpful effects of forests especially benefit poor people. On the other hand, while income from the agriculture that replaces forests can also provide a cushion against the impacts of climate change, this income may or may not especially benefit the poor, as discussed above.

Forest Values Are Invisible to Development Indicators and Efforts

Because the values of forest goods and services are so difficult to measure, they have been systematically excluded from public development planning. A case in point is the flagship macroeconomic indicator for measuring national economic progress—gross domestic product (GDP).

GDP measures the monetary value of all goods and services produced within a country in a given year. The statistic plays a central role in the economic life of national governments. When GDP goes up, the prime minister can take credit for wise economic policies and basks in the glow of adulatory coverage in *The Economist*. When GDP goes down, the minister faces criticism from the opposition party for a sluggish economy. In the short term, a government can prop up GDP by borrowing, printing money, or otherwise diverting resources to inject funds into the economy.[74] But sustained GDP growth requires across-the-board policies, and policies that are expected to affect GDP positively hold a closer place to economic planners' hearts and minds than those that don't.

As an indicator of economic progress, GDP has long faced criticism from many angles.[75] For one thing, it doesn't measure costs and damages. If a vandal breaks a storefront window, the new replacement window is counted in GDP, but the depreciation of the old window isn't. When a child gets sick, the medicine her parents purchase is tallied in GDP, but the child's suffering is not, nor is her stay-at-home parent's bedside labor. Economists have noted that a more appropriate metric of national economic well-being would go beyond gross income to measure net changes in wealth, including natural wealth.[76]

In 1972, Bhutan famously ditched GDP in favor of "gross national happiness"; in 2010, Britain's prime minister David Cameron augmented GDP with similar metrics following the report of a commission led by Nobel Prize-winning economist Joseph Stiglitz and other economic luminaries.[77] Yet enough people see GDP as a good enough proxy for economic well-being that its use endures.

One shortcoming of GDP is particularly salient for a discussion of forests and climate: it does not account for goods and services that do not enter formal markets. Decreases in household charcoal production or natural medicines following forest fires are rarely reflected in national income; increases in sediment retention following reforestation aren't counted, either. As a result, forest conservation is underweighted in national policy decisions relative to farms, mines, and timber concessions, the outputs of which contribute to GDP.

The invisibility of forest values in development statistics extends from the macroeconomic to the microeconomic. Statistical agencies in most tropical countries conduct household surveys to estimate the number of people living in poverty; the estimates are then used by national agencies and international organizations to design and target antipoverty programs. These include national Household Income, Consumption and

Expenditure (HICE) surveys and the World Bank's Living Standards Measurement Study (LSMS).

The details of both questionnaires vary on a country-by-country basis, but forest goods are undercounted, while forest services are left out entirely. Forest foods are usually included, though aggregated with other crops. Fodder, medicine, and building materials from forests are not included. Charcoal is included in the surveys of some countries but not others. As a result, most returns to household welfare from forest conservation pass unnoticed, and forest income is underappreciated as a means of escaping poverty, relative to income from other activities.

Another consequence of the invisibility of forest values is that consideration of forest services is nearly entirely absent from the strategies used to promote development in nonforest sectors. Agricultural programs focus on increasing crop areas and crop yields, for example, but they neglect the services forests provide to agricultural production in the form of pollination, pest control, shade, water, and favorable microclimates. Antimalarial efforts focus on spraying mosquitoes, but not on suppressing them by maintaining forests. Energy efforts focus on building dams but not usually on maintaining the forested watersheds and clean reservoirs that keep those dams functioning. And so on.

Making Forest Services More Visible

A variety of ongoing initiatives are striving to make forest goods and services more visible to development planners. At the macroeconomic level, the World Bank-led partnership known as Wealth Accounting and the Value of Ecosystem Services (WAVES) convenes eight countries that endeavor to incorporate the value of ecosystem services into national accounts.[78] Several of these countries are valuing forests, starting mostly with timber stock assessments, with plans to move on to other goods and services.

At the microeconomic level, a consortium of international development and research institutions has produced guidance on how to measure the socioeconomic contributions of forests to household welfare and livelihoods.[79] The LSMS has already pilot-tested a more detailed forestry module for its questionnaire in Indonesia, which bodes well for its inclusion in future rounds of household surveys.[80]

Then, too, a variety of initiatives are working to inculcate understanding of ecosystems services into development decision making more generally, following on the influential Millennium Ecosystem Assessment commissioned in 2000 by U.N. Secretary-General Kofi Annan.[81] The Economics of Ecosystems and Biodiversity (TEEB) initiative seeks to "make nature's values visible" through sector-, country-, and biome-specific studies of ecosystem service values.[82] Meanwhile, the Natural Capital Project provides software tools and analysis to integrate nature's values into specific decisions of governments, companies, and development finance institutions.[83] The World Bank's Program on Forests (PROFOR) is studying how forests can help the agriculture, water, and energy sectors adapt to climate change.[84]

Still, institutional inertia is powerful. Inclusion of forest values in national accounts, household surveys, and public decisions remains the exception rather than the rule.

Part of the problem may stem from a failure to communicate on the part of the scientists and economists conducting research on forest values. Researchers have tended to express their topline results in terms of dollars per hectare. This metric is intended to speak to a hypothetical land user who is deciding whether it is more profitable to clear or conserve forest. But the dollars-per-hectare metric is poorly aligned with the respective professional objectives of sectoral experts contemplating how to improve health, energy, or food outcomes. These objectives are more commonly expressed in disability-adjusted life years (DALYs, for public health professionals), kilowatt hours (kWh) of electricity (for hydroelectric engineers), or tons of agricultural output (for food security planners). As a result of this misalignment, ecosystem services are not as well known or understood by sectoral development professionals as they should be.

Awareness is only part of the reason the values of forest services are slow to be included in public decisions. An arguably greater factor is stove-piped institutional responsibilities across sectors. Energy planners in Sub-Saharan Africa already know charcoal is a major source of energy for their populations; public works officials in Indonesia are well aware flooding and landslides due to deforestation impose huge costs. But if they don't see forest management as part of their institutional mandates, integration has to come at a higher political level—for example, at a ministry of planning or finance. The same can be said for professionals working in bilateral aid agencies and multilateral development banks.

Forest Services Are Largely Intangible to Land-Use Decision Makers

Forest services often pass unnoticed by another influential group of people—the local land users who decide whether to clear or maintain forests. Of course, local people making use of land have a highly attuned awareness of the forest goods they harvest. But because many services of forests accrue downwind, downriver, or downhill, people living nearby may not notice them. Even if they are aware that forest services provide benefits to others, they may have little incentive to take these values into consideration themselves.

Efforts to make the value of forests' goods and services more tangible to private land users stretch back decades. The history of tropical conservation in recent years has largely been an ongoing campaign to make forests worth more alive than dead. If forest goods and services can be monetized as hard income for private land users, so the thinking goes, local land users will be more likely to conserve those forests voluntarily. This approach to conservation runs parallel, and is often in deliberate response, to a "fortress conservation" approach centered on excluding access to natural resources—for example, by putting up fences and enforcing laws against poaching.[85]

Attempts to monetize forest values in private land-use decisions have included the promotion of sustainable forest products, bioprospecting, ecotourism, and payments for ecosystem services. Some of these initiatives have had scattered successes, but as a whole they have not slowed the rate of tropical deforestation. It is worth recounting the hurdles such projects have encountered before considering some important reasons to think carbon is different and, therefore, why international carbon payments might avoid the same pitfalls.

Sustainable Timber and Forest Products

As mentioned several times above, people harvest a wide range of goods from tropical forests, including timber, charcoal, foods, and medicines. Those who rely on forests for all or some of their livelihoods can be a strong constituency in support of their conservation. Rubber tappers in Brazil, for example, played an early and pivotal role in advocating for protection of the Amazon forest; more information on this is in chapters 7 and 10.[86] Boosting the economic fortunes of forest-dependent people—for example, by providing marketing support for their products—might make them better able to resist the lure of converting forest to cash crops or to attract government support to repel others who would do so.

One of the earliest iterations of efforts to make forests worth more alive than dead came through efforts to promote certified-sustainable timber. Conventional logging in the tropics generally involves extracting high-value trees as quickly as possible before abandoning the residual land or selling it off for conversion.[87] Logging potentially offers an economically viable middle path, however, between total preservation and complete conversion. Even while logging degrades forest carbon stock and threatens some species, it may be compatible with the survival of other species, and it allows for the continued provision of ecosystem services.[88]

Furthermore, logging practices vary in their potential to mitigate harmful impacts.[89]

The idea behind sustainable timber production is that high-value trees are replanted or regenerated within natural forests at the same rate they are harvested, thereby ensuring a continual supply of timber.[90] Since this type of timber production is more expensive than conventional logging,[91] incremental costs need to be covered by educated consumers willing to pay a price premium for the maintenance of biodiverse forest.

The area of forest certified by either the Forest Stewardship Council or the Program for the Endorsement of Forest Certification has expanded rapidly in the past two decades, from 3 million hectares in 1995 to 180 million hectares as of 2013—an area the size of Indonesia.[92] The vast majority of certified-sustainable timber production, however, takes place in temperate or boreal countries; considerably less than 10 percent of the area under certification is in the tropics.[93] Tropical forests have lagged due in part to demanding requirements and high costs of certification in developing countries.[94] Whether it is even possible for sustainable management practices to maintain the persistence of valuable timber species for more than a few harvest cycles has been disputed.[95]

Furthermore, green consumer sentiment has proved elusive outside of a few pockets. Price premiums have failed to materialize, although fears of reputational damage and lost market access have turned out to be salient,[96] as discussed further in chapter 8. Even where certified forest operations have used better social and environmental practices, the extent to which certification has led to the changes in practices, as opposed to merely recognizing companies whose operations were sustainable to begin with, is unclear. Rigorous impact evaluations of forest certification are rare.[97]

In the early 2000s, a review characterized sustainable timber certification as having failed in its original ambitious goal of saving tropical biodiversity but as having succeeded in raising awareness of environmental issues in both tropical forest countries and consumer countries.[98] A 2016 meta-analysis concluded that, while certification rarely has led to price premiums, it has had benefits with regard to learning, community empowerment, and reputation.[99]

Concurrent with the sustainable timber initiative came an effort to make forests worth more alive than dead through attempts to increase the value of nontimber forest products by expanding their markets from local subsistence communities to consumers more broadly. The idea is that income from sustainably harvested products could make the sustainable exploitation of forests competitive with destructive conventional logging and agriculture or, at the very least, could provide incomes sufficient to maintain dignified livelihoods.[100] Nontimber forest products for which increased commercialization has been promoted as a livelihood and conservation strategy include seeds, flowers, fruits, leaves, roots, bark, latex, resins, and other nonwood plant parts.[101] Rainforest-sourced Brazil nuts were an advertised ingredient in Rainforest Crunch, the short-lived Ben and Jerry's flavor mentioned in chapter 1.

Some boutique successes have been achieved, such as in the marketing of shea nuts (a West African tree product used in cosmetics).[102] By and large, however, attempts to market nontimber forest products have met one of two opposite fates. Either they failed to take off, due to market barriers or competition from substitute plantation production (such as production of chicle, a Central American gum used to make chewing gum),[103] or they were victims of their own success, leading to overexploitation of the product in the wild (e.g. rattans in Kalimantan and Vietnam; paper mulberry in Laos; wild mushrooms in Korea).[104]

Bioprospecting

Hodgkin's lymphoma, a cancer of the immune system, once resulted in death in more than half of cases. Survival rates improved, however, from 40 percent in the early 1960s to 88 percent by the first decade of the 2000s,[105] thanks in large part to a drug called vinblastine. Vinblastine is one of four life-saving cancer medications, along with vincristine, vinorelbine, and vindesine, derived from the rosy periwinkle, a rainforest plant from Madagascar. The second most-used class of anticancer drugs, these medicines are also used to treat diabetes and high blood pressure.[106]

Tropical forests are the sources for many other lifesaving medications, too. Quinine, widely used to treat malaria, comes from the *Cinchona* tree in the Peruvian Andes. Tubocurarine, a muscle relaxant used before surgeries, comes from an Amazonian liana and was first used in poison arrows.[107] Progesterone, an active ingredient in birth control pills, is derived from Mexican wild yams.[108]

Pharmaceuticals are a global $300 billion a year industry, and many of these drugs have their origins in traditional plant-based medicines. Of all the thousand or so chemicals approved by the U.S. Food and Drug Administration in the past twenty-five years, 70 percent have biological origins.[109]

The link between tropical forest conservation and the development of new medicines makes intuitive sense. Lose the forests, and potential new lifesaving drugs will go undiscovered. The race against the clock was brought home in 1987, when researchers from the U.S. National Cancer Institute discovered anti-HIV properties in a compound called Calanolide A, collected from a rare rainforest tree in Malaysian Borneo. Upon this discovery researchers dashed back to Sarawak in search of another specimen, only to find that the *Calophyllum* tree from which the original sample had been collected had been cut down. No further trees of the species could be found. Relief came only when the tree turned up in the Singapore Botanic Garden, collected by British colonists more than a century earlier.[110]

That forests are the source of so many medicines led to optimism around the possibility of financing the conservation of forests through bioprospecting—the search for plants and animals from which medicinally valuable compounds might be obtained. But even as some rainforest plants are the source of highly sought-after and lucrative medicines, translating this market demand into a funding stream for forests has proved difficult. The open-access nature of most tropical forests meant that for years, drug companies were able to obtain plants from them without paying anyone, and often without the awareness of anyone in the forest countries. As a result, forest countries leveled charges of "biopiracy,"

and Brazil clamped down on foreign researchers' access to the Amazon.[111] Charges receded after the official adoption of the Nagoya Protocol on access to genetic resources and fair and equitable sharing of benefits under the Convention on Biological Diversity, which was adopted in 2010 and entered into legal force in 2014.

The medicinal value of rainforest plants has been difficult to monetize for another reason, too. Once a few plants have been extracted, they need no longer be collected from the wild, rendering the forest where they were first found of little residual value. Plants found to have medicinal value can be grown in greenhouses, or their chemicals can be synthesized in labs. These days rosy periwinkle is grown in greenhouses, not gathered from forests; and of those plants that are still collected from the wild for medicinal use, dozens are threatened with extinction due to overharvesting.[112]

Furthermore, the pharmaceutical value of forest plants yields diminishing returns. Due to the patent system, the most lucrative medicinal properties are those not already found in existing drugs. Consequently, each successful discovery reduces the value to pharmaceutical companies of additional plants with that property.[113]

Excitement around bioprospecting as a forest conservation strategy hit a high-water mark in 1991, when the pharmaceutical giant Merck paid $1.1 million to Costa Rica for the exclusive right to test biological samples of the nation's plants and animals for pharmaceutical properties, plus royalties from any resulting drugs. But no new drugs ever came of it. This type of deal was never replicated, and the program was quietly shuttered in

2008. Drug companies shifted their search for new drugs away from natural plants and toward high-volume screening of chemical compounds, which, ironically, hasn't yielded any new drugs, either.[114]

Ecotourism

Africa's oldest national park, Virunga, in the Democratic Republic of Congo, offers tourists the trip of a lifetime: the chance to get up close to a mountain gorilla, of which fewer than nine hundred remain in the wild.[115] A permit to view these gentle giants costs $400 for one hour as of 2015, and every year thousands of tourists pay for this privilege.[116] The economic contribution of gorilla tourism to the communities around Virunga extends far beyond park entrance fees to hotels, restaurants, transportation, and souvenirs.

Countries across the tropics have been able to monetize the value of forests by selling visits to unique wild areas, in a business known as ecotourism. Malaysia's Taman Negara, Peru's Manu National Park, and India's Gir Forest are all major tourist attractions. Costa Rica's largest industry and foreign exchange earner is tourism, resting on a foundation of protected wild forests.[117]

Most tropical forests have difficulty replicating these successes, however. Demand for rainforest tourism is limited, and largely saturated. While going to see gorillas may be the trip of a lifetime, it's not a trip one takes every weekend nor even every year. And for every European or American who makes the trek to the tropics, many more will see rainforests only in nature documentaries. Tourism is not viable as a conservation strategy for the entirety of the world's 20 million square kilometers of tropical forests.

Furthermore, rainforest tourism has a serious drawback as a conservation strategy: a park's profitability may be only loosely correlated with its conservation value. Côte d'Ivoire's Luxembourg-sized Taï National Park protects the largest remaining block of primary rainforest in West Africa, along with large populations of chimpanzees and highly endangered pygmy hippos. Yet this World Heritage Site receives few tourists. Meanwhile, the Kakum Rainforest in neighboring Ghana is just one-tenth the size of Taï, but it receives more than a hundred thousand tourists a year due to its excellent tourism infrastructure and easy proximity to Cape Coast. For tourists seeking a guaranteed sighting of wildlife, the best bet is often a small wildlife sanctuary or rescue center rather than a vast tract of dense wilderness. Tourists generally flock to the accessible, comfortable, and predictable; most remote tropical forests in their natural state are none of these.

Payments for Ecosystem Services

Rather than boosting incomes from selling forest goods or tourism, why not pay landowners directly for the services their forests provide? That's the idea behind "payments for ecosystem services" (PES), in which beneficiaries of forest services, or governments acting on their behalf, pay forest landowners contingent upon the provision of the service. Conditionality is key to the concept: payments are made only if ex post monitoring shows the service flow, or the forest area as a proxy for the service flow, has been maintained.[118]

As in so many other areas of forest conservation, Costa Rica has been a pioneer in PES. In 1997, its government began signing contracts with landowners in selected regions who agreed not to deforest their land in exchange for payments of $42 per hectare per year. The program has since expanded to nearly one million hectares, and, as of 2013, it paid up to $80 per hectare per year for forest conservation and up to $300 per hectare per year for reforestation.[119] The concept has been adapted in various forms by Colombia, Ecuador, Mexico, Vietnam, and other countries.

Payments for ecosystem services are conceptually appealing. Downstream beneficiaries of a service (for example, public utilities that depend on clean water for hydropower) pay upstream providers of that service (landowners whose forest conservation provides cleaner water). The buyers benefit from greater production of the service; the sellers benefit from a new source of income. In principle, PES can be applied to any forest service for which there is demand: clean water, clean air, carbon storage, or biodiversity conservation. Some have objected that paying for forests' services may undermine intrinsic reasons to value nature; indeed, monetary benefits have been shown to crowd out the effectiveness of moral suasion in some other contexts.[120] But since monetary motivations frequently drive deforestation, it seems reasonable to think they might be harnessed to drive forest conservation, too.

Payments for ecosystem services have an Achilles' heel, however: land rights are unclear or insecure across much of the forested tropics. As most intact forest areas have few formal landowners, the costs of establishing the property rights necessary for PES to function can be very high. As a result, PES simply hasn't been tried in that many places. In the Poverty and Environment Network study cited at the beginning of this chapter, revenue from PES comprised less than 0.4 percent of income in the forest households studied.[121]

Where payments for ecosystem services have been made, deforestation has been lower, as discussed more in chapter 7. But the question of causality lingers. In the early years of Costa Rica's PES program, much of the money went to farms that wouldn't have cleared their forests anyway, resulting in less cost-effective conservation than if payments had been targeted better.[122] More recently, payments have been targeted for greater impact.[123]

In many of the PES programs to date, dollar values are often modest relative to alternative land uses. Ecuador pays landowners $10 to $30 per hectare per year for forest protection; Mexico pays $27 to $36; Vietnam pays about $15 to $20.[124] When PES recipients choose to maintain forests, they may be motivated to do so by nonpecuniary aspects of the program, such as formal recognition of property rights or the newly heightened presence of forest monitors.[125] And income from PES can supplement other forest-based income, such as well-managed extraction of timber and nontimber forest products; it doesn't need to stand alone.

An intriguing twist on PES is the "ecological fiscal transfer," in which public funds are transferred from one level of government to another based on indicators of environmental performance. In both Brazil and Portugal, the national or state governments transfer funds to municipalities based on the extent of their protected areas.[126] A very large ecological fiscal transfer mechanism specifically for forests was recently enacted by India, as described in box 6.1.

Can Concern for the Climate Make Carbon Values Visible and Tangible?

As described above, most forest values are hard to quantify, and the success of most previous efforts to make them tangible has been limited. Yet, hope is on the horizon in the form of concern about climate change. The service forests provide by absorbing and storing carbon is relatively easy to value, and carbon payments have great potential to succeed where previous efforts have fallen short.

Forests' climate service is easier to value than other services for a few reasons. For one thing, the chain of cause and effect is straightforward. As explained in chapter 2, forests that are burned release their carbon to the atmosphere, causing climate change, while standing forests absorb carbon dioxide, combating it. As described in chapter 4, changes in forest carbon stocks are becoming ever easier to measure. In contrast, assessing the role of forests in suppressing diseases, or promoting favorable weather patterns at continental scales, is highly complex.

Box 6.1: Innovation in Paying for Ecosystem Services: India's Pro-Forest Tax Revenue Distribution

Ever since the country achieved independence in 1947, the central government of India has distributed tax revenue to states according to a formula that includes their populations, poverty levels, and other criteria. In 2015, India's Finance Commission added forest area to this formula, with changes monitored by satellite, as part of India's long-running Forest Survey.[a]

As a result, states that deforest will now lose tax revenue, and states that regrow forest will gain it. Roughly $7 billion to $12 billion a year will be distributed to states on the basis of their forest cover.[b] Assuming future Finance Commissions keep the criterion in the tax revenue distribution formula, this will be the world's largest source of performance-based finance for forest conservation.[c]

According to India's official climate pledge to the United Nations Framework Convention on Cliamte Change (UNFCCC), the tax revenue distribution reform gives a "massive boost" to afforestation, a central component of India's climate goals.[d] The forest-based revenue transfer works out to about $174 per hectare per year.[e] That's larger than the payments made to individual landowners under PES programs, and it should get the attention of officials in state governments.

a. "The Fourteenth Finance Commission," Ministry of Finance, Government of India, January 2, 2013, http://finmin.nic.in/14fincomm/14fcrengVol1.pdf.

b. "India's Intended Nationally Determined Contribution: Working towards Climate Justice," submitted by the Government of India to the United Nations Framework Convention on Climate Change, 2015, http://www4.unfccc.int/submissions/INDC/Published%20Documents/India/1/INDIA%20INDC%20TO%20UNFCCC.pdf.

c. J. Busch, "India's Big Climate Move," Views from the Center blog, February 27, 2015, Center for Global Development, Washington, DC, http://www.cgdev.org/blog/indias-big-climate-move.

d. "India's Intended Nationally Determined Contribution: Working towards Climate Justice," submitted by the Government of India to the United Nations Framework Convention on Climate Change, 2015, http://www4.unfccc.int/submissions/INDC/Published%20Documents/India/1/INDIA%20INDC%20TO%20UNFCCC.pdf.

e. Ibid., 28.

For another thing, every ton of carbon counts equally. The first ton of carbon stored in a forest is just as valuable in preventing climate change as the thousandth, which is not the case for, say, storm wave attenuation. And a ton of carbon stored in trees is just as valuable today as it was yesterday or will be tomorrow. The same can't be said about water purification, the value of which varies between the wet and dry seasons, or air quality, as the damage from forest fires shifts with the direction of the wind.

Furthermore, because carbon dioxide mixes globally, the value of a ton of carbon doesn't depend on whether the forest in which it is stored is in a remote wilderness or on the outskirts of a city. Proximity of potential beneficiaries simply doesn't matter for carbon storage, as it does for pollination or flood control.

Forests' climate service is also easier to value because of how its value is communicated. As mentioned above, the values of forest services are rarely communicated using the metrics familiar to sectoral development planners—kilowatt hours, disability-adjusted life years (DALYs), and the like. Forests' climate services, however, are routinely expressed in terms well known to the climate policy community: tC/ha, tCO$_2$/ha, and \$/tCO$_2$. Expressing forest values in familiar language, as in chapter 5, arguably is partly responsible for the relatively seamless discussion of forests within climate policy forums.

There are also very good reasons to think carbon payments have a better chance of being successful than previous efforts to make forests worth more alive than dead. Most of the challenges that have handicapped sustainable forest products, bioprospecting,

ecotourism, and PES do not apply to REDD+.

First, even if nontimber forest products or ecotourism ventures were successful locally, demand for these goods and services would simply be too small to turn the tide on deforestation globally or even nationally. But potential global demand for the carbon storage provided by tropical forests is practically limitless. If and when the world gets serious about limiting global warming to well below 2 degrees Celsius, as agreed to in the Paris Agreement of 2015,[127] it would swallow in one sitting all the emission reductions from ending tropical deforestation, before going back for seconds with forest restoration.

Second, previous approaches have fought project-by-project battles; they've been bystanders to nationwide policy wars.[128] But international carbon payments under REDD+ would be transacted with national or state governments. These governments, unlike site-specific projects, have the authority to address many of the root causes of deforestation (by, for example, enacting and enforcing laws). Governments would have the responsibility of sharing benefits and responsibilities among stakeholders in a way that prevents deforestation and respects agreed-on international safeguard principles. They might decide to contract with individual households, as with PES, but this is by no means a necessity.

Third, many previous approaches faced diminishing marginal returns. A large amount of tourism or medicinal plants could be produced from a small amount of forest, with limited rationale to conserve forest thereafter. But there are no diminishing returns to carbon. The value of the carbon that one forest stores doesn't diminish if another forest stores carbon, too.

Fourth, some previous approaches promoted income from exploiting rather than maintaining forests. Ensuring a long-term flow of revenue from forest products or tourism requires self-restraint. Overexploitation can quickly destroy the resource, killing the goose that lays the golden egg. Carbon, however, presents no such challenge. Carbon revenue, like revenue from PES, is directly tied to the maintenance of forests rather than their exploitation, and, as with revenue from PES, it can supplement other forest-based income; it doesn't need to stand alone.

Still, while the idea of translating demand for forests' climate services into tangible income seems promising, it is no slam dunk. International carbon payments face their own set of challenges. As recounted in chapter 9, international negotiations around technical issues associated with paying for forest carbon have taken a decade. Even when government-to-government payments arrive, forest countries may have difficulty translating national income opportunities into local incentives to conserve forests.[129] Even if payments increase the value of standing forests, efforts to conserve them may encounter political resistance from entrenched interests, as elaborated in chapter 10. And while political support within rich countries for conserving tropical forests is broad, opposition to the specifics of paying for that conservation is vocal, as explained in chapter 11.

The largest challenge by far is that carbon payments depend on external funding. That funding has been low, slow, and wrapped in bureaucracy, as described in chapter 12. While all of these challenges are real, the later chapters of this book document the progress being made in overcoming them.

Side Benefits of Carbon Conservation

As evidenced above, forests offer far more than just sticks of carbon. They provide clean water and protection from storms; they produce medicines and other valuable goods; they provide local cooling. Many people value forests for nonutilitarian reasons as well: for the habitat they provide to plants and animals, or for intrinsic sentimental or cultural reasons. Supposing international payments are successful in conserving forests based on their carbon value, where does this leave other forest services?

Some have worried that carbon-focused conservation will come at the expense of biodiversity or other ecosystem services.[130] To a large degree, however, forests' goods, services, and intrinsic values are bundled and inseparable; protecting a natural tropical forest for its carbon value ensures that many other services are provided as "co-benefits" by default.[131]

Plus, there's nothing about a carbon conservation policy that prevents governments or land users from going even further in promoting noncarbon benefits of forests. People can use the finance from carbon payments to prioritize forest conservation where biological or hydrological benefits are greatest;[132] or they can use the payment infrastructure set up for carbon to make supplemental payments for noncarbon services;[133] or they can complement carbon payments with distinct policies for other services.[134]

Another side benefit of setting up carbon payments brings the chapter full circle: they help place a dollar value on forest services. Real-world transactions, such as PES or REDD+, have a big advantage over the techniques discussed earlier in this chapter: price discovery. Researchers no longer need to model hypothetical markets to estimate forest values; they can look at evidence from how much real buyers have paid and real sellers have accepted in actual purchases.

Protecting a natural tropical forest for its carbon value ensures that many other services are provided as "co-benefits" by default.

Conclusion

Forests provide myriad goods and services, from medicinal plants and clean water to storm protection and suppression of fires. While the values of some services in some places and times have been quantified, many more have not. The difficulty of valuing tropical forest services renders them all but invisible from public policies and development strategies and private land-use decisions. Nevertheless, these values exist, and they are particularly important to poorer households.

A long-standing goal of forest conservation initiatives has been to make the value of forest services tangible to land users, thereby making forests worth more alive than dead. Initiatives to promote sustainable forest products, bioprospecting, ecotourism, and payments for ecosystem services have had scattered successes, but they have not turned the tide on deforestation at the national or pantropical scales.

Forests' climate services, however, may be able to overcome both challenges. They are easier to value than other services, and their values are often larger relative to both alternative land uses and alternative climate actions. There are a variety of reasons to think international carbon payments, if financed, will be able to succeed where previous enterprises have fallen short.

International carbon payments can put in place financial incentives to conserve forests, but deciding to reduce deforestation, and figuring out how to do so, is squarely the prerogative of forest countries. A tremendous example of how to reduce deforestation is provided by Brazil. In the decade since 2004, Brazil reduced deforestation in the Amazon by around 80 percent, even while increasing the production of soy and cattle. We tell this story in chapter 7.

Notes

1. P. Tyson, *The Eighth Continent: Life, Death, and Discovery in the Lost World of Madagascar* (New York: William Morrow & Company, 2000).

2. C. D. Golden et al., "Rainforest Pharmacopeia in Madagascar Provides High Value for Current Local and Prospective Global Uses," *PLOS ONE* 7, no. 7 (2012): e41221.

3. Ibid.

4. P. Rasoanaivo, "Traditional Medicine Programmes in Madagascar," *Biodiversity & Health: Focusing Research to Policy*, published as the proceedings of the international symposium held in Ottawa, Canada, October 25–28, 2003.

5. G. J. Harper et al., "Fifty Years of Deforestation and Forest Fragmentation in Madagascar," *Environmental Conservation* 34, no. 4 (2007): 325–33.

6. R. A. Kramer, D. D. Richter, S. Pattanayak, and N. P. Sharma, "Ecological and Economic Analysis of Watershed Protection in Eastern Madagascar," *Journal of Environmental Management* 49, no. 3 (1997): 277–95; J. Carret and D. Loyer, "Madagascar Protected Area Network Sustainable Financing: Economic Analysis Perspective," (paper presented at the World Park's Congress, Durban, South Africa, September 2003).

7. L. Starke, ed., *State of the World 2006: A Worldwatch Institute Report on Progress toward a Sustainable Society* (Washington, DC: W. W. Norton & Company, 2006).

8. M. M. Robinson and X. Zhang, "The World Medicines Situation 2011: Traditional Medicines—Global Situation, Issues and Challenges," World Health Organization, Geneva, 2011, http://digicollection.org/hss/documents/s18063en/s18063en.pdf.

9. Ibid.

10. U. Schippmann, D. J. Leaman, and A. B. Cunningham, "Impact of Cultivation and Gathering of Medicinal Plants on Biodiversity: Global Trends and Issues," in Food and Agriculture Organization of the United Nations (FAO), Biodiversity and the Ecosystem Approach in Agriculture, Forestry and Fisheries, satellite event on the occasion of the Ninth Regular Session of the Commission on Genetic Resources for Food and Agriculture, Rome, October 12–13, 2002, Inter-Departmental Working Group on Biological Diversity for Food and Agriculture, Rome, 2002, ftp://ftp.fao.org/docrep/fao/005/aa010e/AA010E00.pdf; N. Myers et al., "Biodiversity Hotspots for Conservation Priorities," *Nature* 403, no. 6772 (2000): 853–58.

11. P. Vedeld, "Counting on the Environment: Forest Incomes and the Rural Poor," Environmental Economic Paper Series, no. 98, Environment Department, World Bank, Washington, DC, 2004.

12. A. Angelsen et al., "Environmental Income and Rural Livelihoods: A Global-Comparative Analysis," *World Development* 64 (2014): S12–28.

13. See for instance, Food and Agriculture Organization of the United Nations (FAO), "The World of Forestry: Declaration of the Eight World Forestry Congress," 8th World Forestry Congress, Jakarta, 1978, http://www.fao.org/docrep/l2680e/l2680e06.htm#the%20world%20of%20forestry.

14. S. Aksornkoae and E. Bird, "Thailand Andaman Sea Coast," in *Encyclopedia of the World's Coastal Landforms*, ed. E. Bird (Dordrecht, Heidelberg, London, New York: Springer Science Business Media, 2010).

15. K. Ewel, R. Twilley, and J. Ong, "Different Kinds of Mangrove Forests Provide Different Goods and Services," *Global Ecology & Biogeography Letters* 7, no. 1 (1998): 83–94.

16. H. Yanagisawa et al., "Tsunami Damage Reduction Performance of a Mangrove Forest in Banda Aceh, Indonesia, Inferred from Field Data and a Numerical Model," *Journal of Geophysical Research: Oceans* 115, no. C6 (2010): C06032; J. C. Bayas et al., "Influence of Coastal Vegetation on the 2004 Tsunami Wave Impact in West Aceh," *Proceedings of the National Academy of Sciences* 108, no. 46

(2011): 18612–17; A. L. McIvor et al., "Mangroves as a Sustainable Coastal Defence" (paper presented at 7th International Conference on Asian and Pacific Coasts, The Nature Conservancy, University of Cambridge, and Wetlands International, Bali, Indonesia, September 2013), 8; M. B. Samarakoon, N. Tanaka, and K. Iimura, "Improvement of Effectiveness of Existing Casuarina Equisetifolia Forests in Mitigating Tsunami Damage," *Journal of Environmental Management* 114 (2013): 105–14.

17. S. Aksornkoae and T. Ruangrai, "Overview of Shrimp Farming and Mangrove Loss in Thailand," in *Shrimp Farming and Mangrove Loss in Thailand*, ed. E. B. Barbier and S. Sathirathai, 37–51 (London: Edward Elgar, 2004).

18. Ibid.

19. E. Barbier, "Valuing Ecosystem Services as Productive Inputs," *Economic Policy* 22, no. 49 (2007): 177–229.

20. Over a twenty-year period at a 10 percent discount rate.

21. Barbier, "Valuing Ecosystem Services as Productive Inputs."

22. S. Sathirathai and E. Barbier, "Valuing Mangrove Conservation in Southern Thailand," *Contemporary Economic Policy* 19, no. 2 (2001): 109–22.

23. M. Kinver, "Sri Lanka First Nation to Protect All Mangrove Forests," BBC News, May 12, 2015, http://www.bbc.com/news/science-environment-32683798.

24. P. H. Gleick, "Three Gorges Dam Project, Yangtze River, China," in *The World's Water 2008–2009: The Biennial Report on Freshwater Resources*, ed. P. H. Gleick and M. J. Cohen, 139–50 (Washington, DC: Island Press, 2009).

25. U.S. Geological Survey, "Three Gorges Dam: The World's Largest Hydroelectric Plant," U.S. Department of the Interior, 2016, http://water.usgs.gov/edu/hybiggest.html; European Space Agency (ESA), "Three Gorges Dam, China," 2016, https://earth.esa.int/web/earth-watching/image-of-the-

week/content/-/article/three-gorges-dam-china-landsat.

26. Agence France-Presse, "China's Three Gorges Dam 'Breaks World Hydropower Record,'" January 1, 2015.

27. China Three Gorges Corporation, *Annual Report 2013*, 2013.

28. Z. Guo et al., "Hydroelectricity Production and Forest Conservation in Watersheds," *Ecological Applications* 17, no. 6 (2007): 1557–62.

29. Ibid.

30. BBC, "China's Three Gorges Dam Reaches Operating Peak," BBC News, July 5, 2012, http://www.bbc.com/news/world-asia-china-18718406.

31. Y. Yuexian, "Impacts and Effectiveness of Logging Bans in Natural Forests: People's Republic of China," in *Forests Out of Bounds: Impacts and Effectiveness of Logging Bans in Natural Forests in Asia–Pacific*, 81–102 (Bangkok: Food and Agricultural Organization of the United Nations, 2001).

32. L. Sáenz at al., "The Role of Cloud Forest Restoration on Energy Security," *Ecosystem Services* 9 (2014): 180–90.

33. Ibid.

34. F. Bernard, R. S. de Groot, and J.J.Campos, "Valuation of Tropical Forest Services and Mechanisms to Finance Their Conservation and Sustainable Use: A Case Study of Tapantí National Park, Costa Rica," *Forest Policy and Economics* 11, no. 3 (2009): 174–83,

35. I. Porras et al., *Learning from 20 Years of Payments for Ecosystem Services in Costa Rica* (London: International Institute for Environment and Development, 2013).

36. S. Page et al., "The Amount of Carbon Released from Peat and Forest Fires in Indonesia during 1997," *Nature* 420 (2002): 61–65.

37. E. Frankenberg, D. McKee, and D. Thomas, "Health Consequences of Forest Fires In Indonesia," *Demography* 42, no. 1 (2005): 109–29; N. Sastry, "Forest Fires, Air Pollution, and Mortality in Southeast Asia," *Demography* 39, no. 1 (2002): 1–23; S. Jayachan-

dran, "Air Quality and Early-Life Mortality Evidence from Indonesia's Wildfires," *Journal of Human Resources* 44, no. 4 (2009): 916–54; K. Anaman and N. Ibrahim, "Statistical Estimation of Dose-Response Functions of Respiratory Diseases and Societal Costs of Haze-Related Air Pollution in Brunei Darussalam," *Pure and Applied Geophysics* 160, no. 1–2 (2003): 279–93.

38. World Bank, "Indonesia Economic Quarterly: Reforming amid Uncertainty," World Bank Group, December 2015, http://pubdocs.worldbank.org/pubdocs/publicdoc/2015/12/844171450085661051/IEQ-DEC-2015-ENG.pdf.

39. K. Mullan, "The Value of Forest Ecosystem Services to Developing Economies," CGD Working Paper 379, Center for Global Development, Washington, DC, 2014.

40. D. Núñez, L. Nahuelhual, and C. Oyarzún, "Forests and Water: The Value of Native Temperate Forests in Supplying Water for Human Consumption," Ecological Economics 58, no. 3 (2006): 606–16; E. Figueroa and R. Pasten, "Forest and Water: The Value of Native Temperate Forests in Supplying Water for Human Consumption: A Comment," *Ecological Economics* 67, no. 2 (2008): 153–56.

41. M. Ahlheim et al., "Landslides in Mountainous Regions of Northern Vietnam: Causes, Protection Strategies and the Assessment of Economic Losses," Institut fur Volkswirtschaftslehre 520, Stuttgart, Germany, 2009.

42. R. A. Kramer, D. D. Richter, S. Pattanayak, and N. P. Sharma, "Ecological and Economic Analysis of Watershed Protection in Eastern Madagascar," *Journal of Environmental Management* 49, no. 3 (1997): 277–95.

43. J. Barkmann et al., "Confronting Unfamiliarity with Ecosystem Functions: The Case for an Ecosystem Service Approach to Environmental Valuation with Stated Preference Method," *Ecological Economics* 65, no. 1 (2008): 48–62.

44. S. K. Pattanayak and R. A. Kramer, "Worth of Watersheds: A Producer Surplus Approach for Valuing Drought Mitigation in Eastern Indonesia," *Environment and Development Economics* 6, no. 1 (2001): 123–46.

45. R. Naylor and M. Drew, "Valuing Mangrove Resources in Kosrae, Micronesia," *Environment and Development Economics* 3, no. 4 (1998): 471–90.

46. Mullan, "The Value of Forest Ecosystem Services to Developing Economies."

47. B. Maas, Y. Clough, and T. Tscharntke, "Bats and Birds Increase Crop Yield in Tropical Agroforestry Landscapes," *Ecology Letters* 16, no. 12 (2013): 1480–87.

48. S. Pattanayak and K. J. Wendland, "Nature's Care: Diarrhea, Watershed Protection, and Biodiversity Conservation in Flores, Indonesia," *Biodiversity and Conservation* 16 no. 10 (2007): 2801–19.

49. K. Arrow et al., "Report of the NOAA-Panel on Contingent Valuation," *Federal Register* 58, no. 10 (1993): 4601–14.

50. Mullan, "The Value of Forest Ecosystem Services."

51. M. Fourcade , E. Ollion, and Y. Algan. "The superiority of economists." *Revista de Economía Institucional* 17, no. 33 (2015): 13-43.

52. Mullan, "The Value of Forest Ecosystem Services."

53. Golden et al., "Rainforest Pharmacopeia."

54. E. Barbier et al., "Coastal Ecosystem-Based Management with Nonlinear Ecological Functions and Values," *Science* 319, no. 5861 (2008): 321–23.

55. Mullan, "The Value of Forest Ecosystem Services."

56. Ibid.

57. See, for example, A. Ghermandi et al., "Values of Natural and Human-Made Wetlands: A Meta-Analysis," *Water Resources Research* 46, no. 12 (2010): W12516, and R. De Groot et al., "Global Estimates of the Value of Ecosystems and Their Services in Monetary Units," *Ecosystem Services* 1, no. 1 (2012): 50–61.

58. R. Costanza et al., "The Value of the World's

Ecosystem Services and Natural Capital," *Nature* 387 (1997): 253–60.

59. R. Costanza et al., "Changes in the Global Value of Ecosystem Services," *Global Environmental Change* 26 (2014): 152–58.

60. See, for instance, N. Bockstael et al., "On Measuring Economic Values for Nature," *Environmental Science & Technology* 34, no. 8 (2000): 1384–89; M. Toman, "Special Section: Forum on Valuation of Ecosystem Services: Why Not to Calculate the Value of the World's Ecosystem Services and Natural Capital," *Ecological Economics* 25 no. 1 (1998): 57–60; and D. Pearce, "Auditing the Earth: The Value of the World's Ecosystem Services and Natural Capital," *Environment: Science and Policy for Sustainable Development* 40, no. 2 (1998): 23–28.

61. L. Carrasco et al., "Economic Valuation of Ecosystem Services Fails to Capture Biodiversity Value of Tropical Forests," *Biological Conservation* 178 (2014): 163–70.

62. Mullan, "The Value of Forest Ecosystem Services."

63. Ibid.

64. S. Jayachandran, "Air quality and early-life mortality evidence from Indonesia's wildfires." *Journal of Human Resources* 44, no. 4 (2009): 916-954.

65. L. Rodriguez et al., "Local +B65:B76Identification and Valuation of Ecosystem Goods and Services from Opuntia Scrublands of Ayacucho, Peru," *Ecological Economics* 57, no. 1 (2006): 30–44; Y. Sawada, "The Impact of Natural and Manmade Disasters on Household Welfare," Agricultural Economics 37, no. s1 (2007): 59–73; S. De Mel, D. McKenzie, and C. Woodruff, "Enterprise Recovery Following Natural Disasters," *The Economic Journal* 122, no. 559 (2012): 64–91.

66. See, for example, R. Elmhirst, M. Siscawati, and C. J. Pierce Colfer, "Revisiting Gender and Forestry in Long Segar, East Kalimantan, Indonesia: Oil Palm and Divided Aspirations," in *Gender and Forests: Climate Change, Tenure, Value Chains, and Emerging Issues*, eds. C.

J. Pierce Colfer, B. S. Basnett, and M. Elias (Abingdon and New York: Routledge, 2016).

67. F. Contente, "Differing Perspectives of Forest Value by Men and Women," box text in P. Shanley, F. C. Da Silva, and T. MacDonald, "Brazil's Social Movement, Women and Forests: A Case Study from the National Council of Rubber Tappers," *International Forestry Review* 13, no. 2 (2011): 239.

68. L. Aguilar, foreword to C. J. P. Colfer, B. S. Basnett, and M. Elias, eds., *Gender and Forests*, xxvii (New York: Routledge, 2016), xxvii.

69. S. Myers et al., "Human Health Impacts of Ecosystem Alteration," *Proceedings of the National Academy of Sciences* 110, no. 47 (2013): 18755.

70. Ibid., 18756.

71. L. German et al., "The Local Social and Environmental Impacts of Biofuel Feedstock Expansion: A Synthesis of Case Studies from Asia, Africa and Latin America," CIFOR Infobrief 34, Center for International Forestry Research, Bogor, Indonesia, 2010.

72. H. Purnomo, B. Shantiko, H. Gunawan, "Political Economy Study of Fire and Haze" (paper presented at the International Seminar toward a Sustainable and Resilient Community: Co-Existence of Oil Palm Plantation, Biodiversity and Peat Fire Prevention, University of Riau, Riau, Indonesia, August 5, 2015); World Bank, "Indonesia Economic Quarterly."

73. K. Chomitz, *At Loggerheads? Agricultural Expansion, Poverty Reduction, and Environment in the Tropical Forests* (Washington, DC: World Bank, 2007).

74. Enrique Rueda-Sabater, personal communication with one of the authors, July 22, 2015.

75. E. Dickinson, "GDP: A Brief History," *Foreign Policy*, January 3, 2011.

76. K. Hamilton and C. Hepburn, "Wealth," *Oxford Review of Economic Policy* 30, no. 1 (2014): 1–20; I. Serageldin, "Sustainability and the Wealth of Nations," World Bank, Washington, DC, 1995.

77. J. Stiglitz, A. Sen, and J. Fitoussi, "Report by the Commission on the Measurement of Economic Performance and Social Progress," 2010, http://www.insee.fr/fr/publications-et-services/dossiers_web/stiglitz/doc-commission/RAPPORT_anglais.pdf.

78. World Bank Group, "Wealth Accounting and the Valuation of Ecosystem Services," last modified 2016, http://www.wavespartnership.org/en. The eight countries are Botswana, Colombia, Costa Rica, Guatemala, Indonesia, Madagascar, the Philippines, and Rwanda.

79. Food and Agriculture Organization of the United Nations (FAO), "National Socio-economic Surveys in Forestry," *Forests and Poverty Reduction*, 2016.

80. R. Bakkegaard, N. Hogarth, and A. Bosselmann, "Measuring the Contribution of Forests in Household Surveys: A Case from Indonesia," Center for International Forestry Research, Bogor, Indonesia, 2015, http://www.ifriresearch.net/wp-content/uploads/2015/09/BAKKEGAARD.pdf.

81. Millennium Ecosystem Assessment, "Overview of the Millennium Ecosystem Assessment," http://www.millenniumassessment.org/en/About.html#.

82. The Economics of Ecosystems and Biodiversity, "The Initiative," 2016, http://www.teebweb.org/about/the-initiative/.

83. See the Natural Capital Project website at http://www.naturalcapitalproject.org/.

84. Program on Forests, "How Forests Enhance Resilience to Climate Change," last modified October 2015, http://www.profor.info/node/2032.

85. See, for example, D. Brockington, *Fortress Conservation: the Preservation of the Mkomazi Game Reserve, Tanzania* (Bloomington: Indiana University Press, 2002).

86. S. Schwartzman, "Social Movements and Natural Resource Conservation in the Brazilian Amazon," in *The Rainforest Harvest: Sustainable Strategies for Saving the Tropical Forests*, ed. S. Counsell and T. Rice, 207–12 (London: Friends of the Earth Trust, 1992).

87. R. Rice, R. E. Gullison, and J. W. Reid, "Can Sustainable Management Save Tropical Forests?" *Scientific American* 276, no. 4 (1997): 44–49.

88. E. Meijaard et al., "Life after Logging: Reconciling Wildlife Conservation and Production Forestry in Indonesian Borneo," Center for International Forestry Research and United Nations Educational, Scientific and Cultural Organization, Jakarta, Indonesia, 2005; D. P. Edwards et al., "Maintaining Ecosystem Function and Services in Logged Tropical Forests," *Trends in Ecology & Evolution* 29, no. 9 (2014): 511–20.

89. F. E. Putz et al., "Reduced-Impact Logging: Challenges and Opportunities," *Forest Ecology and Management* 256, no. 7 (2008): 1427–33.

90. Rice, Gullison, and Reid, "Can Sustainable Management."

91. D. Pearce, F. E. Putz, and J. K. Vanclay, "Sustainable Forestry in the Tropics: Panacea or Folly?" *Forest Ecology and Management* 172, no. 2 (2003): 229–47.

92. Biodiversity Indicators Partnership, "Indicator Facts," updated 2013, http://www.bipindicators.net/forestcertification.

93. E. Rametsteiner and M. Simula, "Forest Certification—An Instrument to Promote Sustainable Forest Management?" *Journal of Environmental Management* 67, no. 1 (2003): 87–98; J. Siry, F. W. Cubbage, and M. Rukunuddin Ahmed, "Sustainable Forest Management: Global Trends and Opportunities," *Forest Policy and Economics* 7, no. 4 (2005): 551–61; Biodiversity Indicators Partnership, "Indicator Facts"; P. B. Durst et al., "Challenges Facing Certification and Eco-Labelling of Forest Products in Developing Countries," *International Forestry Review* 8, no. 2 (2006): 193–200.

94. P.B. Durst et al., "Challenges Facing Certification and Eco-Labelling of Forest Products in Developing Countries."

95. B. L. Zimmerman and C. F. Kormos, "Prospects for Sustainable Logging in Tropical Forests," *BioScience* 62, no. 5 (2012): 479–87.

96. E. Rametsteiner and M. Simula, "Forest Certification—An Instrument to Promote Sustainable Forest Management?" *Journal of Environmental Management* 67, no. 1 (2003): 87–98

97. See, for example, P. Cerutti et al., "Social Impact of the Forest Stewardship Council Certification: An Assessment in the Congo Basin," CIFOR Occasional Paper 103, Center for International Forestry Research, Bogor, Indonesia, 2014; D. Miteva, C. J. Loucks, and S. K. Pattanayak, "Social and Environmental Impacts of Forest Management Certification in Indonesia," *PLOS ONE* 10, no. 7 (2015): e0129675.

98. Rametsteiner and Simula, "Forest Certification."

99. A. Carlson and C. Palmer, "A Qualitative Meta-Synthesis of the Benefits of Eco-Labeling in Developing Countries," *Ecological Economics* 127 (2016): 129–45.

100. See, for example, C. Peters, A. H. Gentry, and R. O. Mendelsohn, "Valuation of an Amazonian Rainforest," *Nature* 339 (1989): 655–56; B. Cordes, "Evaluating an Enterprise-Oriented Approach to Community-Based Conservation in the Asia/Pacific Region," Biodiversity Conservation Network, Biodiversity Support Program, Washington, DC, 1995, http://www.fao.org/docrep/X5336E/x5336e13.htm.

101. T. Ticktin, "The Ecological Implications of Harvesting Non-Timber Forest Products," *Journal of Applied Ecology* 41, no. 1 (2004): 11–21.

102. K. Schreckenberg, "The Contribution of Shea Butter (Vitellaria Paradoxa CF Gaertner) to Local Livelihoods in Benin," in *Forest Products, Livelihoods and Conservation: Case Studies of Non-Timber Forest Product Systems* 2, ed. T. Sunderland and O. Ndoye, 91–113 (Bogor: Center for International Forestry Research, 2004).

103. B. Belcher and K. Schreckenberg, "Commercialisation of Non-Timber Forest Products: A Reality Check," *Development Policy Review* 25, no. 3 (2007): 355–77.

104. Forest Products, Livelihoods and Conservation: Case Studies of Non-Timber Forest Product Systems 2, ed. T. Sunderland and O. Ndoye, 91–113 (Bogor: Center for International Forestry Research, 2004).

105. N. Howlader et al., eds., "SEER Cancer Statistics Review, 1975–2012," National Cancer Institute, Bethesda, MD, http://seer.cancer.gov/csr/1975_2012/, based on November 2014 SEER data submission, posted to the SEER website, April 2015.

106. M. Moudi et al., "Vinca Alkaloids," *International Journal of Preventive Medicine* 4, no. 11 (2013): 1231.

107. K. Springob et al., "Chapter 1," in *Plant-Derived Natural Products: Synthesis, Function, and Application*, ed. A. Osbourne and V. Lanzotti (New York, Springer-Verlag: 2009).

108. R. E. Marker, and J. Krueger, "Sterols. CXII. Sapogenins. XLI. The Preparation of Trillin and Its Conversion to Progesterone," *Journal of the American Chemical Society* 62, no. 12 (1940): 3349–50.

109. D. Newman and G. M. Cragg, "Natural Products as Sources of New Drugs over the 30 Years from 1981 to 2010," *Journal of Natural Products* 75, no. 3 (2012): 311–35.

110. R. Butler, "Anti-HIV Drug from Rainforest Almost Lost before Its Discovery," Mongabay.com, September 13, 2005, http://news.mongabay.com/2005/09/anti-hiv-drug-from-rainforest-almost-lost-before-its-discovery/.

111. B. Ellsworth, "Brazil to Step Up Crackdown on 'Biopiracy' in 2011," Reuters, December 22, 2010.

112. R. Conniff, "A Bitter Pill," *Conservation*, Spring 2012, 18–23.

113. R. D. Simpson, R. A. Sedjo, and J. W. Reid, "Valuing Biodiversity for Use in Pharmaceutical Research," *Journal of Political Economy* 104, no. 1 (1996): 163–85.

114. Conniff, "A Bitter Pill."

115. M. M. Robbins et al., "Bwindi Mountain

Gorilla Census 2011—Summary of Results," Government of Uganda, Uganda Wildlife Authority, 2011, http://uganda.wcs.org/DesktopModules/Bring2mind/DMX/Download.aspx?EntryId=16545&PortalId=141&DownloadMethod=attachment.

116. Virunga National Park, "Treks," updated 2016, http://visitvirunga.org/treks/; World Wide Fund for Nature and Dalberg Global Development Consultants, "The Economic Value of Virunga National Park," World Wide Fund for Nature International, Gland, Switzerland, 2013, http://awsassets.panda.org/downloads/the_economic_value_of_virunga_national_park_lr_2.pdf.

117. A. Hernández and J. C. Picón, "Protected Wild Areas and Eco-Tourism in Costa Rica," in *Tourism in Latin America*, ed. A. Panosso Netto and L. G. G. Trigo, 127–41 (Cham, Heidelberg, New York, Dordrecht, London: Springer International Publishing, 2015).

118. S. Wunder, "Payments for Environmental Services: Some Nuts and Bolts," CIFOR Occasional Paper 42, Center for International Forestry Research, Bogor, Indonesia, 2005.

119. Porras et al., "Learning from 20 Years of Payments for Ecosystem Services in Costa Rica."

120. See, for example, J. Silvertown, "Have Ecosystem Services Been Oversold?" *Trends in Ecology & Evolution* 30, no. 11 (2015): 641–48; S. Bowles, *The Moral Economy: Why Good Incentives Are No Substitute for Good Citizens* (New Haven: Yale University Press, 2016).

121. Angelsen, "Environmental Income," S18.

122. G. A. Sanchez-Azofeifa et al., "Costa Rica's Payment for Environmental Services Program: Intention, Implementation, and Impact," *Conservation Biology* 21, no. 5 (2007): 1165–73.

123. Porras et al., "Learning from 20 Years."

124. Climate and Development Knowledge Network, "INSIDE STORY: Ecuador's Socio Bosque Programme," January 2016, http://cdkn.org/resource/private-conservation-agreements-support-climate-action-ecuadors-socio-bosque-programme/;

International Institute for Environment and Development, "Case Studies: Mexico National–PSAH Programme," Payments for Watershed Markets Schemes in Developing Countries, 2012, http://www.watershedmarkets.org/casestudies/Mexico_National_PSAH_eng.html; P. Thu Thuy et al., "Payments for Forest Environmental Services in Vietnam: From Policy to Practice," CIFOR Occasional Paper 93, Center for International Forestry Research, Bogor, Indonesia, 2013.

125. R. A. Arriagada et al., "Do Payments Pay Off? Evidence from Participation in Costa Rica's PES Program," *PLOS ONE* 10, no. 7 (2015): e0131544.

126. I. Ring, "Integrating Local Ecological Services into Intergovernmental Fiscal Transfers: The Case of the Ecological ICMS in Brazil," *Land Use Policy* 25, no. 4 (2008): 485–97; S. Irawan and L. Tacconi, Intergovernmental Fiscal Transfers, Forest Conservation and Climate Change (Cheltenham, UK, and Northampton, MA: Edward Elgar Publishing, 2016); S. Mumbunan, "Ecological Fiscal Transfers in Indonesia," PhD dissertation, Universität Leipzig, 2011.

127. United Nations Framework Convention on Climate Change (UNFCCC), "Adoption of the Paris Agreement," Conference of the Parties to the United Nations Framework Convention on Climate Change, Twenty-First Session, Paris, France, December 12, 2015.

128. We credit Arild Angelsen for the phrase, "Projects can win battles, but policies win wars."

129. J. Busch et al., "Structuring Economic Incentives to Reduce Emissions from Deforestation within Indonesia," *Proceedings of the National Academy of Sciences* 109, no. 4 (2012): 1062–67.

130. See, for example, G. Paoli et al., "Biodiversity Conservation in the REDD," *Carbon Balance and Management* 5, no. 1 (2010): 7.

131. J. Busch, F. Godoy, W. R. Turner, and C. A. Harvey, "Biodiversity Co-Benefits of Reduc-

ing Emissions from Deforestation under Alternative Reference Levels and Levels of Finance," *Conservation Letters* 4, no. 2 (2011): 101–15.

132. T. A. Gardner et al., "A Framework for Integrating Biodiversity Concerns into National REDD+ Programmes," *Biological Conservation* 154 (2012): 61–71.

133. J. Busch, "Supplementing REDD+ with Biodiversity Payments: The Paradox of Paying for Multiple Ecosystem Services," *Land Economics* 89, no. 4 (2013): 655–75.

134. J. Busch and H. S. Grantham, "Parks versus Payments: Reconciling Divergent Policy Responses to Biodiversity Loss and Climate Change from Tropical Deforestation," *Environmental Research Letters* 8, no. 3 (2013): 034028; M. Potts, L. C. Kelley, and H. M. Doll, "Maximizing Biodiversity Co-Benefits under REDD+: A Decoupled Approach," *Environmental Research Letters* 8, no. 2 (2013): 024019.

Livestock graze in the Brazilian Amazon.

Credit: edsongrandisoli/iStock.com

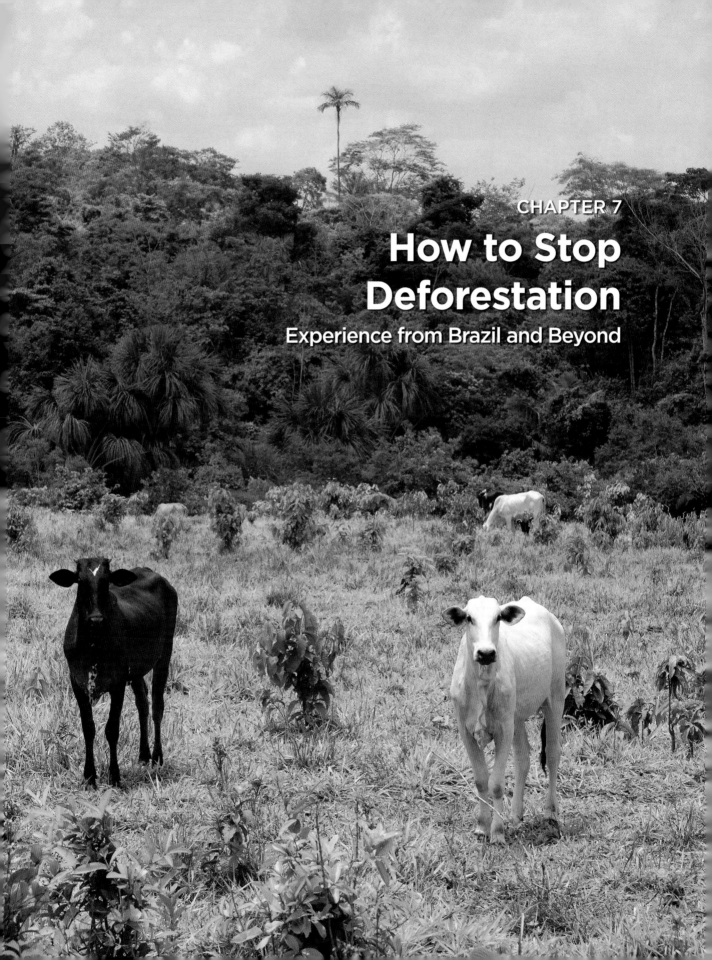

CHAPTER 7

How to Stop Deforestation

Experience from Brazil and Beyond

orto do Moz, Brazil, 2002. The hot season was approaching in Porto do Moz, a rainforest town of a few thousand people in the Brazilian state of Pará, where the mighty Xingu River empties into the even mightier Amazon, as shown in figure 7.1. Inside a tin-roofed shed, Tarcísio Feitosa da Silva gathered with two dozen men and women he knew well: fishermen, farmers, members of a women's cooperative, three members of the clergy.[1] For decades their community had relied on the surrounding forest and the rivers flowing through it for a modest living. Feitosa's grandfather was a rubber tapper; his father was a crab fisherman.[2]

But now their forest was beset by threats on all sides. To the south, loggers were scouring for mahogany along the Xingu River. They were felling the valuable trees and floating them in rafts downriver to the sawmills of Porto do Moz, where they were sawn into lumber and shipped out to international markets.[3] To the east, the muddy Trans-Amazon highway constructed in the 1970s was being paved, as was Highway BR-163 to the west.[4]

Feitosa and his neighbors knew that freshly laid tarmac would hasten the arrival of outsiders seeking land. These *"grileiros"* would log, burn, and clear the forest, just as they had along every other paved highway through the Amazon. Brazilian law allowed squatters to establish ownership by clearing forest and grazing a few cattle. Landgrabbing *grileiros* exploited this system en masse, speculating that the land they stripped bare

of trees could later be sold at a profit to large ranchers and farmers.[5] Their nickname came from *grilo*, the Portuguese word for cricket, from their practice of falsifying land titles by putting new documents in boxes full of crickets until they appeared old.[6]

The *grileiros* were backed by powerful ranchers and farmers who had tacit or active supporters scattered within the federal government, the state governments, the police, and the courts, and they were not afraid to use violence to intimidate other claimants to the land.[7] Fourteen years after the rubber tapper and union leader Chico Mendes was slain in the state of Acre, more than two thousand kilometers to the west of Porto do Moz, for trying to protect his community's forest and its rubber trees from ranchers, threats of murder and other violence to the families of these activists were commonplace along Brazil's vast, lawless frontier.[8] Land grabbers were known to maintain a hit list of hundreds of men and women who, in one way or another, stood in the way of their designs. In Pará state alone, 475 activists were assassinated between 1985 and 2002.[9]

Now Feitosa and his neighbors were fighting to have their region at the confluence of the Xingu and Amazon Rivers declared an extractive reserve. This federal designation would let them continue small-scale farming and harvesting of fruits, nuts, and wood but would prohibit the penetration of industrial-scale logging and agriculture into the forest. It was a fight for their livelihoods, and perhaps their lives.

Feitosa and his colleagues chose a courageous course of action. In September 2002, four hundred local men and women set up a

This chapter draws heavily on a background paper by Kalifi Ferretti-Gallon and Jonah Busch on determinants of deforestation.

blockade across one of the tributaries of the Xingu to prevent logging barges from carrying illegal timber to export.[10] When the police who arrived seized the cargo and issued fines to the logging company, the loggers retaliated with death threats and physical attacks on the blockaders.[11] Feitosa and several of his colleagues were driven into hiding.[12] Despite this violent opposition, the activists persisted, and in 2004 the federal government officially designated their forest as an extractive reserve the size of Brunei. Its name, *Verde para Sempre*, means "Green Forever."

Feitosa and his neighbors had won this battle, but all across the Brazilian Amazon similar communities were losing the war. An "Arc of Deforestation" stretched four thousand kilometers from Acre, near the Peruvian border, to Belém at the mouth of the Amazon River. From 1988 to 2004, more than 312,000 square kilometers of Brazil's forest—an area the size of Poland—were destroyed.[13] A seemingly endless expanse of verdant rainforest was rapidly replaced by vast soy fields, large ranches, and "spectacularly lonely cattle."[14] The destruction of the Amazon rainforest during this decade and a half alone was responsible for releasing to the atmosphere nearly 1 percent of all the carbon dioxide humans have emitted since the Industrial Age.[15]

Outside groups cast Brazil as an "environmental villain,"[16] while inside the country the

Figure 7.1: Map of Pará.

ever-expanding swath of destruction seemed as inevitable as the rising tide. In 2004, Brazil's space agency reported that annual deforestation had reached a new peak of 28,000 square kilometers—an area the size of Albania.[17]

But, then, something began to happen that absolutely nobody had predicted: Brazil's deforestation rate began to fall. This chapter tells the story of how this remarkable turnaround came about. In the first half, we describe the rapid-fire series of policy measures Brazil put into place after 2004 to slow deforestation: protected areas and indigenous lands, stepped-up law enforcement, and economic incentives for forest conservation, alongside voluntary measures by soy and beef producers. We describe the conditions that enabled Brazil to enact these policies successfully: a world-class system for forest monitoring and plentiful low-carbon land on which to increase agricultural production. While political factors were important as well, we reserve discussion of politics for chapter 10. We conclude the first half of the present chapter by discussing the prospects for replicating Brazil's success in other tropical countries, as well as for continued success within Brazil.

While Brazil's success puts it in a class of its own, many other tropical countries have also enacted policies to reduce deforestation. Evaluations of these policies contribute further valuable lessons on what's worked and what hasn't. In the second half of this chapter we describe the results of a meta-analysis undertaken by Kalifi Ferretti-Gallon and Jonah Busch of the Center for Global Development for *Why Forests? Why Now?* that synthesizes lessons from more than one hundred published studies on what stops deforestation and what doesn't.[18] Many of the same policies underlying success in Brazil have succeeded in reducing deforestation in other countries, albeit on a smaller scale.

As explained in chapter 1, the purpose of this book is twofold: first, to raise awareness of the critical importance of tropical forests to achieving both climate and development objectives and, second, to challenge rich countries to do their part in supporting successful efforts to reduce tropical deforestation. We do not presume to tell developing countries how to achieve that goal; indeed, an attractive feature of payment for performance is the "hands-off" role of the financier. Nevertheless, we include this chapter to build confidence that deforestation *can* be slowed, with an ever-increasing set of monitoring tools, policy approaches, experiences, and analytical evidence that can be brought to bear on the problem.

Brazil's Dramatic Drop in Deforestation

In mid-2004, few would have predicted Brazil's deforestation rate was about to drop precipitously, but, as is often the case, things looked darkest just before the dawn. On February 12, 2005, Sister Dorothy Stang, a seventy-three-year-old Catholic nun born in Dayton, Ohio, and a naturalized Brazilian citizen, was walking to a meeting with peasant farmers who were trying to protect their forest, much the same way as Feitosa and his neighbors had done a few years earlier. On her way to the meeting she was ambushed by ranchers who shot her six times and left her to die on the roadside.[19]

The brazen murder of a nun sparked worldwide outrage and condemnation. The government of President Luiz Inácio Lula da Silva declared the act "intolerable"[20] and responded with a vengeance. Two thousand federal troops poured into Pará, arresting and convicting perpetrators of deforestation-related crimes.[21] President Lula decreed a moratorium on recognizing new land claims and granting logging permits in the region, shutting down land speculators overnight.[22] Brazil's environmental protection agency, IBAMA (Instituto Brasileiro do Meio Ambiente e dos Recursos Naturais Renováveis), was given the authority and the budget to prosecute deforestation-related crimes, identified by using near-real-time monitoring by satellite, and dozens of new protected areas and indigenous territories were designated in the region.[23]

In the following years, these actions were bolstered by credit restrictions on farmers and ranchers in high-deforestation municipalities.[24] Under public pressure and threat of prosecution, the soy and beef industries voluntarily imposed moratoriums on the selling of agricultural products from recently deforested land, while a number of public and private initiatives started to provide positive incentives to landowners for forest conservation.[25]

As a result of this combination of policies, Amazon deforestation fell year after year. From an Albania-sized 28,000 square kilometers in 2004, deforestation dropped by more than 50 percent, to 13,000 square kilometers in 2008, and by more than 80 percent, to just 4,600 square kilometers, in 2012, where it has roughly remained since.[26] The slide persisted through upward and downward fluctuations in commodity prices[27] and waxes and wanes in international attention.

Brazil's near-miraculous drop in Amazon deforestation was all the more remarkable because it was accompanied by a simultaneous increase in overall agricultural production, as shown in figure 7.2. Over the same 2004–13 period, Brazil increased nationwide cattle production by 21 percent and soy production by 65 percent, with only a comparatively small increase in deforestation outside the Amazon region. The country's overall economy grew by an enviable 4 percent per year.[28]

The Pará of today is very different from the lawless frontier of the early 2000s. The state is now blanketed by a patchwork quilt of protective reserves. Rubber tappers and small farmers earn livings from the trees protected in extractive reserves. Indigenous peoples, such as the Kayapo, maintain their traditional lifestyles within recognized and respected territorial boundaries. And tourists pay hundreds of dollars a night to marvel at the ancient trees and abundant wildlife in world-class national parks.

Pará is still a dangerous place, as exemplified by the ongoing killings of indigenous and environmental activists.[29] But these days the hired guns are on the wrong side of the power structure. Land regulations protect the forests and the people that depend on them, not the land grabbers and their hired guns. The environmental police are robust and well funded.

The transformation of Pará is emblematic of Brazil's success in forest conservation across the entire Amazon. Brazil has inspired the rest of the world by proving that slow-

Figure 7.2: Brazil reduced deforestation and increased agricultural production at the same time.

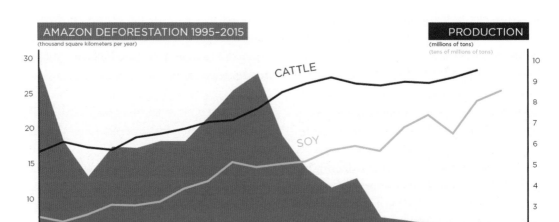

Source: Food and Agriculture Organization of the United Nations (FAO), Statistics Division, "Production quantities by country," updated 2015, http://faostat3.fao.org/browse/Q/*/E; National Institute for Space Research (INPE), "Projeto Prodes: Monitoramento da Floresta Amazônica Brazileira Por Satélite," updated 2016, http://www.obt.inpe.br/prodes/index.php.

ing deforestation is not just feasible but fully compatible with economic growth. By keeping the carbon in the Amazon forests out of the atmosphere, Brazil has been lauded in international circles as the country that has done more than any other to stem climate change.[30] In the space of a decade, the country has transformed from environmental villain to environmental hero. For his part, Tarcísio Feitosa da Silva was awarded the prestigious Goldman Environmental Prize in 2006 in recognition of his actions.[31]

No single policy was solely responsible for Brazil's success in cutting deforestation; rather, it was the result of a combination of public policies and private measures. According to ecologist Daniel Nepstad and his colleagues, policies that contributed to the decline of deforestation can be grouped into three categories related to the profitability of agriculture: supply, risk, and demand.[32] First, the establishment of protected areas and indigenous territories and delays in road construction reduced the supply of land potentially available for deforestation. Second, law enforcement actions, fines, embargoes, and suspension of rural credit increased the risks associated with undertaking deforestation. Third, moratoriums on the clearing of forest by the soy and cattle industries reduced demand for new agricultural land. Table 7.1 shows the policies in these three categories, which we describe in greater depth in the remainder of this section.

Table 7.1: How To Stop Deforestation: Policy Recommendations and Examples from Brazil

Policy category	Factors identified by pantropical meta-analysis	Policy recommendation for slowing deforestation	Example from Brazil
Reducing supply of available land for deforestation	Protected areas	Establish protected areas in regions where forests face higher threat.	New protected areas slowed the advance of the "Arc of Deforestation" in the Amazon.
	Indigenous peoples	Support indigenous peoples, the best allies in the effort against deforestation.	The effectiveness of the Xingu Indigenous Reserve in stopping deforestation is visible from space.
	Roads	Minimize intrusion of new roads into remote forested areas.	While new roads continue to allow access to remote forested areas, law enforcement has increased along roads and some paving has been delayed.
Increasing risk associated with deforestation	Law enforcement	Enforce laws, which are often already on the books, against clearing forests.	A successful crackdown on illegal trade in mahogany in 2003 (described in chapter 10) was an early confidence builder for efforts to control deforestation.
Reducing demand for deforestation	Agriculture	Insulate forested land from pressures to convert to meet demand for agricultural commodities, e.g., through supply-chain interventions.	Traders imposed moratoriums on sourcing soy and beef from recently deforested areas; credit to high-deforestation municipalities was restricted; many companies committed to deforestation-free supply chains.
	Incentives	Link support for rural incomes to the maintenance of forest resources, e.g., through payment for ecosystem services (PES) programs.	Brazil's Bolsa Floresta program provides monthly payments for ecosystem services to families committed to protecting forest.

Notes: Policy categories were defined by D. Nepstad et al., "Slowing Amazon Deforestation through Public Policy and Interventions in Beef and Soy Supply Chains," *Science* 344, no. 6188 (2014): 1118–23. Factors were identified by K. Ferretti-Gallon and J. Busch, "What Drives Deforestation and What Stops It? A Meta-Analysis of Spatially Explicit Econometric Studies," CGD Working Paper 361, Center for Global Development, Washington, DC, 2014, http://www.cgdev.org/publication/what-drives-deforestation-and-what-stops-it-meta-analysis-spatially-explicit-econometric.

Reducing the Supply of "Deforestable" Land by Protecting Threatened Forest Areas

From 2003 to 2008, Brazil expanded the area of Amazon forest designated as protected areas or recognized as indigenous lands by 640,000 square kilometers—an area the size of France.[33] By 2010, these areas covered 2.2 million square kilometers—44 percent of the Amazon, an area larger than Greenland.[34]

> Brazil's success in cutting deforestation was the result of a combination of public policies and private measures.

These areas were of several different types. Some were national parks and wilderness areas. Others were extractive reserves, a type of protected area rubber tappers had successfully petitioned to have created in 1985. Still others were indigenous peoples' reserves, held under collective tenure and designated for sustainable management, with the right to exclude outsiders.[35] What all these areas had in common were delineating geographical boundaries beyond which ranching and soy could not legally spread.

As important as their total size was the location of the new protected areas. Most previously protected areas and indigenous territories in the Amazon were in remote places. In contrast, many of the new areas were created on active frontiers under imminent threat of deforestation. Park guards and local people with the right to exclude outsiders effectively choked off the available supply of open land for new squatting and speculation across much of the Arc of Deforestation.

Making Deforestation Riskier by Enforcing Forest Laws

Deep in the Amazon, along the highways that led to the frontier, the law would come late or not at all. The Brazilian constitution allowed squatters who settled on small plots of unused land to claim ownership after five years. In some cases these unused forests were public; in others, they already belonged to someone else. *Grileiros*, often financed by large logging and ranching companies, could increase the size of their holdings by forging documents, corrupting notaries, and threatening violence against small landowners.[36] In the face of these land grabbers, even legitimate landowners were under pressure to assert their ownership by preemptively clearing their land. [37]

The primary legal mechanism for controlling deforestation on private property was the 1965 Forest Code, amended in 1996 to restrict private landowners to clearing no more than 20 percent of the forest from their property. But this law proved difficult to enforce, largely because it was nearly impossible to catch remote landowners in the act of deforestation. As a result, the Forest Code was often violated. A 2012 revision to the code acknowledged as much by granting amnesty to some landowners for past deforestation. The revised code also mandated a return of forest cover to 80 percent across properties, with provisions for doing so through regional trading mechanisms.[38]

In 2005, the lack of law enforcement at the frontier changed. A satellite system launched the previous year called DETER (described in chapter 4 and below) finally allowed police to observe deforestation within a week or two of its happening and to catch deforesting landowners in the act. It allowed federal prosecutors to bring high-profile lawsuits against politically powerful large property owners and confiscate illegally harvested logs and cattle raised in protected areas.[39] Property-level enforcement abilities were improved still further in 2009 when landholders were required for the first time to submit their property boundaries to a registry.[40]

In 2008, the Ministry of the Environment increased the scale of its enforcement actions from the property to the municipality level. It blacklisted 36 of the Amazon's 547 municipalities that together had accounted for 45 percent of Amazon deforestation the previous year.[41] Farms within blacklisted municipalities were subjected to heightened monitoring and fines and lost access to subsidized agricultural credit from the Central Bank. They would soon lose market access for their meat, as well.[42] The consequences of blacklisting prompted collective action at the municipality and even state levels to return to good graces.[43]

Reducing Demand for Deforestation by Shifting Agricultural Sourcing Elsewhere

A Greenpeace report released in 2006[44] was damning in its criticism: deforestation for soy was a crime, commodity traders trafficking in soybeans were criminals, and restaurants in Europe that sold meat from cows and chickens raised on that soy were accomplices. Greenpeace pointed fingers at Cargill, Archer Daniels Midland, Bunge, McDonald's, and the state of Mato Grosso, where 90

percent of deforestation for soy in Brazil was taking place.

Brazil's soy industry responded swiftly. Within weeks the businesses targeted by Greenpeace decided to stop purchasing soy grown on land where forest had been cleared after July 2006. These buyers had market power, so farmers were forced to follow. Soy growers' two main trade associations in Brazil declared a voluntary moratorium on deforestation, monitored by satellite. The associations extended the moratorium annually until 2016, when they extended it indefinitely.[45]

The soy moratorium has been heralded as a resounding success. Defying expectations, soy production continued to expand in the Amazon, but no longer at the expense of forest. Between 2006 and 2013 the area of soy expansion grew by 50 percent, but the proportion of new cropland coming at the expense of forest dropped from 30 percent to less than 1 percent as new soy fields shifted elsewhere.[46]

The soy moratorium was the first of its kind. It provided a template for subsequent commodity supply-chain commitments around the world, as described further in chapter 8. In 2009, the Brazilian beef and leather industry followed suit with a "cattle agreement," in which meat packers agreed to buy cattle only from ranchers in jurisdictions that had not been blacklisted and who had registered their property boundaries in the State Environmental System (CAR) online registry. Like the soy moratorium, the cattle agreement was self-imposed, but it came as a result of external pressure and was designed to preempt threatened regulatory action. This time the pressure came not just from advocacy organizations, but also from the Ministry of the Environment and state-level federal prosecutors, who put pressure on bank lenders, supermarkets, and slaughterhouses.[47] When meat packers signed the cattle agreement, federal prosecutors agreed to drop legal action.

Adherence to the cattle certification program has been high by both farms and slaughterhouses.[48] By 2013, more than seventy-two thousand properties comprising 20 million hectares had registered for the agreement, comprising nearly 80 percent of the privately owned land area in the state of Pará.[49] Observers have suggested that the program "sets higher standards for sustainability than any existing policy or incentive mechanism and participation in the program may generate significant indirect financial and nonfinancial benefits."[50]

In addition to restrictions making it more expensive for farmers and ranchers to convert forests to agriculture, the Brazilian Amazon also saw fledgling initiatives making it more lucrative to keep land in forests. One, Bolsa Floresta, made monthly payments to hundreds of families in the state of Amazonas in return for keeping forest standing.[51] Funding sources included the Amazon Fund, which channelled international payments for reducing deforestation, and private voluntary carbon offsets.[52]

Payment initiatives such as Bolsa Floresta are too recent and too small to have contributed much to Brazil's big decline in deforestation, but payments and other, nonmonetary, positive incentives can play a much larger role in combating deforestation in the future.[53] Even if such payments on their own are insufficient to protect forest, they can help make restrictive measures more palatable.

How Brazil Did It: Enabling Conditions

Two fortuitous conditions were in place in Brazil by the first decade of the 2000s that made possible the implementation of the policy actions described above. First, Brazil's world-class system of forest monitoring using satellites enabled it to detect deforestation in real time and track national progress annually; and, second, Brazil had an enormous backlog of cleared land available for planting, which allowed it to decouple food production from further deforestation. We discuss these enabling conditions in more detail here. As mentioned previously, we save for chapter 10 a discussion of political factors underlying Brazil's success, which included pressure from civil society coalitions, political leadership, high-level government coordination, and international endorsement from performance-based payments into the Amazon Fund.

Monitoring Forests by Satellite

The ability to monitor forest loss by satellite, discussed in detail in chapter 4, was fundamental to Brazil's success in reducing deforestation. For many years the enforcement of forest laws in the Amazon relied on voluntary reports of deforestation. That changed in May 2004, when Brazil's National Institute for Space Research (INPE) launched the Real-Time System for Detection of Deforestation (DETER). DETER captured images of the entire Amazon forest every two weeks, automatically identified recent hotspots of deforestation, and triggered alerts so law enforcement officials could catch deforesters red-handed.[54] Later these alerts would be used to enforce the soy and cattle moratoriums, as well. Economist Juliano Assunção and his colleagues estimate that without the DETER program, deforestation in the Amazon would have been 59 percent higher.[55]

A second, world-class satellite system, Program for the Estimation of Deforestation in the Brazilian Amazon (PRODES), had been providing annual estimates of total Amazon deforestation since 1988.[56] The numbers were followed closely—and trusted—both inside and outside Brazil. When deforestation rose, as in 2004 and 2008, the federal government was able to respond forcefully with new policies. When it fell to unprecedented lows in the 2010s, Brazil could showcase its achievement to the rest of the world.

The precise yearly measurements of deforestation provided by PRODES were also instrumental in galvanizing public opinion. Geographer Eugenio Arima and his colleagues have suggested that "as the public learned that 75 percent of Brazil's carbon dioxide emissions were coming from changes in land cover and that large increases in agricultural output could feasibly be achieved by making better use of the 70 million hectares that had already been deforested, they grew increasingly supportive of conservation efforts."[57]

Decoupling Agriculture and Deforestation

While deforestation was tumbling over the past decade, soy and cattle production continued to grow apace by increasing yields on already cleared land. This low-cost decoupling of agriculture from deforestation was enabled by two ironies. First, vast areas of cleared land had been made available by decades of rampant deforestation in the recent past. Second, the ability to grow more soy on the same amount of land, the result of investment by the Brazil-

ian Agricultural Research Corporation (Embrapa), was what brought soy to the Amazon to begin with.[58] And yet the decoupling of agricultural growth from deforestation involved foresight as well: areas where new agricultural expansion could and couldn't take place were delineated through protected areas, indigenous lands, and state-level Ecological and Economic Zoning (EEZ) plans.[59]

Some researchers have raised the possibility that forest protection policies in the Amazon could cause agricultural expansion to shift into neighboring countries[60] or into the biologically diverse woody savannas of the Cerrado, through "leakage," or "indirect land-use change."[61] Indeed, the area of the Cerrado under cropland doubled between 2003 and 2013, with three-quarters of this Montenegro-sized expansion coming at the expense of native vegetation.[62] To put this expansion in perspective, though, this was less than one-tenth of the area deforested in the Amazon over the same time period.[63] It is difficult to know how much of this expansion was the result of workers or investors shifting their operations from the Amazon. One study of Mato Grosso state between 2006 and 2010 found little evidence of leakage of soy farms from the Amazon to the Cerrado.[64]

Maintaining Brazil's Success

It's anybody's bet whether Brazil's deforestation rate will stay low relative to historical levels or revert toward its historical mean. But recent history has been on the side of those betting it will stay low. Some believed the fall in deforestation rates after 2005 was just a symptom of low commodity prices, but when the world economy and commodity prices rebounded after the Great Recession, deforestation kept falling. Some believed an uptick in deforestation in 2013 portended further increases, but it fell again in 2014.[65] In 2015, deforestation in the Amazon again ticked upward by 16 percent, as shown in figure 7.2, though it remains nearly 80 percent below 2004 levels.

Some worrisome signs are on the horizon. Brazil's forest faces continued threats from road paving, hydroelectric dams, and growth in global demand for commodities.[66] How the political coalitions upholding forest conservation policies will be affected by economic and political turbulence also remains to be seen. Furthermore, the Brazilian government has been criticized for pledging to eliminate *illegal* deforestation by 2030, rather than *all* deforestation, as dozens of other governments pledged in the 2014 New York Declaration on Forests.[67]

Reasons also exist, however, to think Brazil's success can be maintained for many decades to come and can even be improved upon. The Amazon has several decades' worth of already cleared land available for farming and ranching and considerable scope for continuing to improve yields on it. In fact, Brazil has so much degraded land that economist Bernardo Strassburg and his colleagues estimate that, with modest increases in agricultural productivity, it can continue increasing food production without cutting another tree until after 2040.[68]

Furthermore, while punitive measures have been pushed hard, there is tremendous room to complement these "sticks" with "carrots" in the form of positive incentives to farmers who maintain forests on their land.[69] In addition to pay-for-performance funds (for example, PES), these might include accelerated land titling for legitimate claimants and jurisdiction-level certification of zero-deforestation beef.[70]

And while it's true that other governments have made stronger promises to curb deforestation in the future, so far they are only that—promises. Brazil has already made dramatic cuts to deforestation while other countries' rates are still increasing.

Whether or not Brazil's lower rates of deforestation persist, it's worth emphasizing that its emission reductions since 2004 are just as real and permanent as reductions from any other sector. Just as if Brazil had cut its coal consumption by 80 percent over a decade, a large stock of carbon is left in the ground or in the forest where it might—or might not—be burned later.

Replicating Brazil's Success

Can Brazil's success be replicated elsewhere? Some believe Brazil was exceptional in its conditions. Geographer Ruth DeFries and her colleagues argue that since few other tropical countries have the same capacities for governance and monitoring as Brazil, few can expect to follow in its footsteps.[71]

We're more optimistic, for a few reasons. First, national governance indicators disguise a great deal of internal variation. Brazil's Amazon frontier was arguably once as lawless, violent, and corrupt as anywhere else in the tropics. That changed, rapidly, with presidential political will. Second, while Brazil's monitoring program is proudly world class, forest monitoring systems don't need to be homegrown. They can be imported in whole or in part, as in the case of Guyana, described in box 4.4. DETER-like and PRODES-like data are now available worldwide through the Global Forest Watch platform.[72] Third, offers of performance-based funding might accelerate the development of institutional capacities even where they are currently low.

The other enabling condition we identified—a backlog of cleared land available for planting—is also present in many places around the world. Although most countries don't have as large a stock of deforested land as Brazil, farmable low-carbon land exists throughout the tropics.[73] So, too, does the potential to achieve greater yields from currently farmed land.[74]

Furthermore, there is clearly more to success than simply having the same enabling conditions as Brazil. DeFries and her colleagues mentioned two countries as having rule of law at the national level equal to or better than Brazil: Costa Rica and Malaysia.[75] While Costa Rica has, indeed, been a world leader in forest conservation for three decades, Malaysia has one of the world's highest deforestation rates,[76] driven by logging and palm oil interests. Malaysia's conspicuous absence from participation in international REDD+ programs makes it nearly unique among tropical countries.

Finally, only in hindsight can Brazil's circumstances be considered preconditions for success. No one would have suggested in 2004 that Brazil's conditions meant the Amazon was about to undergo the rapid transformation it did. While Brazil offers valuable lessons, we should be cautious about extrapolating too much from the experiences of a single country. Success stories of reducing tropical deforestation in other countries[77] may result from policies and enabling conditions different than those of Brazil, reflecting the wide diversity of tropical countries.

For that reason, we now turn to an analysis of the factors that generally drive or deter deforestation across the entire tropics, including but not limited to Brazil. No other country has yet succeeded in reducing deforestation on the scale Brazil has, yet policies in many others have lessened it relative to what would have happened otherwise. Many of the most successful are the same ones employed on a larger scale by Brazil.

Understanding What Drives and Stops Deforestation: A Pantropical Meta-Analysis

When Amazon deforestation skyrocketed in the 1980s, the international community "discovered" the problem of tropical deforestation. Since then, forest researchers and practitioners have amassed substantial knowledge and experience about the causes of deforestation and how to address them through policy actions, technological interventions, economic incentives, and governance reforms. Such inquiry has been galvanized by the availability of low-cost, high-resolution spatial data on changes in forest cover, described in chapter 4, and by the advent of REDD+, described in chapter 9.

For *Why Forests? Why Now?* Ferretti-Gallon and Busch conducted a meta-analysis of 117 studies to identify systematically the key factors that drive or deter deforestation.[78] The meta-analysis, described in box 7.1, together with the findings of previous reviews, provide the basis for the section that follows. As noted above, we save for chapter 10 a discussion of political factors that enable or inhibit policies to address deforestation.

Box 7.1: What Drives and Stops Deforestation? The Methods

People's decisions to deforest are influenced by a number of factors, or "drivers." These include the following:

- *Proximity to built infrastructure* such as roads and towns
- *Demand for market commodities* such as beef, soy, palm oil, paper, and timber
- *Demographic and socioeconomic characteristics* of households or communities
- *Land ownership and management rights*, ranging from protected public lands, to open access, to leased concessions, to private ownership rights with varying degrees of tenure security
- *Biophysical characteristics* of land, such as slope, elevation, and soil suitability

Researchers use a statistical technique called spatially explicit econometrics to determine the effect of individual drivers while controlling for the influence of other potentially confounding factors. This task is more sophisticated than simply comparing deforestation rates before and after a policy, or inside and outside of affected areas. It often involves estimating policy impacts relative to what would have happened to deforestation without the policy—a so-called "counterfactual."

Here is a summary of the method used by Ferretti-Gallon and Busch to conduct a systematic review of spatially explicit econometric studies of factors that drive and stop deforestation.

Step 1: Search for studies. Ferretti-Gallon and Busch attempted to compile all published academic studies that analyze the determinants of deforestation using spatially explicit econometrics. They did so by searching academic databases for keywords, including deforestation, causation, and econometrics.

Step 2: Filter studies. They included studies only if they met five predetermined methodological criteria. The application of these criteria yielded 117 studies, shared in an online database.[a]

Step 3: Categorize variables. They categorized more than six thousand explanatory variables into forty categories of drivers, such as elevation, proximity to roads, greater timber activity, and so forth.

Step 4: Code variables. They coded every explanatory variable in every study based on its sign (positive or negative) and the significance of its relationship with deforestation: negative and significant, positive and significant, or not significant.

Step 5: Count variables. They counted the number of times explanatory variables within each category were associated with significantly less or significantly more deforestation. If the ratio of these two results was different from what would be expected by repeatedly flipping a coin, they termed the variables in that category "consistently associated" with higher or lower deforestation, as shown in figure 7.3.

Step 6: Analyze the sensitivity of results. They disaggregated their results based on study region, study scale, and other characteristics to address the well-known potential for the findings of meta-analyses to be skewed by the characteristics of the underlying studies. For example, more than half the studies in the meta-analysis were performed in just six countries (Brazil, China, Costa Rica, Indonesia, Mexico, and Thailand); Sub-Saharan Africa in particular was underrepresented.

Selected caveats. Ferretti-Gallon and Busch's analysis looked only at factors that had been mapped in within-country studies. Their lumping and splitting of variables into categories was subjective and, in some cases, combined relatively disparate variables into single categories. Sample sizes for some categories of variables were small, making findings for those categories more uncertain. Their analysis also did not distinguish results based on study quality or effect size. Finally, their study did not analyze the drivers of forest degradation, which may include logging, charcoal production, fires, grazing, and hunting. Methods and caveats are discussed in more detail in Ferretti-Gallon and Busch (2014).[b]

a. The online database is available at http://www.cgdev.org/publication/data-set-what-drives-deforestation-and-what-stops-it-meta-analysis-spatially-explicit.
b. Ferretti-Gallon and Busch (2014). An updated analysis is forthcoming as Busch and Ferretti-Gallon (2017).

Figure 7.3: Various factors were consistently associated with less or more deforestation.

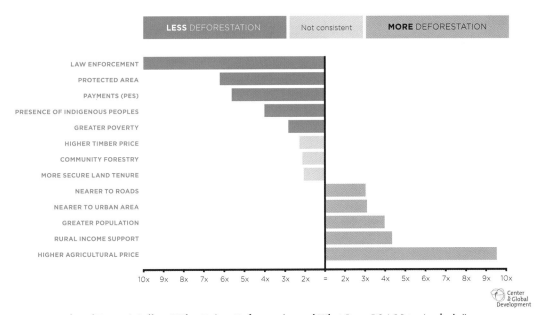

Source: Busch and Ferretti-Gallon, "What Drives Deforestation and What Stops It? A Meta-Analysis."

Note: For example, a ratio of 4x indicates that a variable is associated with less deforestation four times as often as it is associated with more deforestation.

Roads: Dodging the Point of the Lance

When roads are built or paved, deforestation generally follows. The Trans-Amazon Highway and National Highway BR-163 through Pará, mentioned above, were just two of many roads that have crisscrossed the Amazon, leaving behind a spiderweb of cleared land. Highways in the Amazon built to connect distant regions have a tendency to spawn side roads built by loggers or miners to reach their quarries. Sideroads spawn even smaller roads, leading to the "fishbone" pattern of deforestation shown in figure 7.4.[79] Ninety-five percent of the deforestation in the Brazilian Amazon has taken place within five and a half kilometers of a road or one kilometer of a navigable river.[80] Elsewhere, logging and mining roads may penetrate deep into remote forests even before highways are built. They make land more accessible to new migrants, who clear roadside land for pasture or crops. In the absence of roads, land often remains inaccessible and preserved largely in its natural state.

The meta-analysis found roads are consistently associated with higher deforestation—that is, they are associated with higher far more often than lower deforestation. To some extent, deforestation caused by roads can be limited through protected areas or

Figure 7.4: Deforestation in the Brazilian Amazon often follows a "fish-bone" pattern near roads.

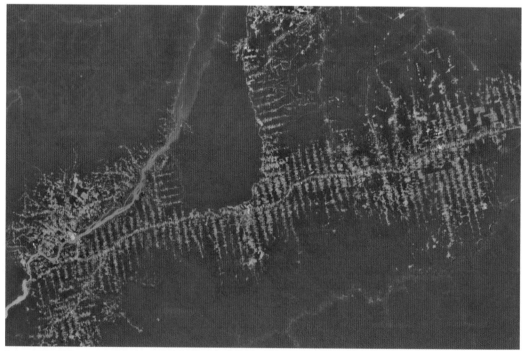

Source: World Resources Institute, "Global Forest Watch."

law enforcement. But the most certain way to reduce deforestation is to minimize the intrusion of new roads into remote forested areas to begin with.

In forests where few people currently live, avoiding opening up a new frontier is perhaps one of the easiest ways to avoid deforestation, as there are no existing claimants to the resources who have their wealth reduced as a result. In contrast, in populated rural areas, new roads improve people's lives by reducing the time and costs of travel to markets and public services, so pressure to build and upgrade roads is strong. Still, transportation networks, potentially including railways and rivers in addition to roads, can be built and upgraded along routes that avoid the most valuable forests in terms of carbon, biodiversity, or other values.[81] The Bank Information Center, for example, praises a World Bank–financed project to improve three thousand kilometers of roads in the Democratic Republic of Congo for its sensitivity to forest-dependent communities and forest values, as well as its participatory planning process.[82]

Protecting the Right Areas

On March 1, 1872, U.S. President Ulysses S. Grant signed the Yellowstone Act, preserving for the public nine thousand square kilometers of land in northwest Wyoming "from injury or spoilation, of all timber, mineral deposits, natural curiosities, or wonders within."[83] Since then, hundreds of millions of visitors have toured the geysers, canyons, mountains, and wildlife of Yellowstone National Park.

The idea caught on, big time. Today more than 150,000 protected areas exist world-wide, in every country on Earth. They span from Australia's Uluru to Zambia and Zimbabwe's Victoria Falls; from postage stamp–size reserves to the United States' vast Papah Naumoku Kea Marine National Monument, which, at 1.51 million square kilometers, is nearly the size of Mongolia.

Only some of these protected areas are preserved in a wilderness state. Many are multiple-use areas that allow economic activities such as hunting, fishing, grazing, or logging while prohibiting full-scale land conversion.[84] Some are mere "paper parks" that exist on the books but have little in the way of effective management.

The meta-analysis found that protected areas are consistently—that is, far more often than not—associated with lower deforestation, partly as a result of their legal status and partly because of their geographical remoteness and low agricultural potential. A disproportionate number of the world's protected areas are "high and far," protecting lands that are scenic but unlikely to be put to agricultural use due to their high altitude, steep terrain, and/or distance from population centers.[85] Lands that are potentially valuable for growing crops are less often set aside in reserves.

Remote, marginal forests may be prized for their scenic beauty or their biodiversity, but for protected areas to prevent deforestation in the near term, they need to be placed where forests are actually under threat, as along Brazil's Arc of Deforestation.[86]

Indigenous Peoples: The Original Forest Defenders

Straddling the states of Pará and Mato Grosso in Brazil and following the Xingu River is a keyhole-shaped area of forest the size of Greece. The fires and chainsaws of deforestation have long raged beyond its perimeter, as shown in figure 7.5, including inside some nominally protected areas. They do not enter the keyhole, however, which is made up of a dozen or so legally recognized Indigenous Areas: Bau, Kayapo, Menkragnoti, Xingu, and others. The tribes that have called this area home for centuries guard their forests vigilantly against intruders.

The meta-analysis found the presence of indigenous peoples consistently associated with lower deforestation rates, spanning areas with and without officially recognized territorial rights. Supporting indigenous peoples is a justifiable agenda in its own right, so strengthening legal recognition of their rights to forests would seem to represent a simultaneous win for people and for forests. But since indigenous peoples' forests incur significantly lower deforestation even where their territorial rights are not legally recognized, more research is needed to understand the conditions under which stronger legal recognition of these rights also results in lower deforestation. To capture its full win-win potential, legal recognition may need also to be monitored, backed up by law enforcement, and complemented by economic opportunities compatible with forest protection.[87]

Enforcing Forest Laws

Many tropical countries have laws on the books protecting forests, but far from the seat of government, these laws may be applied selectively or not at all. Protected areas without protection are just paper parks; restrictions on where agricultural crops can be grown are

Figure 7.5: Deforestation in Pará, Brazil, has been far greater outside indigenous territories.

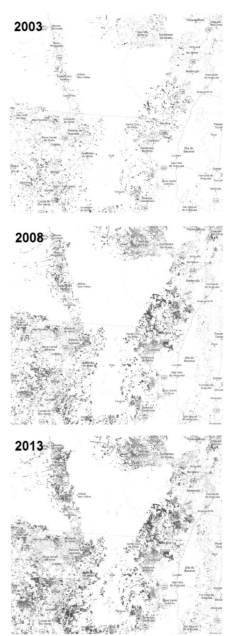

Source: World Resources Institute, "Global Forest Watch."

only as good as their application in practice. Effective forest protection requires not just laws, but law enforcement.

The meta-analysis found law enforcement activity consistently associated with lower deforestation, based on limited evidence to date. This was true of lands spanning all tenure types. On private lands in Brazil, fines by environmental police for illegal clearing reduced deforestation, as did evictions of illegal squatters from national parks in Sumatra, Indonesia, and communal penalties for cases of agricultural encroachment on communal *ejido* forestlands in Mexico.[88] The authors of the studies that yielded these findings emphasized the importance of supplementing law enforcement with positive economic incentives, in order to increase impact or to maintain effectiveness during turbulent times.

While law enforcement has great potential to slow deforestation, would-be forest law enforcers should take care to avoid unjust or repressive actions. Many remote communities rely on forests for much of their livelihoods,[89] and the distinction between legal and illegal can often be blurry and contested. Where one person sees "illegal squatters," another may see "unclear land tenure" or "failure to recognize customary rights." Contested claims may even be codified in law; in some countries, the laws governing rights to forestland conflict with those governing rights to agricultural land.[90] Anthropologist Marcus Colchester and his colleagues have warned against the potential for laws to be enforced selectively, cracking down on the poor and vulnerable while turning a blind eye to the crimes of the rich and politically connected.[91]

Agriculture: Decoupling Commodity Production from Deforestation

The primary cause of tropical deforestation is the expansion of cropland and pasture.[92] More than half of new agricultural land in the tropics during the 1980s and 1990s came at the expense of intact forest.[93] As described further in chapter 8, tropical forest is largely being converted for the production of soy, beef, palm oil, and fast-growing timber for pulp and paper, as well as coffee, cocoa, maize, and sugar.[94] Many people's image of a deforester is a logger with an ax or a saw, but perhaps it should be a farmer with a tractor.

The meta-analysis found agriculture (that is, higher agricultural prices and greater agricultural activity) consistently associated with higher deforestation. Feeding a hungry planet while maintaining a safe and stable climate requires, among other things, decoupling the link between commodity production and deforestation.[95] This means shifting the expansion of cropland and pasture away from forests and peatlands toward lands with less carbon, while considering other social and environmental criteria, as well. A recent study, for example, found 125 million hectares of low-carbon lands in the tropics suitable for oil palm.[96]

Most tropical countries do not have as much open deforested land as Brazil on which to grow crops, suggesting the importance of increasing agricultural yields. Support for increasing yields is politically attractive because it aligns with the existing goals of farmers and agribusinesses. Higher yields on their own are unlikely to reduce deforestation, however. In the absence of direct forest conservation policies, they can increase profitability and thus increase the incentive to clear new land.[97] A cohesive food and forest policy requires direct forest conservation measures, in addition to increasing agricultural yields away from the forest frontier.

A great deal of tropical deforestation takes place to produce commodities that are traded on world markets and consumed in distant countries. As a result, recent years have seen heightened interest in actions that can be taken along commodity supply chains to insulate the forest frontier from the effect of high commodity prices, as described in chapter 8. Some policies have been implemented by governments of forest countries, such as moratoriums on granting new licenses to clear forests for agricultural plantations in Indonesia or restrictions on agricultural credit for farmers in Brazilian municipalities that are blacklisted due to high deforestation.[98] As described further in chapter 11, some policies, such as the European Union's Timber Regulation and 2008 amendments to the U.S. Lacey Act, have been put into place by importing countries. Other measures have been implemented industrywide, such as the commitments by the Brazilian soy and beef industries not to source products from recently deforested land. Still others, including corporate zero-deforestation commitments and voluntary certification schemes, are at the level of individual companies.[99]

Researchers are just beginning to analyze the effectiveness of these various measures. We discuss the role of trade, consumption, and supply-chain measures in driving or deterring deforestation at greater length in chapter 8.

Payments for Ecosystem Services

People typically clear forests because they expect to profit from growing and selling beef, soy, palm oil, or other commodities. Their calculations may include the costs of removing forests from the land, planting crops, and transporting those crops to market. But they probably don't include the costs of dirtier water, hotter air, and greater vulnerability to storms, as we described in chapters 3 and 6. These are often borne by people living downstream, downwind, or downhill of the lost forests.

To the people clearing forests, these other costs are an externality—a deterioration of a public good that is an incidental by-product of their private decision to clear land. Like other activities where benefits are private but costs are passed along to the public, too much deforestation occurs. The public services from forests are underprovided.

The concept of "payments for ecosystem services" (PES), described in chapter 6, aims to right this equation by internalizing the environmental costs in land users' clearing decisions. This logic also underpins efforts to channel international carbon payments to individual landowners to internalize the costs of their forest-based carbon emissions.

As defined by economist Sven Wunder, a PES is a voluntary transaction in which a well-defined environmental service or a land use likely to secure that service is purchased from at least one provider if and only if the service is provided.[100] The environmental service in question is often clean water, and the purchaser is often a municipal water utility, a hydroelectric facility, or a government acting on behalf of water users. The upstream service providers are often landowners.

The world's oldest and most famous PES program, established in 1997, is in Costa Rica. Between 1997 and 2012, Costa Rica's National Forestry Fund (FONAFIFO) paid $340 million to forest owners in ex post payments in exchange for the protection of more than 860,000 hectares of forest.[101] Other PES programs exist in Brazil, China, Ecuador, Mexico, Vietnam, and elsewhere, as mentioned in chapter 6.

Some PES programs, such as later iterations of Costa Rica's, target payments to a few highly threatened areas to maximize additional forest conserved per dollar spent.[102] Others, such as Ecuador's SocioBosque, aim to spread benefits broadly across many recipients in a sort of green rural income-support program, with the amount of deforestation avoided a secondary consideration.[103]

The meta-analysis found PES programs consistently associated with lower deforestation—a combined result of payments lowering deforestation and payments being made to places that had low deforestation to begin with. A separate review study of PES programs found them most effective when payments are targeted to higher threat areas, enrollment is high, recipients are monitored for compliance, and the link between land use and the desired ecosystem service is well established.[104]

The biggest advantage of PES programs over more heavy-handed policies is that they are one of only a few carrots in a policy toolbox full of sticks. PES programs have the potential to create a broad class of winners from forest protection policy, potentially improving the political popularity and equity of conservation measures that would otherwise

result only in losers. They can also be used in conjunction with more restrictive policies, such as in Costa Rica, where PES was introduced at the same time as a ban on all conversion of established forest.[105]

PES programs must be regarded as a "sophisticated and demanding tool," however, because of several preconditions needed for their use: a payment culture and good organization from service users, a trustful negotiation climate, and well-defined land- or resource-tenure regimes for providers.[106] A 2010 study by economist Jan Börner and his colleagues found only one-quarter of threatened forests in the Brazilian Amazon were then under land tenure appropriate for PES.[107] No wonder, then, that the growth of PES programs to date has been largely confined to some regions of some middle-income countries. A $150 million letter of intent between Liberia and Norway for forest conservation and agricultural development mentions plans to experiment with PES to communities;[108] if scaled up, this would make it one of the first national PES programs in Sub-Saharan Africa.[109]

A relative of PES is a tax on deforestation. Like PES, deforestation taxes can internalize public costs in private land-use decisions. Deforestation taxes have not been applied as often, or with such fanfare, as PES, but they do exist. Since 1996, Bolivia has officially required landowners wishing to deforest to pay a permit fee of $15 per hectare to do so, though enforcement of this law has been weak.[110] Levies on logging, as in Indonesia, have typically been applied to collect royalties rather than impede forest degradation.[111]

Revisiting Conventional Wisdom

The effects described by the meta-analysis of the six factors discussed above—roads, protected areas, indigenous peoples, law enforcement, agriculture, and PES—are broadly in agreement with conventional wisdom, as well as with the previous review studies shown in figure 7.6. For the three factors we discuss next, however—poverty, logging, and local land rights—elements of conventional wisdom may need to be revisited in light of the meta-analysis findings and those of other review studies.

Does Poverty Cause Deforestation?

As the conventional thinking has long gone, deforestation is driven by poor and desperate people who must resort to slashing and burning forests to put food on the table. This has some basis in fact; local and subsistence farmers are responsible for around a quarter of deforestation in Latin America and around 40 percent in Africa and Asia.[112] As we elaborate in chapter 8, however, poor smallholders are no longer the most responsible for deforestation overall. Large agricultural interests now drive far more,[113] as evidenced by the big ranchers and soy growers in Brazil and the oil palm kings of Indonesia. The meta-analysis found poverty consistently associated with less—not more—deforestation.

And having more money is probably not just correlated with higher deforestation; it causes higher deforestation. Where people's incomes increase for reasons that have nothing to do with forests, deforestation has followed. Jennifer Alix-Garcia and her

Figure 7.6: Multiple review studies broadly agree on which factors are associated with more or less deforestation.

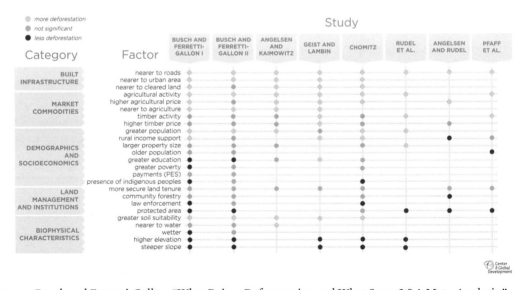

Source: Busch and Ferretti-Gallon, "What Drives Deforestation and What Stops It? A Meta-Analysis."

colleagues showed that Mexico's famously randomized Opportunidades antipoverty program increased deforestation in communities that received cash transfers.[114] The meta-analysis found rural income support programs such as Opportunidades consistently associated with higher deforestation.

Perhaps it is no surprise that people who have more money deforest more. They are better able to purchase equipment and hire labor to clear forests and are more likely to make longer-term investments in agriculture. They also demand more deforestation-intensive commodities, such as beef.

The idea that poverty is the root cause of deforestation has often been paired with an appealing proposition termed the Environmental Kuznets Curve: make countries richer, and they'll automatically shift their preferences to a cleaner environment, including a preference for less deforestation. It's true that there is no shortage of countries where economic growth has paralleled a transition from rapid deforestation to a return in forest cover: the United States in general and New England in particular; Europe; Costa Rica; maybe China.

While growing income over time creates the potential for a middle-class constituency that supports forest conservation, however, there is no guarantee it will do so, or will do so before forests are largely depleted. New England reversed deforestation because railroads and refrigerator cars allowed local agriculture to be undercut by imports of cheaper, higher-yielding produce from the U.S. Midwest, not because its citizenry became particularly wealthy or enlightened. A meta-analysis of studies of the "Environmental Kuznets Curve for deforestation" found the evidence supporting the theory to be mixed and diminishing over time.[115]

None of this justifies keeping people in poverty as a pro-forest program; antipoverty programs are defensible on their own merits. Rather, if deforestation is to be slowed as countries develop, antipoverty programs will need to be complemented by forest conservation policies.

Does Logging Accelerate Deforestation?

As mentioned above, in most parts of the tropics the amount of forest cleared for timber is small relative to wholesale clearing for agriculture.[116] Even where logging does take place, its effect on the forest is complicated. On one hand, logging activity degrades forests. Once valuable timber species are logged out, the remaining forest is often abandoned.[117] In addition, the construction of new roads into remote areas invites deforestation later on. On the other hand, the economic returns forests provide through timber harvest can lead to longer-term management and may forestall more rapid conversion of these forests to agriculture.[118]

On the whole, the meta-analysis found logging was associated with lower rates of deforestation about as often as higher. This finding has some caveats. The satellites used to detect large-scale deforestation may not detect all the fine-scale forest degradation caused by logging, as described in chapter 4. Plantation forests for timber production may be directly replacing natural forests that are more biodiverse and richer in carbon. In addition, logging practices can vary widely in their sustainability;[119] some operations may be devastating to forests while others are well managed and forestall a worse fate.

Do Local Land Rights Prevent Deforestation?

In "The Tragedy of the Commons,"[120] the classic 1968 parable by human ecologist Garrett Hardin, a pasture that belongs to everyone and no one is torn to shreds by overgrazing cattle. Hardin intended the overgrazed pasture to serve as a metaphor for the tragic fate of many "open-access resources": over-fished seas, over-polluted rivers, over-visited national parks, and ultimately, an overpopulated planet.

The way to avoid the tragedy, per Hardin, is to restrict access to the commons. This could be achieved by privatizing it or keeping it public with restricted access, allocated by auction, merit, queues, or lottery. These Hardin took to be "all the reasonable possibilities."

Thus, the belief that granting land rights to local communities would result in greater forest conservation has a theoretical basis, as well as social appeal. A 2014 study by researchers at the World Resources Institute and Rights and Resources Initiative, for example, reviewed evidence that legally protected forest rights for communities tend to lower deforestation.[121]

Unfortunately, while open access to forests encourages over-exploitation, simply granting rights to some people and excluding others does not necessarily result in the resource's being used more sustainably. The meta-analysis found stronger local property rights, in the form of more secure individual land tenure or community forest management, consistently associated with neither higher nor lower rates of deforestation.

Most other review studies of local land rights have come to similar conclusions. While one found land tenure security to be associated with less deforestation, regardless of the form of tenure, studies of the devolution of forest rights to local communities found evidence limited, limited in quality, or difficult to synthesize, or that it was too soon to draw a strong general conclusion.[122]

Perhaps this shouldn't be surprising. More secure property rights reduce the risk that forests will be expropriated by others, thereby increasing the value of leaving them standing to harvest in the future and leading to less deforestation. On the other hand, more secure property rights also increase the incentive for property owners to invest in agriculture, resulting in more deforestation.

In the end, whether or not devolving land rights to local people results in greater forest conservation probably depends on to whom the rights are granted. As mentioned above, the presence of indigenous peoples is associated with lower deforestation far more often than not; but many communities, given the legal right to post a "no trespassing" sign, may choose to plant oil palm or soy fields or sell the rights to do so to others. Nobel laureate economist Elinor Ostrom described eleven attributes of forests and forest users that increase the likelihood a forest will be managed sustainably.[123] These include forest users who trust one another, are concerned about the future, and are already organized, as in the case of Tarcísio Feitosa da Silva and his neighbors.

Not every driver of deforestation need be addressed through policy

One driver is far more often than not associated with faster deforestation, but policies to address it are probably still misplaced: population growth. The meta-analysis found greater population consistently goes hand in hand with faster deforestation. Which causes which is a classic chicken and egg problem, however. On the one hand, a larger population has more workers to clear forest and more people demanding food, leading to more deforestation (the chicken). On the other, more deforestation means more land to grow crops, which can support a larger economic base and a greater population (the egg).

Complicating matters further, new agricultural land can attract both people and deforestation. Brazil's military dictator Emílio Garrastazu Médici announced the building of the Trans-Amazon Highway in 1970 with the intention to "move men without lands to lands without men." Indonesia's decades-long resettlement program, called "transmigration," had a similar intent. Tellingly, in both cases the destinations were already inhabited by indigenous peoples, albeit at low population densities. Thus, the observed relationship between population growth and deforestation may be due as much or more to in-migration as natural population increase.

Even where a growing population does cause deforestation, the relationship may not be straightforward. The first migrants to an area may have a far larger impact on deforestation than later ones.[124] Beyond a certain point, a growing population could cause land to be used more intensively, as Danish economist Ester Boserup theorized in 1965, which could either lead to more deforestation or less.[125] And demand for agricultural products by increasingly wealthy urbanites may be a larger driver of deforestation than demand from local populations, meaning that out-migration from rural areas to cities might decrease deforestation locally, but not regionally or globally. [126]

Given the much broader societal issues regarding population growth and migration, population policies are not a priority for addressing deforestation. Expanding access to family planning services to meet existing demand can be justified on its own merits regardless of its effect on deforestation.

Countries seeking to slow deforestation may or may not use the same mixture of policies Brazil did; they have a wide array of tested policy tools to choose from.

Conclusion

The Brazilian Amazon once had the highest rates of deforestation in the world. For indigenous peoples, rubber tappers, and small farmers, conserving the forest in the face of pressure from loggers, ranchers, and large soy growers once seemed impossible. Yet, when the federal government found political will, Brazil brought down the rate of deforestation in the Amazon by 80 percent in six years. It showed the world that slowing deforestation can be accomplished without sacrificing agricultural production or economic growth.

Brazil reduced deforestation using a broad suite of restrictive policies applied in combination: protected areas, indigenous peoples' reserves, law enforcement, and diversion of agricultural supply chains away from recently deforested lands. It was able to enact them successfully thanks to satellite monitors and plentiful already deforested land. Payments for keeping forests standing were too recent and small to have contributed much to the big decline in deforestation, but they can potentially play a much larger role in combating deforestation in the future, including by helping to make restrictive measures more palatable. Other countries seeking to slow deforestation may or may not use the same mixture of policies Brazil did; they have a wide array of tested policy tools to choose from.

It is tempting to think the ability to curb deforestation lies entirely within the control of forest countries. Yet, to a large extent, deforestation is being driven by market forces that transcend national borders. A large and rising share of tropical forest clearing takes place to supply globally traded commodities such as beef, soy, palm oil, paper, and timber. We discuss the forest footprint of private commodity traders and consumers, as well as public policies in rich countries such as those promoting biofuels, in chapter 8.

Notes

1. P. Symmes, "Blood Wood," *Outside Magazine*, October 1, 2002.
2. L. Rohter, "Struggling to Save His Amazon, from the Top of a Death List," *New York Times*, December 30, 2006.
3. Symmes, "Blood Wood."
4. P. M. Fearnside, "Brazil's Cuiabá-Santarém (BR-163) Highway: The Environmental Cost of Paving a Soybean Corridor through the Amazon," *Environmental Management* 39, no. 5 (2007): 601–14.
5. C. Araujo et al., "Property Rights and Deforestation in the Brazilian Amazon," *Ecological Economics* 68, no. 8 (2009): 2461–68.
6. L. Rohter, "Brazil's Lofty Promises after Nun's Killing Prove Hollow," *New York Times*, September 23, 2005.
7. Ibid.
8. Symmes, "Blood Wood"; C. Simmons et al., "The Changing Dynamics of Land Conflict in the Brazilian Amazon: The Rural-Urban Complex and Its Environmental Implications," *Urban Ecosystems* 6, no. 1–2 (2002): 99–121.
9. Comissão Pastoral da Terra, "Assassinatos e Processos Pará—1985–2011," August 9, 2012, Goiás, Brazil, http://www.cptnacional.org.br/index.php/component/jdownloads/send/26-documentos/296-cpt-para-assassinatos-e-processos-para-1985-2011, as reported in Symmes, "Blood Wood."
10. Greenpeace, "State of Conflict: An Investigation into the Land Grabbers, Loggers and Lawless Frontiers in Pará State, Amazon," Greenpeace, Amsterdam, 2004.
11. Ibid.; S. Sauer, "Human Rights Violations in the Amazon: Conflict and Violence in the State of Pará," Comissão Pastoral da Terra, Justiça Global, and Terra de Direitos, Rio de Janeiro, 2005, http://www.fdcl-berlin.de/fileadmin/fdcl/Publikationen/relatoriopara ingles.pdf.
12. Symmes, "Blood Wood."
13. National Institute for Space Research, "Projeto Prodes: Monitoramento da Floresta Amazônica Brazileira Por Satélite," http://www.obt.inpe.br/prodes/index.php.
14. N. Stern, speech at Forest Day 3, Center for International Forestry Research, Copenhagen, Denmark, December 13, 2009, http://www.cifor.org/publications/pdf_files/cop/cop15/stern-speech.pdf.
15. Authors' calculations based on 555 GtC cumulative emissions, 1750–2013 (Ciais 2013) and an assumed average carbon density of 150 tC/ha.
16. L. Barbosa, "Save the Rainforest! NGOs and Grassroots Organisations in the Dialectics of Brazilian Amazonia," *International Social Science Journal* 55, no. 178 (2003): 583.
17. National Institute for Space Research, "Projeto Prodes: Monitoramento da Floresta Amazônica Brazileira Por Satélite," http://www.obt.inpe.br/prodes/index.php.
18. K. Ferretti-Gallon and J. Busch, "What Drives Deforestation and What Stops It? A Meta-Analysis of Spatially Explicit Econometric Studies," CGD Working Paper 361, Center for Global Development, Washington, DC, 2014.
19. "Sister Dorothy's Killers," op-ed, *New York Times*, March 2, 2005.
20. L. Rohter, "Brazil Promises Crackdown after Nun's Shooting Death," *New York Times*, February 14, 2005.
21. L. Rohter, "World Briefing | Americas: Brazil: 2,000 Troops to Amazon Region," *New York Times*, February 17, 2005; BBC, "Cowboys and Land-Grab," in Amazon: Bruce Parry Explores the Greatest River on Earth, 2008, http://www.bbc.co.uk/amazon/sites/cowboys/pages/content.shtml.
22. M. Campos and D. Nepstad, "Smallholders, the Amazon's New Conservationists," *Conservation Biology* 20, no. 5 (2006): 1553–56.
23. J. C. Assunção, C. Gandour, and R. Rocha, "DETERring Deforestation in the Brazilian Amazon: Environmental Monitoring and Law Enforcement," Climate Policy Initiative and Pontifical Catholic University of Rio de Janeiro, Rio de Janeiro, 2013; A. Veríssimo et al., "Protected Areas in the Brazilian Am-

azon: Challenges and Opportunities," IMA-ZON, Belém, Brazil, 2011.

24. E. Cisneros, S. Lian Zhou, and J. Börner, "Naming and Shaming for Conservation: Evidence from the Brazilian Amazon," *PLOS ONE* 10, no. 9 (2015): e0136402; J. Assunção, C. Gandour, and R. Rocha, "Does Credit Affect Deforestation? Evidence from a Rural Credit Policy in the Brazilian Amazon," Climate Policy Initiative and Pontifical Catholic University of Rio de Janeiro, Rio de Janeiro, 2013, http://climatepolicyinitiative.org/wp-content/uploads/2013/01/Does-Credit-Affect-Deforestation-Executive-Summary-English.pdf.

25. H. K. Gibbs et al., "Brazil's Soy Moratorium," *Science* 347, no. 6220 (2015): 377–78; P. Newton, H. N. Alves-Pinto, and L. Fernando Guedes Pinto, "Certification, Forest Conservation, and Cattle: Theories and Evidence of Change in Brazil," *Conservation Letters* 8, no. 3 (2015): 206–13; H. K. Gibbs et al., "Did Ranchers and Slaughterhouses Respond to Zero-Deforestation Agreements in the Brazilian Amazon?" *Conservation Letters* 9, no. 1 (2016): 32–42.

26. National Institute for Space Research, "Projeto Prodes: Monitoramento da Floresta Amazônica Brazileira Por Satélite," http://www.obt.inpe.br/prodes/index.php.

27. E. Arima et al., "Public Policies Can Reduce Tropical Deforestation: Lessons and Challenges from Brazil," *Land Use Policy* 41 (2014): 465–73; J. Assunção, C. Gandour, and R. Rocha, "Deforestation Slowdown in the Brazilian Amazon: Prices or Policies?" *Environment and Development Economics* 20, no. 6 (2015): 697–722.

28. World Bank Group, "GDP Grown (Annual %)," World Bank Global Development Indicators, http://data.worldbank.org/indicator/NY.GDP.MKTP.KD.ZG.

29. Global Witness, "Deadly Environment: The Dramatic Increase in Killings of Environmental and Land Defenders," London, 2014; "Murder in the Amazon:

30. C. Springer and M. Wolosin, "Who Cut The Most? Brazil's Forest Protection Has Achieved Twice US Emissions Reductions," Climate Advisers blog, Washington, DC, http://www.climateadvisers.com/who-cut-the-most-brazils-forest-protection-has-achieved-twice-us-emissions-reductions/.

31. The Goldman Environmental Prize, "Tarcisio Feitosa: 2006 Goldman Prize Recipient, South and Central America," http://www.goldmanprize.org/recipient/tarcisio-feitosa/.

32. D. Nepstad et al., "Slowing Amazon Deforestation through Public Policy and Interventions in Beef and Soy Supply Chains," *Science* 344, no. 6188 (2014): 1118–23.

33. Environmental Defense Fund, "Brazil National and State REDD," November 2009.

34. Veríssimo et al., "Protected Areas in the Brazilian Amazon."

35. D. Boucher et al., *Deforestation Success Stories: Tropical Nations Where Forest Protection and Reforestation Policies Have Worked* (Cambridge, MA: Union of Concerned Scientists, 2014).

36. C. Araujo et al., "Property Rights and Deforestation in the Brazilian Amazon," *Ecological Economics* 68, no. 8 (2009): 2461–68.

37. Ibid.

38. B. Soares-Filho, "Cracking Brazil's Forest Code," *Science* 344, no. 6182 (2014): 363–64; Nepstad et al., "Slowing Amazon Deforestation."

39. Boucher et al., "Deforestation Success Stories"; Arima et al., "Public Policies Can Reduce Tropical Deforestation."

40. Nepstad et al., "Slowing Amazon Deforestation."

41. J. Assunção and R. Rocha, "Getting Greener by Going Black: The Priority Municipalities in Brazil," technical paper, Climate Policy Initiative, Rio de Janeiro, Brazil, 2014.

42. Ibid.; Nepstad et al., "Slowing Amazon Deforestation"; Arima et al., "Public Policies Can Reduce Tropical Deforestation."

43. Cisneros, Lian Zhou, and Börner, "Naming and Shaming for Conservation."

44. Greenpeace, "Eating Up the Amazon," Greenpeace.org, Amsterdam, 2006.

45. R. Butler, "Brazilian Soy Industry Extends Moratorium on Deforestation Indefinitely," Mongabay.com, May 9, 2016, https://news.mongabay.com/2016/05/brazilian-soy-industry-extends-moratorium-deforestation-indefinitely/.

46. Gibbs et al., "Brazil's Soy Moratorium."

47. Boucher et al., "Deforestation Success Stories"; Arima et al., "Public Policies Can Reduce Tropical Deforestation"; J. Tollefson, "Prosecutor Takes on Beef Industry to Put Brakes on Deforestation in the Amazon," *Inside Climate News*, June 11, 2014.

48. Gibbs et al., "Did Ranchers and Slaughterhouses Respond?"

49. Arima et al., "Public Policies Can Reduce Tropical Deforestation."

50. P. Newton, H. N. Alves-Pinto, and L. Fernando Guedes Pinto, "Certification, Forest Conservation, and Cattle: Theories and Evidence of Change in Brazil," *Conservation Letters* 8, no. 3 (2015): 206.

51. Börner et al., "Promoting Forest Stewardship."

52. Fundação Amazonas Sustentável, "Amazon Fund Approves Support for Bolsa Floresta," December 9, 2009, http://fas-amazonas.org/2009/12/fundo-amazonia-aprova-apoio-ao-programa-bolsa-floresta/?lang=en; Fundação Amazonas Sustentável, "Emission Offset," http://fas-amazonas.org/projeto-rds-do-juma/carboneutralizacao/?lang=en.

53. Nepstad et al., "Slowing Amazon Deforestation."

54. Assunção, Gandour, and Rocha, "DETERring Deforestation in the Brazilian Amazon," 2013, http://climatepolicyinitiative.org/wp-content/uploads/2013/05/DETERring-Deforestation-in-the-Brazilian-Amazon-Environmental-Monitoring-and-Law-Enforcement-Executive-Summary.pdf.

55. Ibid.

56. National Institute for Space Research (INPE), "Projeto Prodes: Monitoramento da Floresta Amazônica Brazileira Por Satélite," updated 2016, http://www.obt.inpe.br/prodes/index.php.

57. Arima et al., "Public Policies Can Reduce Tropical Deforestation," 471.

58. "The Miracle of the Cerrado," *The Economist*, August 26, 2010.

59. V. Vasconcelos, R. M. Hadad, and P. P. Martins Junior, "Methodologies for Integrated Studies of Natural Resources: A Discussion on Ecological-Economic Zoning," *Pesquisas em Geociencias* 40 (2013): 21–30.

60. Y. le Polain de Waroux, "Land-Use Policies and Corporate Investments in Agriculture in the Gran Chaco and Chiquitano," *Proceedings of the National Academy of Sciences* 113, no. 15 (2016): 4021–26.

61. E. Arima et al., "Statistical Confirmation of Indirect Land Use Change in the Brazilian Amazon," *Environmental Research Letters* 6, no. 2 (2011): 465–73.

62. S. Spera et al., "Land-Use Change Affects Water Recycling in Brazil's Last Agricultural Frontier," *Global Change Biology* 22, no. 10 (2016): 3405–13.

63. National Institute for Space Research, "Projeto Prodes."

64. M. Macedo et al., "Decoupling of Deforestation and Soy Production in the Southern Amazon during the Late 2000s," *Proceedings of the National Academy of Sciences* 109, no. 4 (2012): 1341–46.

65. National Institute for Space Research, "Projeto Prodes."

66. Arima et al., "Public Policies Can Reduce Tropical Deforestation."

67. Federative Republic of Brazil, "Intended Nationally Determined Contribution: Towards Achieving the Objective of the United Nations Framework Convention on Climate Change," submission to the United Nations Framework Convention on Climate Change, 2015, http://www4.unfccc.int/

submissions/INDC/Published%20 Documents/Brazil/1/BRAZIL%20 iNDC%20english%20FINAL.pdf; United Nations, "Forests: Action Statements and Action Plans," New York, September 23, 2014, http://www.un.org/climatechange/ summit/wp-content/uploads/ sites/2/2014/07/New-York-Declaration-on- Forest-%E2%80%93-Action-Statement-and- Action-Plan.pdf.

68. B. Strassburg et al., "When Enough Should Be Enough: Improving the Use of Current Agricultural Lands Could Meet Production Demands and Spare Natural Habitats in Brazil," *Global Environmental Change* 28 (2014): 84–97.

69. Nepstad et al., "Slowing Amazon Deforestation"; J. Börner et al., "REDD Sticks and Carrots in the Brazilian Amazon: Assessing Costs and Livelihood Implications," CCAFS Working Paper 8, Consortium of International Agricultural Research Centers Program on Climate Change, Agriculture and Food Security, Copenhagen, Denmark, 2011.

70. S. Stokes, M. Lowe, and S. Zoubek, "Deforestation and the Brazilian Beef Value Chain," Datu Research, 2014, http://www. daturesearch.com/wp-content/uploads/ Brazilian-Beef-Final_Optimized1.pdf.

71. R. DeFries et al., "Export-Oriented Deforestation in Mato Grosso: Harbinger or Exception for Other Tropical Forests?" *Philosophical Transactions of the Royal Society of London B: Biological Sciences* 368, no. 1619 (2013).

72. World Resources Institute, "Global Forest Watch," 2014, www.globalforestwatch.org.

73. E. Dinerstein et al., "Guiding Agricultural Expansion to Spare Tropical Forests," *Conservation Letters* 8, no. 4 (2015): 262–71.

74. R. Licker et al., "Mind the Gap: How Do Climate and Agricultural Management Explain the 'Yield Gap' of Croplands around the World?" *Global Ecology and Biogeography* 19, no. 6 (2010): 769–82.

75. DeFries et al., "Export-Oriented Deforestation in Mato Grosso."

76. M. C. Hansen et al., "High-Resolution Global Maps of 21st-Century Forest Cover Change," *Science* 342, no. 6160 (2013): 850–53.

77. Boucher et al., "Deforestation Success Stories."

78. J. Busch and K. Ferretti-Gallon, "What Drives Deforestation," *Review of Environmental Economics and Policy* (2017), forthcoming.

79. J. P. Metzger, "Effects of Deforestation Pattern and Private Nature Reserves on the Forest Conservation in Settlement Areas of the Brazilian Amazon," *Biota Neotropica* 1 (2001): 1–14.

80. C. P. Barber et al., "Roads, Deforestation, and the Mitigating Effect of Protected Areas in the Amazon," *Biological Conservation* 177 (2014): 203–9.

81. W. F. Laurance et al., "A Global Strategy for Road Building," *Nature* 513, no. 7517 (2014): 229–32.

82. L. Puzio, "Analysis of World Bank Finance & Forests: The Impact of Development Projects on Tropical Forests and Forest Peoples," Bank Information Center, 2015, http://www.bankinformationcenter.org/ wp-content/uploads/2015/09/Analysis_of_ WB_finance_and_forests.pdf.

83. History.com Staff, "Yellowstone Park Established," *This Day in History*, History. com, A&E Networks, 2009, http://www. history.com/this-day-in-history/ yellowstone-park-established.

84. International Union for Conservation of Nature and United Nations Environment Programme World Conversation Monitoring Center, "The World Database on Protected Areas (WDPA)" (Cambridge, UK: UNEP-WCMC, 2016), www.protectedplanet.net,

85. L. N. Joppa and A.Pfaff, "High and Far: Biases in the Location of Protected Areas," *PLOS ONE* 4, no. 12 (2009): e8273.

86. Campos and Nepstad, "Smallholders."

87. A. Larson et al., *Forests for People* (London and Washington, DC: Earthscan, 2010).

88. J. Hargrave and K. Kis-Katos, "Economic

Causes of Deforestation in the Brazilian Amazon: A Panel Data Analysis for the 2000s," *Environmental and Resource Economics* 54, no. 4 (2013): 471–94; D. Gaveau et al., "Three Decades of Deforestation in Southwest Sumatra: Effects of Coffee Prices, Law Enforcement and Rural Poverty," *Biological Conservation* 142, no. 3 (2009): 597–605; J. Alix-Garcia, A. De Janvry, and Elisabeth Sadoulet, "A Tale of Two Communities: Explaining Deforestation in Mexico," *World Development* 33, no. 2 (2005): 219–35.

89. A. Angelsen et al., "Environmental Income and Rural Livelihoods: A Global-Comparative Analysis," *World Development* 64 (2014): S12–S28.

90. M. Colchester et al., *Justice in the Forest: Rural Livelihoods and Forest Law Enforcement* (Bogor, Indonesia: Center for International Forestry Research [CIFOR], 2006).

91. Ibid.

92. N. Hosonuma et al., "An Assessment of Deforestation and Forest Degradation Drivers in Developing Countries," *Environmental Research Letters* 7, no. 4 (2012): 4009.

93. H. K. Gibbs et al., "Tropical Forests Were the Primary Sources of New Agricultural Land in the 1980s and 1990s," *Proceedings of the National Academy of Sciences* 107, no. 38 (2010): 16732–7.

94. T. Rudel et al., "Changing Drivers of Deforestation and New Opportunities for Conservation," *Conservation Biology* 23, no. 6 (2009): 1396–1405; Hosonuma et al., "An Assessment of Deforestation."

95. See, for example, J. Foley et al., "Solutions for a Cultivated Planet," *Nature* 478, no. 7369 (2011): 337–42.

96. Dinerstein et al., "Guiding Agricultural Expansion to Spare Tropical Forests."

97. For contrasting views on this point, see A. Angelsen and D. Kaimowitz, eds., *Agricultural Technologies and Tropical Deforestation* (Wallingford, UK: CAB Intl, 2001), and T. Hertel, N. Ramankutty, and U. L. C. Baldos, "Global Market Integration Increases Likelihood That a Future African Green Revolution Could Increase Crop Land Use and CO_2 Emissions," *Proceedings of the National Academy of Sciences* 111, no. 38 (2014): 13799–804.

98. J. Busch et al., "Reductions in Emissions from Deforestation from Indonesia's Moratorium on New Oil Palm, Timber, and Logging Concessions," *Proceedings of the National Academy of Sciences* 112, no. 5 (2015): 1328–33; Cisneros, Lian Zhou, and Börner, "Naming and Shaming for Conservation"; J. Assunção, C. Gandour, R. Rocha, and R. Rocha, "Does Credit Affect Deforestation?" Climate Policy Initiative, Rio de Janeiro, 2013, http://climatepolicyinitiative.org/wp-content/uploads/2013/01/Does-Credit-Affect-Deforestation-Evidence-from-a-Rural-Credit-Policy-in-the-Brazilian-Amazon-Technical-Paper-English.pdf.

99. Gibbs et al., "Brazil's Soy Moratorium"; Newton, Alves-Pinto, and Guedes Pinto, "Certification, Forest Conservation, and Cattle"; Gibbs et al., "Did Ranchers and Slaughterhouses Respond?"; D. Miteva, C. J. Loucks, and S. K. Pattanayak, "Social and Environmental Impacts of Forest Management Certification in Indonesia," *PLOS ONE* 10, no. 7 (2015): e0129675.

100. S. Wunder, "Payments for Environmental Services: Some Nuts and Bolts," CIFOR Occasional Paper 42, Center for International Forestry Research, Bogor, Indonesia, 2005.

101. I. Porras et al., "Learning from 20 Years of Payments for Ecosystem Services in Costa Rica," International Institute for Environment and Development, London, 2013.

102. Ibid.

103. F. De Koning et al., "Bridging the Gap between Forest Conservation and Poverty Alleviation: The Ecuadorian Socio Bosque Program," *Environmental Science & Policy* 14, no. 5 (2011): 531–42.

104. S. Pattanayak, S. Wunder, and P. J. Ferraro, "Show Me the Money: Do Payments Supply Environmental Services in Developing

Countries?" *Review of Environmental Economics and Policy* 4, no. 2 (2010): 254–74.

105. Porras et al., "Learning from 20 Years."

106. S. Wunder, "When Payments for Environmental Services Will Work for Conservation," *Conservation Letters* 6, no. 4 (2013): 230–37.

107. J. Börner et al., "Direct Conservation Payments in the Brazilian Amazon: Scope and Equity Implications," *Ecological Economics* 69, no. 6 (2010): 1272–82.

108. Governments of Norway and Liberia, "Letter of Intent: Cooperation on Reducing Greenhouse Gas Emissions from Deforestation and Forest Degradation (REDD+) and Developing Liberia's Agriculture Sector," 2014, https://www.regjeringen.no/contentassets/b8b93fa03bda4ac893d065d26d64075b/letterofintentliberia.pdf.

109. J. Austin, "Payments for Ecosystem Services in Rural Africa," Ecosystem Marketplace, March 15, 2006, http://www.ecosystemmarketplace.com/articles/payments-for-ecosystem-services-in-rural-africa/.

110. R. Müller et al., "Policy Options to Reduce Deforestation Based on a Systematic Analysis of Drivers and Agents in Lowland Bolivia," *Land Use Policy* 30, no. 1 (2013): 895–907.

111. C. Barr, A. Dermawan, H. Purnomo, and H. Komarudin, "Financial Governance and Indonesia's Reforestation Fund during the Soeharto and Post-Soeharto periods, 1989–2009: A Political Economic Analysis of Lessons for REDD+," CIFOR Occasional Paper 52, Center for International Forestry Research, Bogor, Indonesia, 2010.

112. Hosonuma et al., "An Assessment of Deforestation."

113. Rudel et al., "Changing Drivers of Deforestation"; Hosonuma et al., "An Assessment of Deforestation."

114. J. Alix-Garcia, C. McIntosh, K. Sims, and J. R. Welch, "The Ecological Footprint of Poverty Alleviation: Evidence from Mexico's Oportunidades Program," *Review of Economics and Statistics* 95, no. 2 (2013): 417–35.

115. J. Choumert, P. C. Motel, and H. K. Dakpo, "Is the Environmental Kuznets Curve for Deforestation a Threatened Theory? A Meta-Analysis of the Literature," *Ecological Economics* 90 (2013): 19–28.

116. Hosonuma et al., "An Assessment of Deforestation."

117. R. Rice, R. E. Gullison, and J. W. Reid, "Can Sustainable Management Save Tropical Forests?" *Scientific American* 276, no. 4 (1997): 44–49.

118. See F. E. Putz and C. Romero, "Futures of Tropical Production Forests," CIFOR Occasional Paper 143, Center for International Forestry Research, Bogor, Indonesia, 2015.

119. S. López, R. Sierra, and M. Tirado, "Tropical Deforestation in the Ecuadorian Chocó: Logging Practices and Socio-Spatial Relationships," *Geographical Bulletin* 51, no. 1 (2010): 3.

120. G. Hardin, "The Tragedy of the Commons," *Science* 162, no. 3859 (1968): 1243–48.

121. C. Stevens, R. Winterbottom, J. Springer, and K. Reytar, "Securing Rights, Combating Climate Change: How Strengthening Community Forest Rights Mitigates Climate Change," World Resources Institute, Washington, DC, 2014, 56.

122. B. Robinson, M. B. Holland, and L. Naughton-Treves, "Does Secure Land Tenure Save Forests? A Meta-Analysis of the Relationship between Land Tenure and Tropical Deforestation," *Global Environmental Change* 29 (2014): 281–93; D. Miteva, S. K. Pattanayak, and P. J. Ferraro, "Evaluation of Biodiversity Policy Instruments: What Works and What Doesn't?" *Oxford Review of Economic Policy* 28, no. 1 (2012): 69–92; M. Ojane, et al., "Environmental Impacts of Different Property Regimes in Forests, Fisheries and Rangelands: Preliminary Findings from a Systematic Review" (paper presented at the 15th Biannual International Conference of the International Association for the Study of the Commons, Alberta, Canada, May 25–29, 2015); D. Bowle et al., "Does

Community Forest Management Provide Global Environmental Benefits and Improve Local Welfare?" *Frontiers in Ecology and the Environment* 10, no. 1 (2011): 29–36; R. Yin et al., "Empirical Linkages between Devolved Tenure Systems and Forest Conditions: Challenges, Findings, and Recommendations," *Forest Policy and Economics* (2016), in press.

123. E. Ostrom, "Self-Governance and Forest Resources," CIFOR Occasional Paper 20, Center for International Forestry Research, Bogor, Indonesia, 1999.

124. A. Pfaff, "What Drives Deforestation in the Brazilian Amazon? Evidence from Satellite and Socioeconomic Data," *Journal of Environmental Economics and Management* 37, no. 1 (1999): 26–43.

125. E. Boserup, *The Conditions of Agricultural Growth: The Economics of Agrarian Change under Population Pressure* (London: Transaction Publishers, 2005); H. Story, "Malthus vs. Boserup," *Big Picture* educational resource, June 2014, http://bigpictureeducation.com/malthus-vs-boserup; D. Carr, L. Suter, and A. Barbieri, "Population Dynamics and Tropical Deforestation: State of the Debate and Conceptual Challenges," *Population and Environment* 27, no. 1 (2005): 89–113.

126. R. S. DeFries, T. Rudel, M. Uriarte, and M. Hansen, "Deforestation Driven by Urban Population Growth and Agricultural Trade in the Twenty-First Century," *Nature Geoscience* 3, no. 3 (2010): 178–81.

An aerial view shows the imprint of a palm oil plantation in Malaysia.
Credit: Jaggat Rashidi/Shutterstock

CHAPTER 8

Global Consumer Demand

A Big Footprint on Tropical Forests

yberspace, March 17, 2010. A Greenpeace video on the Internet portrays a bored office worker opening up a Nestlé Kit Kat candy bar, tearing into its distinctive red wrapper. He fails to notice that instead of chocolate, he is biting into the severed finger of an orangutan, to the horror of his officemates. Blood drips down his chin and splatters onto his computer keyboard. After cutting to scenes of an orangutan surveying a devastated forest to the sound of revving chainsaws, the video presents its message against a bright red background: "Stop Nestlé buying palm oil from companies that destroy the rainforests."[1]

The video immediately went viral. Nestlé reacted by issuing a copyright complaint against Greenpeace, prompting YouTube to remove it the same day. The company's attempt to suppress the video served to add fuel to the fire of the social media campaign.[2] Reposted on Vimeo for four days and returned to YouTube on March 21, 2010, the video attracted 1.5 million viewers and generated hundreds of thousands of responses over a two-month period.[3] On May 17, Greenpeace declared victory when Nestlé executive vice president José Lopez announced a commitment to remove deforestation from the company's supply chain.[4]

Although only one minute in length, the Kit Kat video graphically made the linkage between branded consumer goods purchased in rich countries and the production of globally traded commodities, such as palm oil, at the expense of tropical forests. The Greenpeace campaign targeted at Nestlé and similar campaigns have raised public awareness of the increasingly commercialized and globalized drivers of tropical deforestation. It also demonstrated the power of a social media campaign to tarnish a major brand and the impotence of a large corporation to stop it without agreeing to change its behavior. The campaign's impacts continue to reverberate in corporate boardrooms around the world.

In this chapter, we focus on the large and increasing role of globally traded commodities as drivers of deforestation and associated climate emissions and, in particular, its implications for public policies and private sector actors in consumer countries. Chapter 7 presented the proven policy tools available to forest-rich developing countries to reduce deforestation and described how Brazil's success resulted from a combination of law enforcement, the establishment of protected areas and indigenous territories, and restrictions on credit to high-deforestation jurisdictions, complemented by private sector supply chain initiatives, in response to advocacy campaigns mounted by NGOs such as Greenpeace. Success in other countries will require similar domestic policy efforts, which could be enhanced by the prospect of reward through financial transfers from rich countries under REDD+.

Because the share of agricultural production destined for export is large and increasing, however, consumers, governments, corporations, and financiers based outside of producer countries can also help break the link to deforestation through "demand-side" policies and practices. As elaborated on fur-

---

This chapter draws heavily on two background papers, one by Martin Persson, Sabine Henders, and Thomas Kastner on the forest emissions embodied in globally traded commodities, and one by Kimberly Elliott on biofuel policies in the European Union and the United States.

ther below, such policies include regulations that restrict the import of goods produced through illegal or unsustainable means that destroy forests. They also include public procurement policies and sourcing practices of private corporations that privilege goods certified to be legally and sustainably produced. In addition, sovereign wealth funds, international banks, and other public and private financial institutions can influence behavior through their investment decisions.

We begin by establishing that clearing for commercial-scale agriculture is the single largest driver of tropical deforestation globally, with forests replaced by cattle pastures, soybean fields and plantations of fast-growing timber, oil palm, and other crops. While smallholder farmers continue to be responsible for significant forest conversion in many areas, the conventional wisdom that poor people are the primary agents of tropical forest loss globally is simply no longer true, if it ever was.

Next, we present the results of an analysis commissioned for this book on the extent to which the emissions caused by tropical deforestation are embodied in products consumed elsewhere.[5] The results confirm that the forest footprint of global consumer demand for commodities produced in the tropics is considerable and likely to grow. We then summarize the evidence that much forest clearing to meet global demand for those commodities is illegal.

In the second half of the chapter, we turn our attention to how perverse policies exacerbate the problem of demand for commodities that are "too cheap" because the emissions they cause are unpriced. We focus on how biofuel subsidies in the European Union and the United States have increased pressure on tropical forests, while also threatening food security in developing countries through higher and more volatile food prices. Those policies also provide a bad example for developing-country governments, many of which have already put their own perverse policies in place.

Finally, we describe the recent wave of commitments by private companies to break the link between commodity production and forest clearing. Nestlé has now been joined not only by dozens of other manufacturers and retailers and leading multinational banks, but also by a number of traders and even a few major producers of products associated with deforestation. Such globally recognized brands as Unilever, Archer Daniels Midland, and Asia Pulp and Paper have all pledged to eliminate deforestation from their supply chains.

We conclude that, in addition to such commitments by the private sector to "no-deforestation" supply chains, feasible policy tools are at the disposal of rich countries to reduce demand for commodities that are illegally and unsustainably produced. Such voluntary pledges and public policies can be complementary. Furthermore, public and private initiatives focused on removing deforestation from commodity supply chains offer synergies with international transfer payments endorsed by the December 2015 Paris Agreement on climate change designed to reward developing countries for reducing emissions from deforestation.

Drivers of Deforestation Are Increasingly Commercialized and Globalized

A generation ago, conventional wisdom supported a view that poor people were the primary agents of deforestation. If you had picked up a United Nations report about tropical deforestation in the mid-1980s, you would have read that it was being carried out by smallholder farmers engaging in "slash-and-burn" agriculture "mainly to satisfy the basic subsistence needs of poor rural communities."[6] A decade later, in 1994, the World Wide Fund for Nature placed an advertisement showing an image of an indigenous person in the Amazon with the headline, "He's destroying his own rainforest," with text describing how "some native peoples are felling their forest for cash."[7]

The largest share of deforestation is now attributed to large-scale commercial agricultural enterprises responding to demand for globally traded commodities.

But the conventional wisdom is no longer true, if it ever was. Over the past thirty years, our understanding of the principal causes of forest loss has changed, even as our ability to attribute deforestation to various direct and indirect causes has improved. And in tropical countries, especially in those with the highest rates of forest loss, the largest share of deforestation is now attributed to large-scale commercial agricultural enterprises responding to demand for globally traded commodities.[8]

Small-scale agriculturalists and informal-sector harvesters of forest products continue to be important contributors to deforestation and forest degradation in some countries and regions, especially in Sub-Saharan Africa. But, overall, most tropical deforestation can no longer be blamed on poor people. As described in chapter 7, poorer areas are associated with less, rather than more, deforestation. Instead, the drivers of deforestation are increasingly commercialized and globalized.

Within this broader picture, significant regional variation and dynamism exists among the drivers of deforestation:

- In Latin America, expanding cattle pastures to produce beef has been the primary cause of deforestation in the Amazon rainforest and the Chaco region of Paraguay, while clearing new areas to plant soybeans has been the leading cause of deforestation in the Chaco region of Argentina and a significant contributor to the loss of dry forests in the Cerrado region of Brazil.
- In Southeast Asia, where logging and clearing for tree crops including rubber, coffee, and cacao have all contributed to deforestation, land-use change most recently has been dominated by the conversion of forests to commercial-scale, fast-growing pulpwood plantations to feed the paper industry and oil palm plantations to produce palm oil.
- In the Congo Basin, where deforestation rates remain comparatively low, forest loss is currently driven by a mixture of localized, small-scale activities, including agriculture, fuelwood and charcoal collection, and informal timber extraction; but development of large-scale plantations looms on the horizon.[9]

Global trade in tropical timber and the commodities whose production damages or replaces forests is nothing new. Appetites in temperate latitudes for precious metals, spices, and beverage crops such as coffee and tea were important motivations for early exploration by Europeans and colonial enterprises across the tropics. What's different now is the scale of the demand. Worldwide, a growing and increasingly wealthy population is demanding more food and fiber. Between 1963 and 2005, a 30 percent increase in cropland globally was driven mostly by increases in demand for the meat and vegetable oils associated with richer diets.[10] And perverse government policies are adding to that demand by encouraging consumption, including by subsidizing biofuels that use food grains and edible oils as feedstocks. While speculative land clearing—especially for cattle pasture in Latin America—has been an important contributor to forest loss,[11] investors in forest conversion can increasingly depend on ready global markets for their products.

Thus, a fixed land base is under pressure to produce ever-increasing volumes of commodities to meet soaring global appetites for beef, soybeans, palm oil, pulp and paper, and other products. In the 1980s and '90s, more than 80 percent of new agricultural land came at the expense of intact and disturbed forests, and more than two-thirds of recent forest loss has been due to agricultural expansion.[12] And while about half of increased agricultural production in the tropics has been met by increasing yields from land already under cultivation, elastic demand from global markets has provided incentive to cultivate more hectares, even as more crops are produced per hectare.[13] Expansion of production into poorly regulated forest frontiers has continued to provide an attractive alternative or complement to intensification for producers in many countries.

Emissions from Deforestation Are Embodied in Globally Traded Goods

Imagine a family in Milan sitting down to a sumptuous holiday meal in 2009 featuring pork chops stuffed with beef sausage. For this hypothetical dinner, the pork was imported to Italy from the Netherlands, where the pigs had been fattened with soy cake originating from Argentina. In Argentina, vast areas of forest had been converted to commercial soybean fields over the previous twenty years. The beef came from Brazil, where rates of forest clearing were the highest in the world, mostly for cattle pasture and soybean cultivation. Paper napkins on the table originated in Indonesia, where large expanses of Sumatran peatswamp forest had been cleared to plant fast-growing acacia to feed the world's largest pulp and paper mills. The gelato served for dessert included a palm oil derivative that originated in an oil palm plantation on previously forested land in Malaysia. The table itself was made from high-quality timber logged in the Democratic Republic of Congo.

How significant were the carbon emissions from deforestation embodied in the imported products on and in that hypothetical dinner table in Milan—and millions of other dinner tables across the rich world? Determining that was the task undertaken by a research team led by economist and environmental scientist Martin Persson for a background paper commissioned for this book.[14] The paper represents the most recent of several attempts to quantify the size of the impact, or "footprint," of rich-country consumption as a driver of tropical deforestation. The European Commission, for example, supported a forest footprint analysis to determine the impact of European consumption on deforestation in developing countries. The study concluded that, over the period 1990 to 2008, the production of commodities consumed in Europe was responsible for 36 percent of deforestation embodied in globally traded crop and livestock products.[15] The method used by Persson and others to conduct their study is summarized in box 8.1.

The study mapped the linkages between tropical deforestation and the consumption of four "forest-risk" commodities—beef, soybeans, palm oil, and wood products (including timber, pulp, and paper)—that are increasingly being traded internationally. It focused on eight producer countries: Argentina, Bolivia, Brazil, the Democratic Republic of Congo (DRC), Indonesia, Malaysia, Papua New Guinea, and Paraguay. Together they represent 83 percent of beef and 99 percent of soybean exports from Latin America and 97 percent of global palm oil exports. They also account for roughly half of the official trade in tropical wood products (although it should be noted that the official data do not capture the significant portion of such trade that is illegal).

The study estimated that in 2009, the four selected commodities in the eight countries

---

Box 8.1: Calculating Emissions from Deforestation That Are Embodied in Traded Goods

In a paper commissioned by CGD as a contribution to this book, Martin Persson and colleagues used a novel "bottom-up" method to produce a snapshot of the key sources and destinations of what they termed "forest-risk" commodities and to calculate both the deforestation (in hectares) and the emissions (in tons) embodied in each ton of product exported.[a] Their approach can be summarized as follows:

- First, the researchers selected a limited number of commodities identified by previous studies as key drivers of deforestation and a limited number of countries with high deforestation rates that are also major producers and exporters of the selected commodities: Argentina, Bolivia, Brazil, and Paraguay for beef and soybeans; Indonesia, Malaysia, and Papua New Guinea for palm oil; and a combination of these plus the Democratic Republic of Congo for wood products. The selected countries accounted for the preponderance of global production and exports of the selected commodities. Furthermore, the four commodities accounted for more than three-fourths of deforestation in those countries in the first decade of the 2000s—more than 40 million hectares.

- Second, for each country and commodity pair, the researchers used remote sensing data, complemented by agricultural statistics at national and subnational levels, to calculate a "deforestation footprint" and a "carbon footprint"—that is, the amount of deforestation and associated emissions attributable to the production of one ton of each commodity in each year. For all commodities except timber from natural forests, the analysis took into account deforestation in the ten years prior to measurement of production, dating back to 1990. In other words, a one-time forest clearing event was amortized over ten years of commodity production on the cleared area.

- Third, the researchers used physical trade data to trace commodity flows from producer countries to ultimate consumer countries, taking into account intermediate processing and re-export of selected products. The data included major secondary products, such as soybean cake, palm kernel oil, and paper products, but not highly processed wood products, like furniture. Using the most recent official trade data then available from FAO, their analysis covered the period 2000 to 2009.

- Fourth, the researchers combined the deforestation footprints with the trade data to calculate the area of deforestation and associated carbon emissions attributable to consumption in different countries and regions.

Taken together, the steps in this approach allowed the researchers to quantify the extent to which international market demand for the selected commodities drove deforestation during the decade studied; which countries and regions were the principal consumers of the emissions embodied in those products; and changes over time.

a. Persson et al., "Trading Forests." An updated analysis was subsequently published as S. Henders, U. M. Persson, and T. Kastner, "Trading Forests: Land-Use Change and Carbon Emissions Embodied in Production and Exports of Forest-Risk Commodities," *Environmental Research Letters* 10, no. 12 (2015): 125012. The methods are described in U. M. Persson, S. Henders, and C. Cederberg, "A Method for Calculating a Land-Use Change Carbon Footprint (LUC-CFP) for Agricultural Commodities: Applications to Brazilian Beef and Soy, Indonesian Palm Oil," *Global Change Biology* 20, no. 11 (2014): 3482–91; and T. Kastner, M. Kastner, and S. Nonhebel, "Tracing Distant Environmental Impacts of Agricultural Products from a Consumer Perspective," *Ecological Economics* 70, no. 6 (2011): 1032–40.

were produced at the cost of 3.9 million hectares of forest, or roughly one-third of the deforestation that took place globally that year. Of that amount, approximately 1.2 million hectares of deforestation could be traced to products exported from forest-rich countries and consumed in countries other than those where they were produced—equivalent to an area more than sixteen times the size of Singapore. The 0.62 billion tons of carbon emissions embodied in those exported products was greater than the total greenhouse gas emissions from Australia in 2009.[16]

Figure 8.1 illustrates the largest cross-continent flows of embodied emissions between the countries that produce and the countries and regions that consume the four

forest-risk commodities included in the analysis of data from the period 2000 to 2009.

The results of the analysis for each commodity are summarized below.

Beef

Beef production was the main driver of forest loss in the four Latin American countries studied (Argentina, Bolivia, Brazil, Paraguay), associated with more than 28 million hectares of deforestation and 7.8 billion tons of CO_2—by far the largest source of emissions among the four commodities. The carbon footprint of beef production (tons of CO_2 per ton of commodity produced) was as high as an astonishing 203 tons of CO_2 per ton of beef produced in Bolivia, equivalent to burning 472 barrels of oil.[17] Deforestation added to

Figure 8.1: Emissions from deforestation are embodied in globally traded commodities.

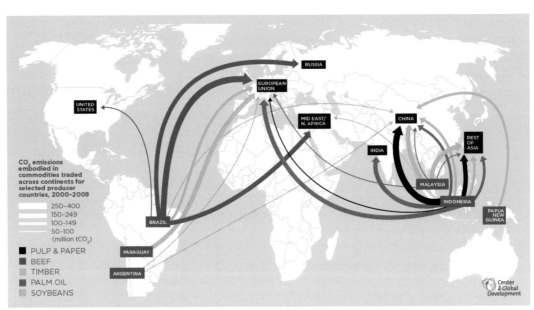

Source: Persson et al., "Trading Forests."

Note: Figure does not depict large flows of emissions embodied in soybeans exported from Paraguay and Bolivia to the rest of Latin America, nor smaller flows embodied in soybeans exported from Paraguay to the rest of the world and in beef exported from Brazil to the rest of Latin America. "Russia" includes other countries of the former Soviet Union.

the other emissions associated with the life cycle of beef production in Latin America (beyond those caused by land-use change), which averaged almost 50 tons of CO_2 per ton of beef. Among the countries studied, Brazil accounted for roughly 85 percent of deforestation for cattle pasture. Although most beef produced was consumed domestically, emissions exported from Brazil nevertheless amounted to more than 1 billion tons of CO_2 over the decade, consumed mostly in the EU, Russia, and countries in the Middle East and North Africa.

Soybeans

In the four Latin American countries studied, soybeans were associated with 4.8 million hectares of deforestation carried out and 1.4 billion tons of CO_2 produced from 2000 to 2009. Most of the production was for export to China, the EU, or elsewhere in Latin America. Although soybeans had a higher deforestation footprint than palm oil (see below), associated carbon emissions were lower due to the lower carbon density of the dry forests in South America compared to that of the humid and peatland forests in Southeast Asia. Since 2009, soybean exports to China have boomed while deforestation rates due to soybean expansion have declined (in part due to a shift of expansion toward pasture land), so the implications for embodied emissions cannot be extrapolated forward.

Palm Oil

Between 2000 and 2009, oil palm plantations were responsible for more than 1.1 million hectares of deforestation in Indonesia—an area half the size of New Jersey. Oil palm plantations in Malaysia and Papua New Guinea brought about an additional 800,000 hectares of deforestation. Palm oil production from Indonesia destined for export markets, principally China, the EU, and India, translated into 752 million tons of CO_2 emissions embodied in palm oil exports—an annual average comparable to the total emissions from the Philippines in 2009.[18] Since 2009, the conversion of forests and carbon-rich peatlands to export-oriented palm oil production (and wood products, see below) has continued. This means the emissions intensity of Indonesia's and Malaysia's palm oil sectors—which takes into account deforestation in the ten years prior to production—has likely increased, and it will remain high as recently deforested lands come into production.

Wood Products

A similarly large amount of CO_2 emissions—more than 2 billion tons—was embodied in officially reported wood products (including timber, pulp, and paper) exported from Indonesia, Malaysia, and Papua New Guinea over that decade.

Overall, more than one-third (37 percent) of total carbon emissions embodied in the forest-risk commodities from the countries studied were consumed outside the tropics in 2009, principally in China and the EU. Some of the most significant emission flows were found in palm oil exported from Indonesia to China, the EU, and India; in wood products exported from Malaysia to China and the rest of Asia; and in Brazilian beef exported to the EU, the Middle East, and Russia.

The share of total production exported varied by commodity and region, with higher shares of soybeans and palm oil than of beef and wood products. Nevertheless, production for export markets was the dominant driver of deforestation during the period in all but two of the eight countries studied: Bolivia and Brazil. Fully one-third of the emissions embodied in all commodities and countries included in the analysis were consumed in Brazil, largely due to the country's high domestic consumption of beef. Indeed, if Brazil's beef consumption were excluded from the analysis, the average share of national production exported across selected countries and commodities would rise from 32 percent to 57 percent. In other words, including beef produced in Brazil drives down the average share of commodities exported and, thus, the average share of forest-based emissions embodied in exports.

The analysis by Persson and colleagues was subsequently updated through 2011 (excluding the DRC), and showed increasing trends in the share of deforestation and emissions attributable to commodity production for export. For the period 2000 to 2011, the four commodities and seven countries accounted for 40 percent of total deforestation and associated emissions across the tropics, and more than one-third of those were embodied in exports.[19]

Without a change in course, commodity-driven deforestation and emissions will continue. According to a Chatham House study, double-digit increases in global production of both palm oil and soy and about 5 percent for beef are projected over the next decade. In the absence of dramatic increases in productivity, the study warns, further expansion into the forest is "inevitable."[20]

But, as described in chapter 7, the governments of forest-rich countries have a number of policy levers they can pull to slow deforestation. And because a demand for imported "forest-risk" commodities by global consumers is an increasingly important driver, assessing what developed and emerging-market countries can do to shift demand toward more forest-friendly consumption is critical. In the remainder of this chapter, we describe how policies and practices in consumer countries can be shifted from being part of the problem to being part of the solution.

Perverse Policies in Rich Countries Exacerbate the Problem

Conspicuously absent from figure 8.1 are large flows of embodied emissions from the tropics to the United States. That's because the United States is itself a major producer of beef, soybeans, and wood products, and it also produces vegetable oils that are substitutes for palm oil.[21] Nevertheless, consumption of these commodities in the United States contributes to tropical deforestation; it's just that the contribution takes place indirectly through market effects rather than via direct imports. Lower domestic demand for the beef, soybeans, wood products, and edible oils produced in the United States might reduce their prices, and those products might substitute for forest-risk commodities on world markets. This indirect effect is not captured in the Persson analysis, which thus likely underestimates the effect of consumption in rich countries on deforestation and associated emissions in the tropics.

What's more, the United States and other rich-country governments lavish direct and indirect subsidies on domestic agricultural producers. The domestic costs of agricultural subsidies in rich countries are considerable, and the distortions they impose on international trade are well documented.[22] To the extent that the resulting increased production substitutes for import of tropical products, increases exports, or lowers prices, the effect could be to reduce deforestation.

But in some cases, subsidies serve to drive domestic consumption of forest-risk commodities higher than it would otherwise be. Under U.S. federal legislation, for example, almost all the taxes collected on beef are channeled to the National Cattlemen's Beef Association, which uses the proceeds to fund advertising campaigns to encourage Americans to eat more beef.[23] Such policies increase pressure on tropical forests through their impact on overall demand, which is already distorted due to the lack of a price on carbon.

In the next two sections, we discuss the case of biofuel mandates and subsidies and their unintended consequences for deforestation.

The Case of Biofuel Mandates and Subsidies

Biofuels—fuels made from recently grown plant materials or organic waste—are thought by many policymakers and the general public to be a climate-friendly alternative to fossil fuels. People assume the plants harvested to produce fuel can grow back, reabsorb carbon from the atmosphere, and thus constitute a "carbon-neutral" feedstock. Unfortunately, the reality is often quite different.[24]

Reviewing the history of support for biofuels in the EU and the United States and the implications of that support for development and climate change, our CGD colleague, economist Kimberly Elliott, concludes that American and European policies to promote so-called "first generation" or "conventional" biofuels—those that depend on food-based feedstocks such as corn and vegetable oils—"are failing to significantly contribute toward any objective other than providing additional subsidies to relatively well-off farmers in rich countries."[25] At the same time, such policies come at the expense of food security (by raising prices) and climate protection (by raising emissions), with impacts felt most acutely by poor people in developing countries. The remainder of this section and the following one summarize Elliott's analysis.

The initial catalyst for interest in biofuels as a possible substitute for gasoline was the oil price shocks of the 1970s. The only country to pursue a biofuels strategy seriously, however, was Brazil, which succeeded in developing a domestic ethanol industry based on sugar cane. As recently as 2000, annual global production and consumption of biofuels remained below 20 billion liters, compared to more than a trillion liters of gasoline produced that year.[26] In the 1990s and early 2000s, low commodity prices led policymakers in the EU and the United States to consider boosting consumption of biofuels as a way of supporting agricultural incomes. But in both places, the rationale for such policies evolved to include providing support not only to rural producers, but for energy security and climate protection as well.

In the absence of direct or indirect subsidies, the economics of producing biofuels depends on the relative prices of food-based feedstocks (which determine the cost of production) and fossil fuel-based energy sources (which determine the biofuels' competitiveness). If the price of feedstocks is too high, biofuel production is too expensive. If the price of fossil fuels is too low, there will be no demand for biofuel. Governments have stepped in to counter these market forces through a variety of direct and indirect subsidies to encourage biofuel production and consumption. They have included "blending mandates," requiring that biofuels make up a certain percentage of transport fuels; tax credits for biofuel production; and direct payments to biofuel producers.

In the EU, policies to support the production of biodiesel fuel began as a way of compensating oil-seed producers for the loss of earlier subsidies, following settlement of a trade dispute with the United States. Policymakers justified a 2003 biofuels directive—which established a progressively increasing target for blending biofuels into transport fuels—in part as a way of meeting commitments to reduce greenhouse gas emissions under the Kyoto Protocol. In 2009, the EU Renewable Energy Directive (RED) raised the biofuel target to 10 percent of transport fuels by 2020.

In the United States, concern about energy security reemerged around the same time. In 2005, Congress established a Renewable Fuel Standard (RFS) mandating rising levels of ethanol in gasoline as a response to concerns about the possible effects of instability in the Middle East on oil prices. The RFS was only subsequently linked to its potential to reduce the emissions that cause climate change.

These policies quite effectively increased demand for biofuels. Between around 2000 and 2010, global consumption of biofuels increased by a factor of five, mostly due to dramatic increases in the use of corn-based ethanol in the United States and vegetable oil-based biodiesel in the EU. Significant volumes of domestically produced corn and soybeans in the United States and rapeseed and sugar beets in Europe were diverted to meet the new source of demand. These increases were entirely policy-driven, with the United States, Brazil, and the EU consuming almost 90 percent of biofuels in 2011.

The resulting surge in demand for biofuel feedstocks—principally food crops (corn and sugar) and oil-seeds (palm oil, rapeseed oil, soybean oil)—has been associated with escalating and increasingly volatile global food prices. That's because the biofuel industry added a relatively large and inelastic new source of demand at a time when commodity prices were already rising. Demand for biofuel contributed to the spike in food prices in 2007 to 2008, causing hardship for poor people in developing countries who were net food consumers.[27] One analysis goes so far as to assert that allocating cropland to grow feedstocks for biofuels poses a fundamental threat to a food-secure future.[28]

Biofuels Drive Deforestation and Emissions

Not only does evidence indicate demand for biofuels increases food prices; it shows demand for certain biofuel feedstocks drives deforestation and associated emissions. Analysis by Chatham House singles out biofuel support policies as one of three main reasons

(along with population growth and changing diets) that global production and consumption of soy and palm oil have doubled since 2000.[29] The link to deforestation to produce biofuel feedstocks undermines the "climate-friendly" rationale for the promotion of biofuels as a way of reducing greenhouse gas emissions.

Two papers published in *Science* magazine in 2008 were early harbingers of a large body of data and analysis linking biofuel production to tropical deforestation and associated emissions.[30] According to research summarized by the IPCC, the "carbon debt" incurred when tropical forests are cleared to expand production of most biofuel feedstocks exceeds the carbon emissions from fossil fuels spared through substitution for fifty years or longer. In other words, it takes decades of emissions savings from not using fossil fuels to make up for the emissions released by the initial deforestation event. At the extreme, when peatlands in Indonesia or Malaysia are drained for oil palm plantations to produce palm oil for biodiesel, the "payback" period to retire the carbon debt could be six hundred to nine hundred years, depending on crop yields.[31]

Studies[32] suggest the increasing use of domestically produced oilseeds as a feedstock for biodiesel—including rapeseed oil in the EU and soybean oil in the United States—has raised the price and created new markets for imported vegetable oils, especially palm oil from Southeast Asia. Use of domestic feedstocks can induce what is termed "indirect land-use change." When a ton of rapeseed oil, for example, is diverted to produce biofuel, increased prices could induce greater production of vegetable oils to meet demand, which could include both soybeans in Latin America and palm oil in Southeast Asia.

As shown in figure 8.2, the EU biofuels directive in 2003 led to a rapid rise in biodiesel consumption and, with it, an increased consumption of vegetable oils. Imports of palm oil also increased sharply, mostly for industrial purposes, but also for food uses. Palm oil surpassed soybean oil and waste oil as a biodiesel feedstock and was second only to rapeseed oil in 2014 (although waste oil was projected to move slightly ahead in 2015 and 2016).[33]

Use of domestic crops for biofuel, in turn, has implications for tropical deforestation; as described in chapter 7, higher agricultural commodity prices are the single most potent factor associated with increased forest loss.[34] The result, in contrast to the stated objective of helping achieve emission reduction targets, is that biofuel mandates can actually increase total emissions compared to the fossil fuels they are designed to replace, when total product life cycles and indirect land-use change are taken into account. Increased EU demand for vegetable oil to fuel automobiles, for example, raised the price of palm oil, which in turn increased pressure to expand production, including into carbon-rich forests and peatlands in Southeast Asia. A recent study that did take into account indirect land-use change estimated the use of biodiesel in the EU transport sector would increase emissions by almost 4 percent by 2020—about

Figure 8.2: European Union biofuel policy increased demand for palm oil, a driver of deforestation.

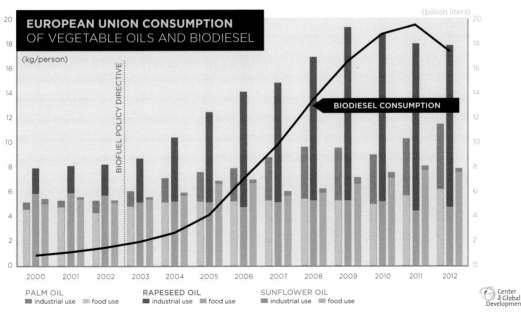

Source: Elliott, "Biofuel Policies: Fuel versus Food, Forests and Climate."

as much as 12 million additional cars on Europe's roads would generate.[35]

There are other reasons to question the wisdom of subsidizing biofuels. In addition to failing to reduce emissions, biofuel policies in the EU and the United States have run into technical, fiscal, and political challenges. In the United States, older models in the motor vehicle fleet are not equipped to use fuels with a higher proportion of ethanol, and gasoline retailers have no incentive to duplicate gas pump infrastructure to accommodate multiple fuel blends. In both the EU and the United States, the costs of tax credits for biofuels have become untenable in a time of budget austerity, and, in the United States, livestock producers have complained about the competition for feed grains.

Attempts to impose sustainability criteria on policy-driven biofuel demand in the EU and the United States have been limited in aspiration and impact. Several years of debate over the impacts of biofuel policies on climate change, and on food prices and forests in developing countries, led the EU in 2015 to cap under the Renewable Energy Directive the proportion of biofuels that come from food-based feedstocks.

To protect jobs, the compromise level of 7 percent set for the cap was significantly higher than the 5 percent the European Commission had proposed. U.S. legislation attempted to address the impacts of biofuel production on direct land-use change, but it did so in a way that protected existing investments and so had no impact on demand for feedstocks from the less-efficient processing capacity in place at the time the RFS was amended. And even when biofuel feedstocks are covered by standards to limit the adverse environmental impacts of renewable fuels, the indirect impacts of oils and grains produced to replace food uses are not. Finally, targets to produce so-called "second generation" or "advanced" biofuels from nonfood precursors such as switchgrass, seaweed, or waste products—which would have little or no impact on increasing deforestation—remain weak and nonbinding.

In part in reaction to the reasons that have surfaced in rich countries to reconsider biofuel policies, consumption in the EU and the United States plateaued in the 2010s, and it may slow further with the withdrawal of EU support for land-based biofuels after 2020.[36] In contrast, consumption in developing and emerging-market countries is on the rise, as their governments follow in the rich world's footsteps and impose associated deforestation footprints on tropical forests. Several initiatives to support biofuels in developing countries were accelerated by protectionist policies in rich countries. In 2013, for example, the EU responded to competition from biodiesel exporters with a series of protectionist trade remedies, including imposition of antidumping duties. As a result, countries such as Argentina and Indonesia imposed their own biodiesel mandates or increased their blending targets to absorb excess production caused by EU trade barriers.

The number of countries that have established biofuel support policies—including mandates that gasoline or diesel fuel be blended with biofuels, tax incentives, or indicative targets for biofuel use—rose from just ten in 2005[37] to at least sixty-four by 2014.[38] In 2015, responding to domestic political interests in propping up palm oil prices, Indonesia imposed a new levy on palm oil exports to finance a Crude Palm Oil Fund, with early indications that some of the proceeds would be used to subsidize biodiesel production. Even while many such targets for production and consumption of biofuels in developing countries are not yet being met, they are likely creating vested interests in maintaining these policies at the expense of the world's forests and climate.

Much Deforestation to Meet Global Demand Is Illegal

In 2012, a Brazilian ecologist joined a study tour to the island of Sumatra in Indonesia. Having had a distinguished career promoting conservation and sustainable development in Latin America, she was eager to learn about the dynamics of tropical forest destruction and protection in Southeast Asia.

A stop on the study tour was Tesso Nilo National Park in the province of Riau, one of the most species-rich tropical forests in the world. Promoted by WWF and established by the government of Indonesia in 2004, Tesso Nilo was designed to protect a remnant of lowland forest habitat for critically endangered Sumatran tigers and elephants. After disembarking from their bus at the camp where they were to spend the night, the ecologist from Brazil and other study tour participants were taken around the park, mounted on elephants that had been trained to assist park guards in their patrols.

Over the next two hours, the lumbering grey chariots carried the ecologist and her colleagues past one depressing scene after another: scrubby stands of fast-growing timber species in a corporate plantation that encroached on the park's boundaries; large areas of maturing oil palm; a recently burned plot planted with rubber; the stump of a tree that had been illegally felled within the past twenty-four hours. When local conservation authorities were questioned as to why this illegal activity could not be controlled by setting up checkpoints on the few roads and waterways providing access to the park, they replied, "Yes, we tried that, but our guards were taken hostage at the point of automatic weapons."

Back at the camp, the ecologist's eyes welled up with tears as she expressed her disappointment at seeing scorched earth and scraggly secondary forest rather than the majestic intact rainforest she had dreamed about. "All my life I've heard about the beautiful Indonesian rainforest. I never imagined it would be like this," she said.[39]

Global demand for commodities helped drive the illegal forest destruction witnessed by participants in the 2012 study tour to Sumatra. Unknown to them, the conservation organization WWF had completed in the previous month a long-term investigation of illegal activity within the park. Following behind company trucks on their motorcycles, WWF researchers documented where the fresh palm fruit from inside the park was ending up. They found it was being purchased by mills associated with Asian Agri, one of Asia's largest exporters of palm oil, and Wilmar International, the world's largest palm oil trader, destined for the international market.[40]

A significant portion of the tropical forest clearance in Indonesia and elsewhere for commodity production to meet global demand is illegal. In some cases, such as Tesso Nilo National Park, forest clearance takes place in protected areas where agricultural cultivation is strictly prohibited but law enforcement is weak. In others, permits to clear forested land are obtained through corrupt payments; two recent governors of Riau Province have been convicted of corruption related to the allocation of such land.[41] In yet other cases, forest clearance begins without the necessary permits in hand, or prohibited methods such as burning are used. Sometimes, bulldozers roll before required environmental impact assessments are completed or without consent from local communities claiming rights to the same land.[42] Not only does illegal forest clearance increase greenhouse gas emissions; associated corruption effectively facilitates theft of state or local assets, and social conflict frequently erupts in violence.[43]

As will be described in chapter 11, one of the factors that kept tropical deforestation on the political agenda in rich countries in the first decade of this century was concern about illegal logging as a driver of forest loss and a source of unfair competition with domestic producers of wood products. Wood producers in these countries joined with environmental advocates to support legislation and regulations prohibiting the import of illegally produced timber into rich-country markets. The Lacey Act (as amended) in the United States, the European Union's Timber Regulation, and Australia's Illegal Logging Prohibition Act were all designed to achieve this objective. (Japanese initiatives to promote sourcing of legally verified wood products are voluntary, and considerably weaker.)

But even while those initiatives were being shaped in the capitals of consumer countries, the nature of the deforestation problem in many producer countries was shifting. Although commercial logging of dubious legality continued to be a significant driver of forest degradation in some, the wholesale conversion to pasture and plantations to produce globally traded commodities was rapidly emerging as the primary threat to the most rapidly disappearing tropical forest ecosystems.

Much of that conversion is illegal, too. In 2014, Forest Trends published a study by analyst Sam Lawson that represented the first attempt to quantify the extent of the illegality.[44] Lawson started by estimating the share of deforestation attributable to commercial agriculture for each country and ended with an estimate for how much illegal forest conversion and associated emissions are embodied in exports. While Lawson addressed many of the same questions and "forest-risk" commodities as the study by Persson and colleagues described earlier in this chapter, the numbers generated by the two studies cannot be compared due to differences in the number of countries, in time periods, and in data sets analyzed.

The key contribution of the Lawson study is its estimate of the share of forest conversion for agriculture that was illegal during the period 2000 to 2012. The study defined "illegal" forest conversion to include licensing or operations that violate "the written laws, policies, and regulations in the concerned country . . . regardless of whether illegalities concerned have been identified or prosecuted by the relevant government authorities or have since been formally forgiven."[45] The study estimated that 68 to 90 percent of deforestation for agriculture in Brazil during the period examined was illegal due to failure to comply with the "legal reserve" requirement of the country's Forest Code, although a 2012 amnesty had retroactively legalized about half the illegal conversion that had taken place through 2007.[46] The study estimated 80 percent of deforestation for commercial agriculture and timber plantations in Indonesia during the period was illegal, with the use of fire to clear land and irregularities in permitting the most frequently cited infractions.[47]

As shown in figure 8.3, the Lawson study estimated illegal conversion for commercial agricultural enterprises was responsible for 49 percent of tropical deforestation over the period 2000 to 2012.[48] Furthermore, based on the share of total production of each com-modity destined for export, the study found half of this illegal clearing—24 percent of total deforestation during the period—was carried out to serve global markets.[49] This bolstered the contention that demand in consumer countries contributes to tropical deforestation and associated emissions.

A New Wave of Supply Chain Commitments

Concerns about commodity-driven tropical deforestation have fueled a surge in civil society advocacy directed at private companies involved in all aspects of commodity production, trade, manufacture, retailing, and finance. Advocates have not limited their focus to the environmental implications of deforestation for global biodiversity and climate

Figure 8.3: Illegal conversion of forests to produce agricultural exports accounted for almost one quarter of recent deforestation.

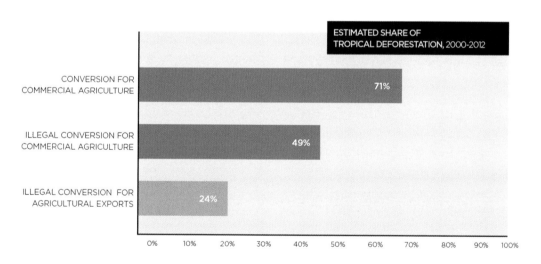

Source: Lawson et al. (2014), using gross forest canopy loss greater than 51% based on satellite data from Hansen et al. (2013).

objectives; they have also trained their campaigns on the associated costs to the rights and livelihoods of local communities and on the abuse of workers' rights.

Frustrated at the limited regulatory and enforcement measures taken by governments in producer countries and the slow pace of voluntary certification initiatives, activists have taken aim at corporate buyers based in rich countries, as exemplified by the Greenpeace campaign against Nestlé described in the opening of this chapter. So successful have they been that government policy initiatives to rein in demand for commodities produced at the expense of tropical forests have been far outpaced by a recent wave of voluntary "no deforestation" commitments undertaken by private companies. A timeline of selected commitments is presented in figure 8.4.

As mentioned in chapter 7, the earliest example of effective pressure exercised through commodity supply chains comes from Brazil. In June 2006, following a Greenpeace campaign, major players in the soybean supply chain—including McDonald's (which sourced chicken fattened on soy), Cargill (one of the world's largest commodity traders), and the Brazilian Vegetable Oil Industry Association (ABIOVE)—agreed to a "soy moratorium." Under the terms of the agreement, companies pledged not to purchase soybeans originating from areas of the Brazilian Amazon that had been cleared after July of that year. The moratorium, in conjunction with a number of other policy initiatives, was largely effective in removing soybeans as a driver of deforestation in the Amazon[50] and, following repeated annual extensions, was extended indefinitely in 2016.[51] Major Brazilian beef producers

agreed to a similar moratorium, intended to have a similar impact, in 2009.[52]

Nestlé's pledge to get deforestation out of its palm oil supply chain heralded a second generation of such commitments and a broadening of activists' focus to include the commodities driving deforestation in Southeast Asia. Such commitments snowballed among manufacturers and retailers based in rich countries starting in 2010, when the board of the Consumer Goods Forum (CGF), representing some four hundred companies, approved a resolution to achieve zero net deforestation in soybeans, beef, palm oil, and paper by 2020.[53]

Financiers also began taking on commitments, with the French bank BNP Paribas adopting a policy prohibiting the financing of plantations in high-conservation-value forests.[54] The Banking Environment Initiative (BEI), subsequently launched in support of the CGF commitment, comprised eleven multinational banks as of 2015. Under the "BEI-CGF Soft Commodities Compact," members pledged to direct their lending to activities that achieve zero net deforestation, increase yields, and support sustainable livelihoods.[55] The collective also supports engagement with financial regulators, with a view toward reforms that would encourage more investment in "green" assets and better management of environmental risks.[56]

In 2011, a pledge by Singapore-based Golden Agri Resources (GAR) marked a milestone as the first "no-deforestation" commitment by a major palm oil producer.[57] The product of negotiations with Greenpeace brokered by a former U.S. ambassador to Indonesia, the commitment established

Figure 8.4: More and more companies and banks are committing to zero deforestation.

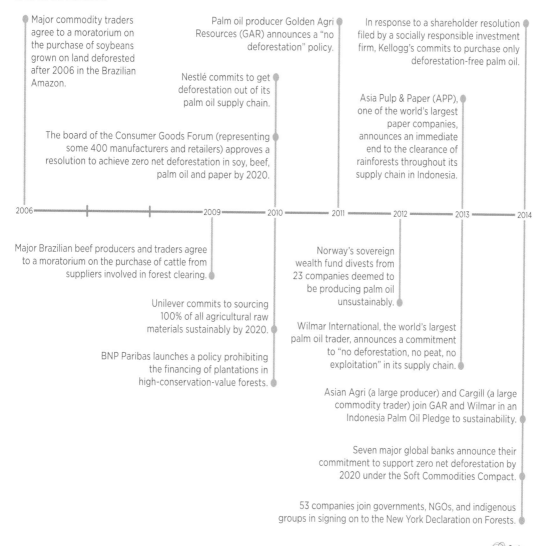

Major commodity traders agree to a moratorium on the purchase of soybeans grown on land deforested after 2006 in the Brazilian Amazon.

Palm oil producer Golden Agri Resources (GAR) announces a "no deforestation" policy.

In response to a shareholder resolution filed by a socially responsible investment firm, Kellogg's commits to purchase only deforestation-free palm oil.

Nestlé commits to get deforestation out of its palm oil supply chain.

Asia Pulp & Paper (APP), one of the world's largest paper companies, announces an immediate end to the clearance of rainforests throughout its supply chain in Indonesia.

The board of the Consumer Goods Forum (representing some 400 manufacturers and retailers) approves a resolution to achieve zero net deforestation in soy, beef, palm oil and paper by 2020.

2006 — 2009 — 2010 — 2011 — 2012 — 2013 — 2014

Major Brazilian beef producers and traders agree to a moratorium on the purchase of cattle from suppliers involved in forest clearing.

Norway's sovereign wealth fund divests from 23 companies deemed to be producing palm oil unsustainably.

Unilever commits to sourcing 100% of all agricultural raw materials sustainably by 2020.

Wilmar International, the world's largest palm oil trader, announces a commitment to "no deforestation, no peat, no exploitation" in its supply chain.

BNP Paribas launches a policy prohibiting the financing of plantations in high-conservation-value forests.

Asian Agri (a large producer) and Cargill (a large commodity trader) join GAR and Wilmar in an Indonesia Palm Oil Pledge to sustainability.

Seven major global banks announce their commitment to support zero net deforestation by 2020 under the Soft Commodities Compact.

53 companies join governments, NGOs, and indigenous groups in signing on to the New York Declaration on Forests.

Center for Global Development

Source: Various sources (see www.cgdev.org/forest-sources).

the concept of "High Carbon Stock" (HCS) forests that would be off limits to clearing. Then, in 2013, Asia Pulp & Paper (APP), one of the world's largest paper companies and, like GAR, a member of the Sinar Mas Group, announced an immediate end to forest clearance throughout its supply chain in Indonesia.[58] In December of that year, the world's largest trader in palm oil, Wilmar International, also based in Singapore, announced a "no deforestation, no peat, no exploitation" policy that is recognized as the gold standard for such policies in terms of its scope and ambition.[59]

Pressure from activists, buyers, financiers, and sometimes governments in rich countries has played a key role in prompting the cascade of commitments to stop deforestation.

Although corporate decision making takes place behind closed doors, it's clear that pressure from activists, buyers, financiers, and sometimes governments in rich countries has played a key role in prompting the cascade of commitments to stop deforestation. In the case of Nestlé, Greenpeace's Kit Kat video and the company's own heavy-handed response were damaging its brand with consumers. In the case of Asia Pulp & Paper, buyers such as Disney and Office Depot had withdrawn their business from the company, which was notorious for converting Riau's carbon-rich peat forests to fast-growing acacia plantations. Palm oil industry executives no doubt took note in 2012 when Norway's sovereign wealth fund began divesting from companies deemed to be engaging in "unsustainable" practices.[60] Wilmar International likely felt the heat from the government of Singapore when its suppliers in Indonesia were linked to the forest fires that blanketed the country in a choking haze for weeks in June 2013.

From Pledges to Impact on Deforestation

The effectiveness of the recent wave of corporate commitments in slowing deforestation remains to be seen, as several challenges must be overcome before pledges are translated into real impacts.

First, demand for "deforestation-free" commodities does not yet extend to consumers and retailers in emerging-market countries. The top three countries consuming palm oil in recent years, for example, were India, Indonesia, and China.[61] One analysis projects 80 percent of the growth in purchasing power by the global middle class between 2009 and 2030 will come from Asia.[62] If voluntary supply chain commitments fall short of transforming industry norms, there is a risk that a bifurcated market will emerge, with progressive companies supplying the environmentally sensitive markets in Europe and the United States and business-as-usual producers selling to the rest of the world. From the perspective of impacts on forests, the only difference would be that the former would source products from land deforested (often illegally) before pledged cutoff dates, while the latter would source products grown on more recently cleared land.

Second, if commitments are limited to particular geographical areas or types of ecosystems, there is a danger that "leakage" will affect forests elsewhere in the tropics by redirecting expansion to areas not covered by voluntary pledges. The success of the soy moratorium in reducing deforestation in the Brazilian Amazon, for example, could be counterbalanced by increased deforestation in the Brazilian Cerrado region or in adjacent countries. And although the application of pledges corporation-wide—especially by large multinational trading companies—can help stem such leakage, the vertical integration of supply chains linking deforesting producers (such as medium-sized palm oil producers in Indonesia) to insensitive markets (such as China) could circumvent their efforts. The update of the analysis by Persson and colleagues suggests that unless "nearly all" of the market adopts no-deforestation standards, such leakage is likely to occur.[63]

Third, the effectiveness of voluntary private commitments could be undermined unless they are supported by law, policy, and enforcement in producer countries. At best, lack of enforcement puts law-abiding companies and smallholders at a competitive disadvantage. At worst, perverse policies can actually reverse their efforts to protect forests. In Indonesia, for example, forest areas set aside by progressive companies within concession areas to protect their high conservation value or carbon stock were considered "abandoned lands," subject to reallocation by local government officials to other companies willing to develop them.[64] Only in mid-2015 did the Ministry of Agrarian and Spatial Planning clarify the policy through a circular letter to affected companies.[65]

Fourth, implementation of the commitments could result in unintended negative consequences for smallholders and local communities. To minimize the expense of tracing supplies to their points of production, processors and traders might choose to exclude smallholders from their supply chains. And to ensure no deforestation takes place within their concessions, corporate producers might pressure indigenous communities to surrender rights to land within those concessions,

as is alleged to have happened in a GAR palm oil concession in West Kalimantan.[66]

Finally, companies that have recently pledged to remove deforestation from their supply chains have only just begun to wrestle with implementation challenges. For commodities such as palm oil, tracing an individual liter of oil to its ultimate source is a formidable and costly undertaking, because the produce from many suppliers is successively commingled at each stage in the supply chain, from plantation to mill to refinery to manufacturing facility.

Certification of "sustainable" or "deforestation-free" practice at the level of entire districts or provinces rather than individual farms is being explored as a way of lowering the costs of excluding products from recently deforested land from supply chains. The Malaysian state of Sabah, for instance, is working with the Roundtable on Sustainable Palm Oil to advance this so-called "jurisdictional approach" to sustainable sourcing.[67] A 2015 report published by the International Sustainability Unit of the Prince's Charities describes how a jurisdictional model can combine features of REDD+ finance and monitoring with preferential supply chain sourcing to reduce the transaction costs of reducing emissions from deforestation.[68]

Fortunately, an echo of the data revolution supporting improved forest monitoring (described in chapter 4) is beginning to be felt in commodity supply chain traceability. A platform being developed by the Stockholm Environment Institute and the Global Canopy Programme, for example, is utilizing production and trade data to trace commodities back to their original producer landscapes at the level of subnational jurisdictions, such as municipalities in Brazil.[69] Such mapping will provide an important tool to downstream supply chain actors and investors seeking to implement no-deforestation commitments.

But market incentives alone (such as access to sensitive markets and/or price premiums for certified products) may not be sufficient to alter the calculus of subnational elected officials, especially when compared to the political and financial benefits associated with business as usual. Ultimately, the effectiveness of voluntary supply chain commitments will likely depend on the willingness of participating companies to use their political muscle to advocate for supportive changes in the national regulatory or fiscal environments in which they operate. Such changes could include "sticks," such as increased enforcement of existing law; "carrots," such as financial rewards for low-deforestation jurisdictions through revenue distribution or preferential access to credit; and more general improvements in land governance, such as better spatial planning.

While the most important actions to stem deforestation caused by the expansion of forest-risk commodities will have to take place in producer countries, rich-country governments can also contribute, not only by creating demand for reduced emissions from deforestation through REDD+ finance, but also by reducing demand for commodities produced on recently cleared forestland.

"Demand-Side" Policy Responses

Increasing awareness of the link between deforestation—especially illegal deforestation—and global demand for forest-risk commodities has prompted consideration of so-called "demand-side" policies in rich countries. Such policies are designed to ensure commodities imported into rich-country markets are produced in ways verified as compliant with laws in the source countries, as well as aligned with other social and environmental standards.

As mentioned above, the first generation of such policies between 2000 and 2010 focused on closing rich-country markets to illegally produced timber (the politics of which is described further in chapter 11). Demand-side policy tools used to address trade in illegal wood products have included the following:

- **Import restrictions:** Laws in Australia and the United States and the EU Timber Regulation have made it a crime to sell timber and wood products that were produced illegally in their countries of origin and/or have imposed due diligence requirements on importers.
- **Trade agreements:** The European Union has entered into voluntary partnership agreements with producer countries to license legally produced timber eligible for export to the EU market. The United States has included provisions related to forest law enforcement in free trade agreements. Provisions related to forest governance, for example, were included in the bilateral trade agreement between Peru and the United States in 2007.[70] Subsequent to allegations from advocacy groups that obligations had not been honored,[71] the

Office of the U.S. Trade Representative in February 2016 asked the government of Peru to verify the legality of a 2015 shipment of timber, the first such request since the agreement entered into force in 2009.[72]

- **Procurement policies:** As of 2014, thirteen countries required government purchasers to source only timber that was certified as legally produced.[73]

A 2016 evaluation of the EU's Forest Law Enforcement, Governance and Trade (FLEGT) Action Plan provided an overall mixed review of the effectiveness of these approaches, in part due to the importance of China and other countries in Asia as markets for illegally produced timber and the shift to nonwood commodities as key drivers of deforestation. The evaluation concluded, however, that activities conducted under the plan had led to improvements in forest governance in all partner countries, and public procurement policies had had a "clear positive effect on the market."[74] In August 2016, the EU recognized Indonesia's licensing scheme for exports of verified legal timber, reflecting a large increase in the percentage of exports originating from independently audited forests and processing facilities.[75]

In recognition of the shifting drivers of deforestation from logging to agricultural conversion, governments have begun broadening their approaches to encompass commodities other than timber and wood products. In 2012, for example, the UK government adopted the target of having all the palm oil it purchased be certified sustainable by the end of 2015.[76] In 2015, the U.S.

Global Development Council, which advises the White House on development policy and practice, recommended the president issue an executive order directing federal agencies to implement deforestation-free procurement policies by 2020.[77] And, in 2016, a committee of the Norwegian Parliament announced a commitment to get deforestation out of public procurement.[78]

Designing and implementing such policies to apply to commodities other than timber faces a number of additional challenges. From a practical perspective, these include the difficulty of tracing a product such as palm oil to its area of origin in the absence of segregated supply chains, and the lag time between a deforestation event and export of the product. From a legal perspective, import restrictions would need to have clear definitions and be implemented in nondiscriminatory ways consistent with World Trade Organization rules. Application of standards to biofuels has proved especially contentious, in producer and consumer countries alike.

Nevertheless, consideration of such demand-side policies in rich countries can send an important signal to producer countries and companies that norms are changing, especially if they are accompanied by efforts to extend those norms to middle-class consumers in emerging-market countries. Future markets can be shaped to reward suppliers of products verified to be legally and sustainably sourced. And, as will be described in chapter 10, corporations that have signed on to "no-deforestation" pledges could lend influential voices in support of improved law, policy, and enforcement to protect forests in producer countries.

Conclusion

In summary, global consumers are leaving big footprints on tropical forests. Clearing for export-oriented commercial agriculture has emerged as a primary driver of tropical deforestation, and a large and growing proportion of associated emissions is embodied in globally traded goods. With a rapidly growing global middle class in emerging markets such as China, commodity-driven deforestation is likely to increase. For this reason, consumer behavior, the sourcing decisions of multinational corporations, the financing decisions of international banks and investors, and government trade and procurement policies in rich countries can all exert key influences over the fate of tropical forests, supporting or undermining efforts to stop deforestation.

While reducing deforestation will require policy changes in producer countries, rich countries also have tools available to reduce demand for commodities that are illegally or unsustainably produced. Signals conveyed through access to markets and to finance have proved effective in providing incentives for commodity production that does not come at the expense of tropical forests. In addition, the scaling back of perverse subsidies for first generation biofuels would reduce the direct and indirect land-use changes they currently induce. Refraining from subsidizing the conversion of food to fuel would also benefit the poor in developing countries by removing a source of volatility in food prices.

Demand-side policies in rich countries can also take advantage of actions by other actors. They can reward policy initiatives and support law enforcement efforts to protect forests in producer countries. Actions by rich-country governments can help ensure the recent wave of voluntary corporate commitments to deforestation-free supply chains leads to new global norms of production and consumption. Finally, these actions can set positive rather than negative examples for the governments of emerging-market countries whose share of global consumption continues to grow, and whose biofuel subsidy policies are now overtaking those of rich countries.

In chapters 10 and 11, we'll pick up the story of how the politics of international cooperation to reduce deforestation is playing out in developing and rich countries, respectively. But first, in chapter 9, we describe how the linkage of tropical deforestation to climate change mitigation has changed the international politics of such cooperation, and given birth to REDD+.

Notes

1. Greenpeace UK, "Have a Break?" YouTube, March 17, 2010, https://www.youtube.com/watch?v=VaJjPRwExO8.

2. A. Ionescu-Somers and A. Enders, "How Nestlé Dealt with a Social Media Campaign against It," *Financial Times*, December 3, 2012; S. Houpt, "Kit Kat Spat Goes Viral despite Nestlé's Efforts," *The Globe and Mail*, March 17, 2010.

3. Greenpeace International, "Sweet Success for Kit Kat Campaign: You Asked, Nestlé Has Answered," May 17, 2010.

4. Ibid.; Nestlé, "Nestlé Open Forum on Deforestation, Malaysia," May 17, 2010, http://www.nestle.com/media/mediaeventscalendar/allevents/2010-nestle-open-forum-on-deforestation-malaysia; K. Tabacek, "Nestlé Sets Timetable for Palm Oil Decision," *The Guardian*, March 19, 2010.

5. U. M. Persson, S. Henders, and T. Kastner, "Trading Forests: Quantifying the Contribution of Global Commodity Markets to Emissions from Tropical Deforestation," CGD Working Paper 384, Center for Global Development, Washington, DC, 2014.

6. Food and Agriculture Organization of the United Nations (FAO), Committee on Forest Development in the Tropics, "Tropical Forestry Action Plan," Rome, 1985, http://www.fao.org/docrep/r7750e/r7750e06.htm, 1.

7. Survival International, "Survival Slams Conservation for Violating Tribal Peoples' Rights," February 5, 2015, http://www.survivalinternational.org/news/10657.

8. N. Hosonuma et al., "An Assessment of Deforestation and Forest Degradation Drivers in Developing Countries," *Environmental Research Letters* 7, no. 4 (2012): 044009; T. Rudel and J. Roper, "The Paths to Rain Forest Destruction: Crossnational Patterns of Tropical Deforestation, 1975–1990," *World Development* 25, no. 1 (1997): 53–65.

9. Persson et al., "Trading Forests."

10. T. Kastner et al., "Global Changes in Diets and the Consequences for Land Requirements for Food," *Proceedings of the National Academy of Sciences* 109, no. 18 (2012): 6868–72.

11. D. Kaimowitz, *Livestock and Deforestation in Central America in the 1980s and 1990s: A Policy Perspective*, Center for International Research (CIFOR), Indonesia, 1996; M. S. Bowman et al., "Persistence of Cattle Ranching in the Brazilian Amazon: A Spatial Analysis of the Rationale for Beef Production," *Land Use Policy* 29 (2012) 558–68.

12. H. K. Gibbs et al., "Brazil's Soy Moratorium," *Science* 347, no. 6220 (2015): 377–78.

13. T. K. Rudel et al., "Agricultural Intensification and Changes in Cultivated Areas, 1970–2005," *Proceedings of the National Academy of Sciences* 106, no. 49 (2009): 20675–80.

14. Persson et al., "Trading Forests."

15. D. Cuypers, T. Geerken, L. Gorissen, A. Lust, G. Peters, J. Karstensen, S. Prieler, G. Fisher, E. Hizsnyik, and H. Van Velthuizen, "The Impact of EU Consumption on Deforestation: Comprehensive Analysis of the Impact of EU Consumption on Deforestation," Technical Report 2013–063, European Union, Brussels, 2013, http://ec.europa.eu/environment/forests/pdf/1.%20Report%20analysis%20of%20impact.pdf.

16. Commonwealth of Australia, Department of Climate Change and Energy Efficiency, "Australian National Greenhouse Accounts: National Inventory Report 2009," Canberra, 2011, https://www.environment.gov.au/system/files/resources/012fd8ed-a041-4160-989b-37280ebc9dbf/files/national-inventory-report-2009-vol1.pdf, ix–x.

17. Authors' calculations based on aboveground carbon density of 165 tCO_2/ha, using the U.S. Environmental Protection Agency's greenhouse gas equivalencies calculator at https://www.epa.gov/energy/greenhouse-gas-equivalencies-calculator.

18. Carbon Dioxide Information Analysis Center, Environmental Sciences Division, Oak Ridge National Laboratory, via "Data: CO_2 Emissions (kt)," World Bank, updated 2016, http://data.worldbank.org/indicator/EN.ATM.CO2E.KT/countries?page=1.

19. S. Henders et al., "Trading Forests: Land-Use Change and Carbon Emissions Embodied in Production and Exports of Forest-Risk Commodities," *Environmental Research Letters* 10 (2015): 1.

20. D. Brack, A. Glover, and L. Wellesley, "Agricultural Commodity Supply Chains: Trade, Consumption and Deforestation," Chatham House, London, 2016.

21. In addition, because the official data used for the Persson et al. analysis do not include illegal trade or highly processed wood products, the figure does not capture the emissions embodied in U.S. imports from China and Vietnam.

22. See, for example, J. C. Bureau et al., "Chapter 6: The Subsidy Habit," in *IFPRI 2012 Global Food Policy Report*, International Food Policy Research Institute, Washington, DC, 2013; and K. Elliott, *Delivering on Doha: Farm Trade and the Poor* (Washington, DC: Peterson Institute, 2006).

23. S. Mahanta, "Big Beef," *Washington Monthly*, January/February 2014, http://www.washingtonmonthly.com/magazine/january_february_2014/features/big_beef048356.php?page=all.

24. This section draws heavily on K. A. Elliott, "Biofuel Policies: Fuel versus Food, Forests and Climate," CGD Policy Paper 51, Center for Global Development, Washington, DC, 2014.

25. Ibid., 25.

26. U.S. Energy Information Administration, "International Energy Statistics," http://www.eia.gov/cfapps/ipdbproject/iedindex3.cfm?tid=5&pid=62&aid=1&cid=ww,&syid=1999&eyid=2001&unit=TBPD.

27. K. A. Elliott, "Subsidizing Farmers and Biofuels in Rich Countries: An Incoherent Agenda for Food Security," CGD Policy Paper 32, Center for Global Development, Washington, DC, 2013; U. M. Persson, "The Impact of Biofuel Demand on Agricultural Commodity Prices: A Systematic Review," *Wiley Interdisciplinary Reviews: Energy and Environment* 4, no. 5 (2015): 410–28. For a more extensive discussion on the impacts of biofuels on agricultural prices, see H. de Gorter et al., *The Economics of Biofuel Policies: Impacts on Price Volatility in Grain and Oilseed Markets* (New York: Palgrave-Macmillan, 2015).

28. T. Searchinger and R. Heimlich, "Avoiding Bioenergy Competition for Food Crops and Land," World Resources Institute, Washington, DC, January 2015; see also J. M. DeCicco, "The Liquid Carbon Challenge: Evolving Views on Transportation Fuels and Climate," *Wiley Interdisciplinary Reviews: Energy and Environment* 4, no. 1 (2015): 98–114.

29. Brack, Glover, and Wellesley, "Agricultural Commodity Supply Chains," 50.

30. T. Searchinger et al., "Use of U.S. Croplands for Biofuels Increases Greenhouse Gases through Emissions from Land-Use Change," *Science* 319 (2008), 1238–40; J. Fargione et al., "Land Clearing and the Biofuel Carbon Debt," *Science* 319 (2008): 1235–38.

31. C. B. Field et al., eds., *Climate Change 2014: Impacts, Adaptation, and Vulnerability. Part A: Global and Sectoral Aspects. Contribution of Working Group II to the Fifth Assessment Report of the Intergovernmental Panel on Climate Change* (Cambridge, UK, and New York: Cambridge University Press, 2014).

32. See, for example, C. Charles et al., "Biofuels—At What Cost? A Review of Costs and Benefits of EU Biofuel Policies," International Institute for Sustainable Development, Winnipeg, Canada, 2013, https://www.iisd.org/gsi/sites/default/files/biofuels_subsidies_eu_review.pdf, and C. Malins, S. Searle, and A. Baral, "A Guide for the Perplexed to the Indirect Effects of Biofuels Production," International Council on Clean Transportation, 2014, http://www.theicct.org/guide-perplexed-indirect-effects-biofuels-production.

33. B. Flach et al., "EU-28, Biofuels Annual: EU Biofuels Annual 2015," GAIN Report NL5028, USDA Foreign Agricultural Service, Hague, Netherlands, 2015, 22.

34. K. Ferretti-Gallon and J. Busch, "What Drives Deforestation and What Stops It? A Meta-Analysis of Spatially Explicit Econometric Studies," CGD Working Paper 361, Center for Global Development, Washington, DC, 2014.

35. Transport and Environment, "Globiom: The Basis for Biofuel Policy Post-2020," Brussels, 2016.

36. Brack, Glover, and Wellesley, "Agricultural Commodity Supply Chains," 60.

37. Renewable Energy Policy Network for the 21st Century, "Renewables 2014 Global Status Report," Paris, 2014, 15, as cited in Elliott, "Biofuel Policies," 4.

38. T. A. Wise and E. Cole, "Mandating Food Insecurity: The Global Impacts of Rising Biofuel Mandates and Targets," Global Development and Environment Institute Working Paper 15-01, 2015; J. Lane, "Biofuels Mandates around the World: 2015," *Biofuels Digest*, December 31, 2014.

39. This series of events was personally witnessed by one of the authors; the name of the Brazilian ecologist is withheld upon request.

40. World Wildlife Fund–Indonesia, "Palming Off a National Park: Tracking Illegal Oil Palm Fruit in Riau, Sumatra," World Wildlife Fund, Riau, Indonesia, 2013, http://d2ouvy59p0dg6k.cloudfront.net/downloads/wwf_indonesia_palming_off_a_national_park_tesso_nilo_sumatra_2013.pdf.

41. A. Dipa, "Court Sentences Riau Governor to 6 Years in Prison for Corrupt [*sic*]," *The Jakarta Post*, June 25, 2015; R. Harahap, "Former Riau Governor Gets 14 Years for Graft," *The Jakarta Post*, March 13, 2014.

42. For an analysis of elements of illegality related to the oil palm and pulp and paper sectors in Indonesia, see E. Wakker, "Indonesia: Illegalities in Forest Clearance for Large-Scale Commercial Plantations," *Aidenvironment Asia*, 2014, http://www.forest-trends.org/documents/files/doc_4528.pdf.

43. See, for example, M. Colchester and S. Chao, eds., *Conflict or Consent? The Oil Palm Sector at a Crossroads* (Jakarta, Indonesia: The Forest Peoples Programme, 2013).

44. S. Lawson et al., "Consumer Goods and Deforestation: An Analysis of the Extent and Nature of Illegality in Forest Conversion for Agriculture and Timber Plantations," Forest Trends, Washington, DC, 2014, http://www.forest-trends.org/documents/files/doc_4718.pdf. While not published in a peer-reviewed journal, the study was subjected to peer review managed by Forest Trends.

45. Ibid., xiii.

46. Ibid.

47. Ibid.

48. Ibid.

49. Ibid.

50. Gibbs et al., "Brazil's Soy Moratorium."

51. R. Butler, "Brazilian Soy Industry Extends Moratorium on Deforestation Indefinitely," Mongabay.com, May 9, 2016, https://news.mongabay.com/2016/05/brazilian-soy-industry-extends-moratorium-deforestation-indefinitely.

52. R. Butler, "Brazilian Beef Giants Agree to Moratorium on Amazon Deforestation," Mongabay.com, October 7, 2009, http://news.mongabay.com/2009/10/brazilian-beef-giants-agree-to-moratorium-on-amazon-deforestation; D. Boucher, "Chapter 5: Cattle and Pasture," in *The Root of the Problem: What's Driving Tropical Deforestation Today?* ed. D Boucher et al. (Union of Concerned Scientists, 2011), 41–48.

53. The Consumer Goods Forum, "Consumer Goods Industry Announces Initiatives on Climate Protection," November 29, 2010, http://www.theconsumergoodsforum.com/consumer-goods-industry-announces-initiatives-on-climate-protection.

54. K. Gilbert, "Financial Institutions Play Catch-Up in Deforestation Fight," *Institutional Investor*, January 23, 2015; BNP Paribas, "Corporate Social Responsibility,"

http://www.bnpparibas.com/sites/default/files/ckeditor-upload/files/PDF/RSE/CSR%20-%20Sector%20policy%20-%20Palm%20Oil.pdf.

55. Cambridge Institute for Sustainability Leadership, "Banking Environment Initiative," University of Cambridge, 2015, http://www.cisl.cam.ac.uk/business-action/sustainable-finance/banking-environment-initiative.

56. Cambridge Institute for Sustainability Leadership, "Financial Regulation," University of Cambridge, 2015, http://www.cisl.cam.ac.uk/business-action/sustainable-finance/banking-environment-initiative/programme/Financial-regulation.

57. J. Cheam, "Golden Agri Adopts No Deforestation Policy," *Eco-Business*, February 9, 2011.

58. Asia Pulp and Paper, "Forest Conservation Policy," February 2013, https://www.asiapulppaper.com/sustainability/vision-2020/forest-conservation-policy.

59. Wilmar, "No Deforestation, No Peat, No Exploitation Policy," December 5, 2013, http://www.wilmar-international.com/wp-content/uploads/2012/11/No-Deforestation-No-Peat-No-Exploitation-Policy.pdf.

60. Norges Bank Investment Management, "Government Pension Fund Global: Annual Report 2012," February 27, 2013, http://www.nbim.no/globalassets/reports/2012/annual-report/annual-report-2012.pdf, 19.

61. U.S. Department of Agriculture, Foreign Agricultural Service, "Oilseeds: World Markets and Trade," May 2016, http://apps.fas.usda.gov/psdonline/circulars/oilseeds.pdf. Consumption by the European Union as a whole ranks third.

62. H. Kharas, "The Emerging Middle Class in Developing Countries," Organisation for Economic Co-operation and Development Centre Working Paper 285, 2010.

63. Henders et al., "Trading Forests," 11.

64. See, for example, C. Nugroho, A. Lyons, A. Kusworo, A. Rafiastanto, and D. Liswanto, "Development of Carbon-Finance

Mechanisms for High Conservation Value Forests and Peatlands in Oil Palm-Dominated Landscapes of Kalimantan," Sustainable Palm Oil Transparency Toolkit, September 26, 2012, http://www.sustainablepalmoil.org/case-studies/ffi/.

65. Foresthints, "Agrarian Minister Tells Palm Oil Companies Not to Buy Time in HCVF Areas Registration," March 23, 2016, http://www.d.foresthints.news/agrarian-minister-tells-palm-oil-companies-not-to-buy-time-in-hcvf-areas-registration.

66. M. Colchester et al., "Independent Review of the Social Impacts of Golden Agri Resources' Forest Conservation Policy in Kapuas Hulu District, West Kalimantan," Forest Peoples Programme and TUK Indonesia, 2014, http://www.forestpeoples.org/sites/fpp/files/publication/2014/01/pt-kpc-report-january-2014final.pdf, 42.

67. A. Zwewnert, "Sustainable Palm Oil Body Eyes Broader Approach to Certification," Thomson Reuters Foundation, September 11, 2015, http://www.trust.org/item/20150911114250-2hndb/.

68. International Sustainability Unit, "Tropical Forests: A Review," London, April 2015, http://www.pcfisu.org/wp-content/uploads/2015/04/Princes-Charities-International-Sustainability-Unit-Tropical-Forests-A-Review.pdf.

69. Stockholm Environment Institute, "Transformative Transparency: Harnessing the Power of Data for Supply Chain Sustainability," 2015, https://www.sei-international.org/mediamanager/documents/Publications/sei-gcp-db-transformativetransparency.pdf.

70. Office of the U.S. Trade Representative, "Chapter Eighteen: Environment," in the Peru–United States Trade Promotion Agreement, 2007, https://ustr.gov/sites/default/files/uploads/agreements/fta/peru/asset_upload_file953_9541.pdf.

71. Environmental Investigation Agency, "Implementation and Enforcement Failures in

the US–Peru Free Trade Agreement (FTA) Allow Illegal Logging Crisis to Continue," briefing paper, June 2015.

72. Office of the U.S. Trade Representative, "USTR Requests Peru Timber Verification," press release, Washington, DC, February 2016.

73. D. Brack and R. Bailey, "Ending Global Deforestation: Policy Options for Consumer Countries," Chatham House and Forest Trends, London, 2013; N. Walker et al., "Demand-Side Interventions to Reduce Deforestation and Forest Degradation," International Institute for Environment and Development, London, UK, 2013.

74. European Union, "Evaluation of the EU FLEGT Action Plan 2004–2014," final report, vol. 1 (2016), https://ec.europa.eu/europeaid/sites/devco/files/report-flegt-evaluation.pdf, 152–56.

75. European Commission, "EU Opens Doors to Indonesia's Licensing Scheme for Exports of Verified Legal Timber," press release, Brussels, Belgium, August 18, 2016.

76. R. Brenyon, "UK to Lead Way on Sustainable Palm Oil," UK Department for Environment, Food & Rural Affairs, October 30, 2012, https://www.gov.uk/government/news/uk-to-lead-way-on-sustainable-palm-oil.

77. President's Global Development Council, "Modernizing Development," May 15, 2015, http://www.usaid.gov/sites/default/files/documents/1872/GlobalDevelopment CouncilReportModernizingDevelopment.pdf.

78. M. Gaworecki, "Norway Commits to Zero Deforestation," Mongabay.com, May 26, 2016, https://news.mongabay.com/2016/05/breaking-norway-commits-zero-deforestation/.

The Eiffel Tower is illuminated in green to mark the Paris climate conference in December 2015.

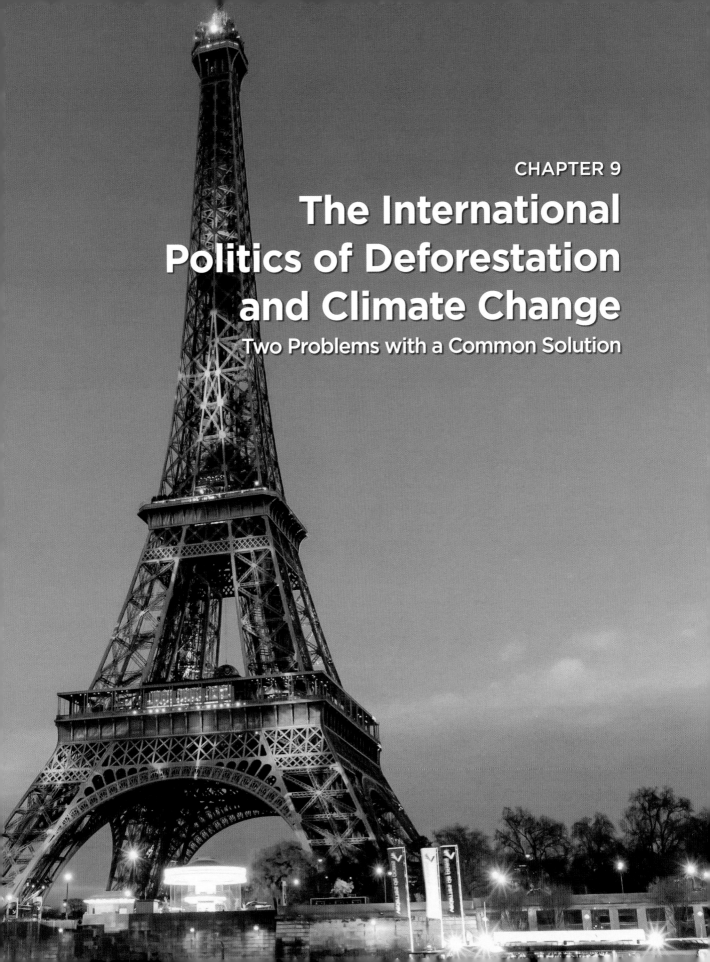

CHAPTER 9

The International Politics of Deforestation and Climate Change

Two Problems with a Common Solution

reat Britain, 1850. Amid alarm about a "denudation crisis," the British Association for the Advancement of Science commissioned a study on the impacts of tropical deforestation, selecting Dr. Hugh Cleghorn, a Scottish surgeon, to lead a team of scientists in conducting it (see figure 9.1).[1] The son of a colonial administrator in Madras and himself a member of the Indian Medical Service, Cleghorn had witnessed and expressed concern about deforestation in southern India. Like many medical professionals of his day, he was also interested in botany and had cultivated expertise in medicinal and economically valuable plants.

The resulting *Report of the Committee Appointed by the British Association to Consider the Probable Effects in an Economical and Physical Point of View of the Destruction of Tropical Forests*, published in 1852, focused mostly on India.[2] Its contents and those of subsequent reports by Cleghorn foreshadowed most of the themes that persist in contemporary debates about international cooperation to improve management of the world's tropical forests.

Cleghorn's report cited the practice of traditional shifting cultivation (described in chapters 2 and 10) by local people as a key cause of forest loss. In later writing, he characterized shifting cultivation as a "wasteful and barbarous system" and successfully argued for the imposition of a policy to ban the practice in government forests with valuable timber. Despite evidence that traditional

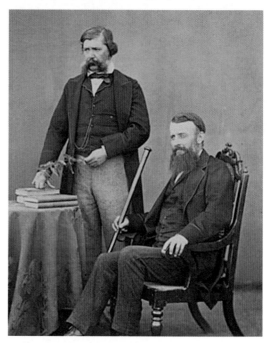

Figure 9.1: Hugh Cleghorn (seated), with John Lindsay Stewart, conservator of forests, Punjab. Photographed in 1864.

Source: Wikimedia.

shifting cultivation practices lag far behind industrial agriculture as a driver of deforestation, policies to stamp them out continue today in a number of tropical countries.

The 1852 report was significant for another reason, too. It was the first to highlight a new cause of deforestation that had suddenly become the most important: the extraction of timber for railroad ties and wood to supply the Indian railway system. The railway system was then rapidly expanding, in part to facilitate the export of agricultural commodities to Britain. Thus, the linkages between economic globalization and deforestation described in chapter 8 continue a story begun more than one and a half centuries ago. And the question of how to provide the infrastructure necessary for economic

This chapter draws heavily on two background papers commissioned for this book, one by Antonio La Viña and Ayala de Leon on the international politics of forests and climate change and one by Sérgio Abranches on the politics of results-based forest finance in Brazil.

growth without destroying forests is still pertinent in development decision making, as described in chapter 7.

A third theme of Cleghorn's report was the potential of tropical forests to serve as an ongoing source of materials and revenue, if managed sustainably. Cleghorn was a believer in the "scientific forestry" practices being introduced in neighboring Burma by Dietrich Brandis, "the father of tropical forestry." In India, Cleghorn promoted active silvicultural treatment to manage natural forests for timber production and the establishment of plantations to provide fuelwood, although demand soon exceeded the yields from those efforts. The proposition that tropical forests can be managed "sustainably" has remained popular—and controversial—to this day.

A fourth theme of the report was the question of who should control forests. Cleghorn viewed state intervention as necessary to counteract the short-term interests of both local populations and private businesses that would lead to forest destruction. This perspective led to the establishment of India's state forest system in 1864 and influenced the design of forest management systems in other tropical countries, as well as in the United States—Gifford Pinchot, founder of the United States Forest Service in 1905, consulted extensively with Dietrich Brandis. The role of the state as a protector of a nation's forests, in relationship both to commercial uses and the rights of local communities, has been a source of considerable contestation ever since.

Finally, anticipating the later science on forest-based ecosystem services presented in chapter 3, the report to the British Association stressed that failure to conserve forests would increase vulnerability to ecological disasters. Cleghorn subsequently downplayed the ecological rationale for reducing deforestation, however, choosing to stress instead forests' role in maintaining a supply of raw material for the railways and generating revenue for the state, which were of more interest to colonial authorities. As detailed in chapter 6, the value of standing forests as providers of development benefits continues to be neglected today.

One theme understandably missing from Cleghorn's report was the connection between tropical deforestation and global climate stability. The linkage between increased carbon dioxide in the atmosphere and global warming was not made until 1896, when Svante Arrhenius, a Swedish scientist, developed the theory of the greenhouse effect.[3] It would be more than a hundred years before Charles Keeling would publish his famous graph showing that carbon dioxide levels were, indeed, rising,[4] and, as recently as 1985, a global strategy to address tropical deforestation would still make no reference to climate change.[5]

The purpose of this chapter is to describe how the linkage to climate change has since precipitated an extraordinary transformation in the international politics of tropical deforestation.

Twenty-five years ago, public awareness of the importance of tropical forests was reaching the first of two contemporary peaks. International cooperation to reverse forest loss was high on the global agenda in the run-up to the United Nations Conference on Environment and Development (UNCED)—popularly known as the Rio Earth Summit—hosted by Brazil in Rio de Janeiro in 1992. Yet negotiations toward a binding international agreement on forests failed amid considerable acrimony, with countries splitting along North–South lines—that is, with industrialized countries on one side and developing countries on the other.

In contrast, negotiations to shape international cooperation to reduce emissions from deforestation and forest degradation initiated in 2007 made significant progress in surmounting the North–South divide where previous initiatives had failed. Clearly, many other changes took place in international politics and in the domestic politics of key forest-rich countries, such as Brazil, in the intervening decade and a half. But reframing tropical forests as an emission mitigation solution for global cooperation under the United Nations Framework Convention on Climate Change (UNFCCC)—rather than framing tropical deforestation as a global problem—made a big difference.

In fact, discussions to design a mechanism to promote financial cooperation on forest protection have been among the most constructive and productive areas of negotiation under the UNFCCC. By the time the final gavel fell at the climate change negotiations in Warsaw in December 2013, the international community had agreed on the main elements of what is now known as "REDD+," for Reducing Emissions from Deforestation and forest Degradation, plus conservation, sustainable management of forests, and enhancement of forest carbon stocks (see box 1.1 in chapter 1). The final dotting of i's and crossing of t's was completed in June 2015, and the results of these prior negotiations were incorporated as Article 5 in the Paris Agreement later that year.[6] Unfortunately, REDD+ has remained hostage to the international community's failure to generate financing of sufficient scale and certainty to reward action to reduce deforestation.

In the sections that follow, we recount the recent history of international forest and climate politics in two parts. First, we trace how the linkage to climate change reshaped forest discussions in the interval between the birth of the Tropical Forestry Action Plan in Rome in 1983 and the 2009 climate negotiations in Copenhagen. We then explain how negotiators addressed the main design challenges to ensuring REDD+ was effective, efficient, and equitable. The domestic politics of international cooperation on reducing deforestation in developing countries and in rich countries, respectively, will be covered in chapters 10 and 11 and REDD+ finance in chapter 12.

From Rome to Bali

As indicated above, interest in tropical forests peaked twice on the international political agenda between the mid-1980s and 2010, framed first with respect to the problem of deforestation, and then in terms of what forests could offer in the way of a solution to climate change. Figure 9.2 provides a timeline of key events described in the following sections.

A Twentieth-Century Deforestation Crisis

One hundred thirty-five years after the British Association for the Advancement of Science commissioned Hugh Cleghorn's report in response to the so-called "denudation crisis," the international community mobilized to address another crisis of tropical deforestation. This time, it was a sharp increase

Figure 9.2: Rome to Bali 1983-2007: Tropical deforestation evolves from political problem to climate solution.

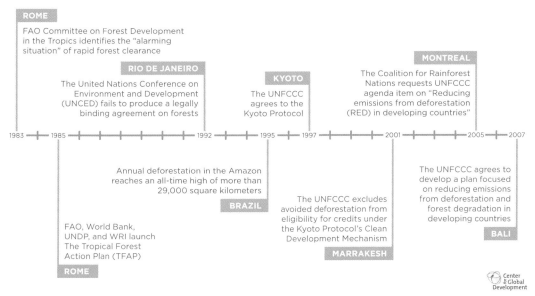

Source: Various sources (see www.cgdev.org/forest-sources).

in deforestation in the Amazon that created a sense of urgency.

In October 1983, a meeting in Rome of the UN Food and Agriculture Organization (FAO) Committee on Forest Development in the Tropics identified the "alarming situation" of rapid forest clearance, which was going on even as funding for tropical forestry programs decreased.[7] In 1985, the FAO joined the World Bank, the UN Development Program (UNDP), and the World Resources Institute (WRI) in launching the "Tropical Forestry Action Plan" (TFAP), which was intended to provide a framework for developing national forestry action plans to reduce deforestation and forest degradation. The TFAP would also coordinate the funding needed to implement those plans, and it called for mobilizing $8 billion to do so over five years.[8]

With its focus strikingly similar to that of Cleghorn's 1852 report, the TFAP set five priority areas for action:

- Forestry in land use (including "the loss of productive forests resulting from . . . shifting cultivation")
- Forest-based industrial development (including "improving the productivity of the forest to ensure that local, regional, national, and export requirements are satisfied")
- Fuelwood and energy
- Conservation of tropical forest ecosystems
- Institutions (including "strengthening the public forest administrations")[9]

The TFAP approach proved controversial, and, by 1990, it faced a crisis of legitimacy.[10]

The World Rainforest Movement, an advocacy group, issued a blistering report alleging the TFAP paid insufficient attention to the rights of forest dwellers, and that its support for industrial logging was accelerating rather than decreasing forest loss. In rapid succession, the FAO and WRI published their own critical reviews. All three reviews agreed the TFAP was failing to address the divergences between international concerns and the interests of developing countries, and they said it was also failing to slow deforestation. The reviews conducted by the FAO and WRI both recommended the initiation of negotiations toward a global convention on forests.[11]

A North–South Divide in Rio

An outcome of the 1990 meeting in Houston of the G7 (an informal block of industrialized countries) was a stated readiness of member countries to begin such negotiations as soon as possible.[12] They commenced during preparations for UNCED, which was to be held in Rio de Janeiro in 1992. The main proponents of a treaty on forests were industrialized countries, not least the European countries and the United States.

Not all countries saw the need for a legally binding agreement on forests. Positions divided along North–South lines, and forests emerged as among the most contentious issues under discussion in the run-up to UNCED. Negotiations at preparatory committee meetings failed to produce even a draft agreement. Ultimately, although UNCED succeeded in concluding conventions on climate change, biodiversity, and desertification, agreement on forests was limited to a non-legally binding statement of principles on the "management,

conservation, and sustainable development of all types of forests."[13]

Why did negotiations toward a forest convention fail? Observers have advanced several reasons—none of them mutually exclusive—to explain the outcome. First, negotiations were complicated by the political necessity of including discussion of all kinds of forests—not just tropical, but temperate and boreal forests as well. Although the industrialized countries were primarily focused on the proposed convention as an instrument for addressing tropical deforestation, negotiating one that applied only to developing countries would not have been politically feasible.

Second, some believed forests were not an appropriate focus for an international agreement. Government and nongovernment voices alike objected to internationalizing the deforestation problem, each with a different reason to resist turning a challenge faced by many countries—forest management—into an issue for global governance. Brazil was particularly outspoken in asserting national sovereignty over natural resources. Others did not believe the linkages between forests and international trade or transboundary impacts were strong enough—at least relative to other issues—to justify an international treaty.[14] (Subsequent initiatives to address trade in illegally felled timber—such as the Forest Law Enforcement, Governance, and Trade [FLEGT] Action Plan discussed in chapters 8 and 11—focused on just such linkages.)

Also opposing a treaty were some nongovernmental organizations (NGOs) and indigenous peoples' groups. Reacting to the injustices inherent in the state-centric forest management systems imposed since Cleghorn's day (and described further in chapter 10), such groups argued that securing local land tenure would be the most effective approach to reducing deforestation.[15]

The third and most compelling explanation for the failure to conclude a convention on forests is that developing countries perceived the proposed treaty as fundamentally unbalanced. From their perspective, they were being asked to accept obligations to reduce deforestation without commensurate sacrifices from industrialized countries. In preparatory committee meetings, India and Malaysia, with the backing of the G77 (a negotiating block of developing countries), took the position that tropical forest countries would have to be compensated for the direct costs as well as the opportunity costs of compliance with the provisions of a convention, an obligation rich countries were unwilling to assume.[16]

Furthermore, political scientist David Humphreys argues the United States, the United Kingdom, and other developed countries were becoming increasingly opposed to legally binding conventions as part of the broader ascendance in the 1980s of a "neoliberal" ideology that favored soft law, volunteerism, and market-based approaches rather than government regulation. According to Humphreys, the neoliberal agenda found particular expression in subsequent international forest governance mechanisms—including the founding of the Forest Stewardship Council in 1993 and the Non-Legally Binding Instrument on All Types of Forests agreed on by the United Nations Forum on Forests (UNFF) in 2007—and its influence is also discernible in the reference to "market forces and mech-

anisms" in the forest principles adopted at UNCED in lieu of a convention.[17]

The same countries that could not agree on a forest treaty in 1992 did, however, agree on a climate change treaty, the UNFCCC. Thus, while the outcomes in Rio de Janeiro noisily marked the slamming of one door to international cooperation on reducing tropical deforestation, they quietly unlocked another.

Forests in the Kyoto Protocol and the Clean Development Mechanism

Following agreement on the UNFCCC at UNCED, the next major milestone in global climate negotiations was the adoption in 1997 of the Kyoto Protocol by parties to the convention. The protocol for the first time imposed legally binding emission reduction targets on industrialized countries, and it included provisions that allowed them to count a portion of domestic forest-related emission reductions toward the achievement of their overall targets. But because the protocol did not require developing countries to set such targets, most potential emission reductions from slowing tropical deforestation were not included in its effective geographical scope.

There was another way, however, in which tropical forests might have been included. The Clean Development Mechanism (CDM) was created under the protocol to allow industrialized countries to "offset" domestic emissions by investing in projects that would reduce emissions in developing countries. In other words, investors in the North could finance initiatives such as renewable energy development in the South in return for credit toward meeting their domestic emission reduction targets. Because developing countries offered cheaper emission reductions, such a "flexibility mechanism" was in theory an attractive way to match the North's demand for emission reductions with the South's demand for development finance.

The degree to which forest-related emission reductions should be eligible as offsets under the CDM proved highly contentious. The question revealed new divisions within and between negotiating blocs and NGO advocacy groups, which sometimes erupted in "shouting matches and bitter rifts" among them.[18] Arguments for and against the inclusion of "avoided deforestation" in the CDM in the late 1990s served as a dress rehearsal for debates that would emerge with respect to REDD+ a decade later.

On the "pro" side, in favor of allowing offsets from avoided deforestation under the CDM, was the "Umbrella Group," which included Australia, Canada, Japan, New Zealand, and the United States, as well as a few Latin American countries.[19] They were joined by some conservation groups, including The Nature Conservancy. Proponents saw the approach as an opportunity to provide financial incentives to developing countries to slow forest loss through the sale of forest carbon credits. They also saw such credits as a potential source of finance for biodiversity conservation projects. The Nature Conservancy was the sponsor of the Noel Kempff Mercado Climate Action Project in Bolivia, one of several pilot projects that had attracted investment from U.S. power companies hoping to get credit for offsetting their fossil fuel-based emissions.[20]

On the other side of the issue, the Association of Small Island States (AOSIS),

Brazil, and the European Union opposed the inclusion of avoided deforestation in the CDM. They were joined by many scientists and NGOs.[21] As described in chapter 4, a key reason for this opposition was a concern that the technology then available was incapable of measuring forest cover change with sufficient accuracy to be confident the emissions from deforestation had actually been avoided. Many believed methodological guidance on how to manage issues of "additionality," "permanence," and "leakage" (described further below) was not yet sufficient to manage the risks they presented and ensure that claimed reductions in forest-based emissions would, in fact, be real.

But opposition to including avoided deforestation in the CDM went beyond scientific and technical concerns. Opponents such as the World Wide Fund for Nature saw adverse political implications for climate protection efforts both within and between countries if forest offsets were allowed. Many groups opposed offsets in general, fearing their availability would lessen the pressure on industrialized countries to reduce emissions at home. The example of U.S. power companies' having already invested in projects such as Noel Kempff perhaps made forest offsets particularly suspect as "an insidious way for polluting industries to continue emitting greenhouse gases by paying poor countries to reduce their own emissions."[22]

Other concerns specific to forest offsets had to do with equity; since only those developing countries with significant forest resources would stand to benefit, smaller countries without significant forest carbon potential were not strong supporters.[23] Finally, some questioned the feasibility of actually achieving reductions in deforestation, given the complexity of the factors driving it.

Ultimately, avoided deforestation was not included in the CDM. The Marrakesh Accords concluded at the 2001 climate negotiations allowed only afforestation and reforestation—that is, tree planting—as eligible forest-related projects. And even those activities were rendered relatively unattractive by decisions to award them less valuable temporary credits (to address the concerns about "permanence," described further below) and cap them at 1 percent of a country's base year emissions (to address concerns about "flooding the market" with cheap credits, also discussed below).[24] The European Union subsequently decided not to allow forest offsets into the European Trading System—the world's largest compliance regime for reducing carbon emissions—launched in 2005. The European Commission's rationale for excluding forests echoed the scientific and technical concerns that arose during the CDM debates, as well as concern that the quantity of potential forest credits could undermine the broader carbon market.[25]

The Evolution of an Idea

The UNFCCC's rebuff to including forest conservation in its negotiations over the CDM sent avoided deforestation as a climate mitigation strategy into a period of hibernation with regard to international negotiations. But the incubation of the concept by Brazilian academics and advocates in the wake of the Rio Earth Summit laid the groundwork for a dramatic change in Brazil's position on including forests in negotiations as a solution to climate change.[26]

At the time of the 1992 summit, Brazil had emerged from authoritarian military rule under a democratic constitution adopted only a few years previously, in 1988. The opening of democratic space in which civil society could operate freely, the global spotlight of the summit, and a number of other factors described in chapter 10 combined to fertilize the blossoming of a domestic environmental movement. It included the founding of a number of new NGOs and think tanks focused on the rights of traditional peoples and forest-related research and policy.[27]

In 1995, Brazil's annual deforestation reached an all-time high of more than twenty-nine thousand square kilometers, an area almost the size of Belgium.[28] Brazilian civil society actors focused their attention on this deforestation in the Amazon and received official encouragement from Rubens Ricupero, an active participant in the UNCED negotiations and leader of Brazil's newly created Ministry for the Environment and the Legal Amazon.[29]

In 2000, a group of NGOs based in the Amazonian city of Belém began a series of discussions questioning why forests were being left out of global climate change negotiations. These groups favored including forests in the climate protection regime, but the idea was at variance with the official position of the government of Brazil and adamantly opposed by other Brazilian NGOs. At an event held on the sidelines of the climate negotiations in Milan in 2003, the Belém coalition internationalized the debate by presenting a proposal for "compensated reduction of deforestation."

The proposal would later be elaborated on in influential articles published in academic journals and a submission to the UNFCCC.[30]

Under the proposed compensated reduction of deforestation mechanism, developing countries would receive financial compensation from industrialized countries for reducing deforestation below an agreed-on baseline, at a price derived from the carbon market. The proposal was brilliant in at least three ways:[31]

- Unlike the CDM, which brokered emission reduction credits on a project basis, the proposed mechanism would operate on a government-to-government basis. Implementation on a national scale would go a long way toward meeting concerns about "leakage"—that is, the problem (discussed below) of reductions in one area simply resulting in increases elsewhere.
- Compensation would be an ex post payment based on verified performance. Without ex ante conditionality, the arrangement would thus respect the national sovereignty of recipient countries.
- Because the mechanism focused only on reduced deforestation, measurement of performance would be simple.

To the surprise of the Brazilian NGOs that organized the event in Milan, the executive secretary (Claudio Langone) to the newly appointed minister of environment (Marina Silva) in Brazil accepted their invitation to participate in a roundtable discussion. Even more surprising, he welcomed their proposal for a compensated reduction of deforestation mechanism, much to the consternation of the diplomats leading Brazil's UNFCCC negotiating team.[32]

Although she harbored concerns about the possible risks entailed by the proposed mechanism, Marina Silva began a series of informal consultations on the NGOs' idea and decided to place it on Brazil's policy agenda. This, in turn, prompted the "prolonged negotiation" within the Brazilian government necessary to reverse a long- and firmly maintained opposition to internationalizing the deforestation issue in the climate change policy arena. In parallel to this domestic policy process, Silva also began conversations with her counterparts in other countries that would contribute to a striking realignment of the politics of forests and climate change over the course of a few short years.[33]

Forest Politics Reframed

At around the same time Brazilian NGOs, academics, and policymakers began debating the proposed compensated reduction of deforestation mechanism in 2003, an alliance of forest-rich developing countries (eventually numbering about forty countries, which notably did not include Brazil) began meeting as the Coalition for Rainforest Nations (CfRN). The coalition was founded in part in reaction to the failure to include avoided deforestation in the CDM. From the coalition's perspective, this exclusion was fundamentally unjust; having cleared their own forests, industrialized countries had set rules that allowed themselves to get credit for planting trees within their own borders, "while asking Developing Nations to conserve the remaining rainforests for free" (although the Kyoto Protocol did not obligate them to do so).[34]

In 2005, at the climate negotiations in Montreal, Papua New Guinea and Costa Rica presented, on behalf of "many supportive Nations," a proposal based on the compensated reduction of deforestation idea.[35] They called it "Reducing Emissions from Deforestation," launching an acronym (RED) that would preoccupy climate negotiators for the following decade. RED would eventually become "REDD+," with an extra "D" appended to connote forest degradation, and the plus sign to connote conservation and regrowth of forest carbon stocks. (Box 1.1 in chapter 1 provides a more complete explanation of the term.)

In their proposal, Papua New Guinea and Costa Rica argued that the convention on climate change was the appropriate forum in which to address emissions from tropical deforestation. They solicited support from industrialized countries, citing a G8 communiqué and a European Commission report that called for global participation in combating deforestation, due to its link to climate change. In addition to Papua New Guinea and Costa Rica, several other countries in Latin America and three Congo Basin countries wrote letters to the UNFCCC Secretariat supportive of the submission.[36] The proposal was a political game changer, precisely because it was put forth by developing countries. Reduction of tropical deforestation was an attractive way for developing countries to contribute to solving the climate change problem and, because participation would be voluntary, to do so in a way that did not infringe on their sovereignty or right to development. Some saw the proposal as "the grease that could lubricate the negotiations on a future climate agreement" by providing developing countries with a meaningful way to participate in the regime.[37] Countries at the Montreal negotiations welcomed the coalition's proposal and referred the RED idea to technical experts for development over the next two years.

Discussions in Montreal in turn forced the government of Brazil to articulate a position on the RED idea. While officials in the Ministry of Foreign Affairs were skeptical, they did not actively oppose RED because they did not think it was feasible as proposed and did not expect it to move forward. They agreed to a nuanced position to be taken by negotiators at the 2006 climate discussions in Nairobi that would accept the idea of developing countries' being paid for past emission reductions. The Brazilian negotiators were instructed, however, to reject any binding commitments, any conditions (including on how the money would be used), and any finance through carbon markets.[38]

In 2007, the stars aligned at the climate negotiations in Bali to thrust international cooperation on conserving tropical forests back into the global spotlight. The negotiations were not always smooth, on forests or more generally. Kevin Conrad, a negotiator for Papua New Guinea and leader of the CfRN, set off a burst of applause in the closing plenary session (and took a star turn on YouTube) when he famously challenged the United States to lead or "get out of the way."[39] But delegates achieved consensus on the Bali Road Map for negotiations toward a new climate agreement that was expected to be concluded in Copenhagen in 2009. The road map included the Bali Action Plan, with international cooperation on reducing deforestation a prominent feature.

The Bali Action Plan initiated a negotiating track focused on "policy approaches and positive incentives on issues related to reducing emissions from deforestation and forest degradation in developing countries." This language suggested financial compensation for avoided forest carbon emissions could be included in the comprehensive climate agreement expected to succeed the Kyoto Protocol in 2012. In the meantime, governments participating in the negotiations were encouraged to move ahead with building capacity to monitor forest-based emissions, to initiate "demonstration activities" to address the drivers of deforestation, and to mobilize resources to support those efforts.[40]

Why Did the Stars Align in Bali?

A number of factors had set the stage for agreement in Bali to bring tropical deforestation into international negotiations on climate change.

The science: The Fourth Assessment Report by the Intergovernmental Panel on Climate Change (IPCC), released in early 2007, had for the first time declared that observed warming was "very likely" due to human-caused greenhouse gases and estimated that deforestation and other land-use change was responsible for more than 17 percent of annual global emissions, exceeding the emissions of the global transport sector—all the world's planes, trains, ships, and automobiles combined. In parallel, advances in remote sensing technologies were gradually eroding one of the main pillars of opposition to including avoided deforestation in the Clean Development Mechanism—that is, that emission reductions could not be accurately measured.

The economics: An authoritative analysis of the economics of climate change published in late 2006 had concluded that reducing emissions from deforestation was one of the most cost-effective mitigation options. The UK-commissioned review by Lord Nicholas Stern stressed that addressing deforestation was one of four key elements of any credible strategy to address climate change.[41] As described further in chapter 11, the potential to use forest offsets as a way to arbitrage between the high costs of domestic emission reductions in industrialized countries and the low costs of reducing deforestation in developing countries was attractive to politicians in rich countries.

The politics: Framing RED as a voluntary mechanism by which rich countries would provide developing countries with financial incentives to reduce deforestation helped complete the transformation of forests from a subject of North–South deadlock in Rio de Janeiro to one of broad-based support in Bali. The proposed mechanism was seen as a "triple win":

- It was a win for the climate in its offering of cost-efficient emission reductions, which were attractive to rich countries.
- It was a win for development in its provision of a new source of development finance, which was attractive to many developing countries and NGOs working to reduce global poverty.
- It was a win for biodiversity conservation and the maintenance of ecosystem services in its provision of incentives

to protect forests rather than convert them to other uses, which was attractive to conservation-oriented NGOs.[42]

The fact that the proposal had been advanced by a coalition of tropical forest countries themselves changed the political dynamic by bridging traditionally opposing North–South alignments. The proposal also blurred the boundaries between established negotiating blocs. While Tuvalu continued its longstanding opposition to a forest-related mechanism, for example (motivated by concerns about the environmental integrity of forest emission reductions), its voice was counterbalanced by that of Papua New Guinea, a fellow member of the Association of Small Island States.[43]

A Virtuous Cycle

The evolution of Brazil's position—from opposition to including forests in climate change negotiations to acceptance of results-based payments for avoided forest emissions—was particularly significant. It illustrated how a positive dynamic between national and international policy arenas became a key factor that caused the stars to align in Bali. In a virtuous cycle, prospective participation in international negotiations impelled leaders within countries to develop and agree on national initiatives that could be showcased to the international community, which, in turn, generated political momentum that could be captured in international agreement. International agreement then stimulated further emission reduction commitments, financing pledges, and other country-level actions.

Figure 9.3 illustrates how actions by Brazil influenced, and were influenced by, partici-

pation in annual international climate talks. The Earth Summit in 1992 not only gave birth to the UNFCCC; it also helped nurture a domestic civil society movement in Brazil focused on deforestation in the Amazon. After avoided deforestation was left out of the CDM, Brazilian civil society organizations used international forums to advance the idea of compensation for reduced deforestation. The concept evolved into REDD+, and the Brazilian position on including forests in climate negotiations evolved, as well. Donor countries also contributed to—and benefited from—such virtuous cycles. Civil society organizations in Norway, for example, leveraged politicians' desire to show international leadership on climate change to prompt a major commitment to forest finance, as described in chapter 11. In what participants experienced as an extraordinary coincidence—although in light of Minister Marina Silva's quiet diplomacy, it was probably less so—domestic policy processes in Brazil and Norway converged on a single day in Bali. At an event on the sidelines of the 2007 climate talks, Tasso Azevedo, head of Brazil's nascent forest service, unveiled a proposed fund to receive payments based on Brazil's success in reducing deforestation. At the last minute, needing a title slide for his PowerPoint presentation, he had decided to call it "The Amazon Fund." In response to the presentation, a member of the audience from the Norwegian delegation stood up to express his government's interest in contributing to the new fund. As it happened, the government of Norway had, that same day, announced a $2.5 billion commitment to fund performance-based finance for rainforest conservation (see chapter 11).[44]

Figure 9.3: International negotiations and national actions to reduce deforestation are mutually reinforcing: Brazil.

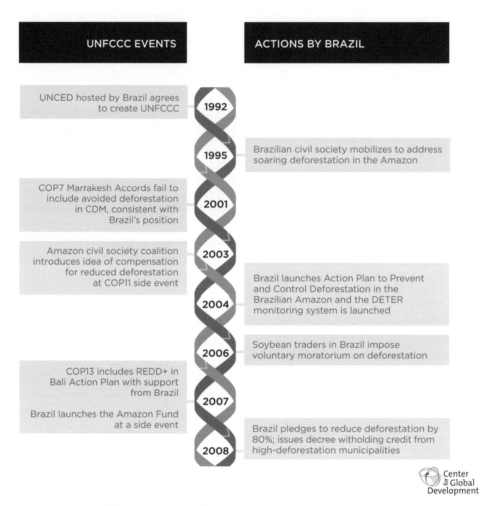

UNFCCC EVENTS

ACTIONS BY BRAZIL

1992 — UNCED hosted by Brazil agrees to create UNFCCC

1995 — Brazilian civil society mobilizes to address soaring deforestation in the Amazon

2001 — COP7 Marrakesh Accords fail to include avoided deforestation in CDM, consistent with Brazil's position

2003 — Amazon civil society coalition introduces idea of compensation for reduced deforestation at COP11 side event

2004 — Brazil launches Action Plan to Prevent and Control Deforestation in the Brazilian Amazon and the DETER monitoring system is launched

2006 — Soybean traders in Brazil impose voluntary moratorium on deforestation

2007 — COP13 includes REDD+ in Bali Action Plan with support from Brazil / Brazil launches the Amazon Fund at a side event

2008 — Brazil pledges to reduce deforestation by 80%; issues decree witholding credit from high-deforestation municipalities

Center for Global Development

Source: S. Abranches, "The Political Economy of Deforestation in Brazil and Payment-for-Performance Finance," CGD Background Paper, Center for Global Development, Washington, DC, 2014, http://www.cgdev.org/sites/default/files/CGD-Climate-Forest-Paper-Series-10-Abranches-Deforestation-Brazil_0.pdf; A. G. M. La Viña and A. de Leon, "Two Global Challenges, One Solution: International Cooperation to Combat Climate Change and Tropical Deforestation," CGD Working Paper 388, Center for Global Development, Washington, DC, 2014, http://www.cgdev.org/publication/two-global-challenges-one-solution-international-cooperation-combat-climate-change-and.

Disappointment in Copenhagen

The level of enthusiasm and excitement that permeated "Forestry World" in 2009 would be hard to exaggerate. Tropical forests had splashed back onto the global agenda in Bali. With the initiation of negotiations on REDD+ in the UNFCCC, political attention to deforestation was securely hitched to meeting the challenge of climate change, and nations of the world seemed poised to conclude a comprehensive climate change agreement that year. Such an agreement was widely expected to unleash unprecedented levels of funding for emission mitigation activities related to tropical forests.

While some elements of "Forestry World" resisted the perceived takeover of "their" issue by "Climate World," many individuals and organizations of all types at all levels raced to position themselves as leaders on forests and climate change in the run-up to the 2009 negotiations:

- President Susilo Bambang Yudhoyono of Indonesia announced the first voluntary emission reduction targets from a developing country, with the understanding that those targets could not be achieved without significantly reduced deforestation, as described in chapter 10.
- The newly elected government in Australia reauthorized a global forests and climate initiative inherited from the previous government and increased its funding, as detailed in chapter 11.
- A coalition of organizations established the Forest Carbon Partnership Facility (FCPF) at the World Bank, while a trio of United Nations agencies set up the UN-REDD Programme. Both were designed to help forest countries get ready for REDD+, as described in chapter 12.

In addition to these cases, among others, public sector agencies, conservation groups, and private entrepreneurs who were encouraged by the Bali Action Plan's call for "demonstration activities" staked out REDD+ pilot projects across the tropics, anticipating a market for the emission reduction credits such projects were designed to supply. Environmental advocates, think tanks, and development-oriented organizations all began staffing up, raising money, and publishing policy analyses and position papers on REDD+, while the new research topic attracted academics. (Ironic, in hindsight, was the great anxiety that demonstration projects would move forward before research teams could be fielded to collect baseline data to support "before and after" comparisons.)

But for reasons having nothing to do with forests, negotiations in Copenhagen failed to reach an agreement. Having made significant investments of time, money, political capital, and passion, proponents of REDD+ were especially crushed by the disappointing outcome. Although negotiations on REDD+ had advanced rapidly, large-scale financing for it was hostage to the achievement of a comprehensive climate agreement and ambitious emission reduction targets.

Although the last-minute collapse of negotiations in Copenhagen pushed the prospect of significant financing for forests far out on the horizon, the clouded outcome had three silver linings. First, REDD+ was, for the first time, formally included in the outcome of negotiations (the Copenhagen Accord, which was only "noted" rather than "agreed" by the conference), and negotiators reached consensus on a number of technical and methodological issues. Developing countries were asked to identify drivers of deforestation and to establish national forest monitoring systems.

Second, the accord encouraged industrialized countries to make substantial financial commitments to help developing countries initiate climate change mitigation and adaptation efforts. It referred to the "crucial role" of REDD+ in abating climate emissions and the need for "scaled up, new and additional, predictable and adequate funding...to enable and support enhanced action on mitigation." Donor countries pledged $30 billion of new and additional "fast-start finance" over the next three years and later reported they had exceeded those pledges, for a total of $35 billion.[45] About 10 percent of those funds were allocated to REDD+ financing. Although this share was small compared to the estimated proportion of total emissions contributed by deforestation, fast-start finance allowed many of the early initiatives prompted by the Bali Action Plan to continue, despite the uncertainty of longer-term support.

The third silver lining was that once the near-term possibility of a global carbon market had evaporated, so, too, did much opposition to REDD+. And the delay in the onset of scaled-up finance gave negotiators and practitioners time to work through a range of technical issues and address concerns about REDD+ one by one. Their efforts are described in the remainder of this chapter.

Negotiations on REDD+ bridged longstanding fissures between developed and developing countries.

From Bali to Paris

The agreement in Bali was a critical milestone toward international consensus on how countries should cooperate to conserve tropical forests, but much work remained to be done. Even the most enthusiastic proponents of REDD+ recognized many questions were unanswered. How would emission reductions from forests be treated, compared to those from other sectors? Which emission reductions would be included within the scope of the framework? How would emission reductions be measured? How would the rights of indigenous peoples be respected? And so on. These questions provided fodder for years of competing proposals, intellectual debate, and high-stakes negotiations among governments, academia, and civil society.

Over the years, the international community ticked off answers to these questions one by one, with the progress made on REDD+ standing out as a perennial bright spot in otherwise bleak international climate negotiations. According to policy expert Michael Wolosin and former REDD+ negotiator for the United States Donna Lee,

> REDD+ was seen throughout the years since COP-13 in Bali as the vanguard of climate negotiations, where developed and developing countries were able to make consistent progress, each year agreeing to a new decision, setting REDD+ apart from the otherwise rancorous and gridlocked debates in other negotiation streams.[46]

Figure 9.4 provides a timeline of events in the UNFCCC negotiations on REDD+.

A number of countries, both North and South, shared leadership on the forest agenda. Individual countries with strong interests at stake were particularly active. Both Brazil and Indonesia, with large forest endowments and high deforestation rates, guarded national sovereignty and, along with African countries, kept attention focused on the need for clarity on finance. Mexico and

Figure 9.4: Bali to Paris, 2007-2015: Climate negotiators reach an agreement on REDD+.

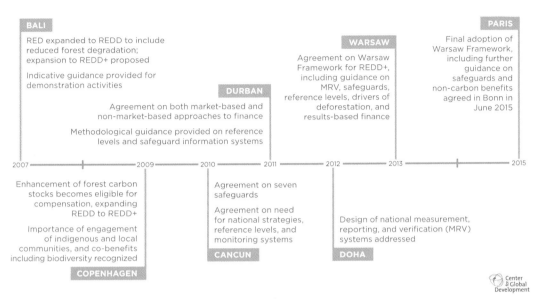

Source: Various sources (see www.cgdev.org/forest-sources).

Peru were especially active in conjunction with their hosting of UNFCCC Conferences of the Parties (COPs) in 2010 and 2014, respectively. Among rich countries from which finance would be expected, delegations from the European Union, Norway, and the United States were especially engaged.

In addition, nongovernment stakeholder groups played key roles in influencing the negotiations. Box 9.1 highlights the interests of indigenous peoples in influencing REDD+ and their strategies to do so.

Negotiations bridged longstanding fissures between developed and developing countries. Negotiators from the Philippines, for example, often found common ground with those from the European Union on the issue of safeguards.[47] One of the more active coa-

litions in REDD+ negotiations was the Environmental Integrity Group, which brought together Mexico and Switzerland, among others.[48] Also noteworthy is that small groups of developing countries, such as the Africa Group and CfRN, played more prominent roles in REDD+ negotiations than the G77 and China, which generally represented common positions among developing countries.[49]

While progress on resolving issues was consistent, it was not without periodic drama. For example, in 2012 at the climate negotiations in Doha, the question of how reported reductions in forest emissions would be verified created an impasse that brought REDD+ negotiations to a standstill. Diplomats from Norway and other European countries argued for international independent

To attend the launch of the Forest Carbon Partnership Facility during the climate negotiations in Bali in December 2007, participants had to step over protesters who had lain down on the sidewalk to block the entrance to the venue. The protesters' slogan, and that of other indigenous rights activists gathered in Bali, was "No Rights, No REDD." The fear was that new revenue streams associated with forest carbon would give governments and corporations an incentive to push aside local communities to capture the funding for themselves.[a] These concerns were not unfounded: as described further in chapter 10, history shows that whenever something valuable is found in the forest —whether timber, minerals, or charismatic wildlife—elites in national and international capitals tend to appropriate the benefits at the expense of local rights.[b]

This threat was of particular concern to indigenous peoples, whose customary territories encompassed much of the forest carbon that REDD+ would infuse with new value.[c] As a result, indigenous rights advocates were especially active stakeholders in international negotiations related to forests and climate change. Their efforts built on an infrastructure of legal principles and forums related to indigenous peoples' rights that had been developed within the United Nations, including the founding of the UN Permanent Forum on Indigenous Issues (UNPFII) in 2000 and the General Assembly's adoption of the Declaration on the Rights of Indigenous Peoples (UNDRIP) in September 2007, only a few months before the UNFCCC COP13 in Bali.

With regard to REDD+ negotiations, indigenous peoples lobbied for recognition of substantive rights to land, territories, and resources, as well as procedural rights, including self-determination and free, prior, and informed consent to climate actions that would affect them.[d] They appealed to moral arguments asserting their status as rights holders, and they advanced instrumental arguments—that is, arguments that the implementation of REDD+ would not succeed without the cooperation of and knowledge provided by the indigenous communities affected.[e]

Beyond participating in public protests staged at annual COPs from Bali to Paris, indigenous advocates employed a variety of tactics to influence REDD+ negotiations. They collaborated with government delegations, among them those from Bolivia and Tuvalu, who were willing to help advance their cause in the negotiations, by, for example, including explicit references to indigenous peoples in their own party submissions. The government of Mexico facilitated consultation with delegations in the run-up to COP16 that contributed to the inclusion of indigenous rights in the Cancun Safeguards.[f]

Indigenous groups themselves made formal submissions to the UNFCCC,[g] issued declarations,[h] organized official side events and parallel outside events (including the "Indigenous Peoples Day," held at COP15 in Copenhagen), and formed coalitions with sympathetic nonindigenous organizations, such as the Accra Caucus created on the sidelines of an August 2009 UNFCCC meeting in Ghana.[i] And they demanded inclusion in multiple REDD+ forums outside the formal negotiations, including the FCPF, the UN-REDD Programme, and the REDD+ Partnership.[j]

Despite the slowness of their progress toward the inclusion in negotiated texts of strong language recognizing indigenous rights, advocates were persistent. In Copenhagen, agreement by negotiators merely to "note" that UNDRIP had been adopted by the UN General Assembly was a compromise between drafts that would have recognized UNDRIP as a source of rights and competing drafts that would have relegated it to a footnote.[k] References to "respect for the knowledge and rights of indigenous peoples" and their "effective participation" as stakeholders were included in an appendix to decisions taken in

Cancun.[l] While the 2015 Paris Agreement made multiple references to indigenous peoples, reference to indigenous rights was included only in the preamble rather than the legally binding text.[m]

Nevertheless, the overall story of indigenous peoples' engagement in REDD+ negotiations is one of effective advocacy based on transnational alliances that shifted the positions of a number of key governments—including the United States government, which had opposed UNDRIP—and influenced the broader normative framework for consideration of indigenous rights within the UNFCCC.[n]

Victoria Tauli-Corpuz, an Igorot from the Philippines, played an especially influential role over the course of many years of REDD+ negotiations. Having participated in drafting UNDRIP, she served as a member of the Philippine delegation to climate negotiations and chair of the UNPFII and went on to become the UN special rapporteur on the rights of indigenous peoples.[o] One of her early contributions was to help organize the 2007 protests in Bali.[p]

a. D. Brown, F. Seymour, and L. Peskett, "How Do We Achieve REDD Co-Benefits and Avoid Doing Harm?" in Moving Ahead with REDD: Issues, Options and Implications, ed. A. Angelsen (Bogor, Indonesia: Center for International Forestry Research [CIFOR], 2008).

b. See, for example, N. Peluso, "Coercing Conservation? The Politics of State Resource Control," Global Environmental Change 3, no. 2, (1993).

c. Environmental Defense Fund and Woods Hole Research Center, "Tropical Forest Carbon in Indigenous Territories: A Global Analysis," 2015, http://www.edf.org/sites/default/files/biomass_map_english.pdf.

d. V. Menotti et al., "Ensuring Indigenous Peoples' and Forest-Dependent Communities' Rights in REDD," summary report and recommendations, International Forum on Globalization, Washington, DC, October 29, 2009, http://ifg.org/v2/wp-content/uploads/2014/05/REDD-Report_Final-10dec09_correx.pdf, 4; L. Wallbott, "Indigenous Peoples in UN REDD+ Negotiations: 'Importing Power' and Lobbying for Rights through Discursive Interplay Management," Ecology and Society 19, no. 1 (2014): 21.

e. Walbott, "Indigenous Peoples."

f. Ibid.

g. See, for example, Coordinating Body of Indigenous Organizations of the Amazon Basin, "SBSTA Submission of the Coordinating Body of Indigenous Organizations of the Amazon Basin (COICA)," Copenhagen, Denmark, February 14, 2009.

h. See, for example, Indigenous Peoples' Global Summit on Climate Change, "The Anchorage Declaration," Anchorage, Alaska, April 24, 2009, http://unfccc.int/resource/docs/2009/smsn/ngo/168.pdf.

i. Menotti et al., "Ensuring Indigenous Peoples."

j. Ibid.; Walbott, "Indigenous Peoples."

k. A. Wiersema, "Climate Change, Forests, and International Law: REDD's Descent into Irrelevance," Vanderbilt Journal of International Law 47, no. 1 (2014): 1.

l. United Nations Framework Convention on Climate Change (UNFCCC), "Addendum to the Report of the Conference of the Parties on its Sixteenth Session, held in Cancun from 29 November to 10 December 2010," Cancun, Mexico, March 15, 2011, http://unfccc.int/resource/docs/2010/cop16/eng/07a01.pdf, 26.

m. United Nations Framework Convention on Climate Change (UNFCCC), "Paris Agreement," Paris, France, 2015, http://unfccc.int/files/essential_background/convention/application/pdf/english_paris_agreement.pdf.

n. Walbott, "Indigenous Peoples."

o. Ibid.; "Biographical Information," Victoria Tauli Corpuz, United Nations Special Rapporteur, http://unsr.vtaulicorpuz.org/site/index.php/en/biography/.

p. Ibid.; "Biographical Information," Victoria Tauli Corpuz, United Nations Special Rapporteur, http://unsr.vtaulicorpuz.org/site/index.php/en/biography/.

verification of reported emissions to ensure transparency and credibility. The Brazilian delegation insisted that such a mechanism would compromise national sovereignty. Over the subsequent months, skillful diplomacy brokered a compromise based on expert review that was acceptable to both parties.

Through the years, an esprit de corps developed among REDD+ negotiators that supported the frank and open discussion necessary to align the divergent positions of different countries. According to Antonio La Viña, a lawyer from the Philippines who frequently chaired the working group charged with negotiating REDD+, sequencing was crucial to maintaining forward momentum, with progress in reaching agreement on more technical issues paving the way for agreement on more politically charged issues, such as reference levels and safeguards.

Broad-based political support for REDD+ would depend on credible approaches to managing risks.

The positions of individual countries such as Brazil and advocacy groups such as the Worldwide Fund for Nature evolved over time as their concerns were addressed, and as they realized the potential of REDD+ to meet their interests. There were also reversals. Bolivia had been a strong supporter of REDD+ until the leftist government of Evo Morales began taking an ideological position against market-based solutions to climate change in 2008. This position hardened into specific opposition to REDD+ in 2010.[50] Australia had

been a leader in REDD+ negotiations and was the first donor country to make a significant financial commitment to the forests and climate agenda in 2007, as described in chapter 11. But when Tony Abbott's coalition replaced Kevin Rudd's Labor government in 2013, the country's delegation to the Warsaw climate negotiations was downgraded and downsized.

In the meantime, various forums outside the formal negotiations provided informal platforms for building consensus. A series of "Forest Days," convened by the Center for International Forestry Research and other members of the UN Collaborative Partnership on Forests on the sidelines of the climate negotiations, served as an annual ideas marketplace for interested stakeholders from 2007 to 2012. An interim "REDD+ Partnership" established in the aftermath of Copenhagen provided a forum for discussions on REDD+ finance among donors and recipient countries. Such forums offered opportunities to build social capital among individuals and institutions working on forests and climate change.

Figure 9.5 illustrates how the virtuous cycle of international negotiations and national actions continued after COP13 in Bali, using the example of the host country, Indonesia. As international negotiators developed guidance on issues such as safeguards, results-based finance, and drivers of deforestation, those same issues were the subjects of innovation in domestic policy and practice.

Aligning Interests and Addressing Risks

As described above, once parties to the UNFCCC accepted the concept of compensating developing countries for reducing emissions from deforestation, a core group of

Figure 9.5: International negotiations and national actions to reduce deforestation are mutually reinforcing: Indonesia.

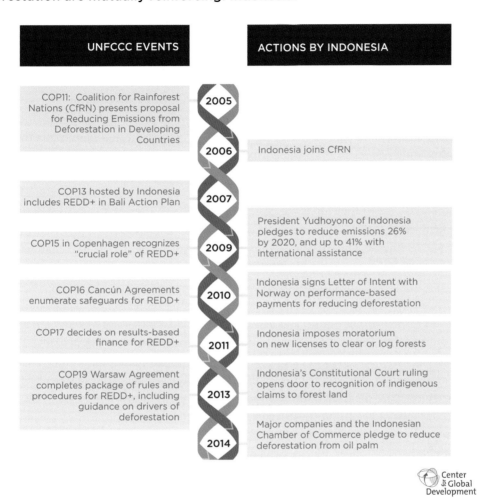

UNFCCC EVENTS		ACTIONS BY INDONESIA
COP11: Coalition for Rainforest Nations (CfRN) presents proposal for Reducing Emissions from Deforestation in Developing Countries	2005	
	2006	Indonesia joins CfRN
COP13 hosted by Indonesia includes REDD+ in Bali Action Plan	2007	
COP15 in Copenhagen recognizes "crucial role" of REDD+	2009	President Yudhoyono of Indonesia pledges to reduce emissions 26% by 2020, and up to 41% with international assistance
COP16 Cancún Agreements enumerate safeguards for REDD+	2010	Indonesia signs Letter of Intent with Norway on performance-based payments for reducing deforestation
COP17 decides on results-based finance for REDD+	2011	Indonesia imposes moratorium on new licenses to clear or log forests
COP19 Warsaw Agreement completes package of rules and procedures for REDD+, including guidance on drivers of deforestation	2013	Indonesia's Constitutional Court ruling opens door to recognition of indigenous claims to forest land
	2014	Major companies and the Indonesian Chamber of Commerce pledge to reduce deforestation from oil palm

Center for Global Development

Source: M. Dharmasaputra and A. Wahyudi, "The Impact of Payment-for-Performance Finance on Political Economy of Deforestation in Indonesia," CGD Background Paper, Center for Global Development, Washington DC, 2014, http://www.cgdev.org/sites/default/files/CGD-Climate-Forest-Series-9-Dhamasaputra-Wahyudi-Indonesia.pdf; A. G. M. La Viña and A. de Leon, "Two Global Challenges, One Solution: International Cooperation to Combat Climate Change and Tropical Deforestation," CGD Working Paper 388, Center for Global Development, Washington, DC, 2014, http://www.cgdev.org/publication/two-global-challenges-one-solution-international-cooperation-combat-climate-change-and.

negotiators worked their way through a long list of questions about how REDD+ would be implemented. Other than how it would be financed (discussed further below and in chapter 12), the main issues facing negotiators were how to ensure efforts to reduce emissions from deforestation would be, respectively, effective, efficient, and equitable.[51]

Different countries and country groupings had different interests as to how these issues would be addressed, as did other stakeholder groups seeking to influence the outcomes of negotiations. Broad-based political support for REDD+ would depend on credible approaches to managing risks associated with achieving these objectives without placing undue burdens on particular interest groups. UNFCCC negotiators reached agreement on the principles to guide such approaches, leaving considerable room for interpretation.

The practical application of those negotiated principles has been advanced through bilateral REDD+ agreements (such as those between Norway and, respectively, Brazil, Guyana, and Indonesia), the governing bodies of various REDD+ financing mechanisms (such as the FCPF Carbon Fund), and deliberations on including international forest offsets in markets such as the state of California's cap-and-trade system. The following sections and tables summarize the issues and the broad political consensus achieved in these various forums regarding how REDD+ should work. We also include some ideas that have been advanced, but not yet negotiated or tried, regarding how various risks could be managed.

Effectiveness: Ensuring Reductions Are Real

Considerable opposition to including forests in the global climate regime has been motivated by fear that doing so would be ineffective in reducing emissions from deforestation or would dilute or distract from efforts to reduce emissions from fossil fuels. Ensuring forest-based reductions are real has been of particular importance to industrialized

countries seeking to maintain the integrity of carbon markets, as well as to those countries most vulnerable to climate change, such as small island states.

The more technical concerns, described earlier and summarized in table 9.1, date back to the debates surrounding the inclusion in the CDM of credits for avoided deforestation. These concerns often march together under the banner of "environmental integrity." They focus on the question of how to ensure purported reductions in deforestation actually result in fewer tons of carbon released into the atmosphere.

Measurement. The first challenge is how to ensure reductions of forest-based emissions are measured with sufficient precision to avoid rewarding reductions that have not actually happened. Until very recently, measurement of deforestation was limited to an international system managed by the FAO, based on countries self-reporting national changes in forest cover every five years. The numbers generated by the system were criticized for inaccuracy stemming from lack of data, inconsistent reporting methods across countries, and incentives for biased reporting.[52] Advances in technology have, however, made available to everyone more precise, frequent, and transparent measurements through satellite imagery, as described in chapter 4.

Climate negotiators have agreed on a common set of standards and methodologies for measurement, reporting, and verification (MRV) of forest-based emissions. These standards are, in turn, based on guidance from the IPCC on such problems as how to estimate the carbon content of different kinds of forests. To deal with remaining uncertainty in the measurements, formulas for determining compensation under various bilateral and multilateral REDD+ financing agreements have been designed to be conservative—that is, more likely to underestimate than overestimate emission reductions eligible for payment. Agreements with Norway use a conservative estimate of one hundred tons of carbon per hectare to calculate payments; the FCPF Carbon Fund anticipates withholding based on the uncertainty of emission reductions.[53]

A related concern is the lack of capacity in developing countries to implement sophisticated MRV systems. This was addressed through the adoption of a step-wise approach, which encourages countries to progress as quickly as possible through stages of increasing precision. Building MRV capacity in developing countries has been a key target of donor funding for "REDD+ readiness." As described in box 4.4 in chapter 4, Guyana established an effective MRV system over the course of a few short years, demonstrating that rapid progress is feasible with international support.

Leakage. What about prevention of "leakage"—that is, the possibility that reductions in one area will simply displace deforestation drivers and result in increases elsewhere? When avoided deforestation was considered for inclusion in the CDM, and ultimately excluded, what was on the table were projects—initiatives limited to small, discrete areas in which emission reduction activities would take place. One could easily imagine forest conservation in one area merely displacing logging or clearing for agriculture to another nearby area not covered by a project.

When tropical forests were reintroduced into international climate negotiations, ne-gotiators concluded that REDD+ should be implemented at the national, rather than at the project, scale. This scaling up reduced the potential for leakage within countries. Some developing countries argued in favor of implementing REDD+ at a subnational scale, citing the need to start small and grow or, in the case of Colombia, the reality of not having de facto control over all of the country's forest territory. Allowing interim implementation of REDD+ at the level of subnational administrative units was a compromise.

Controlling international leakage through a mechanism in which participation is voluntary poses a greater challenge, although one that is not unique to forests: the nonparticipation of some countries—and thus potential leakage—applies to industrial emissions as well as to those from deforestation. By including degradation (the second "D" in "REDD+") and activities that conserve or enhance forest carbon (the "+"), negotiators attempted to make REDD+ attractive to both forest-rich and forest-poor countries, and to both high-deforestation and low-deforestation countries. This approach ensured participation from a wide range of countries, mitigating the risk of leakage across national boundaries, while at the same time responding to equity concerns.

Permanence. Finally, how were negotiators to deal with "permanence"—in other words, how were they to ensure emission reductions in one time period would not be reversed in the next? In theory, the concern about permanence applies equally to forests left standing and fossil fuels left in the ground; and even if reversals take place, having delayed the release of those emissions into the atmosphere remains valuable from a climate change perspective, as it buys time to put other mitigation measures into place. Because of forests' natural carbon capture and storage function, described in chapter 2, even temporary delays in forest clearing provide a double benefit of not only postponing emissions, but of continuing carbon buildup in vegetation and soil in the meantime.

The sensitivity of climate policymakers to reversals has been particularly acute for afforestation and reforestation (A/R) activities under the Clean Development Mechanism, leading them to allow only "temporary" emission reduction credits for these activities, of lower value than those from other sectors. Other options for hedging against reversals include buffers and insurance. With buffers, a portion of avoided emissions credits is set aside and held in escrow for a specified period, so the seller receives the funds only after the forest carbon stock has been maintained for that length of time. Otherwise, the buffer stock

Table 9.1: Concerns about Effectiveness—Ensuring Environmental Integrity

Issue	Risk	How managed
Precision of measurement	Imprecise data on forest cover change or carbon content could lead to overestimates of reduced emissions.	• Take advantage of new forest monitoring technologies. • Adopt standard methodologies and reporting formats for measurement, reporting, and verification (MRV) of emission reductions. • Use conservative approaches to estimating emission reductions. • Improve national monitoring systems over time through a step-wise approach.
Leakage	If deforestation is slowed in one area, it could simply be displaced to another.	• Implement and monitor REDD+ at the scale of political jurisdictions rather than projects. • Provide incentives for broad participation across countries (see also "Equity").
Permanence	Even if forest emissions are prevented today, changes in policy or natural disturbance could cause them to occur tomorrow.	• Note that for standing forests, this risk is no different than that of fossil fuels not consumed today being consumed tomorrow. • Establish buffers to compensate for unexpected forest losses. • Provide public guarantees or commercial insurance. • Implement and monitor REDD+ at the scale of political jurisdictions rather than projects. • Enhance certainty of performance-based finance.

is used to compensate for forest losses. This approach has been adopted by the FCPF Carbon Fund to deal with reversals as well as uncertainty (see below).[54] Commercial insurance could mitigate the risk of natural disasters such as fire, while political risk insurance could hedge the risk of losses due to policy change.

Implementing REDD+ at jurisdictional scales reduces the risk of catastrophic losses in forest carbon associated with the small A/R projects. And, as discussed further below, providing developing countries with more certainty regarding the availability of financial reward for successful efforts to protect forests is likely the best way to ensure those efforts will be sustained.

The issue of reference levels against which to measure reductions, which is also relevant to effectiveness, is discussed below under the section on efficiency.

Effectiveness: Particular Concerns about the Effectiveness of Forest Offsets in Carbon Markets

Concerns about the effectiveness of forest-related emission reductions have not been limited to technical measurement and risk management. What if cheap emission reductions from forests were to undermine emission reduction efforts overall when made available as offsets to emissions in industrialized countries through carbon trading?

Uncertainty. To those who worry emission reductions from forests are less certain than those in other sectors, allowing them to be traded and thus substituted for more certain reductions threatens the overall environmental integrity of the market. A simple and elegant solution is available that is analogous to one in-vented in England in response to King Edward III's ruling in 1266 that every loaf of bread contain a minimum quantity of wheat.[55] Bakers in those days avoided punishment for failing to meet the standard by giving customers thirteen loaves for every twelve purchased—the "baker's dozen"—thus ensuring that even if a small amount of wheat were lost in the baking process, customers would receive at least as much bread as they paid for. Similarly, under REDD+, for every four (for example) forest carbon credits purchased for use as offsets, a fifth would be purchased and "retired"—that is, taken out of the market—an approach included in the Wax-man-Markey climate legislation that passed the U.S. House of Representatives in 2009.[56] In this way, offsetting is not only good for containing costs; it also has a direct net-positive benefit for the atmosphere.

Two additional concerns have motivated opposition to including forest carbon offsets in compliance markets. One is the potential of forest carbon offsets to "flood the market," while the second is the prospect of rich countries and companies being able to "buy their way out" of reducing emissions. In both cases, the issue is not only whether or not a technical solution is available, but also whether or not such a solution is politically viable.

"Flooding the market." If a large supply of inexpensive forest carbon credits were to "flood" into a compliance market without a commensurate increase in demand, the price of credits for emission reductions of any kind would decline. As a result, price signals to stimulate emission reductions and technological change in other sectors, such as energy, would be weakened. Any weakening of incentives for technological change is a valid concern; our

CGD colleagues Nancy Birdsall and Arvind Subramanian have argued that the only way to reconcile climate stability with developing countries' equitable access to energy is through "revolutionary" improvements in the carbon efficiency of production and consumption.[57]

A concern that forest carbon offsets might flood the EU Emissions Trading System with cheap credits has kept REDD+ out of this market. But a simple, practical approach to managing this risk is by capping the portion of emissions that can be offset by forest carbon credits, or by offsets overall. In designing its cap-and-trade system, the state of California capped the amount of allowances that could be offset at less than 8 percent of the total.

"Buying their way out." A final, top-level concern specific to carbon markets is that if rich-country governments or corporations were allowed to offset their own emissions with forest carbon credits from developing countries, they would no longer have sufficient incentive to reduce them. The analysis in chapter 5 makes clear that the world can take on a significantly higher ambition for emission reductions at the same cost if forests are included, in which rich countries would be "buying their way up." But will rich countries take on a higher level of ambition or be satisfied with merely swapping out higher-cost emissions at home for lower-cost emissions abroad?

One way to avoid this risk is to separate

Table 9.2: Concerns about Allowing Forest Offsets in Compliance Markets

Issue	Risk	How managed
Uncertainty	Forest emission reductions of less certain quality could substitute for more certain reductions from other sectors.	• Use strategies outlined above to deal with measurement, leakage, and permanence issues. • Adopt "baker's dozen" discount approach.
"Flooding the market"	Large quantities of cheap forest offsets could depress prices, reducing demand for reductions from other sectors and associated incentives for technological innovation.	• Cap the potential contributions of forest offsets to compliance markets.
Letting rich countries and companies "buy their way out" of reducing fossil fuel emissions	If rich countries can buy cheap forest offsets from developing countries, pressure to reduce emissions from fossil fuel use could be relaxed.	• Make more ambitious mitigation targets by rich countries transparent by implementing a "dual commitments" approach.

domestic emission reductions from those achieved through international cooperation. In this way, industrialized countries can be transparent about the degree to which their total commitments are "both/and"—that is, domestic and international—as opposed to "either/or." Proposals for such "dual commitments" were put forward in the context of the intended nationally determined contributions (INDCs) expected from each country in preparation for the UNFCCC's twenty-first meeting in Paris in late 2015.[58] A striking symmetry is apparent between this approach and the one advanced by Indonesia's president Yudhoyono at the G20 meeting in Pittsburgh in 2009. At that forum, Yudhoyono committed to reducing emissions by 26 percent with Indonesia's own resources and by 41 percent with international support.[59]

Table 9.2 summarizes the risks associated with allowing forest offsets in compliance markets and approaches to managing them.

Efficiency: Getting What You Pay For

Governments of industrialized countries, which would be on the hook for financing an international mechanism to reduce emissions, have been particularly attentive to ensuring they get what they pay for. To get the most tons of avoided forest emissions at the lowest possible cost, they have sought to maximize the efficiency of payments to developing countries for reducing forest-based emissions. Several approaches to achieving this objective have already been discussed with regard to "effectiveness." Donor countries have seen at least three more ways they might "pay too much" for avoided forest emissions: through the too-generous setting of baselines (that

is, the reference emission levels explained in chapter 4); through "excessive" rents (explained below); and through paying twice for the same emission reductions.

Additionality. One of the most hotly debated topics since forests were brought into climate talks has been how to set a baseline, or "reference level," against which to measure performance in reducing emissions. If reference levels are set too high, countries would be paid for emission reductions that would have happened anyway, thus failing the test of "additionality"—that is, resulting in further reductions on top of those that would have occurred in the absence of forest conservation efforts. But if they are set too low, forest countries might walk away from the inadequate incentives on the table.[60]

Should the benchmark be the emission level during a recent base period, analogous to the commitments of developed countries under the Kyoto Protocol, or a future projection that might better reflect what is likely to happen? Is it fair to "reward" countries with high deforestation rates, such as Brazil and Indonesia, by assuming those high rates will continue? Or to "punish" countries with low deforestation rates, such as the Democratic Republic of Congo and Guyana, by assuming those low rates will persist? How often should reference levels be updated? Should the international community be expected to finance *all* of the emission reductions, or should developing countries contribute some portion uncompensated? And should the compensated portion decline over time?

The UNFCCC text on reference levels falls short of providing definitive answers to these questions, specifying only that reference

Box 9.2: Setting Reference Levels in Countries with High Forest Cover and Low Deforestation: the Example of Guyana

Since the very first discussions of the concept of REDD+, one of the most turbulent debates was around how to set the reference levels that determine how much income forest countries would earn for reducing deforestation. A "storm within a storm" brewed in particular over how to set reference levels for a set of countries—mostly in Central Africa and northern South America—that had high levels of forest cover but had historically kept low rates of deforestation. For this set of countries, reference levels equal to historical rates of deforestation would provide little financial incentive to keep the rates low and, thus, no economic alternative to accelerating deforestation in the future.[a]

In 2006, President Bharrat Jagdeo began discussing the possibility of protecting Guyana's forests in return for "the right economic incentives."[b] Instead of prompting economic growth by clearing forests, President Jagdeo sought to earn income by monetizing the climate services provided by the country's vast forest estate. In 2008, his government engaged a consultant from McKinsey & Company to establish a baseline of what would likely happen to Guyana's forests as a result of business as usual. The resulting "apocalyptic scenario"—in which all forests outside of protected areas would vanish within twenty-five years—was rejected by international reviewers as unrealistic.[c]

The reference level to which Guyana and Norway agreed was simple and practical in a way that improved upon the consultant's projection. It was set halfway between Guyana's historical deforestation rate (low) and the average tropical deforestation rate (high). The interim reference level relied on the data on deforestation available at the time and a uniform conservative estimate of forest carbon stock. Norway agreed to fund up to $250 million in results-based payments, with revenues going toward hydropower, fiber optic upgrades, investments in education and tourism, Amerindian community development, and rural electrification.

After a year, monitoring detected a tripling of Guyana's deforestation rate, mostly due to small and unregulated gold mining operations. While the national deforestation rate remained extremely low by global standards, a three-fold increase in a year was enough to attract international attention. In response, Guyana and Norway modified the terms of the agreement. The overall amount of payments would continue to be determined using the previously agreed-on reference level, but payments would only be made as long as deforestation stayed below another, lower, threshold. The modification worked; deforestation stayed below the cutoff threshold. By the most recent year of monitoring deforestation had begun to decline. By May 2015, five payments had been made, totaling $190 million.[d]

Guyana's pragmatic approach to reference levels was codified in December 2014 in its submission to the UNFCCC. The submission used the same approach as the interim reference level, but with much better data on deforestation, degradation, and carbon stocks.[e]

a. G.A.B. da Fonseca et al., "No Forest Left Behind," *PLoS Biology* 5, no. 8 (2007): e216.
b. B. Jagdeo, "Why the West Should Put Money in the Trees," BBC News, September 8, 2008, http://news.bbc.co.uk/2/hi/science/nature/7603695.stm.
c. P. Gutman and N. Aguilar-Amuchastegui, "Reference Levels and Payments For REDD+: Lessons from the Recent Guyana–Norway Agreement," World Wildlife Fund USA, May 2012, http://assets.panda. org/downloads/rls_and_ payments_for_redd__lessons.pdf.
d. PR Newswire, "Guyana Receives US$40 Million Payment from Norway for Climate Services and Continued Low Deforestation," Georgetown, Guyana, May 8, 2015, http://www.prnewswire.com/news-releases/guyana-receives-us40-million-payment-from-norway-for-climate-services-and-continued-low-deforestation-300080282.html.
e. Government of Guyana, "The Reference Level for Guyana's REDD+ Program."

levels should be based on historical data, adjusted for national circumstances. The FCPF Carbon Fund prescribes the use of recent historical emissions as a reference level for most forest countries, with limited upward projections allowed for those with high forest cover and sustained low deforestation rates.

In the absence of a technocratic solution to determining reference levels, early REDD+ agreements have relied on negotiated baselines. In Brazil's partnership with Norway, for example, the annual deforestation rate was compared to the average for the previous ten years, and the ten-year average was updated every five years.[61] Box 9.2 describes how Guyana has adjusted its reference level over time with respect to its bilateral agreement with Norway.

"Excessive" rents. A second efficiency-related concern—raised more by academics than by negotiators—relates to setting the price for avoided forest emissions. If a common price per ton of carbon were set by a market or negotiated through a fund, those suppliers with cheaper emission reduction options would enjoy significant rents. In other words, if the market price were $5 per ton, a project or jurisdiction that could produce emission reductions at a cost of only $2 per ton would reap a profit of $3 per ton. No one questions the profits gained by participants in other markets, but if rich countries wanted their payments to be as close to the marginal costs as possible, they could pursue an approach based on "reverse auctions," in which prospective buyers would specify the quantity of emission reductions they wanted to purchase, and prospective sellers would bid to provide them. When the price is negotiated in the context of public finance, it is, by

definition, based on the buyer's willingness to pay, reflecting the value placed on the carbon storage service provided.

"Paying twice." A third efficiency-related concern, also not the subject of UNFCCC negotiations, has emerged more recently, as developing countries have begun to progress through the phases of REDD+ from readiness to implementation to performance-based payments. Some donor countries have suggested that if they have provided finance for technical assistance and investment to help forest countries reduce deforestation in the first two phases of REDD+ (see chapter 12), they should not have to pay again for results. In other words, investing in inputs and rewarding performance would be "paying twice" for the same outcome. Such a perspective ignores the significant if intangible managerial and political inputs required of forest country governments to achieve success.[62]

Ironically, in light of multiple rich-country concerns about "paying too much," experience to date has, in fact, been the opposite. Brazil, the country that has by far contributed the world's largest emission reductions—from reduced deforestation or, indeed, any other mitigation effort—has been compensated for only about 10 percent of the value of those emission reductions.[63]

Table 9.3 summarizes efficiency-related risks and approaches.

Equity: Ensuring Fairness within and between Countries

A third set of risks faced by negotiators and practitioners alike has to do with ensuring fairness in the design and implementation of a mechanism for rewarding success in reducing forest-based emissions. Concerns about equity across developing countries have focused on what activities would be eligible for reward, the answer to which would, in turn, determine which countries would stand to benefit. Concerns about equity within countries have focused on avoiding harm to forest-dependent communities and ensuring local forest stewards share in any reward. These concerns are described further below.

Scope and eligibility. When Brazilian civil society groups first introduced the concept of "compensated reduced deforestation," it was simple. As the name implied, the concept focused only on change in forest cover, which is relatively straightforward to mea-sure.[64] The initial proposal put forth in 2005 by CfRN—Reduced Emissions from Deforestation (RED)—was similarly simple. But from a political perspective, some countries could perceive the prospect of limiting compensation to reduced rates of deforestation as unfair or even unjust. Countries such as Brazil and Indonesia with large but rapidly shrinking forests had the most to gain from such a model. But what about countries, such as China and India, that had already largely depleted their natural forests? What about countries such as Guyana and countries in the Congo Basin, with large areas of forest but low deforestation rates? What about

Table 9.3: Concerns about Efficiency—Getting What You Pay For

Issue	Risk	How managed
Additionality	If deforestation would have declined anyway, payments might be made without resulting in additional emission reductions.	• Use recent historical data on deforestation rates as a starting point for establishing reference emission levels.
Excessive rents	If payments for forest emission reductions were based on a uniform price rather than the marginal costs, owners of cheap reduction opportunities could capture large rents.	• Recognize that countries that can produce emission reductions cheaply are as entitled to producer surplus as the producers of any other good. • Implement reverse auctions. • Negotiate prices.
Paying twice	If donors financed inputs that helped forest countries reduce deforestation, subsequent payment for results could be seen as "paying twice."	• Recognize that results also require managerial and political investments from forest country governments.

many countries in Sub-Saharan Africa, where forest degradation was a more important dynamic than loss of forest cover?

China and India argued that the benefits of a global mechanism should not be limited to "polluters" but should, rather, also apply to countries engaged in forest restoration and tree planting. CfRN argued that including forest degradation was also important for effectiveness, given it was an important source of emissions and often a first step toward forest clearing.[65] To consolidate a broad base of support, the concept of RED, as described above, was expanded in 2007 to REDD (to include forest degradation) and in 2009 to REDD+ to include "conservation, sustainable management of forests, and enhancement of forest carbon stocks" among the activities for achieving compensable emission reductions. This expansion certainly increased the equity of the mechanism, and perhaps its effectiveness, but possibly at the expense of efficiency; observers have noted that, with its broader scope, REDD+ is now more difficult to implement and monitor.[66]

In addition, equity across countries has been promoted by allowing limited adjustments to reference emission levels for countries with historically low deforestation rates, as was done in the Guyana–Norway agreement. Such an approach widens eligibility for performance-based payments.

Rights and benefit sharing. Although the issue of equity among countries was addressed early on, the conversation about ensuring that the REDD+ mechanism would support equity within countries was less easily resolved. This objective proved a thornier issue for negotiators in light of jealously

guarded national sovereignty on the part of developing country governments on the one hand, and deeply held concerns about threats to human rights on the part of potentially affected communities—especially indigenous peoples—and their advocates on the other.

At the climate talks in Cancun in 2010, negotiators enumerated seven safeguards that must be "promoted and supported" in the implementation of REDD+ activities.[67] The following year in Durban, negotiators agreed countries would implement safeguard information systems that would serve as the basis for periodic reporting to the UNFCCC regarding how safeguards were being addressed and respected. Then, in Warsaw, negotiators made explicit the link between reporting on safeguards and access to results-based finance.

By design, the general guidance provided by text negotiated under the UNFCCC provides significant flexibility in how the safeguard principles are interpreted by each country. As described earlier, a key reason the previous attempts failed to conclude international agreements related to forests was the wariness of developing countries that such agreements would inappropriately intrude into domestic policy making. In REDD+ negotiations overall, many resisted the imposition of one-size-fits-all standards with international oversight in favor of deference to national systems and flexibility to adjust to national circumstances.

Some observers have worried that flexibility, coupled with weak international oversight and standards, blurs accountability for safeguard implementation.[68] To meet concerns of donors and civil society, international REDD+ financing mechanisms have elaborated more detailed normative guidance and/or imposed prescriptive rules regarding safeguard policies and procedures to supplement principles agreed on under the UNFCCC. In early 2013, for example, the UN-REDD Programme published guidelines on how to seek and secure free, prior, and informed consent (FPIC) to ensure that the participation of indigenous and other local communities in REDD+ was truly voluntary.[69] Later that year, the Participants Committee of the FCPF Carbon Fund agreed on a methodological framework of thirty-seven criteria and indicators, with three of the criteria relating to social and environmental safeguards.[70]

Table 9.4 summarizes these risks and the approaches to managing them.

Finance: Markets or Public Funds?

The technical design considerations associated with ensuring the REDD+ mechanism would be effective, efficient, and equitable preoccupied negotiators, analysts, and advocates over the eight years between the debut of the RED concept in Montreal in 2005 to the conclusion of the Warsaw Framework in 2013. At the Bali meeting in 2007, responsibility for developing methodological approaches to deal with issues such as monitoring, baselines, and safeguards were referred to the climate convention's scientific and technological advisory body (SBSTA). The resulting UNFCCC decisions on REDD+ provided an overall framework for what would constitute an internationally accepted emission reduction but

Table 9.4: Concerns about Equity—Fairness within and between Countries

Issue	Risk	How managed
Scope and eligibility	If payments for forest emission reductions were limited to slowing deforestation, only countries with large areas of forest and high deforestation rates would be rewarded.	• Include avoided degradation (the second "D" in REDD+) and conservation and enhancement of existing forest carbon stocks (the "+"). • Allow limited adjustments in reference emission levels for low-deforestation countries.
Rights and benefit sharing	If payments for forest emission reductions were available to forest owners, governments and corporations would have incentives to deny the ownership rights of indigenous and other local communities to capture the benefits.	• Adopt safeguard principles, such as those related to indigenous peoples' rights. • Implement safeguard standards, such as free, prior, and informed consent (FPIC). • Mandate common standards for transparent reporting on national safeguard systems.

begged the question of how such reductions should be paid for. Because the question of how REDD+ would be financed was especially sensitive, a "Working Group on Long-Term Cooperative Action" was established in Bali as the forum for a track of negotiations on funding, separate from but parallel to those on technical and methodological issues.

Whether REDD+ would be paid for through market offsets or public funds was the subject of a long and heated debate. As described above, opponents of market-based finance, such as Bolivia and Brazil, voiced concerns that cuts in emissions from deforestation in poor countries would simply substitute for cuts in emissions from fossil fuels in rich countries, thereby taking the pressure off rich countries to do their part in reducing overall emissions. Advocates of market finance argued that the cost containment provided by REDD+ offsets would allow developed countries to pledge and meet more ambitious targets at lower cost, and that a sufficient volume of finance for REDD+ could never be appropriated from public funds. Market supporters, including Costa Rica and Papua New Guinea, further argued that the scale of international financial flows necessary to address deforestation at a global level would only be feasible if rich countries could receive credit for the fungible asset of emission reductions.

In the end, a debate on "markets or funds" became an agreement on "markets and funds." Even the most pro-market voices recognized the need for fund-based support for the initial readiness and reform phases of REDD+. In Durban in 2011, negotiators agreed results-based finance could come from multiple sources, including both market-based and non-market-based approaches. In Doha in 2012, the most vocal antimarket party standing in the way of consensus—Bolivia—was placated with an agreement to continue discussions on a proposed parallel international mechanism in addition to REDD+ for managing forests for mitigation and adaptation in an integrated manner.

The package of decisions related to REDD+ reached in Warsaw in 2013 provided complete guidance on results-based finance, as well as other technical and methodological concerns. It established an "information hub" at the convention secretariat to keep track of verified emission reductions and results-based payments and emphasized the role of the Green Climate Fund as the vehicle for long-term finance.

The incorporation of the Warsaw Framework on REDD+ into the 2015 Paris Agreement, and the inclusion of reducing emissions from land-use change in dozens of national pledges announced in the run-up to the conference, consolidated the position of forests as a key component of the world's climate protection strategy. Beyond Article 5, which focused on forests, the aspiration included in the agreement to balance greenhouse gas emissions and removals further elevated the need to protect tropical forests. And the agreement's blessing in Article 6 of the voluntary "international transfer of mitigation outcomes" provided further legitimacy for rich countries to purchase emission reductions from developing countries.[71]

But in the absence of compliance markets that include forest carbon credits, and the continuing financing of REDD+ out of constrained development assistance budgets, resolution of the debate about "markets or funds" seems a hollow victory for tropical forests. As explained in chapter 12, the continuing uncertainty of finance is one reason for slow progress in slowing deforestation.

Conclusion

Remarkable changes in the international politics of tropical forests have taken place, not only over the 160 years since Hugh Cleghorn's report but, especially, over the past 30 years, since the international community rediscovered their importance. A United Nations-led Tropical Forestry Action Plan launched in 1985 had ended in recriminations. In the run-up to the 1992 Earth Summit in Rio de Janeiro, a proposed international convention on forests favored by industrialized countries was rejected by developing nations. Subsequent international negotiations on forests failed to yield more than agreement on nonbinding principles. The issue of tropical deforestation gradually slipped off the global agenda.

Yet, by the end of 2013, the international community had agreed on a framework through which rich countries would reward tropical countries financially for conserving their forests. What had changed?

The most important change was the recognition of tropical deforestation as a globally significant source of greenhouse gas emissions and the identification of reducing deforestation as a cost-effective strategy for reducing them. But also essential was the framing of a solution in terms of voluntary cooperation and performance-based reward, rather than binding compliance mechanisms.

Instead of being perceived as an uncompensated obligation in violation of national sovereignty, REDD+ was accepted as a willing partnership among equals to achieve a common goal.

Other changes contributed to the progress made, including the technology-enabled revolution in forest monitoring described in chapter 4 that built confidence among industrialized countries. In key forest-rich countries, especially Brazil, the growth of domestic social and environmental movements helped fuel leadership in solving global problems.

In REDD+, the two problems of stopping deforestation and reducing the emissions that cause climate change found a common solution. While negotiators have achieved remarkable consensus on the broad principles for implementing that solution, much work remains to translate them into concrete actions developing countries can take, backed up by finance of sufficient scale and certainty from industrialized ones.

With political consensus on REDD+ achieved, and the rulebook for managing risks agreed on in Warsaw in 2013 and included in the 2015 Paris Agreement, industrialized countries no longer have an excuse to delay mobilizing the finance needed to move forward. In chapter 11, we illuminate the politics of REDD+ finance in donor countries and, in chapter 12, we show how ill-suited instruments have thwarted the expression of broad-based support for such finance. First, though, we turn our attention in the next chapter to the politics of participation in REDD+ from the perspective of forest-rich developing countries.

Notes

1. The first seven paragraphs of this chapter are based on P. Das, "Hugh Cleghorn and Forest Conservancy in India," *Environment and History* 11, no. 1 (2005): 55–82.

2. H. F. Cleghorn et al. "Report of the Committee Appointed by the British Association to Consider the Probable Effects in an Economical and Physical Point of View of the Destruction of Tropical Forests," *Transactions of the British Academy for the Advancement of Science* (1852): 78–102.

3. J. R. Fleming, *Historical Perspectives on Climate Change* (Oxford: Oxford University Press, 1998); S. Graham, "Svante Arrhenius (1859–1927)," National Aeronautics and Space Administration, Earth Observatory, January 18, 2000, http://earthobservatory.nasa.gov/Features/Arrhenius/arrhenius.php.

4. R. Monroe, "The History of the Keeling Curve," Scripps Institution of Oceanography at UC San Diego, April 3, 2013, https://scripps.ucsd.edu/programs/keeling-curve/2013/04/03/the-history-of-the-keeling-curve/#more-276; C. D. Keeling, "The Concentration and Isotopic Abundances of Atmospheric Carbon Dioxide in Rural Areas," *Geochimica et Cosmochimica Acta* 13, no. 4 (1958): 322–34.

5. Food and Agriculture Organization of the United Nations (FAO), "FAO's Tropical Forestry—Action Plan," *Unasylva* 38, no. 152 (1986): 37–54.

6. Climate Focus, "Forests and Land Use in the Paris Agreement," Climate Focus Briefing Note, Washington, DC, December 22, 2015.

7. Food and Agriculture Organization of the United Nations (FAO), "FAO's Tropical Forestry—Action Plan."

8. Ibid. See also F. W. Burley, "The Tropical Forestry Action Plan Recent Progress and New Initiatives," in *Biodiversity*, ed. E.O. Wilson and F. M. Peter (Washington, DC: National Academies Press, 1988).

9. Food and Agriculture Organization of the United Nations (FAO), "FAO's Tropical Forestry—Action Plan."

10. D. Humphreys, *Forest Politics: The Evolution of International Cooperation* (London: Earthscan, 1996).

11. Ibid.

12. See G7, "Houston Economic Declaration," G7 Economic Summit, Houston, Texas, July 11, 1990, paragraphs 66–68, as cited in A. G. M. La Viña and A. de Leon, "Two Global Challenges, One Solution: International Cooperation to Combat Climate Change and Tropical Deforestation," CGD Working Paper 388, Center for Global Development, Washington, DC, 2014.

13. United Nations Conference on Environment and Development, "Report of the United Nations Conference on Environment and Development," Rio de Janeiro, Brazil, June 14, 1992.

14. D. S. Davenport, "An Alternative Explanation for the Failure of the UNCED Forest Negotiations," *Global Environmental Politics* 5 (2005): 105–30.

15. P. S. Chasek, D. L. Downie, and J. W. Brown, *Global Environmental Politics* (Boulder: Westview Press, 2013), 224.

16. G. Porter and J. W. Brown, *Global Environmental Politics* (Boulder: Westview Press, 1991), 103.

17. D. Humphreys, "Discourse as Ideology: Neoliberalism and the Limits of International Forest Policy," *Forest Policy and Economics* 11 (2009): 319–25.

18. R. Butler, "REDD," Mongabay.com, 2009, http://rainforests.mongabay.com/redd/.

19. P. M. Fearnside, "Saving Tropical Forests as a Global Warming Countermeasure: An Issue that Divides the Environmental Movement," *Ecological Economics* 39 (2001): 167–84.

20. Butler, "REDD."

21. Ibid.

22. Ibid.

23. M. Amano and R. A. Sedjo, "Forest Sequestration: Performance in Selected Countries in the Kyoto Period and the Potential Role of Sequestration in Post-Kyoto Agreements," Resources for the Future, Washington, DC, May 2006.

24. J. Eliasch, *Climate Change: Financing Global Forests: The Eliasch Review* (London: UK Office of Climate Change, 2008).

25. European Commission, "Questions and Answers on the Revised EU Emissions Trading System," EU Emissions Trading System, December 2008, http://ec.europa.eu/clima/policies/ets/faq_en.htm. See also R. O'Sullivan et al., "Should REDD+ Be Included in the CDM? Analysis of Issues and Options Prepared for the CDM Policy Dialogue," Climate Focus and Climate Advisers, Washington, DC, 2012, http://www.cdmpolicydialogue.org/research/1030_Redd.pdf.

26. S. Abranches, "The Political Economy of Deforestation in Brazil and Payment-for-Performance Finance," CGD Background Paper, Center for Global Development, Washington, DC, 2014.

27. Ibid.

28. Ibid.

29. Ibid.

30. M. Santilli et al., "Tropical Deforestation and the Kyoto Protocol," *Climatic Change* 71, no. 3 (2005): 267–76; P. Moutinho and M. Santilli, "Reduction of GHG Emissions from Deforestation in Developing Countries," in *International Submission to the Eighth Convention of Parties to the United Nations Framework Convention on Climate Change*, Instituto de Pesquisa Ambiental da Amazonia, Belém, Brazil, 2005.

31. T. Pistorius, "From RED to REDD+: The Evolution of a Forest-Based Mitigation Approach for Developing Countries," *Current Opinion in Environmental Sustainability* 4, no. 6 (2012): 638–45.

32. Abranches, "The Political Economy."

33. Ibid.

34. Coalition for Rainforest Nations, "Context: Kyoto Protocol & Forests," http://www.rainforestcoalition.org/KyotoProtocol.aspx.

35. Coalition for Rainforest Nations, "Submission by the Governments of Papua New Guinea and Costa Rica," 2015, http://rain-forestcoalition.org/documents/COP-11Agen-daItem6-Misc.Doc.FINAL.pdf.

36. Ibid.

37. Pistorius, "From RED to REDD+."

38. Abranches, "The Political Economy."

39. A. C. Revkin, "Issuing a Bold Challenge to the U.S. over Climate," *New York Times*, January 22, 2008.

40. United Nations Framework Convention on Climate Change (UNFCCC), "Addendum to Report of the Conference of the Parties on its Thirteenth Session, Held in Bali from 3 to 15 December 2007," Bali, Indonesia, March 14, 2007, http://unfccc.int/resource/docs/2007/cop13/eng/06a01.pdf.

41. N. Stern, *The Economics of Climate Change: The Stern Review* (Cambridge: Cambridge University Press, 2007).

42. Pistorius, "From RED to REDD+."

43. C. Betzold, P. Castro, and F. Weiler, "AOSIS in the UNFCCC Negotiations: From Unity to Fragmentation?" *Climate Policy* 12, no. 5 (2012): 591–613.

44. Abranches, "The Political Economy."

45. M. Norman and S. Nakhooda, "The State of REDD+ Finance," CGD Working Paper 378, Center for Global Development, Washington, DC, 2014 (updated 2015).

46. M. Wolosin and D. Lee, "US Support for REDD+," CGD Policy Paper 48, Center for Global Development, Washington, DC, 2014.

47. La Viña and de Leon, "Two Global Challenges."

48. Ibid.

49. Ibid.

50. The REDD Desk, "REDD in Bolivia," updated 2013, http://theredddesk.org/countries/bolivia.

51. The "3 E" framework for analyzing REDD+ was first introduced in A. Angelsen, ed., *Moving Ahead with REDD: Issues, Options and Implications* (Bogor, Indonesia: CIFOR, 2008).

52. See, for example, A. Grainger, "Difficulties in Tracking the Long-Term Global Trend in Tropical Forest Area," *Proceedings of the National Academy of Sciences* 105, no. 2 (2008): 818–23.

53. Forest Carbon Partnership Facility, "ER Program Buffer Guidelines," December 11, 2015, https://www.forestcarbonpartnership.org/sites/fcp/files/2015/December/FCPF%20ER%20Program%20Buffer%20Guidelines.pdf; Government of Guyana, "The Reference Level for Guyana's REDD+ Program," December 2014, https://unfccc.int/files/land_use_and_climate_change/redd/application/pdf/guyana_proposal_for_reference_level_for_redd+.pdf.

54. Forest Carbon Partnership Facility, "ER Program Buffer Guidelines."

55. J. Busch, "The Baker's Dozen: A 748-Year-Old Solution for Climate Offsets," Views from the Center blog, Center for Global Development, November 19, 2014, http://www.cgdev.org/blog/bakers-dozen-748-year-old-solution-climate-offsets.

56. U.S. Congress, "H.R. 2454: American Clean Energy and Security Act of 2009," 2009, https://www.congress.gov/bill/111th-congress/house-bill/2454.

57. N. Birdsall and A. Subramanian, "Energy Needs and Efficiency, Not Emissions: Reframing the Climate Change Narrative," CGD Working Paper 187, Center for Global Development, Washington, DC, 2009.

58. A. Dahl-Jorgensen, "The Billion Ton Solution: Europe's Chance to Lead on Climate Action through International Mitigation Partnerships," Climate Advisers Analysis, February 2015.

59. "Indonesian President Signs Decree to Reduce Projected Emissions 26–41% by 2020," Mongabay.com, September 26, 2011, https://news.mongabay.com/2011/09/indonesian-president-signs-decree-to-reduce-projected-emissions-26-41-by-2020/.

60. For a useful treatment of many issues related to reference levels, see Angelsen, "How Do We Set the Reference Levels for REDD Payments?," in *Moving Ahead with REDD*, chapter 6.

61. Amazon Fund, "Amazon Fund: Project Document," Brasília, Brazil, 2008, http://www.amazonfund.gov.br/FundoAmazonia/export/sites/default/site_en/Galerias/Arquivos/Boletins/Amazon_Fund_-_Project_Document_Vs_18-11-2008.pdf, 9.

62. W. D. Savedoff, "Funders Worry about 'Double Counting'—But What about 'Double Demanding'?" Views from the Center blog, Center for Global Development, March 5, 2015, http://www.cgdev.org/blog/funders-worry-about-double-counting-%E2%80%93-what-about-double-demanding.

63. A. Angelsen, "REDD+ as Performance-Based Aid," UNU-WIDER Working Paper 135, United Nations University UN-UWIDER, 2013, https://www.wider.unu.edu/publication/redd-performance-based-aid; *World Development* 64 (2014): S12–S28.

64. M. Santilli et al., "Tropical Deforestation and the Kyoto Protocol."

65. Pistorius, "From RED to REDD+."

66. A. Wiersema, "Climate Change, Forests, and International Law: REDD's Descent into Irrelevance," *Vanderbilt Journal of International Law* 47, no. 1 (2014): 1–62.

67. United Nations Framework Convention on Climate Change (UNFCCC), "Addendum to the Report of the Conference of the Parties on its Sixteenth Session, held in Cancun from 29 November to 10 December 2010," Cancun, Mexico, March 15, 2011, paragraphs 69 and 2, appendix I, as cited in La Viña and de Leon, "Two Global Challenges."

68. Wiersema, "Climate Change, Forests, and International Law."

69. UN-REDD Programme, "Guidelines on Free, Prior and Informed Consent," January 2013, http://www.unredd.net/index.php?option=com_docman&task=doc_download&gid=8717&Itemid=53.

70. Forest Carbon Partnership Facility, "Carbon Fund Methodological Framework," December 20, 2013, https://www.forestcarbonpartnership.org/sites/fcp/files/2014/MArch/March/FCPF%20Carbon%20Fund%20Methodological%20

Framework%20Final%20Dec%2020%20
2013.pdf.

71. United Nations Framework Convention on
Climate Change (UNFCCC), "Paris
Agreement," Paris, France, 2015, http://
unfccc.int/files/essential_background/
convention/application/pdf/english_paris_
agreement.pdf. See also Climate Focus,
"Forests and Land-Use in the Paris
Agreement," Climate Focus Briefing Note,
2015.

A river carries away timber extracted from
Indonesia's tropical forests.
Credit: A.S. Zain/Shutterstock

CHAPTER 10

Forest Politics in Developing Countries

Tipping the Balance Away from Deforestation as Usual

Brasília, Brazil, 2009. On Wednesday, November 12, a tense meeting took place in the office of the president of Brazil.[1] In a few hours, President Luiz Inácio Lula da Silva would board a plane bound for Paris to work with French president Nicolas Sarkozy on a joint statement for release at the Copenhagen climate negotiations, just a few weeks away. He had gathered top officials in a final attempt to achieve consensus on whether or not Brazil should announce quantitative targets for reducing emissions.

President Lula was impatient. He had already made important decisions to reduce deforestation. He had appointed Marina Silva, a strong environment minister, and he had granted her autonomy in assembling a team independent of coalition politics and supported her disclosure of satellite data on forest loss. After Brazilian academics and advocates from nongovernmental organizations (NGOs) promoted the idea of international compensation for voluntary reductions in emissions from deforestation (which came to be known as Reducing Emissions from Deforestation and forest Degradation, or REDD+), Brazilian negotiators had cautiously accepted it. Then, in 2008, Brazil had signed the first such agreement with Norway. As the president attended meetings with other world leaders, he felt the momentum building toward the climate summit in Copenhagen and needed something more to bring to the table; but his top advisers were divided into two opposing camps.

On one side were those implacably opposed to Brazil's agreeing to any targets for reducing emissions. The Ministry of Foreign Affairs—known as Itamaraty after its headquarters building in Brasília—argued that setting targets meant capitulating to the interests of rich countries that had caused the problem of climate change in the first place. Also opposed to targets was Dilma Rousseff, head of the powerful Gabinete Civil (the office of the president's chief of staff), who was lined up as a presidential candidate to succeed Lula. She strongly believed emission reduction targets would constrain economic growth.

On the other side were those making the case that Brazil was uniquely positioned to undertake emission reduction targets with no regrets. Carlos Minc, who in May 2008 had succeeded Marina Silva as environment minister, argued that, unlike India or China, Brazil's emissions profile was dominated by deforestation, which the country was already bringing under control. Why not capitalize on the opportunity to commit to emission reductions without impairing economic growth? Perhaps surprisingly, the minister of agriculture, Reinhold Stephanes, also supported this view. His team included scientists from the well-regarded Empresa Brasileira de Pesquisa Agropecuária (EMBRAPA, or Brazilian Agricultural Research Corporation), who had persuaded him of the potential for Brazilian agribusiness to sustain gains in productivity and competitiveness from low-carbon agriculture while helping reduce deforestation.

Over the course of four "hot, deadlocked discussions" about emission reduction targets convened by the president in 2009, the team from the Ministry of Science and Tech-

---

This chapter draws heavily on two background papers on the domestic politics of results-based forest finance in forest-rich countries, one by Sérgio Abranches on Brazil, and one by Metta Dharmasaputra and Ade Wahyudi on Indonesia.

nology had been split.[2] Ministerial advisers who had participated in international climate negotiations lined up with Itamaraty against targets. In contrast, scientists from the Instituto Nacional de Pesquisas Espaciais (INPE), the Brazilian space research agency, aligned with the Ministry of Environment in favor.

At the final meeting in November, science and technology minister Sérgio Rezende resolved his agency's split by simply excluding his advisers who opposed targets. The swing of the ministry's position squarely into the camp of those in favor of targets helped to tip the balance. When President Lula called for consensus, the decision was for Brazil to announce quantitative emission reduction targets in Copenhagen. According to journalist Sérgio Abranches, the decision completed an ideological paradigm shift that enabled acceptance of international results-based payments for reduction of emissions from deforestation.

While this decision was driven by domestic actors, it came within the context of international climate negotiations and an agreement with the government of Norway, worth up to $1 billion, for reducing emissions from deforestation. What role did this international agreement play? According to a senior policy maker interviewed in 2014, the promise of international financial support was not decisive in prompting the policy change, "but it was an argument that, within the political context of those tense and frantic days, had its weight."[3]

The purpose of this chapter is to describe how the prospect of financial and political support from rich countries can affect the political economy of forests and climate change in developing countries in ways favorable to reducing deforestation. When he inked the

bilateral agreement with Norway in 2008, President Lula became the first leader of a forest-rich developing country to enter into a transaction in which success in reducing emissions from deforestation would be rewarded with cash.[4] Many others were eager to follow.

In 2009, President Bharrat Jagdeo of Guyana secured a $250 million pledge from Norway in return for maintaining his country's low rate of deforestation. President Susilo Bambang Yudhoyono of Indonesia traveled to Oslo in May 2010 to sign his own billion-dollar deal. In September 2014, Liberia and Peru joined the elite club of countries with national-level agreements to reduce deforestation in return for performance-based payments. At the time, such agreements could still be counted on the fingers of one hand, even though more than fifty countries had signed up to participate in internationally supported REDD+ programs.

The countries participating in REDD+ are astonishingly diverse. Tropical forests themselves come in many forms, ranging from the sweltering peat swamps of Borneo to the high-altitude forests of the Himalaya, from the lush Central African rainforests to the savannah-like Miombo woodlands of southern and East Africa. Today's tropical forests also come in many sizes, ranging from the meager remnants that survived the logging bonanza in the Philippines in the late 1960s and early 1970s to the vast remaining intact forests of the Brazilian Amazon. As described in chapter 9, variations in initial forest endowment and current condition influenced how countries perceived REDD+ when the idea was introduced into international climate negotiations.

This biophysical diversity is compounded by large variation in levels of economic development, population density, and many other economic, social, and cultural characteristics of developing countries. As a result, the political challenges of stopping deforestation—and of enlisting international support for the struggle—also vary significantly across developing countries, and even across different regions within the same country.

Despite this diversity, some commonalities mark the politics of deforestation in the tropics. For example, forests have frequently been treated as sources of wealth to be allocated to political parties or military officials in return for political support. Often, they have been used as land banks to absorb poor populations seeking economic opportunity, with governments passively allowing or actively facilitating migration into forest frontiers. Both commercial exploitation and migration have tended to proceed without regard to the rights of communities with prior claims to forest areas, setting off conflicts with indigenous peoples and other traditional forest users.

> The prospect of performance-based payments can alter the balance between forces that drive and curtail deforestation in material ways.

Another commonality is the tendency of international cooperation related to forest management to be politically sensitive. National governments have restricted foreign access to militarized areas and have attempted to suppress information that would expose rampant rights abuses and illegal exploitation of natural resources. And in countries where the forestry sector generates timber revenues, licensing fees, and opportunities for corruption, forestry agencies and local government officials are not welcoming of donor funding when international engagement challenges business as usual.

Yet in many countries, renewed international attention to forests in the context of climate change is empowering constituencies for reform. Indigenous peoples, advocates of good governance,[5] beneficiaries of forest-based ecosystem services, political leaders seeking legitimacy on the global stage, and private companies seeking access to international markets have all recognized REDD+ as an instrument with the potential to advance their objectives.

In this chapter, we describe the political economy of deforestation and how the availability of payment-for-performance finance has made a difference in a few countries. The analysis complements the evidence presented in chapter 7 (regarding the factors that drive and slow deforestation) by illuminating the underlying political conditions that influence policy choices.

We begin by exploring the forces that have created domestic constituencies for business-as-usual deforestation and the domestic and international forces that are strengthening constituencies for reform. We draw especially on the experiences of Brazil and Indonesia.[6] While not representative of the full range of countries interested in REDD+, together they illustrate many of the political challenges faced by countries attempting to reduce deforestation.

We then focus on the impact of having in hand firm commitments from rich countries to pay for performance in reducing deforestation. We present evidence from the limited number of cases to date, which suggest the prospect of performance-based payments can alter the balance between forces that drive and curtail deforestation in material ways, and we show how uncertainty over financial reward can slow momentum for change.[7]

Conditions Favoring Deforestation as Usual

In many forest-rich developing countries, forests have played an outsized role in the pursuit of national security and economic prosperity. They have also been exploited by a variety of people seeking wealth through legal and illegal means. The extraction of forest resources under conditions of weak governance has resulted in high rates of deforestation and contributed to social conflict.

Forests, Territorial Control, and National Sovereignty

The political economy of forests in a number of countries has been inextricably linked to the pursuit of control, often by the military, over national territory. Framed as a national security imperative, the establishment of state control over forest areas has served as an underlying driver of deforestation. Such framing has also rendered international cooperation politically sensitive, so it is relevant to perceptions of REDD+.

Almost by definition, large areas of intact forest tend to be remote from the concentration of political power in capital cities. Their dense tree cover and poorly mapped terrain have provided havens for many separatist groups and others rebelling against national governments. According to a study of how geographical factors affect civil wars, mountains and forests allow rebel troops to move freely and avoid detection.[8] Forests were the preferred hideouts of the Mau Mau rebellion against the British colonial government in Kenya in the 1950s, the Viet Cong forces fighting the South Vietnamese and United States forces in the 1960s, and the Shining Path insurgency that terrorized Peru in the 1980s. More recently, forests have served as staging areas for combatants in civil wars in Colombia, the Democratic Republic of Congo (DRC), and Nepal.

While armed conflict can temporarily depress pressure on forests—the presence of rebel forces can disrupt economic activity by rendering forest areas too dangerous for non-combatants to enter—it often sows the seeds for deforestation in the long run. In Sierra Leone, for example, areas surrounding rebel bases experienced lower deforestation rates, likely due to the terror experienced by local communities.[9] In Colombia's civil war, the forcible displacement of local communities through violent intimidation opened up areas for commercial or illegal forest exploitation by others and created further conflict when the communities returned. As a result, Colombia's highest rates of deforestation tend to be in areas of past and current conflict.[10]

From the 1950s through the 1970s, forests in Indonesia and, indeed, throughout Southeast Asia were the settings for violent conflict between insurgencies and government counterinsurgency operations that sought to extend state control over forest territories and their populations.[11] For fourteen years after the Dutch government recognized its independence in 1949, Indonesia fought to eradicate the Darul Islam ("Islamic State") insurgency in Aceh, South Sulawesi, and West Java. In the early 1960s, Indonesia's president Sukarno adopted a policy of *konfrontasi*, launching military attacks against Dutch claims to the western half of the island of New Guinea in the east and against the prospective formation of the new state of Malaysia to the north, across the border on the island of Borneo. Under President Suharto (whose New Order regime came to power in 1966), Indonesia battled forest-based separatist movements in Aceh in the far west of the country and in the easternmost province of Papua.

Following the cessation of active hostilities, the Indonesian government viewed state control of remote forested areas as critical to maintaining the territorial integrity of the nation. Forest areas were heavily militarized, and military officials controlled and enjoyed profits from forest exploitation. Indonesia's so-called transmigration program—which relocated ethnic majority households from densely populated Java and Bali to the Outer Islands—was in part an attempt to establish and consolidate state presence and control in remote areas where the loyalty of local populations—often ethnic minorities—was in doubt.[12] And when President B. J. Habibie presided over a radical decentralization of government authority in 1999, decision making was devolved to the regency (*kabupaten*) level—that is, to administrative jurisdictions below the level of province—to reduce the risk of fueling separatist ambitions at the provincial level.[13] The resulting logging activity, forest clearing by migrants, and granting of permits by local authorities have all contributed to Indonesia's high rates of deforestation.

Brazil also saw thinly populated forests on the fringes of national territory as vulnerable peripheries in need of state control. Events dating back to the mid-nineteenth century kindled fears among Brazilians over international interest in the riches of the Amazon's forests. In 1850, for example, the United States Navy had sponsored a scientific expedition to explore the Amazon, and its report to the U.S. Congress caused "an immense sensation throughout the United States."[14] The expedition was proposed by Lieutenant Matthew Maury, who was also a proponent of opening up the Amazon to international navigation and colonization.[15]

More than a century later, the military regime that took power in 1964 advanced a suite of policies to strengthen national sovereignty over the Amazon and to develop its resources during its two decades of rule. It formulated its positions in international forums related to forests amid suspicions that foreigners had designs on the region's economic and biological wealth.[16] In the 1980s, as Brazil made the transition back to democracy, international attention to deforestation in the Amazon was met with skepticism regarding motives. One Brazilian official reflected that common perspective, saying, "This time, the pursuit of economic interests is cloaked in the rhetoric of an environmental crusade."[17]

As a result of these histories, international efforts that see themselves as offering help to reduce deforestation are frequently met with suspicion. Indonesia, for example, has rejected donor-funded forestry initiatives proposed for sensitive provinces.[18] It has also constrained access to spatial data—until recently controlled by the military—needed for developing forest-monitoring systems, although nondisclosure may also serve to shield from international scrutiny corrupt and illegal activities, described further below. In international forest negotiations, Brazil has strenuously argued for protecting national sovereignty. In both countries, national governments have been cool toward provincial-level initiatives to engage international forums on the climate and forest issue.

Development of Forest Areas as a Path to Economic Prosperity

In addition to considerations of territorial control, governments have sought to extend the reach of the state into remote areas in the name of economic prosperity. Building roads to provide access to markets, constructing dams to produce electricity, granting licenses to extract natural resources or establish plantations, and subsidizing credit to smallholders to replace forests with farms and pastures have all been promoted as ways to generate income and employment. But without strong forest protection policies and enforcement, these economic programs are also associated with deforestation and with the loss of all the forest-based goods and services described in chapter 6. Thus, a key challenge of international cooperation to protect forests is to support policies that reduce deforestation without compromising economic development.

The sustainability of Brazil's commitment to reducing emissions from deforestation has rested on the compatibility with economic growth of doing so, as revealed in the debates among President Lula's ministers described above. But achieving the success described in chapter 7 has required political and ideological shifts. During the period of military dictatorship in Brazil, the government invested in road and railroad construction and the expansion of the cattle industry and encouraged migration into the Amazon region. According to Sérgio Abranches, during this period,

> The Amazon seemed to be an El Dorado to be conquered by the people from the southern and southeastern parts of the country, and its occupation would provide food and employment to benefit the impoverished people of northeastern Brazil. This period was characterized by the absence of any concern whatsoever with deforestation and its consequences for biodiversity or the climate. There was, on the contrary, an explicit support for the clearing and occupation of forestland . . . [The] apex was the military government, which set out to finally conquer the "green inferno," and convert the jungle into fertile cropland and vast pastures to feed Brazil and the world. This conquest of the El Dorado mystique fit perfectly the nationalistic and homeland security ideology at the core of the military's geopolitical view.[19]

The narrative that deforestation is necessary for development has been appropriated by contemporary political actors, such as the Ruralista bloc in Brazil's Congress that represents the interests of large farmers. When a law regularizing the illegal occupation of public land in the Amazon was enacted in 2009, legislators spun it as an advance for smallholders, even though most of the land affected was transferred to "large land grabbers."[20] In 2012, ruralistas succeeded in passing legislation to weaken protections in the Forest Code, and they have opposed the recognition of indigenous territories.[21]

Similarly, Indonesia's Suharto regime framed policies to develop the forest-rich Outer Islands as parts of narratives of economic prosperity for local communities and for the nation as a whole. In the 1980s, logging companies were given mandates to promote rural development among communities in and around their concessions. Policies governing oil palm development required a certain percentage of plantation area be developed in collaboration with smallholders.[22] The Mega Rice Project of the mid-1990s, described in chapter 11, targeted the conversion of a million hectares of peat swamp forest into rice fields in the interest of national rice self-sufficiency.

As in Brazil, vested interests in Indonesia have advanced the argument that deforestation serves development objectives. When the palm oil industry and its supporters in government objected to the moratorium on new licenses included in the REDD+ agreement with Norway in 2010, and more recently to the "no-deforestation" commitments made by some companies (as described in chapter 8), they did so on the grounds that such policies would hurt smallholders and constrain economic growth.[23]

In short, the historical presumption that deforestation is the necessary price of economic prosperity has shaped both policies and attitudes that remain relevant today. Accordingly, efforts to reduce deforestation require new, evidence-based narratives that explain how they are compatible with economic growth and food security. REDD+ has been envisioned as an alternative source of revenue that will help narrow the apparent trade-off between forest protection and development.

The Appropriation of Forest Wealth

The previous section outlined how development of forest areas has been treated as an engine for economic growth. But another factor that influences the political economy of deforestation is who actually benefits from the money to be made from exploiting forest wealth. Most often, people think of that wealth in the form of tropical timber and valuable nontimber products, such as rattan. But forests are also cleared to gain access to the oil, gas, coal, and precious metals beneath the forest floor. Forests are converted to pastures for beef and leather production, oil palm plantations, and fields for soybeans and other crops. Without addressing the need for a shift in incentives to keep forests standing—such as that offered by payment-for-performance finance—domestic policies and international cooperation to address deforestation are unlikely to be effective.

Extensive commercial exploitation of Indonesia's Outer Island forests began early in President Suharto's tenure in the late 1960s. Densely packed with the tall, straight trunks of large trees in the *Dipterocarpaceae* family suitable for good quality lumber or plywood, Indonesia's lowland forests were a logger's dream. Forest concessions were distributed to high-ranking military officers and senior bureaucrats in return for political loyalty. Those without operational capacity partnered with private businesses that took the lead in forest exploitation. Conglomerates controlled by personal friends of the president amassed control over vast areas of the nation's forests.[24]

The position of minister of forestry—head of the powerful agency charged with granting and supervising forest utilization permits—was usually awarded to a political party representative rather than someone with relevant technical expertise.[25] While most of the rents from exploiting the nation's forests went to the president's cronies, the Ministry of Forestry still controlled a multibillion-dollar fund accumulated from taxes and fees imposed on logging concessions. Ostensibly to be used for reforestation, the funds were often diverted to finance the regime's pet projects.[26] Funding on offer from donor agencies was modest by comparison.

In the 1970s, timber rose to second place after oil and gas as a contributor to Indonesia's national economy. Following the imposition of a log export ban in 1983 designed to promote downstream processing, the focus shifted to supporting the plywood industry, and Indonesia became the world's largest plywood manufacturer.[27] Plywood, in turn, gave way in the 1990s to support for the pulp and paper industry. Over the course of a decade, Indonesia's installed capacity to manufacture pulp and paper expanded by almost an order of magnitude. When the mills locked in a huge structural demand for wood fiber that could not be met by the country's limited plantations of fast-growing species, natural forests were cut down to feed them, and carbon-rich peat swamps were drained to expand the planted area.[28]

After the fall of Suharto in 1998, a new set of commercial and associated political pressures were brought to bear on the nation's forests, not least being the decentralization in 1999 of many government functions. The appropriate balance of political authority between national and local government can be an important determinant of economic growth by fostering healthy market competition among jurisdictions.[29] But in the absence of strong national regulation, decentralization in Indonesia served to put further pressure on forests, as local officials rushed to issue forest utilization permits and seize their share of the rents.[30]

Subsequently, the clearing of forestland for oil palm plantations skyrocketed, and between 1999 and 2011, revenues from crude palm oil exports increased by 3,000 percent. At the same time, mining for coal was emerging as a locally important driver of forest degradation under a system that granted permits to "borrow and utilize" forests zoned for production and protection. From 2004 to 2014, Indonesia tripled its coal production, becoming the world's largest coal exporter.[31]

Between 2000 and 2010, almost 15 million hectares of land in Indonesia's Outer Islands were deforested, an area almost as large as Florida.[32] Yet, very little forest wealth was captured by the state. A 2015 audit by the Corruption Eradication Commission estimated that, over the twelve years between 2003 and 2014, the government collected just $3.2 billion in timber royalties on an estimated $81 billion worth of timber—at least $9 billion short of what should have been collected.[33]

Governments should be able to manage forest resources more prudently by constraining extraction to sustainable levels or capturing a higher share of revenues for the state.

Instead, government officials more commonly facilitate private appropriation of forest wealth in return for personal wealth and political power. While political scientists have long debated the influence of different political regimes on economic growth, and, in particular, the influence of secure property rights,[34] less attention has been paid to how exploitation of the forestry sector has affected government institutions. One important exception is political scientist Michael Ross's 2001 study of the timber industries in Indonesia, Malaysia, and the Philippines, which describes how government officials responded to rising timber prices by dismantling or thwarting attempts to strengthen regulations that would constrain logging.[35]

In all three countries, permits to log "were distributed to major campaign donors, influential constituents, and the friends, relatives, and cronies of top politicians." Government officials also authorized "logging at unsustainable rates, keeping royalties and taxes low, and failing to enforce logging regulations." Ross concludes that "while weak state institutions may allow rent seeking, rent seeking can weaken state institutions—producing a downward spiral of eroding legal, administrative, and political restraints."[36]

Ross's analysis suggests that, without a fundamental shift in incentives, donor agency programs focused exclusively on building the capacity of government institutions to manage forests more sustainably are unlikely to succeed where there are rents to be seized by political actors.

Weak Forest Governance Leads to Corruption, Conflict, Illegality, and Violence

A fourth feature common to the politics of deforestation in developing countries—which is both a cause and an effect of the three already described—is the weak legal, regulatory, and enforcement environment governing the ownership and use of forest resources. Conditions of weak governance have allowed corruption and illegal activity to flourish and conflict to fester among actors competing for control over natural resources.

In the DRC, for example, logging concessions are governed by complex and opaque regulations, and their boundaries do not line up across maps held by various concessionaires, local communities, or the government. According to one analysis, these conditions promote corruption "as the most direct and sure means of securing the necessary permits to conduct business."[37] At the same time, high levels of illegal logging have undermined the incentives for environmentally and socially responsible behavior on the part of legal concessionaires.[38]

Illegal activity is also associated with violence. Taking advantage of the natural experiment that occurred when Brazil prohibited extraction of and trade in mahogany in 2001, economists Ariaster Chimeli and Rodrigo Soares demonstrated that the shift in logging activity from legal to illegal was associated with an increase in homicides in relevant geographical areas.[39]

Conflict over forest resources is often the result of unclear or contested land tenure and a disjuncture between the forests described by maps in national capitals and the realities on the ground. Most tropical forestland has long been occupied and managed by indigenous and other local communities, yet many forest-rich nations, especially in Asia, claim the preponderance of forestland for the state. An important exception is Papua New Guinea, where local communities' customary rights to forestland are recognized both constitutionally and, largely, in practice;[40] another is Mexico, where post-revolution agrarian reform placed the majority of the country's forests under community management.[41]

The most recent comprehensive study of who controls forestland found that land designated for or owned by indigenous peoples and local communities in selected countries totaled 23 percent in Latin America (largely Brazil and Mexico), 15 percent in Sub-Saharan Africa, and only 1.5 percent in South and Southeast Asia.[42] State-owned forestland is designated for various productive and protective functions, and many of these zones have traditionally excluded or severely limited human habitation and forest use by local communities.

As a result, in many countries, communities that are the most concentrated and direct beneficiaries of the forest goods and services described in chapters 3 and 6 have been actively disempowered as a constituency for forest protection. Throughout Southeast Asia, for example, governments have characterized upland populations as "backward," responsible for environmental degradation, and in need of "development," thus providing a convenient justification for national political and economic elites to exert state control over forest resources for their own benefit.[43]

Governments have also criminalized and attempted to suppress swidden agricultural systems, particularly the use of fire to clear land, despite the limited contribution of such traditional shifting agricultural practices to deforestation.[44] Early campaigns against illegal logging tended to target small-scale chainsaw operators rather than the financiers of large-scale criminal syndicates.[45] At the most extreme, indigenous and local communities have been forcibly resettled out of forest areas, ostensibly to advance biodiversity conservation objectives.[46]

Such conditions breed chronic conflict and, sometimes, acute violence. Agents of national or local governments, corporate actors empowered with state-granted forest concession licenses, and/or recent migrants seeking to exert control over forest resources are pitted against local communities defending their rights to ownership, habitation, and use. In Myanmar, the granting of concessions for large-scale agribusiness development in two forest-rich provinces in 2010–13 was associated with a high incidence of violent conflict over land.[47] In Indonesia, an alliance of indigenous groups recorded 150 new cases of human rights violations related to the customary land of indigenous peoples in 2013 alone.[48]

Furthermore, local contests over rights to forestland have been manipulated by actors on the national stage to gain access to land or votes. In Indonesia, for example, powerful people based in Jakarta who were seeking to build a political base exploited a long-simmering conflict over a former protected forest in Lampung, Sumatra, by supporting the land claims of new settlers and speculators. This exacerbated the conflict and led to violent confrontation.[49]

Clearly, businesses, bureaucrats, and politicians who have benefited from weak forest governance represent an important constituency for business-as-usual deforestation, and one that is resistant to increased transparency and effective law enforcement. But Brazil's success in reducing deforestation provides grounds for optimism that, with the right combination of policies and political will, supported by domestic constituencies for reform, weak governance and other factors enabling deforestation can be overcome.

New Constituencies for Forest Conservation

The characteristics of the forestry sector described above have led some observers to despair of the possibility that international cooperation to conserve forests can ever be effective.[50] And, as will be described in chapter 12, aversion to the "headline risk" of association with corruption or rights violations has led donor agencies to avoid engagement in the forestry sector altogether or to insist on cumbersome safeguard measures and approval processes. Some activists opposed to REDD+ have demanded the improvement of forest governance as a precondition for implementing programs to slow deforestation.

But the evidence suggests a more complex causal sequence toward the twin objectives of better governance and reduced deforestation, as REDD+ programs have themselves contributed to improving forest governance. Early experience with REDD+ initiatives indicates international cooperation can build on and empower a variety of domestic constituencies who favor better governance of forests. International payment-for-performance finance in particular has raised forest issues on national political agendas and expanded the political space for domestic stakeholders to develop appropriate solutions for reducing deforestation.

The convergence of a number of domestic factors—some linked to international politics, finance, and markets—has the potential to create a new political context for protecting forests. According to Sérgio Abranches, the factors that determined Brazil's success in taming deforestation were

> [changes in] governance over deforestation, the emergence of the Ministry of Environment as an international actor on climate change issues, the decisive participation of civil society, the involvement of Amazon states in policy debates, the role of presidential diplomacy, and the gradual engagement of the private sector.[51]

In the following sections, we elaborate on how these and other factors have played out in Brazil, Indonesia, and elsewhere.

Proponents of Strengthening Indigenous and Sustainable Use Rights

An important domestic constituency for reform of forest management is composed of the indigenous and traditional communities that claim rights to forest areas and derive livelihoods and cultural identities from standing forests. In the opening of chapter 9, we saw how the early practitioners of "scientific" forest management in colonial India disregarded the land rights of local communities and suppressed traditional shifting cultivation practices in the interest of timber production. More than a century and a half later, most indigenous and other local communities that rely on forests for their livelihoods around the world do not have legal title to the land. These communities have suffered at the hands of foreign and domestic powers that have taken their lands, exploited their forests, and disregarded their rights.

Thus, it is not surprising that many forest-dwelling communities and their advocates first viewed REDD+ with suspicion—was this another excuse for outsiders to limit the communities' rights to forest resources? Anti-REDD+ activists have asserted as much.[52] Yet, over time, an increasing number of indigenous groups have cautiously embraced REDD+ as an instrument for strengthening their rights to forestland and to gain access to finance for economic development.[53] Because stopping deforestation requires clarity regarding who has the rights and responsibilities for forest management, REDD+ has emerged as an opportunity for such communities to advance their claims.

The modern rainforest conservation movement in Brazil was sparked by conflicts between traditional forest communities and agents of deforestation. In 1988, after raising the profile of the issue internationally, union activist Chico Mendes was murdered for organizing traditional rubber tappers to resist the advance of the cattle ranching frontier. Marina Silva, herself the daughter of a rubber tapper family in Acre State, used her tenure as environment minister to demarcate indigenous territories for indigenous use. Indigenous areas have subsequently been shown to be as or more effective than strictly protected areas in reducing the incidence of forest fire and have experienced a lower rate of deforestation.[54]

Although Indonesia's 1945 constitution recognizes the customary (*adat*) rights of indigenous peoples, the country's 1967 and 1999 Basic Forestry Laws effectively negated those rights by incorporating most territories claimed by indigenous groups within the forest estate (*kawasan hutan*). After the fall of Suharto in 1998, political space opened for the advocacy of indigenous rights. In 2001, the Indigenous Peoples Alliance of Indonesia's Archipelago (AMAN) was founded for that very purpose. Their efforts, however, made little progress before the advent of REDD+. According to Mina Setra, AMAN's deputy secretary-general, it was only when "the international community started talking about forests and REDD+ that we had the opportunity to show that we do exist."[55]

> An increasing number of indigenous groups have cautiously embraced REDD+ as an instrument for strengthening their rights to forestland.

The bilateral REDD+ agreement concluded with Norway in 2010 included a commitment by the Indonesian government to involve indigenous peoples in its implementation. In 2011, the newly appointed head of the national REDD+ Task Force, Kuntoro Mangkusubroto, publicly advocated for recognition of indigenous claims to forestland and invited indigenous groups to submit maps of their territories to be incorporated in the "One Map" initiative launched under his leadership (see below). Encouraged by Kuntoro Mangkusubroto's support, AMAN challenged the 1999 Forestry Law, and, in May 2013, the Constitutional Court issued a ruling that opened the door to recognition of indigenous rights to forestland.[56]

Later, in September 2014, AMAN joined fifteen other indigenous networks and organizations from the Amazon, Central America, and the Congo Basin in signing the New York Declaration on Forests, which promised to conserve 400 million hectares of forests on indigenous territories.[57] In return, the groups articulated three expectations: progress on customary land rights for indigenous peoples; free, prior, informed consent for all decisions that affect them; and access to a fair share of climate finance.[58]

Indigenous groups and other local communities have seen opportunities to advance their interests through the implementation of national REDD+ programs in other countries, as well. Under Guyana's bilateral agreement with Norway, for example, REDD+ funding has been used to make progress on the titling, demarcation, and extension of Amerindian Lands under the Amerindian Act of 2006. Such titling is linked to indigenous communities' ability to "opt in" to participation in REDD+ finance.[59] A trilateral REDD+ agreement among Germany, Norway, and Peru announced in September 2014 includes a specific milestone related to the demarcation and titling of indigenous lands.[60]

Evidence that REDD+ initiatives have advanced indigenous rights in African countries also exists. Research by legal scholar Sebastien Jodoin suggests engagement in REDD+ helped to expand and translate the norm of "Free, Prior, and Informed Consent" (FPIC)

to forest-dependent communities in Tanzania.[61] REDD+ has also generated government support for FPIC in the DRC and contributed to a 2014 decree on allocating forest concessions to local communities, as well as to discussions toward a new law on indigenous peoples under consideration in 2015.[62]

Proponents of Improved Governance

A second domestic constituency for forest-related reform in developing countries is composed of individuals and organizations working to promote better forest governance, as well as good governance more generally. In addition to forest advocates' use of governance tools to advance forest conservation, proponents of more transparent, participatory, and accountable government decision making, anticorruption initiatives, and conflict resolution efforts see initiatives to improve forest management as entry points for prying open political space to advance their broader agendas. In Colombia, for example, some see a role for REDD+ in the complicated transition to peace and sustainable land use in a region emerging from widespread conflict and illegal drug production.[63]

Increased transparency of forest-related information was critical to Brazil's success in reducing deforestation (see chapters 4 and 7). Disclosure of satellite data allowed civil society groups to expose public mismanagement and private misconduct in the nation's forests and allowed independent experts to compare land clearing across states and identify illegal activity on private properties. It was thus resisted by the forces of business as usual.[64]

In Brazil, a confrontation with illegal loggers yielded an important initial victory in the struggle to turn the tide of deforestation. In 2002, the new administration of President Lula was stung by the decision of the Convention on International Trade in Endangered Species (CITES) to list Amazon mahogany on "Annex 2," requiring that all traded mahogany come from sustainably managed forests. An audit of forest management permits associated with the mahogany trade revealed that most logging was occurring on public land, and that most permits were illegal. The government suspended 80 percent of the permits and created a new Brazilian Forestry Service.[65]

The tackling of illegal logging of mahogany demonstrated that success in addressing the causes of forest destruction was possible, built the self-confidence of the incoming technical staff of Environment Minister Marina Silva, and initiated cooperation of the ministry with the powerful Gabinete Civil and the Justice Ministry. This collaboration was subsequently deployed to tackle corruption in the Institute for the Environment and Renewable Natural Resources (IBAMA), the agency responsible for enforcing environmental law. In 2005, Operation Curupira uncovered a multistate network of illegal logging and land grabbing, led to the arrest and prosecution of more than a hundred people, and prompted the firing of dozens of civil servants.[66]

In Indonesia, similar initiatives toward transparency of forest information and investigation of forest-related corruption were initiated as part of or coordinated with the country's REDD+ program. A key commitment contained in the 2010 letter of intent negotiated with the government of Norway—at the suggestion of the Indonesians[67]—was to impose a moratorium on further licensing of exploitation and conversion in the nation's remaining natural forests. The moratorium was delayed and more limited in scope than anticipated, but it still dramatically affected forest governance by forcing increased transparency.[68]

Despite decades of resistance by the Ministry of Forestry to the release of forest condition data, Kuntoro Mangkusubroto authorized online publication of the Indicative Moratorium Map and invited public input through a semiannual review and revision process. Publication of the Indicative Moratorium Map in turn revealed inconsistencies in maps of forest condition, classification, and licensing status across ministries. President Yudhoyono tasked the REDD+ Task Force with launching the so-called "One Map" initiative, which would collect and harmonize all such spatial data.[69]

The national REDD+ Task Force also made common cause with anticorruption forces. In a 2012 study, the highly respected Corruption Eradication Commission found that both the Ministry of Forestry and the permitting process for the release of forestland fell below minimum standards for integrity. In December 2012, Kuntoro Mangkusubroto and the head of the Corruption Eradication Commission were present at the signing of the first of several interagency memoranda of understanding to enhance coordination of law enforcement related to protecting natural resources.[70]

In the meantime, the commission was intensifying its investigations into corrupt practices in the forestry sector. In 2013, for example, the former head of a district in Central Sulawesi and a prominent businesswoman in Jakarta were both sentenced to prison terms for their roles in a scheme in which access to forestlands for oil palm plantations was granted in return for payoffs.[71] According to experts interviewed in 2014, greater public attention to corruption-related deforestation generated by the national REDD+ initiative and associated civil society advocacy compelled forestry officials to be more prudent in their behavior and law enforcement agencies to be tougher on illegal activity.[72]

Although the drivers of deforestation and peatland conversion in Indonesia have not yet been overcome, and no payments for performance from the agreement with Norway have been made, the national REDD+ initiative has clearly made a difference in forest governance.[73] Issues that had long been the focus of traditional donor-funded projects, including increased transparency of forest-related data, progress on recognizing indigenous peoples' rights to forestland, reform of forest licensing, and anticorruption measures, moved forward only through the REDD+ Task Force established under the agreement.[74]

Good governance has been promoted through REDD+ initiatives in other countries, as well. In Guyana, the establishment of a multi-stakeholder committee to advise on the national REDD+ process is associated with

> a move toward greater transparency in government, both from the inclusion on the committee of key civil society actors such as trade union bodies, private sector member associations and environmental and indigenous peoples NGOs, and also from the fact that minutes of this committee were publicly available—an unprecedented step in Guyana.[75]

In Mexico, stakeholders view the planning and implementation of early REDD+ actions as

> one of the most participative, open and inclusive processes in public policy in Mexico, integrating the views and involvement of civil society and academia. This extensive consultation process has created a precedent of including civil society in public policy design and is being replicated in other sectors such as energy.[76]

More generally, internationally supported REDD+ initiatives have succeeded in putting forests squarely on the domestic political agendas of a number of countries.[77] By shining a spotlight on forest mismanagement, they have generated pressure for reform, strengthened the position of environmental agencies, and had positive spillover effects on other sectors. Guyana, since the initiation of REDD+, has established a national protected areas system, and improved forest monitoring under the agreement with Norway has helped make visible deforestation caused by mining.[78] In the DRC, "the REDD+ process has initiated a national conversation about the conservation of forests," strengthened the relative position of the Ministry of Environmental and Sustainable Development, and influenced a new environmental law and revisions to the national mining and agricultural codes.[79]

These examples of the positive impacts of REDD+ on forest governance stand in contrast to the worries of early critics who predicted REDD+ would lead to a number of "bad governance" outcomes in terms of community displacement, recentralization of authority over forests, or widespread corruption in the management of REDD+ funds.[80] Yet even in the few cases where credible reports of harm have emerged, the appropriateness of their attribution to national REDD+ initiatives has been contested.[81] On balance, the potential negative consequences of REDD+ are apparently not being realized.

To the contrary, national REDD+ initiatives are on the whole promoting greater transparency and public participation and are often cited as pushing the frontiers of good governance. The payment-for-performance aspect of REDD+ funding—which requires transparent reporting of change in forest condition—has likely contributed to this outcome. Furthermore, by aligning incentives for achieving outcomes at low cost, performance-based finance can be expected to reduce opportunities for corruption, as described further in chapter 12.[82]

Beneficiaries of Ecosystem Services from Forests

A third domestic constituency in forest-rich countries whose interests align with REDD+ objectives are those who value the ecosystem services forests provide.

Forests are valued not only for their carbon capture and storage functions, but also for local benefits (described in chapters 3 and 6) that are gaining political traction in developing countries. While organized constituencies have seldom coalesced around the cause of maintaining forest-based ecosystem services, awareness among policymakers and the general public is growing. For example, in his speech to a conference commemorating the UN International Year of the Forest in Jakarta in 2011, President Yudhoyono of Indonesia highlighted the domestic benefits of forest-based ecosystem services—such as food security, energy security, and resistance to landslides—as key reasons to manage forests sustainably, before he mentioned climate change mitigation.[83]

In some instances, political mobilization has built on the particular interests of women in protecting forest goods and services. The Chipko movement in India gained international notoriety in the 1970s as village women literally hugged trees to prevent their felling by contractors.[84] The Green Belt Movement, started by Nobel Laureate Wangari Maathai in Kenya, organized rural women to plant trees, in part to restore degraded watershed functions. The movement evolved into a political force that successfully challenged the government's plans to privatize an area of public forestland in 1999.[85]

The degree to which intact forests offer protection against large-scale flooding has been the subject of vigorous debate among researchers, but public sentiment and public policy have tended to accept the connection. [86] Thailand (1989), China (1998), and the Philippines (2004) all issued logging bans in the aftermath of catastrophic floods. More localized flooding—such as the periodic inundations of the city of Jakarta after heavy rains—is typically attributed, at least in part, to changes in land use in upland watersheds.

With the large-scale recurrence of Indonesia's forest fires in 2015, citizens of Indonesia, Malaysia, and Singapore have become more vocal in their complaints about their adverse impacts, as well.[87] In late 2015, President Joko Widodo of Indonesia responded by announcing a ban on further development of peatlands.[88]

The possible linkage between deforestation and loss of ecosystem services has received serious attention in Brazil. Brazilian scientist Antonio Nobre linked the 2013–15 drought in São Paulo to deforestation in the Amazon (see chapter 3).[89] Critics of a major dam under construction in the state of Pará argue that the hydrological effects of deforestation will dramatically reduce the plant's capacity to generate electricity.[90] The strong showing of former environment minister Marina Silva, who garnered more than 20 percent of the vote in the 2014 presidential election despite various liabilities of her candidacy, reflected broad public embrace of her sustainable development agenda.[91]

As appreciation of forest-based ecosystem services has increased, forestry agencies have latched onto their provision as a way to legitimize their roles in forest management. A compelling example is provided by Perum Perhutani, the state forest corporation in Indonesia responsible for managing the colonial legacy of teak and other timber plantations on the island of Java. With the depletion of timber stock due to mismanagement, looting, and encroachment, which intensified during the political turmoil of the late 1990s and early 2000s, declining timber revenues made it increasingly difficult for the corporation to justify its control of 2.4 million hectares of Java's land area. In 2011, it adopted a new strategy emphasizing the role of forests in providing rural livelihoods and ecosystem services and announced a plan to export bottled water to Japan.[92] The company now touts tourism, honey, and bottled water as business lines consistent with the public interest and forest conservation principles.[93]

With growing scientific evidence and public awareness of the linkages between forest health and the benefits of forest-based ecosystem services described in chapter 3, political support for improved forest management and protection from degradation originating from other sectors can be expected to increase.

International Influences Supporting Reform

While domestic factors take center stage in determining the politics of deforestation, international factors can play supporting roles. In this section, we describe how international expectations can align incentives for national leaders and market actors to commit to reducing deforestation.

Desire for International Legitimacy and Reputational Benefits

Since the UN Framework Convention on Climate Change was agreed on in 1992, emissions from developing countries—particularly emerging economies—have significantly increased, and along with them expectations that developing countries would share the burden of reducing emissions. In that context, a desire for international legitimacy has led many heads of state to make commitments to reducing emissions from deforestation, one of the largest sources of emissions from many developing countries. Although such commitments enjoy some domestic support, it is striking that they have been made despite the tacit or overt objections of powerful vested interests in business-as-usual deforestation.

For example, Susilo Bambang Yudhoyono, who assumed office in 2004 as Indonesia's first directly elected president, and his minister of foreign affairs, Marty Natalegawa, were sensitive to Indonesia's status as an international "bad boy" as a result of the periodic forest fires that blanketed the region in suffocating haze. They were eager to reposition Indonesia as a leader in solving regional and global problems.

In this regard, the Thirteenth Conference of the Parties to the UN Climate Convention in Bali in 2007 was a critical milestone both for Indonesia's international policy stance and the development of REDD+. According to Robin Davies,

> Indonesia . . . was looking for a concrete outcome in an area in which it could take an international lead. It had released a National Climate Change Action Plan in February 2007 which specifically called for international support to achieve reduced rates of deforestation and forest degradation, including through a global REDD+ mechanism and bilateral support for pilot activities . . . As custodian of the world's third-largest area of rainforest and largest area of tropical peatlands, and source of some 30 per cent of global land-based emissions, Indonesia was also central in the Coalition of Rainforest Nations, which was gearing up to advocate for action on REDD+ in Bali. Domestic and international concerns about rampant deforestation and, in particular, illegal logging, were also relevant, as were regional concerns about trans-boundary haze resulting from uncontrolled peat fires in Sumatra and Kalimantan. Owing to an El Niño event, fires had been especially severe in 2006, with haze reaching as far as Korea.[94]

In 2009, eager to burnish his reputation as a statesman, President Yudhoyono stepped forward at the G20 meeting in Pittsburgh as the first leader of a developing country to announce a voluntary target for reducing climate emissions. In his speech announcing the commitment, he characterized the target as "entirely achievable, because most of our emissions come from forest related issues, such as forest fires and deforestation."[95] He wished for Indonesia to become part of the solution to global climate change, even though the country still had many domestic challenges to overcome.[96] When his commitment led to the 2010 REDD+ agreement with Norway, the deal was roundly criticized by industry associations, plantation companies, and officials from the Ministry of Forestry.[97]

Brazil provides another example of how the desire for international legitimacy has led heads of state to commit to reducing deforestation. Brazil faced adverse international attention to its mismanagement of forests and associated violence for decades, beginning with the murder of Chico Mendes in 1988, the raging Amazon fires of the 1990s, and the announcement in 1995 that annual deforestation had reached an all-time high of more than 29,000 square kilometers—an area almost the size of Belgium.[98] In response, President Fernando Henrique Cardoso tightened regulations on deforestation in the Amazon, increasing the proportion of private landholdings that had to be maintained as natural forest from 50 to 80 percent.[99]

President Lula was thus well aware of the risks deforestation posed to Brazil's international reputation when he was elected in 2002. While on a trip to the United States as president-elect, he announced the appointment of Marina Silva as environment minister, attracting favorable domestic and international press coverage.[100]

President Lula was especially sensitive to the country's reputation in 2005 after Dorothy Stang, an American-born nun, was murdered for her work to protect forests. Over the next two years, he approved new conservation areas totaling 15 million hectares and supported Ministry of Environment initiatives to repress illegal timber, cattle, and soybean production in the Amazon. Fearing the international visibility that would come with a rebound in deforestation, President Lula signed a decree to deny credit to high-deforestation municipalities and projects in illegally cleared areas.[101]

Brazil's international standing also played a role in the establishment of three additional large protected areas (totaling 13.6 million hectares—an area almost as large as Nepal) across the "Arc of Deforestation"—a forest frontier stretching across the states of Rondônia, Mato Grosso, and Pará, described in chapter 7—as a shield against land grabbing and land clearing that threatened indigenous territories. The protected areas were established despite the fact that in 2005, José Dirceu, head of the Gabinete Civil, resigned in a corruption scandal and was replaced by Dilma Rousseff, who was opposed to setting aside such large tracts.[102]

Facing strong opposition in the cabinet and sensing she was losing the president's backing, Marina Silva strategically resigned in 2008. International dismay over her resignation and concern over an 11 percent increase in Brazilian deforestation strengthened her successor, Carlos Minc, as he appealed to the president for action right before the ninth Conference of the Parties to the Convention on Biological Diversity in Bonn.

Minc convinced President Lula that Brazil's international credibility depended on establishing the new reserves. The president signed the decrees, and Minc unveiled maps of the new conservation units in his opening presentation in Bonn.[103]

Finally, as described earlier, international reputation also played a role in the president's decision to announce quantitative emission reduction targets at the climate talks in Copenhagen in 2009, even in the face of significant opposition from domestic interests and within his own cabinet.

Beyond Indonesia and Brazil, the desire for international legitimacy and reputational benefits has motivated other countries to make commitments to reducing deforestation (although such commitments do not guarantee follow-through). Several experts interviewed for a study by climate policy analyst Charlotte Streck and her colleagues, for example, "pointed to Colombia's desire to build an image as a 'green' country and 'good global citizen' as motivating interest" in efforts to reduce deforestation.[104] Such a reputation would not only attract REDD+ finance; it would also create more welcoming export markets for forest-risk commodities, described below.

Access to Markets and Finance

Signals from world markets can also create domestic constituencies for reform of forest management. The governments of some consumer countries have restricted imports of illegally produced forest goods and committed to procurement of certified sustainable products, as described in chapters 8 and 11. These measures have, in turn, generated pressure for change in producer countries. For example, a World Bank assessment of factors affecting forest sector reform in six African countries found that "harnessing international initiatives" (such as voluntary partnership agreements under the European Union's Forest Law Enforcement, Governance, and Trade initiative) was at least "somewhat influential" in all countries studied, and "very influential" in four.[105]

Civil society activists have enlisted demand-side forces to pressure multinational companies to stop using and financing illegally produced tropical timber and other globally traded commodities—such as soy, beef, palm oil, and pulp and paper—that are produced on recently cleared forestlands. They have cleverly directed their campaigns at retailers such as Home Depot and Lowe's, manufacturers such as Nestlé, and financiers such as HSBC.[106]

Campaigns by Greenpeace and Amigos da Terra against buyers of Brazilian soybeans in 2006 and beef in 2009, for instance, prompted voluntary moratoria on deforestation.[107] Sérgio Abranches describes how these market-oriented campaigns complemented the "Operation Arc of Fire" law enforcement raids directed by Environment Minister Carlos Minc in 2008:

> The first raid of the Arc of Fire Operation was in Tailândia, a city in the state of Pará, and also the first municipality added to the "grey list" of high deforestation municipalities. The raids were met with opposition from local politicians, who mobilized mob riots, and rural producers, who staged demonstrations of opposition and discontent. The operation was aimed at the illegal connections of several formally legal businesses, with the intent to disrupt supply chains that linked legal and illegal parts. Businesses were closed, lumber was sequestered, managers and owners were arrested, and charcoal furnaces were destroyed. Although the operation wasn't something new, it was very encompassing and gave an unprecedentedly strong signal that things were changing. This attracted the attention of both public and private local leaders in the states of Pará and Mato Grosso. Simultaneously, and perhaps even more importantly, the market was becoming less favorable to agricultural products from deforested areas. This language they understood only too well, even better than the signs from repression. If the market, particularly large supermarkets and foreign customers, stopped buying their commodities, they would lose their major source of income.[108]

In short, market-based campaigns reinforced government command-and-control law enforcement efforts to stamp out illegal clearing of forests for soy and beef production in Brazil by changing the politics of deforestation at the local level.

In 2006, Greenpeace established a national presence in Indonesia and started campaigns with local protests, including chaining themselves to heavy equipment belonging to a leading palm oil company.[109] In 2010, the organization was enormously successful with its famous Kit Kat video, which tarnished Nestlé's image by associating the company with shrinking orangutan habitat. Following pressure from Nestlé and other international buyers and financiers, an increasing number of commodity producers and traders with operations in Indonesia took on "no-deforestation" commitments, as described in chapter 8.

In Indonesia, these private sector initiatives have gotten ahead of government-led policies and enforcement efforts, leaving progressive companies, having taken on pledges to adhere to more stringent standards than those applying to their competitors, at a disadvantage. For example, producers of palm oil or fast-growing timber that set aside intact forests within their concessions risked that the government would excise the undeveloped areas as "abandoned land" and reallocate them to less scrupulous companies. As a result, progressive companies became a constituency for changes in government policy. The Indonesian Palm Oil Pledge—announced by the Indonesian Chamber of Commerce and several domestic and international businesses in September 2014—specifically committed participating companies "to engage the Government of Indonesia to encourage development of policies, and legal and regulatory frameworks that promote the implementation of this pledge."[110]

While the companies and governments that supply tropical products have protested that civil society "no-deforestation" campaigns and private initiatives are unfair, many have seen the writing on the wall. Due to changing norms, global markets are increasingly unfavorable to goods that are illegally or unsustainably produced. Thus, a new constituency for protecting forests has emerged—producers and traders based in developing countries who want better policies and improved law enforcement to level the playing field with their competitors.

An additional private sector constituency for reform is composed of those companies that stand to profit from demand for avoided forest emissions. The interests of entrepreneurs in forest countries who placed early bets on the development of global markets for forest carbon are most aligned with the objectives of REDD+. The private companies Biofílica in Brazil and P.T. Makmur Utama in Indonesia, for example, have made significant investments in establishing legal control over carbon-rich forest areas, measuring the carbon content of those areas, and obtaining certification of avoided emissions in compliance with global standards.[111] With the failure of a global carbon market to materialize, the profitability of those investments depends on domestic policies that would create demand for carbon credits.

Factors Affecting the Success of National Initiatives to Reduce Deforestation

In light of the competing forces militating for and against business as usual, what else do we know about the political and institutional factors that have influenced the success of national initiatives to reduce deforestation?

National Leadership and Advocacy Coalitions Help; Conflicting Mandates Hurt

National ownership has long been identified as key to reform processes, and the forestry sector is no exception.[112] In the 2012 World Bank study of six African countries mentioned above, "political will and the leadership role of the state" ranked first among seven political economy factors assessed for their influence on forest sector reforms.[113]

Leadership at the head-of-state level has been key to putting deforestation on national political agendas: Bharrat Jagdeo of Guyana and Susilo Bambang Yudhoyono of Indonesia both adopted forest protection as a signature issue of their presidencies. In a study on climate change governance for the World Bank in 2009, political scientist James Meadowcroft concluded the most important factor influencing success was "engagement (or not) by the top political leadership." He went on, "There is nothing that focuses the minds of officials and external stakeholders more than the knowledge that the prime minister or president is actively interested in a file."[114] Not surprisingly, analysis of early REDD+ experience shows that in national political arenas where power is concentrated, progress on reform depends on the support of the most powerful actors.[115]

Cabinet-level champions have also been essential to reform. One key to Marina Silva's effectiveness in using her tenure as Brazil's minister of environment to advance bold policy initiatives in the Amazon was getting other powerful ministries to back the reform agenda: fourteen ministries participated in the working group that crafted the Action Plan to Prevent and Control Deforestation in the Brazilian Amazon (PPCDAM) over the course of late 2004 and early 2005.[116] In addition, her team structured the Amazon Fund to strengthen the ministry's role by earmarking REDD+ revenues for investments in environmental sustainability.[117] When she sensed her ministry was in danger of losing its grip amid cabinet-level turf wars, she resigned in a way that would force the president to stick with the reform agenda, and her successor Carlos Minc made good use of the resulting political space to do so.[118]

In Indonesia, Kuntoro Mangkusubroto used his strategic position as head of the national REDD+ Task Force based in the Office of the President to push a number of important reforms, including the forest licensing moratorium and disclosure of forest-related data. His ability to move forward, however, was checked by resistance from the powerful Ministry of Forestry, which viewed the establishment of the REDD+ Agency in 2014 as a threat.[119] Political scientist Cecilia Luttrell and her colleagues warned that for the REDD+ agenda to gain traction in Indonesia's political system, presidential leadership would have to be complemented by support from the Parliament, the bureaucracy, and the broader public,[120] and an evaluation of Norway's engagement warned that the REDD+ agency's legal and political base was fragile.[121]

Upon assuming office in late 2014, President Joko Widodo abolished the REDD+ Agency and consolidated the forests and climate agenda in a unit under a new Ministry of Environment and Forests, causing a short-term setback to initiatives launched by the agency.[122] Then, in response to the resurgence of massive forest and peatland fires and resulting "haze" in late 2015, the president announced in January 2016 the creation of a new Peatland Restoration Agency with a mandate to facilitate the mapping, zoning, and restoration of damaged peatlands.[123]

Confusion and conflict over institutional roles are a common constraint on REDD+ across countries. In Peru, for example, finalization of the national REDD+ strategy was delayed by overlapping institutional mandates.[124] This problem is not unique to the forestry sector; a review of experience with "climate compatible development" has shown a common barrier to progress is conflicting roles and responsibilities across ministries, especially when the lead ministry is weak. Prolonged interministerial negotiations and turf wars can cause delays or duplication of effort.[125]

In such conditions, advocacy coalitions play a key role in placing and keeping reform on the national policy agenda. In Brazil, support for international cooperation regarding REDD+ was initiated outside government circles by researchers from independent organizations, as described in chapter 9. They skillfully utilized meetings of the climate convention to form a coalition strong enough to change the government's long-standing resistance to linking deforestation with climate change.[126] Research on national REDD+ policy processes more generally suggests such progress is likely to arise through "bargaining and conflictual relations between reformist non-state actors and business-as-usual interests."[127]

The Role of Payment-for-Performance Finance

Accepting high-level political leadership and advocacy coalitions as pluses and institutional turf wars as a minus, what else do we know about factors that support or constrain national efforts to reduce deforestation? In 2011, a team of social scientists headed by Maria Brockhaus attempted to answer that question in a rigorous way for a sample of twelve countries that had initiated REDD+ programs.[128] The team utilized a method called qualitative comparative analysis, which is used to tease out systematically what factors and combinations of factors cause different policy outcomes when the sample of cases does not support more quantitative analysis. In 2014, the researchers repeated the analysis for thirteen countries, and included a variable to test the significance of having in place a payment-for-performance agreement.[129]

The study found that six of the thirteen countries—Brazil, the DRC, Guyana, Indonesia, Tanzania, and Vietnam—had achieved at least two indicators of success. An important factor distinguishing them from the other seven countries was that they had already initiated climate-related policy reforms and/or were concurrently undertaking broader policy initiatives, such as low-carbon development strategies. These initiatives apparently helped smooth the way for progress on REDD+. Three of the six countries that had made progress (Brazil, Guyana, and Indonesia) also had access to performance-based finance for and strong national ownership of REDD+. Thus, a combination of already initiated policy change, strong ownership of the REDD+ process, and secure access to financial reward was associated with forward progress.

The linkage Brockhaus and her colleagues illuminated among country ownership, availability of payment-for-performance finance, and progress on policy reforms necessary to reduce deforestation lends itself to various interpretations. Did the prospect of a billion dollars in support to Brazil and Indonesia (or $250 million, a sum even larger in the case of Guyana, relative to the size of the national economy) create ownership on the part of governments? Or was Norway simply wise in selecting as partners governments already fully behind the REDD+ agenda? The evidence from the small number of cases available suggests a more nuanced dynamic, in which the prospect of international reward helped consolidate nascent political commitment to reform.

The availability of performance-based finance for reducing deforestation contributed to Brazil's decision to commit to an emission reduction target in Copenhagen in 2009. Although Brazil's decade-long success in bringing down the deforestation rate was well underway before the bilateral agreement with Norway, international finance tied to reducing deforestation helped consolidate the political coalition behind forest-related reforms and enhanced the legitimacy of the Ministry of Environment and other constituencies for conservation.[130]

According to Sérgio Abranches, domestic debate over REDD+ gained momentum with the prospect of the Norwegian agreement, which was "a game changer" in the politics of forest management in Brazil.[131] An official from the Gabinete Civil commented that the agreement with Norway "represented an important encouragement to further pursue deforestation reduction policies in the country."[132] The agreement also legitimized REDD+ as a mechanism for global cooperation in domestic politics, which was a paradigm shift from the previously dominant view of REDD+ as "an undue intervention of foreign interests in domestic policy."[133] It helped that the funds were channeled through a domestic institution, and that the Norwegians adopted a "hands-off" approach to their management.[134]

In Indonesia, the signing of the letter of intent with Norway was a similar "game changer" in the domestic politics of forests, and performance-based finance was a criti-cal element. Never before had forestry issues been discussed in such high government circles for such a long period of time; one former Ministry of Forestry official termed it a "historical breakthrough."[135] Civil society activists welcomed the payment-for-performance approach because they believed it would yield real outcomes and minimize the corruption that had marred previous international development cooperation.[136]

The agreement with Norway succeeded in raising the visibility of deforestation both domestically and internationally, increased transparency of forest information, and created political space for the championing of indigenous rights.[137] The "charismatic" $1 billion commitment had a "flagship effect" that rallied support and provided political leverage for change.[138] The lack of a broad-based constituency for conserving the nation's forests, however, meant that progress was fragile, and the momentum generated by the announcement of the billion-dollar agreement diminished over time.[139]

In Guyana—the only country other than Brazil and Indonesia to have assured access to performance-based REDD+ finance before 2014—a chicken-and-egg dynamic between national commitment and international support was in play, similar to the one that took place in Brazil. President Jagdeo's personal ownership of the REDD+ agenda was doubtless essential to parliamentary and broader public support for the associated Low-Carbon Development Strategy, launched in 2009.[140] Nevertheless, many observers believe "Guyana would not have undertaken such a pathway without the commitment of money on the table from the Norwegians."[141]

In light of the political sensitivities that adhere to the forestry sector, offers of international cooperation on forests must be framed in ways that do not trigger concerns about national sovereignty. One appeal of the payment-for-performance feature of REDD+ is that it offers a way for donors to support reform without being seen as intervening inappropriately in domestic affairs.

In all three countries that concluded early REDD+ payment-for-performance agreements with Norway—Brazil, Guyana, and Indonesia—the importance of framing them as results-based transfers rather than traditional development assistance was revealed in attitudes toward involvement by the World Bank. According to Sérgio Abranches, one reason for Brazil's reluctance to support REDD+ was a suspicion that "any finance controlled by the World Bank would ultimately lead to conditionalities imposed on Brazil and other forest countries within the Climate Convention."[142] Indonesia's traumatic experience with IMF/World Bank conditionality during the 1997–98 financial crisis (see box 10.1) produced an allergic reaction to any suggestion that the Bank serve as the intermediary for REDD+ funds. In fact, the final sticking point in negotiations over the 2010 letter of intent had to do with the criteria for choosing a financial intermediary, with Indonesia insisting on language that opened the possibility of choosing an institution other than an international organization.[143] Guyana's frustration with the World Bank's role as an intermediary for the agreement with Norway is described in chapter 12.

Box 10.1: Changing the Picture of International Support

In 1997, Indonesia experienced catastrophic forest fires that raged for months, blanketing the region in choking haze. The greenhouse gas emissions from the fires caused the spike in total global emissions illustrated in figure 2.1.

But it wasn't only the forests that were in flames; Indonesia's economy was crashing and burning as well. From August 1997 to January 1998, as the Asian financial crisis gained steam, the Indonesian rupiah lost more than 80 percent of its value against the U.S. dollar. Businesses that had borrowed in dollars were driven into bankruptcy, and the savings of families across the archipelago were wiped out.

The International Monetary Fund (IMF), supported by the World Bank, hurriedly cobbled together an emergency stabilization package. The letter of intent (LOI) included a long list of conditions, including a moratorium on further conversion of forests to oil palm, hastily included at the suggestion of World Bank forest experts.[a]

On January 15, 1998, President Suharto signed the LOI. The next morning's newspaper carried a humiliating photograph (see figure 10.1) that was seared into the nation's collective memory: it showed IMF managing director Michel Camdessus standing with his arms crossed, looming over a seated President Suharto as the latter signed the agreement.[b] To the Indonesian public, the image communicated the deeply asymmetrical relationship between the international financial institutions and the government of Indonesia, which allowed the former to dictate terms to the latter. Not surprisingly, the conditions of the LOI attracted very little "ownership" from the Indonesian side, and the moratorium on forest conversion failed to alter the country's trajectory of forest loss.

In May 2010, a ceremony in Oslo produced a photograph in sharp contrast: it showed Prime Minister Jens Stoltenberg of Norway and President Susilo Bambang Yudhoyono of Indonesia standing side by side as their ministers signed an LOI on REDD+ and conveyed a spirit of equal partnership (see figure 10.2). In return for a pledge of up to US$1 billion, the government of Indonesia agreed to a phased program of reforms to reduce emissions from deforestation, with most of the funds to be delivered on a payment-for-performance basis. The agreement included a moratorium on new forest exploitation licenses.

Unlike the 1998 IMF letter of intent that was thrown together in a great rush in Washington, DC, the 2010 LOI was crafted over months of quiet negotiations among small teams from both countries. The legitimacy of the agreement was strong from the Indonesian perspective because it built on a commitment the president had already made. At the G20 meeting in 2009, Yudhoyono had announced the first voluntary emission reduction targets from a developing country, pledging to cut emissions by 26 percent (compared to business as usual) unconditionally, and up to 41 percent conditional on international support. The proposed moratorium was included at the suggestion of the Indonesian side.

On the plane to Oslo, President Yudhoyono had confided to an aide that Indonesia should be embarrassed to be asking for help in reducing deforestation, because it was something the country should be doing anyway. But international attention and the framing of cooperation with Norway as an equal partnership would help to shift the domestic politics of the issue. In contrast to resentment caused by the IMF conditionality imposed in 1998, the 2010 agreement with Norway was welcomed by many Indonesians as supportive of Indonesia's own commitment to protect its forests.

a. F. Seymour and N. Dubash, "The Right Conditions: The World Bank, Structural Adjustment, and Forest Policy Reform," World Resources Institute, 2000, http://www.bankinformationcenter.org/wp-content/uploads/2013/07/iffeforest.pdf.
b. Emmanuel, "Flashback: Camdessus-Suharto Pic," in International Political Economy Zone blog, September 4, 2007, http://ipezone.blogspot.com/2007/09/flashback-camdessus-suharto-pic.html.

Hesitation and Frustration Resulting from Lack of Promised Finance

Although the availability of performance-based transfers has reinforced domestic commitment to forest reform in several countries, the future is unclear. Mixed signals from the international community about its commitment to providing performance payments at scale is having a chilling effect on nascent initiatives in other countries to pursue the REDD+ agenda. Furthermore, the channeling of REDD+ finance through traditional aid channels is leading to frustration among prospective recipients.

For the few countries and subnational jurisdictions that have so far concluded formal agreements with donors for significant levels of performance-based funding, the agreements have contributed to domestic policy shifts. But the political impact has been attenuated by the slow disbursement that has characterized most REDD+ finance, as described in chapter 12. In Guyana, after President Donald Ramotar succeeded Pres-

Figure 10.1: IMF managing director Michel Camdessus watches as Indonesian president Suharto signs the 1998 letter of intent.

Source: Agus Lolong/AFP/Getty Images.

ident Bharrat Jagdeo in 2011, reduced political attention to REDD+ may have been due in part to delays in performance payments "actually hitting the ground."[144] Following the announcement of a bilateral agreement between Liberia and Norway in September 2014, Liberians were kept waiting for almost a year before any money was successfully transferred through the intermediary World Bank trust fund.[145]

Many countries have initiated REDD+ activities, yet do not have commitments to payment for performance in place; for them, the uncertainty of reward has bred hesitation

and frustration, and even erosion of ownership that was built up through participation in "readiness" programs. Mozambique, for example, produced a first draft of its national REDD+ strategy in 2011, but, in light of uncertainty over the future of performance payments, the responsible technical team recommended postponing approval of the strategy "to ensure Mozambique does not embark on something that would not reflect future developments at the global scale."[146] Similarly, a decrease in national ownership of the REDD+ process in Vietnam since 2012 has been attributed partly to uncertainty

Figure 10.2: Prime Minister Stoltenberg and President Yudhoyono witness the signing of the letter of intent between Norway and Indonesia in 2010.

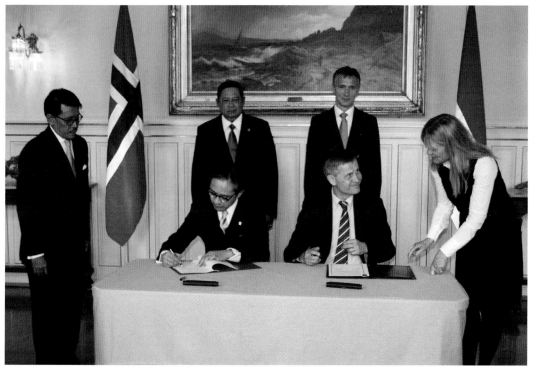

Source: Office of the Norwegian Prime Minister.

surrounding the future of global policies on REDD+.[147]

In the DRC, there is "a sense of restlessness among many domestic actors to move into implementation and leverage the readiness process for the achievement of results-based finance."[148] The lack of donor commitments to its newly established National REDD+ Fund as of mid-2015 reportedly "dampened the momentum created in the country by the engagement of different ministries, and as a consequence the decree to operationalize the Fund has not yet been signed by the Prime Minister."[149] More certainty over the prospect of results-based finance "has the potential to significantly impact political decisions and priorities. But as long as this finance remains small compared to other competing interests such as logging or other extractive industries, its impact will also be limited."[150]

In Mexico, experts believe the country's success in reducing deforestation would be reinforced by performance payments, and that current levels of funding remain

> insufficient to make the transformational changes needed to stop deforestation . . . If international REDD+ finance diminishes just as countries reach readiness, the efforts to date will not pay off . . . "Readiness" does not produce results automatically.[151]

Hesitation and frustration have also been experienced at the subnational level. A 2015 study of twenty-three subnational REDD+ initiatives found that most were "treading water" in the absence of a global agreement that would generate large-scale demand and finance for reduced emissions from deforestation and prompt necessary national efforts to clarify tenure. The authors conclude that "without a substantially larger stream of funding than currently exists, the performance-based mechanism which is at the heart of the REDD+ idea will be too small to perform a meaningful role in bringing deforestation under control."[152]

Frustration has also grown among political leaders at the subnational level. In their 2014 Rio Branco Declaration, governors participating in the Climate and Forests Task Force detailed their actions to date and went on to complain:

> Despite these substantial, globally significant contributions to ongoing efforts to protect forests and climate and despite the $7.3 billion pledged by donor governments for REDD+ since 2009, the GCF states and provinces have received very little financial support through existing pay-for-performance mechanisms and other funding sources. The progress GCF states and provinces have achieved to date is significant but fragile. More support is urgently needed to ensure the economic and political sustainability of these programs.[153]

According to one source, the REDD Early Movers Program—a pilot results-based financing effort initiated by the German government in 2012—was inaugurated precisely "to counter some of the frustration of the countries that have already invested into forest conservation."[154]

Conclusion

The politics of forest use remain contested in developing countries. Despite the rising volume of voices for conservation, constituencies for business as usual persistently push back against reform. In 2014, Brazil elected a new head of state with a pro-growth agenda not necessarily aligned with forest conservation. Similar transitions at the levels of state and provincial government have sometimes knocked REDD+ initiatives off track.

In Indonesia, despite the new president's initiatives to slow forest and peatland conversion, companies that had joined the Indonesian Palm Oil Pledge to "no-deforestation" supply chains in 2014 were forced to disband under government pressure less than two years later.[155] New narratives of sustainable rural development necessary to legitimize low-carbon growth strategies have not yet coalesced into the kinds of clear political messages and policy agendas that make for durable political platforms and private initiatives.

The outcomes of these teetering contests over the future of tropical forests will be determined in domestic policy arenas and be based primarily on national interests. But the examples of Brazil, Guyana, and Indonesia show how international engagement can help tip the balance in favor of forest conservation. While funding is needed to finance the costs of adjusting to a new paradigm of forest management, the political role of such finance is to signal a new kind of international partnership in the context of climate change.

The payment-for-performance feature of REDD+, which distinguishes it from prior decades of development cooperation and conditionality, is essential to its political legitimacy in recipient countries. By putting developing countries in the driver's seat for determining how to reduce emissions, performance-based finance minimizes political sensitivities over external intervention in issues related to military security, economic nationalism, corruption, and conflict. Domestic champions of reform are in a better position than donor agencies to figure out how to address complex forest governance problems, rendering the payment-for-performance approach more attractive than traditional project-based interventions.

And by elevating forest management on the political agenda, payment-for-performance agreements can create political space for a range of constituencies to advance agendas linked to forest protection, including respect for indigenous rights, maintenance of ecosystem services, and the securing of access to international markets.

The climate agreement reached in Paris in December 2015 provides a new opportunity to reinforce nascent efforts to reduce deforestation in developing countries. As described in chapter 9, the agreement itself endorses REDD+, and dozens of countries already participating in REDD+ programs have included reduced deforestation in their nationally determined emission reduction targets. The agreement further allows rich countries to benefit from supporting implementation through the international transfer of mitigation outcomes. Will rich countries step up to the opportunity, or will developing countries once again be disappointed?

In the next chapter, we turn our attention to the politics of REDD+ finance in donor countries.

Notes

1. The first seven paragraphs of this chapter are adapted from S. Abranches, "The Political Economy of Deforestation in Brazil and Payment-for-Performance Finance," CGD Background Paper, Center for Global Development, Washington, DC, 2014.

2. Ibid.

3. Ibid.

4. Norway also signed a REDD+ agreement with Tanzania in 2008, but funding was not on a payment-for-performance basis.

5. In this chapter, we use the term "good governance" as shorthand for transparency and accountability, rule of law, and respect for human rights, to include Principle 10 of the 1992 Rio Declaration: public access to information, participation, and justice in decision making related to the environment. For a review and critique of how "good governance" has been used in development policy and practice, see R. M. Gisselquist, "Good Governance as a Concept, and Why This Matters for Development Policy," United Nations University World Institute for Development Economics Research, working paper 2012/30, 2012.

6. Abranches, "The Political Economy of Deforestation in Brazil and Payment-for-Performance Finance"; M. Dharmasaputra and A. Wahyudi, "The Impact of Payment-for-Performance Finance on Political Economy of Deforestation in Indonesia," CGD Background Paper, Center for Global Development, Washington, DC, 2014.

7. We also draw on the findings of country case studies commissioned by the Climate and Land Use Alliance on Colombia, the Democratic Republic of Congo, Ghana, Guyana, Mexico, and Vietnam, which are synthesized in D. Lee and T. Pistorius, "The Impacts of International REDD+ Finance," Climate and Land Use Alliance, 2015, http://www.climateandlandusealliance.org/wp-content/uploads/2015/09/Impacts_of_International_REDD_Finance_Report_FINAL.pdf.

8. H. Buhaug and S. Gates, "The Geography of Civil War," *Journal of Peace Research* 39, no. 4 (2002): 417–33.

9. See, for example, R. Burgess, E. Miguel, and C. Stanton, "War and Deforestation in Sierra Leone," *Environmental Research Letters* 10, no. 9 (2015): 095014.

10. L. Fergusson, D. Romero, and J. F. Vargas, "The Environmental Impact of Civil Conflict: The Deforestation Effect of Paramilitary Expansion in Colombia," National University of Rosario, Argentina, working paper 165, September 2014, http://repository.urosario.edu.co/bitstream/handle/10336/10988/12158.pdf.

11. N. Peluso and P. Vandergeest, "Political Ecologies of War and Forests: Counterinsurgencies and the Making of National Natures," *Annals of the Association of American Geographers* 101, no. 3 (2011): 587–608.

12. Ibid.

13. S. Usman, "Indonesia's Decentralization Policy: Initial Experiences and Emerging Problems," SMERU Research Institute Working Paper, Jakarta, 2001.

14. D. M. Dozer, "Matthew Fontaine Maury's Letter of Instruction to William Lewis Herndon," *Hispanic American Historical Review* 28 (1948): 212–28; M. Kiemen, "Review of the Book *The Exploration of the Valley of the Amazon*, by William Lewis Herndon, edited by Hamilton Basso," *The Americas* 10 (1953): 376.

15. C. Mann, *1493: Uncovering the New World Columbus Created* (New York: Alfred A. Knopf Incorporated, 2011).

16. T. Nordhaus and M. Shellenberger, *Break Through: From the Death of Environmentalism to the Politics of Possibility* (New York: Houghton Mifflin Harcourt, 2007).

17. H. Mattos de Lemos, "Amazônia: In Defense of Brazil's Sovereignty," *Fletcher Forum of World Affairs* 14, no. 2 (1990): 307.

18. R. Davies, "The Indonesia-Australia Forest Carbon Partnership: A Murder Mystery," CGD Policy Paper 60, Center for Global Development, Washington, DC, 2015.

19. Abranches, "The Political Economy of Deforestation in Brazil," 5–6.

20. E. T. Paulino, "The Agricultural, Environmental and Socio-Political Repercussions of Brazil's Land Governance System," *Land Use Policy* 36 (2014): 136.

21. J. Tollefson, "Brazil Set to Cut Forest Protection," *Nature* 485, no. 7396 (2012): 19; Paulino, "The Agricultural, Environmental and Socio-Political Repercussions."

22. J. F. McCarthy, P. Gillespie, and Z. Zen, "Swimming Upstream: Local Indonesian Production Networks in 'Globalized' Palm Oil Production," *World Development* 40, no. 3 (2012): 555–69.

23. D. Murdiyarso et al., "Indonesia's Forest Moratorium: A Stepping-Stone to Better Forest Governance?" CIFOR Working Paper 76, Center for International Forestry Research, Bogor, Indonesia, 2011; H. Jong, "Govt Opposes Zero-Deforestation Pledge by Palm Oil Firms," *The Jakarta Post*, August 29, 2015.

24. Dharmasaputra and Wahyudi, "The Impact of Payment-for-Performance Finance."

25. Ibid.

26. C. Barr, A. Dermawan, H. Purnomo, and H. Komarudin, "Financial Governance and Indonesia's Reforestation Fund during the Soeharto and Post-Soeharto Periods, 1989–2009: A Political Economic Analysis of Lessons for REDD+," CIFOR Occasional Paper 52, Center for International Forestry Research, Bogor, Indonesia, 2010.

27. M. Brockhaus et al., "An Overview of Forest and Land Allocation Policies in Indonesia: Is the Current Framework Sufficient to Meet the Needs of REDD+?" *Forest Policy and Economics* 18 (2012): 30–37.

28. Ibid.

29. B. Weingast, "The Economic Role of Political Institutions: Market Preserving Federalism and Economic Development," *Journal of Law, Economics, and Organizations* 11, no. 1 (1995): 1–31.

30. B. P. Resosudarmo, ed., *The Politics and Economics of Indonesia's Natural Resources* (Institute of Southeast Asian Studies, 2005).

31. Dharmasaputra and Wahyudi, "The Impact of Payment-for-Performance Finance."

32. Ibid.

33. M. Taylor, "Indonesia Loses Up to US$9 Billion from Timber Clearing—Anti-Graft Body," Reuters in Channel News Asia, October 9, 2015.

34. A. Przeworski and F. Limongi, "Political Regimes and Economic Growth," *Journal of Economic Perspectives* 7, no. 3 (1993): 51–69.

35. M. Ross, *Timber Booms and Institutional Breakdown in Southeast Asia* (Cambridge, UK: Cambridge University Press, 2001).

36. Ibid., 203.

37. T. Johns, "The Impacts of International REDD+ Finance: DRC Case Study," Climate and Land Use Alliance, San Francisco, July 2015, 17.

38. Ibid.

39. A. Chimeli and R. Soares, "The Use of Violence in Illegal Markets: Evidence from Mahogany Trade in the Brazilian Amazon," Institute for the Study of Labor, Discussion Paper 5923, 2011.

40. See C. Filer, "The Double Movement of Immovable Property Rights in Papua New Guinea," *Journal of Pacific History* 49, no. 1 (2014): 76–94.

41. See D. Bray et al., "The Mexican Model of Community Forest Management: The Role of Agrarian Policy, Forest Policy and Entrepreneurial Organization," *Forest Policy and Economics* 8 (2006): 470–84.

42. Rights and Resources Initiative, "Who Owns the World's Land? A Global Baseline of Formally Recognized Indigenous and Community Land Rights," September 2015, http://www.rightsandresources.org/wp-content/uploads/GlobalBaseline_web.pdf.

43. F. Seymour and P. Kanowski, "Forests and Biodiversity," in *Handbook of the Environment in Southeast Asia*, ed. P. Hirsch (London: Routledge, 2016). See also, for example, G. Lestrelin, "Land Degradation in the Lao PDR: Discourses and Policy," *Land Use Policy* 27, no. 2 (2010): 424–39.

44. C. Padoch and M. Pinedo-Vasquez, "Saving Slash-and-Burn to Save Biodiversity," *Biotropica* 42, no. 5 (2010): 550–52.

45. M. Colchester, *Justice in the Forest: Rural Livelihoods and Forest Law Enforcement* 3 (Center for International Forestry Research, 2006).

46. F. Seymour, "Conservation, Displacement, and Compensation," in *Compensation in Resettlement,* ed. M. Cernea and M. Mathur (Delhi: Oxford University Press, 2008).

47. K. Woods, "Commercial Agriculture Expansion in Myanmar: Links to Deforestation, Conversion Timber, and Land Conflicts," Forest Trends, Washington, DC, 2015.

48. L. Bell, "Indonesia to Hear Indigenous Peoples' Grievances on Land Disputes," Mongabay.com, August 22, 2014, http://news.mongabay.com/2014/08/indonesia-to-hear-indigenous-peoples-grievances-on-land-disputes/.

49. S. Jones, "Mesuji: Anatomy of an Indonesian Land Conflict," Institute for Policy Analysis of Conflict Report No. 1, 2013.

50. See, for example, A. Karsenty and S. Ongolog, "Can 'Fragile States' Decide to Reduce Their Deforestation? The Inappropriate Use of the Theory of Incentives with Respect to the REDD Mechanism," *Forest Policy and Economics* 18 (2012): 38–45.

51. Abranches, "The Political Economy of Deforestation in Brazil," 4.

52. J. Lueders, C. Horowitz, A. Carlson, S. Hecht, and E. Parson, "The California REDD+ Experience: The Ongoing Political History of California's Initiative to Include Jurisdictional REDD+ Offsets within Its Cap-and-Trade System," CGD Working Paper 386, Center for Global Development, Washington, DC, 2014.

53. See, for example, La Coordinadora de las Organizaciones Indígenas de la Cuenca Amazónica, "Reducir la deforestación global con Territorialidad Indígena y Planes de Vida Plena," and Alianza Mesoamericana de Pueblos y Bosques (AMPB), "Carta/

Declaración de Interés," presented at the Governors' Climate and Forests Taskforce meeting, Barcelona, Spain, June 16, 2014.

54. A. Nelson and K. Chomitz, "Effectiveness of Strict vs. Multiple Use Protected Areas in Reducing Tropical Forest Fires: A Global Analysis Using Matching Methods," *PLOS ONE* 6, no. 8 (2011): e22722; B. Soares-Filho et al., "Role of Brazilian Amazon Protected Areas in Climate Change Mitigation," *Proceedings of the National Academy of Sciences* 107, no. 24 (2010): 10821–26; A. Verissimo et al., "Protected Areas in the Brazilian Amazon: Challenges and Opportunities," Imazon, 2011, http://imazon.org.br/publicacoes/protected-areas-in-the-brazilian-amazon-challenges-opportunities-2/?lang=en.

55. L. MacDonald, "A Surprising Indigenous View of REDD+—Mina Setra and Frances Seymour," Center for Global Development podcast, 2014, http://www.cgdev.org/blog/surprising-indigenous-view-redd-mina-setra-and-frances-seymour.

56. Dharmasaputra and Wahyudi, "The Impact of Payment-for-Performance Finance."

57. R. Butler, "Leaders Pledge to End Deforestation by 2030," Mongabay.com, September 24, 2014, http://news.mongabay.com/2014/0924-new-york-declaration-on-forests.html#ixzz3e0z4J9kv.

58. New York Declaration on Forests Action Statement and Plan, http://www.un.org/climatechange/summit/wp-content/uploads/sites/2/2014/07/New-York-Declaration-on-Forest-%E2%80%93-Action-Statement-and-Action-Plan.pdf, United Nations, last modified 2014.

59. T. Laing, "The Impacts of International REDD+ Finance: Guyana Case Study," Climate and Land Use Alliance, San Francisco, 2015, http://www.climateandlandusealliance.org/uploads/PDFs/Impacts_of_International_REDD_Finance_Case_Study_Guyana.pdf.

60. "Joint Declaration of Intent between the Government of the Republic of Peru, the

Government of the Kingdom of Norway and the Government of the Federal Republic of Germany on 'Cooperation on Reducing Greenhouse Gas Emissions from Deforestation and Forest Degradation (REDD+) and Promote Sustainable Development in Peru,'" September 23, 2014, https://www.regjeringen.no/contentassets/b324ccc0cf88419fab88f2f4c7101f20/declarationofintentperu.pdf.

61. As presented by B. Cashore et al., "Championing the Diffusion of Community Forestry through Pathways of Influence: Toward the Co-Generation of Strategic Insights" (PowerPoint presentation, Global Landscapes Forum, Lima, Peru, December 6, 2014).

62. Johns, "The Impacts of International REDD+ Finance." See also United Nations-REDD Programme, "Guidelines on Free, Prior, and Informed Consent," 2013, http://www.uncclearn.org/sites/default/files/inventory/un-redd05.pdf.

63. C. Streck et al., "The Impacts of International REDD+ Finance: Colombia Case Study," Climate and Land Use Alliance, San Francisco, 2015, http://www.climateandlandusealliance.org/wp-content/uploads/2015/08/Impacts_of_International_REDD_Finance_Case_Study_Colombia.pdf.

64. Abranches, "The Political Economy of Deforestation in Brazil."

65. Ibid.

66. Ibid.

67. A. Purnomo, *Protecting Our Forests: Moratorium on Forests and Peatlands, A Radical Policy* (Jakarta: Kepustakaan Populer Gramedia, 2012).

68. Murdiyarso et al., "Indonesia's Forest Moratorium."

69. Dharmasaputra and Wahyudi, "The Impact of Payment-for-Performance"

70. Ibid.

71. N. Setuningsih, "Hardaya Inti Plantation President Director Sentenced to 2 Years for Buol Corruption," *Jakarta Globe,* December 17, 2013.

72. Dharmasaputra and Wahyudi, "The Impact of Payment-for-Performance Finance."

73. F. Seymour, N. Birdsall, and W. Savedoff, "The Indonesia-Norway REDD+ Agreement," CGD Policy Paper 56, Center for Global Development, Washington, DC, 2015.

74. LTS International, "Real-Time Evaluation of Norway's International Forest and Climate Initiative: Synthesizing Report 2007–2013," Government of Norway, Norwegian Agency for Development Cooperation, August 2014, https://www.norad.no/en/toolspublications/publications/2014/real-time-evaluation-of-norways-international-climate-and-forest-initiative.-synthesising-report-2007-2013/.

75. Laing, "The Impacts of International REDD+ Finance," 12.

76. P. Bauche, "The Impacts of International REDD+ Finance: Mexico Case Study," Climate and Land Use Alliance, San Francisco, 2015, http://www.climateandlandusealliance.org/wp-content/uploads/2015/08/Impacts_of_International_REDD_Finance_Case_Study_Mexico.pdf, 11.

77. Lee and Pistorius, "The Impacts of REDD+ Finance."

78. Laing, "The Impacts of International REDD+ Finance"; J. Busch and N. Birdsall, "Assessing Performance-Based Payments for Forest Conservation: Six Successes, Four Worries, and Six Possibilities to Explore of the Guyana-Norway Agreement," CGD Note, Center for Global Development, Washington, DC, 2014.

79. Johns, "The Impacts of International REDD+ Finance," 16.

80. See, for example, J. Phelps, E. Webb, and A. Agrawal, "Does REDD+ Threaten to Recentralize Forest Governance?" *Science* 328, no. 5976 (2010): 312–13.

81. See, for example, B. Beymer-Farris and T. Bassett, "The REDD Menace: Resurgent Protectionism in Tanzania's Mangrove Forests," Global Environmental Change,

2011, and the response by N. Burgess et al., "REDD Herrings or REDD Menace," *Global Environmental Change*, 2013, https://www.academia.edu/10647256/The_REDD_Menace_Resurgent_Protectionism_in_Tanzanias_Mangrove_Forests.

82. C. Kenny and W. Savedoff, "Can Results-Based Payments Reduce Corruption?" CGD Working Paper 345, Center for Global Development, Washington, DC, 2013.

83. S. B. Yudhoyono, "Speech by President Susilo Bambang Yudhoyono" (Forests Indonesia Conference: Alternative Futures to Meet Demands for Food, Fibre, Fuel and REDD+, September 27, 2011), http://www.cifor.org/fileadmin/fileupload/media-release/27_Sep_SBY_Speech.pdf.

84. V. Shiva and J. Bandyopadhyay, "The Evolution, Structure, and Impact of the Chipko Movement," *Mountain Research and Development* 6 (1986): 133–42.

85. J. M. Klopp, "Pilfering the Public: The Problem of Land Grabbing in Contemporary Kenya," *Africa Today* 47, no. 1 (2000): 7–26; J. Muthuki, "Challenging Patriarchal Structures: Wangari Maathai and the Green Belt Movement in Kenya," *Agenda: Empowering Women for Gender Equity* 69 (2006): 82–91.

86. See, for example, Food and Agriculture Organization of the United Nations (FAO) and Center for International Forestry Research, *Forests and Floods: Drowning in Fiction or Thriving on Facts*, 2005, http://www.fao.org/3/a-ae929e.pdf, and C. J. A. Bradshaw, N. S. Sodhi, K. S.-H. Peh, and B. W. Brook, "Global Evidence that Deforestation Amplifies Flood Risk and Severity in the Developing World," *Global Change Biology* 13, no. 11 (2007): 2379–95.

87. J. Cochrane, "Southeast Asia, Choking on Haze, Struggles for a Solution," *New York Times*, October 8, 2015.

88. R. Butler, "Indonesia Bans Peatland Destruction," Mongabay.com, November 10, 2015, https://news.mongabay.com/2015/11/indonesia-bans-peatlands-destruction.

89. D. Chiaretti, "Nobre liga a seca em SP com desmatamento de florestas na Amazônia," *Valor Economico*, October 31, 2014; A. Nobre, "The Future Climate of Amazonia: Scientific Assessment," São José dos Campos SP, Brazil, 2014, http://www.ccst.inpe.br/wp-content/uploads/2014/11/The_Future_Climate_of_Amazonia_Report.pdf.

90. C. M. Stickler et al., "Dependence of Hydropower Energy Generation on Forests in the Amazon Basin at Local and Regional Scales," *Proceedings of the National Academy of Sciences* 110, no. 23 (2013): 9601–6.

91. Sergei Soares, personal communication, December 15, 2015. See also J. Watts, "Will Brazil Elect Marina Silva as the World's First Green President?" *The Guardian*, August 30, 2014.

92. Kompas.com, "Perhutani Ekspor Air Minum ke Jepang," *Kompas*, December 7, 2014, nasional.kompas.com/read/2011/12/07/0341365/Perhutani.Ekspor.Air.Minum.ke.Jepang.

93. Perhutani, "Company Profile," http://perhutani-commerce.co.id/profile.php, last modified 2016.

94. Davies, "The Indonesia-Australia Forest Carbon Partnership: A Murder Mystery."

95. S. B. Yudhoyono, "Intervention by H. E. Dr. Susilo Bambang Yudhoyono, President of the Republic of Indonesia on Climate Change," Forest Climate Center, September 25, 2009, http://forestclimatecenter.org/files/2009-09-25%20Intervention%20by%20President%20SBY%20on%20Climate%20Change%20at%20the%20G-20%20Leaders%20Summit.pdf, 2.

96. Ibid.

97. Dharmasaputra and Wahyudi, "The Impact of Payment-for-Performance Finance."

98. Abranches, "The Political Economy of Deforestation in Brazil."

99. Ibid.

100. Ibid.

101. Ibid.

102. Ibid.

103. Ibid.

104. Streck, "The Impacts of International REDD+ Finance," 9.

105. N. Kishor et al., "The Political Economy of Decision-Making in Forestry: Using Evidence and Analysis for Reform," Program on Forests Working Paper, 2015, http://profor.info/sites/profor.info/files/docs/PROFOR_WrkingPaper_PoliticalEconomy.pdf, 47.

106. "Home Depot, Lowe's Selling Illegal Wood from Papua New Guinea," Mongabay.com, March 23, 2006, http://news.mongabay.com/2006/03/home-depot-lowes-selling-illegal-wood-from-papua-new-guinea-report/; Global Witness, "In the Future, There Will Be No Forests Left," 2012, https://www.globalwitness.org/sites/default/files/hsbc-logging-briefing-gw.pdf.

107. D. Boucher, "How Brazil Has Dramatically Reduced Deforestation," *Solutions Journal*, 2014.

108. Abranches, "The Political Economy of Deforestation in Brazil," 32.

109. Greenpeace, "Down to Zero: How Greenpeace Is Ending Deforestation in Indonesia, 2003–2013 and Beyond," 2013, http://www.greenpeace.org/international/Global/international/publications/forests/2013/Down-To-Zero.pdf, 53.

110. Indonesian Palm Oil Pledge, http://www.palmoilpledge.id/wp-content/uploads/2015/09/IPOP_ExecutedPledgeAddendum.pdf, 2.

111. See Biofilica (http://www.biofilica.com.br/) and Katingan (http://www.katinganproject.com/).

112. F. Seymour and N. Dubash, *The Right Conditions: The World Bank, Structural Adjustment, and Forest Policy Reform*, World Resources Institute, 2000; M. Brockhaus and M. Di Gregorio, "National REDD+ Policy Networks: From Cooperation to Conflict," *Ecology and Society* 19, no. 4 (2014).

113. Kishor et al., "The Political Economy of Decision-Making in Forestry," 8.

114. J. Meadowcroft, "Climate Change Governance," Policy Research Working Paper 4941, World Bank, 2009, 12.

115. Brockhaus and Di Gregorio, "National REDD+ Policy Networks."

116. Abranches, "The Political Economy of Deforestation in Brazil," 22.

117. N. Birdsall, B. Savedoff, and F. Seymour, "The Brazil-Norway Agreement with Performance-Based Payments for Forest Conservation: Successes, Challenges, and Lessons," CGD Brief, Center for Global Development, Washington, DC, 2014.

118. Abranches, "The Political Economy of Deforestation in Brazil."

119. Dharmasaputra and Wahyudi, "The Impact of Payment-for-Performance Finance."

120. C. Luttrell et al., "The Political Context of REDD+ in Indonesia: Constituencies for Change," *Environmental Science and Policy* 35 (2012): 67–75.

121. LTS International, "Real-Time Evaluation of Norway's International Climate and Forests Initiative."

122. Seymour et al., "The Indonesia-Norway REDD+ Agreement."

123. Republic of Indonesia, Cabinet Secretariat, "President Jokowi Establishes Peat Land Restoration Agency," January 14, 2016, http://setkab.go.id/en/president-jokowi-establishes-peat-land-restoration-agency-brg/.

124. M. Brockhaus, K. Korhonen-Kurki, J. Sehring, and M. Di Gregorio, "Policy Progress with REDD+ and the Promise of Performance-Based Payments: A Qualitative Comparative Analysis of 13 Countries," CIFOR Working Paper 196, Center for International Forestry Research, Bogor, Indonesia, 2015.

125. K. Ellis, A. Cambray, and A. Lemma, "Drivers and Challenges for Climate Compatible Development," Climate and Development Knowledge Network Working Paper, 2013.

126. Abranches, "The Political Economy of Deforestation in Brazil."

127. Brockhaus and Di Gregorio, "National REDD+ Policy Networks," 10.

128. K. Korhonen-Kurki et al., "Enabling Factors for Establishing REDD+ in a Context of Weak Governance," *Climate Policy* 14 (2014):

167–86. The twelve countries were Bolivia, Brazil, Burkina Faso, Cameroon, Democratic Republic of Congo, Indonesia, Nepal, Papua New Guinea, Peru, Mozambique, Tanzania, and Vietnam.

129. Brockhaus et al., "REDD+, Transformational Change and the Promise of Performance-Based Payments: A Qualitative Comparative Analysis," *Climate Policy* 0 (2016): 1–14. Ethiopia and Guyana were added to the original twelve countries studied, and Bolivia was removed.

130. Birdsall et al., "The Brazil-Norway Agreement with Performance-Based Payments."

131. Abranches, "The Political Economy of Deforestation in Brazil," 7.

132. Ibid., 9.

133. Ibid.

134. Birdsall et al., "The Brazil-Norway Agreement with Performance-Based Payments."

135. Dharmasaputra and Wahyudi, "The Impact of Payment-for-Performance Finance," 34.

136. Ibid.

137. Seymour et al., "The Indonesia-Norway REDD+ Agreement."

138. LTS International, "Real-Time Evaluation of Norway's International Climate and Forests Initiative," 270.

139. Seymour et al., "The Indonesia-Norway REDD+ Agreement."

140. See Government of Guyana, "Low Carbon Development Strategy," http://www.lcds.gov.gy/, last modified 2016.

141. Laing, "The Impacts of International REDD+ Finance," 7.

142. Abranches, "The Political Economy of Deforestation in Brazil," 13.

143. A. Purnomo, *Protecting Our Forests: Moratorium on Forests and Peatlands, A Radical Policy* (Jakarta: Kepustakaan Populer Gramedia, 2012); Seymour et al., "The Indonesia-Norway REDD+ Agreement."

144. Laing, "The Impacts of International REDD+ Finance," 16.

145. Government of Liberia official, personal communication, September 2015.

146. Brockhaus et al., "Policy Progress with REDD+," 17.

147. Ibid.

148. Johns, "The Impacts of International REDD+ Finance: DRC Case Study," 17–18.

149. Ibid., 10.

150. Ibid., 8.

151. Bauche, "The Impacts of International REDD+ Finance: Mexico Case Study."

152. W. D. Sunderlin et al., "REDD+ at a Critical Juncture: Assessing the Limits of Polycentric Governance for Achieving Climate Change Mitigation," *International Forestry Review* 17, no. 4 (2015): 400–413.

153. Governors' Climate and Forests Task Force, "Rio Branco Declaration: Building Partnerships & Securing Support for Forests, Climate and Livelihoods," Rio Branco, Brazil, August 11, 2014, http://www.gcftaskforce.org/documents/2014_annual_meeting/GCF_2014_RioBrancoDeclaration_26_Members_EN.PDF, 2.

154. Interview quoted in T. Pistorius and L. Kiff, "The Politics of German Finance for REDD+," CGD Working Paper 390, Center for Global Development, Washington, DC, 2014.

155. J. Vit, "Under Government Pressure, Palm Oil Giants Disband Green Pledge," Mongabay.com, July 1, 2016, https://news.mongabay.com/2016/07/under-government-pressure-palm-oil-giants-disband-green-pledge/.

Rainforest foliage creates a dense mosaic of greens.

Credit: Barbra Brands/Shutterstock

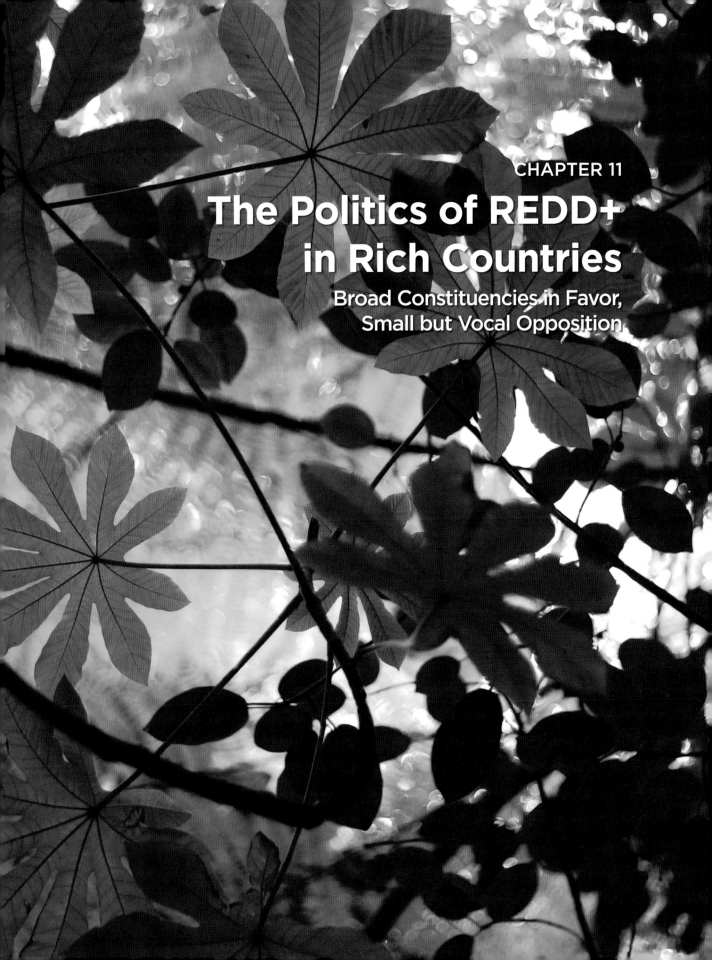

CHAPTER 11

The Politics of REDD+ in Rich Countries

Broad Constituencies in Favor, Small but Vocal Opposition

O *slo, Norway, 2007.* On September 27, 2007, the leaders of two environmental NGOs in Norway—both named Lars—sent a letter to their government that would have global ramifications.[1] Lars Løvold, head of Rainforest Foundation Norway, and Lars Haltbrekken, head of the Norwegian Society for the Conservation of Nature/Friends of the Earth Norway, had discerned a window of opportunity to take advantage of the domestic politics of climate change in a way that would result in a windfall for tropical forests under the emerging rubric of REDD+.[2]

A long-simmering political dilemma in Norwegian climate policy was becoming acute. Aside from a few parliamentary skirmishes in the 1990s, when environmental NGOs and political parties from the left and center advocated for more ambitious actions to address climate change, the issue had not boiled over. But in 2006 and 2007, in Norway as in other countries, the release of the Stern Review and the Intergovernmental Panel on Climate Change Fourth Assessment Report combined with other factors to push the issue of climate change higher on the political agenda.

Norway's greenhouse gas emissions were rising, especially from oil and gas, the nation's most important economic sector. Virtual self-sufficiency in hydroelectric power, and the already substantial emission reductions

from heavy industry, meant no cheap and easy opportunities were left for further cuts.

Prime Minister Jens Stoltenberg, an economist who chaired the pro-industry Labour Party, had long been a proponent of emissions trading and other "flexible mechanisms" under the United Nations Framework Convention on Climate Change (UNFCCC) that would enable substituting less costly reductions abroad for more painful cuts at home. But in his New Year's Day speech on January 1, 2007, the prime minister instead announced a major effort to develop commercially viable carbon capture and storage (CCS) technology as Norway's gift to the world; and when, in June, Stoltenberg's coalition government released a draft "white paper" on climate policy, the opposition parties disparaged it as too weak.

In this setting, "Lars & Lars"[3] made their move. In their September letter addressed to Stoltenberg and key ministers, they proposed Norway foot the bill for 10 percent of the estimated annual costs of reducing emissions from deforestation worldwide, or about $1 billion. The letter highlighted forest conservation as a cost-effective option for reducing emissions that was available now. It also touched on the co-benefits of protecting biodiversity, reducing poverty, and increasing adaptation capacity, all of which would be consistent with Norway's international development objectives. As a clincher, the letter pointed to Norway's moral obligation to act on climate change in light of the oil exports that were the source of the country's wealth.

The NGO leaders amplified the letter's message through the media, parliamentary hearings, and meetings with government officials. Especially effective in lending credi-

This chapter draws heavily on six background papers on the politics of REDD+ finance in rich countries: on Australia by Robin Davies; on Germany by Till Pistorius and Laura Kiff; on Norway by Erlend Hermansen and Sjur Kasa; on the United Kingdom by Kate Dooley and Charlie Parker; on the United States by Michael Wolosin and Donna Lee; and on California by Jesse Lueders, Cara Horowitz, Ann Carlson, Sean B. Hecht, and Edward A. Parson.

bility to their proposal was involving visitors from Brazilian civil society and government agencies, including Minister of Environment Marina Silva, in such meetings.

In November, leaders from opposition parties coalesced around the idea of a parliamentary "climate settlement"—an idea floated back in January by Lars Haltbrekken. When the opposition prepared its response to the government's white paper, the Conservative Party picked up on the NGOs' rainforest idea, and proposed 2 billion kroner (then about $368 million) in annual funding. Not to be outdone, the Liberal Party proposed 3 billion kroner, the figure eventually accepted by the government. Proponents overcame misgivings in the Labour Party and the conservative Ministry of Finance by funding the initiative from growth in the aid budget, which was increasing along with the soaring Norwegian economy as part of Norway's commitment to allocate 1 percent of gross national income to overseas development assistance. The results-based approach embodied in Reducing Emissions from Deforestation and Forest Degradation (REDD+) appealed to Labour and the ministry, as well.

The rapid gestation process sparked by the NGO letter culminated with Stoltenberg's dramatic announcement at the December 2007 UNFCCC conference in Bali of a commitment to REDD+ of $2.5 billion over five years. Broad domestic support for a Norwegian response to the challenge of climate change, combined with constraints on action at home, had given birth to Norway's International Climate and Forests Initiative (NICFI), often referred to as the "Rainforest Billions."

The story of the birth of NICFI illustrates several dynamics behind political support in a few rich countries for financing tropical forest conservation as a strategy for mitigating the emissions that cause climate change. The purpose of this chapter is to illuminate those dynamics and to describe how the politics of commitments to REDD+ finance have played out in selected donor countries.

The chapter draws on insights from six case studies commissioned for this book, covering the five countries and one U.S. state that have been most prominent as actual or prospective sources of REDD+ finance: Australia, Germany, Norway, the United Kingdom, the United States, and the state of California. The analysis yields three key conclusions:

- International cooperation to conserve tropical forests appeals to a broad range of constituencies in rich countries. These include civil society interests in conserving biological and cultural diversity and private sector interests in reducing the costs of climate action and maintaining the competitiveness of domestic products that substitute for those associated with tropical deforestation.
- The promise of REDD+ as an effective climate mitigation strategy and the attractiveness of payment-for-performance approaches have provided compelling rationales to increase substantially international forest finance in selected countries.
- Organized opposition to REDD+ in rich countries has been limited to a small but vocal set of activists who have broader objections to carbon markets and concerns about the adverse impacts that putting a price on forest carbon may have on forest peoples and vulnerable ecosystems in developing countries.

The chapter is organized as follows. First, we inventory the sources of long-standing support in rich countries for forest conservation in developing countries. Next, we describe how such support—and its translation into financial commitments—has been augmented by the linkage of deforestation to climate change, with particular reference to Australia and Norway. We further note the political attractiveness of payment-for-performance approaches and how more recent corporate commitments to deforestation-free supply chains have created new constituencies for government action. We then analyze sources of opposition to REDD+, with a particular focus on controversy over the inclusion of forest carbon offsets in the state of California's cap-and-trade program.

Finally, we provide a transition to the next chapter on REDD+ finance by explaining why, despite its broad ramifications, the politics of the issue has tended to play out within the confines of a small circle of experts in each donor country. The low profile of financing tropical forest conservation as a climate protection strategy contrasts with the prominent political debates that have focused on other emission mitigation options. Whether or not the 2015 Paris Agreement—which directly and indirectly highlights the role of forests in achieving climate goals—will lead to greater political attention to REDD+ in industrialized country capitals remains to be seen.

Rich-Country Constituencies for Tropical Forest Conservation

"Saving the rainforest"—at least if that forest is in another country—tends not to be contro-versial among voters in industrialized countries. Indeed, public and political support for tropical forest conservation was widespread long before deforestation was linked to climate change. Drawing on case studies of Australia, Germany, Norway, the United Kingdom, and the United States, the following sections summarize some of the sources of that support.

The Importance of Domestic and Colonial Forest Histories

The role of forests in the histories of many rich countries underpins public support for tropical forest conservation. In countries such as Finland and Sweden, proud traditions of sustainable forest management at home motivate a desire to share expertise abroad. Elsewhere, colonial ties to tropical countries have served as a precursor to international cooperation related to forest conservation. As described in the opening of chapter 9, British concern about tropical deforestation emerged in the middle of the nineteenth century with the nation's focus on colonial India. French commercial and scientific interests in West and Central Africa's forests dating to the colonial period continue to the present.

In several donor countries, the establishment of national forest management systems and expertise that serve as a basis for international cooperation was preceded by one or more episodes of severe forest resource depletion at home. Rules about how to manage the forests of France were codified in 1669 in response to centuries of overexploitation.[4] Japan, also in the late seventeenth century, responded to a "forest crisis" by improving the management of secondary forests and establishing plantations to meet the demand for wood.[5]

In the United States today, larger-than-life statues of the mythical lumberjack Paul Bunyan and Babe, his blue ox, loom over crossroads in small towns from North Carolina to Oregon, reminding motorists of the role of forests in American history as a frontier for agricultural expansion. In the early 1960s and 1970s, following the forest devastation incurred during the Korean War, the Republic of Korea mobilized public participation in a massive reforestation program that established tree planting as a patriotic duty.[6] Norwegians' utilitarian view of their forests was revealed in 2011, when a book on chopping, stacking, and drying firewood became a runaway hit, and in 2015 the English translation reached second place on bestseller lists in the United Kingdom.[7]

But as described by forest policy experts Till Pistorius and Laura Kiff, it is perhaps in Germany where the psychological weight of a country's own domestic and international forest histories and cultural affinity to forests most powerfully combines with contemporary concerns about climate change to animate development cooperation today.[8] Forests figure prominently in German literature, fairy tales, music, and art. These cultural expressions are informed by German society's two experiences in overcoming forest loss.

The first German "forestry crisis" took place in the aftermath of the Thirty Years' War (1618–48). Rapid economic recovery and population growth in Germany during the latter half of the seventeenth century resulted in the depletion of forest resources.[9] In particular, the need for timber and fuelwood to support mining for silver and the smelting of ores decimated forests at increasing distances from the mines, leading to shortages that threatened the livelihoods of thousands of miners.[10] Amid these circumstances, Hanns Carl von Carlowitz, son of a forest master, became the royal chief officer for mining in the Saxonian Ore Mountains. Among his responsibilities was ensuring the timber supply. His 1713 book, *Sylvicultura Oeconomica*, was the first treatise on the management of forests for sustainable yield.[11]

Building on Carlowitz's approach, Germany took the lead in developing the science and practice of sustainable forest management, which had a lasting effect on the forestry profession throughout the world. When the British became concerned about deforestation in the empire, they turned to German foresters to introduce scientific forest management. In 1856, they recruited Dietrich Brandis to manage the teak forests in a part of what is now Myanmar and, in 1864, appointed him the first inspector general of forests for the government of India.[12] Brandis became known as the "father of tropical forestry."

But back home in Germany, wood shortages faced by emerging industry and local populations persisted until coal replaced wood as a source of energy.[13] Ironically, the large-scale use of coal set the stage for Germany's more recent forest crisis. By the 1980s, it became apparent that acid rain was affecting large areas of German forest. This so-called *Waldsterben* (forest death) led to a mobilization of public concern and policy measures to overcome the problem. Legislation imposing strict regulation of sulfur dioxide emissions was passed over industry objections in 1983, when the issue featured in the national election that saw the rise of the Green Party, and was successful.[14] The German response to the *Waldsterben* crisis illustrates the extent to which valuation of forests had gone beyond the sustainable yield of timber to encompass a broader range of ecosystem services in the twentieth century.

In interviews conducted by Pistorius and Kiff in 2014, German forestry experts consistently referred to the German "special relationship" with forests as a source of support for REDD+ finance.[15] Public awareness of the value of forests for timber and ecosystem services, both locally and globally, combined with pride in the nation's achievements in overcoming domestic deforestation crises and a sense of responsibility for helping address global climate change to shape Germany's robust commitments to funding and the provision of technical support for REDD+.

A Desire to Protect Biological and Cultural Diversity

In addition to having a broad-based public affinity for forest protection based on domestic or colonial histories, rich countries host specific constituencies for engaging in tropical forest protection. Among the most visible are civil society organizations whose missions focus on biodiversity and/or cultural preservation. A fascination with the people and wildlife of the "jungle" has predisposed the public in rich countries to be supportive of international cooperation related to tropical forests, providing fertile ground for the fundraising and advocacy efforts of such organizations.

Tropical plants and animals have long captured the imaginations of scientists and the broader public in temperate latitudes. Although the habitat of the giant panda—featured in the logo of the World Wide Fund for Nature (WWF) since its founding in 1961[16]—is now limited to mountainous bamboo forests in central China, many of the other charismatic species used to draw popular attention in rich countries to conservation issues—toucans and jaguars in Latin America, chimpanzees and gorillas in Africa, tigers and orangutans in Asia—are found in tropical forests.

In nineteenth century England, the proceedings of natural history societies dominated by "gentlemen amateurs" included "long descriptive accounts of the flora and fauna of exotic and domestic locales."[17] In 1897, on the occasion of the Brussels international exhibition, Belgian King Leopold II constructed a special palace in Tervuren to showcase stuffed animals, live freshwater fish, and entire reconstructed villages from his new colony of the Congo. The popularity of the exhibit, visited by more than 1.2 million people, led the king to establish on the site a permanent museum focused on Central Africa.[18] Theodore Roosevelt, who as president had created the U.S. Forest Service in 1905, called American popular attention to tropical forests when he joined Brazilian Colonel Candido Rondon in 1913–14 on a scientific expedition to explore the River of Doubt, a tributary of the Amazon.[19]

The attraction of tropical forest themes in popular culture never really waned. Dozens of books and movies based on Edgar Rice Burroughs' creation Tarzan of the Apes—"one of the most popular fictional characters of all time"[20]—were enjoyed for decades in the twentieth century. A resurgence of interest in tropical forests in the 1980s, however—as described in the first chapter to this book—took place among rich-country constituencies who were captivated by their biological and cultural wealth.

In 1979, Norman Myers, a British biologist based in Kenya, published *The Sinking Ark: A New Look at the Problem of Disappearing Species*.[21] The book sounded the alarm about extinction, with a particular focus on the species richness of tropical forests and the threat posed to it by loss of habitat to economic development. Thomas Lovejoy, an American biologist whose research focused on the forests of the Amazon, is widely credited with coining the term "biological diversity" in 1980,[22] and, in 1985, Walter Rosen used the contraction "biodiversity" when planning a forum sponsored by the U.S. National Research Council.[23] *Biodiversity* was, in turn, used as the title of E. O. Wilson's edited volume of conference proceedings in 1988.[24]

Public concern was also sparked by the discovery of transcontinental impacts of tropical deforestation. In 1962, the U.S. environmental movement had been detonated by Rachel Carson's *Silent Spring*, a book documenting the decimation of bird populations from ingestion of the pesticide DDT. A generation later, in 1989, scientific articles began to appear that linked the decline in songbird populations in North America with the loss of winter habitat in tropical forests.[25]

Concern about the threat posed by tropical deforestation to cultural diversity, and the imperative of protecting the rights of indigenous peoples and other traditional forest communities in developing countries, also

came to the fore in the 1980s. Again, the interest rose on a foundation of previous events at home: in 1973, a violent confrontation between the American Indian Movement and the Federal Bureau of Investigation at Wounded Knee, South Dakota, had increased global public awareness of social injustice experienced by Native Americans.[26]

In the mid- to late 1980s, rising awareness of tropical deforestation led to the first efforts to address it. In 1987, Indonesian activist Emmy Hafild testified before the U.S. Congress about World Bank loans that had caused deforestation and harmed indigenous peoples, and, in 1988, Chico Mendes was assassinated in front of his home in Acre, Brazil, as described in chapter 7. Mendes, a poor rubber tapper, had risen to prominence as an effective activist who organized rubber tappers to resist deforestation caused by cattle ranchers clearing forests for pasture. In the year before his murder, Mendes had won international awards for his environmental protection efforts and traveled to the United States to speak about deforestation.[27]

Political support in rich countries for doing something to protect biodiversity and indigenous and traditional peoples from the ravages of deforestation (although the two objectives were not always linked) prompted allocations of development aid funds for tropical forest conservation. As described in chapter 9, a coalition of international organizations launched the ill-fated Tropical Forestry Action Plan (TFAP) in 1985, attracting support from more than 40 aid agencies and $1 billion in annual funding by 1988.[28] Although forest-related funding from some countries (notably Japan) dropped off significantly in later years, concern about tropical deforestation was sufficient to maintain a steady level of funding from some donors for the two decades until the link to climate change provided a new rationale for forest finance.

In the United States, for example, conservation of tropical forests, championed by U.S. nongovernmental organizations (NGOs) such as the World Wildlife Fund, drew bipartisan support. Amendments to the U.S. Foreign Assistance Act in 1986 made forest management and conservation an important part of the mission of the U.S. Agency for International Development (USAID). In addition, the 1998 Tropical Forest Conservation Act authorized "debt-for-nature" swaps as a way of generating conservation finance in developing countries that owed money to the U.S. government. These mandates translated into funding for activities related to tropical forests at a level averaging almost $100 million per year, regardless of which party held the White House or the most seats in Congress. In the fiscal year before the reframing of forestry assistance as a climate mitigation strategy in 2009, almost 90 percent of USAID's forest-related spending was thematically and geographically targeted toward biodiversity conservation.[29]

Germany's support for tropical forest conservation was similarly robust, and also strongly linked to concern about biodiversity. Funding for forestry-related investments and technical assistance as a part of German development cooperation has remained consistent over decades, through changing constellations among the four major political parties in government.[30] An uptick in Norwegian support for tropical forest conserva-

tion in the first decade of the 2000s, justified mostly on the grounds of biodiversity conservation, indigenous peoples' rights, and poverty reduction, preceded commitment of the "Rainforest Billions" focused on reducing climate emissions.[31]

Interest in Fighting Illegal Logging

As the twenty-first century began, concern about unfair competition from illegally or unsustainably produced wood products and growing consumer awareness began creating new constituencies in rich countries in support of improved forest management in developing ones. Legislation to restrict illegal imports—which was built on the addition of improved forest governance to the list of development assistance objectives—served the interests of domestic wood producers in donor countries. Coalitions linking environmental NGOs and industry associations in this common cause sometimes made for strange bedfellows in the political arena.

In September 2001, the first in a series of ministerial-level meetings on Forest Law Enforcement and Governance (FLEG) took place in Indonesia. With this conference, co-convened in Bali by the World Bank and attended by ministers of forestry from several developing countries, the previously taboo topic of illegal logging entered the official international discourse on tropical deforestation. A paper commissioned in preparation for the conference estimated that illegal logging was causing more than $10 billion in annual losses of public assets and revenues.[32]

The stage for the FLEG ministerials had been set by rich-country governments when they included illegal logging among five areas covered by the G8 Action Programme on Forests, which was agreed on at the Foreign Ministers' Meeting in the run-up to the 1998 summit hosted by the United Kingdom.[33] The action program and successor agreements have served as an umbrella for a wide range of bilateral and multilateral initiatives to improve transparency and combat illegal logging and trade in countries that produce tropical timber.[34]

Advocates for tropical forest conservation had long recognized the role of trade as a driver of deforestation. As described in chapter 8, rich-country consumers provide markets for low-cost tropical timber, as well as for commodities that replace forests to the detriment of price levels and market share enjoyed by domestically produced alternatives. In the 1990s, many conservationists focused their efforts on establishing a system for certifying timber as responsibly produced, with the hope that environmentally sensitive consumers would reward certified timber with price premiums and enhanced market share.

The idea of harnessing market forces through certification was hatched at a meeting that brought together civil society and industry representatives in California in 1990, and the Forestry Stewardship Council (FSC) was formally established at its first assembly in Toronto in 1993.[35] The FSC label now verifies the sustainability of one-sixth of the global industrial roundwood market, but, as described in chapter 7, only a small percentage of certified timber is from the tropics.[36]

Frustrated by the slow uptake of certification by producers in the tropics and the limited reward offered by rich-country markets for certified timber, in the early 2000s NGOs and timber industry interests joined forces to advocate the use of trade policy to stop imports of illegally harvested wood. Political scientist Benjamin Cashore dubbed this coalition an example of "bootleggers and Baptists," referring to an idea in regulatory economics named for a twentieth century alliance that was in favor of banning alcohol sales on Sundays, albeit for very different reasons.[37] Environmentalists in the new alliance were interested in protecting the rainforest abroad, while domestic producers were interested in protecting their markets at home.

The coalition was quite successful in translating its objectives into law and regulation in rich countries, and it often served as a catalyst for complementary allocations of development aid for implementation of legality initiatives in producer countries, as well. By 2003, the launch of the EU Action Plan for Law Enforcement, Governance, and Trade had added a "T" to "FLEG," in recognition of the complicity of consumer countries (as buyers of stolen goods) in tropical forest crime. Within ten years, enactment of the 2013 EU Timber Regulation made it a crime to import illegally produced timber into the European Union.[38] Over the same period, the action plan was accompanied by some €300 million in FLEGT-related grants to thirty-five producer countries.[39]

The United Kingdom was a particular leader in international initiatives focused on improving forest governance during this period. The UK Department for International Development (DfID) was a key player in ensuring followup to the 1998 G8 Summit and the development of EU initiatives to address illegal logging. From 1997 to 2010, under a center-left Labour government, reforming governance and securing the rights and livelihoods of forest communities became the guiding principles of DfID's work in the forestry sector. This rationale was sufficient to maintain funding for forests at an average of around 0.5 percent of official development assistance or £50 million per year, until climate change emerged as a new reason for investing in tropical forests.[40]

In the United States during this same period, a "President's Initiative Against Illegal Logging," launched in 2003, brought together U.S. government agencies, conservation-oriented NGOs, and industry associations to help countries such as Indonesia and Liberia combat illegal logging and related trade.[41] International efforts were soon complemented by domestic action, in part stimulated by a 2004 report commissioned by an industry group, the American Forest and Paper Association (AF&PA).[42] The Seneca Creek Associates report made headlines with startling claims about the extent of the global trade in illegal wood products.[43]

Efforts to restrict the import of illegal timber into the United States focused on amending the Lacey Act. Named after Congressman John Lacey of Iowa, the legislation was first enacted in 1900 with the primary purpose of banning interstate commerce in illegally hunted wildlife, especially insectivorous birds, whose feathers were then popular as women's clothing accessories.[44] Amendments passed in 2008 expanded the legislation's scope to make it illegal to import products made from wood that had been logged in violation of laws in the country of origin.[45] Backing from a coalition that included NGOs (led by the Environmental Investigation Agency), industry associations (led by the AF&PA), and labor unions made it easy for the legislation to attract bipartisan support in Congress.[46]

Meanwhile, forest-related industries in Australia were also growing increasingly concerned about being undercut by imports of illegal timber. In November 2006, the Australian Department of Agriculture, Fisheries, and Forestry published a discussion paper entitled "Bringing Down the Axe on Illegal Logging," which repeated a consultancy firm's estimate that some 9 percent—or A$400 million worth—of the country's forest product imports were suspected of being illegally sourced.[47] The report recommended Australia cooperate with exporting countries within the Asia-Pacific region to improve their sustainable forest management practices. Government action on reducing deforestation abroad could respond to the interests of domestic producers, as a complement to legislative action eventually taken with Australia's Illegal Logging Prohibition Act of 2012.[48]

Illegal logging has also been of concern in Japan, a major timber importer and host of the International Tropical Timber Organization (ITTO), where attention has been paid to the issue by environmental NGOs and the wood products industry periodically since the late 1990s. Internationally, Japan adopted high-profile leadership on the issue, launching the Asia Forest Partnership—a multi-stakeholder forum to discuss illegal logging and trade—as a signature initiative at the 2002 Rio Plus Ten Summit in Johannesburg.[49] The government response on the demand side, however, has been limited to encouraging industry participation in national programs, starting with the *Goho* ("legal") wood system, a voluntary scheme started in 2006 that allowed Japanese companies to demonstrate compliance with guidelines for ensuring legality through industry associations or even self-verification. In 2012, meetings of a Committee on Studying Forestry in Japan, convened at the behest of environmental NGOs, led to a campaign promise by the Liberal Democratic Party (then in opposition) to act on illegal logging by strengthening public procurement instruments.[50] In 2016, Japan promulgated an Act on the Promotion of Distribution and Use of Legally Logged Wood Products that encouraged private companies to register as complying with trading practices that meet government standards.[51]

In short, before the emergence of climate change mitigation as a compelling rationale for protecting tropical forests, donor countries had already committed significant financial resources and political attention to forest conservation initiatives. These initiatives drew on domestic and colonial forest histories and served various constituencies interested in conserving biological and cultural diversity, promoting good governance,and protecting domestic wood industries. Such support was uncontroversial, was championed by leaders and legislators from across the political spectrum, and was supported by NGOs and private sector interests alike.

Climate Mitigation: A New Rationale for Tropical Forest Finance

The recognition of the potential of tropical forests to provide a solution to climate change, starting around 2005, strengthened rich-country constituencies in support of international forest finance. The forests–climate linkage and negotiation toward a mechanism in which rich countries would pay developing ones for reduced emissions from deforestation and forest degradation layered an additional rationale on top of the longstanding and broad-based support for tropical forest conservation. Furthermore, many hoped the performance-based feature of REDD+ finance would lead to greater success than previous funding for reducing deforestation. The new justification both reenergized existing constituencies and brought new interests to the table to support funding for REDD+.

For some constituencies, the linkage to climate change served to deepen previously held positions. Conservation-oriented organizations in rich countries, already proponents of protecting topical forests, understood climate change as a new threat to the wildlife and landscapes on which their missions focused. They also recognized healthy forest ecosystems as a source of resilience to climate change. Organizations with projects underway in developing countries, such as The Nature Conservancy, World Wildlife Fund, and Conservation International in the United States, also saw in REDD+ a prospective source of new funding to advance their objectives. Such organizations have been among the most persistent voices in favor of funding for REDD+.

In some countries, the linkage between forests and climate change simply added another reason to a long list of reasons to support international cooperation to reduce deforestation. Where support for development assistance was strong, and concern about climate change was widespread, the alignment of political constituencies behind finance for REDD+ was relatively straightforward. In Germany, public awareness about the problem of climate change was high, as was a sense of responsibility for doing something about it. When fighting deforestation was framed as a contribution to combating climate change, public support and media attention helped further legitimize international forest finance.[52] In addition, Germany considered REDD+ investments as yielding biodiversity benefits and thus complementing its commitments under the Convention on Biological Diversity.[53]

But not all countries that had been traditional donors to the forestry sector put their weight behind REDD+. What were the influential factors in those countries that did do so, or came close to doing so, such as the United States? Table 11.1 summarizes those

Table 11.1: Factors that Supported REDD+ Finance 2007-2010: Highlights from Case Studies of Selected Rich Countries

	Australia	Germany	Norway	United Kingdom	United States (Federal)	United States (California)
Financing Instrument	GIFC	Various	NICFI	Various	Various, including international forest offsets proposed in ACES legislation	Proposed international forest offsets in AB 32 legislation
Appeal of REDD+ Payment for Performance	Developing "incentive-based pilot approaches" a key component of initiative	Seen as potentially more effective than traditional aid and as an approach for achieving impact at scale	Attractive across the political spectrum	Consistent with increased emphasis on results in aid portfolio	Consistent with cost containment as a key issue in proposed legislation	Promoted as opportunity to demonstrate viability of mechanism to encourage forest protection
High-level Individual Champions	Parliamentary Secretary to Foreign Minister Greg Hunt, Prime Minister Kevin Rudd		Prime Minister Jens Stoltenberg, Environment/ Development Minister Erik Solheim, Finance Minister Kristin Halvorsen	HRH The Prince of Wales		Governor Arnold Schwarzenegger

	Australia	Germany	Norway	United Kingdom	United States (Federal)	United States (California)
Supportive NGO Advocacy			Rainforest Foundation Norway and FOE-Norway, supported by other environmental NGOs		NGO members of US Climate Action Partnership, Forest Carbon Dialogue, and Tropical Forest and Climate Coalition	The Nature Conservancy, Environmental Defense Fund, Conservation International
Business Engagement				Financial sector	Emissions intensive industry	Emissions intensive industry, carbon management and investment firms
Budget Space	Growing aid budget		Growing aid budget	Aid budget protected from austerity-driven cuts	Increasing climate budget, particularly for "fast-start finance"	
Partisan Politics	Coalition government sought advantage over Labour Party in 2007 elections		Social-democratic government and conservative opposition coalition competed on climate ambition		Democratic control of both houses of Congress and Presidency allowed climate ambition	
Public Awareness		Strong support for action on climate change and protecting forests	Strong support for action on climate change	Support for action on tropical rainforests cultivated by Prince's Rainforest Project		

Sources: Davies, "The Indonesia-Australia Forest Carbon Partnership"; Pistorius and Kiff, "The Politics of German Finance for REDD+"; Hermansen and Kasa, "Climate Policy Constraints"; Dooley and Parker, "Evolution of Finance"; Wolosin and Lee, "US Support for REDD+"; Lueders et al., "The California REDD+ Experience."

Note: Table includes positive factors only; an empty cell connotes factor not highlighted in case studies, and not necessarily absence of the factor.

highlighted in the case studies commissioned for this book of the politics of REDD+ finance in selected rich countries.[54]

The Imperative for Climate Action and the Prospect of Cheap Emission Offsets

In some countries, the prospect of cheap emission offsets from tropical forests as a response to the imperative for climate action was a powerful supplement to more altruistic motives for funding conservation efforts abroad, and it created new public and private sector constituencies. Government ministries and legislators seeking financially feasible and politically palatable solutions to climate change found REDD+ attractive, as did private companies that might face new regulations on emissions or that sought to profit from new carbon markets. New motives for maintaining developing-country forests as stores of carbon now eclipsed colonial-era interests in extracting tropical timber.

> The prospect of cheap emission offsets was a powerful supplement to more altruistic motives for funding conservation efforts abroad.

The Stern Review of the economics of climate change, commissioned by the UK government and published in late 2006 (as described in chapter 1), had a powerful impact on thinking in many donor-country capitals, especially in its conclusion that low-cost reductions in emissions from deforestation were key to any strategy to address climate change.[55] If, as elaborated by political scientist Robert Keohane, the framing of climate change as a problem that imposes the costs of mitigation on current voters leads to a bias toward inaction, then a framing that includes cheaper international action could do the opposite.[56] And, indeed, where domestic emission cuts would be expensive, the potential of forests to provide low-cost offsets was a key driver of political interest in helping tropical countries reduce deforestation by allowing governments to show leadership on climate change at lower domestic cost.

First to act on this interest was Australia. In March 2007, the conservative government of Prime Minister John Howard surprised audiences at home and abroad by announcing a Global Initiative on Forests and Climate (GIFC).[57] With a budget of A\$200 million, the initiative was, at the time, the largest commitment by a donor country to what would come to be known as REDD+. A joint press release by Australia's ministers of environment and foreign affairs stated that the GIFC would "pilot approaches to providing real financial incentives to countries and communities to encourage sustainable use . . . and reduce destruction of forests."[58]

Domestic and international politics were aligned to support Australia's initiative. In 2006, the Howard government had begun exploring the feasibility of a domestic carbon market as a way to reduce climate emissions. Greg Hunt, who as parliamentary secretary to the foreign minister helped shape the GIFC, had coauthored a university thesis on emissions trading.[59] Including inexpensive international offsets in such a market was an attractive option for lowering the overall cost of reductions due to the high cost of domestic emission abatement options. A Task Group on Emissions Trading commissioned by the prime minister supported the international offsets approach and observed that, by demonstrating offset methodologies, "Australia would be well positioned to influence the evolution of international rules in this area in a direction that would provide a positive incentive for engagement by developing countries." The task group's report highlighted the particular importance of including trade in avoided deforestation.[60]

A political benefit was also possible: by being seen to exercise leadership on the forests and climate agenda, the coalition government could inoculate itself from the opposition Labor Party's use of the environment as a wedge issue to attract green votes in the election scheduled for later in 2007. Itself a nation with rainforests, Australia in the early 2000s was bitterly divided over the logging of old-growth forests in Tasmania, an issue Prime Minister Howard had faced in the run-up to the 2004 elections.[61]

In parallel, the leader of the Labor Party, Kevin Rudd, commissioned an Australian version of the Stern Review by economist Ross Garnaut. The resulting Garnaut Climate Change Review, published in 2008 after Rudd had become prime minister in a new Labor government, strongly endorsed the aims of the coalition government's forest and climate initiative.[62] The Rudd government continued the initiative virtually unchanged but gave greater emphasis to its relevance to UNFCCC negotiations.[63]

In the United Kingdom, the link to climate change led to a "huge rise in prominence of forests on the political agenda."[64] London's financial sector, interested in the prospect of new business in the trading of forest carbon credits, emerged as a new constituency. The political standing of forests in the run-up to the 2009 climate negotiations in Copenhagen was greatly enhanced by the patronage of Prince Charles. The Prince's Rainforests Project (now part of the International Sustainability Unit of the Prince of Wales's Charitable Foundation) convened a series of high-profile meetings among politicians, financiers, celebrities, and religious leaders that "cemented views in the U.K. that tropical forest loss was a critical issue of immediate urgency."[65] Funding for forests was singled out as a separate pillar of the UK's £800 million International Climate Fund, announced in 2007, alongside the pillars for more general approaches to climate change mitigation and adaptation.[66]

As for the United States, when climate change legislation was being debated in Congress in 2009, "cost was arguably *the* single most important concern of legislators in the political center whose votes would determine the eventual outcome."[67] The potential of international forest offsets to limit the costs of emission abatement efforts also attracted the interest and support of powerful private sector constituencies in favor of the legislation. Large power companies with huge emission profiles, such as American Electric Power and Duke Energy, were very supportive of including international offsets in the climate legislation being debated in 2009–10. They were specifically supportive of REDD+ and influential when they decided to deploy their political clout in its favor.[68] When $74 million of USAID funding was earmarked to help develop capacity in forest countries, one of the six criteria for determining geographical focus was the potential of a particular country or subnational jurisdiction to participate eventually in REDD+ carbon markets.[69]

The Appeal of Payment for Performance

The fact that REDD+ finance was to be based on results increased its political appeal, whether such finance was to be provided from public funds or from carbon markets. An inconvenient truth was that prior decades of donor funding for tropical forest conservation had failed to affect demonstrably the trajectory of deforestation. The resilience of such support in light of the limited evidence of its effectiveness is striking, but the possibility of paying only for results provided a much-needed freshening up of the case for international forest finance.

German development professionals, for example, are proud of the long and deep relationships with developing countries nurtured over three decades of cooperation in the forestry sector. But even they recognized that the limited success of their efforts in actually reversing deforestation required a shift to a results-based logic as a rationale for continued support. According to Till Pistorius and Laura Kiff, "This inherent paradigm change towards performance-based payments generated new enthusiasm and support by many key actors in Germany."[70]

In some countries, the payment-for-performance feature of REDD+ was helpful in the wake of the 2008 global financial crisis, when new claims on development assistance budgets came under particular scrutiny. Even in the United Kingdom, where DfID's budget was one of the few government accounts to be protected from cuts, the atmosphere of austerity led to "an increased appetite across government for a more results-based approach to aid."[71]

In the United States, prospects for large-scale REDD+ finance rested on the American Clean Energy and Security Act. The so-called Waxman-Markey bill, which passed the House of Representatives in June 2009, would have provided demand for up to 1.5 billion tons of CO_2 offsets from forest-based emission reductions annually, plus separate funding from auctions of emission allowances of about $3 billion a year.[72] The REDD+ provisions were part of the legislation's broader objective to address climate change though a national cap-and-trade system. The results-based finance included in the bill for reducing emissions from forests would have been aligned with an emerging focus on results in U.S. development aid that spanned the administrations of George W. Bush and Barack Obama.[73] Furthermore, the payment-for-performance approach would appeal to fiscal conservatives.[74]

Waxman-Markey drew support from an unusual coalition known as the U.S. Climate Action Partnership (USCAP), which united big business CEOs with environmental NGOs; its 2009 Blueprint for Legislative Action recommended incentives to reduce emissions from deforestation.[75] Nevertheless, hopes that the United States would be a major source of REDD+ finance were dashed in July 2010, when the bill failed to move in the Senate.

According to political scientist Theda Skocpol, the "insider bargaining" strategy pursued by USCAP—akin to the "bootleggers and Baptists" approach that was successful in amending the Lacey Act —was no longer viable in the increasingly polarized U.S. political landscape.[76] Mobilization of the "Tea Party" faction within the Republican Party proved fatal to any prospect of bipartisan compromise on environmental issues in general[77] and, likely, with respect to climate change and international cooperation in particular. In Skocpol's view, changing the politics of climate change in the United States would require a counter mobilization of popular support from the center-left, with deeper public understanding of the issue and coordination by national-level advocates with state and local organizations.[78]

Thus, large-scale REDD+ finance from the United States fell victim to the broader politics of climate change and international cooperation. As described by policy expert Michael Wolosin and former REDD+ negotiator for the United States Donna Lee,

> Advocates in Washington glumly observe that, in some corners of Congress at least, "international climate finance" is a phrase with three dirty words put together. It touches on international transfers (some believe the United States cannot afford to send money abroad when there are domestic needs), climate change (some do not believe it is happening, or is beneficial, or is not a priority), and spending (in a tight and limited budget environment).[79]

Reflecting longstanding skepticism regarding sending taxpayer dollars overseas, the conservative newspaper *The Washington Times* characterized the Waxman-Markey bill with the headline, "Bill gives billions to save trees in other nations."[80]

The country that actually *did* decide to "give billions to save trees in other nations" was Norway, as the altruistic motives of civil society leaders and political interest in low-cost emission reductions came together in a dramatic and unexpected way, with NGOs playing a catalytic role.

Norway's Rainforest Billions

As described in the opening of this chapter, Norwegian prime minister Jens Stoltenberg made headlines during the 2007 climate talks in Bali by pledging an eye-popping $2.5 billion over five years to reduce tropical deforestation.[81] Since then, Norway has remained the multi-billion-dollar gorilla when it comes to putting money on the table for mitigating climate emissions from tropical deforestation. Through 2014, as illustrated in figure 11.1, Norway's pledges to REDD+ surpassed those of the next nine countries combined.

Although Lars Løvold and his colleagues at Rainforest Foundation Norway had been raising public awareness of rainforest issues since the organization's founding in 1989, Norway had not previously been as prominent in the fight against tropical deforestation as countries such as Germany, the United Kingdom, and the United States. What domestic political factors aligned to precipitate Prime Minister Stoltenberg's bold pledge in Bali? And why, in contrast to Australian prime minister Howard's forests and climate initiative announced earlier in 2007 (described further in chapter 12), has the Norwegian commitment proved resilient to domestic and international setbacks?

According to political scientists Erlend Hermansen and Sjur Kasa, a number of factors came into play. First, public concern

Figure 11.1: Norway leads in pledges of REDD+ finance.

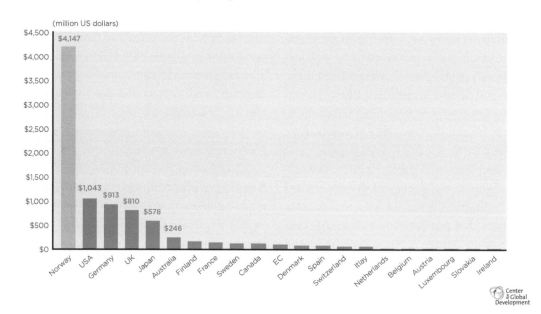

(million US dollars)

Norway $4,147, USA $1,043, Germany $913, UK $810, Japan $578, Australia $246

Center for Global Development

Source: REDD+ Partnership, "Voluntary REDD+ Database- Graphs & Stats," http://reddplusdatabase.org/#graphs_and_stats; M. Norman and S. Nakhooda, "The State of REDD+ Finance," CGD Working Paper 378, Center for Global Development, Washington, DC, 2014 (updated 2015), http://www.cgdev.org/publication/state-redd-finance-working-paper-378.

Note: Numbers current as of December 2014.

about climate peaked in 2007, feeding into a growing consensus in Norwegian society and politics regarding the need to take action on climate change. Norway's foreign policy was distinguished for its leadership on issues related to the protection of human rights and peacemaking, and avoiding the catastrophic impacts of climate change was emerging as a moral imperative. For the society of a major producer and exporter of oil, leadership on rainforest conservation met a need for a "political offset."[82]

The second factor was Norway's limited options for low-cost domestic emission reductions. Emission-intensive industries, particularly in the oil and gas sectors, are politically influential, and Norway had supported so-called "flexible mechanisms" to allow it to "do mitigation abroad" since the beginning of international climate negotiations under the UNFCCC. Rapid policy development on REDD+ following the 2005 proposal by the Coalition for Rainforest Nations at negotiations in Montreal (described in chapter 9) provided an attractive new opportunity for mitigation abroad by reducing emissions from tropical deforestation. Early investment was seen as building a bridge to a future global carbon market.

The third factor was the softness of Norway's budgetary constraints. A growing economy, combined with a target of 1 percent of gross national income for overseas development assistance, allowed the new rainforest commitment to be incorporated into growth in the aid budget, thus circumventing the fiscal conservatism of the largest political party and the Ministry of Finance.

The fourth factor was one of personalities. The forest and climate initiative enjoyed a strong proponent in Erik Solheim, who from 2007 was simultaneously playing the roles of minister of environment and minister of international development. The minister of finance, Kristin Halvorsen, also supported the initiative early on, and the prime minister himself, an economist who had been inspired by the analysis of the Stern Review, championed the idea. Also backing the initiative were the environmental spokespersons of three opposition parties, who proposed it as part of the policy package when they challenged the government to enter into a cross-party parliamentary climate settlement.

A fifth factor was the framing of the commitment as performance-based finance, which increased its palatability across the political spectrum. Erik Solheim has frequently commented that parliamentary support for the pledge was strongly enhanced by the payments' being contingent on results.

But without a sixth factor—the policy entrepreneurship on the part of NGOs, as described in the opening of this chapter—Norway's Rainforest Billions commitment would not have been realized. The importance of this factor provides just one example of how civil society constituencies have played an outsized role in the politics of REDD+ in key countries and at key moments. The advocacy of NGOs for the establishment

of the initiative in the first place helps explain the relative absence of domestic controversy over the program in Norway, even in the face of subsequent allegations of corruption and violations of land rights in the countries receiving financial support. In addition, observers speculate that the initiative's "very generous funding for civil society projects"—channeled through the Norwegian Agency for Development Cooperation (Norad), from which NGOs inside and outside Norway have benefited—might also have dampened criticism.[83]

In other countries, however, a small but vocal cadre of REDD+ skeptics has also been influential, as described below.

The Subsidiary and Insider Politics of REDD+

While the broader politics of climate change and development assistance has influenced the timing and amounts of donor-country commitments to REDD+, in no country apart from Norway has REDD+ funding per se risen to the level of a contested national political debate. In Norway, where rainforest conservation is a key element in a parliamentary climate settlement, parties initially competed to increase proposed funding levels.

The low profile of international forest finance as a climate mitigation strategy contrasts with political fights at the national level surrounding other mitigation options in rich countries, such as the phasing out of nuclear energy in Germany and the regulation of emissions from coal-fired power plants in the United States.[84] Indeed, despite the significant sums of money Germany has allocated to REDD+, discussion has been confined to an "experts' discourse," without attracting significant attention or criticism from the Parliament, the media, or academia.[85]

Instead, international cooperation related to forests has been subsidiary—and vulnerable—to broader political currents driving debates about climate change and international engagement. Although external events (such as climate change summits) have helped trigger donor pledges to REDD+, the amount and sustainability of funding has depended on the vagaries of domestic politics and budget constraints rather than global need.

In Australia, for example, the coalition parties elected in 2013 dismantled both the national emissions trading scheme and the national development assistance agency (AusAID), thus dimming the chances of renewed support from the first country to have made a major financial commitment to REDD+.[86] In Norway, the imperative to reallocate funding to deal with the refugee crisis in Europe in late 2015 against a backdrop of decreasing oil prices led to a minor cut in the budget for the climate and forests initiative.[87]

The lack of high-level political debate on REDD+ has meant that, with the partial exception of Norway, insider politics within and between government bureaucracies have determined the contours of REDD+ finance in terms of the specific objectives of investments, the vehicles through which funding has been channeled, and the geographical allocation of resources across countries. These politics have, for the most part, played out among a small group of protagonists in each donor country. In several instances the ambitions of ministries of environment wanting to deploy new forest finance in new ways have been tempered by the norms of aid agencies

bound by more traditional ways of programming funds. By creating a new Climate and Forests Secretariat under the Norwegian Ministry of Environment, NICFI was able to bypass the cautiousness and many of the norms of Norad.

We describe the process of the "aidification" of REDD+ finance in chapter 12.

Supply Chain Commitments Yield New Private Sector Constituencies

As described in chapter 9, the post-Copenhagen dropoff in expectations for large-scale, market-based climate finance dampened the initial enthusiasm for REDD+ as a potent tool to reduce tropical deforestation. No longer having interests at stake, private sector constituencies that had lobbied in favor of REDD+—including those seeking cheap emission offsets and those poised to make money from a market in forest carbon—disengaged. Their withdrawal left tropical forest conservation without strong private sector champions, especially in comparison to those enjoyed by other mitigation options, such as the deployment of renewable energy technologies.

At about the same time, however, advocacy groups in rich countries were realizing their strategies focused on restricting imports of illegal timber were being undercut by rising demand from emerging-market countries and a shift in the drivers of deforestation to commercial agriculture.[88] Disappointment in the slow pace of REDD+ and the limited scope of timber legality initiatives contributed to a change in focus among rich-country advocacy groups—and some donor agencies—from public sector reform to direct engagement with agents of forest loss in the private sector.

In chapter 8, we described how this civil society advocacy has prompted a wave of commitments to "no deforestation" by companies across the supply chains of commodities that put forests at risk. Realizing they are unlikely to be successful in meeting their commitments in the absence of governance reform, such companies have, in turn, become advocates for donor countries to invest in REDD+ finance.

In a June 2014 "call for action," for example, in the run-up to the 2015 Paris Climate Summit, the leaders of a broad coalition of manufacturers and retailers that had committed to achieving zero net deforestation in their supply chains by 2020 explicitly endorsed REDD+ finance. The statement by the board of the Consumer Goods Forum, which represents some four hundred companies, urged governments to make REDD+ "a priority for supporting appropriate local and national policies that protect forests and support livelihoods" and committed its members to working with governments and other stakeholders "to create funding mechanisms . . . that will incentivise and assist forested countries to conserve their natural assets."[89]

Such support was further reflected in the list of companies based in rich countries that signed onto the New York Declaration on Forests in September 2014; they included traders such as Cargill, manufacturers such as Johnson & Johnson, retailers such as Walmart, and financiers such as Barclays.[90] The declaration represented a convergence of public and private constituencies for reducing deforestation and recognized their interdependence in achieving that goal. Such recognition, however, has not yet translated into a willingness to go to bat for REDD+ finance in the national capitals of donor countries.

In the meantime, donor agencies began to broaden forests-and-climate finance to include complementary support for initiatives to rid commodity supply chains of deforestation. In 2012, the United Kingdom began developing a new facility, initiated in late 2014, to fund public–private partnerships to direct private investment toward sustainable land use.[91] Similarly, NICFI began to support organizations promoting public–private partnerships in REDD+ countries to break the link between commodity production and deforestation.[92]

Opposition to REDD+

As described in chapter 9, some developing countries voiced opposition to linking forests with climate change in international forums at various points during the evolution of REDD+. Many were concerned about the potential diluting effect of REDD+ on overall emission reduction efforts and/or possible infringements on national sovereignty, while Bolivia denounced it as the "commodification of nature."[93]

Within rich-country policy arenas, political opposition to REDD+ (which is ongoing) has, for the most part, been confined to a subset of the advocacy-oriented NGO community. A number of academics in industrialized countries published unfavorable articles about REDD+; however, among the countries covered by the case studies commissioned for this book, only in Australia was academic criticism highlighted as influential in national decision making. And while some elements of

"Forestry World" within donor governments resisted the takeover of "their" agenda by "Climate World," these debates played out within the insider politics to be described in chapter 12. Compared to other climate mitigation options, it's notable that REDD+ did not draw organized opposition from within government or from particular agricultural or industrial lobbies or labor unions.

Environment- and development-oriented NGOs in rich countries generally aligned with conservation organizations in promoting donor-country support for tropical forest conservation. But the coalition splintered when it came to the prospect of using financial incentives to promote tropical forest protection for many of the same reasons described in chapter 9, including disagreements about the role of carbon markets in reducing overall emissions and the risk of adverse social and environmental impacts from placing monetary value on forest carbon. The main lines of argument are summarized below.

Concerns about Carbon Markets

Environmental and social justice campaigners in donor countries have advanced two arguments against forest carbon markets. First, they have claimed the availability of cheap forest carbon credits will not lead to greater overall emission reductions than would otherwise occur. In other words, they do not trust lower cost will lead to increased overall climate ambition. The objection would apply to any offset mechanism, but opponents have highlighted what they believe to be particular risks to the "environmental integrity" of forest carbon markets, as described in chapter 4. They worry, for example, that politically defined reference levels and other sources of uncertainty described in chapter 9 will result in avoided emissions that are credited but not real. Chapter 9 summarizes the measures advanced in negotiations and other international forums to deal with these concerns.

Second, opponents have raised concerns about the vulnerability of forest carbon markets to fraud and manipulation. The idea of forest carbon transactions was tainted early on by a rash of sensational reports that "carbon cowboys" were swindling developing-country governments and local communities out of their rights to forest carbon. In June 2010, City of London police arrested Mike Foster, director of a firm called Carbon Harvesting Corporation, on bribery charges stemming from his pursuit of a 400,000-hectare carbon concession in Liberia on terms highly unfavorable to the Liberian government.[94] In 2012, *60 Minutes Australia* aired an expose of David Nilsson, a Queensland businessman who had convinced illiterate tribespeople in the Peruvian Amazon to sign away rights to their forests for two hundred years.[95] Such stories have provided rich fodder for anti-REDD+ activists and made donor governments nervous, although project-level scams by unscrupulous entrepreneurs are largely avoided when REDD+ is implemented by governments at jurisdictional scale.

Furthermore, in 2011, a consulting firm's study concluded that, due to design flaws, proposed forest carbon markets would be unacceptably risky, and they would, like other commodity markets, benefit traders rather than producers.[96] The study was picked up by NGO activists to support their arguments against financing REDD+ through carbon markets.[97]

Based on these concerns, many NGOs in the United Kingdom and other EU member states focused their advocacy efforts on EU climate policies, to ensure emission reduction targets do not include forest carbon offsets, and forest carbon credits are excluded from the EU Emissions Trading System (ETS).[98] Those efforts have been effective, and they have been made easier by the oversupply of emission allowances granted under the ETS and the collapse of the carbon price.[99]

In the United States, arguments that REDD+ "doesn't work" (in terms of actually reducing total emissions) have been influential in debates at the federal level, as well as at the state level in California (described below).[100] Figure 11.2 illuminates how conservation and environment NGOs in the United States have been positioned in climate policy debates across a spectrum, ranging from seeing REDD+ as an opportunity to seeing it as a risk.

Despite the differences in their positions on offsets, many such groups were able to reach a "negotiated détente" in the debate over the Waxman-Markey legislation in the form of a "Tropical Forest and Climate Unity Agreement," brokered by Avoided Deforestation Partners.[101] A few left-leaning groups, including Greenpeace and Friends of the Earth, did not join the agreement, as their oppo-

Figure 11.2: The bulk of American environmental groups have seen REDD+ as an opportunity.

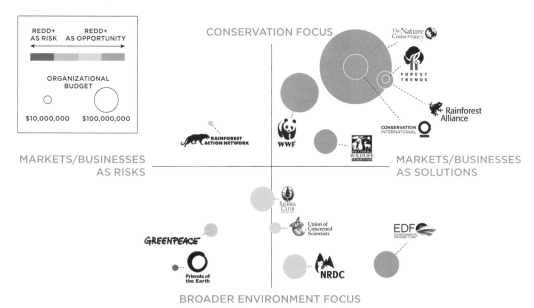

Source: Climate Advisers analysis adapted from M. Wolosin and D. Lee, "US Support for REDD+: Reflections on the Past and Future Outlook," CGD Policy Paper 48, Center for Global Development, Washington, DC, 2014, http://www.cgdev.org/publication/us-support-redd-reflections-past-and-future-outlook.

Note: Placement on main axes based on authors' judgment and expert review in Wolosin and Lee (2014). Conservation/Environment placement based on core mission. Market/Business axis aligns closely with position on offsets.

sition to forest offsets was part of a broader disagreement with USCAP's pro-business strategy. In their view, that strategy had resulted in too many compromises and concessions to industry.[102]

Concerns about Unintended Harm

A second set of arguments advanced against REDD+ is based on fears that placing a value on forest carbon—even through initiatives funded outside of carbon markets—will have negative environmental or social impacts on vulnerable ecosystems and communities in developing countries. Some advocacy has focused on the risk of an exclusive focus on the carbon benefits of forests leading to diversion of agricultural expansion to low-carbon ecosystems that are nevertheless valuable for biodiversity or ecosystem services.[103]

Continued concern about possible unintended negative consequences for forest peoples has been a key factor in restraining enthusiasm for REDD+ in rich countries.

But the civil society argument that has proved the most toxic to political support in donor countries is the assertion that REDD+ poses unacceptable risks to the rights and livelihoods of indigenous and other local communities in developing countries. The fear is that, if standing forests are given new value as carbon stocks, governments and private companies will have incentives to take them away from the forest stewards who have protected them up to now.

As described in chapter 10, such concerns are entirely appropriate in light of the history of national and international elites' appropriating forest wealth at the expense of local rights and welfare. And as described in chapters 9 and 10, the advent of REDD+ has prompted a healthy debate about the need for safeguards, along with consensus on the substantive and procedural principles to be respected. REDD+ policy arenas have also provided openings for indigenous advocates to assert their rights and interests.

Nevertheless, continued concern about possible unintended negative consequences for forest peoples has been a key factor in restraining enthusiasm for REDD+ in rich countries. In the United States, for example, "The NGOs and indigenous groups objecting on these grounds have had the ear of several important policymakers in Congress and in the Administration, and often added enough doubt about REDD+ that potential allies instead remained on the sidelines."[104]

In Australia, the Green Party echoed concerns initially voiced by Friends of the Earth–Indonesia regarding the impact of the Kalimantan Forest Carbon Partnership (described further in chapter 12) on the access of indigenous communities to forestland. Although such allegations were not substantiated by subsequent independent field research,[105] the silence of project proponents allowed the criticism to stand unchallenged and contributed to the erosion of political support for the project.[106] As described further in chapter 12, donor agency sensitivity to the "headline risks" of potential unintended negative consequences of REDD+ have generated an abundance of caution—and delay—in programming funding.

The timing and targets of civil society opposition to REDD+ suggest it is primarily driven by a rejection of carbon markets and the use of forest carbon credits as offsets for rich-country emissions. A brief flurry of NGO advocacy about REDD+ in Germany vanished as soon as the failed 2009 negotiations in Copenhagen took away the prospect of a global carbon market.[107] In the United Kingdom, following the crash of carbon prices in 2011, the focus of NGOs' advocacy shifted from sources of finance for REDD+ to the definition of "results" against which results-based payments would be applied.[108] In the United States, arguments about offsets reached a "rapid boil" while legislation that would have set up a national cap-and-trade system was under discussion in 2009 and 2010, but they were subsequently reduced to a simmer.[109] Only in the state of California, where international forest offsets remain a near-term possibility, is the debate still heated.[110]

The politics of REDD+ in California has also featured a final line of argument against REDD+, one that is unique to debates in rich countries. Social justice-oriented groups have asserted that by letting emission-intensive industry get off the hook through cap-and-trade mechanisms, forest offsets condemn communities to living with the other pollutants and associated environmental destruction that accompany the continued release of greenhouse gas emissions from fossil fuels produced and consumed in rich countries. The objection would apply to any offset, not just those from tropical forests.

Forest Carbon Offsets in California

On November 18, 2008, California governor Arnold Schwarzenegger convened a Governors' Climate Change Summit in Los Angeles that was attended by the leaders of forest-rich provinces from Brazil and Indonesia.[111] The governors signed a memorandum of understanding to cooperate on forests and climate issues, thus sprinkling Schwarzenegger's celebrity stardust on the nascent REDD+ agenda.

The background for the summit was the California Global Warming Solutions Act (known as AB 32) that Governor Schwarzenegger had signed into law two years earlier. Under the new legislation, the California Air Resources Board was in the process of designing a cap-and-trade program as a mechanism to meet emission reduction targets. Policy entrepreneurs saw an opportunity to marry the state's need for low-cost emission reduction options with the potential to supply such reductions through conservation of tropical forests at the subnational scale.

Before long, the possibility of financing REDD+ through "jurisdictional" forest offsets at the subnational level was one of the hottest topics in forest and climate change circles. A potential California market was one of the few rays of hope for REDD+ finance following the crushing disappointment of the UNFCCC's inability to reach an overall climate agreement in Copenhagen in 2009 and the subsequent failure of the U.S. Senate to pass the Waxman-Markey legislation, which had included a large share of emission reductions from international offsets. The Governors' Climate and Forest Task Force initiated by Governor Schwarzenegger grew to include additional states and provinces from Brazil, Indonesia, Mexico, Nigeria, and Peru.

REDD+ proponents argued that by including international forest offsets in its cap-and-trade program, California could spur broader reductions in emissions from tropical deforestation, a key element of any strategy to protect the global climate and one with significant co-benefits for biodiversity and ecosystem services. Cost-effective forestry offsets were also seen as a way to contain compliance costs for regulated businesses in the state. Pro-REDD+ forces were led by a group of environmental and conservation organizations, including The Nature Conservancy, the Environmental Defense Fund, and Conservation International, with some mild support from the private sector.

Opposition to the inclusion of international forestry offsets in California's emission reduction strategy was led by a few large environmental organizations, including Friends of the Earth and Greenpeace, that also opposed forest carbon offsets in national legislation. The national organizations made common cause with smaller groups from California's environmental justice community and international environmental and social justice movements. Their objections focused on the three issues outlined above.

First, they were skeptical of the environmental integrity of forest-based emission reductions, which AB 32 requires to be "real, additional, quantifiable, permanent, verifiable, and enforceable." Second, they were concerned REDD+ initiatives could result in adverse social and environmental consequences in developing countries, including the violation of indigenous peoples' rights to

forests. Finally, they wanted to give priority to in-state emission cuts, so that low-income communities could benefit from associated reductions in local air pollution.

Neither side put forward rigorous analyses to justify their positions. The "pro" side, for example, failed to advance a comprehensive, publicly available analysis of the potential impact of forest carbon offsets on California's overall compliance costs under the cap-and-trade system. On the "anti" side, claims of harm allegedly caused by REDD+ projects appeared to be based more on potential, rather than already realized, risks to vulnerable communities and ecosystems, as well as on the past performance of international forest conservation efforts that looked very different from those being contemplated by California.[112] California's unfortunate choice of the Mexican state of Chiapas—site of a Zapatista rebellion—as an early partner had the effect of associating REDD+ with governmental counterinsurgency efforts in rural areas.[113]

According to environmental law expert Jesse Lueders and his colleagues, it was difficult, in November 2014,

> to tell how much traction either side has made with policymakers. Outwardly at least, those in California government have maintained a mostly neutral stance, acknowledging the merits of both sides of the debate while declining either to move forward on REDD+ offsets or to abandon the idea.[114]

While the door to including international forest offsets in California's cap-and-trade program remained open in mid-2016, with the Air Resources Board having issued a proposal and held a series of public workshops, much uncertainty prevailed as to whether, and how soon, that might happen. The linkage of California's cap-and-trade program to Quebec's in 2014 suggested a potential for other U.S. states and Canadian provinces to piggyback onto California's investment in overcoming legal and technical hurdles and to increase demand for forest offsets. In 2015, Governor Jerry Brown, who replaced Governor Schwarzenegger in 2011, increased the ambition of California's emission reduction targets.[115] The combination of Governor Brown's increased ambition and California's multiyear drought—which has reduced the state's hydropower potential[116]—could generate increased demand for cost containment through offsets.

Other key actors include the Chair of the Air Resources Board, members of the state legislature, and leaders from the regulated business community. According to Lueders and colleagues, if the last were to be more vocal in their support for international forest offsets, they could make a big difference. Also said to have changed key minds in the governor's office have been visits organized by pro-REDD+ NGOs for state officials to meet with indigenous communities in Brazil and Mexico whose voices had been strengthened through REDD+ initiatives.[117]

But delay in moving forward has eroded momentum in California and partner jurisdictions in forest-rich developing countries alike. Over time, the voices of those opposing REDD+ have gotten louder, and they have garnered more political attention than those of supporters. At a December 2015 event hosted in Paris by the Governors' Climate and Forest Task Force in association with the climate summit, Governor Brown was heckled by protestors from California yelling, "No REDD!"[118]

Nevertheless, as of mid-2016, the Air Resources Board was still set to publish rules for international forest carbon offsets in accordance with plans laid out in an October 2015 staff white paper.[119] But the fact that the board delayed further action until after the legislature voted to extend climate targets beyond 2020 suggests continuing opposition prompted a cautious approach to moving forward on REDD+.[120]

In short, organized opposition to REDD+ has been limited to a small but vocal group of NGOs, primarily concerned about the environmental and social risks of creating a market for forest carbon. The engagement of the private sector in the politics of REDD+ (in the form of industries seeking forest carbon credits for offsets or banks and brokers that would profit from their trade) has been largely opposite from—but seldom equal to—the civil society campaigns against offsets. And in the cases where NGO opposition has contributed to a retreat from REDD+ on the part of public officials—Australia and California—supporters have not stepped up forcefully to make the case that risks can be effectively managed through application of the safeguard principles negotiated internationally.

Conclusion

International cooperation to protect tropical forests as a climate mitigation strategy has enjoyed broad support across the political spectrum in several rich countries, building on long-standing historical ties as well as contemporary interests unrelated to climate change. The mitigation potential of reducing deforestation reenergized existing constituencies among conservation organizations and added new constituencies interested in low-cost emission reduction options. These interests combined to prompt large new forest initiatives featuring prominently in climate change mitigation strategies in Australia and Norway, as well as pledges for increased funding from other donor countries.

Finance for reducing forest-based emissions has attracted political support in rich-country policy arenas. With the exception of NGOs that have objected to forest carbon offsets, no organized constituencies have emerged to oppose it. Coalitions of "strange bedfellows" spanning environmental NGOs and private companies have come together to support relevant legislation. Where forest-related funding has failed to materialize, as in the case of cap-and-trade legislation in the United States, or has faced reversals, as in the case of Australia's retreat from its early initiative, it has been a casualty of broader rightward political currents opposed to action on climate change and to international agreements. At the same time, the case of California demonstrates the potential potency of the small but vocal opposition from the left to carbon offsets as a source of forest finance.

The failure to reach an overall climate agreement in Copenhagen in 2009 shifted the politics of REDD+ in rich countries to an experts' discourse within and between government bureaucracies charged with programming aid funds, decribed further in chapter 12. The receding possibility of a global market for forest carbon offsets defanged the primary opposition to REDD+, but it also prompted the withdrawal of active support from emission-intensive industries and those poised to profit from trade in forest carbon credits. Advocacy groups shifted their attention to direct engagement with companies in commodity supply chains, thereby creating a new rich-country constituency for finance of REDD+ among companies needing to deliver on no-deforestation commitments.

The bottom line is that political support for international cooperation to conserve tropical forests is broadly favorable in most rich countries, although only a handful have provided substantial financing for REDD+. The success of "Lars & Lars" in prompting a large financial commitment from Norway has not been repeated elsewhere. Broader public mobilization around climate change, more vocal support from private sector constituencies, and further steps to assuage the legitimate concerns of opponents who focus on the risks of forest offsets to communities at home and abroad would all increase the chances of doing so.

In the next chapter, we turn to the problems inherent in funding REDD+ through development assistance agencies, and we explain why new fit-for-purpose vehicles are needed to deliver timely and effective finance.

Notes

1. The first eight paragraphs of this chapter are based on E. A. T. Hermansen and S. Kasa, "Climate Policy Constraints and NGO Entrepreneurship: The Story of Norway's Leadership in REDD+ Financing," CGD Working Paper 389, Center for Global Development, Washington, DC, 2014.

2. REDD+ stands for Reducing Emissions from Deforestation and forest Degradation plus conservation, sustainable management of forests, and enhancement of forest carbon stocks. Further information on REDD+ is included in box 1.1.

3. Hermansen and Kasa, "Climate Policy Constraints and NGO Entrepreneurship: The Story of Norway's Leadership in REDD+ Financing."

4. W. Tissot and Y. Kohler, "Integration of Nature Protection in Forest Policy in France," INTEGRATE Country Report, EFICENT-OEF, Freiburg, 2013, http://www.eficent.efi.int/files/attachments/eficent/projects/france.pdf.

5. G. Marten, "Environmental Tipping Points: A New Paradigm for Restoring Ecological Security," *Journal of Policy Studies (Japan)* 20 (2005): 75–87.

6. Korea Forest Service, "Leveraging Public Programmes with Socio-Economic and Development Objectives to Support Conservation and Restoration of Ecosystems: Lessons Learned from the Republic of Korea's National Reforestation Programme," Republic of Korea, Daejeon, Korea, 2015, https://www.cbd.int/ecorestoration/doc/Korean-Study_Final-Version-20150106.pdf.

7. S. Morris, "How a Book about Norwegian Wood Has Become a Global Hit," *The Independent*, November 24, 2015. A. Flood, "'Armchair Woodchoppers' Make DIY Timber Guide Surprise Bestseller," *The Guardian*, November 16, 2015.

8. T. Pistorius and L. Kiff, "The Politics of German Finance for REDD+," CGD Working Paper 390, Center for Global Development, Washington, DC, 2014.

9. C. H. Parker, *Global Interactions in the Early Modern Age, 1400–1800* (Cambridge: Cambridge University Press, 2010), cited in Pistorius and Kiff, "The Politics of German Finance for REDD+."

10. F. Schmithüsen, "Three Hundred Years of Applied Sustainability in Forestry," *Unasylva* 240, no. 64 (2013): 5–6.

11. H. C. von Carlowitz, *Sylvicultura Oeconomica: Hausswirthliche Nachricht und Naturmäßige Anweisung zur Wilden Baum-Zucht* (Leipzig: Faksimile der Erstauflage, 1713), 2013 reprint with an introduction by J. Huss and F. von Gadow (Remagen: Verlag Kessel, 2013), http://www.forstbuch.de/Carlowitz_1713_Informationen.pdf, cited in Pistorius and Kiff, "The Politics of German Finance for REDD+."

12. I. M. Saldanha, "Colonialism and Professionalism: A German Forester in India," *Environment and History* 2, no. 2 (1996): 195–219.

13. Parker, *Global Interactions*.

14. F. Wätzold, "SO2 Emissions in Germany: Regulations to Fight Waldsterben," in *Choosing Environmental Policy: Comparing Instruments and Outcomes in the United States and Europe*, eds. W. Harrington, D. Morgenstern, and T. Sterner, 23–40 (Washington, DC: Resources for the Future, 2004).

15. Pistorius and Kiff, "The Politics of German Finance for REDD+."

16. World Wildlife Fund, "WWF in the 60's," http://wwf.panda.org/who_we_are/history/sixties/.

17. R. England, "Natural Selection before the Origin: Public Reactions of Some Naturalists to the Darwin-Wallace Papers (Thomas Boyd, Arthur Hussey, and Henry Baker Tristram)," *Journal of the History of Biology* 30, no. 2 (1997): 267–90.

18. Royal Museum for Central Africa, "History," http://www.africamuseum.be/museum/about-us/museum/history/Congomuseum.

19. C. Millard, *The River of Doubt: Theodore Roosevelt's Darkest Journey* (New York: Broadway Books, 2005).

20. R. B. Browne and P. Browne, *The Guide to*

United States Popular Culture (London: Popular Press, 2001).

21. N. Myers, *The Sinking Ark: A New Look at the Problem of Disappearing Species* (Oxford: Pergamon Press, 1979).

22. K. Dennehy, "Lovejoy, 'Godfather' of Biodiversity, Reflects on 50 Years in the Amazon," *Yale School of Forestry & Environmental Studies News*, February 17, 2016.

23. New World Encyclopedia, s.v. "Biodiversity," http://www.newworldencyclopedia.org/p/index.php?title=Biodiversity&oldid=685139.

24. E. O. Wilson, *Biodiversity* (Washington, DC: National Academy Press, 1988).

25. C. S. Robbins, J. R. Sauer, R. S. Greenberg, and S. Droege, "Population Declines in North American Birds That Migrate to the Neotropics," *Proceedings of the National Academy of Sciences* 86, no. 19 (1989): 7658–62.

26. Minnesota History Center, "American Indian Movement: Overview," 2016, http://libguides.mnhs.org/aim/ov.

27. Encyclopedia of World Biography, s.v. "Chico Mendes," http://www.encyclopedia.com/doc/1G2-3404707413.html.

28. R. Winterbottom, "Taking Stock: The Tropical Forestry Action Plan after Five Years," World Resources Institute, 1990, 10, 16.

29. M. Wolosin and D. Lee, "US Support for REDD+: Reflections on the Past and Future Outlook," CGD Policy Paper 48, Center for Global Development, Washington, DC, 2014.

30. Pistorius and Kiff, "The Politics of German Finance for REDD+."

31. Hermansen and Kasa, "Climate Policy Constraints."

32. A. Contreras-Hermosilla, "Law Compliance in the Forestry Sector: An Overview," WBI Working Paper 37205, World Bank Institute, Washington, DC, 2002.

33. G8 Foreign Ministers, "G8 Action Programme on Forests," May 9, 1998, http://www.g8.utoronto.ca/foreign/forests.html.

34. Government of Japan, Ministry of Foreign Affairs, "The G8 Forest Experts' Report on Illegal Logging," May 2008, http://www.mofa.go.jp/policy/environment/forest/report0805.pdf.

35. Forest Stewardship Council, "History," https://ic.fsc.org/en/about-fsc/our-history.

36. Forest Stewardship Council, "The Global Volume and Market Share of FSC-Certified Timber," August 28, 2015, https://ic.fsc.org/en/news/id/1234.

37. B. Cashore and M. W. Stone, "Does California Need Delaware? Explaining Indonesian, Chinese, and United States Support for Legality Compliance of Internationally Traded Products," *Regulation & Governance* 8, no. 1 (2014): 49–73; B. Yandle, "Bootleggers and Baptists: The Education of a Regulatory Economist," *Regulation* 7, no. 3 (1983): 12.

38. The European Parliament and the Council of the European Union, "Regulation (EU) No. 995/2010 of the European Parliament and of the Council of 20 October 2010 Laying Down the Obligations of Operators Who Place Timber and Timber Products on the Market Text with EEA relevance," October 20, 2010, http://eur-lex.europa.eu/legal-content/EN/TXT/HTML/?uri=CELEX:32010R0995&from=EN, as cited in K. Dooley and C. Parker, "Evolution of Finance for REDD+ in the UK: A History and Overview of the UK Government's Engagement with REDD+ Finance, with a Focus on Performance-Based Payments for REDD+," CGD Policy Paper 55, Center for Global Development, Washington, DC, 2015.

39. European Court of Auditors, "EU Support to Timber-Producing Countries under the FLEGT Action Plan: Special Report," European Union, 2015, http://www.illegal-logging.info/sites/files/chlogging/SR_FLEGT_EN.pdf.

40. Dooley and Parker, "Evolution of Finance."

41. U.S. Department of State, Bureau of Oceans and International Environmental and Scientific Affairs, "The President's Initiative Against Illegal Logging," State Department Factsheet, Washington, DC, 2008, http://2001-2009.state.gov/documents/organization/103493.pdf.

42. Seneca Creek Associates, LLC, "'Illegal' Logging and Global Wood Markets: The Competitive Impacts on the US Wood Products Industry," American Forest & Paper Association, Poolesville, Maryland and University Place, Washington, DC, 2004.

43. A. J. Dieterle, "The Lacey Act: A Case Study in the Mechanics of Overcriminalization," *Georgetown Law Journal* 102 (2013): 1279.

44. Ibid., 1286; Rep. John Lacey, 33 Congressional Record, statement of Rep. John Lacey, (1900): 4871.

45. U.S. Fish and Wildlife Service, "Lacey Act," http://www.fws.gov/international/laws-treaties-agreements/us-conservation-laws/lacey-act.html.

46. S. Leipold and G. Winkel, "Divide and Conquer—Discursive Agency in the Politics of Illegal Logging in the United States," *Global Environmental Change* 36 (2016): 38.

47. Government of Australia, "Bringing Down the Axe on Illegal Logging: A Practical Approach," Canberra, Australia, 2007, http://www.unece.lsu.edu/responsible_trade/documents/2007July/rt_4aAP_04.pdf.

48. Government of Australia, Department of Agriculture and Water Resources, "Illegal Logging," http://www.agriculture.gov.au/forestry/policies/illegal-logging, 4.

49. Government of Japan, Ministry of Foreign Affairs, "International Cooperation of Japan to Promote Sustainable Forest Management in Developing Countries," November 21, 2003, http://www.mofa.go.jp/policy/environment/forest/coop0211.html.

50. M. Momii, "Trade in Illegal Timber: The Response in Japan: A Chatham House Assessment," Chatham House, November 2014.

51. S. Umeda, "Japan: Act Aims to Promote Trade in Legally Produced Timber," Global Legal Monitor of the Library of Congress, July 28, 2016, http://www.loc.gov/law/foreign-news/article/japan-act-aims-to-promote-trade-in-legally-produced-timber/.

52. Pistorius and Kiff, "The Politics of German Finance for REDD+."

53. M. Norman and S. Nakhooda, "The State of REDD+ Finance," CGD Working Paper 378, Center for Global Development, Washington, DC, 2014 (updated 2015).

54. R. Davies, "The Indonesia-Australia Forest Carbon Partnership: A Murder Mystery," CGD Policy Paper 60, Center for Global Development, Washington, DC, 2015; Pistorius and Kiff, "The Politics of German Finance for REDD+"; Hermansen and Kasa, "Climate Policy Constraints"; Dooley and Parker, "Evolution of Finance"; Wolosin and Lee, "US Support for REDD+"; J. Lueders, C. Horowitz, A. Carlson, S. Hecht, and E. Parson, "The California REDD+ Experience: The Ongoing Political History of California's Initiative to Include Jurisdictional REDD+ Offsets within Its Cap-and-Trade System," CGD Working Paper 386, Center for Global Development, Washington, DC, 2014.

55. N. Stern, *The Economics of Climate Change: The Stern Review* (Cambridge: Cambridge University Press, 2007).

56. R. Keohane, "The Global Politics of Climate Change: Challenge for Political Science," *PS: Political Science & Politics* 48, no. 1 (2015): 19–26.

57. J. Howard, "Australia to Lead the World: Global Initiative on Forests and Climate," joint press release from the Hon. John Howard MP (prime minister of Australia), the Hon. Alexander Downer MP (minister for foreign affairs), and the Hon. Malcolm Turnbull MP (minister for the environment and water resources), March 29, 2007, http://www.cifor.org/publications/pdf_files/media/Howard%20Downer%20Turnbull%20Release.pdf.

58. Howard, "Australia to Lead the World," 2.

59. Davies, "The Indonesia-Australia Forest Carbon Partnership."

60. Department of the Prime Minister and Cabinet of Australia, Prime Ministerial Task Group on Emissions Trading and P. R. Shergold, "Report of the Task Group on Emissions Trading," 2007, http://pandora.

nla.gov.au/pan/72614/20070601-0000/ www.pmc.gov.au/publications/emissions/ docs/emissions_trading_report.pdf, 118.

61. See, for example, M. Matherell, S. Peatling, and A. Darby, "Howard Chips Away in Tasmania," *Sydney Morning Herald*, October 7, 2004.

62. R. Garnaut, *The Garnaut Climate Change Review* (Cambridge: Cambridge University Press, 2008).

63. Davies, "The Indonesia-Australia Forest Carbon Partnership."

64. Dooley and Parker, "Evolution of Finance," 9.

65. Ibid., 23. The International Sustainability Unit later published a useful report synthesizing the state of knowledge and policy regarding tropical forests: International Sustainability Unit, "Tropical Forests: A Review," London, April 2015, http://www.pcfisu.org/wp-content/ uploads/2015/04/Princes-Charities-International-Sustainability-Unit-Tropical-Forests-A-Review.pdf.

66. Ibid., 8.

67. Wolosin and Lee, "US Support for REDD+," 13.

68. Ibid.

69. Ibid., 44.

70. Pistorius and Kiff, "The Politics of German Finance," 27.

71. Dooley and Parker, "Evolution of Finance," 2.

72. U.S. Congress. House of Representatives. Committees on Science and Technology; Energy and Commerce; Foreign Affairs; Financial Services; Education and Labor; Transportation and Infrastructure; Natural Resources; Agriculture; Ways and Means. American Clean Energy And Security Act of 2009. 111th Cong., 1st sess., 2009. H. Rep., 111–137.

73. M. Gerson and R. Shah, "Foreign Assistance and the Revolution of Rigor," in *Moneyball for Government*, 2nd ed., ed. J. Nussle and P. Orszag (New York: Disruption Books, 2015).

74. Wolosin and Lee, "US Support for REDD+."

75. United States Climate Action Partnership, "A Blueprint for Legislative Action: Consensus Recommendations for U.S. Climate Protection Legislation," 2009, http://www.

merid.org/~/media/Files/Projects/USCAP/ USCAP-A-Blueprint-for-Legislative-Action.

76. T. Skocpol, "Naming the Problem: What It Will Take to Counter Extremism and Engage Americans in the Fight against Global Warming" (paper presented at the Symposium on the Politics of America's Fight against Global Warming, Harvard University, Cambridge, MA, January 2013).

77. Ibid., 94.

78. Ibid., 119–30.

79. Wolosin and Lee, "US Support for REDD+," 25.

80. A. DeBard, "Bill Gives Billions to Save Trees in Other Nations," *Washington Times*, June 25, 2009, as cited in Wolosin and Lee, "US Support for REDD+."

81. This section draws heavily on Hermansen and Kasa, "Climate Policy Constraints."

82. A. Angelsen, "REDD+ as Performance-Based Aid," UNU-WIDER Working Paper 135, United Nations University UNU-WIDER, 2013, https://www.wider.unu.edu/ publication/redd-performance-based-aid; A. Angelsen, "Kan norske oljemilliarder redde tropisk regnskog?" PowerPoint presentation at Universitetet for miljø-og biovitenskap , 2012, http://samfunnsokonomene.no/wp-content/uploads/2012/10/Arild-Angelsen. pdf, slide 17.

83. Hermansen and Kasa, "Climate Policy Constraints," 22.

84. Pistorius and Kiff, "The Politics of German Finance."

85. Ibid.

86. Davies, "The Indonesia–Australia Forest Carbon Partnership."

87. "Norway Makes Deep Aid Cuts to Fund Refugee Costs Next Year. Targets Ngos, UN," *Development Today*, October 30, 2015, http://www.development-today.com/ magazine/Frontpage/norway_makes_deep_ aid_cuts_to_fund_refugee_costs_next_ year_targets_ngos_and_un_agencies.

88. A. Hoare, "Tackling Illegal Logging and Related Trade: What Progress and Where Next?" Chatham House Report, London, 2015.

89. Consumer Goods Forum, "The Forum Board

Statement on Climate Change," 2015, http://www.theconsumergoodsforum.com/the-forum-board-statement-on-climate-change.

90. United Nations, "Forests: Action Statements and Action Plans," New York, September 23, 2014, http://www.un.org/climatechange/summit/wp-content/uploads/sites/2/2014/07/New-York-Declaration-on-Forest-%E2%80%93-Action-Statement-and-Action-Plan.pdf.

91. Dooley and Parker, "Evolution of Finance," 17–18; Government of the United Kingdom, Department for International Development, "Investments in Forests and Sustainable Land Use," updated 2015, https://devtracker.dfid.gov.uk/projects/GB-1-202745/.

92. See, for example, the Sustainable Trade Initiative and Norwegian Agency for Development Cooperation, "Norway Partners with IDH to Conserve Forests," press release, December 11, 2015.

93. See, for example, World People's Conference on Climate Change and the Rights of Mother Earth, "Letter from President Evo Morales to Indigenous Peoples: Nature, Forests and Indigenous Peoples are Not for Sale," November 7, 2010, https://pwccc.wordpress.com/2010/10/07/presidents-letter-to-the-indigenous-peoplesnature-forests-and-indigenous-peoples-are-not-for-sale/.

94. F. Carus, "British Deal to Preserve Liberia's Forests 'Could Have Bankrupted' Nation," *The Guardian*, July 23, 2010.

95. L. Bartlett, "The Carbon Cowboy," *Sixty Minutes*, July 6, 2012, http://sixtyminutes.ninemsn.com.au/stories/8495029/the-carbon-cowboy.

96. L. Munden, "REDD and Forest Carbon: Market-Based Critique and Recommendations," the Munden Project, March 7, 2011, http://www.rightsandresources.org/wp-content/exported-pdf/reddandforestcarbonv10.pdf.

97. See, for example, Friends of the Earth, "State of the Forest Carbon Market: A Critical Perspective," 2011, Friends of the Earth Report, http://www.foe.org/system/storage/877/a1/9/872/State_of_the_forest_carbon_

market_a_critical_perspective_2011.pdf.

98. Dooley and Parker, "Evolution of Finance."

99. Fern, "Will Carbon Markets Ever Deliver for Southern Governments, Forests and People?" 2015, http://www.fern.org/sites/fern.org/files/carbonleaflet_2015.pdf.

100. Wolosin and Lee, "US Support for REDD+"; Lueders et al., "The California REDD+ Experience."

101. Ibid.; J. Horowitz, "Nobel Peace Prize Laureates Oscar Arias and Wangari Maathai Endorse the Tropical Forest and Climate Unity Agreement," Avoided Deforestation Partners, May 20, 2009, http://adpartners.org/news/tropical-forest-and-climate-unity-agreement-reached-new-forest-protection-coalition-formed/.

102. Skocpol, "Naming the Problem," 99–100; M. Gaworecki, "Greenpeace, Friends of the Earth, Public Citizen Decry Weakening of Waxman-Markey Bill," Greenpeace, May 13, 2009, http://www.greenpeace.org/usa/greenpeace-friends-of-the-earth-public-citizen-decry-weakening-of-waxman-markey-bill/.

103. Conservation International, "Advice on REDD+ Safeguards," Conservation International Position Paper, Hyderabad, India, 2012, http://www.conservation.org/global/japan/initiatives/biodiversity/Documents/COP11REDDplus_positionpaper_FINAL.pdf.

104. Wolosin and Lee, "US Support for REDD," 24.

105. S. Atmadja et al., "Kalimantan Forests and Climate Partnership, Central Kalimantan, Indonesia," in *REDD+ on the Ground: A Case Book of Subnational Initiatives across the Globe* (Bogor, Indonesia: Center for International Forestry Research, 2014).

106. Davies, "The Indonesia-Australia Forest Carbon Partnership."

107. Pistorius and Kiff, "The Politics of German Finance for REDD+."

108. Dooley and Parker, "Evolution of Finance."

109. Wolosin and Lee, "US Support for REDD+."

110. Lueders et al., "The California REDD+ Experience."

111. This section draws heavily on Lueders et al., "The California REDD+ Experience."

112. Lueders et al., "The California REDD+ Experience."

113. T. Osborne, "Fixing Carbon, Losing Ground: Payments for Environmental Services and Land (In)security in Mexico," *Human Geography* 6, no. 1 (2013): 119–33.

114. Lueders et al., "The California REDD+ Experience."

115. Office of Governor Edmund G. Brown Jr., "Governor Brown Establishes Most Ambitious Greenhouse Gas Reduction Target in North America," April 29, 2015, https://www.gov.ca.gov/news.php?id=18938.

116. M. Bowman, "California's Continued Drought, Reduced Snowpack Mean Lower Hydropower Output," Energy Information Administration (EIA), 2015, http://www.eia.gov/todayinenergy/detail.cfm?id=20732; P. H. Gleick, "Impacts of California's Ongoing Drought: Hydroelectricty Generation," Pacific Institute, Oakland, CA, 2015, http://pacinst.org/wp-content/uploads/sites/21/2015/03/California-Drought-and-Energy-Final1.pdf.

117. Anonymous, personal communication with the authors, October 28, 2015.

118. D. Siders, "Jerry Brown Heckled in France, with Video," *Sacramento Bee*, December 8, 2015.

119. State of California Air Resources Board, "Scoping Next Steps for Evaluating the Potential Role of Sector-Based Offset Credits under the California Cap-and-Trade Program, Including from Jurisdictional 'Reducing Emissions from Deforestation and Forest Degradation' Programs," Sacramento, Califormia, October 19, 2015, https://www.arb.ca.gov/cc/capandtrade/sectorbasedoffsets/ARB%20Staff%20White%20Paper%20Sector-Based%20Offset%20Credits.pdf.

120. J. J. Cooper, "California Lawmakers Approve Extension of Climate Change Law," Associated Press, August 24, 2016.

Tropical forests ring the seven cascades of Tamarin Waterfall in Mauritius.

Credit: Quality Master/Shutterstock

CHAPTER 12

Finance for Tropical Forests

Too Low, Too Slow,
Too Constrained as Aid

UN *Headquarters, New York, 1989.* A few years after tropical deforestation was placed on the international agenda through the Tropical Forestry Action Plan, described in chapter 9, UK prime minister Margaret Thatcher delivered a prescient speech to the United Nations General Assembly in anticipation of the 1992 UN Conference on Environment and Development. Long before the importance of forests to climate change mitigation gained traction more widely, she observed,

> We are seeing a vast increase in the amount of carbon dioxide reaching the atmosphere … At the same time as this is happening, we are seeing the destruction on a vast scale of tropical forests which are uniquely able to remove carbon dioxide from the air.[1]

Not previously known as an environmentalist, the prime minister no doubt had noted that the Green Party had attracted some 15 percent of the vote in UK elections for the European Parliament that June. In her November speech, Thatcher announced a commitment of £100 million over three years for tropical forest conservation, "a previously unprecedented amount for such an issue."[2]

Among those surprised by the size of the prime minister's commitment was Andrew Bennett, a senior civil servant at the Overseas Development Administration (ODA, which was later renamed the Department for International Development, DfID). In prepa-

ration for Thatcher's speech, Bennett had been asked to formulate an international forestry initiative, but the assignment had been accompanied by a caution to keep in mind constraints on the development aid budget. Accordingly, he had submitted a proposal with a £10 million price tag.

After Thatcher added a zero to the figure in her speech, Bennett was told it would be his job to convince ODA offices around the world to come up with the £90 million balance from existing budget allocations. His challenge was further complicated the following year, when the prime minister joined other G8 leaders in Houston in announcing a pilot program to save the Brazilian rainforest that would have first claim on the earmarked funds.[3] The aid agency's ability to respond to the new political initiative was constrained by existing allocations.

Twenty years later, history would repeat itself, as many (but not all) donor commitments to Reducing Emissions from Deforestation and forest Degradation (REDD+) funding turned out to amount to less like new and additional pledges than they initially appeared.

The purpose of this chapter is to describe the landscape of REDD+ funding and analyze its implications for the potential of performance-based finance as an instrument for reducing tropical deforestation.

We begin by summarizing the state of finance for REDD+ in terms of amounts, sources, vehicles, and destinations of public sector pledges during the period 2006–14. We describe how funding has been low relative to the mitigation potential of forests and concentrated among a limited number of donors. We contrast the supply of REDD+ fi-

---

This chapter draws heavily on a background paper by Marigold Norman and Smita Nakhooda on REDD+ finance, and on five country case studies on the politics of REDD+ finance: by Robin Davies on Australia; by Till Pistorius and Laura Kiff on Germany; by Erlend Hermansen and Sjur Kasa on Norway; by Kate Dooley and Charlie Parker on the United Kingdom; and by Michael Wolosin and Donna Lee on the United States.

nance with potential demand: many developing countries have lined up to initiate REDD+ programs and offered to make more ambitious commitments to reduce forest emissions in return for more certain payment.

Second, we examine the consequences of relying on aid budgets and organizations as the primary source of REDD+ finance in the absence of market-based demand for forest carbon credits. We describe how the programming of funds through traditional aid channels has resulted in tensions among government agencies with different mandates, a reluctance to program funds on a payment-for-performance basis, and slow disbursement of available funds. Limited, slow, and uncertain finance has dampened enthusiasm for REDD+ in developing countries, many of which have gotten stranded in an extended phase of getting ready to qualify for a reward that is not yet bankable.

Finally, we sketch three alternative sources of finance for REDD+, including forest carbon markets, climate finance instruments, and private investment leveraged by the creditworthiness of rich countries.

We begin with a look at the numbers.

The Landscape of REDD+ Finance

When the idea of REDD+ first caught fire in the run-up to the 2007 climate negotiations in Bali, it was widely assumed large-scale finance would be provided through a global market in carbon credits.[4] At the time, many people expected an agreement in Copenhagen in 2009 would create such a market by establishing a global limit on total greenhouse gas emissions. The market could gen-

erate demand for reduced emissions from deforestation as well as from other mitigation options. Estimates of the level of funding needed were in the range of $21.4 billion to $35.7 billion, total, to cut deforestation rates by 25 percent by 2015[5] and $17 billion to $33 billion per year to cut them in half by 2030.[6]

The two sections below describe how initial enthusiasm for REDD+ and the prospect of carbon markets prompted a surge of financial pledges from the public sector and interest from the private sector, followed by a leveling off in 2010 and beyond once the post-Copenhagen reality set in.

A Fast Start to REDD+ Finance

Rich countries saw the potential to lower the overall cost of climate protection by financing cheaper reductions internationally and were eager to help get REDD+ efforts up and running in advance of a global climate deal. Australia and Norway were early movers in committing significant funds to the forests and climate change agenda in 2007; Australia's pledge of A$200 million seemed large until it was overshadowed by the Norwegian rainforest billions described in chapter 11.

Other bilateral donors scrambled to line up pledges for REDD+ as part of the so-called fast-start finance agreed to in Copenhagen in 2009, with the United States announcing a billion-dollar package of support and the United Kingdom a pledge of £300 million.[7] While discussions under the United Nations Framework Convention on Climate Change (UNFCCC) always envisioned financing from both market and nonmarket sources, it is important to remember that at the time these pledges were developed, they were understood to function for the most part as bridges to the much larger-scale finance expected to be generated by a global carbon market.

Multilateral organizations moved quickly to position themselves as vehicles for new funding flows associated with REDD+. Even before the 2007 UNFCCC negotiations in Bali endorsed a road map for including tropical forests in climate mitigation strategies, such organizations were competing to set up REDD+ financing facilities. In Bali, the Forest Carbon Partnership Facility (FCPF)—with the World Bank as trustee—was launched with an initial $160 million in contributions from nine donor country governments and The Nature Conservancy, a U.S.-based conservation organization.[8] The FCPF Readiness Fund eventually attracted seventeen donors and $365 million.[9] It became operational in June 2008 and, by 2009, thirty-seven developing countries had applied and been accepted to receive initial grants for capacity building. Such programs would be a first step toward eligibility for performance-based finance from the FCPF's Carbon Fund, which would become operational in 2011.[10]

In June 2008, three agencies of the United Nations—the Food and Agriculture Organization (FAO), the UN Environment Programme (UNEP), and the UN Development Programme (UNDP)—joined to launch the UN-REDD Programme, also dedicated to supporting national REDD+ readiness efforts. Within a year, initial contributions from Norway were underwriting a $19 million portfolio of agreements with the Democratic Republic of Congo (DRC), Indonesia, Papua New Guinea, and Vietnam.[11] Funding for the program from six countries and the European Union totaled $215 million by early 2016.[12] Meanwhile, the Global Environment Facility (GEF)—established as a financing mechanism to service international conventions on biodiversity, climate, desertification, and other environmental issues—pivoted in 2008 to direct $25 million earmarked for "sustainable forest management" toward enhancing institutional capacity for REDD+ in Brazil, Colombia, and the Congo Basin.[13]

This mushrooming of various vehicles for REDD+ finance happened in the absence of clarity regarding the global architecture that would emerge from the climate negotiations in 2009 or consensus on what would be a desirable framework. To inform those negotiations, the government of Norway, the David and Lucile Packard Foundation (a U.S.-based philanthropy), and the Meridian Institute (a nonprofit facilitator) cosponsored an expert-led assessment.[14] The resulting Options Assessment Report (OAR)[15] was widely credited for articulating a phased approach to REDD+ finance, which was first advanced by the Coalition for Rainforest Nations[16] and ultimately adopted by the UNFCCC.[17] The three phases are described in box 12.1.

With readiness funding for phase 1 REDD+ activities to be administered by the FCPF and the UN-REDD Programme and prospects for phase 3 performance-based funding from the FCPF Carbon Fund (and eventually carbon markets), governments identified a "missing middle" of finance for REDD+ phase 2, the implementation phase for policies and measures to reduce deforestation. To fill the gap, the Forest Investment Program (FIP) was created in 2009 as a financing window of the multilateral Climate Investment Funds (CIFs) based at the World Bank and by 2015 had attracted $787 million

As detailed in chapter 9, negotiations to shape REDD+ unfolded over the course of several years under the climate convention, supported by dialogue in other forums. One subject of discussion was how countries with limited capacity and resources could gain access to funds for capacity building and investment before becoming eligible for results-based finance. Agreement on how to address the challenge was crystalized in a decision made at the climate talks in Cancun in 2010.[a] Negotiators agreed REDD+ should be implemented in three overlapping phases, with the UNFCCC referring to capacity-building phases 1 and 2 and to demonstration activities "evolving" into results-based actions in phase 3.

The activities and financing that have characterized the three phases are as follows:

- **Phase 1, or "Readiness" Phase**—In phase 1, countries assemble the building blocks of a national initiative to reduce deforestation and to account for avoided emissions. They develop a national strategy and undertake associated public consultations, and they establish systems for measuring, reporting, and verifying (MRV) emission reductions and for providing information on how safeguards have been addressed and respected. Donors have provided grants to support these activities, including via the Forest Carbon Partnership Facility (FCPF) Readiness Fund and the UN-REDD Programme.

- **Phase 2, or "Implementation" Phase**—In phase 2, countries implement policies, make investments, and undertake other activities designed to reduce deforestation. Donors have provided both grants and loans to support these activities, including via the multilateral development banks' Forest Investment Program.

- **Phase 3, or "Results-Based" Phase**—In phase 3, countries are rewarded for verified emission reductions on a payment-for-performance basis. Results-based transfers have been made within bilateral agreements (such as those concluded by Norway and by Germany's REDD Early Movers Program) and are expected from the FCPF Carbon Fund.

a. United Nations Framework Convention on Climate Change (UNFCCC), "Report of the Conference of the Parties on Its Sixteenth Session, Held in Cancún from 29 November to 10 December 2010, Addendum Part Two: Action Taken by the Conference of the Parties at Its Sixteenth Session," March 15, 2011, 1/CP.16 Para 73, http://unfccc.int/resource/docs/2010/cop16/eng/07a01.pdf.

in donor funding.[18] Developing countries had to compete for access to FIP funds because the program was initially limited to pilots in eight countries, although it was subsequently expanded.[19] The FIP was designed to promote "transformational change" in recipient countries that would be "of a nature and scope necessary to help significantly shift national forest and land use development paths."[20]

Much early REDD+ finance was targeted to support either local demonstration projects or "readiness" activities at the national level. The first three bilateral payment-for-performance agreements concluded between Norway and, respectively, Brazil (2008), Guyana (2009), and Indonesia (2010) all focused on national implementation. Subsequently, additional sources of REDD+ finance became operational, targeting the subnational "jurisdictional" scale at the level of states and provinces. In 2012, Germany launched the REDD Early Movers (REM) initiative, with an initial commitment of €67 million, to bridge the gap in results-based finance pending development of a mechanism under the UNFCCC;[21] and, in 2013, the World Bank's BioCarbon Fund established a $280 million Initiative for Sustainable Forest Landscapes (ISFL), with support from Norway, the United Kingdom, and the United States.[22] The ISFL was designed to provide technical assistance and grants, as well as payment-for-performance finance.[23]

In addition to these public sector commitments and institutional innovations, the years leading up to the 2009 climate summit in Copenhagen witnessed a flourishing of private sector interest and entrepreneurship in anticipation of growing markets for forest carbon credits. Both brand-name investors and consulting firms saw the potential to profit. The global consulting firm McKinsey & Co. sought to position itself as an adviser to governments on REDD+, producing the marginal abatement cost curves described in chapter 5; Eco Securities, an Ireland-based firm that had pioneered the development and trade in carbon credits under the Kyoto Protocol's Clean Development Mechanism, embraced the prospect of REDD+ as a new business opportunity; and, as described in chapter 11, fly-by-night operators also sought to get in on the carbon trading action.

Would-be suppliers of forest carbon credits rushed to establish projects to generate forest emission reductions. In 2008, Merrill Lynch began raising $100 million in equity to purchase voluntary carbon offsets expected from a project developed jointly by a private firm, a conservation organization, and the provincial government in Aceh, Indonesia.[24] Meanwhile, Australia's Macquarie Bank began prospect-

ing for REDD+ project investments, eventually establishing an equity fund of $25 million with support from the International Finance Corporation.[25] As of 2009, several hundred "first generation" REDD+ projects were in various stages of development, with entrepreneurs betting on eligibility to participate under the rules of carbon markets yet to be created.[26]

The Post-Copenhagen Reality

The failure of the 2009 climate negotiations in Copenhagen to achieve a binding global agreement to reduce emissions dramatically changed expectations regarding the landscape of future REDD+ finance. Without the prospect of demand from compliance markets for forest carbon credits, financing from rich countries was essentially limited to only two sources: the nascent voluntary carbon market and development assistance budgets. Both were affected by the economic downturn resulting from the 2008 financial crisis, which reduced demand for carbon credits and constrained public purses. According to a background paper commissioned for this book by climate finance experts Marigold Norman and Smita Nakhooda of the Overseas Development Institute (ODI), those two sources generated just short of $10 billion, total, between 2006 and 2014. Box 12.2 summarizes the composition of REDD+ finance during that period.

The relatively modest amount of less than $9 billion in public funding comprised promised bilateral aid and national contributions to multilateral trust funds. The total was not so different from the $8 billion in pledges solicited for the Tropical Forestry Action Plan back in Margaret Thatcher's era, before the importance of forests to climate change prevention was widely appreciated.

International finance for REDD+ over the period 2006 to 2014 had the following characteristics:

- Total available: US$9.8 billion
- Share from public sector pledges: 90 percent
- Share from voluntary carbon markets: 10 percent
- Largest sources: Bilateral aid (51 percent); multilateral funds (33 percent)
- Five donor countries provided more than three-quarters of available finance (ranked by amount): Norway, United States, Germany, Japan, United Kingdom
- Brazil and Indonesia shared 35 percent of total funding and an even larger share of total forest emissions.
- Portion programmed on a payment-for-performance basis: Less than half (at most 42 percent)

Source: M. Norman and S.Nakhooda, "The State of REDD+ Finance," CGD Working Paper 378 (2014, updated May 2015).

Policy expert Michael Wolosin and former REDD+ negotiator for the United States Donna Lee describe how donor countries determined their pledges to REDD+ as part of their fast-start finance commitments in 2009:

> While there were multiple analyses about the scale of need for REDD+ funding—driven mostly by opportunity cost analysis that generated large numbers in terms of future needs—this analysis was not the driving factor in the level of funding commitments made for REDD+ by any of the major donors. Pledges were made, firstly, in the context of current ODA budget allocations and what additional amounts were domestically feasible; and secondly in the context of the expected fast start finance commitment from each country, and how REDD+ might comprise a portion. Each developed country was, at that time, calculating its own perception of its "fair share" of the fast start commitment and considering how to meet that commitment in the context of domestic budget limitations.[27]

Also in question is whether or not REDD+ has received its fair share of overall public funding allocated to climate finance. As illustrated in figure 12.1, out of the total $35 billion pledged for fast-start finance, only 10 percent was allocated to forests. This proportion is far short of forests' potential to mitigate up to 30 percent of current annual global emissions, as described in chapter 2.

Furthermore, while the role of forests in bolstering resilience to climate change is increasingly appreciated (as described in chapter 3), funding for forest conservation as an adaptation strategy has not featured prominently in the portfolios of adaptation finance mechanisms. In the $1.2 billion portfolio of the Pilot Program for Climate Resilience (PPCR) of the Climate Investment Funds, only a few projects have focused on it.[28] And, despite recognition of the value of ecosystem-based approaches, the Adaptation Fund—the mechanism created by the UNFCCC to finance adaptation projects—had, as of 2015, supported only a handful of forest-related projects, most of which included forest restoration as a minor element of broader efforts to improve management of productive landscapes.[29]

Figure 12.1: Tropical forests' share of climate finance is small relative to their mitigation potential.

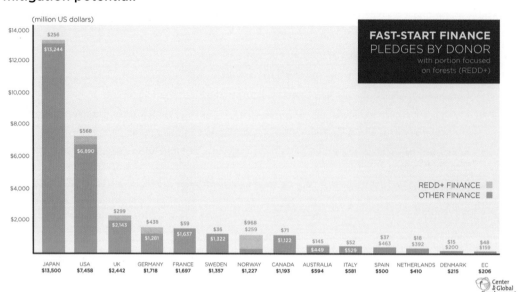

Source: S. Nakhooda, T. Fransen, T. Kuramochi, A. Caravani, A. Prizzon, N. Shimizu, H. Tilley, A.Halimanjaya, and B.Welham, "Mobilising International Climate Finance: Lessons from the Fast-Start Finance Period," Overseas Development Institute, World Resources Institute, Institute of Global Environmental Strategies and Open Climate Network, 2013, https://www.odi.org/sites/odi.org.uk/files/odi-assets/publications-opinion-files/8687.pdf.

Note: Fast-start finance commitments include both grants and loans, which may distort comparisons of the value of finance across countries and sectors.

While a chronic lack of appreciation of forests' potential contribution to emission mitigation and adaptation to climate change likely explains some of the gap, other factors also contributed. Significant portions of some countries' fast-start finance pledges were in the form of loan financing, which is easier to invest in clean energy projects than in forest conservation initiatives. In addition, much of the new funding was programmed as extensions of existing aid portfolios in which forest-related activities were underrepresented, having fallen out of fashion in the previous decade.

But even the amount of REDD+ finance reported was less than meets the eye. No doubt, much of the funding counted against

REDD+ pledges was not truly "additional," in the sense that, as happened after Margaret Thatcher's 1989 commitment, funds already budgeted were reallocated to meet new commitments. Furthermore, funding for forests and climate was often broadly defined. For example, USAID's "Sustainable Landscapes" program, under which REDD+ was funded, was expanded in 2013 to include all landscapes, including farmlands and wetlands, although most funding was reserved for forests.[30] And even though average annual U.S. funding for forests in 2010–14 was more than double its average during the previous five years, Michael Wolosin and Donna Lee report a perception among other donors that the amount of U.S. REDD+ funding is much smaller than it should be and, in relation to the size of its economy, relatively smaller than what many other donors provide; that it is scattered both in terms of strategic focus and implementation; and that it is not truly additional but rather is just relabeled from previous uses.[31]

Private finance was insufficient to take up the slack, as cumulative funding for REDD+ generated by the voluntary carbon market between 2006 and 2014 totaled about $1 billion. Without the near-term prospect of a significant compliance-driven carbon market, demand for forest carbon credits was, for the most part, limited to corporations such as Microsoft and Walt Disney, which purchased them as a way of meeting their voluntary targets for corporate social responsibility. One study estimates that under a "status quo" scenario, the supply of forest carbon credits will outstrip the demand on the voluntary market by more than 500 percent in the period 2015–25.[32]

Both public pledges and private finance for REDD+ surged in the run-up to and immediate aftermath of the Copenhagen climate conference in 2009 and subsequently dropped off or stagnated. One explanation for the drop-off in new public funding was the slow disbursement of funds already pledged, for reasons described further below. It is difficult for donors to justify pledging additional funds when those already on offer are backing up in the pipeline.

A modest uptick in 2014 pledges presaged a reinvigoration of the REDD+ agenda in anticipation of the 2015 climate negotiations in Paris. And on the first day of the summit, the governments of Germany, Norway, and the United Kingdom announced a joint commit-

ment of $5 billion over six years (2015–20).[33] But as of mid-2016, REDD+ finance remained largely captive to the constraints that encumber development aid, to which we return in the latter half of this chapter.

Fifty Shades of REDD+

As of 2016, more than fifty countries were participating in internationally supported REDD+ programs—a great many more than the handful that had secured a payment-for-performance agreement. National REDD+ initiatives spanned the range from ambitious, integrated strategies under implementation in some countries to more nascent planning efforts in others.

Figure 12.2 shows the countries participating in the FCPF Readiness Fund, the UN-REDD Programme, and/or the FIP, which together encompass most of the world's remaining tropical forests. Many participate in two or more programs; for example, Mexico takes part in all three and is also a prospective recipient of phase 3 finance from the FCPF Carbon Fund. The many countries participating in phases 1 and 2 stand in contrast to the few that have agreements for performance-based finance. As a result, most countries are still stuck in an extended phase of preparation, or "readiness," for REDD+.[34]

> Modest levels of funding cannot be expected to constitute meaningful incentives for reform.

By signing up to participate in one or more of these phase 1 or phase 2 REDD+ financing programs, recipient country governments

Figure 12.2: More than fifty countries have initiated REDD+ programs, but only a few have access to performance-based finance.

COLOMBIA (2015)
ECUADOR (2014)
GUYANA (2009)
LIBERIA (2014)
PERU (2014)
BRAZIL (2008)
INDONESIA (2010)

■ COUNTRIES THAT HAVE
INITIATED REDD+ PROGRAMS WITH INTERNATIONAL FUNDING

■ COUNTRIES WITH PERFORMANCE-BASED
FINANCE AGREEMENTS SIGNED

Center for Global Development

Sources: Forest Carbon Partnership Facility, "FCPF Dashboard," March 31, 2016, https://www.forestcarbonpartnership.org/sites/fcp/files/2016/May/PC21%20FCPF%20Readiness%20Progress__MASTERec.pdf; Forest Investment Program, "Forest Investment Program Factsheet," June 2016, https://www-cif.climateinvestmentfunds.org/sites/default/files/knowledge-documents/fip_factsheet_6-2016_web.pdf; UN-REDD, "Status of National Programmes," updated 2016, http://www.unredd.net/index.php?option=com_national_programme&view=nationalprogramme overview&Itemid=484.

Note: "Countries that have initiated REDD+ programs with international funding" refers to countries that have signed a Preparation Grant with the Forest Carbon Partnership Facility, have active, closed or pipeline national programs with the UN-REDD Program, and/or participate in the Forest Investment Program, but did not yet have a payment-for-performance agreement in place as of December 2015. "Countries with performance-based finance" refers to countries that had a payment-for-performance agreement in place as of December 2015.

signal an intention to address deforestation and forest degradation. But initiatives supported by the modest levels of funding available through such programs cannot be expected to alter domestic forest politics fundamentally on their own, detached from firm commitments to phase 3 finance sufficient to constitute meaningful incentives for reform.

The first round of grants for readiness activities from the FCPF Readiness Fund and UN-REDD Programme, for example, averaged less than $4 million per country to pay for activities such as developing a national strategy and forest monitoring system and associated public consultations. The finance available to the first eight pilot countries participating in the FIP was also small, with the largest packages of grants and concessional lending approved topping out at about $70 million each for Brazil and Indonesia, an amount unlikely to initiate transformational policy change in such large economies.[35] And to get access to even relatively small amounts of money, developing country governments must jump through a number of hoops set up by donors that have delayed final approval and disbursement of funding, as described further below.

Because the finance available through such input-based programs is not much different than traditional foreign aid to the forestry sector in terms of funding volumes or vehicles, it is unlikely to prompt a different result on its own. According to Heru Prasetyo, who served as head of Indonesia's REDD+ Agency, the "pot of gold at the end of the rainbow"—that is, results-based finance—is what motivates the efficient and effective use of funds provided ex ante.[36]

"Show Us the Money"

Increasingly, forest-rich countries and leaders of subnational jurisdictions have been challenging donor countries to make phase 3 commitments by stepping forward with quantitative pledges of their own to reduce emissions from deforestation in return for performance-based finance.

Indonesia's president Susilo Bambang Yudhoyono pioneered the structuring of this kind of contingent pledge, as described in chapter 10. At the G20 meeting in Pittsburgh in September 2009, he announced the first voluntary emission reduction target from a developing country, pledging to reduce Indonesia's emissions by 26 percent relative to business as usual by 2020 using the nation's own resources. With international support, he was confident the amount could rise to 41 percent.[37] Given that the composition of Indonesia's emissions was dominated by land-use

change, President Yudhoyono's pledge was tantamount to a commitment to reduce emissions dramatically from deforestation and peatland conversion.

Governors of subnational jurisdictions in forest-rich developing countries have advanced commitments of their own. As early as April 2007, in anticipation of the climate negotiations in Bali later that year, the governors of the Indonesian provinces of Aceh, Papua, and West Papua declared their intentions to reduce emissions from deforestation using a variety of policy tools. These included imposing a temporary moratorium on logging in Aceh and, in Papua and West Papua, prohibiting log exports and revoking timber concessions that did not benefit local communities. In their declaration, the governors made clear that, in return for their efforts, they expected new revenues above and beyond aid, derived from carbon finance mechanisms.[38]

In the following year, 2008, governors from Aceh and Papua joined four governors from Brazil and three from the United States in signing a memorandum of understanding establishing the Governors' Climate and Forest Task Force, described in chapter 11. Six years later, in August 2014, participating governors signed onto the Rio Branco Declaration, committing themselves to reducing deforestation by 80 percent by 2020, in exchange for "adequate, sufficient, and long-term performance-based funding . . . whether through market or non-market sources."[39]

Later in 2014, on the sidelines of the climate negotiations in Lima, fourteen developing countries issued a joint ministerial announcement endorsing the so-called Lima Challenge. The signatories stated their will-

Figure 12.3: Many developing countries and states have offered additional reductions in deforestation in return for guaranteed performance-based payments.

■ COUNTRIES ENDORSING THE LIMA CHALLENGE (2014)
■ DEVELOPING COUNTRY STATES ENDORSING
   THE RIO BRANCO DECLARATION (2014)

Center
& Global
Development

Sources: Signatory countries, "Lima Challenge"; Rio Branco Declaration.

ingness to do their fair share to promote climate stability through domestic emission reductions supportive of sustainable development goals. But they also challenged developed countries to match with international support their ambition to achieve additional emission reductions through REDD+, land restoration, and landscape-scale mitigation.[40] Figure 12.3 illustrates the breadth of subnational jurisdictions and countries whose leaders had, through the Rio Branco Declaration or the Lima Challenge, respectively, challenged rich countries to increase incentives to reduce emissions from deforestation.

Over the course of 2015, these and other countries began quantifying their ambitions to reduce emissions in their so-called Intended Nationally Determined Contributions (INDCs), submitted to the UNFCCC in preparation for the twenty-first round of climate negotiations in Paris. According to one estimate, if international support motivated all forest-rich developing countries to cut their deforestation-related emissions by 40 percent by 2020—that is, half of what Brazil has achieved (as described in chapter 7)—the avoided emissions would close about half the gap between the sum of expected emission reduction pledges in Paris and what is needed to avoid crossing the two-degree warming threshold.[41]

In sum, political leaders of these countries and provinces need certainty of financial reward to help overcome the political challenges they face in following through on their commitments. Shifting the political economy factors that drive deforestation and forest degradation is a daunting task, one that is difficult to initiate and to sustain. Firm international financial commitments can help tip the balance.

The "Aidification" of REDD+ Finance

On December 8, 2010, during the climate negotiations in Cancún, a capacity crowd of six hundred packed a hotel ballroom to hear world leaders talk about forests at an event convened by a U.S. nonprofit organization called Avoided Deforestation Partners (ADP). Political figures, including UN secretary-general Ban Ki Moon and Norwegian prime minister Jens Stoltenberg, were joined by philanthropists such as George Soros and private sector leaders such as Rob Walton, chairman of the board of Walmart.[42] Jane Goodall, joining by video, serenaded the audience with her signature chimpanzee greeting.

In tone, the event was a pep rally for international cooperation to reduce deforestation. It built on a similar event organized by ADP the previous year in Copenhagen, at which Prime Minister Stoltenberg and President Bharrat Jagdeo of Guyana had highlighted their recently concluded $250 million performance-based agreement on REDD+.[43]

But the atmosphere of the 2010 event changed abruptly when President Jagdeo took the microphone and used the opportunity to complain bitterly about delays in receiving the money. According to one account,

> "The international community has a very poor track record of delivering help," he

said, adding that he appreciates Norway's generosity. "But I can't get the money." In an interview after the panel discussion, Jagdeo explained that, while his government proved in January it had fulfilled the first part of its commitment to Norway, it was just on the verge of getting the first $30 million of Norway's pledge. He placed the blame for the delay squarely on the World Bank, which he said has repeatedly stalled in handing over the money.[44]

What were the reasons behind President Jagdeo's frustration? The commitment of Norwegian finance in return for reduced emissions from deforestation had become entangled in the internal bureaucratic machinery of multilateral development banks and external political constraints on Norway's foreign aid. From President Jagdeo's perspective, the payment should have been a straightforward fee-for-service business transaction between two equal parties. But because the Norwegian funds were governed by the legal and political constraints that apply to development assistance, the World Bank had been asked to serve as a trusted intermediary. As a result, disbursement of funds was held up by standard World Bank (and later, Inter-American Development Bank) fiduciary safeguards designed to reduce the risk of corruption.[45]

While the Guyana case has its unique features, it exemplifies one aspect of the broader phenomenon of what has been termed the "aidification" of REDD+ finance.[46] As described in the previous section, the failure to create market demand for reduced forest emissions has meant that most REDD+ finance has to come from development assistance budgets and through institutions designed to program development aid. This change in the envisioned source of most funds for REDD+ has had adverse consequences for the scale and speed of delivery. Financing REDD+ with aid money has influenced how funds have been programmed, and it has created tensions within and between participating organizations when the needs of REDD+ and the norms of development assistance have diverged. Like putting new wine in old wineskins, channeling REDD+ funds through development agencies and projects has proved problematic for both.[47]

New Wine, Old Wineskins

In the first instance, the objectives of REDD+ and development assistance are related, but they are not the same. The objective of REDD+ is to reduce emissions, while the main objective of development assistance is to reduce poverty. As described in earlier chapters, poor households and communities suffer first and most from climate instability and deforestation. But the geographies of tropical deforestation and poverty diverge: the largest potential reductions in deforestation-related emissions are currently from middle-income countries, especially Brazil and Indonesia, rather than the low-income countries on which development assistance is commonly focused.[48] In Norway, the emergence of Brazil as the country receiving the most Norwegian aid caused discomfort among those arguing that such aid should be directed to the poorest countries.

Beyond dealing with geographical misalignment, a refocusing of forest-related investments on emission reductions also requires changes in partners and adjustments to approaches. USAID was slow to embrace the reframing of U.S. forest-related development assistance as a climate mitigation tool, in part because traditional forestry sector partners in recipient countries are different than those leading new REDD+ programs. Many development professionals in the European Union who were focused on leveraging forestry sector reform through the Forest Law Enforcement, Governance and Trade initiative (described in chapter 8) were skeptical of the potential of REDD+ performance-based payments to effect meaningful change in forest governance.

In some cases, REDD+ financing agencies have faced pressure to bridge the gap between climate mitigation and other development objectives by giving more weight to the "co-benefits" of REDD+, such as poverty reduction and biodiversity conservation. Germany's International Climate Initiative, for example, puts a heavy emphasis on biodiversity,[49] while the REDD Early Movers program insists a large portion of funds be channeled to communities in partner jurisdictions.[50]

A third challenge is that aid agencies have developed policies and procedures to govern forest-related investments at the project level and lack familiarity with working at the scale of broader jurisdictions and advancing associated policy reforms. As a result, they tend to direct REDD+ funds to specific, often place-based, activities and give less attention to bringing about structural change at broader scales. The Congo Basin Forest Fund (CBFF), for example, chose to "sprinkle" its funding across many projects in amounts insufficient to attract political support.[51] Even the FIP has targeted fully half of its finance to site-specific investments, and the associated investment plans have been criticized for failing to articulate how such projects will lead to the "transformational change" the program is mandated to promote.[52]

In his study of Australia's flagship REDD+ project in Indonesia (described in box 12.3, below), former Australian government official Robin Davies argues that place-based demonstration activities were essential to building confidence that performance-based incentives could work. But he also describes the impact of insufficient engagement of government officials at provincial and district levels, who were key to the planning and implementation of emission reduction measures. The payments local villagers received for participating in project activities did not constitute a trial of payment-for-performance incentives as an approach to reducing deforestation.[53]

The mismatch between systems designed for projects and the need for jurisdictional-scale implementation has also posed difficulties in the application of various safeguard policies. Implemented effectively, such policies are tools for managing risks of social and environmental harm and necessary for the legitimacy of foreign aid in response to the concerns of donor country taxpayers. But safeguard policies are not easily applied at the level of entire countries or provinces,[54] and safeguard advocates are not confident that domestic procedures are sufficiently robust to achieve the necessary standards of protection. The World Bank has struggled for a decade to introduce a "country systems" approach in its lending,[55] and operations considered to be "high risk" (such as those

involving forests and indigenous peoples) are excluded from its Program-for-Results instrument, which supports sector-wide and regional initiatives.[56]

A fourth challenge arising from the use of aid agencies to manage REDD+ funds is the agencies' strong aversion to "headline risk." While all public sector institutions seek to avoid negative publicity, aid agencies may be particularly vulnerable to scandals, particularly those related to corruption.[57] In rich countries where political support for development assistance is tepid, bureaucratic incentives are aligned to minimize the chances of something going wrong and, when it does, to reduce the chances of the story getting into the newspaper. Advised one retired multilateral development bank official in a discussion of REDD+ finance, "If you want an institution that can absorb reputational risk, don't come to the World Bank."[58]

A key design feature of Norway's first three bilateral payment-for-performance agreements was the choice of financial intermediaries that could manage fiduciary risk. Brazil's proposal to have the Brazilian Development Bank (BNDES) manage the funds provided a politically acceptable option for Norway.[59] In Guyana, utilizing first the World Bank and then the Inter-American Development Bank as intermediaries caused significant tensions between the donors and the government.[60] In Indonesia, the government proposed channeling funds through UNDP on an interim basis while developing its own financial mechanism, but its slow progress contributed to a loss of momentum.[61]

Contributing to the death by a thousand cuts of the Australian flagship project was adverse press attention stemming from NGO allegations of harm to local communities and the publication of a critique by two Australian academics who focused on the project's lack of results relative to its initial ambition.[62] Lack of transparency on the part of the government—which could have helped communicate the progress and benefits of the project—allowed negative press to remain unchallenged, even though subsequent independent analysis showed the allegations of harm to local communities to be unfounded. According to Robin Davies,

> In the absence of any strong countervailing voices urging patience and defending the potential value of REDD+ demonstration activities, this authoritative academic critique and the more strident NGO critiques combined to create the impression that [the project] could not, or even should not, succeed in its aims. It began to be perceived within AusAID as a "problem project."[63]

A fifth challenge, detailed below, was posed by the different mandates and institutional cultures of the various agencies within rich-country governments that had to work together to program REDD+ funds.

Challenges of Coordination across Agencies in Donor Countries

As described in chapter 11, the relative lack of controversy over funding for tropical forests as a climate mitigation strategy has meant that decision making about REDD+ has played out among a small group of experts and agency staff in each donor country. The absence of high-level political attention (other than in Norway) has meant many of the protagonists in the bureaucratic politics

of REDD+ in donor countries have been government officials below the political level, spread across ministries responsible for climate change, environment, development assistance, and/or foreign policy, in addition to treasury departments.

As climate finance has been mobilized for forest conservation, agencies with different mandates and modes of operation have had to learn to work together. Policy analysts Kate Dooley and Charlie Parker describe the situation in the United Kingdom:

> The establishment of the International Climate Fund (ICF) and the changing institutional landscape that this entailed, required coordination across three government departments that had previously not worked together on the disbursement of international forest finance. In addition, each of these departments had vastly different experiences to contribute to the ICF. DfID, as the sole historical donor to forests internationally had the most expertise in project/program implementation, but had relatively little experience in climate change mitigation and prioritizing interventions based on emissions from tropical deforestation. DECC, on the other hand, had the most experience in climate change and the international negotiations on REDD+, but relatively little experience in the implementation of tropical forest conservation. Finally, DEFRA had a vast amount of experience in the conservation of national forests and biodiversity but no experience in the tropics.[64]

In the rich countries covered by the case studies commissioned for this book—Australia, Germany, Norway, the United Kingdom, and the United States—and described in chapter 11, ministries with a mandate to address climate change have been more focused on climate-related objectives (including measuring emission reductions), more impatient to move forward, and, in some cases, more tolerant of risk than aid agencies, even as (or perhaps because) they have had less practical experience with forests. By contrast, aid agencies, with more in-country and sectoral experience, have been more focused on development objectives, slower moving, and more concerned about managing risk directly rather than shifting it to multilateral institutions.

In Germany in 2014, interviews conducted by forest policy experts Till Pistorius and Laura Kiff with forest and climate experts across government agencies revealed an "astonishingly clear common story line and a wide consensus about the needs, the issues and the risks" related to investment in REDD+.[65] Nevertheless, some differences of opinion across ministries surfaced as new funding for forest-related activities under Germany's International Climate Initiative (ICI) were added to long-standing streams of development cooperation funding for improved forest management. While interagency cooperation was smooth in general, the differences in objectives, experience, and expectations between BMZ (the Federal Ministry for Economic Cooperation and Development, which manages development assistance funds) and BMUB (the Federal Ministry for the Environment, Nature Conservation, Building, and Nuclear Safety, which manages climate-related funds) were evident, especially in the early years of the International Climate Initiative.[66]

Norwegian funding of REDD+ with official development assistance has brought with it its own interagency politics. As mentioned above, the emergence of Brazil—hardly a poor country—as the largest recipient of Norwegian aid has been controversial. Initially, the climate and forests initiative was insulated from environment versus development agency tensions because at the time it was created with a separate unit in Norway's Ministry of Environment, Erik Solheim simultaneously held both portfolios and had the confidence of Prime Minister Stoltenberg. If a conflict between the two agencies arose, Solheim was well placed to resolve it. Continued strong leadership of the initiative has managed ongoing frictions arising from the aid agency's somewhat divergent priorities and operational norms.[67]

Robin Davies describes how interagency dynamics played out in the management of Australia's Kalimantan Forests and Climate Project (KFCP) and the Indonesian National Carbon Accounting System (INCAS) program:

> As for the two public service agencies concerned, AusAID and the Department of Climate Change, each had a bias: one toward economic and community development, and localised payment-for-environmental-services approaches; the other toward national-level carbon accounting and generalised payment-for-performance approaches. AusAID led on the overall program of bilateral cooperation and on KFCP; the Department of Climate Change on support for INCAS. The two agencies tended to shadow each other carefully in order to protect their ministers' or agencies' interests but essentially divided labour. Where they felt unsure of each other's actions, the default response was to delay or block.[68]

In some case study countries, political leadership of aid agencies showed a preference for bilateral funding, which provided greater flexibility and opportunity to demonstrate to taxpayers how their money was being spent.[69] In Australia, the environment ministry was keener on bilateral funding to showcase its leadership in this field internationally.[70] In either instance, the focus on meeting donor-country interests might have come at the expense of recipient-country priorities. According to perceptions gleaned from interviews conducted by Michael Wolosin and Donna Lee,

> Implementation of bilateral REDD+ assistance is burdensome (too much overhead and requirements), rigid (has to be spent "their way" and not clear that it will be applied where actually needed), and insufficiently consultative with important forest-country constituents.[71]

The case studies suggest that, without significant operational experience or capacities of their own, climate and environment ministries tend to have more appetite for channeling funds through multilateral initiatives, which offer economies of scale and the potential to harmonize approaches with other donors and across recipient countries.[72] Multilateral initiatives also offer bureaucratic incentives to donor-agency staff to contribute: money is recorded as disbursed when it is deposited in the multilateral fund, thus relieving pressure to spend. Furthermore, responsibility for program management is offloaded onto the fund's secretariat.[73] Such management responsibility includes taking on the challenge and reputational risk associated with assuring compliance with safeguard policies.

The five challenges described above posed by the use of development assistance as a source of REDD+ finance—divergent objectives, different partners and approaches, mismatched policies and procedures, low risk tolerance, and interagency coordination— have caused headaches for donor agencies and recipient countries alike. But the most important way that traditional development assistance is not "fit for purpose" is the difficulty it has in operationalizing the key distinguishing feature of REDD+: payment for performance.

Constraints on Payment for Performance

As described in chapter 11, the payment-for-performance feature of REDD+ was among the factors that made tropical forest conservation an attractive climate mitigation option in rich-country political arenas.

Ideas about payment for performance as a new approach to development assistance originated at about the same time as the idea of REDD+.[74] In 2005, the linking of aid resources to results was one of the five pillars of the widely endorsed Paris Declaration on Aid Effectiveness.[75] In 2006, scholars at the Center for Global Development (CGD) published an initial working paper on the subject that was elaborated on in a 2010 book entitled *Cash on Delivery: A New Approach to Foreign Aid*.[76] Its basic proposition was that donors should pay for progress toward agreed-upon outcomes—such as the number of additional girls educated or the number of maternal deaths averted—rather than micromanage the inputs necessary to achieve such outcomes.

According to the CGD analysis, payment for performance fundamentally shifts accountability relationships between donor and recipient governments by linking funding commitments to independently verified results. By making progress more transparent, it also increases the accountability of recipient governments to their own citizens. In addition, with donors adopting a more "hands-off" role, recipient governments have greater ownership of initiatives and greater flexibility to design and adjust methods for achieving results in a learning-by-doing approach.[77]

The two communities advancing payment-for-performance ideas in "Development World" and "Forestry World," respectively, remained separate for a number of years, with scholars and practitioners in Development World focused on sectors such as health, education, and energy and largely unaware that results-based payments were the central idea of REDD+. Forestry World policy arenas were similarly remote from discussions about the potential of results-based aid in other sectors. But the evolutionary paths of the two concepts were following similar trajectories.

For example, while the idea of cash-on-delivery aid built on various results-based aid instruments aimed at households or private service providers, its focus was on national-level government-to-government transfers. The premise was that such transfers would provide incentives to remove policy barriers and constraints originating outside of a particular sector. Similarly, REDD+, while conceptually related to earlier site-specific "payments for environmental services" (PES) schemes (described in chapter 6), made a transition from its initial focus on project-level demonstration activities to greater emphasis on measuring performance at the level of national or subnational jurisdictions. As economist Arild Angelsen elaborated, both practitioner communities have wrestled with such issues as how best to establish baselines against which

to measure performance, but sharing of experience between the two has been limited.[78]

General Constraints on Payment for Performance

Proponents of payment for performance in other sectors and with regard to REDD+ have also shared the experience of running up against donor agency constraints on providing results-based finance. Some of these are legal and regulatory. In the United States, for example, the annual budget appropriations process precludes making multiyear funding commitments unless the entire amount is counted in the year it is pledged. In addition, according to Michael Wolosin and Donna Lee, "It is only in rare cases that the U.S. is willing to engage in direct budget support and to make cash transfers to governments."[79]

But even in the absence of legal and regulatory constraints, donor agencies have been very cautious about moving to results-based finance. Among concerns typically raised is the greater vulnerability of performance-based funds to corruption, even though making payments contingent on results should reduce incentives to misuse funds. In the words of our CGD colleague William Savedoff, "To steal money from a pay-for-results program, corrupt officials have to achieve success so efficiently that they can skim money from the final disbursements."[80] In fact, Savedoff proposes the more frequent use of payment-for-performance approaches as a component of a more general strategy to reduce corruption.[81]

Furthermore, Savedoff and our CGD colleague Charles Kenny argue that traditional "input-tracking" approaches to controlling diversion of aid funds through elaborate procurement procedures, oversight, and audits are costly and often ineffective and do not address the costs of failure to achieve development impact. By contrast, in a results-based payment model, the potential for corruption is limited to forms of it with little impact on long-term results (otherwise payments would stop) and to the fraudulent reporting of results (which is difficult with independent satellite-based monitoring of deforestation). Their analysis concludes that, under circumstances in which a good indicator of performance exists, the results-based approach is likely to be preferable to the inputs-based approach even if the "production function" (in the case of REDD+, how to reduce deforestation and degradation) is unknown.[82]

Other concerns include worries that the prospect of financial reward will distort public policy decisions that promote the objective while undermining other interests, that a focus on short-term outcomes will come at the expense of long-term sustainability, and that monitoring and verification will entail high transaction costs.[83] As a result, very few experiments with true payment-for-performance finance—that is, ex post payments to governments based on outcomes—have, in fact, moved forward. Indeed, when Savedoff and another CGD colleague, Rita Perakis, set out in 2013 to identify examples of results-based aid, they could find only six instances in which donor agencies paid governments for outcomes—and three of them involved Norwegian agreements to pay for reduced deforestation.[84]

Although several of the cases studied by Perakis and Savedoff diverged from "pure" payment for performance—for example, by having too much funder involvement in program design or insufficient transparency to enable domestic constituencies to hold governments accountable—they nevertheless generated positive outcomes, mainly by focusing the attention of staff in the relevant agencies on results. None of the cases exhibited the problems of performance-based finance commonly raised by skeptics.[85]

At the end of the day, many of the constraints on paying for performance appear to stem from the reluctance of aid bureaucracies to consider stepping back from their accustomed involvement in the detailed planning of and budgeting for development interventions. With payments for performance, donors lose much of their influence over the timing, location, and other characteristics of the activities implemented to achieve the desired outcome.[86] Such loss of donor control is the flip side of the expected benefits of results-based finance, which include giving more autonomy to recipient governments to figure out how best to achieve agreed-on objectives.[87]

Forest-Specific Constraints on Payment for Performance

The more general reluctance of donor agencies—and, in the case of multilaterals, of the governments represented on their governing boards—to adopt a payment-for-performance approach seems to be particularly acute when it comes to the forestry sector. At first glance, this is puzzling; from the perspective of measuring performance, a results-based payment approach is arguably easier to implement for reduced deforestation than for other development objectives, such as those related to health or education outcomes. Even in light of remaining limitations, the rapidly advancing capabilities of satellite-based monitoring technologies described in chapter 4 are sufficient to support conservative estimates of changes in forest carbon stock.

But donors have been especially hesitant to move forward with payment-for-performance approaches related to forests because of legitimate concerns about the poor governance conditions and weak institutions characteristic of the sector in most developing countries.[88] The UK government agency DfID, for example, which works mostly in poorer countries with weak institutions and profound governance challenges, has hesitated to experiment with unproven results-based payments in the forestry sector and instead has focused on supporting governance reform and capacity building. By contrast, DECC, which was closer to international negotiations and focused on the capacity of middle-income countries to reduce emissions in the short term, saw an opportunity to build the case for performance-based finance through REDD+.[89]

Many aid agency officials are skeptical that payment-for-performance incentives will be sufficient to overcome forest-related governance challenges and capacity constraints; proponents of cash on delivery counter that aid agency staff are unlikely to know better than colleagues in recipient governments how to do so. In any case, demand-driven technical assistance is more likely to be used well.[90]

Donors also wonder how countries with little financial and institutional capacity will be able to reverse increasing deforestation trends without upfront funding for capacity building and investment, although proponents of cash on delivery characterize performance-based payments as complementary to, rather than substitutes for, other aid programs.[91] Furthermore, a firm contract promising payment for performance could be used to leverage financing for upfront costs, on the model of development impact bonds.[92] Impact bonds differ from other kinds of bonds in that investors receive repayment and return only if desired outcomes are achieved.[93] Environmental finance expert Rupert Edwards and colleagues at Forest Trends have proposed "Jurisdictional REDD+ Bonds" to finance transitions to zero-deforestation agricultural development at the subnational scale.[94]

Other concerns of donors regard the possible negative consequences of steps governments might take to reduce deforestation, such as restricting local access to forests or infringing on the rights of indigenous communities. Potential harm to vulnerable communities and ecosystems has led to risk aversion and an insistence on the design and implementation of safeguard systems as a prerequisite to commitments of results-based finance.

Such concerns about the potential for unintended harm are well founded. But the avoidance of the risks of actions to protect forests has sometimes come at the expense of due attention to the risks of no action or lengthy delay. As described in chapter 2, tropical forests in many countries are rapidly being converted to other land uses, often involving the theft of public assets and generating severe social and environmental impacts. Global Witness documented a record

185 murders in 2015 of people defending their land from encroachment by mining, agribusiness, hydroelectric dams, and logging, with 40 percent of the victims indigenous people.[95]

Such conditions call for forest protection initiatives that manage both kinds of risk. The Joint Declaration of Intent to cooperate on REDD+ concluded among Germany, Norway, and Peru in 2014—which specified that results-based payments would be contingent on adherence to relevant UNFCCC safeguards, while also setting a milestone for demarcation and titling of indigenous territories—suggests a promising way forward.[96]

Nevertheless, an abundance of caution has led donor agency officials to invest relatively more in the "readiness" activities associated with the first of the three phases of REDD+ rather than commit funds for performance-based payments, with support earmarked for such activities as institutional capacity building, strategic planning, and consultation. Many donors have been particularly attracted to the more apolitical aspects of readiness, investing tens of millions of dollars in the development of forest measurement, reporting, and verification (MRV) systems. When Australia launched its Indonesia National Carbon Accounting System (INCAS) project, for example, such donor-funded MRV initiatives were already plentiful in Jakarta.[97]

In the absence of donor coordination, such crowding of funds has diminished the effectiveness of REDD+ finance more generally, as documented in a set of case studies commissioned by the Climate and Land Use Alliance. A case study on REDD+ in Colombia described how donors failed to harmonize their support for readiness activities,[98] while a case study on REDD+ in Ghana revealed that more than twenty uncoordinated streams of funding for developing monitoring systems and reference levels had failed to produce either.[99]

Thus, aversion to risks specific to the forestry sector has led to overinvestment in certain readiness activities at the expense of commitments to results-based finance. Even with a project explicitly designed to test payment-for-performance modalities in anticipation of a future forest carbon market—Australia's Kalimantan Forests and Climate Partnership—this fundamental objective got eclipsed by an overemphasis on readiness and, in particular, precise measurement of emission reductions. In 2009, Australian advisers had assisted in the preparation of an Indonesian Ministry of Finance "Climate Change Green Paper," which promoted the concept of a "regional incentive mechanism," with cascading payments from the national level rewarding emission reductions achieved at the provincial or district level.[100] Australia's REDD+ initiative in Indonesia was just getting started at the time the report was being produced. Yet over the course of six years and despite expenditure of A\$65 million, the project never managed to focus on payment for performance, the key feature distinguishing REDD+ from previous attempts to reduce deforestation. The story is summarized in box 12.3.

As a result of these donor funding preferences, 42 percent at most of REDD+ pledges had been made on a payment-for-performance basis as of the end of 2014, as shown in figure 12.4. The payment-for-performance portion mostly comprised Norway's bilateral agreements, followed by Germany's REDD Early

Box 12.3: The Fate of Australia's Flagship REDD+ Project in Indonesia

Following Prime Minister John Howard's March 2007 announcement of a Global Initiative on Forests and Climate (described in chapter 11), the Australian government moved rapidly to program the funds, with a special focus on Australia's neighbor to the north, Indonesia. In September, on the occasion of Australia's hosting of the Asia-Pacific Economic Cooperation (APEC) meeting, an allocation of A$30 million for a Kalimantan Forests and Climate Partnership (KFCP) was announced in the presence of Howard and Indonesian president Susilo Bambang Yudhoyono.

The November 2007 Australian elections brought a change of government from the right-leaning Coalition to the left-leaning Labor government led by Kevin Rudd. Commitment to the forests and climate agenda remained strong and even intensified. In early 2008, the new government renamed the program the International Forest Carbon Initiative (IFCI) and aligned its goals more closely with development of the REDD+ mechanism that had just set sail as a prospective new vehicle for international cooperation on forests at the December 2007 climate negotiations in Bali, as described in chapter 9.

In June 2008, the Indonesia–Australia Forest Carbon Partnership (IAFCP) was launched as an umbrella encompassing support for the previously announced KFCP, a proposed second demonstration project in Sumatra, and an Indonesian National Carbon Accounting Scheme (INCAS). The total commitment of IFCI funds to Indonesia grew to A$70 million by late 2009 and to A$100 million by May 2010, fully half of the original A$200 million global pledge.

The site chosen for the demonstration project in Kalimantan was a 120,000-hectare portion of the Ex-Mega Rice Project, an ill-fated scheme by President Suharto to improve food security by converting a million hectares of peat swamp to rice paddies. About 50,000 hectares of the future KFCP project area had been cleared and drained before the scheme was abandoned. The resulting wasteland was prone to chronic burning—the fires had been especially severe in 2006—and provided an opportunity to showcase restoration of degraded land. The remaining 70,000 hectares had relatively intact peat forest and thus provided an opportunity to demonstrate avoided deforestation. As described in chapter 2, disturbed peatlands are a particularly potent source of the emissions that cause climate change.

In early 2007, President Yudhoyono had issued a presidential decree mandating the area's rehabilitation and revitalization. As a member of the Coalition for Rainforest Nations, and especially in its role as host of the climate negotiations in Bali, the government of Indonesia was eager to demonstrate success in reducing deforestation.

With two governments with converging objectives, support from two heads of state—both thinking of their legacies—and a generous financial commitment with bipartisan support in the donor country, what could possibly go wrong?

Many things, it turned out. They included difficult relationships among multiple agencies with decision-making authority in both the donor and the recipient countries; technical challenges and delays in developing methods to measure emissions from peat swamps; failure to engage governments of relevant subnational political jurisdictions in between the national and the project levels; and adverse publicity from NGOs championing indigenous peoples' rights and from academics alleging waste.

But perhaps the most important reason for the KFCP's limited success was the failure to focus on payment for performance. The project's managers put off planned experimentation with results-based payments and benefit-sharing arrangements pending development of more accurate methods of measuring peatland emissions and greater clarity on national and international REDD+ policy frameworks. According to Robin Davies,

> Once one assumes that performance-based payments cannot be made without a high degree of measurement precision and without certainty about the wider REDD+ payment architecture, and indeed that trialing performance-based payment for emission reductions is a second order priority, it is natural for a project implementation agency, which in this case was an international development agency, to shift into local economic development and capacity-building mode—to get on with what it knows how to do.

Although A$8.4 million of project funds earmarked for performance-based incentives were placed in a World Bank trust fund in 2009, the fund could not be activated until completion of a regional environmental and social assessment, which in turn depended on completion of an environmental management and monitoring plan by the government of Indonesia. These safeguard processes were not finished until 2012, and the funds were eventually reprogrammed for activities unrelated to forests.

Within five years of its official launch in 2008, Australia's aid agency quietly decided to close down the climate and forests partnership with Indonesia as quickly as it could, having achieved only a small portion of its original ambitions. In effect, REDD+ was declared a failure before it had ever been tried.

Source: R. Davies, "The Indonesia-Australia Forrest Carbon Partnership: A Murder Mystery," CGD Policy Paper 60, Center for Global Development, Washington, DC, 2015.

Movers program and the UK's contributions to multilateral funds. The balance of funding—at least 58 percent—was programmed as traditional input-based grant funding, not contingent on reducing emissions from deforestation and forest degradation.[101] Although few developing countries have progressed to the stage of eligibility for phase 3 finance by, in fact, achieving such reductions, the certainty of results-based reward would help motivate efforts to do so.

Furthermore, even those donor funds committed to payment for performance have gotten hung up in the policies and procedures of traditional aid institutions. As described above, President Jagdeo's outburst on the stage in Cancún was an expression of his frustra-

tion with delays in the transfer of Norwegian funds. Although the funds were pledged on a payment-for-performance basis, Norway's choice to channel the money through a World Bank trust fund meant their disbursement would be subject to a full array of safeguard requirements, especially fiduciary controls on procurement. Similarly, as described in box 12.3, Australian funds earmarked for performance-based payments under the KFCP were held up for three years pending completion of various safeguard procedures.[102]

While bilateral funds committed to payment for performance have been slow to disburse, multilateral funds have been slow to reach even the commitment phase. Established to serve as a channel for multilat-

Figure 12.4: Less than half of pledged finance for REDD+ from 2006–14 was results-based.

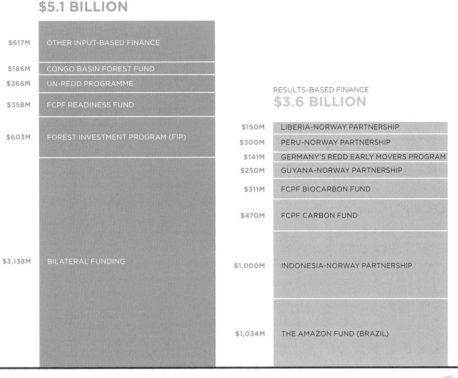

Source: Compilation of reported public sector data from the REDD+ Partnership Voluntary REDD+ Database and ODI HBF Climate Funds Update, covering REDD+ financial commitments for 2006 to 2014. Private foundation data from Forest Trends' REDDX initiative data, as of December 2014. Adapted from Norman and Nakhooda, "The State of REDD+ Finance."

eral performance-based finance, the FCPF Carbon Fund had received $692 million in contributions and commitments as of 2016.[103] But the fund's ability to strike payment-for-performance deals with forest-rich countries and jurisdictions has been both delayed and constrained, in part by donors' aversion to risk. A methodological framework of thirty-eight criteria and associated indicators to govern such transactions was finalized six years after the carbon fund was proposed, just as climate negotiations in Warsaw sewed up consensus on the rules governing REDD+ more generally in December 2013.[104]

The application process through which countries become eligible for performance-based finance from the fund is difficult to distinguish from more traditional input-based aid: in addition to completing a required "readiness" phase and producing strategies to reduce deforestation and comply with safeguards, a country must submit for donor approval a design document detailing how it will achieve results.[105] In June 2016, Costa Rica and the DRC became the first two countries to have their emission reduction program documents approved by the Carbon Fund Board,[106] the sixth step in an eight-step process that has been compared to the Indian board game, "Snakes and Ladders," in which players must roll the dice to advance toward a treasure if they land on a ladder and risk sliding backward if they land on a snake.[107]

Beyond erecting such hurdles for prospective recipients to surmount before they become eligible for REDD+ finance, several donor governments have also insisted they account for how the performance-based payments are subsequently used. What Savedoff calls "double demanding"[108]—that is, requiring recipients to earn the funds through performance in reducing emissions, as well as insisting they then spend the money on donor-approved activities—has been among the many causes of slow disbursement, described further below.

The Problem of Slow Disbursement

One outcome of the channeling of REDD+ finance through traditional development finance institutions has been the slow disbursement of both results-based and other funding.

In the case of Norway's bilateral payment-for-performance agreements, the source of delay in moving the money was different for each country. In Brazil, the agreement specified money would be transferred from Norway to the Amazon Fund upon request when project funding for grants administered by the fund was needed. As a result of delays in populating the project pipeline, sizable chunks of funding remained in Norwegian bank accounts even after deforestation reductions made Brazil eligible for performance-based payments. With Norway in danger of missing its target for official development assistance funding under OECD Development Assistance Committee accounting rules, a transfer was hastily arranged in late 2013.[109]

In Guyana, as mentioned above, delays in disbursement of Norwegian finance were an artifact of channeling funds through multilateral development banks and of dispute over the application of the World Bank's safeguard policies to revenues earned on a performance basis under the agreement. Slow disbursement not only threatened to undermine political support for the partnership; the lack of funds constrained the government's ability to respond to the emergence of mining as the main cause of deforestation.[110]

In Indonesia, failure to move to performance-based payments after initial funding for "readiness" activities has been due to the government's slow pace in establishing agreed-upon institutional infrastructure and a lack of performance in reducing emissions. Yet even without disbursement of funds earmarked for performance-based payments, the Norwegian agreement has contributed to a number of significant reforms in forest governance in Indonesia (described in chapter 10), suggesting the important role of "patient capital" in such agreements.[111]

Delays in disbursing bilateral REDD+ funds not committed on a payment-for-performance basis have been mostly due to protracted programming processes, on top of the time needed to get new funding mechanisms up and running. In the United Kingdom, for example, first the ICF had to be created, then proposed investments had to undergo detailed economic analysis, and then a complex decision making process had to accommodate the involvement of multiple agencies. As a result, only 20 percent of funds allocated to forests had been disbursed midway through the ICF's funding cycle in November 2013, and two-thirds of this amount was "disbursed" in the form of transfers to multilateral funds.[112]

Yet disbursement from multilateral REDD+ funds has also been quite slow, and not just those focused on results-based finance. As shown in figure 12.5, of the $2.2 billion pledged to multilateral development banks, 70 percent had been deposited as of the end of 2014, 41 percent had been committed to specific countries or projects, 29 percent had been formally approved, and only 11 percent had actually been disbursed.[113]

Figure 12.5: Disbursement of multilateral REDD+ funding has lagged far behind pledges.

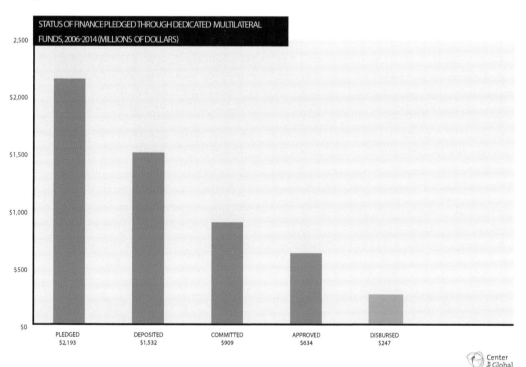

Source: Adapted from M. Norman and S.Nakhooda, "The State of REDD+ Finance," CGD Working Paper 378 (2014, updated May 2015). http://www.cgdev.org/sites/default/files/CGD-Norman-Nakhooda-Climate-Forests-5-REDD-Finance.pdf, based on data for the Forest Investment Program, the Forest Carbon Partnership Facility Carbon Fund, the Congo Basin Forest Fund, the BioCarbon Fund, and the UN-REDD Programme, as of December 31, 2014.

According to interviews conducted for a case study on REDD+ implementation in the DRC, for example,

> Several respondents noted that the burden on early action projects is great, and the flow of finance is hindered by the bureaucratic demands of the donors or multilateral funding institutions. Tensions around the implementation of the Congo Basin Forest Fund (CBFF) were also highlighted as having significant impacts on the ability of actors to successfully demonstrate impacts. The CBFF, which finances most of the pilot projects in the country through the African Development Bank (AfDB), has been the source of significant friction due to bureaucratic delays and problems with disbursement, which have hindered and jeopardized the full implementation of project activities.[114]

Disbursement by the CBFF was also constrained by poor financial management in funded projects and civil unrest that suspended AfDB operations in some countries. In 2014, the CBFF began winding down its operations after its major donors, Norway and the United Kingdom, gave notice they would not be replenishing the fund nor fulfilling remaining pledges to it.[115]

Programming of funds for even the least controversial activities has been slow. The $50 million Development Grants Mechanism (DGM) of the Forest Investment Program managed by the World Bank was established as a way to channel funding directly to indigenous groups to strengthen their roles in REDD+-related decision making and implementation. The DGM was first conceived during the FIP design process in 2009,[116] yet it was six years before the first funds from it were disbursed—to an executing agency for indigenous groups in Brazil.[117]

As described further below, delays in translating pledges into payments have drained momentum from the implementation of REDD+ initiatives in forest countries, and they have created political challenges on the donor side as well. It is difficult to make the case for additional finance when funds already pledged remain stuck in the funding pipeline. In justifying 2014 investments in multilateral REDD+ funds, for example, the UK Department of Energy and Climate Change noted that a number of existing funds had a "considerable tranche of funds from previous donations still to disburse [which means that the funds] are not currently accepting a new round of projects and investments."[118] But the traditional logic of aid replenishment does not apply to the "patient capital" needed for performance-based finance.

Some REDD+ funders and practitioners, observing the slow disbursement of pledged funds and the number of countries not yet "ready" for results-based finance, have questioned the need for further financial commitments. Such a position ignores the potential of certain financial reward to motivate the political and pecuniary investments necessary to tackle the drivers of deforestation. It's a classic chicken-and-egg problem. Which comes first, the promise of performance-based finance or the performance necessary to gain access to it? We believe the former can motivate and accelerate the latter.

It is, thus, ironic that slow disbursement of available funds has dampened the prospects of mobilizing additional funds sufficient to attract high-level political attention in forest countries. The result is a risk that forest-rich countries will choose "non-performance for non-payment."[119]

An alternative risk is performance without payment. Some REDD+ proponents in donor countries are nervous about being put on the spot if forest-rich developing countries succeed in reducing deforestation before adequate finance is available. Two REDD+ experts in Germany interviewed by Till Pistorius and Laura Kiff in 2014 described the situation as follows:

> The expectation we all had a few years ago was that the carbon market would deliver the huge amount of finance required for phase III. However, now this is not very likely to happen. I have an uncomfortable feeling about the availability of funding for phase III, and I foresee already that REDD+ countries may become very impatient and frustrated if they see that the funding we promised a few years ago for phase III is not yet available.
>
> In Warsaw we closed REDD+ negotiations on the REDD+ rule book, so the rules are there now, and they can be implemented. Like in Brazil—they did it. However, if more countries follow their example they will put us, the donors, in a very uncomfortable situation. They will say, so we are here now, where is the predictable stable finance you promised for result-based payments?[120]

Are There Alternatives to Aid?

An initial attraction to developing countries of the idea of REDD+, as described in chapters 9 and 10, was that it reframed their traditional recipient–donor relationships with rich countries as transactions among equal partners to address a global challenge jointly. Yet the mostly disappointing track record of REDD+ finance channeled through aid budgets and institutions constitutes a failure to deliver on the promise of that reframing.

But what are the alternatives? Certainly, some scope exists within the framework of development assistance to increase the number of rich countries allocating substantial amounts of funds to REDD+, and to designate a greater part of such funds for rewarding developing countries on the basis of performance.

Alternatives are available outside of traditional aid budgets and agencies for generating and channeling payment-for-performance finance for reduced emissions from forests.

But in light of broader constraints and other demands on aid budgets, imagining that source as anything other than complementary to larger volumes of finance generated in other ways is unrealistic. And while the example of India described in box 6.1 illustrates the large potential of domestic fiscal policies to provide incentive for forest conservation, surely rich countries should be expected to co-finance such efforts in light of the global public goods tropical forests produce. Reallocation of just 5 percent of the amount that advanced economies spend annually on fossil fuel subsidies[121]—which generate a global "public bad" in the form of emissions—would represent a tripling of funding for REDD+.

Fortunately, a number of possible alternatives are available outside of traditional aid budgets and agencies for generating and channeling payment-for-performance finance for reduced emissions from forests. In 2014–15, CGD convened the Working Group on Scaling Up Performance-Based Transfers for Reduced Tropical Deforestation, and its report identifies several proposals.[122] A 2015 analysis of REDD+ financing options for the European Union by climate policy analysts Charlotte Streck and Andreas Dahl-Jørgensen also provides a useful inventory of options.[123]

We highlight three of the most promising possibilities viable at the time of our writing. One focuses on the potential of emissions trading, one describes an option for channeling results-based finance through new institutions, and one illustrates how rich countries could use public guarantees to leverage private finance. These ongoing discussions provide a source of optimism that, as governments, corporations, and civil society get serious about addressing the challenge of climate change in the wake of the agreement reached in Paris, they will find tools available to generate the necessary finance for forests.

Markets for Forest Carbon

Much of the pre-Copenhagen enthusiasm for REDD+ in 2007–9 was based on the expectation that an international climate agreement would lead to a global market for forest carbon credits. While a global market remains in the distant future, many smaller markets are under development, and the Paris Agreement gives renewed life to the idea that countries can meet their nationally determined emission reduction targets through "internationally transferred mitigation outcomes."[124] The provision allows rich countries to obtain credit for emission reductions generated by

tropical forests, either through emissions trading or results-based payments.[125]

In mid-2016, the state of California was developing rules that would open the door to the first compliance market demand for international forest offsets.[126] Although such inclusion has generated opposition, as described in chapter 11, the staff of the Air Resources Board determined in 2015 that the state should pursue passage of the necessary regulatory amendments to include REDD+ offsets in the third compliance period of its cap-and-trade system, scheduled to begin in 2018.[127] They identified the state of Acre in Brazil as the jurisdiction most advanced toward a position from which it could issue compliance-grade credits.[128]

If California were to pioneer the inclusion of REDD+ offsets in its program, it could set a high standard for such transactions and build confidence that the various risks identified by opponents can be managed effectively; this would make more likely the inclusion of international forest offsets in other emissions trading systems currently under development. It would also rekindle hope among officials in Acre and other forest-rich states and provinces that their efforts to conserve forests will be rewarded.

The world's airlines also might soon become large-scale buyers of market-based REDD+ credits. Unlike greenhouse gas emissions that emanate from activities within national boundaries, which are covered under the UNFCCC, emissions from international flights fall under the auspices of the International Civil Aviation Organization (ICAO), a consortium of national governments and airlines. As of mid-2016, ICAO members were negotiating whether airlines could use offset credits, potentially including REDD+, to meet a global industry-wide emission reduction target.[129]

At the time of writing, much remained uncertain about whether ICAO would adopt such a "market-based measure," whether forest credits would be allowed, and what form these credits would take; but the magnitude of the aviation industry's potential demand for forest offsets would constitute a material increase in REDD+ finance. Michael Wolosin estimates that while California's market could generate $150 million in demand for forest offsets per year during 2018–20, ICAO's demand could be in the range of $3.2 billion to $4 billion per year in the 2020s.[130]

Climate Finance Instruments

The second option for freeing REDD+ finance from the constraints of aid is to channel funds through climate finance institutions rather than aid agencies. Although the Paris Agreement did not specify targets for the amount or timing of climate finance, it did note the importance of public funds and ask developed countries to "take the lead."[131] Furthermore, the decision accompanying the agreement specifically calls for REDD+ funding and refers to the Green Climate Fund (GCF, the official climate finance mechanism under the UNFCCC), "dispelling any doubts on whether the GCF could play a role in providing financing for REDD+."[132]

In October 2014, the GCF board adopted a "logic model" to guide results-based payments for REDD+,[133] and, as of mid-2016, GCF staff were conducting informal discussions on how the fund could operationalize such finance. This fresh start provides an opportunity to design a genuine payment-for-performance funding procedure that would avoid some of the causes of delay and frustration characterizing REDD+ finance administered by organizations designed to deliver development assistance.

In a 2016 policy paper, William Savedoff elaborates on the GCF's opportunity to develop a funding modality closer to a pure cash-on-delivery approach. He proposes the GCF make an "open offer" to sign five-year, renewable agreements with a limited number of tropical forest countries. The fund would commit to paying for avoided emissions, verified by satellite monitoring, up to a certain level each year and at a certain price. It would reserve the right to suspend payments if a participating country were found to be failing to implement social and environmental safeguards by a previously agreed-upon international organization or panel.[134]

If the GCF board were willing to experiment with such an approach, it could provide a meaningful incentive to forest-rich countries to conserve their forests, as well as valuable experience with results-based finance more generally. In 2014, the New Climate Economy Commission recommended that developed countries provide $5 billion per year in REDD+ financing from 2015 to 2030—and a shift to performance-based payments—as a component of the $100 billion in annual climate finance rich countries pledged to mobilize from public and private sources by 2020.[135] In light of the analysis presented in previous chapters, this amount should be considered a lower bound.

Leverage Private Finance through Rich-Country Creditworthiness

A third non-aid option for REDD+ finance involves leveraging the balance sheets of rich countries to generate funding outside of development assistance budgets. Rich-country backing for "green bonds" has long been promoted as a tool for attracting private finance to climate-friendly investments in general,[136] and to forests in particular,[137] but to date application to the land-use sector has been limited.[138]

An annex to the CGD working group report mentioned above proposes a different way for rich countries to use their AAA ratings to generate REDD+ finance, building on an idea promoted by Kenneth G. Lay, a former treasurer of the World Bank. It outlines a mechanism in which sponsor governments would extend deposit guarantees to domestic retail and institutional investors in a $100 billion "Forest Foundation Fund" endowment. The aggregated funds would be managed as a single global fund and invested in long-term assets, similar to the way in which university endowments are managed. Eligible forest-rich countries would be granted returns on shares in the net earnings of the fund commensurate with their verified emission reductions. If such a fund had been operational in the decade before 2015, it would have generated more than $5 billion per year for distribution to those countries.[139]

If the political hurdles to establishing such an endowment fund could be overcome, it could deliver on the promise of long-term finance not dependent on the whims of annual appropriations processes. Such certainty would be a major step forward in providing developing countries with meaningful incentives for forest protection.

Conclusion

Early discussions of REDD+ were animated by the potential of carbon markets to unleash finance on the scale needed to alter fundamentally the calculations of developing countries regarding the optimal rate of deforestation. Although a few donor countries have made significant allocations of funding to REDD+ as part of their contributions to financing climate mitigation, such funding overall has been too low, too slow, and too encumbered by bureaucratic processes to represent meaningful incentives to forego business as usual in forest-rich countries or to demonstrate results at scale.

Specifically, these funds have suffered from "aidification" in terms of their size, bureaucratic procedures, and speed of disbursement. The volume of funding available for REDD+ has been determined by the broader politics of climate and development finance rather than the needs of forest countries or the mitigation potential of forests. Channeling funds through traditional bilateral and multilateral aid agencies has allowed internal politics within and among such agencies to shape REDD+ investments. The result has been an excessive focus on avoiding the risks associated with initiatives to protect forests rather than avoiding the risks of continuing deforestation as usual. It has also led to greater emphasis on funding "readiness" activities and place-based projects rather than on guaranteeing payment for performance at jurisdictional scale—the key and unique attribute of REDD+.

The absence of markets for forest carbon credits and the reluctance of most donors to commit to genuine payment-for-performance finance have left the compelling idea of REDD+

largely untested a decade after it first captured the world's imagination as a solution to climate change. And although scope for increasing aid-based funding is limited, a number of possibilities exist for generating and channeling funds outside the framework of development assistance and creating market demand for forest emission reductions.

In short, although payment for performance was the feature of REDD+ that distinguished it from previous efforts toward international cooperation to reduce deforestation, experience has so far been limited to a handful of bilateral agreements and a group of prospective multilateral agreements still in the pipeline. It thus remains, for the most part, a great idea that hasn't been tried. Like a bride left waiting at the altar, Forestry World has gotten all dressed up and ready to formalize her marriage to Climate World (as negotiated under the UNFCCC, as described in chapter 9), but the groom's family has so far failed to show up with the dowry of large-scale performance-based finance so the wedding can take place.

In our concluding chapter, we assert the necessity, feasibility, and urgency of reviving commitment to the promise of REDD+.

Notes

1. M. Thatcher, "Speech to the United Nations General Assembly," United Nations, New York, November 8, 1989, http://www.margaretthatcher.org/document/107817.

2. K. Dooley and C. Parker, "Evolution of Finance for REDD+ in the UK: A History and Overview of the UK Government's Engagement with REDD+ Finance, with a Focus on Performance-Based Payments for REDD+," CGD Policy Paper 55, Center for Global Development, Washington, DC, 2015, 4.

3. Andrew Bennett, personal communication, February 26, 2016.

4. This section draws heavily on M. Norman and S. Nakhooda, "The State of REDD+ Finance," CGD Working Paper 378, Center for Global Development, Washington, DC, 2014 (updated 2015).

5. Informal Working Group on Interim Finance for REDD+, "Report of the Informal Working Group on Interim Finance for REDD+ (IWG-IFR): Discussion Document," 2009, http://www.illegal-logging.info/sites/default/files/uploads/ReportoftheInformalWorkingGrouponInterimFinanceforREDDIWGIFRFinal.pdf, using an exchange rate of 1 USD=.7 Euro.

6. J. Eliasch, *Climate Change: Financing Global Forests: The Eliasch Review* (London: Office of Climate Change, 2008), https://www.gov.uk/government/uploads/system/uploads/attachment_data/file/228833/9780108507632.pdf.

7. M. Wolosin and D. Lee, "US Support for REDD+: Reflections on the Past and Future Outlook," CGD Policy Paper 48, Center for Global Development, Washington, DC, 2014.

8. World Bank, "Forest Carbon Partnership Facility Launched at Bali Climate Meeting," World Bank press release 2008/142/SDN, December 11, 2007.

9. Forest Carbon Partnership Facility, "About FCPF," Washington, DC, 2016 https://www.forestcarbonpartnership.org/about-fcpf-0.

10. Forest Carbon Partnership Facility, "Forest Carbon Partnership Facility: Demonstrating Activities That Reduce Emissions from Deforestation and Forest Degradation," Washington, DC, 2009, https://www.forestcarbonpartnership.org/sites/fcp/files/New%20FCPF%20brochure%20--%20low%20resolution%20051809_0.pdfu_8_z_0.pdf.

11. United Nations Programme on Reducing Emissions from Deforestation and Forest Degradation, "UN-REDD Programme Multi Donor Trust Fund Semi Annual Update," United Nations Collaborative Program on Reducing Emissions from Deforestation and Forest Degradation (REDD) in Developing Countries, Geneva, 2009, http://www.unredd.net/index.php?option=com_docman&view=list&slug=global-programme-documents-596&Itemid=134.

12. United Nations Programme on Reducing Emissions from Deforestation and Forest Degradation, "UN-REDD Programme Donors," 2008–2016, http://www.un-redd.org/Donors_and_Partners/tabid/102612/Default.aspx.

13. Global Environment Facility, "The GEF Incentive Mechanism for Forests: A New REDD+ Multilateral Finance Program," Washington, DC, 2010, https://www.thegef.org/gef/sites/thegef.org/files/publication/REDDEnglish.pdf.

14. E. Schadler, "Case Study: The Development of the REDD Options Assessment Report," Institute for Environmental Diplomacy & Security, University of Vermont, 2012, http://www.uvm.edu/ieds/sites/default/files/OAR_casestudy.pdf.

15. A. Angelsen et al., "Reducing Emissions from Deforestation and Forest Degradation (REDD): An Options Assessment Report," Meridian Institute, Washington, DC, 2009, http://www.redd-oar.org/links/REDD-OAR_en.pdf.

16. J. Leber, "A Plan to Save Rainforests Gains International Momentum," *ClimateWire*, September 24, 2009, http://www.eenews.net/stories/82590.

17. United Nations Framework Convention on Climate Change (UNFCCC), "Report of the

Conference of the Parties on Its Sixteenth Session, Held in Cancún from 29 November to 10 December 2010," March 15, 2011, http://unfccc.int/resource/docs/2010/cop16/eng/07a01.pdf.

18. Climate Investment Funds, "Forest Investment Program—FIP Factsheet," Washington, DC, November 2015, https://www-cif.climateinvestmentfunds.org/sites/default/files/knowledge-documents/fip_factsheet_nov2015_web.pdf.

19. Ibid.

20. Climate Investment Funds, "Design Document for the Forest Investment Program: A Targeted Program under the SCF Trust Fund," Washington, DC, 2009, http://www.climateinvestmentfunds.org/cif/sites/climateinvestmentfunds.org/files/FIP_Design_Document_July_final.pdf, 4.

21. E. von Pfeil, "REDD Early Movers: Rewarding Pioneers in Forest Conservation," Federal Ministry for Economic Cooperation and Development, Bonn, Germany, September 2015, https://unfccc.int/files/cooperation_and_support/financial_mechanism/standing_committee/application/pdf/rem_wfc_09_15_final.pdf; Deutsche Gesellschaft für Internationale Zusammenarbeit (GIZ), "REDD Early Movers," Bonn, Germany, https://www.giz.de/en/worldwide/33356.html.

22. A. Aquino, "BioCarbon Fund Launches $280 Million Initiative for Sustainable Forest Landscapes," World Bank, Washington, DC, November 20, 2013.

23. BioCarbon Fund, "What Is the Initiative for Sustainable Forest Landscapes?" BioCarbon Fund Initiative for Sustainable Forest Landscapes, Washington, DC, http://www.biocarbonfund-isfl.org/about-us.

24. S. Zwick, "Painting the Town REDD: Merrill Lynch Inks Massive Voluntary Forest Deal," Ecosystem Marketplace, February 8, 2008, http://www.ecosystemmarketplace.com/articles/painting-the-town-redd-merrill-lynch-inks-massive-voluntary-forest-deal/.

25. D. Fogarty, "Macquarie, IFC Agree Forest Carbon Investment Fund," Reuters, July 7, 2011.

26. A. Angelsen, ed., *Realising REDD+: National Strategy and Policy Options* (Bogor, Indonesia: Center for International Forestry Research, 2009), 19.

27. M. Wolosin and D. Lee, "US Support for REDD+: Reflections on the Past and Future Outlook," CGD Policy Paper 48, Center for Global Development, Washington, DC, 2014, 11.

28. Climate Investment Funds, "Pilot Program for Climate Resilience," https://www-cif.climateinvestmentfunds.org/fund/pilot-program-climate-resilience.

29. Adaptation Fund, "Projects and Programmes," 2015, https://www.adaptation-fund.org/projects-programmes/.

30. USAID, "Sustainable Landscapes: Reducing Emissions from Tropical Deforestation," GCC Brief, 2013, https://www.climatelinks.org/resources/gcc-brief-sustainable-landscapes.

31. Wolosin and Lee, "US Support for REDD+," 51.

32. N. Linacre et al., "REDD+ Supply and Demand 2015–2024, Forest Carbon, Markets and Communities Program," FCMC Program, U.S. Agency for International Development, January 2015, https://rmportal.net/library/content/fcmc/publications/redd-supply-and-demand-2015-2025/at_download/file, 19.

33. K. Barrett and A. Goldstein, "Norway, Germany, UK Pledge $5 Billion to Combat Tropical Deforestation," Ecosystem Marketplace, November 30, 2015, http://www.ecosystemmarketplace.com/articles/norway-germany-uk-pledge-5-billion-to-combat-tropical-deforestation/.

34. M. Brockhaus and M. Di Gregorio, "National REDD+ Policy Networks: From Cooperation to Conflict," *Ecology and Society* 19, no. 4 (2014): 14.

35. ICF International, Independent Evaluation of the Climate Investment Funds (Washington, DC: World Bank, 2014), http://www.cifevaluation.org/docs/cif_evaluation

_final.pdf?utm_source=website&utm_medium=homepage&utm_content=full_eval&utm_campaign=cifevaluation.

36. Heru Prasetyo, personal communication, October 2013.

37. S. B. Yudhoyono, "Intervention by H. E. Dr. Susilo Bambang Yudhoyono, President of the Republic of Indonesia, on Climate Change," Forest Climate Center, September 25, 2009, http://forestclimatecenter.org/files/2009-09-25%20Intervention%20by%20President%20SBY%20on%20Climate%20Change%20at%20the%20G-20%20Leaders%20Summit.pdf.

38. "Declaration of the Governors of Aceh, Papua and Papua Barat on Climate Change," Nusa Dua, Bali, April 26, 2007, http://webcache.googleusercontent.com/search?q=cache:XKWBgyoNHeoJ:siteresources.worldbank.org/INTINDONESIA/Resources/GovernorsDeclaration.doc+&cd=1&hl=en&ct=clnk&gl=us.

39. Signatory countries, "Lima Challenge," Peru, September 2014, http://www.un.org/climatechange/wp-content/uploads/2015/05/LIMA-CHALLENGE.pdf; Governors' Climate and Forests Task Force, "Rio Branco Declaration: Building Partnerships & Securing Support for Forests, Climate, & Livelihoods," Rio Branco, Brazil, August 11, 2014, http://www.gcftaskforce.org/documents/2014_annual_meeting/GCF_RioBrancoDeclaration_August_5_2014_EN.pdf, 3.

40. Climate Advisers, "Forest Countries Challenge World to Increase Climate Ambition," Washington, DC, September 2014, http://www.climateadvisers.com/forest-countries-challenge-world-to-increase-climate-ambition/.

41. M. de Nevers and J. Engelmann, "Reducing Deforestation Is Key to Closing the Paris Gap," Views from the Center blog, Center for Global Development, June 4, 2015, http://www.cgdev.org/blog/reducing-deforestation-key-closing-paris-gap.

42. Avoided Deforestation Partners, "In Cancún, World Leaders Call for Quick Action on Forests," December 8, 2010, http://adpartners.org/news/in-cancun-world-leaders-call-for-quick-action-on-forests/.

43. "President Jagdeo Meets Key World Leaders as Efforts Intensify in Copenhagen," Guyana Chronicle, December 17, 2009, http://guyanachronicle.com/president-jagdeo-meets-key-world-leaders-as-efforts-intensify-in-copenhagen/.

44. J. Eilperin, "At Cancún Conference, Blunt Talk on Forests," Washington Post, December 8, 2010.

45. J. Busch and N. Birdsall, "Assessing Performance-Based Payments for Forest Conservation: Six Successes, Four Worries, and Six Possibilities to Explore of the Guyana-Norway Agreement," CGD Note, Center for Global Development, Washington, DC, 2014.

46. F. Seymour and A. Angelsen, "Summary and Conclusions: REDD+ without Regret," in Analysing REDD+: Challenges and Choices, ed. A. Angelsen (Bogor, Indonesia: Center for International Forestry Research, 2012).

47. The remainder of this section and subsequent sections rely heavily on five background papers on the politics of REDD+ finance in donor countries commissioned for this book: Wolosin and Lee, "US Support for REDD+"; Dooley and Parker, "Evolution of Finance for REDD+ in the UK"; T. Pistorius and L. Kiff, "The Politics of German Finance for REDD+," CGD Working Paper 390, Center for Global Development, Washington, DC, 2014; E. Hermansen and S. Kasa, "NGOs as Climate Policy Entrepreneurs: The Surprising Story of NICFI and Norwegian Leadership in REDD+ Financing," CGD Working Paper 389, Center for Global Development, Washington, DC, 2014; and R. Davies, "The Indonesia-Australia Forest Carbon Partnership: A Murder Mystery," CGD Policy Paper 60, Center for Global Development, Washington, DC, 2015. The

sections also draw from a set of country case studies on international REDD+ finance commissioned by Donna Lee and Till Pistorius, with support from the Climate and Land-Use Alliance: T. Johns, "The Impacts of International REDD+ Finance: DRC Case Study," Climate and Land Use Alliance, San Francisco, July 2015, http://www.climateandlandusealliance.org/wp-content/uploads/2015/08/Impacts_of_International_REDD_Finance_Case_Study_DRC.pdf; C. Streck, D. Conway, J. P. Castro, and T. Varns, "The Impacts of International REDD+ Finance: Colombia Case Study," Climate and Land Use Alliance, June 2015, http://www.climatefocus.com/sites/default/files/Impacts_of_International_REDD_Finance_Case_Study_Colombia.pdf; R. Asare, "The Impacts of International REDD+ Finance: Ghana Case Study," Climate and Land Use Alliance, May 2015, http://www.climateandlandusealliance.org/wp-content/uploads/2015/08/Impacts_of_International_REDD_Finance_Case_Study_Ghana.pdf; T. Laing, "The Impacts of International REDD+ Finance: Guyana Case Study," Climate and Land Use Alliance, July 2015, http://www.climateandlanduse alliance.org/wp-content/uploads/2015/08/Impacts_of_International_REDD_Finance_Case_Study_Guyana.pdf; and T. Pistorius, "The Impacts of International REDD+ Finance: Vietnam Case Study," May 2015, http://www.climateandlandusealliance.org/wp-content/uploads/2015/08/Impacts_of_International_REDD_Finance_Case_Study_Vietnam.pdf.

48. Wolosin and Lee, "US Support for REDD+."

49. Government of Germany, Federal Ministry for the Environment, Nature Conservation, Building and Nuclear Safety, "The International Climate Initiative," https://www.international-climate-initiative.com/en/about-the-iki/iki-funding-instrument/.

50. KfW Development Bank and Deutsche Gesellschaft für Internationale Zusammenarbeit GmbH, "Rewarding REDD+ Action and Supporting Low-Deforestation Development in the Colombian Amazon," Government of Germany, Federal Ministry for Economic Cooperation and Development (BMZ), Frankfurt/Eschborn, Germany, December 2015, https://www.kfw-entwicklungsbank.de/PDF/Entwicklungsfinanzierung/Themen-NEU/20151128-REM-Colombia-agreement-summaryFINAL.pdf.

51. M. Norman, "Where Has Funding for Forest Protection in Central Africa Gone Wrong? UK and Norway Back Out of a Major Climate Fund Set Up to Protect Congo Basin Forests, as New Initiative Is Launched," Thomson Reuters Foundation News, November 10, 2015.

52. Climate Investment Funds, "FIP Semi-Annual Operational Report," Washington, DC, November 19, 2014, https://www.climateinvestmentfunds.org/cif/sites/climateinvestmentfunds.org/files/FIP_13_3_FIP_semi_annual_operational_report_rev.1.pdf; ICF International, Independent Evaluation, 41.

53. Davies, "The Indonesia-Australia Forest Carbon Partnership."

54. Pistorius and Kiff, "The Politics of German Finance for REDD+."

55. J. D. Quintero, A. Ninio, and P. J. Posas, "Use of Country Systems for Environmental Safeguards," analytical background paper for the World Bank, World Bank, Washington, DC, 2010.

56. World Bank, "Program-for-Results: Two-Year Review," March 17, 2015, http://www-wds.worldbank.org/external/default/WDSContentServer/WDSP/IB/2015/03/19/000477144_20150319141327/Rendered/PDF/951230BR0R2015020Box385454B00OUO090.pdf, 28.

57. See, for example, W. Savedoff, A. Glassman, and J. Madan, "Global Health, Aid and Corruption: Can We Escape the Scandal Cycle?" CGD Policy Paper 86, Center for

Global Development, Washington, DC, 2016.

58. Comment by Warren Evans at a Center for Global Development event, Working Group Report Launch: "Look to the Forests, How Performance Payments Can Slow Climate Change," Center for Global Development Headquarters, Washington, DC, October 13, 2015.

59. N. Birdsall, B. Savedoff, and F. Seymour, "The Brazil-Norway Agreement with Performance-Based Payments for Forest Conservation: Successes, Challenges, and Lessons," CGD Brief, Center for Global Development, Washington, DC, 2014.

60. Busch and Birdsall, "Assessing Performance-Based Payments."

61. F. Seymour, N. Birdsall, and W. Savedoff, "The Indonesia-Norway REDD+ Agreement," CGD Policy Paper 56, Center for Global Development, Washington, DC, 2015.

62. E. Olbrei and S. Howes, "A Very Real and Practical Contribution? Lessons from the Kalimantan Forests and Climate Partnership," *Climate Law* 3, no. 2 (2012): 103–37.

63. Davies, "The Indonesia-Australia Forest Carbon Partnership," p. 38.

64. Dooley and Parker, "Evolution of Finance for REDD+ in the UK," 11.

65. Pistorius and Kiff, "The Politics of German Finance for REDD+," 42.

66. Pistorius and Kiff, "The Politics of German Finance for REDD+."

67. Not-for-attribution interviews conducted by one of the authors in Oslo, September 2014.

68. Davies, "The Indonesia-Australia Forest Carbon Partnership," p. 54.

69. Pistorius and Kiff, "The Politics of German Finance for REDD+."

70. Robin Davies, personal communication, March 31, 2016.

71. Wolosin and Lee, "US Support for REDD+," 51.

72. Norman and Nakhooda, "The State of REDD+ Finance."

73. Dooley and Parker, "Evolution of Finance for REDD+ in the UK."

74. F. Seymour, "Separated at Birth? COD Aid and REDD+," Views from the Center blog, Center for Global Development, October 2013, http://www.cgdev.org/blog/separated-birth-cod-aid-and-redd.

75. Organisation for Economic Co-operation and Development, "The Paris Declaration on Aid Effectiveness and the Accra Agenda for Action," Paris, France, 2005.

76. O. Barder and N. Birdsall, "Payments for Progress: A Hands-Off Approach to Foreign Aid," CGD Working Paper 102, Center for Global Development, Washington, DC, 2006; N. Birdsall and W. Savedoff, *Cash on Delivery: A New Approach to Foreign Aid* (Washington, DC: Center for Global Development Books, 2010).

77. Ibid.

78. A. Angelsen, "REDD+ as Performance-Based Aid: General Lessons and Bilateral Agreements of Norway," United Nations University World Institute for Development Economics Research Paper No. WP2013/135, 2013.

79. Wolosin and Lee, "US Support for REDD+," 34.

80. W. Savedoff, "How the Green Climate Fund Could Promote REDD+ through a Cash on Delivery Instrument: Issues and Options," CGD Policy Paper 72, Center for Global Development, Washington, DC, 2016, 13.

81. Ibid.

82. C. Kenny and W. Savedoff, "Can Results-Based Payments Reduce Corruption?" CGD Working Paper 102, Center for Global Development, Washington, DC, 2013.

83. R. Perakis, and W. Savedoff, "Does Results-Based Aid Change Anything? Pecuniary Interests, Attention, Accountability and Discretion in Four Case Studies," CGD Policy Paper 53, Center for Global Development, Washington, DC, 2015.

84. Ibid.

85. Ibid.

86. Pistorius and Kiff, "The Politics of German Finance for REDD+."

87. Birdsall and Savedoff, *Cash on Delivery.*

88. Wolosin and Lee, "US Support for REDD+."

89. Dooley and Parker, "Evolution of Finance for REDD+ in the UK." DECC was disbanded by the new government led by Prime Minister Theresa May in July 2016.

90. Birdsall and Savedoff, *Cash on Delivery*.

91. Ibid.

92. M. de Nevers, "Look to the Forests: How Performance Payments Can Slow Climate Change," CGD Working Group Report, Center for Global Development, Washington, DC, 2015; see also Center for Global Development, "Development Impact Bonds Briefing Note," Center for Global Development, Washington, DC, 2014.

93. Norman and Nakhooda, "The State of REDD+ Finance."

94. R. Edwards, D. Tepper, and S. Lowery, "Jurisdictional REDD+ Bonds: Leveraging Private Finance for Forest Protection, Development, and Sustainable Agriculture Supply Chains," Forest Trends, 2014, http://www.forest-trends.org/documents/files/doc_4208.pdf.

95. Global Witness, "On Dangerous Ground," London, UK, June 2016, https://www.globalwitness.org/documents/18482/On_Dangerous_Ground.pdf.

96. "Joint Declaration of Intent between the Government of the Republic of Peru, the Government of the Kingdom of Norway and the Government of the Federal Republic of Germany on 'Cooperation on Reducing Greenhouse Gas Emissions from Deforestation and Forest Degradation (REDD+) and Promote [sic] Sustainable Development in Peru,'" New York, September 23, 2014, https://www.regjeringen.no/contentassets/b324ccc0cf88419fab88f2f4c7101f20/declarationofintentperu.pdf.

97. Davies, "The Indonesia-Australia Forest Carbon Partnership."

98. Streck et al., "The Impacts of International REDD+ Finance."

99. Asare, "The Impacts of International REDD+ Finance."

100. Government of Indonesia, Ministry of Finance, "Ministry of Finance Green Paper: Economic and Fiscal Policy Strategies for Climate Change Mitigation in Indonesia," Republic of Indonesia and Australia-Indonesia Partnership, Jakarta, 2009, http://www.fiscalpolicyforclimatechange.depkeu.go.id/pdf/var/green_paper_final.pdf.

101. Norman and Nakhooda, "The State of REDD+ Finance."

102. Davies, "The Indonesia-Australia Forest Carbon Partnership."

103. Forest Carbon Partnership Facility, "About FCPF."

104. Forest Carbon Partnership Facility, "Carbon Fund Methodological Framework," December 20, 2013, https://www.forestcarbonpartnership.org/sites/fcp/files/2014/MArch/March/FCPF%20Carbon%20Fund%20Methodological%20Framework%20Final%20Dec%2020%202013.pdf.

105. Forest Carbon Partnership Facility, "The Carbon Fund," https://www.forestcarbonpartnership.org/carbon-fund-0.

106. World Bank, "Taking Climate Action from Paris to the Rainforests," *World Bank News*, June 22, 2016.

107. J. Busch, "Snakes or Ladders at the Carbon Fund?" Views from the Center blog, Center for Global Development, June 17, 2016, http://www.cgdev.org/blog/snakes-or-ladders-carbon-fund.

108. W. Savedoff, "Funders Worry about 'Double Counting'—But What about 'Double Demanding'?" Views from the Center blog, Center for Global Development, March 5, 2015, http://www.cgdev.org/blog/funders-worry-about-double-counting-%E2%80%93-what-about-double-demanding.

109. "OECD Rejects Norway's Reporting of Brazil Forest Aid," *Development Today*, October 9, 2012; Brazilian Government, Brazilian Development Bank (BNDES), Brazilian Ministry of Development, Industry, and Foreign Trade, Brazilian Ministry of the

Environment, "Amazon Fund: Activity Report 2013," Rio de Janeiro, Brazil, June 2014, http://www.amazonfund.gov.br/FundoAmazonia/export/sites/default/site_en/Galerias/Arquivos/Relatorio_Atividades/RAFA_Virtual_English_2013.pdf.

110. LTS International, "Evaluation of Norway's International Climate and Finance Initiative," annex 9, Guyana, 2013, https://www.norad.no/globalassets/import-2162015-80434-am/www.norad.no-ny/filarkiv/vedlegg-til-publikasjoner/annexes-real-time-evaluation-of-norways-international-climate-and-forest-initiative.-synthesising-report-2007-2013.pdf, 249 and 256.

111. Seymour, Birdsall, and Savedoff, "The Indonesia-Norway REDD+ Agreement." See also LTS International, "Real-Time Evaluation of Norway's International Forest and Climate Initiative Synthesizing Report 2007–2013," Government of Norway, Norwegian Agency for Development Cooperation, August 2014, https://www.norad.no/en/toolspublications/publications/2014/real-time-evaluation-of-norways-international-climate-and-forest-initiative.-synthesising-report-2007-2013/.

112. Dooley and Parker, "Evolution of Finance for REDD+ in the UK," 15.

113. Norman and Nakhooda, "The State of REDD+ Finance."

114. Johns, "The Impacts of International REDD+ Finance," 8.

115. M. Norman, "Where Has Funding for Forest Protection in Central Africa Gone Wrong? UK and Norway Back Out of a Major Climate Fund Set Up to Protect Congo Basin Forests, as New Initiative Is Launched," Thomson Reuters Foundation News, November 10, 2015.

116. Climate Investment Funds, "Design Document for the Forest Investment Program, a Targeted Program under the SCF Trust Fund," Washington, DC, 2009, http://www.climateinvestmentfunds.org/cif/sites/climateinvestmentfunds.org/files/FIP_Design_Document_July_final.pdf.

117. World Bank, "BR DGM for Indigenous People and Traditional Communities (P143492)," World Bank Implementation Status & Results Report, December 2015.

118. UK Department of Energy and Climate Change, "An International Climate Fund Business Case for DECC investment in the BioCarbon Fund and the Forest Carbon Partnership Facility-Carbon Fund," 2014, quoted in Norman and Nakhooda, "The State of REDD+ Finance," 21.

119. Seymour, Birdsall, and Savedoff, "The Indonesia-Norway REDD+ Agreement," 14.

120. Pistorius and Kiff, "The Politics of German Finance for REDD+," 27–28.

121. The Organisation for Economic Co-operation and Development (OECD) estimates that member countries provided about $60 billion in support for fossil fuels in 2014. OECD, "OECD Companion to Inventory of Support Measures for Fossil Fuels 2015," OECD Publishing, Paris, 2015, http://dx.doi.org/10.1787/9789264239616-en, 43.

122. De Nevers, "Look to the Forests."

123. C. Streck, A. Dahl-Jørgensen, and P. Bodnar, "Options for the EU to Generate Adequate, Predictable and Sustainable Financing for Emission Reductions from REDD+," Meridian Institute, Washington, DC, 2015, http://www.climatefocus.com/sites/default/files/REDD%2B%20Finance%20paper_jun24.pdf.

124. United Nations Framework Convention on Climate Change (UNFCCC), "Paris Agreement," Conference of the Parties to the United Nations Framework Convention on Climate Change, Twenty-First Session, Paris, France, December 12, 2015, http://unfccc.int/files/essential_background/convention/application/pdf/english_paris_agreement.pdf.

125. Climate Focus, "The Paris Agreement Summary," Climate Focus Briefing Note, December 28, 2015, http://www.climatefocus.com/sites/default/files/20151228%20COP%2021%20briefing%20FIN.pdf.

126. Ecosystem Marketplace, "Is California Getting Serious about REDD?" April 7, 2016, http://www.ecosystemmarketplace.com/articles/california-getting-serious-redd/.

127. California Air Resources Board, "Scoping Next Steps for Evaluating the Potential Role for Sector-Based Offset Credits under the California Cap-and-Trade Program, including from Jurisdictional 'Reducing Emissions from Deforestation and Forest Degradation' Programs," staff white paper, Sacramento, California, October 19, 2015, 44.

128. Ibid., 43.

129. International Civil Aviation Organization, "Market-Based Measures," http://www.icao.int/environmental-protection/Pages/market-based-measures.aspx; International Civil Aviation Organization, "Global Aviation Dialogues on Market-Based Measure to Address Climate Change" (presented at ICAO Global Aviation Dialogues [GLADs] meeting in Lima, Peru, April 9, 2015), http://www.icao.int/Meetings/GLADs-2015/Documents/Presentations/Lima/20150409_GLADs_P1_V33_LIMA.pdf.

130. M. Wolosin, "Domestic and International Options for Results-Based Finance: Reasons for Optimism?" (presentation at Oslo REDD Exchange, Oslo, Norway, June 2016).

131. United Nations Framework Convention on Climate Change (UNFCCC), "Paris Agreement," article 9.3; Climate Focus, "The Paris Agreement Summary."

132. Climate Focus, "Forests and Land Use in the Paris Agreement," Climate Focus Briefing Note, December 22, 2015, http://www.climatefocus.com/sites/default/files/20151223%20Land%20Use%20and%20the%20Paris%20Agreement%20FIN.pdf, 3.

133. Green Climate Fund, "Decisions of the Board—Eighth Meeting of the Board, 14–17 October 2014," Bridgetown, Barbados, October 14–17, 2014, http://www.greenclimate.fund/documents/20182/24946/GC F_B.08_45_-_Decisions_of_the_Board_-_Eighth_Meeting_of_the_Board__14-17_October_2014.pdf/1dd5389c-5955-4243-90c9-7c63e810c86d?version=1.1, 10.

134. Savedoff, "How the Green Climate Fund Could Promote REDD+."

135. Global Commission on the Economy and Climate, Better Growth, "Better Climate: The New Climate Economy Report," 2014, http://newclimateeconomy.report/2014/, chapter 3, 27, and chapter 8, 6.

136. See, for example, Climate Bonds Initiative, "Scaling Up Green Bond Markets for Sustainable Development: A Strategic Guide for the Public Sector to Stimulate Private Sector Market Development for Green Bonds," consultation paper, 2015, http://www.climatebonds.net/files/files/GB-Public_Sector_Guide-Final-1A.pdf.

137. See, for example, M. Cranford et al., "Unlocking Forest Bonds: A High-Level Workshop on Innovative Finance for Tropical Forests," workshop report, WWF Forest & Climate Initiative, Global Canopy Programme and Climate Bonds Initiative, 2011, https://www.climatebonds.net/files/uploads/2011/10/FBWorkshop_report_web_A.pdf.

138. Streck, Dahl-Jorgensen, and Bodnar, "Options for the EU."

139. De Nevers, "Look to the Forests," annex 6, 43–46.

CHAPTER 13
Conclusion
A Closing Window
of Opportunity

In the preceding chapters of this book, we have presented many answers to the questions embedded in the title, *Why Forests? Why Now?* In short, conservation of tropical forests is critical to achieving both climate and development objectives. The science, the economics, and the politics are aligned to support ambitious international cooperation to capitalize on the potential contribution of tropical forests to meeting those objectives. Paying developing countries for their performance in forest conservation is among the most promising approaches to climate change mitigation and development alike. But the big money is missing, and the window of opportunity is closing.

In this concluding chapter, we summarize the answers to *Why Forests?* and, especially, *Why Now?* We explain why recent initiatives to meet this challenge have fallen short and close by outlining an agenda for action by governments and other actors in rich countries.

Why Forests?

The world's remaining tropical forests are essential to global prosperity, both as a cost-effective buffer against catastrophic climate change and a contributor to many sustainable development goals.

Climate change is a fundamental threat to development. As each year brings record-breaking temperatures and unprecedented extreme weather events, the potential for climate change to impede and even unravel global development gains becomes increasingly evident. As described in chapter 1, the poorest countries and the poorest households within those countries face immiseration as temperatures and sea levels creep upward. Climate change inflicts chronic hardships, such as heat stress and water shortages, as well as the acute hardship that results as natural disasters such as fires and floods become more frequent and severe. With limited assets, insurance, and mobility, poor people are suffering climate-related misfortunes first and worst.

Achieving climate stability requires conservation of tropical forests. At the climate summit in Paris in December 2015, 195 countries agreed to keep global temperature rise well below two degrees Celsius and to aspire toward a more ambitious limit of one and a half degrees. As described in chapter 2, realistic hopes of achieving such goals will depend on a dramatic reduction in tropical deforestation. Forest loss is currently a major contributor to overall global greenhouse gas emissions, while forests are a safe and natural carbon capture and storage technology.

The way emissions from the forestry sector are reported conveys a misleadingly small sense of forests' potential contribution to climate stability. Forests' share of total emissions is reported as a net number, which is derived by subtracting carbon removed by forest growth from the gross emissions caused by deforestation. This number masks the true potential of forests as a climate solution. Halting tropical deforestation while allowing damaged forests to recover—and, in so doing, maintaining forests' ability to pull carbon from the atmosphere into vegetation and soils—could secure an amount of carbon equivalent to almost one-third of current annual emissions from all sectors.

Tropical forests provide a myriad of ecosystem goods and services beyond carbon storage that are essential to meeting sustainable development goals. While forest conservation makes a vital contribution to averting catastrophic climate change at the global level, tropical forests promote human well-being in developing countries through many other pathways, as described in chapters 3 and 6. On average, rural communities in and around forests derive more than one-fifth of household income from gathering wild forest products, such as fuelwood, food, and medicinal plants. Forested watersheds constitute a green infrastructure that supplies the water for irrigating agricultural crops, generating hydroelectric power, and providing clean drinking water and sanitation. Intact forest vegetation increases resilience to the impacts of extreme weather events, including those exacerbated by climate change, such as landslides on steep slopes and storm waves that batter coastlines. Forests thus contribute to health and safety as well as to food and energy security.

Yet the quest to internalize these multiple values of forests into economic decision making has so far fallen short. Income from forest goods is seldom captured in the statistics used by economic policy makers and rarely enters into the economic calculus of the decision making that drives land-use change. Even less visible to development decision makers are the forest-based ecosystem services that underpin progress toward sustainable development goals.

Protecting tropical forests could lower the overall costs and accelerate the achievement of global climate stability. Early forest-related agreements between industrialized and developing countries have been concluded at a price per ton of avoided emissions far lower than the costs of alternative options to reduce emissions. In particular, forests offer a path to achieving the balance between carbon emissions and sequestration called for in the Paris Agreement that is dramatically cheaper than other carbon capture and storage technologies.

As described in chapter 5, economic modeling simulating a price on forest carbon shows that slowing forest loss from agricultural conversion could account for more than half of the lowest-cost emission reductions in developing countries other than China. Translating the economic value of forest carbon into tangible financial incentives is one of the most attractive and affordable approaches—both within and between countries—to mitigating the emissions that cause climate change. Including this cost-effective action in the global portfolio of responses to climate change could enable faster progress in reducing emissions and result in a substantially cooler planet.

We know what drives and what slows deforestation. As described in chapter 7, a rapidly accumulating body of evidence and experience illuminates the factors that drive deforestation and the policy tools that can slow it. Among others, we know expansion of industrial agriculture has become a more important cause of forest loss than poor people's seeking to make a living; indigenous communities are eager for governments to defend their rights to forest territories against commercial pressures.

The evidence confirms some elements of the conventional wisdom but confounds others. High prices for agricultural commodities are consistently associated with accelerated deforestation, along with road building and rural income support, while protected areas, law enforcement, and the presence of indigenous peoples are more often than not associated with maintaining forest cover. Perhaps surprisingly, the presence of poor people (who lack the means to clear large areas of forest) and logging activity (which can provide incentives to maintain forests as forests) are not consistently associated with higher rates of deforestation.

Brazil's dramatic success in reducing deforestation in the Amazon by some 80 percent over the course of a decade illustrates that deforestation can be arrested without sacrificing agricultural production. It further suggests the package of policies and incentives that work: establishment of protected areas, delineation of indigenous territories, responsive law enforcement based on near-real-time monitoring through remote sensing technologies, and access to credit and markets that discriminate between high- and low-deforestation jurisdictions.

Key constituencies in developing countries support international cooperation to conserve tropical forests. For many developing countries, emissions from deforestation constitute the largest contribution to climate change, and elected leaders at national and subnational levels have stepped forward to offer more ambitious reductions in return for international finance. Those commitments are bolstered by domestic constituencies whose interests are aligned with efforts to conserve forests. As described in chapter 10, they include indigenous peoples seeking recognition of their customary land rights, anticorruption forces, and the broader public that suf-

fers from the private appropriation of forest assets and the loss of forest-based ecosystem services.

In rich countries, concern about climate change has layered yet another justification on top of long-standing support for efforts to conserve tropical rainforests. As described in chapter 11, such support is rooted in domestic and colonial histories intertwined with forests, desires to conserve biological and cultural diversity, and a growing recognition that global consumption patterns are a key driver of deforestation in the tropics. Finance to conserve tropical forests through development aid has drawn support spanning political parties and administrations in several donor countries, and the prospect of paying only for results enhances its attractiveness. While forest carbon offsets have drawn opposition from a small but vocal set of advocacy groups, the idea of paying developing countries to reduce emissions from deforestation as a way to lower the overall costs of achieving global climate stability has enjoyed broad support.

Consumer countries and transnational corporations can either exacerbate or attenuate the role of globally traded commodities in driving tropical deforestation. As described in chapter 8, global demand for forest-risk commodities such as beef, soy, palm oil, and wood products is a leading cause of tropical deforestation and associated greenhouse gas emissions. Production to supply export markets is often the result of illegal land conversion, while some of the demand is artificially inflated by rich-country policies, such as subsidies and mandates for biofuels. Recent innovations in consumer government policies—such as limiting market access and public procurement to products certified as legally and sustainably produced—have begun to show an impact in producer countries. Brazil's effective public policies have been complemented by voluntary efforts by private corporations to avoid sourcing commodities from recently deforested land.

Why Now?

A constellation of factors has aligned in ways that render international action urgently needed, as well as technically and politically feasible.

The last decade has witnessed a revolution in technology to monitor changes in forest cover. As recently as 2013, any attempt to estimate the rate of tropical deforestation globally was hobbled by data that were incomplete and inconsistent over time and space, expensive to obtain, and time consuming to analyze. Within a few short years, astonishingly rapid advances in remote-sensing technology and computing power and new norms of transparency have changed everything. As described in chapter 4, it is now possible not only to assess global changes in tree cover annually at a resolution of thirty meters, but also to detect deforestation events (such as clearing and fires) with sufficient frequency to enable response in a matter of days. Furthermore, new technologies and analytical techniques now make possible the production of maps of carbon density to support increasingly accurate estimation of emissions from deforestation and forest degradation.

The increasing accuracy, frequency, and availability of information on forest cover change have also changed the politics of deforestation, both within countries and inter-

nationally. Key enablers of Brazil's success in slowing deforestation were civil society organizations empowered to engage in evidence-based advocacy and government authorities empowered by the spatial data necessary to apply law enforcement and policy incentives. Internationally, the ability to measure changes in forest carbon emissions has toppled objections that kept avoided deforestation out of earlier climate change mitigation mechanisms.

New science shows tropical forests are even more important for climate and development objectives than previously known, but also that they are disappearing more quickly. Research continues to expand new understanding of the scope and scale of forest benefits, as described in chapter 3. While the beneficial effects of tropical forests on microclimates were noted by colonial foresters in the mid-nineteenth century, for example, only recently has sophisticated modeling revealed the degree to which tropical forests influence weather patterns—and thus agricultural production—at continental and even transcontinental scales. And the newly available data on forest cover change are ushering in a new era of spatial econometric analysis that promises to substantiate further the emerging evidence that forests are essential to hydrological regulation, control of disease, and resilience to natural disasters.

Yet new science is also undermining complacency that tropical deforestation is being brought under control. National statistics compiled by the FAO had suggested global deforestation had slowed between 2000–2005 and 2005–10, but more recent analysis of tree cover change enabled by satellite imagery revealed the rate of tropical deforestation had actually been increasing. Brazil's success in controlling deforestation in the Amazon was counterbalanced by the acceleration of forest loss elsewhere.

Climate negotiators have agreed on a framework for action on forests. The rules for international cooperation to reduce deforestation have now been agreed on within the United Nations Framework Convention on Climate Change (UNFCCC). With negotiations on forests among the most productive negotiating streams, consensus on a framework for reducing emissions from deforestation and forest degradation and enhancing forest carbon stocks (REDD+) was essentially achieved at climate talks in Warsaw in 2013. As described in chapter 9, over the course of several years, a unique assemblage of countries systematically addressed issues related to the effectiveness, efficiency, and equity of providing international performance-based payments for reduced forest emissions. In so doing, they achieved a breakthrough in international cooperation on forests that had been stuck in a North–South divide since negotiations toward a global forest convention had failed more than two decades previously.

In December 2015, REDD+ was enshrined in Article 5 of the historic climate agreement reached at the climate summit in Paris, and other provisions of the agreement bolster the prospects for scaling up international cooperation on forests as well. The balance between emission sources and sinks called for by the agreement can only be achieved by maintaining and enhancing the natural carbon uptake provided by forests. And the agreement's provision for the international transfer of

mitigation outcomes opens the door to rich countries' achieving some portion of their national emission reduction targets by financing reductions in developing countries. For their part, dozens of developing countries included reduced emissions from deforestation in the national climate pledges they lodged in advance of the summit.

Initial experience with performance-based finance is now available to inform scaled-up action. A few rich countries led by Norway, in cooperation with a handful of developing countries, starting with Brazil, Guyana, and Indonesia, have pioneered international REDD+ payment-for-performance agreements. As described in chapter 10, agreements such as these helped consolidate political will behind Brazil's program to reduce deforestation in the Amazon and, in Indonesia, served as a catalyst for unprecedented steps to improve forest governance. Guyana demonstrated it is possible to create a sophisticated forest monitoring system in a few short years.

Early experience has also generated cautionary lessons. The decision to tie financial transfers from Norway to the Amazon Fund's expenditure needs, for example, led to a temporal decoupling of payment from performance in Brazil. In Guyana, the rigid application of fiduciary safeguards by multilateral development banks serving as financial intermediaries caused delays and frustration. In Indonesia, a $1 billion reward has not proved a sufficient incentive for all the actions necessary to reverse business-as-usual deforestation. These experiences and others emerging from more recent bilateral and trilateral deals in Colombia, Liberia, and

Peru, subnational agreements under Germany's REDD Early Movers program, and some twenty-two pending agreements under the Forest Carbon Partnership Facility (FCPF) Carbon Fund will provide further insight into the design features of effective REDD+.

A wave of corporate commitments to get deforestation out of commodity supply chains creates a powerful new constituency for policy change and capacity for action. Thanks to hard-edged civil society advocacy and changing norms of corporate accountability, recent years have seen a cascade of "no deforestation" commitments from companies that buy, trade, or produce commodities whose production replaces forests. From Cargill to Nestlé to Walmart, corporations have responded to socially conscious consumers and financiers by pledging that commodities such as beef, cocoa, palm oil, paper, and soy will no longer be sourced from deforestation frontiers. Many of the pledges also include commitments to improve performance on social concerns, such as respect by commodity producers for the rights of indigenous peoples and labor and the inclusion of smallholders in supply chains.

As described in chapter 8, such corporate commitments alone will not be sufficient to end tropical deforestation. They are not feasible to implement in the absence of favorable enabling environments that only governments can provide through, for example, support for clear land tenure and consistent law enforcement. And without broader regulation, producers that serve markets not yet sensitive to legality and sustainability criteria will continue to clear forests. But recent corporate pledges have transformed major ben-

eficiaries of business-as-usual deforestation into constituencies for better forest governance policy and practice. And commitments made in 2015 in Paris by a few corporations to begin preferential sourcing from "green" jurisdictions provide opportunities for synergies with REDD+ initiatives. The current moment offers an unprecedented opportunity to complement private initiative with public action to secure tropical forests at jurisdictional scales.

The Window for Action Is Closing

Just when the world's appreciation of tropical forests has never been higher, and tools for international cooperation have never been more available, the window for action is rapidly closing. For scientific, economic, and political reasons, the opportunity to harness forests as a climate mitigation strategy and ensure a continuous flow of development benefits is a time-limited offer. Due to the factors described below, the alignment of possibilities available now is unlikely to persist much longer.

Current forest losses are effectively irreversible from a climate perspective. With every hectare of forest cleared, more carbon is released into the atmosphere, and nature's capacity to absorb carbon is reduced. While restoring the carbon stock of cleared and damaged forests is possible and necessary, it requires a time scale measured in decades, while the time frame to avoid catastrophic climate change is measured in years. Reliance on reforestation alone would be much more expensive than protecting the forests currently standing and would result in the loss of the many other development benefits of forest goods and services in the meantime. Current trends in deforestation are transforming the world's forests into a wasting asset in the fight against climate change.

Tropical forests are themselves at risk from climate change. As depicted in figure 1.1 in the introduction, deforestation fuels a pernicious feedback loop. The emissions from deforestation and forest degradation accelerate climate change, which in turn renders tropical forests more vulnerable to drought, fires, and storm damage. The longer action to slow and eventually reverse deforestation is delayed, the more forest-based emissions will contribute to climate change, and the greater the frequency and severity of adverse climate impacts on forests are likely to be. As a result, the potential for forests to be mobilized as a solution to climate change is declining as climate change itself progresses.

Without countervailing economic incentives and improvements in forest management and governance, tropical forests will continue to disappear. Every day, about 260 square kilometers of tropical forest are cleared. In part because public policies and private markets fail to capture the value of most forest goods and services, tropical forests continue to be converted to other land uses. As described in chapter 5, current trends suggest an area of tropical forest about the size of India will be lost by 2050 unless policy interventions alter the decisions of millions of land users regarding whether or not to clear forests for agriculture.

Forest-rich countries are getting tired of waiting for a signal that action will be rewarded. As described in chapter 10, the link to climate change, along with the potential for payments for performance in reducing deforestation, has contributed to nascent shifts in the political economy of forests in many developing countries; and, as described in chapter 12, more than fifty forest-rich countries have initiated national REDD+ programs, signaling they are willing partners to international transactions to reduce emissions from forests. Through the Governors' Climate and Forests Task Force, some twenty forest-rich states and provinces have pledged to reduce deforestation up to 80 percent in return for financial support.

But for most countries, the time lag between initial excitement over the concept of REDD+ and the certainty of financial reward is stretching toward a decade. Many political leaders who were early champions of REDD+ have been replaced in the course of election cycles before their investments of political capital began to pay off in the form of bankable guarantees of performance-based finance for conserving forests. A narrative of disappointment has begun to take hold, and the REDD+ "brand" has begun to tarnish.

The post-Paris political momentum on forests won't last forever. The current alignment of political factors in support of a major international initiative on forests is unique. In 2015, a target for ending deforestation was included in the Sustainable Development Goals, and REDD+ was enshrined in the Paris Agreement. Dozens of developing countries included forests in their national emission reduction pledges, while the number of companies that signed up to get deforestation out of commodity supply chains reached critical mass. Indigenous peoples' groups effectively used the Paris process to claim their rights and roles as forest stewards as never before. Commitments made in Paris provided civil society advocates and researchers with benchmarks against which to apply newly available forest monitoring technologies, leaving bad actors with no place to hide.

Without ambitious action, the current window of opportunity will inevitably close. Developing-country governments that have invested in REDD+ will be susceptible to the narrative of disappointment if expected financial commitments do not materialize. Private corporations attempting to implement their commitments in good faith will be frustrated by the lack of complementary public sector support, while laggards will happily continue business as usual. Progress in arresting deforestation in some countries will be undermined by increased rates in others.

What's the Hold-Up?

If mobilizing forests in the service of climate stability and development is so necessary, so affordable, so politically attractive, and so urgent, what's the hold-up in committing the necessary results-based finance to drive the agenda forward? The process has stalled for several reasons.

Forest finance has been a casualty of the broader failure of the international community—and key rich countries such as the United States—to act on the threat of climate change. When the idea of REDD+ was first taking shape a decade ago, firm targets for limiting global emissions were widely expected to result in strong demand for reductions in forest-based emissions, and regulation of industrial emissions was expected to generate

high levels of finance through demand for forest-carbon offsets.

When negotiators failed to conclude the anticipated global climate agreement in Copenhagen in 2009 and U.S. climate legislation failed to pass in 2010, near-term funding prospects for tropical forest conservation shriveled to those available from aid budgets and voluntary carbon markets. As described in chapter 12, in contrast to the estimates of tens of billions of dollars needed annually to provide adequate incentives to forest-rich countries to reduce deforestation, actual funds made available have since stubbornly hovered around one billion dollars per year.

Concerns about forest governance have intensified risk aversion. As described in chapter 10, forestry sectors in developing countries are fraught with governance challenges. For the most part, the rights of indigenous peoples over forestlands remain unrecognized, commercial exploitation poorly regulated, corruption rife, and conflict over resources inadequately addressed. As described in chapter 11, allegations by a small but vocal set of groups that valuing forest carbon could exacerbate these problems have led to wavering political support for including forest offsets in the few carbon markets up and running, and they have constrained results-based finance due to donor aversion to "headline risk."

Ironically, the result has been that even REDD+ finance targeted to indigenous groups has been mired for years in a morass of procedural checks. In the meantime, financial flows to support expansion of commercial agriculture, infrastructure, and extractive industry—often at the expense of forests as well as the rights and welfare of forest communities—have proceeded largely unimpeded.

The "aidification" of REDD+ finance has rendered funding too low, too slow, and insufficiently based on performance. Disappointment generated by the evaporation of hopes for large-scale climate finance has been compounded in recipient countries by excruciatingly slow disbursement of pledged development assistance funds and heavy bureaucratic processes necessary to get access to those funds. Well-meaning attempts by bilateral and multilateral donor agencies to avoid risk have strangled the potential for return.

REDD+ is a great idea that remains largely untried.

As described in chapter 12, the key feature that was intended to differentiate REDD+ finance from prior decades of development assistance funding to the forestry sector—payment for performance—was an early casualty of this aidification. Payment for performance has large potential to reframe climate finance from charity to partnership. It can empower forest-rich countries to take the lead in figuring out how best to address complex forest governance challenges in ways consistent with globally agreed-upon safeguard principles. Yet the preponderance of funding for REDD+ to date has been programmed through traditional project-based, input-defined channels. Even those funds earmarked for performance-based payments have been encumbered by stringent eligibil-

ity requirements, procedural hurdles, and requirements for donor approval of how earned payments will be spent.

As a result, REDD+ is a great idea that remains largely untried.

What Next?

The decisions needed to slow and eventually reverse current trends in tropical deforestation and forest degradation are squarely in the hands of political leaders in developing countries. While local communities and private sector actors can play important roles in forest conservation, only the public sector can enact and enforce the laws, regulatory frameworks, and economic incentives necessary to legitimize and support their efforts. Many national and subnational governments have announced intentions to take steps in this direction by making voluntary commitments through the New York Declaration on Forests and the Governor's Climate and Forests Task Force and by pledging nationally determined contributions to addressing climate change under the UNFCCC.

While developing countries are in the driver's seat when it comes to conserving tropical forests, rich countries can and should do everything they can to ensure efforts in developing countries succeed. The evidence assembled in this book justifies a massive and immediate mobilization of international financial and political support for stopping and reversing deforestation.

Broad frameworks for action are already in place through commitments made under the UNFCCC Paris Agreement, the UN Sustainable Development Goals, and the New York Declaration on Forests. A number of worthy initiatives are already underway and should be continued. These include financing for satellite monitoring of global forest cover change, support for more research on the role of forests in both climate mitigation and adaptation, support for building the capacity of civil society organizations, and partnerships to end illegal logging and trade in commodities produced at the expense of forests and forest peoples.

But without a new surge of international finance and policy support, ambitious commitments to reduce deforestation are unlikely to succeed. Nascent policy reform efforts in developing countries are vulnerable to reversal, and commodity supply chain initiatives are insufficient on their own.

In advance of the major international mobilization called for above, rich countries can make a serious contribution toward marshaling tropical forests as a solution to climate change and maintaining their many services to development in at least three ways.

Rich countries and international organizations should aggressively develop new sources of forest finance outside of development assistance budgets and institutions. Aid budgets alone will not be sufficient to close the gap between existing sources of finance and meaningful incentives to developing countries to conserve their forests. Furthermore, the nature of forest carbon storage as a global public good suggests a reframing of related financial transactions is in order. Payments for performance in reducing forest-related emissions are closer to trade in services between equal partners than to charitable contributions from donor to recipient, and aid instruments are not fit for that purpose. New sources of finance at the appropriate scale, and new institutions able to commit to and implement genuine payment-for-performance agreements, are needed now.

> The evidence assembled in this book justifies a massive and immediate mobilization of international financial and political support for stopping and reversing deforestation.

Chapter 12 highlights several possibilities for mobilizing the necessary finance. First, rich-country governments should allow international forest offsets in current and future compliance markets. The provision in the Paris Agreement for internationally transferred mitigation outcomes allows countries to cooperate to reduce emissions as part of overall progress on mitigation. The state of California is considering adoption of an approach to forest carbon offsets at the jurisdictional scale as part of its cap-and-trade system. California's initiative could provide important early experience on which to base confidence in REDD+, a model for other carbon trading schemes on which to build, and standards other jurisdictions could adopt for rapid replication.

In addition, rich-country governments should pursue using their creditworthiness to attract private sector finance to forests. Proposals to use public guarantees for "green" bonds and to extend deposit guarantees to capitalize an international forest fund could provide the needed scale and certainty of reward needed by developing countries for their forest protection efforts.

Within existing flows of climate finance, a larger share should go to forests, and more of that share should be allocated to results-based finance. Only a few countries have made significant pledges to performance-based REDD+ finance. Within the constraints of climate finance allocated from development assistance budgets, forests merit a larger share of available funding from additional countries on at least four grounds:

- The large potential of forests to contribute to cost-effective global climate mitigation, especially within the portion of emissions from developing countries (as described in chapters 2 and 5)
- The role of forests in providing resilience—and options for adaptation—to the impacts of climate change (as described in chapters 3 and 6)
- The many contributions of forests to the achievement of sustainable development goals related to food, water, and energy (as described in chapters 3 and 6)
- The alignment of many of the actions needed to address deforestation in an equitable fashion with broader development objectives, such as clarifying property rights and reducing corruption (as described in chapter 10)

On the basis of the first justification alone—the potential of forests to provide cost-effective emission reductions—more than half of climate finance available to developing countries other than China should be invested in conserving forests, as described in chapter 5.

Furthermore, a larger share of the larger slice of the funding pie allocated to forests should be programmed through streamlined payment-for-performance mechanisms, consistent with the original value proposition for REDD+. While developing countries will continue to need complementary funding for "readiness" activities and upfront investment, the use of such funding will likely be more efficient and effective if recipient governments are certain a pot of gold will, indeed, be waiting at the end of the rainbow. And donor country support for continuation of such funding will likely be more robust if politicians can assure taxpayers that payments will only be made for verified results. A near-term opportunity is the design and generous funding of a results-based REDD+ financing window at the Green Climate Fund.

Consumer countries and multinational corporations should accelerate implementation of public and private initiatives to ensure the legality and sustainability of globally traded commodities. With global demand for forest-risk commodities driving a large and increasing share of tropical deforestation, "demand-side" measures are an important complement to in-country "supply-side" initiatives and performance-based payments for conserving forest carbon. As a first threshold of doing no harm, bioenergy subsidies and mandates should be adjusted to remove perverse incentives to clear forests to produce fuel.

As described in chapter 8, efforts to promote legality in the international timber trade have demonstrated how limiting market access for illegally produced forest products can be linked to domestic law enforcement efforts in producer countries. Commitments by globally branded manufacturers and retailers to get deforestation out of their supply chains for commodities such as soy, beef, and palm oil as well have, in turn, prompted changes in behavior from major traders and producers. Public procurement standards, private commodity sourcing decisions, and public and private investment screens all have the potential to alter incentives to clear forests by signaling changing norms in global markets and finance. Criteria and indicators of legality and sustainability need to be developed and enforced at the level of producer countries or subnational jurisdictions, as has been pioneered through timber legality agreements.

The confluence of international agreement on REDD+ and corporate supply chain commitments provides an unusual opportunity to marry complementary public and private initiatives at scales ranging from entire countries to district-level jurisdictions. Institutional infrastructure developed for REDD+—such as systems for monitoring forest cover change and demarcating indigenous territories—can be mobilized to provide indicators of progress to inform the commodity sourcing and investment decisions of multinational buyers, traders, and financiers. Preferential access to markets and finance can reward countries and subnational jurisdictions that establish systems for the legal and sustainable production of commodities that put forests at risk.

Diverging Paths

Like the traveler in Robert Frost's famous poem, rich countries stand at a point where two forest roads diverge. The more worn road starts with press releases trumpeting large-sounding commitments of financial support for tropical forest conservation, followed by more modest follow-through and disappointing results. It's a path that leads to more storms like Hurricane Mitch in Honduras, more floods like those in Haiti, more erosion like that in Madagascar, more fires like those in Indonesia.

The less-traveled road encourages more successes like the one in Brazil, where a lawless frontier with the world's highest rate of deforestation was transformed in a matter of years to one where a package of policy tools effected an 80 percent reduction in the rate of forest loss. While Brazil's success was the result of domestic leadership and political will, the international community played an important supporting role. International policy arenas focused on climate change and biodiversity created expectations for improved performance. Global buyers of beef and soy signaled that association with deforestation could result in loss of market access.

And, not least, results-based finance for reducing emissions helped consolidate support inside and outside government to protect forests. This road less traveled holds promise in other countries, as well, but time is of the essence. International support could make all the difference.

Abbott, Tony, 268

Abranches, Sérgio, 289, 293, 298, 307, 311, 312

Accra Agenda for Action (2008), 12

Additionality, test of, 275

ADP (Avoided Deforestation Partners), 347, 371

AF&PA (American Forest and Paper Association), 334

AfDB (African Development Bank), 386

Africa: deforestation and forest degradation in, 47–48, 206; ecotourism in, 171; factors affecting forest reform in, 307, 308; forest income in, 151; indigenous lands in, 300; malaria in, 74; palm oil plantations in, 106; peatlands of, 36; in REDD+ negotiations, 264, 265; Sahel region of, 9, 39; wild food species used in, 71. *See also specific regions and countries*

African Development Bank (AfDB), 386

Agriculture: decoupling deforestation and, 195, 203–04; deforestation due to, 21, 34, 47, 203, 234–35, 403–04; demand reduction for deforestation by shifting of, 193–94; in developing countries, 69; ecosystem services in, 166; greenhouse gas emissions from, 34; peatland draining for, 2–3; pollination and pest control in, 70–71; subsidies for, 228; swidden, 28, 35, 42, 43–44, 297; tropical forest contributions to, 7, 69–73; weather patterns impacting, 69–70. *See also* Plantations

Aguilar, Lorena, 163

Aidification of REDD+ finance, 371–76, 390, 410

Airlines, carbon market offsets for,

388–89

Air pollution: from coal plants, 122, 126; deaths from, 73, 75; and deforestation, 134; from forest fires, 7, 73, 75, 162

Albedo effect, 38–39

Alcántara-Ayala, Irasema, 76

Alix-Garcia, Jennifer, 206–07

Alto Mayo Protected Forest, 123–24, 126, 131

AMAN (Indigenous Peoples Alliance of Indonesia's Archipelago), 299, 300

Amazon dieback, 49–50

Amazon Fund, 194, 261, 309, 384, 406

Amazon rainforest: biodiversity of, 66; climate change effects on, 49–50; conservation efforts in, 8, 9, 21; deforestation in, 2, 62, 69, 70, 187, 253; fisheries in, 72; international interest in, 292; medicinal plants of, 169; weather patterns in, 70

American Clean Energy and Security Act. *See* Waxman-Markey Bill of 2009

American Electric Power, 339

American Forest and Paper Association (AF&PA), 334

Angelsen, Arild, 377

Angola, deforestation in, 49

Annan, Kofi, 62, 166

AOSIS (Association of Small Island States), 256, 261

APP. *See* Asia Pulp & Paper

Archer Daniels Midland, 193, 221

Arc of Deforestation, 187, 192, 201, 306

Argentina: biofuel mandates in, 232; deforestation in, 222, 223

Arima, Eugenio, 195

Arrhenius, Svante, 251

Arrow, Ken, 159

Asia: deforestation in, 47, 206; financial crisis in, 312; forest income in, 151; land-use change in, 38; malaria in, 74; wild food species used in, 71. *See also specific regions and countries*

Asia Forest Partnership, 334

Asia Pulp & Paper (APP), 221, 237, 238

Association of Small Island States (AOSIS), 256, 261

Assunção, Juliano, 194–95

At Loggerheads? (Chomitz), 164

Australia: Bush-Tender program in, 129; carbon monoxide levels in, 75; development assistance from, 344; fast-start finance by, 361, 364; fisheries in, 73; global forests and climate initiative in, 263, 338–39, 341, 381; import restrictions in, 240; interagency dynamics in, 375, 376; in Kalimantan Forests and Climate Partnership, 348, 375, 380, 381–82; logging regulations in, 234, 334; on REDD+, 268, 345, 348, 373–74; satellite-based mapping programs in, 97

Avoided Deforestation Partners (ADP), 347, 371

Avoided deforestation projects: demand for forest carbon offsets from, 14, 256; as emission mitigation strategy, 19, 90; inclusion in CDM, 90–91, 93, 113, 256–57

Azevedo, Tasso, 261

Bali Action Plan (2007), 259–60, 263, 264

Ban Ki Moon, 371

Banking Environment Initiative (BEI), 236

Barbier, Ed, 154, 160
Barclays, 345
Barder, Owen, 124
Beef industry: cattle agreement by, 193–94; deforestation due to, 47, 222, 225; emissions due to, 225–26; moratorium on deforestation by, 188, 189, 236, 307; productivity of, 130; supply chain commitment to zero deforestation, 204
BEI (Banking Environment Initiative), 236
Benefit sharing, 131, 279–80
Bennett, Andrew, 360
Bernard, Florence, 156
Bhutan, gross national happiness metric in, 165
Biodiversity: and climate change, 140; conservation of, 18, 105–09, 256; and forest foods, 71; monitoring, 94, 102, 107, 109; as motivation for donor countries, 330–32; origins of term, 331; of tropical forests, 39, 64–66
Biofuels: blending mandates for, 229; defined, 228; as driver of deforestation and emissions, 230–33; first generation, 229, 242; global consumption of, 230; import restrictions for, 241; second generation, 232; subsidies for, 23, 221, 229, 231–32, 242
Biomass, 64
Biomass mission (European Space Agency), 101
Biopiracy, 170
Bioprospecting, 169–71, 176
Biotic pump theory, 68–69
Birdsall, Nancy, 274
Blending mandates, 229
Bolivia: beef production in, 225; deforestation in, 49; greenhouse gas emissions in, 48; household income from wild products in, 20; Madidi National Park in, 66; Noel Kempff Mercado Climate Action Project in, 256; in REDD+ negotiations, 268, 281,

345; taxation on deforestation in, 205
Bolsa Floresta program, 194
Bonn Challenge, 47
Boreal forests, 36, 38, 39, 254
Börner, Jan, 205
Boserup, Ester, 209
Brandis, Dietrich, 251, 329
Brazil: agricultural production in, 189, 190; antideforestation policies in, 130, 136; beef production in, 188, 189, 193, 204, 226, 307; biofuel production and consumption in, 229, 230; cattle certification program in, 193–94; deforestation in, 42, 49, 187–88, 192, 201, 222, 235; democratic transition in, 13, 292; disbursement delays in, 384; drought in, 70, 304; ecological fiscal transfer in, 172; economic development in, 293–94; on emission reduction targets, 288–89; enabling conditions for reducing deforestation in, 194–95; forest conservation efforts in, 8, 9, 21, 189; greenhouse gas emissions in, 48; illegal forest activities in, 9, 109–10, 296; international negotiation and national action in, 261, 262; land registration system in, 129; leadership and advocacy coalitions in, 308–09, 310; livestock in, 185; mapping technologies in, 9, 93, 96–97, 98, 107; monitoring capabilities in, 192–93, 194–95; national sovereignty in, 254, 292, 293; Pará region of, 186–87, 189–90, 201–02; partnership with Norway, 277, 288, 289; payment for ecosystem services in, 205; performance-based finance for, 310–12, 363, 368, 373, 406; plantations in, 121; policy recommendations from, 190–94, 257–58; property registry in, 110, 193; in REDD+ negotiations, 264, 268, 281; reduced deforesta-

tion in, 188–96, 209–10, 299, 300–01, 413; reforestation by, 47, 104; replicating success of reduced deforestation in, 196–97; reputation and international legitimacy concerns, 305–06; soy industry in, 8, 121, 130, 189, 193, 307; weather patterns in, 69
Brazilian National Institute for Space Research (INPE), 96, 97, 98, 109, 194, 289
British Association for the Advancement of Science, 250, 252
Brown, Jerry, 351
Budgetary costs of forest conservation, 128–29
Bukit Lawang village, 149
Bunge, 15, 193
Burma (Myanmar), agribusiness development in, 297
Burroughs, Edgar Rice, 330–31
Busch, Jonah, 124, 132–34, 136–37, 139, 142–43, 188, 197, 198–99
Bushmeat, 71–72

Calanolide A, 170
California: cap-and-trade system in, 270, 274, 328, 349–51, 388; drought in, 351; forest carbon offsets in, 349–51, 388, 411; REDD+ debates in, 347, 349
Calima Dam, 155–56, 159, 161
Cambodia: fisheries in, 72; greenhouse gas emissions in, 48; reforestation efforts in, 47
Camdessus, Michel, 312, 314
Cameron, David, 165
Cancer medications, 74, 169
Cancún Safeguards, 106, 107, 266
Cap-and-trade system, 14, 270, 274, 328, 349–51, 388
Carbon capture and storage (CCS): industrial methods for, 45; technological developments for, 326; by tropical forests, 6, 20, 22, 33, 94, 272
Carbon debt, 230
Carbon density: defined, 36, 99; gains and losses within forests,

102; laser technologies for assessment of, 12; mapping, 92–93, 97–101, 102, 104–05; of tropical forests, 36, 38

Carbon dioxide: atmospheric levels of, 32; common equivalents for tons of, 30; deforestation and release of, 6, 33–34, 39–41; extraction in clean coal technology, 122; in fossil fuel emissions, 32, 39; natural uptake by tropical forests, 32, 33, 34; net emissions of, 40–43; in ocean acidification, 32–33; price per ton in payments for forest conservation, 7

Carbon fertilization, 49

Carbon market offsets: for airlines, 388–89; in avoided deforestation projects, 14, 256; cap-and-trade system for, 14, 270, 274, 328, 349–51, 388; donor country perceptions of, 338–45, 346–48; effectiveness of, 273–75; in emissions trading systems, 388–89; flooding concerns, 273–74; fraud and manipulation in, 346; purchases from developing countries, 90; in REDD+, 94, 388–89, 411; uncertainty of, 273

Carbon monoxide, 75

Carbon payments: advantages of, 173–76; challenges of, 153, 175; cost effectiveness of, 124, 143; funding for, 175; reduced deforestation resulting from, 133, 135, 138; results-based, 44

Carbon pricing policies, 129, 137–39

Carbon stocks. *See* Carbon density

Cardoso, Fernando Henrique, 305

Cargill, 15, 193, 236, 345, 407

Carlowitz, Hanns Carl von, 329

Carson, Rachel, 331

Cash on Delivery: A New Approach to Foreign Aid (CGD), 376

Cash on delivery financing, 12, 376, 377, 379, 389. *See also* Performance-based finance

Cashore, Benjamin, 333

Cattle certification program, 193–94

CBERS (China-Brazil Earth Resources Satellite), 96

CBFF. *See* Congo Basin Forest Fund

CCS. *See* Carbon capture and storage

CDC (Centers for Disease Control and Prevention), 61

CDM. *See* Clean Development Mechanism

Center for Global Development (CGD): cash on delivery approach proposal from, 12, 376; marginal abatement cost curve from, 124, 132; meta-analysis on reduced deforestation, 188; working group on performance-based finance, 388, 390

Center for International Forestry Research (CIFOR), 151, 163, 268

Centers for Disease Control and Prevention (CDC), 61

CfRN. *See* Coalition for Rainforest Nations

CGD. *See* Center for Global Development

CGF (Consumer Goods Forum), 236, 345

Charles (prince of Wales), 339

Chatham House, 227, 230

Chimeli, Ariaster, 296

China: emission reduction goals in, 141–42; flooding in, 303; Logging Ban in, 155; palm oil consumption in, 238; payment for ecosystem services in, 205; reforestation efforts in, 20, 42, 47, 104, 279; Three Gorges Dam in, 154–55, 161

China-Brazil Earth Resources Satellite (CBERS), 96

Chipko movement, 303

Choice modeling, 159

Chomitz, Ken, 164

CI. *See* Conservation International

CIFOR. *See* Center for International Forestry Research

CIFs (Climate Investment Funds), 362–63, 365

CITES (Convention on International Trade in Endangered Species), 301

Clean coal technology, 122, 124, 126

Clean Development Mechanism (CDM), 19, 90, 91, 113, 255–57, 272

Cleghorn, Hugh, 250–51, 252, 253, 282

Climate and Forests Task Force, 316

Climate and Land Use Alliance, 380

Climate change: adaptation to, 77–78; adverse effects of, 4, 140, 402; deforestation as factor in, 2–3, 6, 16–18, 34–35, 251; economic development as influenced by, 4, 5; forest-based emissions accelerating, 5, 6–7, 16; international negotiations on, 257–61; natural disasters impacted by, 2, 4, 402; politics of, 9, 258, 326, 341; poverty influenced by, 3, 4, 5; tropical forests affected by, 49, 77, 408; two-degree limit on, 6, 7, 402. *See also* Fossil fuel emissions; Greenhouse gas emissions; Mitigation of climate change

Climate Investment Funds (CIFs), 362–63, 365

Cloud forests, 36, 65, 68, 155–56

Coalition for Rainforest Nations (CfRN), 258–59, 265, 278, 279, 342, 362

Co-benefits: of forest conservation, 33, 63, 126, 136, 175, 326; of REDD+, 350, 372

Colchester, Marcus, 203

Colombia: Calima Dam in, 155–56, 159, 161; civil war in, 291; greenhouse gas emissions in, 48; hydroelectricity generation in, 155–56; multilateral financing in, 406–07; payment for ecosystem services in, 172; in REDD+, 271, 300, 380; reputation and international legitimacy concerns, 306

Columbus, Christopher, 60
Congo Basin Forest Fund (CBFF), 372, 386
Conrad, Kevin, 259
Conservation International (CI), 123–24, 335, 350
Conservation Reserve Program, U.S., 129
Conservativeness approach to performance payments, 111, 271
Consumer Goods Forum (CGF), 236, 345
Contingent valuation, 159
Convention on Biological Diversity (1992), 170, 306, 336
Convention on International Trade in Endangered Species (CITES), 301
Copenhagen Accord (2009), 263–64
Corruption: forest-related, 296–98, 301–02; in land allocation, 234; in performance-based finance, 311, 377–78
Costanza, Robert, 161
Costa Rica: carbon density mapping in, 105; ecotourism in, 171; forest conservation in, 197; hydroelectric plants in, 156; mapping technologies in, 107; payment for ecosystem services in, 129, 156, 171–72, 205; pest control in, 71; proposal for compensated emission reductions, 93, 259, 384; in REDD+ negotiations, 281
Côte d'Ivoire, ecotourism in, 171
Cyclones, 2, 4, 72, 77

Dahl-Jørgensen, Andreas, 388
David and Lucile Packard Foundation, 362
Davies, Robin, 305, 373, 374, 375, 382
Decarbonization, 141–42, 143
Deforestation: adverse consequences of, 60–62, 63; agricultural causes of, 21, 34, 47, 203; climate change influenced by, 2–3, 6, 16–18, 34–35, 251; commodity-driven, 22–23, 220, 221–28,

230–33, 404–05; cost effectiveness of reductions, 124–28, 136–39, 141, 143–44, 403; decoupling agriculture and, 195, 203–04; definitions of, 35; demand reduction through shifting agricultural sources, 193–94; in developing countries, 291–98; direct restrictions on, 130, 136–37; and diseases, 74–75; distribution and trends in, 47–49; enabling conditions for reducing, 194–95; evolution from political problem to climate solution, 252–61; fishbone pattern of, 200–01; in international negotiations on climate change, 257–61; land use following, 34, 35; MAC curves for estimating costs of reductions in, 125–32, 134, 136; of mangrove forests, 36, 154; mapping, 12, 91–92, 96–97; meta-analysis on drivers of reduced deforestation, 188, 197–205, 206; and natural disasters, 2, 76–77; policy recommendations for slowing, 190–94; politics of, 251, 288–90, 296, 304, 307; and poverty, 3, 20–21, 60, 206–07; rates of, 6, 38, 45, 92, 135, 405–06, 408; real-time detection of, 97, 102, 109–10; risk enhancement through enforcement of forest laws, 192–93, 202–03; supply reduction through protection of forests, 192, 201; taxes on, 205; of temperate forests, 37–38. *See also* Avoided deforestation projects; Forest-based emissions; Forest degradation
DeFries, Ruth, 196, 197
Demand-side policies, 220–21, 240–41, 242, 307, 412
Democratic Republic of Congo (DRC): emission reduction program approval in, 384; fast-start finance for, 362; governance of forests in, 302; greenhouse gas emissions in, 48; indigenous

rights in, 300; logging industry corruption in, 296; performance-based finance for, 310; REDD+ strategy in, 315; road projects in, 201
DETER. *See* Real Time System for Detection of Deforestation
Developing countries, 287–317; access to markets and finance, 306–08; agricultural employment in, 69; antagonism toward forest conventions from, 255; appropriation of forest wealth in, 294–96; beneficiaries of ecosystem services in, 303–04; biofuel initiatives in, 232; carbon market offsets purchased from, 90; conditions favoring deforestation as usual in, 291–98; conflicting mandates in, 309–10; constituencies for forest conservation in, 298–304, 404; diversity of, 290; factors affecting success of initiatives to reduce deforestation, 308–16; forest area development as path to economic prosperity in, 293–94; governance of forestry sectors in, 296–98, 409–10; international influences supporting reform in, 304–08; lack of promised finance for, 313–16; leadership and advocacy coalitions in, 308–09, 310; nonagricultural emissions in, 135, 139; performance-based finance for, 11, 310–12, 313–16, 369–71; politics of deforestation in, 288–90, 296, 304, 307; REDD+ opposition by, 268, 345; reduced deforestation in, 5, 7, 9, 139, 140; reputation and international legitimacy concerns for, 304–06; territorial control and national sovereignty over forests in, 291–93; traditional medicine in, 73, 151; water and energy in, 67. *See also specific countries*
Development Grants Mechanism (DGM), 386

Dilution effect hypothesis, 74

Dipterocarp forests, 28, 65, 99

Dirceu, José, 306

Direct restrictions, 130, 136–37

Disasters. *See* Natural disasters

Diseases: from bushmeat consumption, 72; and deforestation, 74–75; insect-borne, 4, 50, 74; water-borne, 60, 61; zoonotic, 74–75. *See also* Health

Domestic costs of forest conservation, 130–31

Dominican Republic, forest cover in, 60, 61, 78

Donor countries, 325–52; biological and cultural diversity protection as motivations for, 330–32; on carbon market offsets, 338–45, 346–48; climate mitigation as rationale for tropical forest finance from, 335–38; constituencies for forest conservation in, 328–35; coordination challenges across agencies in, 374–76; domestic and colonial forest histories of, 328–30, 404; efficiency concerns of, 275, 277; emission reduction financing by, 264, 326–27, 338–45; logging regulations by, 332–35; performance-based finance from, 340–43, 369–71; pledges to save rainforest from, 9; REDD+ opposition by, 345–51; supply chain commitments by, 344–45; in virtuous cycles, 261. *See also* Finance for REDD+

Dooley, Kate, 374

Double demanding, 384

DRC. *See* Democratic Republic of Congo

Drought: in California, 351; and climate change, 4, 6; and deforestation, 304; forest protection against, 7; in Sahel region, 9; vulnerability to, 3, 49; and weather patterns, 70

Duke Energy, 339

Ecological and Economic Zoning (EEZ), 195

Ecological fiscal transfer, 172, 173

Ecological transitions, 164

Economic development: climate change as factor in, 4, 5; and conservation efforts, 189–90; and ecological transitions, 164; forest area development as path to, 293–94; invisibility of ecosystem services in, 165–66; natural disasters impacting, 2

The Economics of Ecosystems and Biodiversity (TEEB) initiative, 166

Eco Securities, 364

Ecosystem-based adaptations, 77, 78

Ecosystem services: beneficiaries of, 303–04; bioprospecting, 169–71, 176; of cloud forests, 36, 155–56; diversity of, 36; ecotourism, 171, 176; examples of, 152, 402–03; and global health issues, 18; income from, 151, 169; intangibility to land-use decision makers, 167–72; of mangrove forests, 36, 153–54, 160, 164; or riparian forests, 36; poor and vulnerable household dependence on, 162, 164–65; sustainability of, 168–69, 176; and women, 163, 303. *See also* Payment for ecosystem services (PES); Value of ecosystem services

Ecotourism, 171, 176

Ecuador, payment for ecosystem services in, 172, 205

Edward III (king of England), 273

Edwards, Rupert, 379

EEZ (Ecological and Economic Zoning), 195

Eiffel Tower, 249

Electricity, water as source of, 61, 66–67, 154–56

Elliott, Kimberly, 229

El Niño weather pattern, 28, 41, 75, 156

Emissions. *See* Forest-based emissions; Fossil fuel emissions; Greenhouse gas emissions

Emissions Trading System (EU), 257, 274, 347

Endemic species, 66

Engelmann, Jens, 124, 132–34, 136–37, 139, 142–43

EnMAP (Environmental Mapping and Analysis Program), 109

Environmental Defense Fund, 350

Environmental integrity: of forest-based emission reductions, 90, 270, 272, 350; technical challenges related to, 93, 113; threats to, 273, 346

Environmental Integrity Group, 265

Environmental Kuznets Curve, 207

Environmental Mapping and Analysis Program (EnMAP), 109

Environmental Protection Agency, U.S., 7, 75

Erosion, 60, 61, 67

Ethiopia, wild food species used in, 71

European Space Agency, 96, 98, 101

European Union (EU): biofuel subsidies in, 221, 229, 231–32; cost of reducing emissions from industrial sources, 124, 135, 138; emissions generated by, 6, 31, 40, 50; Emissions Trading System, 257, 274, 347; forest law enforcement in trade agreements, 240; on forest offsets, 257; in REDD+ negotiations, 265; Renewable Energy Directive from, 229, 232; Timber Regulation, 204, 234, 240, 333. *See also specific countries*

Evans, Alex, 124

Evapotranspiration, 65, 68, 76

Exxon Valdez oil spill (1989), 159

FAO. *See* United Nations Food and Agriculture Organization

Farming. *See* Agriculture

Fast-start finance, 19, 264, 361–67

FCPF. *See* Forest Carbon Partnership Facility

Feitosa da Silva, Tarcísio, 186–87, 188, 190, 208

Females. *See* Women

Ferretti-Gallon, Kalifi, 188, 197, 198–99

Field plots, 98, 99, 103, 104

Finance for REDD+, 359–91; aidification of, 371–76, 390, 410; alternative sources of funding, 361, 387–90, 391; carbon market offsets, 94, 388–89, 411; climate finance instruments, 389; constraints on, 23, 361, 364, 371, 376–80, 382–84; coordination challenges across agencies, 374–76; disbursement issues, 384–87; fast-start finance, 19, 264, 361–67; green bonds, 390, 411–12; impact bonds, 379; lack of promised finance, 313–16; landscape of, 361–67; leveraging private finance through donor-country creditworthiness, 390, 411–12; markets and public funds in, 280–82; participant countries in, 367–68; phased approach to, 362, 363. *See also* Donor countries; Performance-based finance

Finland, forest management in, 328

FIP. *See* Forest Investment Program

Fires. *See* Forest fires

First generation biofuels, 229, 242

Fishbone pattern of deforestation, 200–01

Fisheries, 36, 69, 72–73, 78

FLEG. *See* Forest Law Enforcement and Governance

Flooding: and climate change, 78; and deforestation, 76–77; destruction caused by, 4; and fisheries, 72; forest protection against, 7, 303; hurricanes resulting in, 2, 76; risk factors for, 61

Fogliano, Felipe Arias, 130

Food and Drug Administration, U.S., 150, 170

Food security: and biofuel subsidies, 221, 229; and climate change, 4, 140; deforestation as

necessity to achieve, 21, 294; and Mega Rice Project, 381; as political consideration, 69; seasonal gaps in, 72

Forest-based emissions: calculation of reductions, 95; climate change accelerated by, 5, 6–7, 16; from degradation, 101, 102, 103; embodied in globally traded commodities, 223–28; from forest fires, 29–30; globally traded commodities as drivers of, 230–33, 404–05; human actions resulting in, 2–3, 8; measurement of, 12, 13, 22, 96–101, 270–71; misperceptions regarding, 18; mitigation efforts, 7, 10–11; monitoring, 9, 12, 95–103; percentage in total annual emissions, 6, 16, 19, 30; permanence of reductions in, 271–73; reference levels for, 95, 130, 275–77; trends in, 134, 135. *See also* Deforestation; Forest degradation

Forest Carbon Partnership Facility (FCPF): Carbon Fund, 111, 271, 273, 277, 362, 383, 407; establishment and launch of, 263, 266, 362; Readiness Fund, 362, 363, 367, 368

Forest Code (Brazil), 192, 235, 294

Forest conservation: affordability of, 6–8; climate scholar perceptions of, 17–18, 19–20; co-benefits of, 33, 63, 126, 136, 175, 326; compatibility with economic growth, 189–90; constituencies in developing countries, 298–304, 404; development agency underinvestment in, 18, 20–22; domestic costs of, 130–31; donor country constituencies for, 328–35; feasibility of, 8–9; framework for international cooperation on, 10–12, 406; governance tools to advance, 300; history and evolution of, 9–16; incentives for, 189; opportunity vs. budgetary costs of, 128–29; private sec-

tor support for, 15; results-based finance for, 9, 10–11, 12–13; in Sustainable Development Goals, 15, 18, 142, 408. *See also* Reforestation

Forest degradation: causes of, 48, 50, 103; climate damage due to, 30; compensated reduction of, 279; defined, 36; monitoring emissions from, 101, 102, 103

Forest fires: air pollution from, 7, 73, 75; economic cost of, 157; greenhouse gas emissions from, 29, 30, 33, 156; health consequences of, 29, 62, 75, 156–57, 160; images of, 27; in Indonesia, 28–30, 36, 156–57, 160, 162–63, 312; in peatlands, 28, 36, 89; poor and vulnerable households impacted by, 162–63; risk factors for, 28, 49

Forest Investment Program (FIP), 362–63, 367, 368, 372–73, 386

Forest Law Enforcement and Governance (FLEG), 241, 332, 333, 372

Forest Monitoring for Action (FORMA), 93, 97, 110

Forest Resources Assessment (FRA), 91, 92

Forests. *See specific types of forests*

Forest services. *See* Ecosystem services

Forest Stewardship Council (FSC), 168, 255, 333

Forest Trends, 234, 379

Fortress conservation approach, 167

Fossil fuel emissions: carbon dioxide in, 32, 39; history of, 31–32, 38; percentage in energy consumption, 142; reduction of, 4–5, 142

Foster, Mike, 346

FRA (Forest Resources Assessment), 91, 92

France, forest management in, 328

Francis (pope), 15

Free, prior, and informed consent (FPIC), 266, 280, 300

Friends of the Earth, 347–48, 350
FSC. *See* Forest Stewardship Council

GAR (Golden Agri Resources), 15, 236–37
Garnaut, Ross, 339
GCAM (Global Climate Assessment Model), 133
GCF. *See* Green Climate Fund
GDP (gross domestic product), 153, 165
GEDI. *See* Global Ecosystem Dynamics Investigation
GEF (Global Environment Facility), 362
Geoscience Laser Altimetry System (GLAS), 99
Germany: conservation funding from, 15, 330, 332, 336; forest management in, 329–30; interagency dynamics in, 375; performance-based finance from, 340, 363–64, 372, 387, 407
Ghana: ecotourism in, 171; mapping technologies in, 107; in REDD+, 380
GIFC (Global Initiative on Forests and Climate), 338–39, 381
GLAS (Geoscience Laser Altimetry System), 99
Global Canopy Programme, 239–40
Global Climate Assessment Model (GCAM), 133
Global Ecosystem Dynamics Investigation (GEDI), 97, 99, 101
Global Environment Facility (GEF), 362
Global Forest Watch, 91, 92, 97, 110, 197
Global Initiative on Forests and Climate (GIFC), 338–39, 381
Globally traded commodities, 219–42; demand-side policies for, 220–21, 240–41, 242, 307, 412; as drivers of deforestation, 22–23, 220, 221–28, 230–33, 404–05; emissions from deforestation embodied in, 223–28; illegality

of deforestation to meet demand for, 233–35, 412–13; jurisdictional approach to sustainable sourcing of, 239. *See also* Beef industry; Biofuels; Palm oil and palm oil plantations; Soy industry; Supply chains; Wood products
Global positioning system (GPS), 110
Global warming. *See* Climate change
Global Witness, 379–80
Glover, David, 157
Golden, Chris, 150
Golden Agri Resources (GAR), 15, 236–37
Goodall, Jane, 371
Gorilla tourism, 171
Governors' Climate and Forest Task Force, 349–50, 351, 369, 408, 410
GPS (global positioning system), 110
Grant, Ulysses S., 201
Grassi, Giacomo, 111
Green Belt Movement, 303
Green bonds, 390, 411–12
Green Climate Fund (GCF), 127, 133, 139, 143, 281, 389, 412
Greenhouse effect, 251
Greenhouse gas emissions: in agriculture, 34; in clean coal technology, 122; from forest fires, 29, 30, 33, 156; land-use changes responsible for, 38; monitoring, 113; from peatlands, 36, 37; reducing, 7, 50, 94, 136. *See also* Forest-based emissions
Greenpeace: Nestlé campaign by, 220, 236, 238, 307; opposition to forest offsets, 347–48, 350; on soy and beef industry, 193, 307
Grileiros (land grabbers), 186, 192
Gross domestic product (GDP), 153, 165
Gross national happiness, 165
Guo, Zhongwei, 155
Guyana: disbursement delays in, 384; governance of forests in, 302; indigenous lands in, 300;

MRV system in, 271; performance-based finance for, 112, 276, 289, 310–14, 363, 373, 406; reference levels for, 276, 277

Habibie, B. J., 292
Hafild, Emmy, 331
Haiti: deforestation in, 60–62, 78; electricity consumption in, 61; hookworm outbreak in, 61; poverty in, 60
Haltbrekken, Lars, 326, 327
Halvorsen, Kristin, 343
Hansen, Matthew, 91–92
Hardin, Garrett, 208
Harris, Nancy, 40
HCS (High Carbon Stock) forests, 237
Headline risk, 298, 348, 373, 409
Health: fires affecting, 29, 62, 75, 156–57, 160; forest contributions to, 7, 62, 73–75; medicinal plants for, 73–74, 150, 151, 160, 169–70; Sustainable Development Goals related to, 73. *See also* Diseases
Hectares, common equivalents of, 28, 30
Hermansen, Erlend, 341–42
HICE (Household Income, Consumption and Expenditure) surveys, 165–66
High Carbon Stock (HCS) forests, 237
High-resolution satellites, 97, 103, 107
Hobbes, Thomas, 91
Hodgkin's lymphoma, 169
Honduras: deforestation in, 2; reforestation efforts in, 47
Hookworm, 61
Houghton, Richard, 44
Household Income, Consumption and Expenditure (HICE) surveys, 165–66
Howard, John, 338, 339, 341, 381
Humphreys, David, 255
Hunt, Greg, 338
Hurricane Mitch (1998), 1–2, 3, 4, 8, 76, 77

Hydroelectric dams, 60, 66–67, 154–56

Hyperspectral Infrared Imager (HyspIRI), 109

Hyperspectral remote sensing, 109

IAFCP (Indonesia–Australia Forest Carbon Partnership), 381–82

IBAMA (Institute for the Environment and Renewable Natural Resources), 189, 301

ICAO (International Civil Aviation Organization), 388–89

ICESAT-1 satellite, 97, 99

ICF. See International Climate Fund

Ikonos satellite, 97

Illegal Logging Prohibition Act of 2012 (Australia), 234, 334

Imaging spectroscopy, 109

IMF (International Monetary Fund), 312, 313

Impact bonds, 379

Import restrictions, 240

INCAS. See Indonesian National Carbon Accounting System project

INDCs (intended nationally determined contributions), 275, 370

India: Chipko movement in, 303; deforestation in, 9, 250; ecological fiscal transfer in, 172; ecotourism in, 171; fisheries in, 73; palm oil consumption in, 238; reforestation efforts in, 42, 47, 104, 279; satellite-based mapping programs in, 97; state forest system of, 251; tsunamis affecting, 77; wild food species used in, 71

Indigenous peoples: deforestation and impacts on, 13; delineation of territory by, 110, 192; as factor in reduced deforestation, 201–02, 208, 299; forest conservation by, 152; recognition of rights of, 10–11, 21, 266, 298–300, 408–09; in REDD+ negotiations, 21, 265, 266–67, 299, 348

Indigenous Peoples Alliance of Indonesia's Archipelago (AMAN), 299, 300

Indirect land-use change, 195, 230–31

Indonesia: biofuel mandates in, 232–33; conservation efforts in, 157–58; deforestation in, 28, 42, 49, 67–68, 235, 294–95; democratic transition in, 13; disbursement delays in, 384; economic development in, 294, 295; emission reduction targets for, 13, 263, 275, 305, 313, 369; enforcement of forest laws in, 203, 239, 307–08; fast-start finance for, 362; financial crisis in, 312; forest fires in, 28–30, 36, 156–57, 160, 162–63, 312; governance of forests in, 301–02, 304, 309, 316; greenhouse gas emissions in, 48; illegal forest clearing in, 110, 334; indigenous peoples of, 297, 299–300; insurgencies in, 291–92; international negotiation and national action in, 268, 269; in Kalimantan Forests and Climate Partnership, 348, 375, 380, 381–82; mapping technologies in, 110; national sovereignty in, 292–93; palm oil consumption in, 238; peatland draining in, 2–3, 230; performance-based finance for, 310–12, 313, 363, 368, 373, 406; pest control in, 71; plantations in, 106, 107, 164, 227, 287, 295; poverty surveys in, 166; in REDD+ negotiations, 264; reputation and international legitimacy concerns, 304–05; Tesso Nilo National Park in, 233–34; transmigration program in, 209, 292; tree-planting campaigns in, 20, 45, 46; tsunamis affecting, 77; wood products exported from, 227, 241

Indonesia–Australia Forest Carbon Partnership (IAFCP), 381–82

Indonesian National Carbon Accounting System (INCAS) project, 375, 380, 381

Indonesia's Fires and Haze: The Costs of Catastrophe (Glover & Jessup), 157

Initiative for Sustainable Forest Landscapes (ISFL), 364

INPE. See Brazilian National Institute for Space Research

Insects: diseases spread by, 4, 50, 74; forest degradation due to, 50; pest control measures for, 62, 69, 70–71

Institute for the Environment and Renewable Natural Resources (IBAMA), 189, 301

Intended nationally determined contributions (INDCs), 275, 370

Intergovernmental Panel on Climate Change (IPCC): on adverse effects of climate change, 4, 140; on Amazon dieback, 50; on carbon debt incurred from biofuel feedstocks, 230; carbon measurement guidance from, 270; net emission calculations by, 6, 16, 42, 43; on reversal of deforestation, 31; statistical reports generated by, 19–20, 136, 260

International Civil Aviation Organization (ICAO), 388–89

International Climate Fund (ICF), 339, 374, 385

International Monetary Fund (IMF), 312, 313

International Space Station, 97, 99, 102, 103, 104, 105

International Tropical Timber Organization (ITTO), 334

IPCC. See Intergovernmental Panel on Climate Change

ISFL (Initiative for Sustainable Forest Landscapes), 364

Jagdeo, Bharrat, 112, 276, 289, 308–09, 311, 314, 371

Japan: forest management in, 328–29; logging regulations in, 334–35; promotion of legally verified wood products in, 234; tsunamis affecting, 77

Jessup, Timothy, 157

Jet Propulsion Lab (NASA), 92–93, 99

Jodoin, Sebastien, 300

Johnson & Johnson, 345

Joko Widodo, 303, 309

Kakum Rainforest, 171

Kalimantan Forests and Climate Partnership (KFCP), 348, 375, 380, 381–82

Kasa, Sjur, 341–42

Keeling, Charles, 251

Kenny, Charles, 377–78

Kenya: ecosystem-based adaptations in, 78; Green Belt Movement in, 303; wild food species used in, 71

Keohane, Robert, 338

KFCP. See Kalimantan Forests and Climate Partnership

Kiff, Laura, 329, 330, 340, 375, 387

Kuntoro Mangkusubroto, 299–300, 301, 309

Kyoto Protocol (1997), 19, 90, 229, 255–57

Lacey Act Amendments of 2008, 204, 234, 334, 341

Land-cover change vs. land-use change deforestation, 35

Landsat: in detection of plantations, 106–07; evolution of, 91, 96; features of, 97; in forest mapping, 101, 102, 104, 112; in PRODES, 96, 98

Landslides: and climate change, 78; and deforestation, 76; forest protection against, 7; risk factors for, 4, 60

Langone, Claudio, 258

Laser technologies, 12

Latin America: beef production in, 225–26; community management of forests in, 297; deforestation in, 47, 206, 222, 223; electricity production in, 66;

forest income in, 151; palm oil plantations in, 106; soybean production in, 226. See also specific countries

La Viña, Antonio, 90, 268

Lawson, Sam, 234–35

Lay, Kenneth G., 390

Leakage, 48, 195, 238–39, 258, 271

Lee, Donna, 264, 341, 365, 366–67, 376, 377

Leopold II (king of Belgium), 330

Lépissier, Alice, 124, 133–34, 139, 142–43

Liberia: illegal logging in, 334; multilateral financing in, 406–07; performance-based finance for, 205, 289, 314

Life expectancy, 73

Light Detection and Ranging (Lidar), 97, 99–100, 102, 103, 104–05, 109

Lima Challenge, 15, 369–70

Living Standards Measurement Study (LSMS), 166

Local land rights, impact on deforestation, 208–09

Locatelli, Bruno, 68, 69

Logging: deforestation due to, 197; emissions due to, 94; forest degradation due to, 47, 199, 207; illegal, 300–01, 332–35; permits for, 296; roads created for, 36, 200; rotational sites for, 42; sustainability of practices in, 168, 207–08. See also Timber plantations; Wood products

Lopez, José, 220

Lovejoy, Thomas, 331

Løvold, Lars, 326, 341

LSMS (Living Standards Measurement Study), 166

Lubowski, Ruben, 141

Lueders, Jesse, 350, 351

Lula da Silva, Luiz Inácio, 13, 189, 288, 289, 301, 305–06

Lund, Gyde, 35

Luttrell, Cecilia, 309

Maathai, Wangari, 303

MAC curves. See Marginal abatement cost curves

Madagascar: biodiversity in, 66, 150; deforestation in, 150–51, 164; Makira National Park in, 150, 160; Mantadia National Park in, 157; medicinal plants of, 73, 74, 150, 160, 169; wild food species used in, 72

Madidi National Park, 66

Makira National Park, 150, 160

Malaria, 62, 73, 74, 169

Malawi, wild food species used in, 71

Malaysia: biodiversity in, 66; deforestation in, 49, 197; ecotourism in, 171; greenhouse gas emissions in, 48; medicinal plants in, 170; peatland draining in, 230; plantations in, 106, 107, 164, 219, 227; wood products exported from, 227

Mangrove forests: biodiversity of, 65; carbon dioxide emissions from, 40; deforestation of, 36, 154; as fishery breeding grounds and nurseries, 36, 72–73, 78; hurricane damage to, 2, 3; sedimentation reduction by, 67; services provided by, 36, 153–54, 160, 164; tsunami protection from, 36, 77

Mantadia National Park, 157

Mapping: carbon density, 92–93, 97–101, 102, 104–05; commodity supply chains, 239–40; deforestation, 12, 91–92, 96–97; forest cover gains and losses, 101–02; satellite-based, 96–97

Marginal abatement cost (MAC) curves, 124–39; carbon pricing policies in, 129, 137–39; defined, 126; for emission mitigation assessment, 22; in estimating costs of reduced deforestation, 125–32; evidence-based, 132; limitations of, 128–32; from McKinsey and Company, 126–27, 128; methodology for, 132,

Marginal abatement cost (MAC) curves (*cont.*)
133–34; price incentive considerations in, 124; projections of tropical deforestation from, 132, 134, 136; usefulness of, 126–28

Market feedback, 131

Marrakesh Accords (2001), 257

Maury, Matthew, 292

McDonald's, 15, 193, 236

McKinsey and Company, 126–27, 128, 276, 364

Meadowcroft, James, 309

Measured, reported, and verified (MRV) emissions, 95, 270, 271, 363, 380

Médici, Emílio Garrastazu, 209

Medicinal plants, 73–74, 150, 151, 160, 169–70

Mega Rice Project, 294, 381

Mendes, Chico, 186, 299, 305, 331

Merck, 170

Meridian Institute, 362

Merrill Lynch, 364

Methane gas, 31, 33, 34

Mexico: antipoverty program in, 207; community management of forests in, 297; enforcement of forest laws in, 203; greenhouse gas emissions in, 48; landslides in, 76; mapping technologies in, 107; medicinal plants of, 169; payment for ecosystem services in, 172, 205; pest control in, 71; in REDD+, 264–65, 266, 302, 367; reduced deforestation in, 315

Micro-satellites, 110

Microsoft, 367

Millennium Ecosystem Assessment, 62, 166

Minc, Carlos, 288, 306, 307, 309

Mitch, Hurricane (1998), 1–2, 3, 4, 8, 76, 77

Mitigation of climate change: clean coal technology in, 122, 124, 126; cost effectiveness in, 124–28, 136–39, 141, 143–44, 403; economic analysis of, 16–17, 260; fossil fuel reductions in, 4–5;

nonmonetary benefits in, 131; as rationale for tropical forest finance, 335–38; REDD+ initiatives in, 10, 11, 123; reforestation in, 19–20, 42, 44; trajectory predictions for, 44; tropical forests in, 5, 6, 16–18, 42–44, 402, 412

Moderate Resolution Imaging Spectroradiometer (MODIS), 93, 97, 98, 99, 102, 106–07

Monitoring tropical forests, 90–113; advancements in, 91–94, 113; biodiversity, 94, 102, 107, 109; carbon density, 92–93, 97–101, 102, 104–05; challenges associated with, 19, 91; current and near-future status of capabilities for, 101–02; data revolution in, 91–94, 405; distinguishing forests from plantations, 92, 94, 102, 106–07, 108; emissions, 9, 12, 95–103; forest cover gains and losses, 101–02; Guyana-Norway partnership, 111, 112; illegal forest clearing, 9, 109–10; importance of, 110–11, 113; laser technologies for, 12; mapping capabilities, 12, 91–92, 96–97; real-time detection, 97, 102, 109–10, 192–93, 194–95; regrowth, 104; safeguards on conservation of natural forests and biodiversity, 105–09; usefulness of, 94. *See also* Mapping; Remote sensing technologies; Satellite technology

Morales, Evo, 268

Mozambique, REDD+ strategy in, 314

MRV emissions. *See* Measured, reported, and verified emissions

Mullan, Katrina, 157, 158, 159

Myanmar, agribusiness development in, 297

Myers, Norman, 331

Myers, Samuel, 164

Nagoya Protocol (2010), 170

Nakhooda, Smita, 364

Natalegawa, Marty, 305

National Aeronautics and Space Administration (NASA), 91, 92, 96, 97

National Cancer Institute, U.S., 170

National Cattlemen's Beef Association, 228

National Oceanic and Atmospheric Administration (NOAA), 2, 159

Natural Capital Project, 166

Natural disasters: climate change as influence on, 2, 4, 402; and deforestation, 76–77; economic impact of, 2; forest protection against, 7–8, 75; mitigation of, 162–63; Sustainable Development Goals on, 75. *See also specific types of natural disasters*

The Nature Conservancy, 256, 335, 350, 362

Nelson, Tia, 90

Neoliberal ideology, 255

Nepstad, Daniel, 190

Nestlé, 220, 221, 236, 238, 307, 407

New York Declaration on Forests (2014), 15, 142, 196, 300, 345, 410

NICFI. *See* Norway's International Climate and Forests Initiative

Nilsson, David, 346

Nitrous oxide, 33, 34

NOAA (National Oceanic and Atmospheric Administration), 2, 159

Nobre, Antonio, 70, 304

Noel Kempff Mercado Climate Action Project, 256

Norad (Norwegian Agency for Development Cooperation), 343, 344

Norman, Marigold, 364

North–South divide on forest conventions, 252, 254–55, 406

Norway: civil society organizations in, 261; conservation funding from, 15, 332; development assistance from, 344; disbursement delays by, 384; emission reduction financing by, 326–27; fast-start finance from, 362; forest management in, 329; greenhouse gas emissions in, 326; in Initiative for Sustainable Forest Landscapes, 364; interagency dynamics in, 375; partnership with Brazil, 277, 288, 289; performance-based finance from, 112, 276, 289, 310–12, 341–43, 363, 373; in REDD+ negotiations, 265

Norway's International Climate and Forests Initiative (NICFI), 327, 344, 345

Norwegian Agency for Development Cooperation (Norad), 343, 344

Ocean acidification, 32–33
Office Depot, 238
Oil palm plantations. *See* Palm oil and palm oil plantations
One Map initiative, 110, 299, 301
Operation Arc of Fire, 307
Opportunity costs of forest conservation, 128–29
Organization for Economic Co-operation and Development (OECD), 66
Ostrom, Elinor, 208

Palm oil and palm oil plantations: for biofuels, 230, 231; carbon storage in, 45–46; deforestation for, 47, 106, 164, 221, 222, 227; distinguishing forests from, 106–07, 108; emissions due to, 227; imprint of, 219; low-carbon lands suitable for, 203; monitoring, 106–07; peatland draining for, 3, 28, 230; sedimentation and, 67–68; supply chains, pledges to remove deforestation from, 15, 236–38, 239
Pan, Yude, 40
Papua New Guinea: community management of forests in, 297; fast-start finance for, 362; plantations in, 227; proposal for compensated emission reductions, 93, 259; in REDD+ negoti-

ations, 281; wood products exported from, 227
Paraguay, deforestation in, 49, 222
Paris Agreement (2015): implementation efforts, 16, 389; on indigenous peoples, 267; objectives of, 42, 136, 141, 142, 174; provision for internationally transferred mitigation outcomes, 411; REDD+ incorporated into, 10–11, 12, 252, 281, 317, 406; role of tropical forests in, 9, 15, 328, 403
Paris Declaration on Aid Effectiveness (2005), 12
Parker, Charlie, 374
Patient capital, 384, 386
Payment for ecosystem services (PES): advantages of, 205; benefit sharing in, 131; carbon pricing policies in, 129; defined, 204; ecological fiscal transfers, 172, 173; history of, 205; limitations of, 172; objectives of, 156, 171, 204
Payment-for-performance finance. *See* Performance-based finance
Peatlands: carbon dioxide emissions from, 40, 101, 103; characteristics of, 36; draining for agricultural use, 2–3, 28; forest fires in, 28, 36, 89; greenhouse gases released by, 36, 37
Péligre Dam, 61
PEN (Poverty and Environment Network), 151, 172
Perakis, Rita, 378
Performance-based finance: applicability of, 12–13; availability of, 20; benefits of, 21, 291, 298, 312, 316–17, 410; cautionary lessons from, 406–07; conservativeness approach to, 111, 271; constraints on, 376–80, 382–84; corruption in, 311, 377–78; for developing countries, 11, 310–12, 313–16, 369–71; disbursement issues, 384; from donor countries, 340–43, 369–71; financial transactions reframed

as, 13; growth of, 9; lack of promised finance, 313–16; qualifications for, 11; tenets of, 17, 376–77
Persson, Martin, 223–24, 227, 234, 239
Peru: Alto Mayo Protected Forest of, 123–24, 126, 131; conflicting mandates in, 309; ecotourism in, 171; greenhouse gas emissions in, 48; mapping technologies in, 107; multilateral financing in, 407; performance-based finance for, 289; in REDD+ negotiations, 264–65; trade agreement with U.S., 240–41
PES. *See* Payment for ecosystem services
Pest control, 62, 69, 70–71
Pharmaceuticals, 73–74, 169–70
Philippines: flooding in, 303
Photosynthesis, 33, 49
Pilot Program for Climate Resilience (PPCR), 365
Pinchot, Gifford, 251
Pistorius, Till, 329, 330, 340, 375, 387
Planetary carbon budget, 136
Plantations: disease in, 74; distinguishing forests from, 92, 94, 102, 106–07, 108; regrowth of, 40. *See also* Palm oil and palm oil plantations; Timber plantations
Politics: of climate change, 9, 258, 326, 341; of deforestation, 251, 288–90, 296, 304, 307; of REDD+, 343–44, 349, 352
Pollination, 7, 21, 65, 69, 70–71
Pollution. *See* Air pollution; Water pollution
Population growth, impact on deforestation, 209
Portugal, ecological fiscal transfer in, 172
Poverty: climate change as influence on, 3, 4, 5; and deforestation, 3, 20–21, 60, 206–07; surveys for estimation of, 165–66

Poverty and Environment Network (PEN), 151, 172
PPCR (Pilot Program for Climate Resilience), 365
Prasetyo, Heru, 369
Procurement policies, 15, 221, 241, 242, 413
Progesterone, 169
Program for the Endorsement of Forest Certification, 168
Program for the Estimation of Deforestation in the Brazilian Amazon (PRODES), 96, 98, 195
Program on Forests (PROFOR), 166

Qualitative comparative analysis, 310
Quickbird satellite, 97
Quinine, 169

Radiowave Detection and Ranging (radar), 98, 100–01, 104
Rainforest. *See* Amazon rainforest
Ramotar, Donald, 313–14
Rapid-Eye satellite, 97, 112
Real Time System for Detection of Deforestation (DETER), 97, 102, 109–10, 192–93, 194–95
RED (Renewable Energy Directive), 229, 232
REDD Early Movers Program (REM), 316, 363–64, 372, 407
Reducing Emissions from Deforestation and forest Degradation (REDD+): benefit sharing in, 279–80; carbon market offsets in, 94, 273–75; climate mitigation as rationale for funding, 335–38; cost effectiveness of, 126; defined, 10, 11; effectiveness concerns regarding, 270–75; efficiency considerations, 275–77, 278; equity concerns, 277–80; good governance promotion through, 300, 301, 302–03; incorporation into Paris Agreement, 10–11, 12, 252, 281, 317, 406; indigenous influences on, 21, 265, 266–67, 299, 348; insti-

tutional infrastructure developed for, 413; international agreement on, 15, 19, 23, 93, 252, 265, 406; jurisdictional approach to, 93, 273, 390; leadership as factor for success of, 309; misperceptions regarding, 20; negotiations on, 264–65, 268–70, 271, 281, 282; operationalization of elements in framework for, 94, 95; opposition to, 21, 268, 298, 327, 345–51; origins and evolution of, 93, 259, 261; participants in, 289–90, 367, 368, 408; pilot projects, 256, 263; political framing of, 260–61; results-based finance in, 10–11, 13–14; site-specific projects, 123, 372–73; stepwise approach to, 111, 271; subsidiary and insider politics of, 343–44, 349, 352; time constraints on opportunity for implementation, 408–09; transaction purchase prices under, 130, 131–32; unintended harm from, 348–49, 379–80; Warsaw Framework for, 11–12, 280, 281. *See also* Finance for REDD+
Reference levels, 95, 130, 275–77
Reforestation: carbon sequestration through, 45–46; constraints on, 44; mitigation of climate change through, 19–20, 42, 44; tree-planting campaigns for, 18, 20, 31, 45–47, 257; UNFCCC pledges for, 47. *See also* Forest conservation
REM. *See* REDD Early Movers Program
Remote sensing technologies: advances in, 260; in biodiversity monitoring, 109; in carbon density mapping, 99–101; development and advancement of, 8, 9, 12, 13, 19; emissions measurement with, 12, 13, 22; in forest degradation monitoring, 103; hyperspectral, 109; Lidar, 97,

99–100, 102, 103, 104–05, 109; limitations of, 101; types of, 97–98. *See also* Satellite technology
Renewable Energy Directive (RED), 229, 232
Renewable Fuel Standard (RFS), 229, 232
Report of the Committee Appointed by the British Association to Consider the Probable Effects in an Economical and Physical Point of View of the Destruction of Tropical Forests (Cleghorn et al.), 250–51
Results-based finance. *See* Performance-based finance
Reverse auctions, 129, 277
Rezende, Sérgio, 289
Ricupero, Rubens, 257
Rights and Resources Initiative, 208
Rio Branco Declaration (2014), 316, 369, 370
Rio Earth Summit. *See* United Nations Conference on Environment and Development (UNCED)
Riparian forests, 36, 67
Roads, deforestation caused by, 200–01
Rondon, Candido, 330
Roosevelt, Theodore, 330
Rose, Steven, 141
Rosen, Walter, 331
Ross, Michael, 296
Rosy periwinkle, 74, 169, 170
Rotational forestry, 35, 38, 42, 43–44
Rousseff, Dilma, 288, 306
Rudd, Kevin, 268, 339, 381

Sáenz, Leo, 155, 156, 161
Safeguard policies: Cancún Safeguards, 106, 107, 266; on conservation of natural forests and biodiversity, 105–09; defined, 95, 373; of World Bank, 384
Safeguards information system (SIS), 11
Sahel region (Africa), 9, 39
Sarkozy, Nicolas, 288

Satellite technology: availability of, 12; biodiversity monitoring with, 94, 102; in carbon density mapping, 99, 101, 102; China-Brazil Earth Resources Satellite, 96–97; deforestation monitoring with, 6, 48–49, 93, 96–97; high-resolution, 97, 103, 107; illegal forest clearing monitoring with, 9, 109–10; micro-satellites, 110; MODIS, 93, 97, 98, 99, 102, 106–07. *See also* Landsat

Savedoff, William, 377–78, 384, 389

Schwarzenegger, Arnold, 349–50, 351

Scientific forestry, 251

SDGs. *See* Sustainable Development Goals

Second generation biofuels, 232

Sedimentation, 7, 61, 67–68

Seneca Creek Associates, 334

Sentinel missions (European Space Agency), 96, 98, 103

Setra, Mina, 299

Sierra Leone, civil war in, 291

Silent Spring (Carson), 331

Silva, Marina: on compensated reduction of deforestation, 258; diplomacy by, 261; as environment minister, 288, 301, 305, 309, 327; indigenous territories demarcated by, 299; in presidential election, 304; resignation of, 306, 309

The Sinking Ark: A New Look at the Problem of Disappearing Species (Myers), 331

SIS (safeguards information system), 11

Skocpol, Theda, 340–41

SkyShares model, 124, 134, 140

Soares, Rodrigo, 296

Solheim, Erik, 343, 375

Solow, Robert, 159

Soros, George, 371

South America: carbon density of dry forests in, 226; forest fires in, 75; malaria in, 74; peatlands of, 36. *See also specific countries*

Southeast Asia: commodities driving deforestation in, 236; community management of forests in, 297; deforestation in, 39, 222, 231; distinguishing forests from plantations by mapping in, 107; fisheries in, 73; forest fires in, 62; insurgencies in, 291–92; sequestration by forest regrowth in, 104. *See also specific countries*

Southern Company, 122, 124

Soy industry: and biofuels, 230, 231; deforestation due to, 47, 121, 164, 187, 221, 222, 226; emissions due to, 226; moratorium on deforestation by, 8, 188, 189, 190, 193, 236, 307; productivity of, 70, 130, 176, 195; supply chain commitment to zero deforestation, 204

Spatial econometric analysis, 198–99, 405

Spot-5 satellite, 97

Sri Lanka: ecosystem-based adaptations in, 78; mangrove forests in, 154

Stang, Dorothy, 188, 306

Stephanes, Reinhold, 288

Stern, Nicholas, 16–17, 260

Stern Review, 126, 326, 338

Stewart, John Lindsay, 250

Stiglitz, Joseph, 165

Stockholm Environment Institute, 239–40

Stoltenberg, Jens, 112, 142, 313, 315, 326, 341, 371

Strassburg, Bernardo, 196

Streck, Charlotte, 306, 388

Subramanian, Arvind, 274

Sub-Saharan Africa: community management of forests in, 297; deforestation in, 222; energy planning in, 167; payment for ecosystem services in, 205. *See also specific countries*

Subsidies: for agriculture, 228; for biofuels, 23, 221, 229, 231–32, 242

Suharto, 28, 45, 292, 294–95, 312, 314, 381

Sukarno, 292

Supply chains: donor country commitments to zero deforestation in, 344–45; industry pledges to remove deforestation from, 204, 220, 221, 235–40, 407; mapping, 239–40

Sustainable Development Goals (SDGs): clean water and access to energy, 67; forest conservation, 15, 18, 142, 408; global nature of, 125; health-related, 73; hunger elimination, 69; natural disaster assistance, 75; role of tropical forests in achievement of, 62

Sweden, forest management in, 328

Swidden agriculture, 28, 35, 42, 43–44, 297

Sylvicultura Oeconomica (Carlowitz), 329

Taï National Park, 171

Tamarin Waterfall, 359

Tanzania: indigenous rights in, 300; performance-based finance for, 310

Tauli-Corpuz, Victoria, 267

Taxes, deforestation, 205

TEEB (The Economics of Ecosystems and Biodiversity) initiative, 166

Teleconnections, 70

Temperate forests: biomass conversion by, 64; carbon density of, 36, 38; conventions for, 254; deforestation of, 37–38; regeneration of, 38; timber plantations in, 35, 38

Tesso Nilo National Park, 233–34

TFAP. *See* Tropical Forestry Action Plan

Thailand: flooding in, 303; forest fires in, 27; mangrove forests in, 153–54, 164

Thatcher, Margaret, 360, 366

Thomas, Jean François, 61

Three Gorges Dam, 154–55, 161

Timber plantations: carbon storage in, 45–46; deforestation for, 47, 106, 207–08, 221; illegal, 234; income from, 151; monitoring, 106–07; peatland draining for, 3, 28; regrowth cycle for, 42; rotational, 35, 42; sustainable practices of, 168–69, 207–08; in temperate forests, 35, 38. *See also* Logging; Wood products

Timber Regulation (EU), 204, 234, 240, 333

Trade agreements, 240–41

Traditional medicines, 73, 150, 151, 170

"The Tragedy of the Commons" (Hardin), 208

Trans-Amazon Highway, 186, 200, 209

Transmigration programs, 209, 292

Transparent World, 107

Tree-planting campaigns, 18, 20, 31, 45–47, 90, 257

Tropical Forest and Climate Unity Agreement, 347–48

Tropical Forest Conservation Act of 1998, 332

Tropical Forestry Action Plan (TFAP), 9, 253–54, 282, 331, 360

Tropical forests: in achievement of SDGs, 62; adaptation to climate change, 77–78; in agricultural production, 7, 69–73; biomass conversion by, 64; carbon capture and storage system of, 6, 20, 22, 33, 94, 272; carbon density of, 36, 38; climate change effects on, 49, 77, 408; cloud, 36, 65, 68, 155–56; density of foliage in, 325; diversity of, 289; functions and benefits of, 7–8, 33, 36, 62–63, 78, 405; as haven for rebels and separatist groups, 291; health benefits of, 7, 62, 73–75; misperceptions regarding, 20; in mitigation of climate change, 5, 6, 16–18, 42–44, 402, 412; natural uptake of carbon dioxide by, 32, 33, 34; North–South divide on conven-

tions for, 252, 254–55, 406; physical structure and biodiversity of, 39, 64–66; political reframing of, 258–61; regeneration of, 35, 39, 44; riparian, 36, 67; safety role of, 75–76; time constraints on opportunity for change, 407–09; in water use and energy, 66–69. *See also* Deforestation; Ecosystem services; Forest-based emissions; Forest conservation; Forest degradation; Mangrove forests; Monitoring tropical forests; Reforestation

Tsunamis: and deforestation, 62, 77; poor and vulnerable households impacted by, 163; protection from, 36, 77

Tubocurarine, 169

Umbrella Group, 256

UNCED. *See* United Nations Conference on Environment and Development

UNDP (United Nations Development Program), 60, 253

UNDRIP (United Nations Declaration on the Rights of Indigenous Peoples), 266, 267

UNFCCC. *See* United Nations Framework Convention on Climate Change

Unilever, 221

United Kingdom: conservation funding from, 15, 339; disbursement delays by, 385; fast-start finance by, 361; forest governance initiatives of, 333–34; in Initiative for Sustainable Forest Landscapes, 364; interagency dynamics in, 374, 379; neoliberal ideology in, 255; on performance-based finance, 340; sustainable land use initiatives, 345

United Nations Conference on Environment and Development (UNCED), 251, 254, 255, 257

United Nations Declaration on the Rights of Indigenous Peoples

(UNDRIP), 266, 267

United Nations Development Program (UNDP), 60, 253

United Nations Food and Agriculture Organization (FAO), 91, 132, 225, 253–54, 270, 405

United Nations Forum on Forests (UNFF), 255

United Nations Framework Convention on Climate Change (UNFCCC): classification of forests under, 106; deforestation as defined by, 35; failure to produce binding agreement to reduce emissions, 14; indigenous rights within, 266, 267; Kyoto Protocol to, 19, 90, 229, 255–57; Lima Challenge endorsements at, 15, 369–70; origins of, 261; on reference levels, 275, 277; reforestation pledges by member countries, 47; reframing tropical forests as emission mitigation solution, 252; safeguard on natural forests and biodiversity, 106. *See also* Reducing Emissions from Deforestation and forest Degradation (REDD+)

United Nations Permanent Forum on Indigenous Issues (UNPFII), 266, 267

United Nations-REDD Programme, 263, 266, 280, 362, 367, 368

United States: agriculture in, 228; biofuel subsidies in, 221, 229, 232; conservation funding from, 332, 339–40; consumption of globally traded commodities in, 228; cost of reducing emissions from industrial sources, 7, 124, 135, 138; emissions generated by, 28, 40; failure to act on climate change threat, 409; fast-start finance by, 361, 366–67; forest law enforcement in trade agreements, 240–41; import restrictions in, 240; in Initiative for Sustainable Forest Landscapes, 364; logging regulations in, 334;

neoliberal ideology in, 255; on performance-based finance, 340–41, 377; protected areas in, 201; on REDD+, 265, 347–48, 349; role of forests in history of, 329. *See also* California

UNPFII (United Nations Permanent Forum on Indigenous Issues), 266, 267

U.S. Agency for International Development (USAID), 332, 339–40, 366, 372

U.S. Climate Action Partnership (USCAP), 340, 341, 348

U.S. Forest Service, 251, 330

U.S. Geological Survey (USGS), 91, 96, 97

Value of ecosystem services, 151–67; carbon capture and storage, 173–74; chain of cause and effect in, 159, 173; challenges of quantifying, 157–65; extrapolating and aggregating, 161–62; infrequent occurrence of large values, 162, 163; initiatives for promoting visibility of, 166–67; international, 156–57; invisibility of, 20, 151–53, 165–67, 176; local, 153–54; marginal vs. average, 159–60; market considerations in, 158–59; monetization of, 22, 167, 171; regional, 154–56; regressive nature of, 162–65; space and time fluctuations in, 160–61

Védrine, Emmanuel, 60

Very high-resolution satellites, 97, 103, 107

Vietnam: fast-start finance for, 362; payment for ecosystem services in, 172, 205; performance-based finance for, 310; REDD+ strategy in, 314–15; reforestation efforts in, 47, 157; rice fields in, 59

Vignola, Rafaele, 68, 69

Vinblastine, 74, 169

Vincristine, 74, 169

Vindesine, 169

Vinorelbine, 169

Virtuous cycles, 261, 262, 268, 269

Virunga National Park, 171

Waldsterben (forest death), 329–30

Walmart, 345, 407

Walt Disney Company, 123–24, 238, 367

Walton, Rob, 371

Warsaw Framework (2013), 11–12, 280, 281

Water: availability of, 68–69; as electricity source, 61, 66–67, 154–56; importance of, 66; quality of, 67–68; scarcity of, 4, 68

Water cycle, 65

Water pollution, 67, 73, 134

Waxman-Markey Bill of 2009, 14, 273, 340–41, 347, 349

Wealth Accounting and the Value of Ecosystem Services (WAVES), 166

Weather patterns: agriculture impacted by, 69–70; deforestation in alteration of, 34, 70; El Niño, 28, 41, 75, 156; maintenance of, 65. *See also* Climate change

West Africa: deforestation in, 9; ecotourism in, 171; sequestration by forest regrowth in, 104. *See also specific countries*

Wild foods, 71–72

Wilmar International, 15, 233, 237–38

Wilson, E. O., 331

Wolosin, Michael, 264, 341, 365, 366–67, 376, 377, 389

Women: ecosystem services valued by, 163, 303; fishery harvests by, 72

Wood products: carbon stored in, 46–47; deforestation due to, 224; demand-side policies to address illegal trade of, 240–41; emissions due to, 227–28; forest income from, 151. *See also* Logging; Timber plantations

Woods Hole Research Center, 92–93, 99

World Bank: assessment of factors affecting forest reform, 307, 308; BioCarbon Fund, 364; Climate Investment Funds, 362–63; on cost of Indonesian forest fires, 157; country systems approach to lending by, 373; disengagement from forestry sector, 9; Inspection Panel, 21; Living Standards Measurement Study, 166; Program-for-Results instrument, 373; in REDD+ finance, 312, 371; on relationship between deforestation and poverty, 17; road projects undertaken by, 201; safeguard policies, 384; Tropical Forestry Action Plan launched by, 253; as trustee of Forest Carbon Partnership Facility, 362

World Health Organization, 73

World Rainforest Movement, 254

World Resources Institute (WRI), 91, 107, 208, 253, 254

World Trade Organization, 241

World Wide Fund for Nature, 222, 256, 268, 330

World Wildlife Fund, 233, 332, 335

Wunder, Sven, 204

Xi Jinping, 141–42

Yellow fever, 74

Yellowstone National Park, 201

Yudhoyono, Susilo Bambang: on domestic benefits of ecosystem services, 303; emission reduction targets announced by, 13, 263, 275, 305, 313, 369; forest protection initiatives, 308–09; Kalimantan Forests and Climate Partnership authorized by, 381; One Map initiative of, 301; payment-for-performance agreement signed by, 289, 313, 315; reputation and international legitimacy concerns, 304–05; tree-planting campaigns of, 45, 46

Zambia, deforestation in, 49

Zoonotic diseases, 74–75

The Center for Global Development works to reduce global poverty and inequality through rigorous research and active engagement with the policy community to make the world a more prosperous, just, and safe place for us all.

The policies and practices of the rich and the powerful—in rich nations as well as in the emerging powers, international institutions, and global corporations—have significant impacts on the world's poor people. We aim to improve these policies and practices through research and policy engagement to expand opportunities, reduce inequalities, and improve lives everywhere.

By pairing research with action, CGD goes beyond contributing to knowledge about development. We conceive of and encourage discussion about practical policy innovations in areas such as trade, aid, health, education, climate change, labor mobility, private investment, access to finance, and global governance to foster shared prosperity in an increasingly interdependent world.

The Center for Global Development is an independent and nonpartisan research institution. No conditions or limitations on CGD's independence in research, findings, conclusions, or resulting publications are attached to any funding received.

FRANCES SEYMOUR

Frances Seymour is a Senior Fellow at the Center for Global Development, where she leads the Center's work on tropical forests for climate and development. Recognized as an expert on international forest policy, she also serves as an adviser to the David and Lucile Packard Foundation. From 2006-2012 Seymour served as Director General of the Center for International Forestry Research (CIFOR) at its headquarters in Indonesia. For her leadership there, the Government of France awarded her the rank of *Officier* in the Order of Agricultural Merit, citing her "exceptional dynamism" and "visionary thinking." Previously she led research and outreach on mainstreaming environmental considerations into development finance in her roles as founding Director of the Institutions and Governance Program at the World Resources Institute and Director of Development Assistance Policy at the World Wildlife Fund. Early in her career, her work as a Program Officer at the Ford Foundation's office in Indonesia focused on promoting community forestry and human rights. Seymour holds an MPA in Development Studies from Princeton University.

JONAH BUSCH

Jonah Busch is a Senior Fellow at the Center for Global Development. He is an environmental economist whose research focuses on climate change and tropical deforestation. He is the lead developer of the OSIRIS model for analyzing and designing policies for reducing greenhouse gas emissions from deforestation. Busch's scientific publications have appeared in academic journals including *Science*, *Proceedings of the National Academy of Sciences*, *Land Economics* and *Environmental Research Letters*. He serves on the editorial board of *Conservation Letters*. Busch has advised on climate and forests for the President of Guyana, the Government of Indonesia, the United Nations Framework Convention on Climate Change, the Forest Carbon Partnership Facility and other governments and institutions. Previously he worked as the Climate and Forest Economist at Conservation International and taught high school math in Burkina Faso as a Peace Corps volunteer. Busch holds a PhD in Economics and Environmental Science from the University of California, Santa Barbara.